THE IMPACT OF TELEVISION
A Natural Experiment in Three Communities

THE IMPACT
OF TELEVISION
A Natural Experiment in Three Communities

Edited by

TANNIS MACBETH WILLIAMS

Department of Psychology
The University of British Columbia
Vancouver, British Columbia, Canada

WITH A FOREWORD BY ALBERTA E. SIEGEL

1986

ACADEMIC PRESS, INC.
Harcourt Brace Jovanovich, Publishers

Orlando   San Diego   New York   Austin
London   Montreal   Sydney   Tokyo   Toronto

ACADEMIC PRESS, INC.
Orlando, Florida 32887

United Kingdom Edition published by
ACADEMIC PRESS INC. (LONDON) LTD.
24–28 Oval Road, London NW1 7DX

LIBRARY OF CONGRESS CATALOGING-IN-PUBLICATION DATA

Main entry under title:

The Impact of television.

  Includes bibliographies and index.
  1. Television—Influence—Addresses, essays,
lectures.   2. Television—Psychological aspects—
Addresses, essays, lectures.   I. Williams, Tannis
MacBeth.
PN1992.6.I47   1985   302.2'345   85-9213
ISBN 0-12-756290-7 (alk. paper)
ISBN 0-12-756291-5 (paperback)

PRINTED IN THE UNITED STATES OF AMERICA

86 87 88 89   9 8 7 6 5 4 3 2 1

CONTENTS

3 TELEVISION AND COGNITIVE DEVELOPMENT
Linda Faye Harrison and Tannis MacBeth Williams

4 TELEVISION AND OTHER LEISURE ACTIVITIES
Tannis MacBeth Williams and A. Gordon Handford

7 TELEVISION AND CHILDREN'S AGGRESSIVE BEHAVIOR
Lesley A. Joy, Meredith M. Kimball, and Merle L. Zabrack

8 TELEVISION AND ADULTS: THINKING, PERSONALITY, AND ATTITUDES
Peter Suedfeld, Brian R. Little, A. Dennis Rank, Darilynn S. Rank, and Elizabeth J. Ballard

CONTRIBUTORS

Numbers in parentheses indicate the pages on which the authors' contributions begin.

ELIZABETH J. BALLARD (361), Department of Psychology, University of British Columbia, Vancouver, British Columbia, Canada V6T 1W5

MICHAEL C. BOYES (215), Department of Psychology, University of British Columbia, Vancouver, British Columbia, Canada V6T 1W5

RAYMOND S. CORTEEN (39), Department of Psychology, University of British Columbia, Vancouver, British Columbia, Canada V6T 1W5

A. GORDON HANDFORD[1] (143), Department of Psychology, University of British Columbia, Vancouver, British Columbia, Canada V6T 1W5

LINDA FAYE HARRISON[2] (87), Department of Psychology, University of British Columbia, Vancouver, British Columbia, Canada V6T 1W5

LESLEY A. JOY[3] (303), Department of Psychology, University of British Columbia, Vancouver, British Columbia, Canada V6T 1W5

MEREDITH M. KIMBALL[4] (265, 303), Department of Psychology, University of British Columbia, Vancouver, British Columbia, Canada V6T 1W5

BRIAN R. LITTLE[5] (361), Department of Psychology, University of British Columbia, Vancouver, British Columbia, Canada V6T 1W5

---

[1] Present address: Department of Basic Health Sciences, British Columbia Institute of Technology, Burnaby, British Columbia, Canada V5G 3H2.

[2] Present address: Open Learning Institute, Richmond, British Columbia, Canada V6X 1Z9.

[3] Present address: Department of Psychology, Simon Fraser University, Burnaby, British Columbia, Canada V5A 1S6.

[4] Present address: Department of Psychology/Women's Studies Program, Simon Fraser University, Burnaby, British Columbia, Canada V5A 1S6.

[5] Present address: Department of Psychology, Carleton University, Ottawa, Ontario, Canada K1S 5B6.

A. DENNIS RANK[6] (361), Department of Psychology, University of British Columbia, Vancouver, British Columbia, Canada V6T 1W5

DARILYNN S. RANK[6] (361), Department of Psychology, University of British Columbia, Vancouver, British Columbia, Canada V6T 1W5

PETER SUEDFELD (361), Department of Psychology, University of British Columbia, Vancouver, British Columbia, Canada V6T 1W5

TANNIS MACBETH WILLIAMS (1, 39, 87, 143, 215, 395), Department of Psychology, University of British Columbia, Vancouver, British Columbia, Canada V6T 1Y7

MERLE L. ZABRACK[7] (303), Department of Psychology, University of British Columbia, Vancouver, British Columbia, Canada V6T 1W5

[6] Present address: 485 West 59 Avenue, Vancouver, British Columbia, Canada V5X 1X4.
[7] Present address: Department of Psychology, Simon Fraser University, Burnaby, British Columbia, Canada V5A 1S6.

FOREWORD

A valuable set of research projects is reported here. A capable team of investigators conducted the research under the skillful and dedicated leadership of Tannis MacBeth Williams. She is a meticulous and thoughtful psychologist, and I am delighted to commend her work to the reader's thoughtful attention.

No team of research workers, however talented, could compel people to watch as much television as people watch voluntarily. Similarly, no one can compel people to deprive themselves of watching television for any extended period. Further, even if there were people who would let a research team control their leisure time so totally, the researchers would probably refrain from doing so for ethical reasons.

These are the reasons that it is impossible to conduct a truly experimental study of the effects of television-watching. In a true experiment, the investigator controls which persons will watch and which will not, and that decision is based entirely on the toss of a coin or some other random event. We have excellent short-term experiments about television-watching, but none which is truly long term.

Most of the research on the effects of watching television has been forced to compare "light viewers" with "heavy viewers." Like light smokers and heavy smokers, these people differ in many ways other than in their watching habits, and those other differences create difficulties in interpreting what might appear at first glance to be the outcomes of watching a lot or watching relatively little. At least the investigator of the effects of smoking has nonsmokers to study. But not since the late 1940s and very early 1950s, when television was being introduced commercially in North America, have there been nonviewers to study.

Or so we all thought until word of Williams's project reached us. I served on the Scientific Advisory Committee on Television and Social Behavior, which framed the report to the U.S. Surgeon General in 1972. Williams identifies this report as having stimulated her research. That committee met frequently in the years from 1960 through 1971. We often discussed how good it would be to have studies comparing communities with television with other communities not reached by television. Serving on this committee were several research workers and executives with ties to the U.S. television industry. They assured us that no such communities existed any longer. Other committee members certainly knew of none. We were of course unaware of a small town in Western Canada whose location meant the residents could not receive TV. Williams learned of that town and had the good sense to study it before the technological changes that brought television took place. She had the prepared mind which chance favors, and she had the energy and leadership skills to seize the opportunity for research.

The merits of this research go beyond the fact that it utilizes information from a town which had never received television at the time of the initial study and which adapted to television over the course of the research. Information from the residents of this town is compared with information from other towns which had been receiving television for years. The quality of this information is high, and the measures command the respect of serious psychologists.

There is a large literature of research on television and children. Without belaboring the point, I want to comment that frequently it has relied on rough and ready measures. All too often, information has been secondhand. For example, investigators have turned to mothers to report on how much television their children watch. When that secondhand information eventually was compared with firsthand observations in the home about television watching, it was found to be in error; however, much research relies on such estimates. Sometimes the information has been shoddy. For example, when a serious psychologist speaks of a child's IQ, that psychologist is referring to the score reporting the child's performance on an individual test administered in one or two hour-long sessions by a qualified psychologist. The success of the IQ test generated commercial imitations, many of them shoddy. Often schools rely on those imitations, which are paper and pencil tests administered to a group of children and scored by a machine. Reports of research about television have relied on so-called IQs which were merely the results of those group tests, available in school files. "Rough and ready" is a polite term for such measures as part of the research enterprise. To their credit, Williams and her colleagues use research-quality measures of children's intelligence, not commercial-quality tests, when assessing verbal ability (in the chapter on cognitive development). Group test scores were used only as a secondary control.

Similarly, the measure of aggression in the children in the three towns is not some teacher's report or simply the estimate of peers. Rather, qualified observers took the time to observe each child on the playground and to record instances of aggressive acts. This approach is time-consuming and expensive, but it yields information we can understand and depend on.

Another example is the information about reading abilities of the children. It would be easy enough to ask teachers to rank the children in their classrooms on reading ability. Or an investigator could search through the school records to locate scores on some commercial test of reading ability which is administered annually for administrative purposes. Our authors did neither: They administered individual tests of reading ability, using a tachistoscopic apparatus.

Williams and her colleagues have the virtues of serious scientists, including caution and conservatism. They avoid claims they cannot buttress. Other scientific virtues are modesty about one's own contribution and generosity about the contributions of others. I admire these virtues, but I recognize that they could cause the book to be overlooked or under-appreciated. So I am glad to have the opportunity to say clearly that this is an important study. The book merits a wide and attentive readership.

To high-quality research, with a strong architecture and good measures, Williams brings high-quality skills in writing. No reader needs to be told that many excellent scientists lack the ability to talk about their findings in a way nonspecialists can comprehend. Williams is fortunate in having that ability. The book is carefully laid out so that both the intelligent general reader and the specialist can find the information they require. The information needed by the specialist is not allowed to crowd out or obscure the core information for the general reader. The authors deserve our commendation for their successful effort to bring their research findings to a wide readership.

There is so much new information in this book that the authors might be forgiven for thinking their task was done once they had conveyed it. Instead, they have regularly gone beyond their own data. Repeatedly, they turn from their own research to that of others, offering serious and probing discussions of how their own findings augment, refine, or contradict those which had already been known. In this as in other tasks, the tone is serious and respectful. The authors see their task as sharing with the reader the best of what is known, not simply conveying what they have found, ample though that is.

This book will be a landmark in our field. It sets a new standard of excellence for research on our topic, while standing as an accurate record of what is now known. I have learned from reading it, and so will others. On behalf of all its readers, I take pleasure in congratulating Williams and her colleagues on a job well done.

ALBERTA E. SIEGEL
STANFORD UNIVERSITY

PREFACE

Does television affect its child and adult viewers, and if so, how? This question has provoked considerable controversy every since TV first became widely available in the 1950s. Now that most people watch television regularly, the debate is even more difficult to resolve. Do light versus heavy viewers of television differ on some measure because they use television differently, and/or because they differ on some other important characteristic (e.g., intelligence)? Do they differ because they have been influenced by TV? Or is the process of influence transactional? This book describes the results of a large research project based on an unusual opportunity to address these kinds of issues—a natural experiment involving a non-isolated Canadian town which did not obtain TV reception until late 1973. We studied three communities on two occasions, just before one of the towns obtained television for the first time and again 2 years later. The book is not, however, merely a description of who was studied, when, how, and what was found. Our goal is to use this natural experiment to understand the processes involved in television's influence and the complexities of relationships between TV and human behavior.

The first chapter provides an overview of the research, including its context and background, descriptions of the communities and their comparability, and so on. Chapters 2–8 describe the individual studies. Broadly speaking, television theoretically could influence its viewers either indirectly by displacing other activities or directly via its content. Chapters 2, 3, and 4 deal with television's potential displacement effects on children's reading competence, several aspects of children's thinking, and participation in other leisure activities by both adolescents and adults. Chapter 5 discusses the ways in which children and adults in the three communities used TV and other available media. Chapters 6 and 7 deal with effects of television's content on children in two major areas— perceptions of the behavior of females and males (sex-role attitudes) and aggression. Chapter 8 deals entirely with adults, focusing on TV's potential effects on problem-solving behavior, personality, and perceptions of the environment. Chapter 9 summarizes the findings described in Chapters 2–8, speculates about the processes underlying television's influence, and discusses some implications of the results of this natural experiment. The effects of television are of interest to people in many fields, so we have tried to use as little jargon as possible and present the results in such a way that motivated parents, educators, policy makers, advertisers, and people in the television industry will find this book readable. Its primary audience will be researchers, teachers, and students in the fields of communication studies, psychology, education, and sociology. Because readers will vary in their knowledge of research methodology and statistics, we have described our findings as straightforwardly as possible in the text, tables, and figures and provided the statistical details in the appendixes and notes to each chapter. Sufficient detail is provided in the notes that they can be read either in conjunction with or independently of the text. All results discussed in the text are statistically significant, meaning they would occur by chance 5 times or less if the study was repeated 100 times. Occasionally, a finding that would occur more than 5 but less than 10 times in 100 by chance is mentioned as marginally significant if it is of central interest. All analyses and post hoc tests were conducted to three decimals, but means reported in this book have been rounded to two places for numbers greater than 2.

─────── ACKNOWLEDGMENTS

This project was conducted by several faculty members and students in the Department of Psychology at the University of British Columbia, under the direction of Tannis MacBeth Williams. We could not have studied several thousand people in each of three communities on two occasions without considerable assistance, however, and would like to acknowledge that help.

We are especially grateful to the Canada Council/Social Sciences and Humanities Research Council of Canada for funding the research and for leave fellowships which enabled Tannis MacBeth Williams to complete the data analyses and writing; to Mary Morrison for alerting us to the research opportunity represented by Notel; to Mireille Badour, Sheridan Scott, and Susan Scanlon for expediting the grant review process at different stages; to Jo-Anne McFadden Hordo for supervising the first phase of data collection and analysis; to Virginia Green for supervising the computer work from beginning to end; to Liz McCririck for similar dedication to the manuscript; to Toomas Ilves for his work on early phases of the editing of Chapters 1, 2, 6, and 7; to Jacqueline Kampman for preparing the subject index; and to the staff of Academic Press for their assistance during the publication process. All these people were extraordinarily helpful and conscientious.

Many people gave us valuable advice over the course of this project. The suggestions of Dan Anderson, Andrew Arno, Chris Bachen, Albert Bandura, Merry Bullock, Michael Chandler, George Comstock, Jacqueline Goodnow, Bradley Greenberg, Patricia Greenfield, Barrie Gunter, Pedro Hernandez-Ramos, Hilde Himmelweit, Bob Hornik, Bill Husson, Aletha Huston, Jack Lyle, Hilliard MacBeth, Nathan Maccoby, Ken Marchant, Michael Morgan, John Murray, Mabel Rice, Don Roberts, Eli Rubinstein, Gavriel Salomon, Alberta Siegel, Ron Slaby, Harriet Stone, Doug Williams, Mallory Wober, and John Wright were especially useful. Additional thanks go to numerous undergraduate and graduate students, at our own and other universities, who contributed many of the most thought-provoking comments received.

We also appreciate the careful and responsible work done on data collection, coding, and proofreading by Lynne Atchison, Louise Ball, Naomi Barty, Robin Cappe, Nancy Carter, Rachelle Chertkow, Patricia Crawford, Natalie Dickson, Elsie Eccles, Sue Fisk, Margaret Fryer, Jeanne Garber, Brenda Hildebrandt, Stephen Holliday, Ginny McDonald, Tim McTiernan, Fran Moran, Ann Noble, Rebecca Noble, Susan Lee Painter, Giorgio Pastore, Sandra Pauliuk, Norma Pawlowski, Leanne Radford, Linda Rainaldi, Brian Rapske, Una Reid, Alice Sanderson, Kathleen Sun, Adele Thorne, Lisa Travis, Susan Tseng, Rena Urbach, Hugh Westrup, Christine Whittall, Herb Wong, and Helen Zorn.

Last but foremost, we thank the residents and teachers of Notel, Unitel, and Multitel for their cooperation, which ultimately is what made this book possible.

BACKGROUND AND OVERVIEW

Tannis MacBeth Williams

INTRODUCTION

North American children and adults spend most of their leisure time watching television. How, if at all, does this affect children's reading skills, their vocabulary, their creativity, their aggressive behavior, and their attitudes toward sex roles? Does it affect adults? Is TV viewing related to their perception of their environment and their problem-solving skills? How does the availability of television affect the community as a whole? Does it influence the number of community activities available? Does it affect participation in those activities? These and related questions about television and human behavior are the focus of this book.

A natural experiment based on the arrival of television in a Canadian community provided an unusual opportunity to investigate the effects of television. We studied three towns both before and 2 years after reception began in the town originally without TV. This book describes why and how our research was conducted, what we found, and the implications of these results. It is not, however, merely a description of a before and after study of television. Rather, it draws upon the unique methodological advantages of a natural experiment to address important questions about the effects of television and the processes involved in television's influence. Many of these questions are not new; indeed, some have been the focus of volumes of previous research. Almost all such previous research, however, has been conducted on regular viewers, making it difficult to draw causal inferences and conclusions about TV's long-term effects.

HISTORY AND CONTEXT OF THE RESEARCH

This project began in the summer of 1973 when we learned that a community without television was due to acquire it within a year.[1] This town lacked TV because it happened to be in a geographic blind spot, not because it was particularly isolated. Other Canadian communities still without TV are accessible only by sea or by air, and thus differ from most North American towns in a number of other ways. The impact of TV in isolated areas is of considerable interest, but many of the appropriate research questions differ from those one would ask in studying a non-isolated community without television (e.g., Granzberg, 1982; Granzberg & Steinbring, 1980; Williams, 1985). Except for anachronistically lacking television reception in 1973, the town we studied was typical. It was accessible by road, had daily bus service in two directions, and its ethnic mix also was not unusual. The town just happened to be located in a valley in such a way that the transmitter meant to serve the area did not provide television reception for most residents. A few homes did have reception much of the time, although it was poor. Others picked it up occasionally, but most people were unable to watch television on a regular basis in their own homes.

Why was it worth studying a town without television in the 1970s? Weren't all the important questions answered during the 1950s, when television was new? Unfortunately, no. Some outstanding studies have become landmarks in the field, most notably those conducted in England by Himmelweit, Oppenheim and Vince (1958), in North America by Schramm, Lyle, and Parker (1961), and in Japan by Furu (1962). These researchers laid the groundwork of our knowledge regarding television and children. All three groups, however, focused more on the uses and gratifications of television than on its effects. When they did ask about effects, they more often obtained self-report, parent, or teacher ratings than measures of actual behavior. Their studies also covered a restricted age range. Himmelweit et al. (1958) focused on children aged 10–11 and 13–14 years, and Schramm et al. (1961) focused on children in grades 6 and 10, with some attention to first graders as well. Furu modeled his research after the other two investigations. Thus, although these projects contributed immeasurably to our knowledge of children and television, they also left many questions unanswered. In addition, the formulation of some central questions about television's influence depended upon the hindsight afforded by history. Many important questions were not asked until most people in the developed world had become regular viewers. The most obvious example is the relationship between televised violence and aggressive behavior. An extensive body of research on the effects of televised violence on children and youth culminated in the *Report of the [U.S.] Surgeon General's Advisory Committee on Television and Social Behavior* (National Institute of Mental Health [NIMH], 1972). The publication of that report and the publicity surrounding it set the stage for our research in several ways.

The major influence of the Surgeon General's (NIMH, 1972) report on this project was to underline the uniqueness and importance of the opportunity to conduct research in a town without television. This opportunity promised to shed new light on the much-debated question of whether the relationships between TV viewing and other behaviors (e.g., school achievement) obtained in correlational studies occur because television affects those behaviors, because people who already exhibit more of those behaviors tend to watch more television, or both. It also promised to add to the field survey evidence by indicating whether short-term effects observed in the laboratory also occur in natural settings and whether they hold up over the long run.

The U.S. Surgeon General's report focused primarily on the relationship between televised violence and aggressive behavior. It reflected the tenor of the time; there was more interest in the unintended, potentially negative consequences of television than in its potentially positive effects. Earlier researchers (e.g., Furu, 1962; Himmelweit et al., 1958; Schramm et al., 1961), who had initially been more hopeful, by and large concluded that television did not have the positive impact on children's knowledge they had predicted. In the meantime, as the content of television became better documented, the scientific and lay communities had become more vocal in expressing concern about television's potentially negative effects. Our research began relatively soon after the publication of the U.S. Surgeon General's report, and that report was one of the influences on our choice of topics for this project. Other influences and the specific effects we studied are discussed later in this chapter.

More than a decade has elapsed since we began our research. Whereas its design was based on the evidence and thinking extant then, interpretation of our findings and some of the data analyses have benefited from subsequent research. We began with what strike us now as simplistic hypotheses but have moved on, with other researchers in the field, to a more complex view of television and human behavior. It is perhaps timely that the 10-year update of the Surgeon General's report (Pearl, Bouthilet, & Lazar, 1982) was published during the last stages of our work. The update cuts a wider swath; aggression is only one of many topics studied in relation to television. Our research is in that sense typical of its era—we tried to cover as wide a range of behaviors and as broad a range of the life span as possible, given our expertise and budget.

GENERAL DESIGN OF THE NATURAL EXPERIMENT

For simplicity and to preserve the anonymity of its residents, we shall refer to our town without television by the pseudonym "Notel." However, had we collected data only in Notel before (Phase 1) and after (Phase 2) television arrived it would have been impossible to know whether changes occurred because of TV or because of general changes in the society. In other words, if the arrival of television in Notel was to be studied as a natural experiment, some control groups were needed. We knew that within a year Notel would begin to receive one channel, CBC, the Canadian government-owned network. (The content of CBC as well as the networks available in the other towns is described later in this chapter.) Our first control or comparison group, therefore, was chosen to be similar. "Unitel" was about the same size as Notel, located approximately 55 miles away, and had been receiving one channel, CBC, for 7 years. Census data (see Table 1.3) indicated Notel and Unitel were similar, and residents of both communities agreed. We wondered, however, whether television's impact varies according to the number of channels available and whether there are differences between the impact of CBC and the impact of U.S. television. We therefore included a second control town, "Multitel." In 1973, most Multitel residents paid for a cable hookup and had been receiving CBC as well as affiliated stations of the three major U.S. networks, ABC, CBS, and NBC, for 15 years. Good reception on all U.S. networks requires cable service in Canada and is available in small towns only near Canada's border with the United States. Thus, Multitel is much closer to the border than is either Notel or Unitel. As the crow flies, Multitel is about 305 miles from Notel and 245 miles from Unitel. In 1971, 92% of the occupied dwellings in Multitel had television sets and 85–90% of these were on the cable. Residents not on the cable received one U.S. channel (CBS) well, and some were able to pick up a weak Canadian (CBC) signal on occasion if they had an antenna.

To summarize the design of this research (see Table 1.1), in Phase 1 Notel had no television reception, Unitel had one channel (CBC), and Multitel had four channels (CBC, ABC, CBS, NBC). Notel obtained one TV channel (CBC) in November 1973, just after the first phase of data collection. The transmitter bringing CBC to Notel also improved recep-

TABLE 1.1
Design of the Research[a]

Community	Phase 1[b]	Phase 2[c]
Notel	No television reception	One channel: CBC
Unitel	One channel: CBC	Two channels: both CBC
Multitel	Four channels: CBC, ABC, CBS, NBC	Four channels: CBC, ABC, CBS, NBC

[a] CBC is the Canadian government-owned channel; ABC, CBS, and NBC are commercial U.S. channels.
[b] Just prior to television's arrival in Notel.
[c] Two years after Phase 1.

tion for Unitel and brought them a second CBC channel originating in a different city. With the exception of regional news and a few other local programs, the content of the two CBC channels received in Unitel was the same. The quality of reception and the number and types of channels available in Multitel did not change from Phase 1 to Phase 2. All three towns were studied just before television arrived in Notel and again 2 years later.

OVERVIEW OF THE QUESTIONS ASKED AND DATA OBTAINED

The major questions we asked about television's possible effects and the kind of information we obtained to answer these questions are summarized in Table 1.2. For each question, the measures, methods, hypotheses, results, and our conclusions are described in detail in Chapters 2 through 8. In addition, our findings and conclusions are summarized in Chapter 9. In this chapter, the practical and theoretical reasons for our choice of topics and hypotheses are discussed next. Those comments are followed by further information about our general procedures, that is, information applicable to the project as a whole.

Topics Studied

All studies of the effects of television focus on some variables and exclude others. Ours was no exception. The topics shown in Table 1.2 were selected in part on the basis of their salience in the literature when

TABLE 1.2

Summary of Questions Asked and Data Obtained

Chapter	Measures[a]	Age levels	
		Phase 1	Phase 2
	Does TV viewing affect the acquisition and/or maintenance of fluent reading skills?		
2	Individual, time-controlled presentation of standard reading test items[b]	Grades 2, 3, 8	Grades 2, 3, 4, 5, 8, 10
	Group administration of standard reading tests	Grades 1–7	
	How effectively does television teach vocabulary to children?		
3	PPVT, Stanford–Binet, and WISC vocabulary tests	Kindergarten, grades 1, 4, 7[c]	Grades 4, 6, 7, 9
	Does TV viewing affect children's visual-spatial ability?		
3	WISC Block Design task	Grades 4, 7	Grades 4, 6, 7, 9
	Does TV viewing affect performance on creativity tasks for children or adults?		
3	Alternate Uses and Pattern Meanings creativity tasks	Grades 4, 7	Grades 4, 6, 7, 9
8	Duncker Candle Problem	Adults	
	Nine Dot Problem		Adults
	Does the presence of TV in a community affect participation by adolescents and adults in leisure activities?		
4	Behavior settings list of community activities	Grades 7–12, adults	Grades 7–12, adults
	List of private leisure activities	Grades 7–12, adults	Grades 7–12, adults
	How did children and adults in the three towns use the available media?		
5	Television-viewing habits	Grades 1–12, adults	Grades 1–12, adults
	Use of other media		Grades 1–12, adults
	Does TV viewing affect children's sex-role attitudes and perceptions?		
6	Attitudes re peer behavior and characteristics	Grades 6, 9	Grades 6, 9
	Perceptions of own parents' behavior	Grades 6, 9	Grades 6, 9
	Does TV viewing cause aggressive behavior among children?		
7	Observations of behavior on school playgrounds	Grades 1, 2, 4, 5	Grades 1, 2, 3,
	Peer ratings	Grades 1, 2, 4, 5	Grades 1, 2, 3,
	Teacher ratings	Grades 1, 2, 4, 5	Grades 1, 2, 3,
	Does TV viewing affect adults' cognitive style?		
8	Embedded Figures Test	Adults	Adults
	Paragraph Completion Test	Adults	Adults

TABLE 1.2 (*Continued*)

Chapter	Measures[a]	Age levels Phase 1	Phase 2
	Does TV viewing affect adult personality or attitudes?		
8	Adjective checklist of personality characteristics	Adults	Adults
	Cantril personal concern scales		Adults
	Environmental Response Inventory	Adults	Adults
	Thing–Person Orientation	Adults	Adults
	Does intelligence play an important role in the impact of television in other areas?		
3	General IQ, based on group test scores[d]	Obtained from school records for grades 1–12	

[a] Except as indicated in footnote c, each measure was given in all three towns.

[b] A third phase of data also was collected, 2 years after Phase 2, in grade 2 (in all three towns).

[c] Vocabulary scores for children in kindergarten and grade 1 were obtained only in Notel and Unitel and only i Phase 1.

[d] Used as a control in other chapters.

the project was designed, and in part on the basis of our expertise. Our training as psychologists undoubtedly influenced the direction of the research, and the specific topics chosen were ones on which one or more of us had previously worked. Given those caveats, we tried to cover as wide a range as possible, including cognitive and social variables, and variables on which television's influence was expected to be positive, negative, or more difficult to predict. We also selected some variables for which television's impact was likely to occur more directly via its content, and others likely to be affected more indirectly via displacement of other activities. Both children and adults were studied, although as in most other research dealing with television, more emphasis was given to the former than the latter. Whenever possible, we tried to observe behavior rather than rely upon self-reports or ratings by others. This was not always feasible, of course. We did use self-report survey instruments to assess children's sex-role attitudes, participation in leisure activities, and media use by both children and adults, as well as personality and perceptions of the environment of adults. Whenever possible these instruments were given under supervision, for example, in an individual interview or in the classroom.

One of the strengths of this project is that all studies included more than one age level. Of primary consideration in choosing these age levels was the topic under consideration, based on previous literature and common sense. For example, grades 2 and 3 were selected as the focus of the reading skills study because the greatest gains in reading competence are made in those grades (as Chall, 1983, has since discussed). Grade 8 was included because we wanted to assess the influence of television on the maintenance as well as the acquisition of fluent reading skills. The second consideration in selecting age levels was the project as a whole. It was important to spread the research across all age levels and to avoid inundating any particular grades in the schools.

Topics Not Studied

With the benefit of hindsight, we can think of several topics we wish we had studied but did not. Some are discussed in Chapter 9; here, we will mention one. We attempted but failed to obtain time budget or time use data. In Phase 1, adults were sent forms by mail and asked to keep a diary for 1 week indicating how they spent their time. The response rate was so low (12%) that there was no point in analyzing the data or in collecting Phase 2 data. Discussions with people such as the postmaster indicated that many residents thought the information requested was nobody's business and required too much time. They were willing to answer questionnaires about their television use, their hobbies, and their participation in public leisure activities, but they were not willing to provide a diary.

Hypotheses

Our hypotheses about the possible effects of television, like the topics on which they rested, were based almost entirely on prevailing wisdom, that is, the previous literature. Since our research was designed soon after publication of the U.S. Surgeon General's report (NIMH, 1972), and the impetus for funding that investigation of television and social behavior was concern regarding potentially negative effects of television, it is not surprising that a number of our hypotheses were framed negatively. We want to emphasize, however, that this did not mean we began with a particular bias. As is often the case (Hornik, 1981), we were neophytes in research on television. We all had done basic research on the topics chosen for this project, but this was our first venture into the applied realm, so we began, in a real sense, with a clean slate. Our specific hypotheses reflect the literature rather than our personal views; indeed, we were skeptical that results obtained in laboratory or short-term field studies would hold up when examined in three communities over a relatively long time period.

MODES OF TV INFLUENCE

How might television affect its viewers? At a detailed level there are endless possibilities. Viewers might learn specific facts from television. They might gain a general impression of reality, or "world view." They might acquire knowledge of other lands and people. They might become more or less tolerant of behaviors observed on TV. They might acquire certain kinds of information-processing skills. They might spend more time with friends because they watch TV together, or they might spend less time with friends because they are home alone watching TV. They might interact less, more, or differently with others in their family, and so on. These potential effects of television can be grouped conceptually into two broad categories: content effects and displacement effects.

Discussions of television programming—what is shown on TV, the techniques with which it is portrayed, and how it affects viewers—focus on content. Learning specific facts, learning general attitudes, and changing one's tolerance for certain behaviors all are examples of content effects. Most research on television has involved questions about the impact of content, and the majority of these studies have dealt with a negative unintended effect of television, the impact of TV violence on viewers' aggressive behavior. It is a negative effect because in our society violence and aggression generally are discouraged rather than encouraged.[2] It is an unintended effect because although the violence and aggression were intentionally included in the program, this was not done to produce an increase in the aggressive behavior of viewers. Studies designed to assess whether children can learn to share or learn the letters of the alphabet are other examples of content effects research. In this case, however, they are studies of the intended positive effects of educational television or the unintended positive effects of entertainment programming. Investigations assessing whether a child chooses a toy recommended by his or her parent or a toy seen advertised in a TV commercial also are designed to evaluate the intended impact of television's content, although whether these are seen to be positive or negative probably depends on whether you are the manufacturer of the advertised toy or the child's parent. Interestingly, television's unintended effects have been studied more extensively than its intended effects (Siegel, 1980). When we hypothesized that some aspects of television's content would affect residents of Notel, Unitel, and Multitel, we were largely if not entirely concerned with unintended effects. In some cases these were hypothesized to be positive, and in others, negative. We expected on the basis of previous research that regular TV viewing would result in better vocabulary scores (Chapter 3) but that it also would lead to an increase in aggressive behavior (Chapter 7) and more stereotyped sex-role attitudes (Chapter 6).

When television was new, a variety of concerns were expressed about its potential displacement effects (e.g., Himmelweit et al., 1958; Schramm et al., 1961). For example, researchers investigated whether children went to bed later, spent less time on homework, read fewer or different materials, and so on. It is not surprising that concerns about television's content were less evident then, since people lacked the bases of comparison now available, for example, between public and commercial broadcasting within the United States, or between the programming available in the United Kingdom, Australia, or Japan and that available in Canada or the United States. What *is* surprising is that questions regarding displacement effects (other than effects on media use) have received less attention in recent years, especially given evidence that the decision to view takes precedence over what to view (Comstock, 1980). The statement that the average North American child spends more time watching TV than in school has been quoted so often that the source is unclear, but rather than leading to a discussion of the impact of time spent with television, the statement typically ushers in a discussion of the effects of the content to which children are exposed during those hours of viewing. This emphasis on content effects stands in contrast to the widely quoted statement that "the medium is the message" (McLuhan, 1964).

If the average North American child spends 3–4 hours a day with television (Comstock, Chaffee, Katzman, McCombs, & Roberts, 1978) it seems reasonable to believe this has an effect.[3] All children have to sleep, attend school, get to and from school, eat, and dress, and some children have to do homework and chores as well; the amount of discretionary time left for other activities is limited. What are the effects of this time taken away from other activities? This question was a major stimulus to our project. For example, the study dealing with participation in leisure activities (Chapter 4) addressed it specifically. In other instances we were careful to consider the possibility that both displacement and content-effects might account for the findings.

Conceptualization of the effects of television by simply distinguishing between content and displacement would, however, be overly simplistic. In particular, the displacement hypothesis requires considerable refinement. We must ask not only *whether* displacement occurs but more specifically *for whom* and *what* is displaced. In some circumstances the effect may be positive, in others, negative.

Children and adults do other things while "watching television" both in and out of the room. The stereotype of the mesmerized viewer is largely a myth. Anderson (1983; personal communication, April, 1984) and his colleagues have observed children watching television in their laboratories and are now analyzing data from an impressive project involving home observations. Of the 334 families in the study, 106 had time-lapse video equipment in their homes during a 10-day period. Two video cameras in the same room as the family television set were installed so the cameras came on intermittently when the set was turned on and provided a (soundless) picture of the people in the room, the television screen, and a printout of the date and time. Data for 221 children aged 11 years or under (94 of whom were 5-year-olds, the target age for the study), 12 adolescents, and 169 adults yielded the following results. Visual attention to the set by people in the room with television declined from 70% for ages 5–12 to 60% in adulthood. Five-year-olds looked at the set an average of 1.3 hours per day and were in the room with the set on 1.9 hours per day. These figures are lower than viewing estimates obtained by other researchers based on parent or self-reports. Although only 12.4% of the families initially contacted volunteered to have video-recording equipment in their homes, comparisons with control families indicated they were not a special group, so it is unlikely that they watched less television than the norm. Anderson's explanation for the discrepancy is that estimates obtained in previous research may be too high. A month before the videotaped observations, he asked parents to estimate how much television their children watched on average each morning, afternoon, and evening. For 5-year-olds the mean was 3.3 hours per day, which correlated only .21 with actual time spent in the room with the set on and only .14 with time looking at the screen. By contrast, parents' reports of hours of television viewing, based on detailed diaries they kept during the same period, correlated .84 with observations of time in the room and .67 with time looking at the screen. The parents' global estimates (obtained a month earlier) correlated .60 with their diary reports of time in the room.

What implications do these findings carry for studies based on parental and self-reports of amount of television viewing? (See Chapter 5 for further discussion of this issue.) At first glance Anderson's results are discouraging, since the expense and time involved in observations of home viewing are prohibitive, and many people are unwilling to keep diaries. In addition, the low correlations between parental estimates and the videorecorded observations suggest the estimates are not simply off by a constant factor which could be used as a correction. These results may explain in part why correlational studies tend to yield at best low and often nonsignificant relationships between reported hours of TV viewing and other behaviors. Anderson's data underline the strengths of experimental studies in which television exposure is manipulated, albeit only on a short-term basis. They also make clear the importance of natural experiments such as we studied in Notel, Unitel, and Multitel for understanding the long-term effects of television.

What are the implications of Anderson's findings for hypotheses about the displacement effects of television? The evidence that children and adults spend much of their TV-viewing time doing other things, both in the same room and out of it, indicates that we cannot speak simply of displacement of other activities. We must consider what sorts of things people time-share with television. What do they do while they are in the room with the set, and what do they do when they leave the room during periods in which they watch intermittently? Anderson's research will provide important information about the former but not the latter question. Let us speculate about both, in reverse order.

Certain kinds of activities cannot be time-shared with television, in particular, activities outside the home such as sports, attending meetings, dances, and so on. The Murray and Kippax (1978) results for their Australian No-TV, Low-TV, and High-TV towns illustrate this point. Linear decreases in children's involvement in outdoor activities and watching and playing sports occurred with exposure to television and were balanced by increases in playing with friends and toys and sitting around doing nothing. Brown, Cramond, and Wilde (1974) found that following the introduction of TV to a small Scottish village, children reported that indoor activity had become more enjoyable, and rule-governed outdoor activity was regarded less favorably. One of the studies we conducted in Notel, Unitel, and Multitel focused on participation in leisure activities (Chapter 4). We hypothesized that before Notel residents could watch television regularly they would participate in more community activities than would Unitel and Multitel residents, and that participation in Notel would drop following the arrival of television. In contrast, participation in indoor leisure activities might vary less with availability of television.

We shall use the phrase *time spent with television* to acknowledge that when an individual is watching a particular program he or she may do other things while watching the set (e.g., knit); may attend to the set auditorally but not visually (e.g., while eating a meal, perusing a newspaper, or playing a boardgame); and may leave the room intermittently to obtain food or carry out other activities (e.g., household chores, talking on the telephone, supervising children), either during commercial messages or during the program itself. Maybe one of the reasons Anderson obtained a discrepancy between estimates of viewing time and his observations of time in the room with the set on is that people usually think in terms of time spent with television. If I begin viewing a 1-hour program at 8 P.M., I say I have watched TV for an hour when 9 P.M. arrives even if I have checked on the laundry, had a snack, gone to the bathroom, and looked at a magazine during that same period. Since commercials comprise as much as 20 minutes of each program hour, this may be the rule rather than the exception. In addition, there probably are large individual and situational differences in such behavior, which may explain the low correlation between Anderson's parental estimates and his observational data. For example, Anderson's (1983) own findings indicate that young children are typically more "glued to" the set on Saturday morning than on weekday evenings, perhaps because they can more readily comprehend the programming (Anderson & Lorch, 1983).

We have said that time spent with television or watching television precludes activities outside the home. It is our hypothesis that TV also precludes some activities inside the home, in particular, those requiring certain levels of mental concentration or elaboration. An individual may be able to draw, talk, or do certain household chores while watching television, but activities such as problem solving, serious practice of a musical instrument, memorization, and studying are either impossible or less efficient. Again, there undoubtedly are individual differences in the extent to which such activities are precluded by TV viewing, and probably there also are group differences. These are likely to include (but not be limited to) chronological age, intelligence, experience with the activity in question, and television literacy (knowledge of television and its formal properties, i.e., production techniques). In addition to displacing activities which require mental concentration, the format and content of television may discourage mental elaboration, or "mindful" as opposed to "mindless" information processing (Langer, 1982), as Salomon (1983) contends. (See Chapters 3 and 8 for further discussion of this point).

In this project we hypothesized that television would have an impact via displacement on certain activities which require a level of mental concentration largely precluded by TV viewing. These were reading, for children in the process of learning to read (Chapter 2), and creativity and problem solving (Chapters 3 and 8), because performance is dependent on experience with self-generated activities (perhaps when bored), on persistence, and on mindful information processing.

Anderson's own laboratory data (Anderson & Lorch, 1983) help to explain the discrepancy between time spent actually looking at the set and time spent in the room with the television. Viewers auditorally monitor what is going on and look at the set when they hear something which catches their attention. The fact that blind people "watch" television and movies is only one indication that the auditory channel provides considerable information. The home viewing data obtained by Anderson and his colleagues not only provide important information about the uses of television but contribute considerably to our understanding of the processes involved in its impact by forcing us to think about these processes in more complex ways.

In sum, our research was designed to investigate the effects of television via both its content (see Chapter 6 on sex-role attitudes, Chapter 7 on aggressive behavior, and sections dealing with vocabulary in Chapter 3) and via displacement of other activities (see Chapter 4 on participation in leisure activities, Chapter 2 on reading skills, the sections of Chapter 8 dealing with adult problem-solving behavior, and the sections of Chapter 3 dealing with creativity).

COMPARABILITY OF THE THREE COMMUNITIES

It was important that, except for the availability of television, the three towns in this natural experiment be as similar as possible. Random assignment of people to groups is the best method of ensuring that pre-existing group differences do not account for any changes observed in a study. Even with random assignment the groups may differ by chance, particularly if they are not large. In this case random assignment was impossible, so in selecting the towns, we considered as many potentially relevant factors as possible. The demographic information listed in Table 1.3, based on 1971 census figures, was the best available prior to the initial (1973) phase of data collection. Some information about parental occupation obtained during interviews with the school children also is provided in Table 1.3. Additional information about the towns is listed in Table 1.4.

It would be incorrect to say that the communities were identical except for the availability of television. Their origins and histories have been different, and each has a distinct sense of identity and local pride as well as special problems. Nevertheless, although the towns differ in minor ways on one or another variable, the similarities are much more striking. Moreover, the differences are not systematic. For example, one index of socioeconomic status, mean income, favored Multitel in the 1971 census, but another, education, favored Notel.

Two points in Table 1.4 deserve special comment. The first deals with educational facilities. Since the one school in Unitel did not go beyond grade 10 in Phase 1, eleventh and twelfth graders had to attend school elsewhere. Many went to Notel and boarded there during the week (in a school dormitory for that purpose). This meant they could not watch television during the week when they resided in Notel, but they could do so on weekends when at home in Unitel. Had there been more of these students it would have been interesting to study their adjustments as they

TABLE 1.3
Comparability of the Three Towns: Census Information and Interviews

	Notel	Unitel	Multitel
	1971 Canadian census information		
Population within town limits[a]	658	693	872
Town area (acres)	354	N.A.	375
Principal sources of income	Logging, farming, railroad	Logging, railroad	Logging, mining
Mean income, head[b]	$7377	$6854	$8055
Family heads with English as official language	88%	93%	95%
Mother tongue English	74%	81%	83%
Proportion of experienced labor force in blue-collar jobs	62%	72%	77%
Family heads educated beyond high school	37%	23%	21%
Birthplace Canada	77%	90%	77%
	1973 parental occupation[c]		
Professional, business, supervisory	11%	7%	9%
Skilled work, farming	57%	64%	65%
Unskilled work	29%	21%	18%
Unemployed	3%	7%	8%

[a] The population served by each community was about 4 times larger. That is, about 3000 people used the town as a center for stores, schools, and so on.

[b] Canadian dollars.

[c] Based on information obtained in interviews with school children.

moved from living with television on weekends to living without it on weekdays. Such data would be difficult to interpret, however, because the students also had made a number of other life-style changes by living in a dormitory away from home. The absence in Phase 1 of grade 11 and 12 students in Unitel and the presence of experienced TV viewers among the Phase 1, Notel grade 11 and 12 students is one of the reasons we did not focus on this age level in our research. As Table 1.4 indicates, by Phase 2, Unitel had two schools covering the same grades as Notel and Multitel.

The second noteworthy point in Table 1.4 has to do with recreational facilities. One of the Phase 1 differences among the towns was that only Notel had an indoor movie theater. This theater went out of business within about a year of the introduction of television. Drive-in movies were available on summer evenings within an hour's drive to residents of all three towns in both phases of the study. In their study of two Canadian

TABLE 1.4

Comparability of the Three Towns: Descriptive Information

Transportation links	Each town on well maintained highway. Rail freight service to each town. Scheduled daily bus service to each town. Canadian rail passenger service to Notel and Unitel; U.S. rail passenger service to Multitel. Commercial airport 120 miles from Notel, 175 miles from Unitel, 50 miles from Multitel; each town has an unpaved landing strip of about 3000 feet.
Relationship to environs	In each case the village is used as the major center for routine trade, entertainment, and education.
Educational facilities 1973–1974	Notel: grades 1–7 in elementary school, grades 8–12 in junior–senior secondary school. Unitel: grades 1–10 in single school. Most grade 11 and 12 Unitel students boarded and attended school in Notel during the week, returning home on weekends. Multitel: grades 1–7 in elementary school, grades 8–12 in junior–senior secondary school.
1975–1976	In all three towns, grades 1–7 in elementary school, grades 8–12 in junior–senior secondary. (Unitel's new senior school was built between the phases of this project.)
Commercial core	All three towns had a similar complement of essential services with an organized business community and a chamber of commerce.
Medical services 1973–1974	Notel: regional hospital and resident physician. Unitel: no hospital or clinic; residents went to Notel or to another town, both about 55 miles away. Multitel: resident physician's clinic; hospital about 50 miles away. None of the towns had a resident dentist; a traveling dentist visited Notel and Unitel, and Multitel residents went out of town to the dentist.
1975–1976	Unitel had a resident physician; otherwise the situations were unchanged.
Civic government	All towns had a mayor and council, town clerk, Royal Canadian Mounted Police detachment, department of highways yard, and representative of the forestry branch.
Communication links other than television	Post office in each town. Telephone in all towns. Radio reception from outside stations available in each town.
Recreational facilities	Notel: indoor movie theater in 1973–1974 that was out of business by 1975–1976; curling rink; skating arena; ballpark. Unitel: drive-in movie theater (summer only); curling rink; skating arena; ballpark. Multitel: no movie theater; curling rink; skating arena (condemned in late 1973; new arena built by 1975–1976); ballpark; swimming pool.
Newspapers 1973–1974	Notel and Unitel had local weekly newspapers; Multitel had had one but it was no longer functional. Multitel had a section published regularly in the local paper of a community 55 miles away.
1975–1976	All three towns had weekly local newspapers.

TABLE 1.4 (*Continued*)

Arts and culture	Each town had infrequent concerts by visiting groups, usually arranged through a school.
	Each town had a small library with one paid librarian and volunteer assistants.
Industries	For all three towns, an important element of the forestry industry operated in the vicinity.
	Agriculture (mainly cattle ranching) was present in all three towns, to a major extent in Notel, and somewhat less in Unitel and Multitel.
	The railroad was a source of jobs in Notel and Unitel, and in Multitel, some people were employed in mining.

towns, one with and one without television, Schramm et al. (1961) reported that Radiotown had one indoor and one outdoor movie theater. They did not collect follow-up data in either Radiotown or Teletown, but did mention that 2 years prior to their study Teletown had had an indoor and an outdoor theater, which had both closed in the interim. Townspeople attributed the closures to television. Notel residents in our study did likewise, and the owners of the Unitel drive-in theater (which was not their sole source of income) told us that attendance had dropped dramatically following the introduction of television to Unitel. In Australia, Murray and Kippax (1978) found that children in their No-TV town reported spending significantly more of their leisure time at the cinema than did children in their Low- and High-TV towns. In short, the facts that Notel had an indoor movie theater in Phase 1 but not Phase 2 and that indoor theaters in Unitel and Multitel had gone out of business prior to Phase 1 are probably best understood as an economic consequence of the introduction of television, rather than a confounding variable describing an antecedent difference among the towns.

In addition to being similar on the factors described in Tables 1.3 and 1.4, the towns had similar geographical features and climates. All three are in valleys near mountains. The climates are hot and dry in summer and cold and snowy in winter. To our knowledge, there were no major social changes in terms of such things as bus, rail, or plane service during the 2-year period between the first and second phases of data collection. The road linking Notel and Unitel was improved at about the same time as television arrived, but this did not affect Notel's access to the nearest larger community and commercial airport, which are in the opposite direction. For all of these reasons, we feel confident that the availability of television was the overwhelming difference between Notel and the control towns.

NOTEL AS A TOWN WITHOUT TV

As we stated earlier, Notel was not totally without TV in 1973. By vicissitude of the location of their houses, some residents of the area served by the town did receive TV reception on a regular basis prior to installation of the repeating transmitter. Reception was variable, but never good. We heard numerous tales of people watching "Hockey Night in Canada" and never seeing the puck. The presence of people in Notel who were able to watch TV on occasion in their own homes, at friends' homes, or on weekends when they visited friends or relatives in other communities (e.g., Unitel) resulted in a Phase 1 arithmetic mean for Notel students of 4.7 hours of TV viewing per week. This compared with the Phase 1 means for Unitel and Multitel students of 25.1 and 31.2 hours per week, respectively. Most Notel children, however, watched no TV at all in the first phase of the study; the median number of hours per week, that is, the number of hours above and below which 50% of the Notel sample watched, was 0. Fully 76% of the Notel students in grades 1–12 reported watching 0 hours of television per week, by comparison with only 11% of the Unitel sample and 3% of the Multitel sample. The Phase 1 median hours of TV viewing for Unitel (23.5 hours per week) and Multitel (29.3 hours per week) were much closer to the means for those towns, indicating more even distributions around the means. A more detailed discussion of television-viewing habits is presented in Chapter 5. The information reported here is sufficient to confirm that in Phase 1, Notel residents differed radically from Unitel and Multitel residents, and from typical North Americans, in their usual television-viewing habits.

Despite these low figures for actual viewing, Notel residents were not naive about TV. Virtually all had seen television during their travels and most took every opportunity to watch it. One Notel family told us they had a portable TV set in their recreational vehicle and watched on their travels whenever they could pick up reception. Notel residents wanted TV; the vigorous activities of the town's television lobby laid the groundwork for acquisition of the repeating CBC transmitter. In our opinion, the fact that Notel residents knew about TV and watched when they could is a methodological strength rather than weakness. It is difficult to make causal inferences about television's effects by comparing set owners and nonowners in communities with television reception, since ownership varies systematically with a number of other factors, including socioeconomic status. Coffin (1955) and Robinson (1972) have discussed the problems with such research. By contrast, Notel residents were not a special group of people who chose not to own a TV set or not to watch television.

They were typical North Americans, except that unlike other North Americans and unlike residents of Unitel and Multitel, they couldn't watch TV on a regular basis.

DESCRIPTION OF TELEVISION AVAILABLE IN THE TOWNS

Some familiarity with the amount and type of television programming in the three towns will be helpful in interpreting the results. In particular, knowledge of the similarities and differences between CBC television, the Canadian government-owned network, and the television portrayed on ABC, CBS, and NBC, the three major U.S. networks, may be useful.

Hours of Programming

The first distinction between the CBC programming available in Unitel in both phases (and in Notel in Phase 2) and that available in Multitel (ABC, CBC, CBS, and NBC in both phases) is that there was less of it. On weekdays CBC programming did not begin until 9:30 A.M. On Saturday and Sunday it usually began at 8:00 A.M. In contrast, programming began at 6:00 A.M. in Multitel on weekdays and at 6:30 A.M. on weekends. The major implication of this difference is that Unitel children in Phase 1 and Notel and Unitel children in Phase 2 could not watch television on weekday mornings before going to school. Programming ended for the day on CBC with the late movie which began around midnight, except on Saturday, when it began at 1:00 A.M. ABC, CBS, and NBC programming ended at 1:30 A.M. Sunday through Thursday, and at 2:30 or 3:00 A.M. on Friday and Saturday.

The mean number of hours of television typically available per week was 139 in Multitel and 117 in Unitel and Notel (Phase 2 only). The mean daily hours of programming available Monday through Thursday were 19.6 in Multitel versus 16.2 in the other towns; for Friday through Sunday the analogous figures were 20.1 and 17.5, respectively.[4]

In short, a major difference between Multitel and the other towns was the greater amount of television available, in terms of both number of channels and hours of programming. The difference in hours (about 3 hours per day) was smaller, however, than the difference in the Australian study conducted by Murray and Kippax (1977, 1978). The Australian Broadcasting Commission channel was on 59.5 hours per week by comparison with 98.8 hours for the commercial channel, yielding a mean difference of 5.6 hours per day. Note also that there were fewer hours of programming in both Australian communities than in our study. CBC was available 2.6 hours more per day than the Australian commercial channel and 8.2 hours more per day than the Australian government-owned channel. The difference between the hours of television available in Multitel and the two Australian towns was even greater (5.7 and 11.4 hours per day, respectively). The greater availability of television in Multitel was reflected in greater exposure, that is, more hours of reported viewing, but the similarities in exposure between Multitel and Unitel in Phase 1 and all three towns in Phase 2 were more impressive than the differences (see Chapter 5).

Content of CBC versus U.S. Networks:
General Comments

Unfortunately, there is relatively little empirical evidence documenting general similarities and differences among the major North American television channels. We are currently doing content analysis research with that goal in mind; in the meantime, the following comparisons are made cautiously. Although CBC is government owned, its programming probably is more similar to the commercial U.S. networks than to the government-owned networks in the United Kingdom (British Broadcasting Corporation, or BBC) and Australia (Australian Broadcasting Commission, or ABC) or to public television (PBS) in the United States.[5] This statement rests upon several lines of reasoning. First, CBC carries advertisements, as do ABC (U.S.), CBS, and NBC, whereas BBC, ABC (Australia), and PBS do not. Commercials occur on most CBC programs, with the exception of occasional special shows and documentaries and programming aimed at children under 12 years of age. Second, BBC, ABC (Australia), and PBS all have a mandate to provide educational programming for both children and adults. ABC (Australia), for example, devotes fully 34% of its weekly broadcast time to specific instructional programming intended for the schools; this figure stands in contrast to 3% for the Australian commercial channel (Murray & Kippax, 1977). CBC does carry significantly more informative programming than do the commercial U.S. networks or the Canadian commercial network (CTV), but this is not particularly intended for school use (Longstaffe & Williams, 1985). In general, CBC focuses more on entertainment than on education. A final indication that CBC differs from PBS is that Canadians contribute heavily to the financial support of PBS, which is available in Canada via cable.[6]

CBC has a mandate to carry a minimum of 60% "Canadian content." This includes programming produced in Canada as well as programming produced elsewhere which meets a set of guidelines for Canadian content (based on the status of actors, directors, and so on). The remaining 40% of programming is purchased from a variety of sources, including roughly 30% from the United States. The 60% Canadian content rule applies across the broadcast day, so the proportion of programming meeting the guidelines varies by time of day (e.g., evening vs. afternoon). Most imported programs are shown during the evening, between 7:00 and 10:00 P.M. (that is, in prime time).

Content Differences: Children's Programming

Children's programming on CBC differed in at least two ways from that available on ABC, CBS, and NBC. First, CBC has had a policy since September 1974 of no advertising on programming intended primarily for children under 12 years of age. The only exceptions are public service announcements and advertisements for other CBC programs. This difference has no special implication for this particular study, but we do plan to pursue it in the future. Second, CBC does not show many cartoons, except in the context of "World of Disney," special animated programs, and, at the time of our study, "Bugs Bunny." This policy, coupled with the lack of English-language programming early on weekend mornings (see note 4), meant the Saturday morning TV diet of children in Notel (Phase 2) and Unitel (both phases) differed somewhat from that of children in Multitel.

Content Differences: Portrayal of Aggression and Sex Roles

The effects of two specific types of content, aggression and sex-role portrayals, were studied in this project, so we shall briefly describe the available programming in these areas.

Cartoons have been found in several studies to contain high levels of aggression (Comstock et al., 1978; Greenberg, Edison, Korzenny, Fernandez-Collado, & Atkin, 1980; Williams, Zabrack & Joy, 1977, 1982). The relative absence of cartoons on CBC is therefore one indication that CBC may portray less aggression than do ABC, CBS, and NBC. Another indication is that in 1976 CBC carried only two police detective shows per week, "Police Story," produced in the United States, and "Sidestreet," produced in Canada. "Sidestreet" tended to focus on social issues and to contain less aggression than U.S.-produced detective programs (Williams et al., 1977, 1982). Finally, content analyses have shown that English-language programming on CBC contains less aggression than programming on U.S. networks; this was true both overall (Williams et al., 1977; 1982) and when CBC news was compared with CBS news (Singer, 1970).

Williams et al. (1977, 1982) compared 26 programs taped from CBC with 37 programs taped from ABC, CBS, and NBC. Content analyses focused on the portrayal of conflict, with more severe levels (aggression and violence) differentiated from milder forms (argument, nonaggressive conflict). The proportion of program segments containing conflict was remarkably similar; 31.3% for programs taped from CBC and 31.4% for those taped from the U.S. networks.[7] However, the *level* of conflict differed, with greater emphasis on more severe conflict in the U.S. programming. Further, the U.S. networks spent a greater proportion of the program time depicting aggression. They portrayed more aggression in the lead-ins to programs and more often used a technique Williams et al. (1977, 1982) labeled *build-up to aggression* than did CBC. Build-up to aggression prolongs the period devoted to aggression without extending the actual time spent depicting aggression. For example, the audience may be shown an assassin creeping up on an unsuspecting victim; the viewer is waiting for an aggressive act that invariably follows. When the proportionate duration of aggression in the program lead-ins was added to the proportionate duration of build-up to aggression and the proportionate duration of actual aggression, the programs shown on ABC, CBS, or NBC spent almost twice as much time on aggression (16.6% of the program time, exclusive of commercials) as programs shown on CBC (9.3%).

In sum, the available evidence indicates that CBC probably portrays less aggression than do the three major U.S. networks. The documented differences are not large, however, and some of the most violent programming in the sample analyzed by Williams et al. (1977, 1982) occurred in CBC documentaries (e.g., those focusing on war and on terrorists or assassins).

If there has been relatively little content analysis research comparing aggression in Canadian and U.S. television programming, there has been even less research comparing sex-role portrayals. The only study of which we are aware (Halpern & Ethier, 1977) focused on dramatic fiction shown between 7 and 11 P.M. The sample (a subsample of the programming analyzed by Williams et al., 1977, 1982) included shows taped from the three U.S. networks and from CBC as well as two other Canadian channels. The major analyses involved comparison of the sex roles portrayed in commercials produced in Canada with those produced in the

United States. There was no difference in the frequency of female central figures, age of central figures, location of central figures (home vs. occupation), sex of voice-over, sex of product users or authority figures, type of argument, or global sex-role portrayal of adult or teenage figures.[8] However, children were portrayed in traditional (as opposed to nontraditional or neutral) sex roles more often in U.S.-produced than in Canadian-produced commercials. In addition, the proportions of female and male central figures in certain roles differed for the U.S. sample but not the Canadian sample. In U.S.-produced commercials central figures portrayed as parents, homemakers, and sex objects were more often females, whereas central figures portrayed in occupational roles were more often male. There was no difference in Canadian commercials in the type of benefit shown accruing to product users, but in U.S.-produced commercials females more often offered or reaped self-enhancement rewards, whereas males more often were shown in conjunction with practical rewards. U.S. commercials also more often depicted women advertising home products and men advertising business and automotive products. There were no significant differences in this regard in Canadian commercials.

Taken together, these data provide some evidence that Canadian-produced commercials shown in prime time during the 2 weeks sampled in May 1976 portrayed women and men in less stereotyped ways than did U.S.-produced commercials shown during the same period. Commercial messages, however, represent only a small proportion of the sex roles seen on television. Halpern and Ethier (1977) did not ask whether the sexes were portrayed differently in the programs in which these commercials were embedded, but they did conduct some overall analyses on the programs. The sample of 27 programs included 12 taped from ABC, CBS, or NBC and 15 taped from Canadian channels, of which 6 were from CBC. Only 4 of the 27 programs were produced in Canada. For the sample as a whole, almost 3 times as many male as female central characters were portrayed (73% versus 27%), and the pattern for secondary characters was similar (72% versus 28%). Of all central figures coded, 77% were shown in traditional sex roles, 8% were shown in progressive roles, 6% were in reversed roles, and 9% were in neutral roles. The comparable proportions for secondary figures were 63%, 14%, 2%, and 21%. These data are consistent with findings based on analyses restricted to U.S. programming and, therefore, imply that CBC programming did not differ much from that available on the U.S. networks in terms of sex-role portrayals. This is not surprising, since much of evening CBC programming is U.S. produced. The finding that, if anything, Canadian-produced commercials were less stereotyped than those produced in the

United States could be interpreted as an indication that our study of television and sex roles (Chapter 6) provided a conservative test. Note, however, that the data on students' sex-role attitudes were obtained in late 1973 and late 1975, whereas the programs analyzed by Halpern and Ethier were taped in May 1976. It is possible that sex-role portrayals on CBC, ABC, CBS, or NBC changed in the intervening period.

Content Comparisons: Summary

On the basis of their review of Singer's (1970) data for news shown on CBC and CBS, and other research comparing the U.S. networks, Comstock et al. (1978) concluded "that the U.S. networks are indeed more similar to each other than any one is to the Canadian network" (p. 61, referring to CBC). The evidence discussed earlier in this chapter supports this view. It also indicates, however, that CBC is not in the same genre as BBC, ABC (Australia), and PBS. CBC is similar to the commercial U.S. networks in some ways and different in others. This made predictions about the pattern of television's effects involving Unitel and Multitel difficult, and it underscored the importance of including both towns in the project.

INTERVAL BETWEEN FIRST AND SECOND PHASES

One potential problem in before and after studies of TV is the length of time it takes for television to saturate the community. The process of acquiring sets and becoming regular viewers might be slow. More important, speed of acquisition of television sets varies with socioeconomic status; rich people acquire sets sooner, on average, than poor people. This was one of the problems with some studies conducted when television was a new phenomenon in the 1950s. It was not a problem in Notel; virtually everyone acquired a TV set immediately. As we noted, Notel residents knew about television and almost all were keen to have it. Indeed, many people had acquired TV sets in anticipation of the new transmitter and had them hooked up waiting for reception to begin. To our surprise and consternation, when we began collecting data in the schools, 52% of Notel children answered yet to the question, "Is there a TV set in your home?" Then we began asking, "Does your TV set work—can you watch it?" Almost all these children answered no, so we relaxed and continued. We did not document the speed of saturation, but by the time we returned 2 years later, more than 90% of the Notel residents had a working TV set. Moreover, their television-viewing patterns were similar to those of Unitel and Multitel residents, and in the same range as those of other North Americans (see Chapter 5 for further discussion).

If 2 years was a long enough interval for normal viewing patterns to become well established, was it too long? We wanted to study the same individuals before and after the arrival of TV in Notel. Attrition is often a problem in longitudinal research, but in this study, the retention rate was both high and remarkably similar across the towns.[9] The proportions of Phase 1 school children in grades 1 through 10 who were still in the schools 2 years later were 72%, 71%, and 72% for Notel, Unitel, and Multitel, respectively. We also knew this was a period of rapid social change; major changes in economic or social conditions might affect all three towns, either similarly or differently, and make it difficult to relate findings to differences in the availability of television. We chose an interval of 2 years because it was long enough for people to have settled down to regular viewing patterns but not too long to yield problems with attrition or interpretation of the findings in the context of other changes.

CONTACTING THE COMMUNITIES AND OBTAINING COOPERATION

When the research was being planned in July 1973, we understood that television reception would begin in Notel the following summer. In September we learned that the people installing the transmitter were aiming for a mid-November deadline so Notel residents could watch the Grey Cup, the finale of the Canadian football season. This news was startling, to put it mildly, but with considerable effort we managed to obtain the baseline (i.e., Phase 1) data before television arrived in Notel. The first phase of data collection in Unitel and Multitel followed immediately.

How much information should people being studied have about the research in which they are involved? This is a thorny question. Our intention was to walk a middle line. On the one hand, we knew from Rosenthal's (1966) research on experimenter bias that behavior may change in the direction of the hypotheses if the people being studied or those administering the tasks are aware of the hypotheses. On the other hand, we were concerned about research ethics and also were anxious to obtain the continuing cooperation of the three communities. We felt it was important to be well intentioned and honest in our interactions with the residents. We first obtained the cooperation of the elementary and secondary schools in each town, including the necessary approval from the school districts involved. A letter was sent to the parents of each child explaining that some faculty members and students from the University of British Columbia would be in town over the next several weeks to conduct various studies with the school children and adults of the community, and that we were interested in finding out more about life in small communities. It indicated that Notel had been selected for study because it did not yet have television reception, whereas Unitel and Multitel had had it for several years. The town's real names, not the pseudonyms, were used in the letter. Aside from these statements, no further mention of television was made and no explanation of any hypotheses was given. The dissemination of the letters to parents via the schools meant most residents were aware that some people from the university were in town. Other contacts were made on an individual basis, either by mail or in person, depending upon the topic under study. In general, we tried to "keep a low profile" in the communities to diminish the possibility that people would change their behavior because we were studying them (i.e., the Hawthorne effect, Roethlisberger & Dickson, 1939).

Contacts during the initial phase of data collection were made to secure cooperation only for that phase; there was no mention that we might want to return some time hence. We did not plan a follow-up until we had seen that the results of the first phase were sufficiently interesting to warrant a second phase. When the decision to collect more data had been made and new funding obtained, we reestablished contact with the schools and school districts. Again, cooperation was obtained with little difficulty. Our study may be unusual in this regard (Vidich, Bensman, & Stein, 1964).

WHO WAS STUDIED WHEN

Upon returning to all three towns after a 2-year interval, we collected both longitudinal and cross-sectional data (see note 9). For example, before Notel had television we assessed the creativity of children in grades 4 and 7 in all three towns. Two years later, the same children, now in grades 6 and 9, constituted our longitudinal, or panel, sample. In Phase 2 we also assessed the creativity of children in grades 4 and 7, as we had done in Phase 1. These students comprised our across-time sample. We therefore were able to make longitudinal comparisons, cross-sectional comparisons among the towns within each phase of the study, and across-time comparisons between the two phases.

Longitudinal research has several advantages. It enables investigators to examine the processes of change over time and ask questions concerning stability and continuity of development within individuals. It also has disadvantages. Attrition has already been mentioned; people may move and be unavailable for follow-up. Another major disadvantage is that change due to normal development and maturation may be confounded with the changes of major interest. For example, we might have studied longitudinally the aggressive behavior of Notel first graders before television arrived and again 2 years later. If we found an increase in aggression, we would not know whether it occurred because third graders normally behave more aggressively than first graders, whether the arrival of TV led to an increase in aggression for these children, or whether some combination had occurred. We avoided this potential problem of confounding developmental change with changes due to television by studying children at a minimum of two age levels. In addition, by studying three towns we were able to assess *differential change* as evidence of television's impact. We were looking for a change in the behavior of Notel residents relative to change in the behavior of residents of the other towns. Obtaining across-time, cross-sectional data as well as longitudinal data in the second phase of the project provided a further check that any changes observed occurred differentially in relation to television's availability.

MAKING CAUSAL INFERENCES IN NATURAL EXPERIMENTS

Before moving on to the individual studies in the project, some general comments are in order concerning causal inferences in social science research. Such causal statements as "throwing the ball caused the window to break" must be made with care. We usually do not observe the process but instead are in the position of the person who returns home to find a broken window and on the floor a baseball, a hammer, and a rock.

The first problem is to define what constitutes an experiment. In their discussion of the pros and cons of conducting true experiments and quasi-experiments in field settings, Cook and Campbell (1976) defined experiments as "any experimenter-controlled or naturally occurring event (a "treatment") which intervenes in the lives of respondents and whose probable consequences can be empirically assessed" (p. 224). The distinction between true and quasi-experimental designs is that in true experiments people are assigned randomly to treatment groups by the experimenter, whereas in quasi-experiments they are not. Our study of the inception of television in Notel therefore qualifies as a quasi-experiment conducted in a field setting (defined by Cook and Campbell as "any setting which respondents do not perceive to have been set up for the primary purpose of conducting research," p. 224). According to Cook and

Campbell (1976, 1979), the extent to which causal inferences can be made in interpreting the results of such studies depends largely on the extent to which it is possible to rule out alternative hypotheses to explain the obtained results. They outline a number of categories of alternative hypotheses, which they call *threats to internal validity*. We have found it helpful in assessing our research findings to examine the design of our study in relation to each of these potential threats to internal validity. A brief outline is given here; for more detailed information concerning this issue the reader may wish to consult Cook and Campbell (1979).

A spurious causal relationship may be inferred in a quasi-experiment conducted in a field setting due to some quirk of history. In our project, history could pose problems, in general, if some societal change affected all three communities, or locally, if some event coincided with the inception of television in Notel and was actually responsible for the observed changes. To our knowledge no such event occurred. If it did, the outcome probably would not be a sensible pattern of results in relation to the availability of television. It is even more unlikely that such a sensible pattern would occur consistently for different age levels and both sexes.

Maturation between pretest and posttest of the people studied is a potentially spurious explanation of change. As we discussed earlier, children at several age levels were studied both longitudinally and cross-sectionally in all three towns, so we would be able to separate change due to maturation from possible television-related change.

Repeated testing also can be a problem for researchers; people may remember certain questions, or may simply become "test-wise," that is, better at taking tests. This threat to internal validity can be ruled out on several bases. First, all three towns were studied in the same way, so one would have to hypothesize differential test-wisdom in order to explain the patterns of results obtained. Second, some of the measures, for example, observations of aggressive behavior on school playgrounds, did not involve test taking. Third, the relatively long interval between phases of the study and infrequent testing also make this an unlikely explanation of the results. To our surprise, children and adults remembered only vaguely, if at all, that researchers had been around 2 years previously. Fourth, in some cases different tasks were given when longitudinal data were being collected, specifically because of the repeated-testing problem. Finally, the project was designed as a set of interlocking substudies. In selecting grade levels for each of the substudies, we kept in mind the problem of repeated testing and did not inundate the children and teachers at any particular grade level. This meant compromise was sometimes necessary in choosing grade levels for any individual study, but in our opinion, it strengthened the project as a whole.

If there are instrumentation changes between the pretest and posttest, this, rather than the hypothesized factor such as television, may account for the obtained changes. In most of our studies the same measures were employed in both phases. When measures were changed to deal with the testing threat to internal validity, only some measures were changed, so comparisons could be made between performance on the new and old measures. In some cases the personnel administering the measures changed from the first to the second phase of data collection, and, theoretically, this could result in a change in the use of measures. Again, this was one of the reasons we designed our research so as to be able to examine patterns of findings across several ages and towns, rather than relying only on individual pre–post comparisons. The personnel were consistent across ages and towns within each phase of the project.

Selection refers to the problem that preexisting differences among experimental groups may account for any observed effect. This, of course, is the reason for random assignment. It is possible that the kind of people who reside in Notel are different from the kind of people who reside in Unitel and in Multitel, but we have been unable to find evidence of any systematic differences in the census data and other demographic information collected. Attrition between Phase 1 and 2 was low and similar in the three towns, so the arrival of television in Notel did not prompt an exodus of people who had chosen to live there because the town lacked television. Using two towns as controls rather than just one and searching for sensible patterns of difference among them also mitigate against selection as an explanation of the findings.

Mortality or differential dropout from the treatment groups may result in selection bias: The groups may contain different types of people at the posttest even though they were similar at the pretest. This problem can be circumvented to some extent by examining the retention rate of longitudinal subjects, which as we noted earlier was high and remarkably similar across the towns. We also tested to see whether there were town differences in Phase 1 on the measures used in each study among the people who subsequently dropped out, and whether the dropouts differed in Phase 1 from the people retained in the study. In only 1 of more than 20 tests conducted was a statistically significant difference obtained, and this would be expected by chance.

Interactions between selection and other threats to internal validity may produce results erroneously interpreted as treatment effects. The most common problem is the interaction between selection and maturation occurring when experimental groups are composed of different kinds of persons maturing at different rates. The fact that we either included all residents in each town at the age levels we were studying or used the same criteria for selection across towns diminishes the likelihood of this problem in our research. Further, we know from census data that the towns were similar in terms of socioeconomic status, one of the factors most likely to be involved in a selection–maturation interaction. Finally, by studying children at several different age levels in each of the areas of interest we were able to examine the extent to which change occurred in relation to the availability of television at different points in development.

Ambiguity about the direction of causal influence is more likely to be a problem in correlational than in quasi-experimental designs such as ours, where the timing of the treatment, in this case the inception of television, is clear. Indeed, as we have noted, one of the motivations for conducting our research was the opportunity to help arbitrate the direction of influence in the relationship between television viewing and the viewers' behavior.

Diffusion or imitation of the treatment is a problem when the experimental group and the control groups can communicate: The control group(s) may inadvertently receive the treatment. For example, if one child in a family participates in a special program designed to improve certain skills, that child's siblings also may be affected either directly, through teaching by parents or the treated sibling, or indirectly, through changed parental attitudes toward children and what they can accomplish. In our design, Unitel and Multitel already had the treatment, that is, television, so diffusion or imitation could not occur, except as we discussed earlier in the sense that a few Notel residents had access to television. However, this would have had the effect of reducing the likelihood of differences between Notel and the other towns, making comparisons more conservative, and thus add credibility to any significant differences obtained.

Four of the remaining threats to internal validity outlined by Cook and Campbell (1976) are not applicable to the natural experiment we studied: statistical regression toward the mean when groups are preselected on the basis of certain measures; compensatory equalization of treatment because of ethical considerations concerning the availability of potentially positive benefits; compensatory rivalry (wherein control groups make up for being the underdogs); and resentful demoralization of respondents receiving less desirable treatments. It is perhaps worth noting here that resentful demoralization has been a problem for field studies of the relationship between TV and aggressive behavior in which existing groups have been assigned to particular television diets. People assigned to nonaggressive fare typically resent not being able to watch their favorite programs.

In sum, this research project was designed so each of the many potential threats to internal validity described by Cook and Campbell (1979) can plausibly be eliminated, making it "possible to make confident conclusions about whether a relationship is probably causal" (p. 55).

GENERALIZING FROM THE FINDINGS

The question of external validity, or the degree to which findings based on this study of Notel, Unitel, and Multitel are generalizable to other communities, also is important. In a sense, this question boils down to asking whether our towns constitute a sample of a larger population to which the results can be generalized (for example, Canada, North America, or western countries), or whether the towns themselves constitute the population they represent. On the basis of size alone these towns differ from many communities, and the fact that Notel received television reception for the first time in late 1973 probably makes it unique in North America among non-isolated communities. The question of interest, however, is whether the processes involved in television's impact vary dramatically according to the specific characteristics of the affected community, or whether its influence is more consistent and pervasive. Several kinds of evidence are relevant to this question.

The three towns formed a continuum in terms of the availability of TV (none; one channel of CBC; four channels—CBC, ABC, CBS, NBC). If television's impact does vary dramatically with the target group, we would be unlikely to obtain an interpretable pattern of findings in relation to the television continuum. Rather, the data would be very "noisy"; patterns of similarities and differences among the towns would lack consistency.

A second indication of the extent to which generalization would be warranted was expected to come from comparisons between Unitel and Multitel in Phase 1 and all three towns in Phase 2. Finding several or major differences between residents of a town with one Canadian television channel and residents of a town with four channels, including three from the United States, would indicate that the effects of television may be specific. On the other hand, finding that the presence or absence of television is more important than source or number of channels would suggest the effects of television are more general, at least across the range and types of television available in this project.

Another kind of evidence relevant to generalizability is the extent to which Notel, Unitel, and Multitel residents can be considered representative of a larger population. Replication of well-known findings (e.g., sex differences) obtained by other researchers for samples from urban centers would be one indication of similarity. Direct comparisons of the performance of participants in this study with performance on the same measures by other North Americans would be another indication of similarity. In some instances (e.g., the sex-role attitudes study), data from this study could be compared with data obtained from an urban sample. In other instances the performance of residents of the three towns in this study could be compared with the performance of standardization samples used in developing the measures. Standardization samples are selected to be representative of the general North American, Canadian, or U.S. population. To the extent that our sample can be established as representative of a larger population, the possibility of differences in these areas can be ruled out as an argument against generalizability.

Every study is unique, and strictly speaking, researchers can never be sure whether they would have obtained similar results if they had studied a different sample in different circumstances. Evidence from this natural experiment concerning the effects of television which corroborated or converged with evidence obtained with different methods by other researchers, therefore, was expected to be especially important. We were not so much interested in the effects of television in Notel, Unitel, and Multitel, as in what we could learn from studying these communities about the effects of television on children and adults in general. The fact that Notel was not "pure" in its lack of television provided a conservative test of television's effects, making differences between Notel and the other towns less likely.

APPROACH TO DATA ANALYSIS

As much as possible, we have tried to avoid using technical jargon in this book, stating what we did and found as simply as possible. At the same time we have tried to be scientifically accurate and precise in our methods and descriptions. Achieving both goals has not always been easy. Our major tactic is to describe the methods and results in plain English in the text, placing the details of the statistical analyses and results in notes at the end of each chapter. These notes are informative enough to be read either with or without reference to the text. This plan has enabled us to avoid using technical statistical terms in the text and, we hope, will widen the range of potential readers. At this point in the introduction, however, we shall briefly violate our own rules about jargon and provide an overview of the approach taken in analyzing the data.

Appropriateness of Linear Models

Our major vehicle for assessing the potential effects of television was the quasi-experimental nature of the project. We were looking for evidence of the impact of regular TV viewing (in Unitel and Multitel in both phases and Notel in Phase 2) by comparison with no or very little TV viewing (in Notel in Phase 1). Multivariate (MANOVA) and univariate (ANOVA) analyses of variance were used to evaluate this evidence. In addition, however, we obtained information from residents of all three towns at both times concerning their use of television and other media. Questions concerning television-viewing patterns, media diets, and so on fall within the genre of television research known as "uses and gratifications." Such questions were not the major focus of our project, but were an important adjunct to it and are described in Chapter 5.

The reader might expect us to use information about amount of TV viewing to assess the relationship between television exposure and other variables of interest, thereby corroborating the findings revealed through mean comparisons among the towns. In most instances this has been done, largely because it permits comparisons between our findings and those obtained by other researchers who have studied regular TV viewers. In our opinion, however, problems often arise in interpreting data concerning the relationship between amount of TV viewing and other variables (Salomon & Cohen, 1978). When significant correlations are found, interpretation is reasonably straightforward; the relationship exists, although causality cannot be inferred. However, measures of television exposure in terms of hours of TV viewing frequently are found to be unrelated to other variables, or to be related only minimally, so very little of the variation in one can be accounted for by variation in the other. It is important to recognize in these instances that all that has been demonstrated is lack of a linear relationship between hours of TV viewing and that particular variable. As has been argued elsewhere (Hornik, 1981; Williams, 1981), a linear model may not be appropriate; a threshold model of some sort seems more likely. Below some level, television exposure may have relatively little impact. Beyond some level, greater exposure may not necessarily lead to greater impact. Within some middle range the effect may or may not be linear. The inappropriateness of a linear model for the impact of television seems especially likely given typical North American media diets, that is, high levels of exposure to television and the repetitive nature of its content (Hornik, 1981). In addition, television's influence may be positive for one range of exposure and negative for another. A meta-analysis of the literature relating leisure-time television to school learning (Williams, Haertel, Haertel, & Walberg, 1982) supports this argument.

For the reasons just outlined, our analyses of the relationship between self-reported hours of television viewing and the variables we studied are secondary to the major analyses which focused on similarities and differences among the towns.[10] Discussion of the findings concerning hours of television viewing, therefore, is brief, presented secondarily, and located more in notes and appendixes than in the text of each chapter.

Levels of Analysis and Type I Error Rates

As we have indicated, our major approach to data analysis was to compare the towns within each phase of the study and to ask whether scores for each town changed from Phase 1 to Phase 2, using analysis of variance. Unweighted means analyses were used whenever the group sizes were unequal, since this occurred by chance rather than because the populations represented by these groups were unequal, and repeated measures analyses were used whenever longitudinal comparisons were made. When possible, multivariate analyses of variance were used, followed by univariate analyses to detect patterns of differences. In some cases, analyses of covariance were done to partial out the effects of another variable (e.g., intelligence). When statistically significant effects were found in the overall analyses, post hoc planned comparisons were used to determine where these significant effects arose. The source of differences contributing to significant interactions was determined with simple main effect analyses. Tukey tests were used to compare pairs of means when three or more were significantly different in an overall test, but when means differed by Newman–Keuls test and not by Tukey test, that was reported. Scheffé tests also were used in some instances.

In any large project the problem of escalating Type I error must be considered. That is, the probability of finding an apparently statistically significant difference by chance increases with the number of tests conducted. We are well aware of this problem and have dealt with it in several ways. First, we have focused on patterns of results rather than single findings. In no case do the interpretations center on any single piece of data; for each topic and each chapter we have sifted and weighed the evidence and drawn conclusions accordingly. Since each study involved two sexes, two or more age levels, three towns, and two phases, in every case we were evaluating a complex pattern of data points. Second, we have used multivariate analyses wherever possible to reduce the number of tests conducted. Third, we have reduced the amount of data and number of tests by combining items into superordinate scores when that was appropriate (e.g., when a test of internal consistency and Cronbach's coefficient alpha indicated it was warranted). Fourth, we have tried to avoid the "fishing expedition" approach, typical of so many large data sets, by testing specific hypotheses. At the same time we have remained open to alternative conceptualizations and have looked for contradictory evidence. If, for example, a correlation opposite to the relationship we have hypothesized was obtained, and this correlation would be significant with a one-tailed but not a two-tailed test, we have reported it and mentioned that it contradicts the hypothesis. This point is particularly relevant when analyses involving subgroups (e.g., females in one town) are involved, because as the size of the sample decreases, the likelihood of obtaining a statistically significant relationship using a two-tailed test also decreases. In short, we have tried to walk a tightrope by presenting as much evidence on all sides of the questions as possible while remaining aware of the problem that type I error escalates as the number of statistical tests conducted increases.

McLeod and Reeves (1980) divide reviewers of research on media effects into type one worriers and type two worriers. Type one worriers are concerned about drawing inferences that are too strong, so are inclined to accept a null position of no effects. They cite field studies using gross measures and point out that significant correlations are small and account for relatively little shared variance in the two measures. Type two worriers are concerned about overlooking any media effect and are interested in indirect as well as direct effects. They note that communication variables tend to be less reliably measured; hence, correlation coefficients may understate their "true" predictive power. McLeod and Reeves take the view that "neither type of worry is completely foolish or unwise. Perhaps one way out of the dilemma is to use the broad research strategies of the Type Two worrier in combination with the basic caution of the Type One worrier" (p. 35). This is what we have tried to accomplish.

With this overview in hand, we can move on to the individual studies. What *did* Notel, Unitel, and Multitel reveal about the effects of television on human behavior?

NOTES

[1] We are most grateful to Mary Morrison, the psychologist who brought this town without television to my attention.

[2] Researchers who study the relationship between television and aggressive behavior restrict the term aggression to behavior with the potential to harm. The kind of competitive or energetically assertive behavior sometimes labeled aggression by the public, for example, in the business community, has not to our knowledge been studied in relation to television.

[3] Both the mean and the median are between 3 and 4 hours a day.

[4] These figures represent averages for several weeks of programming, based on television-viewing guides. The difference between the amount of television available in the communities we studied was functionally slightly greater than the numbers indicate, because CBC programming early on weekend mornings was entirely in French. This was true from 8:00 until 9:30 at the earliest and 12:00 at the latest on Saturdays, and from 8:00 until 8:30 at the earliest and 9:30 at the latest on Sundays (there were weekly variations in the schedule of French programming). Canada is officially bilingual, but very few residents of Notel, Unitel, or Multitel spoke or understood French.

[5] A complete list of the programming available in each town in each phase of the project can be obtained from the editor.

[6] For example, during their spring 1983 fund-raising campaign, the Seattle PBS station said that 50% of their individual donations came from Canadian residents.

[7] Programs were divided into segments for the purposes of some of the content analyses. With a few explicit exceptions (e.g., commercial interruption, a telephone conversation) a new segment began when either the setting changed or the time changed (even when the setting remained the same).

[8] For skit-like commercials, a central figure was defined as any individual with at least one line of dialogue and prominent visual exposure. For narrative commercials, central figures were individuals with prominent visual exposure. In both cases, a maximum of six central figures was coded for any one commercial. Reliability was established for this and all other aspects of the coding system. The term *voiceover* refers to speech not initiated by figures in the commercial; a maximum of two was coded per commercial. *Type of argument* referred to the reasons given for using the product, categorized as scientific, nonscientific, or no argument (mere display with no verbal description). Each commercial was coded as portraying the sexes, overall, in traditional, progressive, reversed, or neutral sex roles.

[9] *Longitudinal* refers to research in which the same people are studied at two or more points in thier lives. *Cross-sectional* refers to research in which different people in two or more groups are studied at the same point. This project involved both kinds of research. Across-time comparisons involving different people of the same age were also made.

[10] We have used both correlations (including partial correlations) and regressions in analyses involving hours of TV viewing, but have avoided using cross-lagged panel correlations, in keeping with Rogosa's (1980) cautions.

REFERENCES

Anderson, D. R. Home television viewing by preschool children and their families. In A. C. Huston (Chair), *The ecology of children's television use.* Symposium presented at the meeting of the Society for Research in Child Development, Detroit, April 1983.

Anderson, D., & Lorch, E. P. Looking at television: Action or reaction. In J. Bryant & D. R. Anderson (Eds.), *Children's understanding of television.* New York: Academic Press, 1983.

Brown, J. R., Cramond, J. K., & Wilde, R. J. Displacement effects of television and the child's functional orientation to media. In J. G. Blumler & E. Katz (Eds.), *The uses of mass communications: Current perspectives on gratifications research.* Beverly Hills, Calif.: Sage, 1974.

Chall, J. S. *Stages of reading development.* New York: McGraw-Hill, 1983.

Coffin, T. E. Television's impact on society. *American Psychologist,* 1955, *10,* 630–641.

Comstock, G. *Television in America*. Beverly Hills, Calif.: Sage, 1980.
Comstock, G., Chaffee, S., Katzman, N., McCombs, M., & Roberts, D. *Television and human behavior*. New York: Columbia University Press, 1978.
Cook, T. D., & Campbell, D. T. The design and conduct of quasi-experiments and true experiments in field settings. In M. D. Dunette (Ed.), *Handbook of industrial and organizational psychology*. Chicago: Rand McNally, 1976.
Cook, T. D., & Campbell, D. T. *Quasi-experimentation: Design and analysis issues for field settings*. Boston: Houghton Mifflin, 1979.
Furu, T. *Television and children's life: A before–after study*. Tokyo: Japan Broadcasting Corporation, 1962.
Granzberg, G. Television as storyteller: The Algonkian Indians of central Canada. *Journal of Communication*, 1982, *32*(1), 43–52.
Granzberg, G., & Steinbring, J. *Television and the Canadian Indian*. Technical Report, University of Winnipeg, Department of Anthropology, 1980.
Greenberg, B. S., Edison, N., Korzenny, F., Fernandez-Collado, C., & Atkin, C. K. Antisocial and prosocial behaviors on television. In B. S. Greenberg (Ed.), *Life on television: Content analyses of U.S. TV drama*. Norwood, N.J.: Ablex, 1980.
Halpern, S., & Ethier, B. *The portrayal of men and women in Canadian and U.S. television commercials*. Unpublished manuscript, University of British Columbia, Department of Psychology, 1977. (Available from T. M. Williams).
Himmelweit, H. T., Oppenheim, A. N., & Vince, P. *Television and the child*. London: Oxford University Press, 1958.
Hornik, R. Out-of-school television and schooling: Hypotheses and methods. *Review of Educational Research*, 1981, *51*, 193–214.
Langer, E. J. Playing the middle against both ends: The usefulness of adult cognitive activity as a model for cognitive activity in childhood and old age. In S. R. Yussen (Ed.), *The development of reflection*. New York: Academic Press, 1982.
Longstaffe, S., & Williams, T. M. *Content analysis of informative programming on the major English networks available in Canada*. Paper presented at the meeting of the Canadian Communication Association, Montreal, June 1985.
McLeod, J. M., & Reeves, B. On the nature of mass media effects. In S. B. Withey & R. P. Abeles (Eds.), *Television and social behavior: Beyond violence and children*. Hillsdale, N.J.: Erlbaum, 1980.
McLuhan, M. *Understanding media*. New York: McGraw-Hill, 1964.
Murray, J. P., & Kippax, S. Television diffusion and social behaviour in three communities: A field experiment. *Australian Journal of Psychology*, 1977, *29*(1), 31–43.
Murray, J. P., & Kippax, S. Children's social behavior in three towns with differing television experience. *Journal of Communication*, 1978, *30*(4), 19–29.
National Institute of Mental Health. *Report of the Surgeon General's Scientific Advisory Committee on Television and Social Behavior*. Rockville, Md.: Author, 1972.
Pearl, D., Bouthilet, L., & Lazar, J. (Eds.). *Television and behavior: Ten years of scientific progress and implications for the eighties*. Vols. 1 and 2. Rockville, Md.: NIMH, 1982.
Robinson, J. P. Television's impact on everyday life: Some cross-national evidence. In E. A. Rubinstein, G. A. Comstock, & J. P. Murray (Eds.), *Television and social behavior: Vol. 4. Television in day-to-day life: Patterns of use*. Washington, D.C.: U.S. Government Printing Office, 1972.
Roethlisberger, F. J., & Dickson, W. J. *Management and the worker*. Cambridge, Mass.: Harvard University Press, 1939.
Rogosa, D. A critique of cross-lagged correlation. *Psychological Bulletin*, 1980, *88*, 245–258.
Rosenthal, R. *Experimenter effects in behavioral research*. New York: Appleton-Century-Crofts, 1966.

Salomon, G. Television watching and mental effort: A social psychological view. In J. Bryant & D. R. Anderson (Eds.), *Children's understanding of television.* New York: Academic Press, 1983.

Salomon, G., & Cohen, A. A. On the meaning and validity of television viewing. *Journal of Human Communication Research,* 1978, *4,* 265–270.

Schramm, W., Lyle, J., & Parker, E. B. *Television in the lives of our children.* Stanford, Calif.: Stanford University Press, 1961.

Siegel, A. E. Research findings and social policy. In E. L. Palmer & A. Dorr (Eds.), *Children and the faces of television.* New York: Academic Press, 1980.

Singer, B. D. Violence, protest and war in television news: The U.S. and Canada compared. *Public Opinion Quarterly,* 1970, *34,* 611–616.

Vidich, A. J., Bensman, J., & Stein, M. R. *Reflections on community studies.* New York: Wiley, 1964.

Williams, P. A., Haertel, E. H., Haertel, G. D., & Walberg, H. J. The impact of leisure-time television on school learning: A research synthesis. *American Educational Research Journal,* 1982, *19*(1), 19–50.

Williams, T. M. How and what do children learn from television? *Human Communication Research,* 1981, *7*(2), 180–192.

Williams, T. M. Implications of a natural experiment in the developed world for research on television in the developing world. *Journal of Cross-Cultural Psychology,* 1985, *16,* 263–287.

Williams, T. M., Zabrack, M. L., & Joy, L. A. A content analysis of entertainment television programming. In *Report of the Ontario Royal Commission on Violence in the Communications Industry,* Vol. 3. Toronto, 1977.

Williams, T. M., Zabrack, M. L., & Joy, L. A. The portrayal of aggression on North American television. *Journal of Applied Social Psychology,* 1982, *12*(5), 360–380.

2

TELEVISION AND
READING SKILLS

Raymond S. Corteen
Tannis MacBeth Williams

INTRODUCTION

The question of whether television influences school achievement positively, negatively, or even at all has been debated since the medium was invented. We investigated one aspect of this question, the role of television in the development of childrens' reading competence. The natural experiments involving the introduction of television in the 1950s had yielded some information about television's influence on childrens' reading choices, but little or no evidence concerning their reading skills (Furu, 1971; Himmelweit, Oppenheim, & Vince, 1958; Schramm, Lyle, & Parker, 1961). Findings accumulated since then indicate that television may have a slight negative influence on reading competence, but the conclusions are not straightforward. Based on research available prior to the arrival of television in Notel, we speculated that if television has a negative effect on children's reading skills, this occurs because TV displaces reading practice, at least for some children. Our study focused primarily on children in the process of learning to read (grades 2 and 3), since lack of reading practice seems most likely to affect reading competence at that stage. To investigate whether TV affects established reading skills, we also studied students in grade 8.

39

THE PROCESS OF LEARNING TO READ

The acquisition of fluent reading requires considerable practice and, for most children, is difficult. Grades 2 and 3 seemed to us likely to be the period when fluent reading skills are acquired. Chall's (1979, 1983) theorizing supports this view. According to her, the first four stages of reading development are the following:

Stage 0. *Prereading* (birth through kindergarten). Children develop the visual, visual-motor, and auditory-perceptual skills required to begin reading. Individual characteristics, environment, and experience interact to develop prereading skills and ability.

Stage 1. *Initial reading or decoding* (grades 1–2). Children learn letters and how to match them with spoken words: Mastery of the alphabet is a benchmark.

Stage 2. *Confirmation, fluency, ungluing from print* (grades 2–3). Stage 1 is consolidated by reading familiar stories, and this leads to fluency. Practicing decoding with familiar books is critical; children do not yet read to learn or for pleasure. Gaps in reading ability related to socioeconomic status emerge.

Stage 3. *Reading for learning the new* (grades 4–8). Children begin to read for knowledge or information and move from finding it easier to learn from listening or watching to recognizing reading as at least equal to other methods of knowledge acquisition.

Cognitive psychologists use the term *automatic information processing* (LaBerge & Samuels, 1974) to describe the process of obtaining information without conscious effort. Once this automated level of reading is achieved, however, and the individual is "unglued from print" as Chall says, meaning is extracted and recalled with only minimal memory for the actual words. For example, most automated or fluent readers who saw the sentence, "He had ham and eggs for breakfast," and were asked to recall whether they had seen the above sentence or, "He had a breakfast of ham and eggs" would be unable to do so. Effective readers go as quickly as possible to the meaning, and concentrating on individual letters or even words seriously interferes with comprehension. Once meaning has been extracted, the fluent reader tends to discard the specific words or sentence structure in which it was expressed (Marcel & Patterson, 1978; Wilson, 1979; Wilson & Zajonc, 1980).

Television programs such as "Sesame Street" may be effective in teaching rudimentary letter and number recognition skills, although that is a matter of some debate (Ball & Bogatz, 1970; Bogatz & Ball, 1971; Bryant, Alexander, & Brown, 1983; Cook, Appleton, Connor, Shaffer,

Tabkin, & Weber, 1975; Tierney, 1980). "Reading Rainbow" is a relatively new program designed to encourage reading and library use. Such programs were not designed to teach children to read fluently, however. In contrast, "Electric Company" was designed to increase reading competence, especially symbol and sound analysis and meaning. According to Chall, however, these are Stage 0 and 1 reading skills. The finding (Ball & Bogatz, 1973) that gains in reading achievement by viewers over nonviewers were greatest for first graders supports this point. As Roser (1974) noted, a second grader probably would obtain more reading practice while attempting to decipher the rules of a board game. Noninteractive television seems to be an inappropriate medium for improving reading fluency, and, not surprisingly, no television program yet devised has focused on this task.

TELEVISION AND READING HABITS

What is the evidence from previous research concerning our hypothesis that television affects reading skills by displacing activities which otherwise might facilitate reading? The question of quality of reading matter is not directly relevant, since the development of fluent reading skills may be served as well by reading comics or model aircraft assembly instructions as by reading literature of quality.[1] However, since much of the previous research on television and reading has been concerned with quality, or at least with displacement of one kind of reading material for another, we shall look at that evidence as a means of addressing the issue of quantity.

The impact of television on quantity of reading is central to our displacement hypothesis. Unfortunately, the evidence on this point is not entirely clear. For example, how are comics to be compared with books? Murray and Kippax (1978) studied 8–12-year-olds in three Australian communities: No-TV (no television), Low-TV (one channel, the public channel with a mandate to provide educational programming for use in the schools), and High-TV (the public channel and a commercial channel). No-TV children reported reading, on average, 1.08 books and 5.84 comics per week; Low-TV children reported reading 1.61 books and 3.91 comics per week; and High-TV children reported reading 1.85 books and 2.76 comics per week. No-TV children also estimated, however, that they spent a total of 5.51 hours per week reading, in contrast with 4.62 hours for Low-TV children and 4.17 hours for High-TV children. Do these data reflect an increase or decrease in quantity of reading with increased television? Note, too, that this study focused more on students in Chall's third stage of reading development than on students in the process of developing fluency.

Himmelweit et al. (1958) also studied children beyond the decoding stage. Effects of the introduction of television in the United Kingdom on book reading were most marked for children of average intelligence; the brighter students didn't change, and the less intelligent students read little anyway. With time, television seemed to stimulate interest in book reading. This finding at first glance contradicts our hypothesis. However, students in the Himmelweit et al. study were old enough to read for pleasure and information, whereas we were interested in the acquisition of fluency. In addition, comparisons of school marks obtained by nonviewers and matched viewers revealed a slight but nonsignificant trend favoring nonviewers. As Hornik (1978) pointed out, socioeconomic status (SES) indicators favored the viewing sample, so the countertrend in teacher ratings favoring nonviewers may have underestimated an even larger negative relation between viewing and achievement.

Schramm et al. (1961) studied the media habits of students in several North American communities. Most had television, but two Canadian towns were included, one with TV (Teletown) and one without it (Radiotown). They concluded that the reading of books, newspapers, and quality magazines is not affected by television, but the reading of comics and pulp magazines shows a sharp decline. Most of their data is not applicable to the age range in which we are most interested, but information from Radiotown, Teletown, and San Francisco provides a hint that children in the early grades may read fewer comics as television becomes increasingly available. Comstock (1980) reports that "comic-books surrendered many of the action- and humor-seeking young readers to television. Sales were 600 million in 1950; by 1970 they were half that" (p. 35).

Morgan (1980) studied sixth through ninth graders in the eastern United States. For students at the lower end of this age range, heavy television viewing was associated with less reading, but in the later grades, students who had previously indulged in heavy TV viewing, and who continued with heavy viewing, read more than students who had a stable history of light viewing. Despite reporting that they read more, these heavy viewers obtained lower scores than lighter viewers on reading comprehension tests. Morgan can offer no easy explanation for these puzzling results. Since television viewing typically falls off during the adolescent years (Comstock, Chaffee, Katzman, McCombs, & Roberts, 1978), as students become more involved with their peers and with music (Lull, 1983), perhaps the students in Morgan's study who persisted as heavy viewers represented an atypical group. They may have spent more time at home, less time with peers, and thus had more time to spend both watching television and reading. Whether this speculation is correct or not, Morgan's data indicate that a simplistic displacement hypothesis regarding television and reading is not appropriate for all, if any, age groups.

TELEVISION AND READING SKILLS

The research on reading and television most directly relevant to our study has focused on amount of television viewed and performance on tests of reading achievement (Burton, Calonico, & McSeveney, 1979; Fetler, 1982; Gadberry, 1980; Hornik, 1978; LaBlonde, 1967; Medrich, 1979; Morgan, 1982; Morgan & Gross, 1980; Roberts, Bachen, Hornby, & Hernandez-Ramos, 1984; Scott, 1958; Slater, 1965; Starkey & Swinford, 1974; Williams, Haertel, Haertel, & Walberg, 1982; Witty, 1966, 1967; Zuckerman, Singer & Singer, 1980).

If television has the potential to stimulate reading, it would seem most likely to do so for students who have reached the point of reading to learn, that is, Chall's Stage 3. Some results reported by Lee (1980), Solomon (1975), and Himmelweit et al. (1958) are consistent with this hypothesis. Ironically, however, Morgan and Gross's (1982) review of the literature on television and school achievement indicates it is precisely at this point, grade 4, that amount of television viewing has been found in several studies to be *negatively* related to reading achievement. Only two studies focused on younger children.

Burton et al. (1979) assessed the relationship between amount of weekday television viewed during the preschool years and academic performance at the end of grade 1 for children of lower and middle SES in New Orleans. The mother's retrospective estimate of her child's preschool TV viewing was significantly negatively correlated $(-.56)$ with the child's academic achievement and remained so (lowest partial correlation, $-.50$) when a number of other factors were controlled, one at a time. The most important of these was mother's education. Preschool TV viewing explained the largest portion of variance (30%) in grade 1 academic achievement. These results are impressive, but the retrospective nature of the mother's estimate is a serious methodological flaw. The findings may be due more to systematic differences because of selective memory than to any relationship between television and school achievement. The control for maternal education eliminates one potential source of bias, but there may have been others. Evidence from a prospective study using a better assessment of television exposure would be more convincing.

A study by the Singers, conducted in collaboration with Rapaczynski (Singer & Singer, 1983), meets these criteria. They investigated interactions among parental behavior, household routines, and the child's television environment in predicting later cognitive and behavioral patterns. Their measure of television exposure was a TV diary kept for the child by the parent beginning at age 4.

> The best prediction of good reading comprehension by the 2nd or 3rd grade emerges from a combination of a) familial factors such as parental reliance on inductive rather than power-assertive discipline, the mother's own self-description as resourceful (e.g., curious, creative, imaginative), and a more orderly household routine with more hours of sleep, and b) television variables, specifically fewer hours of television watching during the preschool years. This result is particularly clear for the brighter or more middle-class cohorts in our study; for lower SES children, better reading comprehension in the early school years is predicted by a combination of heavier preschool television watching and a mother who reports herself as curious and imaginative. (p. 892)

These findings indicate television is only one of several important aspects of the child's home environment related to performance on reading achievement tests, and may explain in part why the correlations between reading achievement and television exposure, although consistently negative, are often small and become nonsignificant when intelligence (IQ) or SES are included as controls. Further support for this view comes from studies by Fetler (1982) and Roberts et al. (1984).

Fetler (1982) used the 1981 California Assessment Program data to examine the relationship between sixth graders' television habits and their reading, written expression, and mathematics skills. For this large sample (10,603 students), increased television viewing was significantly negatively related to performance in all three aspects of school achievement. The largest and most consistent decreases occurred for students of high SES, high prior achievement, and those who rated school work as easy. For very low SES students (residing in a neighborhood composed primarily of unskilled workers), achievement improved with viewing up to a peak of 3 to 4 hours per day, but declined with additional viewing. Scores declined relatively sharply in all SES groups for heavy viewers (those in the top 10%), who tended to watch light entertainment and to be from lower SES families in which all members watched a good deal of television (and in which conversations often revolved around TV). By contrast, light viewers (bottom 10%) watched more public television, including more public affairs and news shows, and tended to be from higher SES families which placed stricter controls on their television viewing. These results indicate that heavy and light viewers differ not only in school achievement and amount of television they watch but also in what they watch. Intelligence was not assessed, but amount of television viewed contributed significantly negatively to school achievement even after SES (which tends to co-vary with intelligence), prior achievement (grade 3 scores, which were used as a proxy for intelligence), reported ease of school work, and other home environment variables were controlled. Fetler concluded that heavy viewing in and of itself is associated with lower achievement, but for relatively light viewers, educational and informative programming may have the potential to improve achievement.

The correlational nature of Fetler's (1982) data makes it impossible to determine whether TV use influences school achievement, whether TV use varies according to school achievement, or both. This problem does not apply to Hornik's (1978) study in El Salvador. He compared students whose families had obtained a television set between their seventh and ninth grades with students whose families over the entire period either had a TV set (and were of higher SES) or had no TV set (and were of lower SES). Students in families which obtained TV sets did about 10% worse on a reading test relative to the other groups, and this occurred for three different cohorts. Hornik hypothesized that television displaces attention from more intellectually stimulating activities which otherwise might facilitate improvement in reading skill. Although it is difficult to assess the implications of Hornik's results for long-term TV-set owners or for more developed countries, it is noteworthy that the advent of television apparently had a negative influence on the development of reading achievement as late as the junior high school period.

Roberts et al. (1984) have reported results of the first wave of a 3-year panel study involving second, third, and sixth graders. The five sets of measures used to predict reading achievement were SES, the home environment concerning print and television, amount of TV viewing and reading, the child's orientations toward print and television, and level of cognitive involvement with print and television. None of these was related to the reading achievement of second graders, a finding tentatively attributed to problems with measurement and reliability of the children's reports. For third graders, SES, the home environment regarding TV and print, and the child's orientation toward print and television were significant predictors, accounting for 51% of the variance in reading achievement. For sixth graders, SES was no longer a significant predictor, but all four of the other sets of measures contributed significantly to prediction and accounted together for 48% of the variance in school achievement. These results demonstrate the inadequacy of a simple measure of amount of television viewing to account for the TV–reading relationship and underscore the importance of a variety of print-related environmental, attitudinal, and behavioral variables. They also support Chall's emphasis (1979, 1983) on the importance of the home environment for the acquisition of reading skills.

The two California studies (Fetler, 1982; Roberts et al. 1984) under-score the complexity of the relationship between television and school achievement. It is unfortunate that IQ data could not be obtained in either study (because of California law), since other researchers have found that use of print, use of television, and school achievement tend to vary with intelligence. The possibility that IQ is a third variable accounting for much if not all the relationship between television and school achieve-ment therefore must be kept in mind. It also is important to remember that significant prediction in a regression analysis does not necessarily permit causal inferences. In particular, it seems plausible that print use contrib-utes causally to the acquisition of reading skills in the early school years, perhaps mediated strongly by SES and other home environment factors. Children who become fluent readers during this stage subsequently may use both television and print differently than those who do not become fluent readers; that is, amount of television viewed may predict reading achievement in the later years only because children who are better read-ers (and/or more intelligent) watch less TV, watch different television programs when they do watch, read more, are more inclined to use print to learn and to use TV for entertainment, and so on.

OVERVIEW OF OUR STUDY

The design of our research as a natural experiment promised to help unravel the question of whether television use plays a role in the develop-ment of reading skills, whether students with different levels of reading skill use television differently, or both. We assessed all children in each grade we studied in three comparable communities, which made it less likely that SES or IQ variations would account for the results. We also used IQ scores as a control in most analyses.

Reading competence was assessed in two ways. The most important information came from individual administration of the items of a stan-dard reading test under conditions which controlled the amount of time the item was available for the child to read. This part of the study was designed to assess reading fluency or automatic processing. We also gave a different standard reading test under the usual group conditions. This part of the study was designed to assess reading vocabulary and compre-hension skills in the more typical fashion and to provide a context in which to assess the results of our measure of automated reading. Finally, IQ (from school records, the best data available) was used to assess the role of intelligence in the relationship between television and reading.

DESCRIPTION OF MEASURES AND PROCEDURES

Automated Reading Fluency

Before Notel had television, we tested the automated reading skills of 217 students in grades 2, 3, and 8 in the three towns. Two years later, 206 students in the same grades were tested to provide cross-sectional comparisons. In addition, 153 students in grades 4, 5, and 10 who had been tested 2 years earlier were retested. Finally, we returned a third time to all three communities an additional 2 years later (4 years after the arrival of television in Notel) and tested 82 second graders. This was the only study in the project which included a third phase of data collection.[2]

The 153 longitudinal students available for follow-up in Phase 2 (71% of the original sample) had similar Phase 1 reading scores to the students who were not available for follow-up.[3]

The test materials were selected from the Gates–McKillop (1962) Diagnostic Reading Tests. The items were designed for flash presentation and consisted of 20 single words, 26 phrases, and 23 nonsense words, the latter being items which look like words but have no meaning (e.g., sked). Each word, phrase, and nonsense word was mounted on a white 5″ × 8″ card. To control precisely the amount of time the card was available for the child to read, it was presented in a two-channel Cambridge tachistoscope.

The tachistoscope is a square box, completely enclosed and light proof, containing a diagonal half-silvered mirror. At one side of the box is an illuminated presentation field. This is normally "on" and consists of a white card with a light gray X situated just above the center. The image of this card, which is known as the *fixation card,* is reflected off the mirror into a shielded viewing opening. Anyone looking into the opening will see the card as if it were set against the back of the box. At the back of the box, in fact, is another illuminated field. This is normally "off," and it consists of a white card, known as the *stimulus card.* The word, phrase, or nonsense word is centered on the card, and the cards are changed by the experimenter. The cards can be shown to the viewer at any preselected time ranging from ten one thousandths of a second (10 milliseconds) up to 2 seconds (2000 milliseconds). The tachistoscope is activated by a button pressed by the experimenter after the appropriate card has been inserted. When the button is pressed the light above the fixation card goes off and the light above the stimulus card comes on for the preselected time. When that time is over the stimulus card light goes off and the fixation card light comes on again. During the time the stimulus card light is on, that card can be seen clearly through the half-silvered mirror. To the viewer it appears as if the stimulus material flashes briefly onto a single white card which is always in the same place. The tachistoscopes used in this study were reliable and easy to operate. They were checked for calibration before and after each testing session.

The children were tested individually. When asked to look into the "box" and tell the tester what she or he could see, all students reported seeing an X. They were then told to look just below the X because they would see something and they were to tell the tester what it was. A practice word was then presented at the time to be used later for testing. This was 100 milliseconds for grades 2–5 and 30 milliseconds for grades 8 and 10. Students who recognized the practice word and reported it were then ready for testing. Students who failed to report the practice word on the first presentation were shown the same word for longer and longer times until they finally recognized it. Whatever the final duration for the practice word, however, the test words were shown to all students at the times indicated above, namely 100 milliseconds for students in grades 2–5, and 30 milliseconds for grades 8 and 10. No practice was given before the phrases; students were simply told they would now see more than one word. Prior to the first nonsense word, students were given another practice item which was presented in the same way as the practice item used before the single words. Once this nonsense practice item was recognized, testing recommenced using the same presentation time as before. The child was given words until the last word was reached or until six consecutive errors were made, whichever came first. The phrases were then given using the same criteria, and, finally, the nonsense words were given.[4]

Four scores were calculated, namely, the number of words, phrases, and nonsense words accurately read, and the total.

Group Reading Test

In Phase 1, when we asked the schools in each town how we could repay them for their cooperation with our research project, they requested that we administer and score standardized reading achievement tests. In May of that school year we therefore gave the Gates MacGinitie Reading Achievement Tests to the grade 1–7 classes in all three towns. This was approximately 6 months after television arrived in Notel. One version of the test was given to grades 1–3, and a second version to grades 4–7, as the test prescribes. Both yield a variety of scores. Since standard scores take into account the child's grade level, which permits direct comparisons across grades, the data reported in this chapter are based on standard scores.

Group reading test scores were obtained for a total of 813 students, 238 from Notel, 263 from Unitel, and 312 from Multitel. Of these students, 118 participated in Phase 1 of our automated reading study, and 180 participated in Phase 2.

AUTOMATED READING RESULTS

The results for our measure of fluent reading were complex. Whether television affected children's reading competence depended on their sex and grade level. Since the results for words, phrases, and nonsense words were very similar and correlations among these scores were high (Table 2.A1), total scores were used in most of the analyses.

We asked first whether total scores varied according to town, sex, and/ or phase of the study (i.e., before or after the arrival of TV in Notel) for all students who had been tested in the fluent reading task. When possible, we then ran a second set of analyses controlling for IQ. This was done because reading skill tends to vary systematically with intelligence, and it was possible that variations in IQ among groups of students would mask or be confounded with reading differences. Since IQ scores were not available for all students, the sample for which IQ could be controlled was smaller than the sample on which the initial analyses were based, and we therefore have reported both sets of results. They are presented graphically in Figures 2.1–2.7; the means are in Tables 2.A2 and 2.A3.

Cross-Sectional Automated Reading Results

GRADE 2

The cross-sectional results indicated that overall, the average score of grade 2 girls was higher than that for boys, and this was true for all three towns and both phases.[5] We therefore conducted subsequent analyses separately for girls and boys (Figure 2.1 and Table 2.A2).

In Phase 1, Notel boys obtained higher scores than both Multitel and Unitel boys, who did not differ. There was only marginal evidence of differences among the towns in Phase 2, reflecting marginally higher scores for Notel and Multitel, which did not differ, than for Unitel. The scores of both Notel and Unitel grade 2 boys in Phase 1 were higher than those of their Phase 2 counterparts, whereas there was no difference for Multitel.[6]

On average, second-grade girls in Phase 2 obtained significantly lower scores than grade 2 girls in Phase 1.[7] As Figure 2.1 indicates, girls in all three towns obtained high scores in Phase 1 and lower scores in Phase 2.

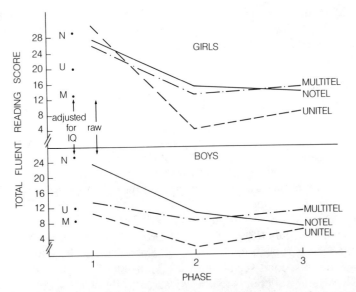

FIGURE 2.1   Grade 2 cross-sectional mean total fluent reading raw scores by town, sex, and phase (1, 2, and 3). Phase 1 means adjusted for IQ are indicated by the dots.

This initial set of results for second graders was both interesting and perplexing. Taken at face value, they indicated that Notel boys who had gone through grade 1 and the first part of grade 2 without access to television had relatively good fluent reading skills. Two years later, Notel boys in grade 2, who had been in kindergarten when television arrived, did no better than children who had grown up with TV and worse than their Phase 1 counterparts. If we had had data only from Notel and Multi-tel we would have left it at that, concluding that the grade 2 results suggest a deleterious effect of television for boys but not for girls.

We decided to conduct further analyses and collect more data because of the perplexing low scores obtained by Unitel girls and boys in Phase 2. We wondered whether the procedures used in administering the task to Unitel second graders in Phase 2 had been faulty, and the best way to resolve the issue was to conduct a third phase of testing in all three towns. This was done 2 years after the Phase 2 data had been obtained.

Before describing the results (Figure 2.1 and Table 2.A2), it is perhaps worth noting that our experience with "noisy" data at the grade 2 level is not unique. Roberts et al. (1984) were able to predict reading achievement scores from a variety of print, television, and family environment variables for third and sixth graders, but not for second graders. Chall (1979,

1983) has commented that it is almost impossible to predict Stage 1 (second-grade) standardized reading test scores using any set of predictors.

Comparison of the Phase 1 and Phase 3 results for grade 2 boys yielded precisely the pattern hypothesized regarding the effects of television.[8] Before they had television, Notel boys obtained significantly higher scores than Unitel and Multitel boys, who did not differ. There were no differences among the towns 4 years later in Phase 3, and the only difference across the phases occurred in Notel, with second-grade boys in Phase 1 obtaining higher scores than those in Phase 3.

For girls, the results based on comparison of Phase 1 and Phase 3 were the same as results based on comparison of Phase 1 and Phase 2; second-grade girls in all three towns obtained lower scores than their counterparts had done 4 years earlier.[9]

Comparison of the Phase 2 and Phase 3 second-grade results (Figure 2.1) revealed the same pattern for both girls and boys.[10] Overall, Unitel students obtained lower scores than students in both Notel and Multitel, who did not differ. The consistency of the findings from Phase 2 to Phase 3 for all three towns gave us confidence in our impression that the procedures used to administer the test had been consistent across the towns and phases. For some unknown reason, the scores of second-grade boys in Unitel were lower than those of boys in the other towns in Phases 2 and 3. This town difference was not large enough to be statistically significant when the Phase 3 data were compared with Phase 1, and it was only marginally significant when Phase 2 was compared with Phase 1, but when Phases 2 and 3 were compared, the pattern was strong enough to be significant.

Since IQ has been found by other researchers to be related to both reading skill and television viewing, we re-analyzed our data using IQ as a control. We wondered, in particular, whether this might clarify the results for girls. Unfortunately, there were not enough second graders in Phase 2 or Phase 3 with IQ scores to permit analyses for those phases. We did, however, re-analyze the data for the subsample of 51 Phase 1 second graders with IQ scores, who represented 72% of the original group. The results can be seen in Figures 2.1 and 2.2 as well as in Table 2.A2.[11] IQ did make a difference, and when it was controlled, the sex difference was only marginally significant. For Phase 1 girls and boys combined, the Notel (pre-TV) mean was higher than the means for Unitel and Multitel, which did not differ.

On the one hand, the results for grade 2 formed a clearer and more readily interpretable pattern when we controlled for variation in the Phase 1 scores related to IQ and when we obtained a third phase of data. We have graphed these results together in Figure 2.2. When IQ was con-

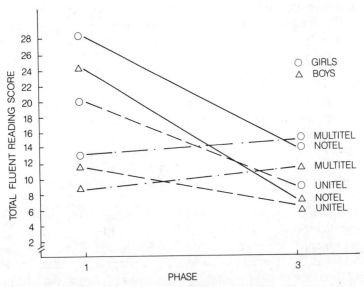

FIGURE 2.2   Grade 2 cross-sectional mean total fluent reading scores by town, sex, and phase. Phase 1 scores are adjusted for IQ; Phase 3 scores are not.

trolled in Phase 1, prior to the arrival of TV, Notel second graders (boys and girls combined) obtained significantly better fluent reading scores than both Unitel and Multitel second graders, who did not differ significantly. In Phase 3, when Notel had had TV for 4 years, there were no significant differences among the towns for either girls or boys.

On the other hand, it is clear that at the grade 2 level, automated reading scores were quite variable. The range (1.86–28.5 for the raw scores) indicates that some second graders have excellent reading skills but that others are able to read very little. Our test of fluent reading apparently was very sensitive to variations in the reading skills of second graders. It seemed possible that, at least for second graders, performance on our automated reading task was almost an all-or-none proposition. At Hornik's (personal communication, May 1983) suggestion, we conducted several analyses designed to ascertain whether performance was characterized more by an interval or threshold sort of scale.[12] The results indicated that the scale was more interval than not, so the analyses on which our findings are based are appropriate.

Taken together, these results provide some evidence that children who grow up without television during their preschool years, kindergarten, grade 1, and the early part of grade 2, are in grade 2 further advanced in the acquisition of fluent reading skills than children who have regular access to television during the same period. This occurred for boys whether or not IQ was controlled. For girls, it occurred only after IQ was controlled. After 2 or 4 years of TV viewing, the fluent reading scores of Notel second graders were similar to those of children who had grown up with TV.

GRADE 3

The scores for third graders were less variable than those for second graders (Figure 2.3 and Table 2.A2). There were no differences related to sex.[13] In Phase 1, Notel and Multitel third graders, who did not differ, obtained higher scores than Unitel third graders. The scores of Unitel and Multitel students did not change from Phase 1 to Phase 2, but Notel third graders in Phase 2 obtained significantly lower scores than their Phase 1 counterparts. Indeed, in Phase 2, Notel third graders obtained significantly lower scores than third graders in both Unitel and Multitel, who did not differ.

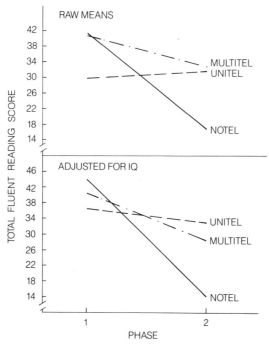

FIGURE 2.3   Grade 3 cross-sectional mean total fluent reading scores, by town and phase.

IQ scores were available for 76% of the third graders. When we controlled for IQ, the pattern of results did not change appreciably, except that the towns no longer differed in Phase 1.[14] The scores of Phase 2 third graders in both Notel and Multitel were lower than scores obtained by their Phase 1 counterparts. Notel third graders obtained lower Phase 2 automated reading scores than third graders in both Unitel and Multitel, who did not differ.

The most notable result for grade 3 students was the very low Notel Phase 2 means. These students were first graders when television arrived. When these results are considered in conjunction with the grade 2 results and the fact that third graders in Notel did not differ from Unitel and Multitel third graders in Phase 1, the combined evidence suggests that the availability of television may slow down the acquisition of automatic processing in reading, but most children do acquire such skills. The results from older students were consistent with this interpretation.

GRADE 8

We studied eighth graders because it seemed unlikely that once automatic processing was firmly established it would be influenced by television viewing, even if TV did displace reading at that point. It was possible, however, that before their town had television, eighth graders in Notel would exhibit better reading skills than their peers in Unitel and Multitel because of their long history with more time available for reading. As it turned out, even with the exposure time for the reading items reduced from 100 milliseconds to 30 milliseconds, the reading test may have been too easy to discriminate among eighth-grade readers. In other words, a "ceiling effect" may have occurred.

There were no differences among eighth graders that involved both the towns and phases of the study. The major finding was that the towns differed significantly overall; Notel and Unitel eighth graders, who did not differ, scored marginally higher than Multitel eighth graders. However, as Figure 2.4 and Table 2.A2 indicate, this was not related to phase.[15]

In Phase 1 and 2, IQ scores were available for 88% of the eighth graders. When we controlled for IQ the pattern of reading results did not change, but the marginally significant differences among the towns became statistically significant.[16] Both Unitel and Notel students, who did not differ, obtained higher scores, averaging across the phases, than Multitel students.

The town differences for grade 8 students are potentially interesting but difficult to explain. Notel eighth graders in Phase 1 had not yet become regular TV viewers, and those in Phase 2 were in grade 6 when television arrived. Multitel eighth graders in both phases had had television avail-

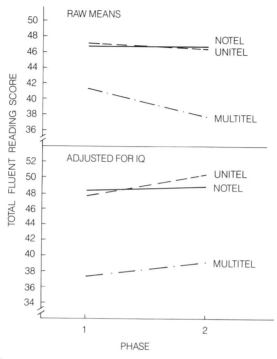

FIGURE 2.4   Grade 8 cross-sectional mean total fluent reading scores, by town and phase.

able since at least the preschool years. Unitel eighth graders in Phase 1 were in first grade when television arrived, and those in Phase 2 were not yet in school. It therefore seems unlikely that the pattern of town differences for grade 8 is related to the availability of television. Multitel students had four channels, including the U.S. networks, by comparison with only CBC in Unitel, and Multitel students watched more TV than did Unitel students in both phases and Notel students in Phase 2. It is difficult to imagine, however, how this could account for the grade 8 results.

Hindsight suggests it might have been more appropriate at the grade 8 level to use a test of comprehension via automatic processing rather than reading skill per se, since we may have encountered a ceiling effect. Hornik (1978) found that acquisition of TV slowed the development of reading ability between grades 7 and 9 for three different cohorts of students in El Salvador. We did, however, have a measure of reading comprehension for students in grades 1–7 as part of the group reading test (discussed later), and there were no town differences beyond the grade 3 level.

CONCLUSIONS BASED ON CROSS-SECTIONAL COMPARISONS FOR AUTOMATED READING

Taken together, the cross-sectional, across-time and within-phase data from grades 2, 3, and 8 suggest that television may interfere with the acquisition of fluent reading skills in the very early grades, but group differences are no longer apparent by grade 8 and may even disappear as early as grade 3 if the television environment is stable.

LONGITUDINAL AUTOMATED READING RESULTS

The longitudinal analysis provided information about stability versus change in the same students' performance over time. We expected that the scores of each group would improve from Phase 1 to Phase 2, since students would have an additional 2 years of reading practice. The main question was whether any superiority in reading skill apparent in Notel in Phase 1 would be maintained or disappear following the introduction of television.

GRADE 2 TO GRADE 4

The analysis of the raw total scores revealed that, as expected, students did better when they were in fourth grade in Phase 2 than when they were in second grade in Phase 1 (Figure 2.5 and 2.A3).[17] On average, girls also obtained higher scores than boys. There was no evidence of differences related to town for the raw scores, but when IQ was controlled, Notel students obtained higher mean scores than students in both Unitel and Multitel, who did not differ. As was the case for the unadjusted means, girls obtained higher scores than boys, and fourth graders in Phase 2 were better readers than when they were second graders in Phase 1.

Apparently, Notel students who in grade 2 had better automated reading skills than their Unitel and Multitel peers maintained their superiority over the next 2 years. This is a bit surprising, since the cross-sectional results indicated that any advantage for students who grew up without television had disappeared by grade 8 (although, as we noted earlier, all students did very well, and a ceiling effect may have obscured potential differences). In addition, the Phase 1 results for third graders did not indicate that Notel students who had grown up without television were more skilled readers than their Unitel and Multitel counterparts. Nevertheless, the longitudinal results for the grade 2 to grade 4 groups provide a small piece of additional evidence that television may play a negative role in the acquisition of fluent reading skills.

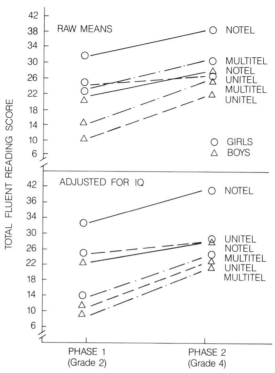

FIGURE 2.5   Grade 2 to 4 longitudinal mean total fluent reading scores, by town, sex, and phase.

GRADE 3 TO GRADE 5

Although gender was not an important factor in the within-phase results for grade 3, there was a sex difference in some towns but not in others for the longitudinal group who went from grade 3 in Phase 1 to grade 5 in Phase 2, and there was a marginally significant evidence of an overall sex difference.[18] We therefore conducted separate analyses for girls and boys (Figure 2.6 and Table 2.A3). Averaging across the phases, the scores of girls varied according to town; both Notel and Multitel girls obtained higher automated reading scores than did Unitel girls. Notel girls' scores also were marginally higher than those of Multitel girls. The raw scores of boys in the longitudinal grade 3 to grade 5 group did not vary according to town or phase.

When we introduced IQ as a control, the results did not change much even though IQ was a significant factor. On average, students obtained

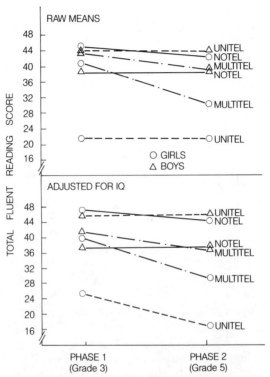

FIGURE 2.6   Grade 3 to 5 longitudinal mean total fluent reading scores, by town, sex, and phase.

lower scores in Phase 2 than in Phase 1, a suprising finding, since they were 2 years older and in Grade 5 rather than Grade 3. There was a significant sex difference in Unitel, but not in the other towns, and not overall. The Unitel boys' mean was similar to that for students of both sexes in the other towns, but for some unknown reason, Unitel girls in this longitudinal group did poorly, significantly more poorly than Notel girls, who performed best.

The most surprising result for the grade 3 to grade 5 group was the lack of improvement in performance from Phase 1 to Phase 2. The analysis of raw scores indicated that the girls' mean decreased marginally from Phase 1 to 2, and the analyses based on the means adjusted for IQ indicated that there was a significant overall decrease, averaging across gender and town. An examination of the means in Table 2.A3 indicates that the decreases occurred primarily in Multitel, but an increase did not occur in any of the towns. If this is a reliable result, the most likely explanation is that this is the stage, according to Chall (1979, 1983), when students have mastered decoding skills and are moving from reading for practice to reading for pleasure and to learn. There may be a period of consolidation or even minor slippage in automatic processing skills as this change occurs. This also tends to be the point in development when amount of reported television viewing peaks (Comstock et al., 1978), and this was true in our towns as well (see Chapter 5). The other possible explanation for the decrease is that the task may have been less interesting to fifth graders than to third graders. That is, perhaps there was a motivational factor involved which was specific to this age level. In sum, the longitudinal results for students who were third graders in Phase 1 and fifth graders in Phase 2 provided a minor piece of evidence that availability of television is related to automated reading skills, but this was specific to girls.

GRADE 8 TO GRADE 10

As we had expected, students in the longitudinal group obtained higher automated raw reading scores in Phase 2 when they were in grade 10 than in Phase 1 when they were in grade 8.[19] This pattern did not vary according to sex, but there was marginally significant evidence that performance in the two phases differed according to town (Figure 2.7). Since the scores at this age level all were high and there was relatively little room for variation, we examined the town variations more closely. The scores of Multitel students increased significantly from grade 8 to grade 10, and the increase for Unitel students was marginally significant. The change for Notel did not even approach significance.

When IQ was controlled, the results became clearer. The towns did not differ in Phase 2, but in Phase 1, Unitel and Notel students, who did not differ, obtained higher fluent reading scores than Multitel students. From Phase 1 (grade 8) to Phase 2 (grade 10) both the Unitel and Multitel students improved, but Notel students did not. The lack of improvement in Notel could not be attributed to lack of room for improvement (a ceiling effect), since Unitel students improved even though their Phase 1 scores were comparable to those of Notel students.

The finding that Notel students' reading scores did not improve from the eighth to the tenth grade is on the one hand surprising, given the reasonable expectation that, on average, all students do so over a 2-year period, and given that Unitel and Multitel students did improve. On the other hand, it is consistent with Hornik's (1978) finding that the development of reading competence between grades 7 and 9 was slowed by the acquisition of TV. We wondered whether the information we had obtained in Phase 2 about the students' usual television-viewing patterns

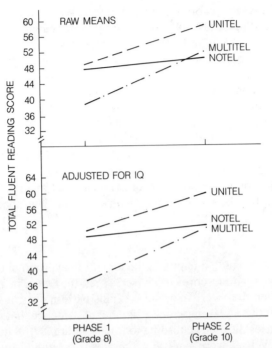

FIGURE 2.7   Grade 8 to 10 longitudinal mean total fluent reading scores, by town and phase.

might shed light on this finding. As other researchers have consistently reported (Comstock et al., 1978), the pattern of TV viewing by grade followed an inverted U-shaped curve (see Chapter 5 for details). This pattern of an increase in hours of TV viewing over the early grades and a decrease in the later grades did not, however, differ by town. Moreover, there was no evidence to suggest that 2 years after the arrival of television Notel tenth graders were watching more television than Unitel and Multi-tel tenth graders. Indeed, averaging across all grades, Notel and Unitel students reported watching significantly fewer hours of TV per week (20.88 and 21.01) than Multitel students (26.9).

It is important to note, however, that we have information about TV-viewing patterns only before and 2 years after the arrival of television in Notel. We do not know how much time students spent with TV during the intervening years. Based on other research and anecdotal evidence, it is likely there was some initial period of undetermined length during which Notel residents watched a great deal of television. It is possible, there-fore, that Notel students who were in grade 8 during Phase 1 watched more television in subsequent months and, even more important, read less than their peers in Unitel and Multitel. This might explain why their reading scores did not improve. Any statements about TV viewing and reading habits between the first and second phases are, however, purely speculative.

Summary and Conclusions Regarding Automated Reading

Our individual test of automatic processing provided several pieces of evidence that TV plays a role in the development of reading competence. Phase 1 second graders in Notel who had grown up without TV were better readers than children who grew up with it in Unitel and Multitel. This was true for both sexes if IQ was controlled but only for boys if it was not. After 2 or 4 years of TV viewing, however, Notel second graders read no better than children who had grown up with TV. The grade 3 Phase 2 results revealed that Notel children who had been in grade 1 when television arrived were poorer readers than Unitel and Multitel children. This finding, coupled with the grade 2 results, points to grades 1 and 2 as especially important for television's potential influence on the acquisition of fluent reading skills. Whether TV makes a difference beyond grade 2 is less clear. On the one hand, the lack of Phase 1 differences among the towns for third graders indicates that if TV slows the acquisition of fluent reading in grades 1 and 2, catch-up occurs by the middle of grade 3. On the other hand, the longitudinal data indicate that television may affect reading competence beyond grade 3. When IQ was controlled, the grade 2–4 Notel children performed better in both phases than Unitel and Multitel children, who did not differ. A similar result occurred for girls in the grade 3–5 group. These findings suggest that, at least in some instances, superior fluent reading skills are maintained despite the advent of TV, and catch-up by regular viewers does not occur. In addition, the grade 8–10 results indicate that the arrival of TV in Notel may have slowed the expected improvement in fluent reading over this period; the scores of Unitel and Multitel students increased, but those of Notel students did not.

The pattern of results from our fluent reading test was far from perfect, but the weight of the evidence indicates that reading development may proceed more slowly in the presence than in the absence of TV, and, as Hornik (1978) also found, the acquisition of TV may have the same effect.

In the next set of analyses we asked whether the better automatic processing skills of Phase 1 Notel children in the early grades were sufficiently robust to be apparent on a group reading test given at the end of the academic year, 6 months after television arrived.

GROUP READING TEST RESULTS

The group reading tests were given at the end of the Phase 1 school year. We analyzed the data separately for students in Chall's (1979, 1983) "initial reading or decoding" stage (grade 1), those in the "confirmation, fluency, ungluing from print" stage (grades 2 and 3), and children in the "reading for learning the new" stage (grades 4–7). The vocabulary, comprehension, and total standard score means are shown in Table 2.A4. IQ was included as a control in all analyses, and it was a significant influence in every case.

For first graders, there was no evidence of a sex difference in performance and no evidence that the vocabulary scores varied according to town.[20] The comprehension mean scores of Multitel and Notel students, which did not differ, were both higher than the mean for Unitel first graders. The same pattern was true of the total scores.

For second and third graders combined, girls obtained higher vocabulary, comprehension, and total scores than boys.[21] The comprehension scores varied significantly by town, with Notel students obtaining higher scores than both Multitel and Unitel students, who did not differ. The same pattern was true of vocabulary scores when specific comparisons were made among the towns, but the set of comparisons overall was not statistically significant. The total scores did not vary by town. When the results for fourth through seventh graders were combined, there were no significant differences related to either town or sex.[22]

These group test results tend to corroborate the findings obtained with our measure of automatic processing. For both measures, IQ was an important consideration, and there was some evidence in both cases that availability of television may be related to reading competence in the early grades. The finding that Notel second and third graders' superiority on the group test was strongest for comprehension scores is interesting, since better automatic processing skills should facilitate comprehension more than vocabulary, and television may even teach vocabulary to some extent. It also should be noted that the group test was given after the first 5–6 months of television reception in Notel, when its displacement effects would be likely to be strongest. This may or may not explain why the difference between Notel and the other towns, although significant for grades 2–3, was small, relative to the differences for the automated reading task.

For students in grades 4 through 7, most of whom would be in Chall's third stage of reading development, there was no evidence of differences among the towns, even for comprehension. It would be interesting in future research to measure comprehension in an automated reading test and assess its relationship to use of both print and television for students beyond the decoding stage of reading development.

Finally, the results for first graders provide a very subtle hint 6 months after the arrival of television in Notel of the findings we obtained 18 months later with our measure of automatic processing. The mean for Notel first graders was lower than that for Multitel first graders for all three scores, although not significantly so in any instance.

Taken together, the results of both the individual and group tests suggest that reading skills are most vulnerable to negative influence when they are being acquired in the early grades. The converging evidence provided by this and other studies points to television as one potential influence. We suspect its role is more indirect than direct, however, as we outline later in this chapter.

CORRELATIONS FOR READING SCORES AND IQ

As we have noted, a major difficulty for researchers interested in reading and television is that brighter students tend to be better readers, to watch less television, and to read more. Sorting out the relationships among reading ability, reading behavior, television use, and intelligence is very difficult. Since IQ proved to be important in interpreting most of our results, we looked more closely at the pattern of relationships among the reading measures, and between reading scores and IQ (see Table 2.A1). Notel correlations are presented separately because they form a slightly different pattern than those for Unitel and Multitel. We will comment first on the similarities, then on the differences.

First, performance on the fluent reading measure was stable for all three towns; students who did well in Phase 1 tended to do well 2 years later. This indicates that administering the Gates–McKillop test in the tachistoscope did not damage its reliability. Second, students who did well on the vocabulary part of the group reading test also tended to do well on the comprehension part, and both subscores were highly correlated with the total score. Again, this was true for all towns. Third, students who obtained high scores on the group reading test also tended to obtain high scores on our individual measure of fluent reading, whether it was given 6 months earlier in the same school year or 18 months later. The correlations within Phase 1 were higher for Notel than for the other towns, but all were statistically significant. This indicates that our fluent reading task provides a valid measure of reading achievement. Overlap between the two sets of scores was by no means complete, however, and performance on our individual measure was more independent of IQ than was performance on the group reading test.

The only surprising finding in Table 2.A1 was the lack of significant correlation between IQ and the fluent reading measure for Notel students in Phase 1. The findings for the group reading test also are interesting. In that case, IQ and reading scores were significantly correlated for all three towns, but the correlations for Notel were significantly lower than those for Unitel and Multitel.[23]

Why would IQ be more strongly related to reading test scores in the presence than in the absence of TV? Chance may be the best explanation, but we shall speculate about others. One possibility is that children who have difficulty learning to read spend more time practicing reading when television is not available, and IQ, therefore, is unrelated to performance on a measure of fluent reading. When television is available, perhaps proportionately more of the brighter children and/or those who find reading a relatively easy skill to acquire spend sufficient time practicing, and proportionately more of the less intelligent children do not, so IQ is related to automated reading scores. Performance on group reading tests is a function not only of reading skill but also general intelligence (quickness, paying attention to the right item, and so on), and this coupled with the fact that brighter children are more likely to read better (because they pick up the decoding skills more quickly, or whatever) means that IQ is related to performance on group tests whether or not television is available. These comments are entirely speculative, of course, and must be put to empirical test.

In a sense what we are suggesting is that the availability of television may increase the proportion of less intelligent children who do not acquire reading skills to the point of automatic processing. This argument rests in part on the assumption that when television is available, reading skill is positively related to use of print and negatively related to amount of television watched. The evidence reviewed earlier from the studies by Roberts et al. (1984) and Fetler (1982) supports these assumptions, but intelligence was not controlled in either case. What did our own results indicate?

RELATIONSHIP BETWEEN READING COMPETENCE AND TV VIEWING: CORRELATIONS AND OTHER ANALYSES

Most of the evidence concerning television and reading has been based on correlations between reported amount of television viewing and performance on group reading achievement tests. Significant but small negative correlations usually are obtained. When IQ and/or SES are controlled, the relationship tends to diminish, sometimes but not always to the point of nonsignificance. Since we obtained information about viewing habits, we conducted correlational analyses to ascertain whether television was implicated in reading skill at the individual level. In general, the results support those based on the natural experiment, and are consistent with findings obtained elsewhere by other researchers.

As Table 2.A5 indicates, reading scores tended to be negatively related to reported hours of television viewing even after the influence of IQ had been controlled. In Phase 1, however, the group reading scores of students in Unitel and Multitel were significantly negatively related to hours of television viewing largely because of Multitel students; the correlations for Unitel were smaller and not statistically significant. Similarly, group reading scores were negatively related to the Phase 2 television-viewing information obtained 18 months later primarily in Multitel; the correlations for Notel and Unitel were not significant. As a result, the correlations for Unitel and Multitel and for all three towns combined, although statistically significant, are small in absolute terms. These combined correlations are more similar to those reported by other researchers (e.g., Morgan & Gross, 1982; P. Williams et al., 1982) than are the ones for Multitel alone, which suggests that the large samples assessed in such studies may contain subgroups for which weaker and stronger relationships hold true. In our sample, TV viewing was significantly (and negatively) related to reading skill only for the group (Multitel) that watched significantly more television on average than the groups for which the TV viewing–reading correlations were nonsignificant (i.e., Unitel in Phase 1 and both Notel and Unitel in Phase 2). This may, of course, be coincidental, but it may also be worth pursuing in research on other samples.

We have omitted the Phase 2 fluent reading scores for second graders in these analyses because of our reservations (see Chapter 5) about the reliability and validity of young children's reports of TV viewing. The Phase 2 automated reading scores of students in grades 3, 4, 5, 8, and 10 were consistently negatively, but not strongly, related to hours of TV viewing. The partial correlations for all three towns were about the same size but significant only when combined.

These results indicate that both our individual and group measures of reading were concurrently negatively correlated with reported hours of TV viewing even after controlling for IQ. In addition, students who obtained higher group reading test scores tended to watch less television 18 months later than students who obtained lower scores. As other researchers have found, however, the relationships were not strong.

We examined the relationship between amount of television viewed and reading skill in another way, based on a report by P. Williams and her colleagues (1982). They conducted a meta-analysis of the literature on school achievement and found that for children who watch up to 10 hours of television per week achievement may be slightly enhanced, between 10 and 35 hours it diminishes with amount watched, and beyond 35 hours there is relatively little additional impact. These results fit with our own view that the relationship between TV watching and many behaviors is unlikely to be linear across the entire range of viewing and with the suggestion that a threshold model may be more appropriate (Hornik, 1981; T. Williams, 1981).

Our study did not include enough students to compute correlations for subgroups, so we examined the data another way. We divided each town into students who watched television 10 or fewer hours per week, those who watched more than 10 but less than 35 hours, and those who watched 35 or more hours per week. We then computed the mean standardized vocabulary, comprehension, and total group reading test scores obtained by each group. In both towns with television in Phase 1 and in all three towns in Phase 2, there was a decrease from the lowest to medium to highest TV-viewing group in all three reading scores, with only one exception (see Table 2.A6). In Phase 1, the differences were statistically significant for Multitel, but not for Unitel, and in Phase 2, for Notel and Multitel, but not Unitel.

The nonlinear pattern of results concerning amount of TV viewing and school achievement reported by Williams et al. (1982) is intriguing, but our own data seem to reflect a more linear relationship. Since other analyses have consistently indicated the importance of intelligence as a mediating variable for TV–achievement relationships, and the Unitel results did not follow a pattern similar to that obtained in Multitel and Notel, we examined the data further by introducing IQ. The reduced size of the sample for which IQ scores were available made it impossible to use three levels of television viewing, so we divided the students in each town into two groups on the basis of hours of TV viewing (25 hours per week or less vs. more than 25 hours per week) and further divided these groups according to IQ (100 or less vs. greater than 100). For each of the resulting four groups (low TV, low IQ; high TV, high IQ; low TV, high IQ; high TV, low IQ) we determined the mean group reading test scores. The results are shown in Table 2.A7. The most consistent finding is that brighter students obtain better reading achievement scores irrespective of how much TV they or their less intelligent schoolmates watch. There is a trend in the Multitel data for the brighter students who watch less than 25 hours per week to obtain higher reading scores than brighter students who watched more than 25 hours per week, but this difference was never statistically significant when the number of comparisons made was taken into account (it was consistently significant when only the individual comparisons in Multitel were considered). There also was a slight trend in Multitel for the less intelligent students who watched television more than 25 hours per week to obtain higher reading scores than their less intelligent classmates who watched less TV, but in this case none of the comparisons was significant regardless of whether or not the number of tests was controlled. The Unitel Phase 1 data indicating that students of above average intelligence who watched more than 25 hours of TV obtained higher reading scores than their similarly intelligent classmates who watched less TV seem to be anomalous, since they are not corroborated by the Unitel Phase 2 data or the pattern obtained in either of the other towns.

In sum, the weight of our evidence indicates there is a significant negative relationship between reading achievement and amount of television watched, even after IQ is controlled. This relationship is more linear than not and doesn't interact with IQ. The relationships among school achievement, intelligence, and use of television are by no means simple, however. They are complicated further by use of print and other non-television media, as well as the family viewing environment and attitudes toward print and television, as Roberts et al. (1984) have documented. Unfortunately, our study was not designed to assess these other important influences.

ALTERNATIVE POSSIBLE EXPLANATIONS OF THE RESULTS

Before drawing conclusions, it is important for all researchers to consider as many relevant factors as possible which might explain or confound the pattern of results obtained. We considered five possibilities which seemed especially important for a study of reading competence. (The general comparability of the towns also is important and is discussed in detail in Chapter 1).

The wide range of mean scores which occurred in some instances on the fluent reading test raises the question of whether the testing technique varied. We feel reasonably confident that it did not. The senior author conducted at least half the tests personally and supervised most of the others. The procedure was highly standardized—almost to the point of automaticity. As we discussed earlier, we were concerned that nonstandard procedures might have been used in Unitel for second graders in

Phase 2; thus, we returned to all three towns to collect a third phase of data. The additional analyses indicate instead that the low grade 2 Unitel Phase 2 scores were not anomalous. Phase 3 Unitel second graders did no better, and the Phase 2 and 3 scores of Multitel and Notel boys were in the same relatively low range. Figure 2.1 indicates that the most aberrant mean for Unitel second graders was the high score for girls in Phase 1, and when IQ was used as a control this mean dropped, as did the Phase 1 Multitel girls' and boys' means. Another indication that variability in the scores was not due to our procedures comes from comparison of the findings across age levels. Variability was highest in grade 2, less in grade 3, and minimal in grade 8, just as would be expected. Finally, the test we used is a well-standardized, respected measure of reading competence.

In our opinion, the differences probably are due to the test's sensitivity in the early grades. Some of the second and third graders read quite well, but many could read very little. We carefully examined the distribution of scores to ascertain whether we were testing a threshold phenomenon, but all the evidence pointed to an incremental interval-type scale. For researchers interested in the development of reading competence, the sensitivity of the test for assessing automatic processing in the early grades is desirable.

The possibility that teaching methods used in the different towns, grades, and/or phases were responsible for the results was sufficiently important that we investigated it carefully. Interviews with the teachers indicated they were using identical or very comparable books, and similar methods. Any stylistic differences seem likely to have been outweighed by the similarities in methods and materials.

Teacher effectiveness is difficult to determine even under the most favorable circumstances, and no attempt was made to assess effectiveness in this study; it would have been neither appropriate nor possible. Changes in teachers and teacher effectiveness theoretically could have produced the results obtained, and readers should scrutinize the results with this possibility in mind. However, much of the data are consistent with what might reasonably be expected following the introduction of television to Notel. In our view, it seems implausible that changes in teacher effectiveness could so fortuitously produce a similar pattern at so many data points.

The fourth possible confounding variable, general intelligence, deserves careful consideration. In his review of research on the relationship between television viewing and school achievement, Hornik (1981) noted that when significant correlations between hours of TV viewing and reading or school achievement scores occur, the relationship has tended to disappear when IQ is controlled. Hornik also argued, however, that this should not be interpreted as indicating that reading and television exposure are unrelated. Rather, the relationship may be obscured for a number of reasons. It may hold for particularly vulnerable subgroups, but not overall. For example, Morgan and Gross (1980) found no relationship between hours of viewing and reading comprehension for low and medium IQ subgroups, but they found an enhanced negative relationship $(-.28)$ for sixth through ninth graders who had high IQ scores. It is difficult to assess the confounding role of intelligence when relatively few people watch small amounts of television, and those who do are a self-selected, atypical group. It was precisely for this reason, of course, that the opportunity to study Notel was so attractive. The natural experiment enabled us to study students whose median level of TV viewing was 0 hours per week and thus avoid the problems involved in interpreting correlational results. In any event, this discussion of the possible confounding role of intelligence is academic, since we did use IQ as a control wherever possible. Doing so tended to make the pattern of results for comparisons among the towns clearer and more readily interpretable. Controlling IQ also was important for the correlational analyses.

The final potentially confounding factor is the family environment. The research by Roberts et al. (1984) and Fetler (1982) underscores the importance of home influences for reading competence. Although such information undoubtedly would have been helpful in interpreting our results, they were informative on their own. Our comparisons among the means based on the natural experiment assume that family environment differences, other than those covarying with television exposure, were distributed randomly across the towns. Since all students present on the testing days were included in the study, and the towns did not differ in SES, this seems a reasonable assumption. In any event, home influences unrelated to the availability of television could not account for changes in Notel.

In sum, we feel reasonably confident that the pattern of results obtained in this study cannot be explained by the factors we have discussed here. As in any experiment it is possible that our results are due to some other factor which has not been considered, but given a pattern of results involving several towns, grades, and two or three phases, this seems unlikely.

CONCLUSIONS

Taken together, our results indicate that television may have a negative effect on reading competence. This effect probably is limited in terms of both who is affected and the period over which it occurs. Our data are consistent with the following hypothetical scenario.

Once a young child has learned letters and numbers during the pre-school years, kindergarten, and grade 1, when our culture informally and formally attempts to teach these things, she or he is faced with the more difficult task of learning to decode print—words, phrases, and sentences. The school system teaches this process, which Chall (1978,1983) calls Stage 2 in reading development, during grades 1–3. Some children catch on quickly (indeed some do so in the preschool years), and some more slowly, but all must practice reading a good deal before it becomes auto-matic. For most children, school does not provide sufficient opportunity for practice to ensure the development of reading fluency. Allington's (1980) review indicates in addition that good readers receive more prac-tice in school than do poor readers, who presumably need it more. More-over, once children are beyond grade 3, the schools spend little time teaching decoding skills, so if fluency has not been acquired by then it becomes more, rather than less, difficult to obtain these skills in school. For all children, reading practice is hard work, but for brighter children (at least, those without a learning disability) it tends to be easier. It also may be more fun than for less intelligent children. Or, it may be equally difficult and unpleasant, but the rewards associated with becoming fluent may occur more quickly. During Stage 2 in reading development, children focus on decoding rather than on meaning and cannot yet read for plea-sure or to learn. This becomes possible only once reading has become automated—once the child is able to go straight to the meaning and is no longer aware of the specific words involved. The extent to which, in later years, children enjoy reading for pleasure and to learn may depend in part on the degree of fluency they have achieved (i.e., how fully automated reading has become), and in part on how long it took them to work their way through Stage 2.

The role of television in this hypothetical scenario begins with letter and number learning, which programs such as "Sesame Street" may facilitate. This process is fun, but the next stage is not; it requires slogging practice. The child may do this alone or by reading to a sibling, a babysit-ter, or a parent. Encouragement from others is not available to some children, and even if it is, watching television is probably more fun. Some children may practice reading while watching TV, not realizing that read-ing is one of many activities requiring too much mental concentration for time-sharing with television, if they are to be done effectively. Even adults who read fluently probably do so less well (more slowly, with decreased comprehension, or both) when their attention is divided, e.g., while watching TV.

Some families have few books with which to practice reading, and some children do not want to bring books home from school or the library if they may be damaged by pets or younger siblings. Some children, including but not only the more intelligent ones, may require relatively little practice over and above the opportunities available in school, whereas others require more practice. Those who require more may find practicing even less pleasant and television even more attractive, much as the prospect of losing 30 pounds seems impossible, whereas the prospect of losing 5 seems manageable. Such children may never really achieve automaticity, and for them, reading may not be an attractive way to spend leisure time. They may, therefore, by comparison with fluent readers, read fewer books, go to the library less often, and so on. Because they read less, they are less likely to develop further their already weak reading skills. These children also may watch more television, but not necessarily a great deal more. What we are suggesting is that the small significant negative correlations between reading achievement and amount of television viewing which appear fairly consistently beginning about grade 4 (Morgan & Gross, 1982) occur primarily because children who are more fluent readers tend to be more intelligent, to read more, and to watch television less. The role of television is, in our opinion, probably more indirect than direct.

In sum, our results do not form a perfect pattern, but the weight of the evidence suggests that television may slow down the acquisition of reading skills. The effect is weak, but the converging results from several sources within this study and from other studies, coupled with the fact that our findings were maintained or strengthened with IQ was controlled, make the effect difficult to ignore. Hornik (1978) reached a similar conclusion, using a different measure of reading achievement in a different country. Like him, we suspect that a displacement process is involved. At least for some children, time spent with television probably displaces reading practice. The absence of reading practice is, in our view, more important than television per se. Correlations between performance on standardized group reading tests and amount of television typically watched are therefore relatively weak even when statistically significant, and sometimes become nonsignificant when intelligence is controlled. Brighter students probably move on to the reading for pleasure stage more quickly. At that point they read more, which in turn facilitates comprehension and vocabulary. Families of higher SES are more likely to emphasize print as a medium for learning, and also may be more likely to provide motivation and encouragement in Stage 2, for example, by reading to the child and listening to the child practice reading. Parents who want their children to read well and to enjoy reading probably would be

better advised to foster a positive attitude toward books and reading and
to ensure that their children practice reading during the early school years
than to focus on television. It may be necessary to reduce amount of
television viewing in order to find sufficient time to practice reading, but
we suspect the latter, not the former, is what counts.

One possibility worth pursuing in further research is that the importance of children's leisure activities for their school achievement varies
with intelligence in a way which varies with level of schooling. More
specifically, it seems plausible that in the early school years, time spent
with television has greater potential to influence school achievement for
less intelligent children because they need the additional reading practice
most, that is, school does not provide sufficient opportunity. Less intelligent children from low SES families will be expecially disadvantaged if
their home environment provides little opportunity or encouragement to
practice reading. During the later school years, television may have a
greater indirect influence on the achievement of more intelligent students
and/or those from higher SES families because they would otherwise be
more likely to value doing well in school, spend their leisure time reading,
play games such as crossword puzzles and Scrabble which facilitate performance on reading tests, and so on. Their favorite TV programs also
tend to be more educationally oriented than those of lower SES students
(Fetler, 1982). In addition, of course, the higher achievers have farther to
fall. The results reported by Fetler (1982) support the notion that by the
sixth grade, television viewing is more strongly negatively related to
school achievement for students who otherwise would be expected to do
well by virtue of aptitude or environment. Findings obtained by Morgan
(1982) and by Roberts et al. (1984) support the hypothesis that how students spend their non-TV leisure time contributes importantly to their
school achievement.

IMPLICATIONS FOR FURTHER RESEARCH

Much remains to be learned about the role of television in reading
development. Although basic reading fluency tests are appropriate for
younger children, there should be more emphasis upon comprehension
during automatic processing in the later grades. This is suggested by the
work of Vipond and his colleagues (Kintsch & Vipond, 1979; Vipond,
1980) on micro- and macroprocessing in reading. It also would be interesting to study literacy in a broader sense, by including assessments of

grammatical knowledge and writing ability. Whether or not a natural experiment such as ours is available, effective automatic processing could be assessed with relatively inexpensive microcomputers, and this might provide a better motivational context than the tachistoscopic method used in this study. Unfortunately, microcomputers were not readily available when our data were collected.

At least in the early grades, analyses of reading competence should be conducted separately by grade level. Very large changes occur in Grades 1–3, and lumping students together may obscure variations. Roberts et al. (1984) found they could predict reading achievement for third and sixth graders, but not for second graders, and the predictions for third graders differed from those for sixth graders.

In addition to conducting analyses separately by grade, researchers ideally should consider sex, intelligence, SES, and the family environment concerning television and print. This unfortunately requires large samples and much time and expense. In addition, investigators may want to consider assessing automated reading fluency rather than relying on group achievement tests. Our results suggest that performance on the latter may be more closely linked to intelligence, and our most interesting results had to do with the development of automatic processing skills. Unfortunately, these probably have to be measured individually, which adds enormously to the time and expense involved.

Finally, as we noted in the introduction, most research on reading, television, and print use has focused on students in grades 6 or beyond. Our own results, as well as those obtained by Singer and Singer (1983) and by Roberts et al. (1984), point to the need for more research in the early grades. In addition, Chall's theory suggests that an important transition (from reading in order to practice decoding, to reading for learning and pleasure) occurs around grades 3–4, which points up the need for much more information about the grade 3 to 5 period. The data reported so far by Roberts et al. (1984) cover only the first of three waves of a panel study, so the students initially in grades 2 and 3 will move through this important phase during the course of their study. Their results should be enlightening.

EDUCATIONAL IMPLICATIONS

At this point the evidence is not sufficient to warrant other than the most muted comments regarding educational implications. It probably is

important for parents and educators to ensure that children spend sufficient time practicing reading to acquire fluency to the point of automatiza-
tion. We suspect that most children find watching television a more appealing alternative, and this may be especially true of the children who are
least competent. It also seems likely to be true of children for whom
television is a novelty. We have in mind here children in countries where
television is not yet endemic, or where the hours it is available increase
dramatically during the periods when children are able to watch. Hornik
(1978) found in El Salvador that the acquisition of TV slowed reading
development well beyond the early grades.

Television itself might be used to encourage children to practice reading, as Solomon (1975) and Lee (1980) have done to some advantage, and
as the program "Reading Rainbow" is designed to do.

As Anderson (1983) has documented, children and adults do many
other things while watching television. Salomon (1983) has emphasized
the importance of amount of mental effort invested in watching television
for children's learning from television. We would suggest that the same
principle applies to other forms of learning, including learning from print,
learning to play a musical instrument, learning problem-solving skills, and
learning to read. Some children practice reading while watching television. Unfortunately, this may not be sufficient, and perhaps the children
for whom it is not, those with less "invested mental effort" in reading, are
the least competent readers and the ones most likely to time-share reading
with TV. There is still much to understand about the relationships among
reading competence, use of print, and use of television, and a simplistic
displacement hypothesis is inappropriate.

Some observers suggest (e.g., Debes, 1974) that the emphasis placed
upon reading by this and other studies is misplaced. They argue, as
McLuhan (1964) did, that the onset of the "hot" media, especially television, has made reading unimportant except to an increasingly irrelevant
minority. Not surprisingly, we disagree with this view. A great deal of
information is conveyed by television, but the majority of significant human decisions are still based upon information and ideas conveyed by
print. We believe this will remain the case into the forseeable future. Any
communication revolution will contain a large component devoted to the
written word. The current proliferation of the significantly named "word
processors" provides a good example. People who read poorly or not at
all remain disadvantaged. Reading is, and will continue to be, an important skill, and all factors influencing it deserve the fullest and most careful
investigation possible.

APPENDIX: TABLES

TABLE 2.A1

Pearson Correlations among Reading Measures and IQ[a]

	Group test				Individual test	
Measure	IQ	Vocab	Comp	Total	Fluent 1	Fluent 2
IQ		.53 (200)	.60 (200)	.60 (199)	.19 (47)	.36 (73)
Vocabulary[b]	.67 (417)		.77 (211)	.94 (210)	.78 (32)	.47 (62)
Comprehension[b]	.68 (416)	.77 (453)		.94 (210)	.71 (32)	.49 (62)
Group test total[b]	.72 (415)	.94 (453)	.94 (453)		.79 (31)	.51 (61)
Fluent total 1[c]	.44 (136)	.43 (84)	.52 (83)	.51 (83)		.73 (41)
Fluent total 2[c]	.41 (165)	.53 (116)	.52 (116)	.57 (115)	.72 (119)	

[a] For all correlations, $p < .001$, two-tailed tests, except for Notel, IQ and Fluent total 1, which was nonsignificant. Correlations for Notel are above the diagonal, those for Unitel and Multitel (combined) are below it. Parentheses enclose the number of students on which each correlation is based.

[b] Standard scores from the group reading test given at the end of the school year.

[c] Standardized scores from the individual test of fluent reading given in Phase 1 to grades 2, 3, and 8 and in Phase 2 to grades 2, 3, 4, 5, 8, and 10. (Not all students had group reading test or IQ scores.)

TABLE 2.A2

Mean Automated Total Reading Scores for the Cross-Sectional Analyses

	Girls			Boys		
	Phase 1	Phase 2	Phase 3[a]	Phase 1	Phase 2	Phase
Grade 2 raw means						
Notel	28.00	15.50	13.84	23.23	10.36	7.18
Unitel	28.50	4.67	8.77	10.00	1.86	6.31
Multitel	26.07	13.31	14.91	13.75	8.68	11.25
Adjusted means, using						
IQ as the covariate[b]						
Notel	28.65	—	—	24.45	—	—
Unitel	20.08	—	—	11.58	—	—
Multitel	13.33	—	—	8.76	—	—
Grade 3 raw means						
Notel	44.60	15.20	—	38.17	19.11	—
Unitel	22.50	35.11	—	37.20	28.64	—
Multitel	37.91	34.91	—	44.08	31.18	—
Adjusted means, using						
IQ as the covariate						
Notel	48.18	12.43	—	40.08	15.86	—
Unitel	29.93	31.38	—	42.65	34.62	—
Multitel	39.76	30.38	—	41.43	26.87	—

(Continued)

TABLE 2.A2 (Continued)

	Girls			Boys		
	Phase 1	Phase 2	Phase 3[a]	Phase 1	Phase 2	Phase 3[a]
Grade 8 raw means						
Notel	46.50	51.56	—	47.18	42.00	—
Unitel	42.86	53.38	—	51.46	39.67	—
Multitel	35.96	41.38	—	46.90	34.40	—
Adjusted means, using IQ as the covariate						
Notel	48,80	53.47	—	47.83	44.44	—
Unitel	43.81	53.87	—	51.59	47.05	—
Multitel	34.78	45.50	—	40.10	33.12	—

[a] Phase 3 scores were obtained only in grade 2.
[b] IQ scores were not available for a sufficient number of grade 2 children in Phase 2 or 3.

TABLE 2.A3
Mean Automated Total Reading Scores for the Longitudinal Analyses

	Girls		Boys	
	Phase 1	Phase 2	Phase 1	Phase 2
Grade 2 to grade 4 raw means				
Notel	31.75	38.50	21.67	27.83
Unitel	24.33	26.67	10.56	21.67
Multitel	23.55	30.55	14.32	25.16
Adjusted means, using IQ as the covariate				
Notel	32.86	39.61	22.33	27.97
Unitel	24.66	27.00	10.50	22.21
Multitel	13.70	24.13	8.89	21.28
Grade 3 to grade 5 raw means				
Notel	44.60	42.00	38.33	38.44
Unitel	21.80	21.60	44.17	44.00
Multitel	40.21	30.71	43.42	39.08
Adjusted means, using IQ as the covariate				
Notel	47.16	44.56	37.57	37.68
Unitel	24.90	17.23	45.75	45.59
Multitel	39.62	30.12	41.26	36.93
Grade 8 to grade 10 raw means				
Notel	46.25	52.75	49.43	48.29
Unitel	48.75	61.25	49.40	55.80
Multitel	36.88	50.81	40.53	52.93
Adjusted means, using IQ as the covariate				
Notel	47.09	53.59	51.16	50.02
Unitel	50.09	62.59	50.81	57.21
Multitel	35.96	49.90	39.65	52.05

TABLE 2.A4

Adjusted Mean Group Reading Test Standard Scores,
Controlling for IQ

	Vocabulary	Comprehension	Total
Grade 1			
Notel	48.83	50.99	50.17
Unitel	45.20	44.68	45.20
Multitel	51.33	52.65	52.28
Grades 2, 3			
Notel	51.12	49.33	49.72
Unitel	48.67	45.07	46.57
Multitel	49.42	46.51	48.21
Grades 4, 5, 6, 7			
Notel	48.23	47.25	48.00
Unitel	47.71	46.19	47.16
Multitel	48.84	46.16	47.70

TABLE 2.A5

Partial Correlations between Reading Scores and Hours of Television Viewing,
Controlling for IQ

	n^a	Group test[b]			Fluent[c] reading total
		Vocab-ulary	Compre-hension	Total	
		Partial correlations with Phase 1 hours of TV viewing per week			
Unitel	75	−.03	−.12	−.09	—
Multitel	164	−.23***	−.24***	−.27***	—
Unitel & Multitel		−.12*	−.18***	−.18***	—
		Partial correlations with Phase 2 hours of TV viewing per week			
Notel	154, 69	−.10	−.06	−.09	−.13
Unitel	135, 43	.01	−.07	−.05	−.16
Multitel	187, 91	−.28***	−.27***	−.31***	−.14
Unitel & Multitel		−.09	−.14***	−.14***	−.16*
Notel, Unitel, & Multitel		−.08*	−.12***	−.12***	−.15**

[a] Sample size for the group test is given first; sample size for the fluent reading test second.

[b] The group reading test was administered to students in grades 1–7 twice: 6 months after Phase 1 TV-viewing data and 18 months before Phase 2 TV-viewing data were collected.

[c] The test of fluent reading was administered individually at approximately the same time as the Phase 1 and Phase 2 TV-viewing data were collected. The sample sizes for which both Phase 1 scores were available were too small to compute correlations. Phase 2 correlations, based on standardized fluent reading scores, are for students in grades 3, 4, 5, 8, and 10, combined.

* $p < .10$; ** $p < .05$; *** $p < .01$; all two-tailed tests.

TABLE 2.A6

Group Reading Test Standard Scores According to Level of TV Viewing, by Phase and Town[a]

| | Hours of TV viewing per week | | | | | |
| | Phase 1 | | | Phase 2 | | |
	<10	10–35	>35	<10	10–35	>35
Notel						
Vocabulary	—	—	—	54.44[b]	49.74[b,c]	46.41[c]
Comprehension	—	—	—	50.00	49.06	45.63
Total	—	—	—	52.67[b]	49.70[b]	46.26[c]
Unitel						
Vocabulary	48.00	45.70	46.64	50.00	46.96	43.73
Comprehension	51.75	43.56	42.91	47.43	45.19	41.77
Total	50.25	44.90	44.91	49.00	46.37	42.89
Multitel						
Vocabulary	62.67[b]	52.42[c]	49.45[b]	58.83[b]	51.73[c]	48.67[d]
Comprehension	58.67[b]	50.30[b]	46.74[c]	55.83[b]	49.65[b]	46.06[c]
Total	61.00[b]	51.63[b]	48.34[c]	57.67[b]	50.91[b]	47.59[c]

[a] For each row of scores within each phase, an overall one-way ANOVA determined whether there were differences according to level of TV viewing reported. If this test was significant at $p < .05$ or less, Scheffé tests were used to compare the pairs of means. Within each set of three means, those which do *not* share the same superscript differ at $p < .05$ or less. The absence of lettered superscripts means the overall F test was not significant.

TABLE 2.A7

Group Reading Test Standard Scores According to Level of TV Viewing and IQ

| | IQ and level[a] | | | |
	Low IQ, high TV	Low IQ, low TV	High IQ, high TV	High IQ, low TV
Phase 1				
Unitel				
Vocabulary	42.21[b]	43.04[b]	58.44[c]	47.40[b]
Comprehension	40.10[b]	40.85[b]	56.22[c]	45.40[b]
Total	41.37[b]	42.19[b]	57.44[c]	46.60[b]
Multitel				
Vocabulary	45.76[b]	46.92[b,d]	53.00[c,d]	58.16[c]
Comprehension	42.08[b]	43.69[b]	51.33[c]	56.63[c]
Total	44.16[b]	45.54[b]	52.39[c]	57.74[c]

TABLE 2.A7 (Continued)

	IQ and level[a]			
	Low IQ, high TV	Low IQ, low TV	High IQ, high TV	High IQ, low TV
Phase 2				
Notel				
Vocabulary	44.76[b]	46.30[b]	52.09[c]	53.79[c]
Comprehension	43.91[b]	44.65[b]	52.76[c]	52.57[c]
Total	44.97[b]	45.43[b]	52.64[c]	53.47[c]
Unitel				
Vocabulary	42.72[b]	43.00[b]	54.62[c]	52.70[c]
Comprehension	40.49[b]	41.14[b]	51.76[c]	52.20[c]
Total	41.94[b]	42.16[b]	53.38[c]	52.70[c]
Multitel				
Vocabulary	45.00[b]	48.42[b,d]	52.88[c,d]	56.22[c]
Comprehension	41.93[b]	44.73[b]	51.44[c]	54.67[c]
Total	43.67[b]	46.88[b]	52.35[c]	55.69[c]

[a] Low IQ, ≤100; high IQ, >100; low TV, 25 hours or less TV viewing per week; high TV, >25 hours TV viewing per week. The overall F tests for each row of four means were all significant at $p < .001$. The paired comparisons were Scheffé tests; within each set of four means, those which do *not* share the same superscript are significant at $p < .05$ or better.

NOTES

[1] Note, however, that Chall (1979, 1983) emphasizes practicing reading with *familiar* material for the development of decoding skills or fluency.

[2] We decided to collect Phase 3 data from second graders on the basis of the pattern of results obtained in Phase 2. Unitel second graders obtained very low scores in Phase 2.

[3] The Phase 1 scores of retained and nonretained students were:

	Retained		Non-retained				
	M	SD	M	SD	t	df	p
Words	10.33	5.01	11.12	5.85	.98	215	ns
Nonsense words	9.76	7.55	10.79	7.28	.89	215	ns
Phrases	12.92	7.09	13.79	6.26	.81	215	ns
Total score	33.02	18.13	35.70	17.68	.97	215	ns

[4] Order of presentation of the subtests was not counterbalanced for two reasons. First, there was no conceptual rationale for comparing performance on the different types of

items. Second, a logical order was implicit in the materials; words were easier to read than phrases, and nonsense words were the most difficult. For motivational reasons it made sense to present the easiest material first and the most difficult material last.

[5] In an unweighted means cross-sectional ANOVA on total scores for Town × Phase (1 vs. 2) × Sex for second graders, the town, $F(2,146) = 4.88, p < .001$; phase, $F(1,146) = 35.74, p < .001$; and sex, $F(1,146) = 14.67, p < .001$ main effects were significant. The Phase × Sex interaction was marginally significant, $F(1,146) = 3.35, p < .07$. Subsequent analyses of the grade 2 results therefore were conducted separately by sex.

[6] In an unweighted means cross-sectional ANOVA on grade 2 boys' total scores for Town × Phase (1 vs. 2), the town, $F(2,86) = 8.17, p < .001$; and phase, $F(1,86) = 15.69, p < .001$ main effects were significant. Scores were higher on average in Phase 1 (15.66) than in Phase 2 (6.97), and the Notel mean (16.79) was higher than that for both Multitel (11.22; $p < .05$ by Newman–Keuls and .10 by Tukey test) and Unitel (5.93; $p < .01$ by Tukey test). The Multitel mean also was higher than the Unitel mean ($p < .05$ by Newman–Keuls test). The Town × Phase interaction was not significant, $F(2,86) = 1.07, p > .10$, but since it was of central interest to the study we conducted simple main effects analyses to see whether they would be helpful in interpreting the significant findings. They indicated that the town means differed significantly in Phase 1, $F(2,86) = 6.44, p < .05$, and marginally in Phase 2, $F(2,86) = 2.81, p < .10$. In Phase 1, Notel grade 2 boys obtained significantly higher total scores (23.23) than boys in both Multitel (13.75; $p < .05$ by Tukey test) and Unitel (10.00; $p < .01$ by Tukey test), who did not differ. In Phase 2, when the towns differed only marginally, the scores of Notel boys (10.36) were marginally higher than those of Unitel boys (1.86; $p < .10$ by Tukey test), as were the scores of Multitel boys (8.68; $p < .10$ by Newman–Keuls test). Notel and Multitel boys did not differ in Phase 2. The scores of both Notel, $F(1,86) = 11.47$, $p < .01$ and Unitel boys, $F(1,86) = 4.59, p < .05$ in Phase 2 were lower than the scores of their Phase 1 age-mates, whereas Multitel boys in the two phases did not differ.

[7] In an unweighted means cross-sectional ANOVA on grade 2 girls' total scores for Town × Phase (1 vs. 2), only the phase main effect, $F(1,60) = 17.56, p < .001$ was significant, reflecting significantly lower scores in Phase 2 than in Phase 1 for all three towns.

[8] In an unweighted means cross-sectional ANOVA on grade 2 boys' total scores for Town × Phase (1 vs. 3), the Town × Phase interaction, $F(2,78) = 3.32, p < .05$ was significant. Simple main effects analyses revealed significant town differences during the first, $F(2,78) = 5.48, p < .05$, but not the third phase. In Phase 1, the mean Notel grade 2 boys' reading score (23.23) was significantly higher than the mean for both Unitel (10.00; $p < .01$ by Tukey test) and Multitel (13.75; $p < .05$ by Newman–Keuls test, $p < .10$ by Tukey). Only the mean score of Notel boys changed from Phase 1 to 3, and it decreased significantly, $F(1,78) = 15.18, p < .001$. The phase main effect, $F(1,78) = 9.71, p < .002$ was also significant (reflecting a decrease), and the town main effect was marginally significant, $F(2,78) = 2.98, p < .10$.

[9] The only significant result in the unweighted means cross-sectional ANOVA on total grade 2 scores for Town × Phase (1 vs. 3) for second-grade girls was the phase main effect, $F(1,63) = 13.00, p < .001$. The overall mean was higher in the first (27.52) than in the third (12.51) phase of the study.

[10] In an unweighted means cross-sectional ANOVA on total grade 2 scores for Town × Phase (2 vs. 3) × Sex, only the sex, $F(1,157) = 6.47, p < .02$; and town, $F(2,157) = 6.77, p < .002$ main effects were significant. Girls obtained higher scores on average (11.83) than boys (7.61). The mean scores in Multitel (12.04) and Notel (11.72) did not differ, and both were higher than the Unitel mean (5.40; $p < .01$ by Tukey test for both comparisons).

[11] In analysis of covariance on the Phase 1 grade 2 total scores, IQ was a significant covariate, $F = 5.56, p < .03$, and the town main effect was significant, $F(2,44) = 6.66, p <$

`.004. Tukey analyses of the adjusted means revealed that Notel second graders obtained a higher mean score (26.54) than both Unitel (15.84; $p < .05$) and Multitel (11.04; $p < .01$) second graders, who did not differ. The sex main effect was marginally significant, $F(1,44) = 3.50$, $p < .07$, reflecting a higher adjusted mean for girls (21.15) than for boys (14.47).

[12] Several analyses were used to determine whether performance on the automated reading task increased gradually or was more of a threshold proposition. First, we looked at the cumulative distribution of scores on each subtest for each grade level to see whether there were one or more sudden jumps. For words, phrases, and total scores, the cumulative proportion of students getting each item correct formed a gradually increasing pattern, and this also was true for nonsense words beyond grade 2. In Phase 1, however, 39% of the second graders in Notel, 78% in Unitel, and 54% in Multitel obtained nonsense word scores of zero; this distribution was only marginally significant, however, $\chi^2(2) = 5.65, p < .06$. The analogous Phase 2 distribution of 42%, 86%, and 63% was significant, $\chi^2(2) = 11.59, p < .01$, but the Phase 3 distribution of 73%, 69%, and 48% was not. Since a number of second graders in each town obtained scores of zero, we re-analyzed the data for each phase using a nonparametric test. The results were similar to the results for the ANOVA. In a Kruskal–Wallis ANOVA the mean ranks of total scores of grade 2 boys differed by town in Phase 1, χ^2 corrected for ties = 9.18, $p < .01$; uncorrected = 7.19, $p < .03$ and in Phase 2, χ^2 corrected = 7.63, $p < .03$; uncorrected = 5.40, $p < .07$. The Phase 1 mean ranks for Notel, Unitel, and Multitel were 29.92, 15.83, and 22.80, respectively. The Phase 2 ranks were 29.25, 17.39, and 25.00, respectively. The towns did not differ in Phase 3 for boys and did not differ in any phase for grade 2 girls.

The wide range of means for second and third graders prompted a second approach to the question of the psychometric nature of the automatic processing task. We are grateful to Bob Hornik for these suggestions. First, we plotted the fluent reading scores against the group reading scores separately for each grade in each phase (if both measures were available). The plots indicated the relationship between the two scores is linear. The second procedure involved going back to the raw data and for each item (e.g., the first word) plotting the proportion of students getting that item correct against the group test scores. This series of curves was spaced evenly along the graph; the plots for the items did not cluster as would be expected if performance followed a threshold rather than interval model. The results of these analyses indicated that our main analyses (ANOVA, correlations) were appropriate for the data.

[13] In an unweighted means cross-sectional ANOVA for Town × Phase × Sex for third graders, there were no significant effects involving sex. The phase main effect, $F(1,117) = 11.36, p < .001$; and the Town × Phase interaction, $F(2,117) = 6.58, p < .002$ were significant. Simple main effects analyses of this interaction revealed that the scores of Notel third graders in Phase 2 were lower (mean 17.16) than those of their Phase 1 counterparts (41.38), $F(1,117) = 22.69, p < .001$, but no differences were found for the other towns. The towns differed in both phases; $F(2,117) = 3.25, p < .05$ for Phase 1; $F(2,117) = 5.88, p < .01$, for Phase 2. In Phase 1, third graders in both Notel (41.38) and Multitel (40.99), who did not differ, obtained marginally higher scores than Unitel third graders (29.85; $p < .10$ by Tukey tests in both cases; the Multitel–Unitel difference was significant at $p < .05$ by Newman–Keuls test). Two years later, Notel third graders obtained significantly lower scores (17.16) than students in both Unitel (31.87; $p < .05$ by Tukey test) and Multitel (33.05; $p < .01$ by Tukey test).

[14] In cross-sectional analysis of covariance on the grade 3 total scores for Town × Phase × Sex, IQ was a significant covariate, $F(1,84) = 23.08, p < .001$. The phase main effect, $F(1,85) = 19.74, p < .001$; and the Town × Phase interaction, $F(2,85) = 6.04, p < .004$ were significant. Simple main effects analyses revealed that the towns differed in Phase 2, $F(2,85)$

= 6.39, $p < .01$, but not in Phase 1. In Phase 2, the adjusted mean for Notel third graders (14.15) was lower than that for both Multitel (28.62; $p < .05$ by Tukey test) and Unitel (33.05; $p < .01$ by Tukey test) third graders. The scores of both Notel, $F(1,85) = 29.36, p < .01$; and Multitel, $F(1,85) = 4.68, p < .05$ students decreased from Phase 1 to Phase 2.

[15] In an unweighted means cross-sectional ANOVA on grade 8 total scores for Town × Phase × Sex, only the town main effect, $F(2,126) = 3.35, p < .04$; and the Sex × Phase interaction, $F(1,126) = 10.40, p < .002$ were significant. Unitel (46.84) and Notel (46.81) eighth graders obtained marginally higher scores than Multitel eighth graders (39.66; $p < .10$ by Tukey test for comparison with Unitel; $p < .10$ by Tukey and $p < .05$ by Newman–Keuls for comparison with Notel).

Simple main effects analyses of the Sex × Phase interaction revealed a sex difference in Phase 2, $F(1,126) = 10.43, p < .01$, with girls obtaining higher scores than boys. There was no sex difference in Phase 1. Looked at the other way, the scores of both sexes differed across the phases. Girls, $F(1,126) = 5.74, p < .05$ obtained higher scores in Phase 2 (50.61) than in Phase 1 (41.77), but the opposite was true for boys, $F(1,126) = 4.68, p < .05$; Phase 1, 46.67; Phase 2, 38.69. We can think of no plausible explanation for this result, and since it is not of central interest to our study, will not discuss it further.

[16] In cross-sectional analysis of covariance on the grade 8 total scores for Town × Phase × Sex, IQ was a significant covariate, $F(1,107) = 25.29, p < .001$. The phase main effect, $F(2,108) = 7.53, p < .001$; and the Phase × Sex interaction, $F(1,108) = 7.25, p < .01$ were significant. The adjusted mean scores of Unitel (49.08) and Notel (48.63) eighth graders were higher than that for Multitel eighth graders (38.38; $p < .01$ by Tukey test in both cases).

Simple main effects analyses of the Phase × Sex interaction revealed that the adjusted mean of girls in Phase 2 (50.95) was higher than that for Phase 1 girls (42.46), $F(1,108) = 5.86, p < .05$, and the sexes differed in Phase 2, but not in Phase 1, $F(1,108) = 7.20, p < .01$. Phase 2 girls had a higher adjusted mean (50.95) than Phase 2 boys (41.54). As we noted earlier, this seems to be a chance finding.

[17] In a repeated measures ANOVA for Town × Sex × Phase using an unweighted means solution on the total scores of students in the grade 2 to 4 longitudinal sample, the sex, $F(1,52) = 4.36, p < .05$; and phase, $F(1,52) = 18.65, p < .001$ main effects were significant. Girls obtained a higher mean score (29.22) than boys (20.20), and scores were higher in Phase 2 (28.40) than in Phase 1 (21.03), as expected.

In analysis of covariance on the same data, IQ was a significant covariate, $F(1,38) = 5.92, p < .02$. The town, $F(2,38) = 5.38, p < .01$; sex, $F(1,38) = 4.42, p < .05$; and phase, $F(1,39) = 19.00, p < .001$ main effects were significant. The adjusted mean for Notel (30.69) was higher than that for both Unitel (21.09; $p < .10$ by Tukey test and $p < .05$ by Newman–Keuls test) and Multitel (17.00; $p < .01$ by Tukey test). The adjusted mean for girls (26.99) was higher than that for boys (18.86), and the Phase 2 mean (27.03) was higher than the Phase 1 mean (18.82).

[18] In a repeated measures ANOVA for Town × Sex × Phase using an unweighted means solution on the total scores of students in the grade 3 to 5 longitudinal group, the Town × Sex interaction was significant, $F(2,45) = 3.53, p < .04$; and the sex main effect was marginally significant, $F(1,45) = 3.36, p < .08$, so similar Town × Phase analyses were conducted separately for girls and boys.

For girls, the town main effect was significant, $F(2,21) = 4.11, p < .04$. The means for both Notel girls (43.30) and Multitel girls (35.46) were higher ($p < .01$ by Tukey test in both cases) than the mean for Unitel girls (21.70), and the Notel mean also was higher than the Multitel mean ($p < .10$ by Tukey test and $p < .05$ by Newman–Keuls test). The phase main effect, $F(1,21) = 3.53, p < .08$ was marginally significant, reflecting a minor decrease rather than an increase from Phase 1 (35.54) to Phase 2 (31.44). The phase main effect also was significant in the analyses reported earlier in which the sexes were combined, $F(1,45) =$ 4.19, $p < .05$, reflecting a higher score in Phase 1 (38.76) than in Phase 2 (35.97). For boys, neither the main effects nor any interaction approached significance.

In analysis of covariance on the same data for Town × Phase × Sex, IQ was a significant covariate, $F(1,42) = 5.93$, $p < .02$. The phase main effect was significant, $F(1,43) = 8.32$, $p < .006$, reflecting a higher mean in Phase 1 (grade 3; 39.38) than in Phase 2 (grade 5; 35.35). The only other significant result was the Town × Sex interaction, $F(2,42) = 3.82$, $p < .03$. Simple main effects analyses indicated there were no differences among the towns for boys, but for girls, $F(2,42) = 5.52$, $p < .05$, the Notel (45.86) mean was higher than the Unitel (21.06) mean, $p < .01$ by Tukey test; Multitel girls were in between (34.87) and not different from either Notel or Unitel. There was no sex difference for Notel or Multitel, but Unitel boys (45.67) obtained a higher mean than Unitel girls (21.06).

[19] In a repeated measures ANOVA for Town × Sex × Phase using an unweighted means solution on the total scores of students in the grade 8 to 10 longitudinal group, the phase main effect was significant, $F(1,45) = 21.41$, $p < .001$, reflecting higher scores in Phase 2 (grade 10 mean, 53.64) than in Phase 1 (grade 8 mean, 45.21). The Town × Phase interaction was marginally significant, $F(2,45) = 2.84$, $p < .07$. Because the scores of this group may have been subject to a ceiling effect and this interaction was of central interest, simple main effects analyses were conducted. The scores of Notel students did not change from grade 8 (47.84) to 10 (50.52); those of Unitel students increased marginally, $F(1,45) = 3.55$, $p < .10$ (from 49.08 to 58.53); and those of Multitel students increased significantly, $F(1,45) = 6.89$, $p < .05$ (from 38.70 to 51.87). The towns did not differ in Phase 2 but differed marginally in Phase 1, $F(2,45) = 2.55$, $p < .10$. The Notel and Unitel means, which did not differ, both were marginally higher in Phase 1 than the Multitel means ($p < .10$ by Tukey test in both cases).

In analysis of covariance on the same data, IQ was a significant covariate, $F(1,44) = 10.45$, $p < .003$. The town main effect, $F(2,44) = 4.23$, $p < .03$; phase main effect, $F(1,45) = 21.41$, $p < .001$; and their interaction, $F(2,45) = 3.47$, $p < .04$ all were significant. Scores were higher overall in Phase 2 (grade 10; 54.23) than in Phase 1 (grade 8; 45.79). Overall, the mean for Unitel (55.17) was higher than that for Multitel (44.39); $p < .05$ by Tukey test; Notel was in between (50.46) and not different from Unitel or Multitel. Simple main effects analyses indicated the towns differed in Phase 1, $F(2,44) = 5.46$, $p < .05$, but not Phase 2. In Phase 1, Unitel (50.45) and Notel (49.13) students, who did not differ, both obtained higher scores than Multitel students (37.81; $p < .01$ by Tukey test for comparison with Unitel; and $p < .05$ by Tukey test for comparison with Notel). The scores of Notel students did not change significantly from Phase 1 to Phase 2, but both Unitel (from 50.45 to 59.90), $F(1,44) = 5.05$, $p < .05$; and Multitel (from 37.81 to 50.98), $F(1,44) = 9.81$, $p < .01$ students improved significantly from grade 8 to 10.

[20] In analysis of covariance for Town × Sex on first graders' Vocabulary group reading test scores, IQ was a significant covariate, $F(1,49) = 40.78$, $p < .001$, but no other effects were significant. For Comprehension scores IQ was again a significant covariate, $F(1,50) = 32.54$, $p < .001$. In addition, the town main effect was significant, $F(2,50) = 4.80$, $p < .02$; both Multitel (52.65) and Notel (50.99) first graders, who did not differ, obtained higher scores than Unitel (44.68) first graders ($p < .01$ by Tukey tests in both cases). IQ also was a significant covariate for Total scores, $F(1,49) = 41.84$, $p < .001$. The Total score town main effect was significant, $F(2,49) = 3.40$, $p < .05$; Multitel (52.28) students obtained higher scores than Unitel students (45.20; $p < .01$ by Tukey test). The same was true for Notel students (50.17; $p < .05$ by Tukey test). Notel and Multitel did not differ.

[21] In analysis of covariance for Town × Sex on second and third graders' group test Vocabulary scores, IQ was a significant covariate, $F(1,155) = 47.38$, $p < .001$. The signifi-

cant sex main effect, $F(1,155) = 4.61$, $p < .04$ reflected a higher adjusted mean for girls (50.87) than for boys (48.61). Notel students (51.12) obtained higher vocabulary scores than Unitel students (48.67; $p < .01$ by Tukey test) and Multitel students (49.42; $p < .10$ by Tukey test and $p < .05$ by Newman–Keuls). The overall town main effect was not, however, significant, $F(2,155) = 1.89$, $p = .16$. IQ was a significant covariate for Comprehension scores, $F(1,155) = 59.74$, $p < .001$. Again, on average, the significant sex main effect, $F(1,155) = 8.54$, $p < .005$ reflected higher scores for girls (48.88) than for boys (45.07). The significant town main effect, $F(2,155) = 3.69$, $p < .03$ reflected a higher mean for Notel (49.33) than for both Multitel (46.51; $p < .05$ by Tukey test) and Unitel (45.07; $p < .01$ by Tukey test), who did not differ. IQ was a significant covariate for Total scores, $F(1,155) = 43.72$, $p < .001$. The significant sex main effect, $F(1,155) = 8.36$, $p < .005$, reflected a higher mean for girls (50.08) than for boys (46.25). No other effects approached significance.

[22] In analyses of covariance for Town × Sex on the group reading scores of fourth through seventh graders, IQ was a significant covariate for Vocabulary, $F(1,392) = 311.04$, $p < .001$; Comprehension, $F(1,391) = 326.04$, $p < .001$; and Total, $F(1,391) = 413.37$, $p < .001$ scores, but no other effects approached significance.

[23] The Pearson correlation between Vocabulary standard scores and IQ for Notel (.53) was significantly lower than that for Unitel and Multitel combined (.67), $Z = 2.55$, $p < .05$. The same was true of the Total standard scores from the group reading test (.60 vs. .72), $Z = 2.97$, $p < .01$. The town difference for the Comprehension–IQ correlations (.60 vs. .68), $Z = 1.875$ was not significant.

REFERENCES

Allington, R. L. Poor readers don't get to read much in reading groups. *Language Arts*, 1980, *57*, 872–876.

Anderson, D. R. Home television viewing by preschool children and their families. In A. C. Huston (Chair), *The ecology of children's television use*. Symposium presented at the meeting of the Society for Research in Child Development, Detroit, April 1983.

Ball, S., & Bogatz, G. A. *The first year of Sesame Street: An evaluation*. Princeton, N.J.: Educational Testing Service, 1970.

Ball, S., & Bogatz, G. A. *Reading with television: An evaluation of the Electric Company*. Princeton, N.J.: Educational Testing Service, 1973.

Bogatz, G. A., & Ball, S. *The second year of Sesame Street: A continuing evaluation, Vol. I and II*. Princeton, N.J.: Educational Testing Service, 1971.

Bryant, J., Alexander, A. F., & Brown, D. Learning from educational programs. In M. J. A. Howe (Ed.), *Learning from television: Psychological and educational research*. London: Academic Press, 1983.

Burton, S. G., Calonico, J. M., & McSeveney, D. R. Effects of preschool television watching on first-grade children. *Journal of Communication*, 1979, *29*(3), 164–170.

Chall, J. S. The great debate: Ten years later, with a modest proposal for reading stages. In L. B. Resnick & P. A. Weaver (Eds.), *Theory and practice of early reading*. Hillsdale, N.J.: Erlbaum, 1979.

Chall, J. S. *Stages of reading development*. New York: McGraw-Hill, 1983.

Comstock, G. *Television in America*. Beverly Hills, Calif.: Sage, 1980.

Comstock, G., Chaffee, S., Katzman, N., McCombs, M., & Roberts, D. *Television and human behavior*. New York: Columbia University Press, 1978.

Cook, T. D., Appleton, H., Conner, R. F., Shaffer, A., Tabkin, G., & Weber, V. S. *Sesame Street revisited*. New York: Russell Sage, 1975.

Debes, J. L. *Mind, languages and literacy.* Paper presented at the annual convention of the National Council of Teachers of English, New Orleans, 1974.

Fetler, M. *Television viewing habits and school achievement.* Paper presented at the meeting of the American Educational Research Association, New York, March 1982.

Furu, T. *The function of television for children and adolescents.* Tokyo: Sophia University, 1971.

Gadberry, S. Effects of restricting first graders TV-viewing on leisure time use, IQ change, and cognitive style. *Journal of Applied Developmental Psychology,* 1980, *1,* 45–47.

Gates, A. I., & McKillop, A. S. *Gates–McKillop Diagnostic Reading Tests.* New York: Teachers College Press, 1962.

Himmelweit, H., Oppenheim, A. N., & Vince, P. *Television and the child.* London: Oxford University Press, 1958.

Hornik, R. Television access and the slowing of cognitive growth. *American Educational Research Journal,* 1978, *15,* 1–15.

Hornik, R. Out-of-school television and schooling: Hypotheses and methods. *Review of Educational Research,* 1981, *51,* 193–214.

Kintsch, W., & Vipond, D. Reading comprehension and readability in educational practice and psychological theory. In L. G. Nilsson (Ed.), *Perspectives in memory research.* Hillsdale, N.J.: Erlbaum, 1979.

LaBerge, D., & Samuels, S. J. Toward a theory of automatic information processing in reading. *Cognitive Psychology,* 1974, *6,* 293–323.

LaBlonde, J. *A study of the relationship between television viewing habits and scholastic achievement of fifth grade Children.* Abstract of unpublished doctoral dissertation, University of Minnesota, 1967.

Lee, B. Prime time in the classroom. *Journal of Communication,* 1980, *30*(1), 175–180.

Lull, J. *The origins and consequences of adolescent mass media use.* Paper presented at the meeting of the International Communication Association, Dallas, May 1983.

Marcel, A. J., & Patterson, K. E. Word recognition and production: Reciprocity in clinical and normal studies. In J. Requin (Ed.), *Attention and Performance, Vol. 7.* Hillsdale, N.J.: Erlbaum, 1978.

McLuhan, M. *Understanding media.* New York: McGraw-Hill, 1964.

Medrich, E. A. Constant television: A background to daily life. *Journal of Communication,* 1979, *29*(3), 171–176.

Morgan, M. Television viewing and reading: Does more equal better? *Journal of Communication,* 1980, *30*(1), 159–165.

Morgan, M. *More than a simple association: Conditional patterns of television and achievement.* Paper presented at the meeting of the American Educational Research Association, New York, March, 1982.

Morgan, M., & Gross, L. Television viewing, IQ, and academic achievement. *Journal of Broadcasting,* 1980, *24,* 117–132.

Morgan, M., & Gross. L. Television and educational achievement and aspiration. In D. Pearl, L. Bouthilet, and J. Lazar (Eds.), *Television and behavior: Ten years of scientific projects and implications for the eighties.* Vol. 2. Rockville, Md.: NIMH, 1982 (pp. 78–90).

Murray, J. P., & Kippax, S. Children's social behavior in three towns with differing television experience. *Journal of Communication,* 1978, *30*(4), 19–29.

Roberts, D. F., Bachen, C. M., Hornby, M. C., & Hernandez-Ramos, P. Reading and television: Predictors of reading achievement at different age levels. *Communication Research,* 1984, *11,* 9–49.

Roser, N. L. "Electric Company" critique: Can great be good enough? *Reading Teacher,* 1974, *27,* 680–681.

Salomon, G. Television watching and mental effort: A social psychological view. In J. Bryant & D. R. Anderson (Eds.), *Children's understanding of television*. New York: Academic Press, 1983.

Schramm, W., Lyle, J., & Parker, E. *Television in the lives of our children*. Stanford, Calif.: Stanford University Press, 1961.

Scott, L. F. Relationships between elementary school children and television. *Journal of Educational Research*, 1958, *52*, 134–137.

Singer, J. L., & Singer, D. G. Psychologists look at television: Cognitive, developmental, personality, and social policy implications. *American Psychologist*, 1983, *38*, 826–834.

Slater, B. R. An analysis and appraisal of the amount of televiewing, general school achievement and socio-economic status of third grade students in selected public schools in Erie County, New York. *Dissertation Abstracts*, 1965, *25*, 5651–5652. (State University of New York at Buffalo Microfilm No. 63-6712)

Solomon, B. To achieve, not to please. *Learning Today*, 1975, *8*, 48–51.

Starkey, J., & Swinford, H. *Reading: Does television viewing time affect it?* De Kalb: Northern Illinois University, 1974. (ERIC Document Reproduction Service No. ED 090 966)

Tierney, J. D. The evolution of televised reading instruction. *Journal of Communication*, 1980, *30*(1), 181–185.

Vipond, D. Micro- and macroprocessors in text comprehension. *Journal of Verbal Learning and Verbal Behavior*, 1980, *19*, 276–296.

Williams, P. A., Haertel, E. H., Haertel, G. D., & Walberg, H. J. The impact of leisure-time television on school learning: A research synthesis. *American Educational Research Journal*, 1982, *19*(1), 19–50.

Williams, T. M. How and what do children learn from television? *Human Communication Research*, 1981, *7*(2), 180–192.

Wilson, W. R. Feeling more than we can know: Exposure effects without learning. *Personality and Social Psychology*, 1979, *37*, 811–821.

Wilson, W. R., & Zajonc, R. B. Affective discrimination of stimuli that cannot be recognized. *Science*, 1980, *207*, 557–558.

Witty, P. Studies of the mass media. *Science Education*, 1966, *50*, 119–126.

Witty, P. Children of the TV era. *Elementary English*, 1967, *44*, 528–535.

Zuckerman, D. M., Singer, D. G., & Singer, J. L. Television viewing, children's reading, and related classroom behavior. *Journal of Communication*, 1980, *30*(1), 166–174.

3

TELEVISION AND COGNITIVE DEVELOPMENT

Linda Faye Harrison
*Tannis MacBeth Williams**

INTRODUCTION

The question of whether television facilitates or inhibits various aspects of children's thinking has been argued since widespread viewing began during the 1950s and 1960s. The answers still are not clear. Schramm, Lyle, and Parker (1961) found that when they started school, children growing up with television had about a 1-year advantage in vocabulary over children growing up without television. This advantage had disappeared by grade 6. The bulk of their evidence led Schramm et al. to conclude, however, as Himmelweit, Oppenheim, and Vince (1958) did in England, that although children think TV helps with school performance (teachers are ambivalent), there is no evidence that it does. Schramm et al. also concluded that television does not markedly broaden children's horizons or stimulate them intellectually or culturally; it may do these things, but probably no more than would happen via other avenues in the absence of TV.

* Order of authors is alphabetical to reflect their equal contribution.

These discouraging statements were made before programs such as "Mister Rogers" became available, but the controversy continues. In particular, the effectiveness of "Sesame Street" (Ball & Bogatz, 1972; Cook, Appleton, Connor, Shaffer, Tabkin, & Weber, 1975; Lesser, 1974) and the impact of television on imaginative thinking (Singer & Singer, 1981; 1983) have been debated. Even with longitudinal panel designs, it is difficult to determine whether watching television leads to a change in performance, since people who score high on measures of cognitive ability use television differently than people who obtain low scores. For example, the National Institute of Mental Health (NIMH) review (Pearl, Bouthilet, & Lazar, 1982) of research done in the 1970s concluded that a negative relationship between TV viewing and IQ has been demonstrated for both children and adults, but the direction of influence cannot be specified. The design of our study as a natural experiment, therefore, promised to shed new light on much-debated issues concerning television and cognitive development. We focused on three aspects of children's thinking: vocabulary, spatial ability, and creativity. These three abilities were chosen in part on the basis of their salience in the literature (Cattell, 1971; French, 1951; Hakstian & Cattell, 1974; Horn, 1968; Thurstone, 1938) and in part because they are considered to be independent aspects of thinking; thus, an impact of television in one area would carry no necessary implications for the others. In addition, we were able to obtain general IQ information from the school records.

CREATIVITY, INTELLIGENCE, AND TELEVISION: THEORY AND EVIDENCE

What Is Creativity, and Is It Related to Intelligence?

Getzels (1975) divided the investigation of creativity and intelligence into three historically overlapping periods, each marked by a salient emphasis: "genius," "giftedness," and "creativity." Systematic work began in 1869 with the publication of Galton's *Hereditary Genius: An Inquiry into Its Laws and Consequences,* and investigations of genius persisted into the twentieth century. With the increasing popularity of the intelligence metric and the publication of Terman's studies of highly intelligent children in the 1920s, the research emphasis shifted to giftedness. In the 1950s the emphasis shifted once more—from giftedness, as measured by the intelligence test, to creativity (Getzels, 1975).

The dominance of research interest in intelligence over the field of mental functioning was sufficiently diminished by the late 1940s that other conceptions, including creativity, emerged (Getzels & Csikszentmihalyi, 1975). There still was neither a clear conceptual distinction between intelligence and creativity, however, nor an operational approach specific to creativity. By introducing his concept of "divergent thinking," Guilford (1950) provided a dialectical foil to the reigning notion of intelligence. The tests he and his associates used (many of which originally were developed by Thurstone and modified over the years by Guilford) provided a methodology (Getzels & Csikszentmihalyi, 1975). Thurstone (1950) also stimulated others to examine possible creativity factors not included in the usual standard intelligence tests. He and one of his students, Taylor (1947), moved away from the "right or wrong answer" approach and identified two fluency factors, fluency of ideas and verbal versatility. However, it was Guilford's (1956) distinction between convergent and divergent thinking as one aspect of his Structure of Intellect (SI) model that seemed to provide the greatest impetus to researchers.

The *operations* dimension of the SI model deals with aspects of thinking which produce information. Within that dimension, convergent thinking involves zeroing in on an answer specified or implied by the information on hand, whereas divergent thinking involves finding an answer or answers more loosely related to what is already known, necessitating a broad-based search (Wallach, 1970). Of course, as Barron and Harrington (1981) point out, divergent thinking goes hand in glove with convergent thinking in every thought process that results in a new idea.

Can creativity be shown to account for thinking beyond what is accounted for by intelligence? Despite criticisms of other aspects of Guilford's SI model (e.g., Butcher, 1973; Horn & Knapp, 1973; Vernon, 1979; Wallach, 1970), there is good evidence that two of its dimensions, namely *ideational fluency* (ability to generate ideas that fulfill particular requirements) and *originality* (ability to generate statistically unique or unusual ideas), are independent of general intelligence (Wallach, 1970). Moreover, people who generate many ideas also are more likely to produce unusual ones. Mednick (1962) proposed that creative thinkers are less fixated on common associations and more capable of reaching distant, less accessible ideas. He defined these as "new combinations which either meet specified requirements or are in some way useful" (p. 221). Whereas Mednick's method of assessing creativity, the Remote Associates Test (RAT), has been widely criticized, the model on which it is based has received empirical support (e.g., Milgram, Milgram, Rosenbloom, & Rabkin, 1978; Wallach & Kogan, 1965).

The usual method of assessing creativity in a test-like atmosphere was criticized by Wallach and Kogan (1965). They contended that an evaluative context lacks face validity; situations which evoke thoughts of correctness probably are not conducive to thinking often described as "going off in different directions." Time limits also seemed inappropriate; freedom and spontaneity rather than speed of responding struck them as important. They argued that substantial correlations between creativity and intelligence sometimes are obtained because creativity has not been properly measured. Performance may reflect method variance more than trait variance (in the sense discussed by Campbell & Fiske, 1959).

Wallach and Kogan (1965) administered creativity tasks (including some of Guilford's ideational fluency measures) to fifth graders in a relaxed, nonevaluative, untimed setting. Creativity scores were independent of conventional intelligence scores, and each constituted a unitary dimension. Subsequent research has supported this distinction (e.g., Cropley & Maslany, 1969; Pankove & Kogan, 1968; Wallach & Wing, 1969; Ward, 1968; Williams & Fleming, 1969; see Barron & Harrington, 1981; and Dellas & Gaier, 1970, for reviews), although Milgram and Milgram's (1976) data for Israeli children suggest that the atmosphere in which tasks are given may make a difference only for children of average or lower intelligence, not for bright children.

In sum, there is considerable evidence to support the contention that creativity, when assessed in terms of ideational fluency and originality, is a concept at the same level of abstraction as intelligence. As Dellas and Gaier (1970) point out, even Thorndike (1966), who severely criticized the work of both Getzels and Jackson (1962) and Guilford, conceded that their data suggest "there is some reality to a broad domain, distinct from the domain of the conventional intelligence test, to which the designation of divergent thinking or 'creative thinking' might be applied" (p. 52). Thorndike did, however, consider the domain of creativity to be looser than the domain of intelligence, with lower correlations among measures within the domain.

Most researchers agree with Guilford's (1976) suggestion that although creativity and intelligence are independent domains of thinking, a certain level of intelligence is a prerequisite to performance on divergent-thinking tasks. For example, both Barron (1963) and McNemar (1964) have suggested that although a low positive relationship between creativity and IQ holds across the total range of creativity and intelligence, beyond some threshold level of intelligence (IQ of 120 or so), the two are unrelated, and creativity is rare among individuals of average or lower intelligence. In general, studies of adults identified as highly creative (artists, scientists, mathematicians, and the like) support this assertion; they tend to score high on general tests of intelligence, but correlations between intelligence and measures of creative achievement range from nonsignificant to mildly and significantly positive (see Barron & Harrington, 1981, for a review).

Do Ideational Fluency Tasks Measure Creativity?

This criterion validity issue was raised by Wallach (1970) as the most important agenda for the psychology of creativity for the next decade. By 1981, Barron and Harrington's (1981) review cited validating evidence at the elementary, junior high, and high school levels. This is encouraging, given the problems involved in judging creativity in children.

The general consensus is that ability to produce numerous and original ideas is a necessary but not sufficient condition for creative functioning. Barron and Harrington (1981) invoke personality characteristics as a factor in determining whether individuals capable of the creative process actually are productive. The view that prediction of creative performance is a multivariate issue (Cattell, 1971; Guilford, 1976) and that many social and psychological factors make an important difference for creative functioning is widely shared (e.g., Andrews, 1975; Torrance, 1975). Like Barron and Harrington (1981), Dellas and Gaier (1970) emphasize the contribution of personality characteristics over and above cognitive factors. In particular, independence, dominance, introversion, openness to stimuli, wide interests, self-acceptance, intuitiveness, flexibility, an asocial attitude, and unconcern for social norms seem to differentiate creative from noncreative adults. There is some evidence that this also holds true for younger people, which suggests to Dellas and Gaier that these traits develop fairly early and may be determinants rather than consequences of creative performance.   In addition to personality characteristics, Dellas and Gaier (1970) review considerable evidence that actual creative production or performance is highly dependent on motivational characteristics, as Golann (1963) has suggested. Inevitably, creative production results from a "long period of purposeful, relentless, organized thought, and motivated persistence" (Dellas & Gaier, 1970). This may be one route through which television viewing has the potential to influence creativity, albeit negatively.

We have seen that ideational fluency, personality characteristics, and motivational characteristics all have been theorized to play a central role in determining creative output. Societal factors also are relevant. As an extreme example, people who must spend their time and energy seeking food, shelter, and safety would be unlikely to produce creative products. This, of course, is what Maslow (1954, 1962) has proposed in his hierarchy of steps toward self-actualization. More subtle societal barriers no doubt also are important. Virginia Woolf's plea on behalf of women for "a room of one's own" (1929) in which to work uninterrupted is an eloquent example.

We focused on ideational fluency in this study because we were interested in the impact of television on creativity in children, and ideational fluency provided the best approach. We are well aware, however, that the problem of identifying creative products or performance, which is difficult enough with adults, is exacerbated in the case of children. Moreover, as Ward (1974) pointed out, there are too many experiences intervening between early childhood and maturity to expect significant prediction of accomplishment in adulthood. He suggested that researchers avoid using the word *creativity* in describing research with young children, and refer instead to what is being measured. We would prefer to follow Ward's suggestion, but unfortunately have found that exclusive use of terms such as ideational fluency leads to confusion rather than clarity. Early reports of our work have been cited as measuring "verbal fluency" or "verbal association," which is inaccurate. In this chapter we therefore have used the term creativity, as well as more specific terms, as a reminder of the conceptual domain of our work.

Relationship between Verbal Ability and Spatial Ability

The literature just reviewed justifies distinguishing creativity from intelligence. The evidence and arguments regarding verbal ability and spatial ability are less clear. On the one hand, people such as McNemar (1964), Vernon (1965), and Thorndike (1963) have argued that no grounds exist in terms of predictive validity for making any further distinction beyond a g factor within the general intelligence domain. On the other hand, Vernon (1979) has stated, "for some purposes, and with some populations, a hierarchical model of g plus specialized group factors seems most appropriate; in other circumstances, multiple factors, showing little or no obliquity, are more effective" (p. 61). He uses the analogy of school achievement—a child's performance could be characterized in terms of average, all-around achievement or in terms of marks in specific subjects, which might be quite varied.

In this study we have distinguished between verbal ability and spatial ability as aspects of intelligence for several reasons. First, they are the two facets of cognitive ability in which a sex difference is most consistently found; girls tend to excel in verbal ability and boys in spatial ability (e.g., Maccoby & Jacklin, 1974). Both experiential and biological hypotheses have been offered to explain these findings. The different pattern of sex differences suggested to us that performance on verbal and spatial tasks might be differentially affected by one aspect of a child's experience, namely exposure to television. Second, although Wechsler (1958, 1974) conceives of intelligence as a global entity (multifaceted and multidetermined), he avoids equating general intelligence with intellectual ability. In particular, his intelligence tests are divided into verbal and nonverbal, or performance, components, with the Vocabulary subtest consituting the single best verbal measure and the Block Design subtest, a measure of spatial ability, constituting the single best performance measure. Children in Wechsler's standardization sample who did well on one of these tests tended to do well on the other, but there still was considerable non-overlap.[1] Finally, empirical evidence from previous research indicates television may have a positive impact on vocabulary, at least for young children (Schramm et al., 1961). We knew of no evidence that television affects performance on spatial ability tasks and could think of no reason why it would when this study was designed. Researchers have become interested, however, in the form as well as the content and impact of the medium, stimulated perhaps by McLuhan's (1964) provocative statement, "the medium is the message," and have since begun to study television's noncontent features and their ramifications (e.g., Greenfield, 1984; Huston & Wright, 1983; Salomon, 1979; Watt & Welch, 1983). It seems possible that the skills involved in decoding information presented on television, comprehending the images, and so on, might facilitate performance on spatial ability tasks, although perhaps on two-dimensional more than three-dimensional ones. Conversely, spatial ability might predict interest in TV viewing.

Previous Research on Television and Cognitive Development

When television was first widely available, Maccoby (1951) suggested that although some time spent with television represents a shift from other mass media, much of it is taken from playtime, practicising musical instruments, and other forms of activity which might be called creative or potentially productive. Himmelweit et al. (1958) found no evidence to support this displacement hypothesis, but they focused more on expressive activities and interests and did not measure creativity. Furu (1971) regarded creativity as a disposition controlling television use. He reported that heavy viewers in the higher grades were inferior to print-oriented students in "intelligence, creativity, positivity, and adaptability, and had less interest in 'thinking' and 'science'" (p. 266). Wade (1971) similarly argued that creative adolescents are committed to a variety of activities in their leisure hours, and therefore limit their use of television. Her findings supported her hypothesis of a negative relationship between performance on creativity tasks and hours per week spent with TV ($r = -.29$, $p <$

.001), but since her data were correlational the alternative possibility that creativity is affected by television cannot be ruled out.

Subsequent research tends to support the hypothesis that television is a less adequate stimulus for imagination than either print or auditory media. Greenfield, Geber, Beagles-Roos, Farrar, and Gat (1981) found that children who heard an incomplete story on radio gave more imaginative story endings than did children who saw the same story on television. Imagination was not simply a negative function of amount of TV viewing, however, since working-class children were more imaginative on average than middle-class children, and other research indicates they are heavier TV viewers. Meline (1976) found that sixth and seventh graders exposed to a story via print or audiotape gave more stimulus-free and transformational ideas than children exposed to the same story via videotape; the videotape group stuck more closely to given facts and concepts.

Singer and Singer (1981) found in a longitudinal study that the children most likely to be imaginative during observed play in the nursery school were the brighter, older preschool boys who scored higher on an Imaginative Play Predisposition Interview and watched more hours of situation comedies but fewer hours of action–adventure shows. Imaginativeness of play in the nursery school was generally not, however, related to frequency of television viewing as reported by the child's parents. Another study linking imagination to content of television viewed at home was conducted by Zuckerman, Singer, and Singer (1983). Imaginative play of third, fourth, and fifth graders, as rated by their teachers, was predicted by higher IQ and home viewing of fewer fantasy–violence television programs. Amount of time spent reading also was inversely related to time spent watching fantasy–violence programs.

In her review of the literature on television and imagination, D. Singer (1982) concluded that empirical evidence supports an inverse relationship between heavy television viewing and self-generated imaginative capacity. Results from a longitudinal study beginning in the preschool years (Singer & Singer, 1983) indicate that "the combined measures of imaginativeness in the 8-year-old are best predicted by less television viewing, less recent viewing of realistic action–adventure programming, greater self-description as imaginative and creative by both parents, and less parental emphasis on power-assertive disciplinary methods" (p. 830).

Intelligence and Television

If there are reasons to hypothesize a negative relationship between television and creativity, what is the evidence concerning intelligence?

Cattell (1971) postulates two factors to account for performance on cognitive tests. Fluid intelligence, or Gf, is the constitutionally determined (not just genetically determined) "total associational or combining mass" of the brain that enables us to solve new problems, whereas crystallized intelligence, or Gc, represents skills and strategies acquired through environmental influences, including education. According to Cattell, conventional verbal tests (either individual or group) of intelligence and achievement are more dependent on crystallized than on fluid intelligence. His theoretical formulation would suggest that television, as an environmental influence, might affect performance on verbal measures of intelligence. It also seems likely, however, that people who differ in intelligence use television differently, in terms of both amount and content of what they watch and perhaps in level of involvement as well (what Salomon, 1983, calls AIME, amount of invested mental effort).

The 1982 NIMH review of research done during the 1970s on television and human behavior concluded there is consistent evidence of a negative relationship between amount of TV viewing and mental ability or IQ; this relationship is stronger for boys than for girls; and there is a difference in the range of IQ scores related to heavy and light viewing, reflecting a wide range of scores for light viewers but less variation for heavy viewers (Pearl et al., 1982, Vol. 1). They also concluded that the correlational nature of the evidence does not make it possible to state whether the relationship between TV viewing and intelligence occurs because individuals with lower IQ scores tend to watch more television or whether being a heavy viewer leads to lower scores. The issues and results regarding school achievement are even more complex, and school achievement is less consistently related to television exposure than is IQ. This occurs in part because it is important to control for intelligence when asking questions about the relationship between TV viewing and school achievement, and this has not always been done. In some instances, for example in California, IQ information is not available.

The picture may be even less clear than has been acknowledged. We will avoid the "what is intelligence and how can it best be measured" argument and consider instead performance on traditional measures of intelligence. Such measures have been the basis of the conclusion that there is a negative relationship between TV viewing and mental ability or IQ. Whether or not they do a good job of assessing intelligence, IQ tests do predict success in the school system. (Vernon estimates correlations as high as .7 to .8 in a heterogeneous group; 1979, p. 51.) We are thus faced with a paradox—television exposure tends to be consistently related to performance on measures of intelligence, which predict success in school, but television exposure is not consistently related to school achievement.

One possible explanation for the inconsistent pattern of relationships among television, intelligence, and school achievement is that researchers have taken vocabulary subtests from IQ tests and used them to measure school achievement. Their interest in television and vocabulary may be prompted by the hypothesis that television is an effective vocabulary teacher for children, or by the hypothesis that television displaces activities which otherwise would be effective vocabulary teachers. In either case, vocabulary is conceptualized as a measure of acquired knowledge. The problem is that the vocabulary subtests of intelligence measures such as the Stanford–Binet (S–B) or Wechsler Intelligence Scale for Children (WISC) typically are the single best predictors of the total score or IQ, and IQ tends to be fairly stable beyond the preschool years. Moreover, for reasons outlined below, to the extent vocabulary tests are viewed as measures of acquired knowledge, one would hypothesize a positive effect of television; but to the extent they are seen as measures of intelligence, one would hypothesize a negative relationship to TV viewing.

If we consider a vocabulary test to measure knowledge about words and objects, then television may function as a teacher. As is the case for television's influence in general, the effect is likely to be greatest when other sources of information and other teachers are lacking (Comstock, Chaffee, Katzman, McCombs, & Roberts, 1978; Hornik, Gould, & Gonzalez, 1980). For example, a child who grows up in a non-English-speaking household in an English-speaking country probably learns more English words from television than a child whose first language is English. A preschool child who is read to relatively infrequently probably acquires more information about words and objects from television than another preschooler who is read to more often, assuming that their spheres of operation in the world are otherwise similar. And a child who is not yet a fluent reader probably acquires more vocabulary from television than a child who reads well, all other things being equal. This is consistent with Schramm et al.'s (1961) finding that first graders who grew up with TV performed better on a vocabulary test than those who grew up without it, but no differences were found in grades 6 or 10.

If, on the other hand, we consider a vocabulary test in its role as a measure of intelligence, then we notice that it assesses some general skills, including strategies of memory search and retrieval, precision in thinking, and so on. These and other cognitive processes develop through experience, including play and games. Most current theories of development emphasize both the active role of humans in their own development and the importance of interactive real-world experience for development. The passive nature of television provides little experience of this sort. Moreover, although TV presents its viewers with a great deal of information, its format may not be optimal for learning. Collins (1982) suggests that the sheer proliferation of information on television and its relatively rapid pace may be counterproductive for effective learning. Reflection and even daydreams are used to organize ideas and plan for future behavior. Salomon (1983) argues that processing information from television requires only encoding and chunking, not mental elaboration. Children may acquire lower level processing skills via TV viewing and then use them to process information from other sources (e.g., print). If that material requires greater mental effort, the children will perform poorly. Time spent with television may displace activities, such as reading, that could be more effective learning experiences because they provide both the information and the opportunity to organize and reflect upon it.

So far we have asked whether and how television affects performance on various measures of intelligence and school achievement. We also need to ask whether children use television differently depending on their level of intelligence and/or school achievement. The theoretical and empirical considerations regarding the relationships among television exposure, intelligence, and vocabulary form a complex web which may prove difficult to untangle.

SUMMARY OF HYPOTHESES

There was very little precedent in the literature concerning the relationship between ideational fluency or originality and television exposure when this study was designed. For the empirical and conceptual reasons outlined earlier, we hypothesized that children who grew up without television would obtain higher mean ideational fluency and originality scores than children who grew up with television. We did not distinguish in our hypotheses between these two creativity measures.

If television can serve as a stimulus for cognitive development, it seems most likely to affect performance on measures related to informational experience. Children growing up in towns with television reception, therefore, were expected to score higher on vocabulary tests than children in a town lacking television. On the basis of Schramm et al.'s (1961) findings, this effect was expected to be strongest in the early elementary grades. On the other hand, to the extent that the vocabulary measure used is an index of general intelligence, for both theoretical and empirical reasons TV would be expected to be negatively related to performance. We designed this study with a positive rather than negative relationship in mind.

We chose to measure spatial ability because, in a sense, it formed a package with the other two primary abilities. Like them, it was an aspect of cognitive functioning, but unlike them, it seemed less clearly related to television exposure. As an aspect of intelligence it is probably in part constitutionally determined, but to the extent that performance is environmentally determined, direct experience with spatial tasks would be likely to be helpful. When we designed this study we thought television would provide little relevant experience; thus, differences on the WISC Block Design subtest in relation to television experience were expected to be minimal. More recent research indicates, however, that TV teaches media literacy. In conducting our analyses we therefore were open to the possibility that television experience would be positively related to spatial ability, either because children high in spatial ability are more attracted to the medium or because television facilitates performance on spatial ability tasks.

When we designed our research the evidence concerning television and general intelligence as reflected in IQ scores was mixed. Several researchers had found consistent negative relationships (e.g., Bailyn, 1959; Himmelweit et al., 1958), but there was some evidence of variation in younger children (Lyle & Hoffman, 1972), and Schramm et al. (1961) found that brighter children (IQ 115 or higher) watched more television than below average children (IQ 100 or less) until 10–13 years, after which the pattern reversed. Later evidence (reviewed by Morgan & Gross, 1982) tends to reflect a negative relationship, but much of that work has been done with older students. We were interested to see, therefore, whether and how IQ was related to amount of television exposure across the grades 1–10 age range for which we obtained data.

DESIGN OF THE RESEARCH

In Phase 1, the WISC Vocabulary subtest, WISC Block Design subtest, and Alternate Uses and Pattern Meanings creativity tasks (all described later in more detail) were administered individually to 160 grade 4 and grade 7 students in the three towns. In addition, the S–B Vocabulary subtest and the Peabody Picture Vocabulary Test (PPVT) were administered to 61 students in kindergarten and grade 1, but only in Notel and Unitel.[2]

In Phase 2, 147 grade 4 and grade 7 students in the three towns were given the same tasks administered to grade 4 and grade 7 students in Phase 1, providing cross-sectional comparisons between the phases. In addition, 137 students in grades 6 and 9 were assessed. This longitudinal sample represented 86% of the 160 fourth and seventh graders tested in Phase 1, and the retention rates for Notel, Unitel, and Multitel were similar (85%, 87%, and 87%, respectively). For the Alternate Uses, Pattern Meanings, and block design tasks there were no significant differences in Phase 1 between students who later were and were not available for follow-up, in terms of either mean scores or variability of scores.[3] There was no difference in variability for the WISC vocabulary scores, but the 23 students tested only in Phase 1 obtained a higher mean vocabulary score than the 137 students tested in both phases. This was due largely to Multitel; there was no difference between retained and nonretained students in Notel and Unitel. We have no ready explanation for this difference. The mean Phase 1 scaled score of the longitudinal group is very close to the norm for the test, whereas the mean for the small group tested only in Phase 1 is two-thirds of a standard deviation higher than the mean for the standardization population. This suggests that the group not available for follow-up was more anomalous than the longitudinal group. We also should note that this was the only significant difference in the entire project between retained and nonretained students. Chance would be expected to produce more than one significant difference, so in keeping with our general strategy of focusing on meaningful patterns of results, we did not pursue this issue further.

MEASURES AND PROCEDURES

Our measures were selected for their psychometric properties; all are widely used and well established.

Vocabulary

The Vocabulary subtest of the WISC requires the child to define a series of words (e.g., nail, alphabet, join); thus, it is a fairly stringent test of vocabulary knowledge. We chose it for several reasons. First, all Wechsler tests provide scaled scores for each subtest. Since scaled scores take into account the child's age, comparisons across age levels are possible. Second, the Vocabulary subtest has strong psychometric properties, showing consistently high correlations across age levels with both the verbal and full scale scores, and high split-half and test–retest reliability.[4] Finally, it was used by Wallach and Kogan (1965), so we could compare our findings concerning the relationship between creativity and intelligence with theirs.

In all three towns, the WISC Vocabulary subtest was given in Phase 1 to students in grades 4 and 7 and in Phase 2 to students in grades 4, 6, 7, and 9. The items are scored as 2, 1, or 0, with the distinction between 2 and 1 depending on the precision of the child's response. For example, in response to the item, "thief," "someone who takes from others" (with no elaboration) would be scored 1, whereas "someone who steals" or "takes without permission" would be scored 2. Following the rules outlined in the WISC scoring manual, two independent scorers eventually reached 94% agreement on the vocabulary scores, although it is perhaps worth noting that several sessions were required, and rules had to be developed to supplement those in the manual.[5]

Vocabulary data also were obtained in Phase 1 by Mary Morrison (the person who alerted us to the research opportunity in Notel). She administered the S–B Vocabulary subtest and the PPVT to children in kindergarten and grade 1. These tests were given only in Phase 1, and only in Notel and Unitel, so the design of this part of the study was comparable to the Radiotown and Teletown study by Schramm et al. (1961). Like the WISC (which would not have been appropriate for children at this age level), the S–B requires the child to define a series of words, but the response is scored only as 1 (acceptable) or 0. The PPVT is less stringent than the WISC and S–B vocabulary tests, since it does not require a verbal definition based on recall. Instead, each item consists of four pictures on one page; the child has to point to the picture describing the word said by the examiner. This involves recognition memory more than recall memory and is a test of receptive vocabulary, or what the child understands. The WISC and S-B are considered to be production measures of vocabulary, although strictly speaking none of these tests assesses whether the child actually uses the vocabulary in speech or writing.

Spatial Ability

The WISC Block Design subtest involves manipulation of a set of blocks to produce a design on the top surface of the set that matches a model. The model initially is another set of blocks manipulated by the examiner, and later, a drawing. The score depends on both the accuracy and speed with which each design is reproduced.

The WISC Block Design subtest has been widely used as a measure of spatial ability. It is the WISC performance measure most highly correlated with the performance score and full scale score (see note 4), and like the Vocabulary subtest it has the advantage of providing scaled scores. It also was one of the tests used by Wallach and Kogan (1965).

In all three towns, the Block Design subtest was given in Phase 1 to students in grades 4 and 7 and in Phase 2 to students in grades 4, 6, 7, and 9.

Creativity

As we explained earlier, ideational fluency, or the generation of many ideas, and ideational originality, or the generation of infrequent ideas, were our measures of creativity.

In Phase 1, fourth and seventh graders received five Alternate Uses items (magazine, knife, shoe, button, key). The child had to think of all the different ways each object could be used, and the researcher wrote down the answers. There were no time limits. This task, one of the early creativity measures developed by Guilford's group, was used by Wallach and Kogan (1965) and is cited by Barron and Harrington (1981) as among the instruments that have dominated divergent thinking research for the past 15 years. Our figural measure of ideational fluency was the Pattern Meanings task, developed by Wallach and Kogan (1965). In Phase 1, drawings a through e in Figure 3.1 were presented, each on a separate card, and the child was asked to think of all the things each complete drawing could be.

In Phase 2, the students in grades 4 and 7 in all three towns were given the same five Alternate Uses and five Pattern Meanings items given in Phase 1. The items given to the longitudinal sample differed somewhat because we were concerned about the possibility of a testing effect (see Chapter 1 for a more detailed discussion of this potential threat to internal validity). In particular, it seemed possible that some students might remember individual items and/or might have practiced the tasks following their administration in Phase 1. If they performed better in Phase 2 than in Phase 1 we would not be able to sort out whether this occurred because of a testing effect, because they were 2 years older, or for some other reason. Accordingly, in Phase 2 the longitudinal sample was given two of the Alternate Uses items from Phase 1 (shoe, button) and two new Alternate Uses items (chair, car tire). Similarly, two of the same Pattern Meanings items (b and d in Figure 3.1) and two different items (f and g in Figure 3.1) were administered. The addition of these new items dealt with the possibility of a testing effect for items, but we also were concerned about the possibility of a testing effect for the tasks. We therefore administered two additional ideational fluency tasks to the longitudinal sample in Phase 2, each consisting of two items. The Similarities task required the child to think of all the ways in which two things are alike or similar (meat and

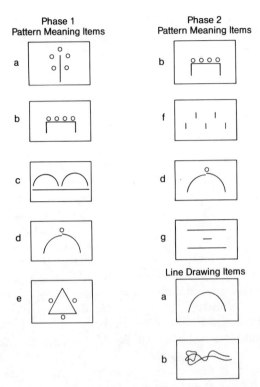

FIGURE 3.1   Pattern Meaning and Line Drawing creativity items given in Phase 1 and Phase 2 to the longitudinal sample. The cross-sectional sample received Pattern Meaning items a through e in both phases.

milk; curtain and rug), and the Lines task required the child to think of all the things a line drawing could be (see Figure 3.1). These new tasks and items were chosen from Wallach and Kogan's (1965) work. As it turned out, our concern about a testing effect was not well-founded; students barely remembered they had participated 2 years earlier, let alone remember what they had done.

For all creativity tasks the major score for the analyses was the total fluency score, that is, the total number of acceptable responses given for each item. Only answers that were repetitions of previous responses to the same item or were so obscure that no relationship could be discerned were excluded, and they were very rare (less than 1%). In each phase, interrater reliability for the fluency scores was established by having two raters independently score the responses of 20 children to all items. They agreed 100% (see note 5).

In Phase 1, the creativity data were scored for quality as well as quantity. One point toward a "uniqueness," or originality, score (Wallach & Kogan, 1965) was given for each answer not given by any other children in the entire Phase 1 sample. Two raters independently scored all responses to the item "magazine"; they reached 95% agreement (see note 5).

The results obtained in Phase 1 for uniqueness were similar to those for total fluency scores; correlations between the two types of scores were consistently high. Scoring the ideational fluency data for uniqueness was extremely time consuming, and research funds were limited, so since the Phase 1 uniqueness and total fluency results were similar, the Phase 2 ideational fluency data were scored only for fluency. More recently, Milgram et al. (1978) obtained findings in Israel with sixth and twelfth graders which, in their opinion, justify scoring for quantity of response only, a simpler and more reliable procedure yielding approximately the same results as scoring for quality. The high correlations we obtained between ideational fluency and uniqueness, therefore, are consistent with the findings of other researchers (including Wallach & Kogan). They support Mednick's (1962) argument that under conditions ensuring the appropriateness of ideas generated, a more creative person by comparison with a less creative individual will produce both more ideas in total and more that are novel.

IQ

IQ scores were obtained from the permanent school records when available. A mean was computed if the child had more than one score on a standardized group test. Such tests are not as reliable as individual tests (e.g., WISC, S–B) administered by an expert, a limitation we readily acknowledge. The fact that the scores came from a variety of tests given at varying points in the children's school careers also may pose a problem. Despite these limitations, group test IQ scores were used as a control in some analyses because of the theoretical and empirical importance of considering the intellectual abilities of the viewer when assessing the effects of television. Computing a mean when possible probably yielded increased reliability. The mean IQ for the 631 students with scores available was 101.7, with a standard deviation of 13.9. These are very close to the mean of 100 and standard deviation of 15 characteristic of almost all standardized tests, indicating that the students in Notel, Unitel, and Multitel constitute a representative sample of North American students, at least in this regard.

Task Administration Procedures

The cognitive ability measures were administered individually in a session lasting about an hour. The creativity tasks always were given first, followed by the WISC Vocabulary and Block Design subtests, in that order, because of Wallach and Kogan's (1965) contention that creativity can be validly assessed only in a nonevaluative, relaxed, untimed situation, that is, the sort of setting in which creative people usually are productive. If the creativity tasks were to be given in a nonevaluative atmosphere they had to precede the intelligence tasks, which clearly produce evaluation pressure. Both involve coming up with a correct answer, and children usually know when they are wrong. In addition, the block design task is timed. Since performance across tasks was not compared, counterbalancing was not required.

OVERVIEW OF ANALYSES

Our major test of the impact of television on vocabulary, spatial ability, and creativity focused on the natural experiment and asked whether groups differing in exposure to television differ in cognitive ability. We began by asking whether the overall pattern (vector) of vocabulary, block design, fluency uses, and fluency patterns scores differed according to town, phase, sex, grade, or combinations of these factors—and it did.[6] We therefore went on to analyze each of the four measures separately.

The second set of analyses focused on individuals rather than groups and asked whether there was correlational evidence of a relationship between TV viewing and cognitive ability. These analyses also addressed the question of stability in cognitive ability and the relationship between creativity and intelligence.

Finally, correlational analyses were used to explore the relationships between cognitive abilities and participation in leisure activities.

CREATIVITY: ALTERNATE USES RESULTS

Cross-Sectional Findings

Comparison of the Alternate Uses total ideational fluency scores of fourth and seventh graders in Phase 1 with their age-mates in Phase 2 revealed the hypothesized pattern of results (Figure 3.2 and Table 3.A1).[7] Before their town had television, Notel grade 4 and grade 7 students

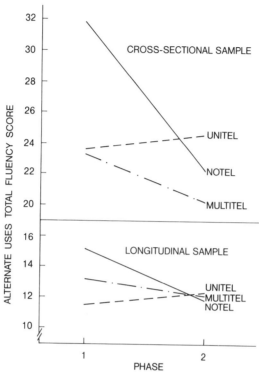

FIGURE 3.2   Alternate Uses mean total fluency creativity scores for the cross-sectional and longitudinal samples, by town and phase. Cross-sectional scores are based on five items in each phase, longitudinal scores are based on three in each phase.

obtained higher Alternate Uses scores than children who had grown up with television in both Unitel and Multitel. After Notel had had television reception for 2 years, however, Grade 4 and grade 7 students there did no better than students in Unitel and Multitel. In addition, the Phase 1 Notel children's creativity scores were significantly higher than the Phase 2 children's scores, but there was no difference for Unitel or Multitel.

The pattern of results for Phase 1 originality scores on the Alternate Uses task was the same as for total fluency scores (see Table 3.A1); Notel uniqueness scores were higher than those in Unitel and Multitel, which did not differ.[8] As we explained earlier, the ideational fluency tasks were not scored for orginality in Phase 2.

We next asked whether the pattern of findings changed when IQ was taken into account, based on the speculation that although creativity and intelligence are independent domains of thinking, only relatively intelli-

gent people may be capable of producing creative products. Although the
sample was smaller (IQ scores were available for 75% of the students), the
mean scores changed only slightly, and the pattern of results was the
same (Table 3.A1 and Figure 3.2). More important, IQ was not a significant covariate for Alternate Uses fluency or originality scores. In other
words, IQ did not play a significant role in the relationship between creativity and television exposure.

Longitudinal Findings

Were differences between Phase 1 and Phase 2 in the performance of
Notel students, as revealed by cross-sectional comparisons, corroborated
by the longitudinal analyses? Dellas and Gaier (1970) argued that creativity is a personality variable or trait influenced by experience. This implies
that changes due to experience will be limited to some range. The problem
of making specific hypotheses for the longitudinal sample was further
complicated by the evidence that creativity scores may drop during the
adolescent years (Kogan & Pankove, 1972; Torrance, 1975). We therefore
were looking for differential evidence of change, that is, a greater decrease in Notel than in Unitel and Multitel for children in the longitudinal
sample. That is what we found, but the analyses were more complicated
than for the cross-sectional sample.

As we noted earlier, children in the longitudinal group received five
Alternate Uses items in Phase 1 and four in Phase 2, of which two were
the same and two were different. Since findings based on a larger number
of items usually are more reliable than findings based on fewer items,
preliminary analyses were used to determine whether we could compare
performance on more than two items from each phase. (The minimum
would be the same two items given at both times.)

We asked whether there were differences in the mean Alternate Uses
scores for the individual items given within each phase, averaging across
the towns. In Phase 1 the scores for shoe, button, and key were comparable, and in Phase 2, scores for shoe, button, and chair were comparable.
In addition, correlations among scores on these sets of items were high,
and there was strong evidence that each three-item scale was internally
consistent and reliable.[9] Since the items were assessing the same theoretical construct, and since performance was empirically consistent, longitudinal analyses were based on the sum in each phase for three items.

The pattern of longitudinal results obtained with the Alternate Uses
task[10] mirrored that found for the cross-sectional sample (Figure 3.2 and
Table 3.A2). Only the scores of Notel students changed from Phase 1 to

Phase 2, and they decreased significantly. The towns differed before television came to Notel, but not 2 years later. In Phase 1, Notel students scored highest, and obtained significantly higher scores than students in Unitel, who scored lowest. Notel scores also were higher than those of students in Multitel, but not significantly so.

The only other significant result was that overall, averaging across the towns, the Alternate Uses scores of students originally in grade 4 were not different 2 years later when they were in grade 6, but the scores of the older group decreased significantly from grade 7 to grade 9 (see note 10). This replicates the decline in creativity scores during the adolescent years reported by other researchers (Kogan & Pankove, 1972; Torrance, 1975) and indicates that, at least in this sense, our sample was representative of North American students.

We did not conduct a second set of longitudinal analyses controlling for the effects of IQ, since the longitudinal and cross-sectional analyses of the Alternate Uses data yielded the same conclusions and IQ did not contribute significantly to the cross-sectional results.

On both the Similarities and Lines tasks (given in Phase 2 to longitudinal students), there were no differences related to town, sex, or grade, whether or not IQ was controlled (IQ contributed significantly to Similarities scores but not to Lines scores).

Summary of Alternate Uses Creativity Results

The results from the cross-sectional and longitudinal samples for the Alternate Uses task both indicated that exposure to television has a negative effect on creativity. In the absence of television, Notel children obtained higher ideational fluency scores than children in Unitel and Multitel. This was true for both total number of responses and originality. Two years after the arrival of TV, the total scores of Notel children had fallen, and the towns did not differ. We have no direct evidence concerning the processes involved, but we are inclined to suspect, along with Salomon (1983) and Collins (1982), that television affects information-processing skills in ways which may not be optimal for creative thinking. In addition, we suspect that children who do not regularly watch television spend more time in activities that facilitate creativity than do regular viewers. The kinds of responses given by Notel children before their town had television suggested they had a wider variety of experiences than Unitel and Multitel children. For example, they more often mentioned activities such as camping, hiking, building crafts, and projects. The results in Chapter 4 concerning participation in community activities tend to corroborate this impression. In later sections of this chapter we describe some exploratory analyses which provide tentative support for the hypothesis that use of leisure time is related to performance on creativity tasks.

CREATIVITY: PATTERN MEANINGS RESULTS

Results for the Pattern Meanings task were less clear cut than those concerning the Alternate Uses task.

The major finding for the cross-sectional data was that seventh graders obtained higher total Pattern Meanings scores than fourth graders (Table 3.A1).[11] This analysis also indicated that total scores varied according to town and phase, but not in a meaningful way. The towns did not differ significantly in either phase. The scores of Notel and Multitel students did not change from Phase 1 to Phase 2, but Unitel students' scores were higher in Phase 2 than in Phase 1. When we re-analyzed the Pattern Meanings fluency scores using IQ to partial out the effects of intelligence, IQ did make a difference; the relationship between town and phase disappeared and the only significant finding was a higher score in Phase 2 than in Phase 1.

The Phase 1 Pattern Meanings uniqueness scores were higher in grade 7 than in grade 4, but this was due mainly to Multitel.[12] There was only a marginally significant difference in the same direction in Notel, and no grade difference in Unitel. IQ did not contribute significantly to the Pattern Meanings uniqueness scores.

As we had done for the Alternate Uses longitudinal data, preliminary analyses were used to determine whether comparisons could be made for more than the two items given in both phases of the study. The mean Pattern Meanings scores did not differ for three of the patterns (a, b, and c in Figure 3.1) given in Phase 1 or for three (a, b, and d) given in Phase 2. Two of these were given at both times (a and b). Correlations among the three patterns in each set were high, and each three-item scale was internally consistent and reliable.[13] Longitudinal analyses for the Pattern Meanings task therefore were conducted on these two sets of three items each.

The only significant result was a sex difference that varied according to town.[14] Boys in Multitel obtained higher scores than boys in Unitel. Notel boys fell in between and did not differ from boys in either Unitel or Multitel. The girls' scores did not vary by town. Since neither the cross-sectional nor the longitudinal analyses of the Pattern Meanings data yielded readily interpretable findings, we did not conduct longitudinal analyses partialling out the influence of intelligence.

Summary of Figural Creativity Results

The lack of interpretable differences for the Pattern Meanings creativity task coupled with the clear-cut pattern of findings for the Alternate Uses creativity task is puzzling in view of the fact that for individual children, performance on the two tasks tended to be related. Children who obtained high scores on the Pattern Meanings task also tended to obtain high scores on the Alternate Uses task in both phases, as well as across the phases.

The simplest explanation of the figural creativity findings is that performance on the Pattern Meanings task is not related to TV exposure. Alternatively, or perhaps in addition, the Pattern Meanings task may not be as reliable or valid a measure as the Alternate Uses task, which certainly is better established as a measure of creativity (Barron & Harrington, 1981). A more complex possibility is that television may have both positive and negative effects. Television might in general negatively affect performance on creative thinking, as we have hypothesized, and as our Alternate Uses data indicate. At the same time, experience with television and becoming literate in the visual techniques of the medium may facilitate performance on figural tasks. As several researchers have demonstrated (e.g., Huston & Wright, 1983; Salomon, 1979; Wright & Huston, 1981), viewers must decipher the meaning of visual images on the screen and ascertain what they represent. This is true of all images shown, since they arise from a limited number of lines, but it is even more true for drawings (for example, cartoons). It is possible, therefore, that in the case of figural ideational fluency, television has a positive impact on interpretation of visual images but a negative impact on elaboration of ideas, producing the result of no differences among children in the three towns in this study. Although this seems to be an unnecessarily complicated possibility, we mention it because it would explain how we could obtain a different pattern of findings for the Pattern Meanings and Alternate Uses ideational fluency tasks and, at the same time, find that performance on the two tasks was related. Individuals might perform well or poorly on both tasks, but the mean level for the town could be affected by exposure to TV in one case and not the other.

INTELLIGENCE: SPATIAL ABILITY RESULTS

The cross-sectional block design data yielded no evidence that the availability of television is related to spatial ability (Table 3.A3).[15] The only finding was a sex difference, reflecting a higher mean Block Design scaled score for boys than for girls. This is consistent with previous findings for both the WISC Block Design subtest in particular and spatial ability in general (see Maccoby, 1966, and Maccoby & Jacklin, 1974, for reviews of this literature) and provides another indication of the representativeness of our sample.

The longitudinal block design data corroborated the cross-sectional findings in that the only statistically significant result was a sex difference favoring boys.[16] However, there was a marginally significant indication that this sex difference varied by town, and since town differences were of primary interest, we looked at it more closely. There was a strong sex difference in Multitel and a marginally significant sex difference in Unitel; in both cases the mean for boys was higher than the mean for girls. There was no sex difference in Notel, and Notel girls scored highest, obtaining a marginally higher mean score than Multitel girls. Unitel was in between and not different from Notel or Multitel. We mention this finding only because a similar pattern, namely no sex difference in a town without television coupled with a sex difference in towns with television, occurred in three other studies in this project (reading skills, sex-role attitudes, and participation in community activities). Results for sex role attitudes obtained in this project and in previous research described in Chapter 6 indicate that one of the effects of the content of television is to reinforce traditional sex-role stereotypes. It is interesting, therefore, to find that students who have grown up without television are less differentiated by sex in spatial ability, sex-role attitudes, reading ability, and leisure activity patterns than students who have grown up with TV.

The longitudinal analyses of the spatial ability data also revealed a marginally significant indication that scores differed according to town and phase, but the pattern was not readily interpretable (see note 16). The towns did not differ in Phase 1. In Phase 2, they differed only marginally; Unitel students obtained significantly lower block design scores than students in Notel, and marginally lower scores than students in Multitel (who were in between).

In sum, the major finding for the spatial ability task was a sex difference favoring boys, with a hint in the longitudinal data that this sex difference was more characteristic of children who grew up with television than those who grew up without it.

INTELLIGENCE: VOCABULARY RESULTS

In general, the Phase 1 data obtained by Mary Morrison for kindergarteners and first graders in Notel and Unitel did not support our hypothesis that television enhances children's vocabulary in the early grades (Table 3.A4). The pattern of findings for kindergarten was in the predicted direction; Unitel children obtained slightly higher mean raw S–B and PPVT raw scores and a higher PPVT mean IQ score than Notel children. The differences were small, however, and only the raw S–B vocabulary score reached even marginal statistical significance, based on a liberal (one-tailed) test. In grade 1, the opposite pattern occurred, and again, none of the differences was statistically significant. The different pattern of results and generally nonsignificant findings cannot be attributed to age, since the towns did not differ in age at either grade level (Table 3.A4). Moreover, multivariate tests of the vectors of results revealed that the pattern of findings was not significant at either grade level. In sum, the results for children entering school provide only a very slight hint of support for the hypothesis that television has a positive impact on vocabulary. This is when the effect would be expected to be strongest, based on both theoretical grounds and previous research (Schramm et al., 1961).

When the vocabulary scores of fourth and seventh graders in the cross-sectional sample were analyzed, the pattern for the three towns varied according to phase (Figure 3.3 and Table 3.A3).[17] In Phase 1 the means were ordered as hypothesized, with Multitel highest, Unitel next, and Notel lowest. The difference between the Multitel and Notel scores was

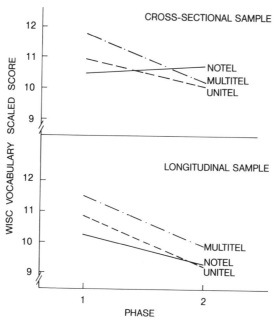

FIGURE 3.3   Wechsler Intelligence Scale for Children (WISC) mean Vocabulary scaled scores for the cross-sectional and longitudinal samples, by town and phase.

statistically significant, and the difference between the Multitel and Unitel means was marginally significant. However, the lack of differences among the towns in Phase 2 was not due to an increase in the Notel vocabulary scores following the inception of television, as had been hypothesized. Instead, there was a signficant decrease in Multitel scores and a marginally significant decrease in Unitel scores. These decreases resulted in an overall lower score in Phase 2 than in Phase 1.

An unexpected result was a grade difference in the WISC Vocabulary scaled scores, reflecting a higher mean scaled score for grade 4 than grade 7 (see note 17). This finding surprised us because we had used scaled scores rather than raw scores in the analyses, which should have meant that variation across towns in the children's ages would not influence the results and that analyses could be based on the combined data from the two grades. The finding that fourth graders scored higher than seventh graders does not mean that they obtained higher scores in absolute terms, but that fourth graders in our sample obtained higher vocabulary scores relative to the sample of fourth graders on whom the test was standardized than did seventh graders in our sample vis-à-vis the grade 7 standardization sample. Because of this grade difference in performance and because Schramm et al.'s (1961) data suggested that the relationship between television exposure and vocabulary might be different for fourth and seventh graders, we analyzed the cross-sectional data separately by grade. The results did not illuminate further the findings from the combined analysis.

In sum, although the cross-sectional findings for grades 4 and 7 from Phase 1 were consistent with Schramm et al.'s (1961) conclusion that television may have a positive impact on vocabulary scores, the cross-sectional findings from Phase 2 indicate that such a conclusion probably would be in error.

The longitudinal vocabulary results were consistent with the cross-sectional results. When the two groups (grades 4 to 6 and 7 to 9) were combined, the only significant differences were first, a decrease in mean scaled scores from Phase 1 to Phase 2; second, a different pattern of town differences for the two sexes (Table 3.A3); and third, the same overall grade difference as occurred in the cross-sectional sample, with the younger (grades 4 to 6) group scoring higher than the older (grades 7 to 9) group.[18] Town differences occurred only for boys, with Multitel boys obtaining higher vocabulary scores than Notel boys. Unitel boys were in between and not different from Notel or Multitel. In Multitel, boys scored significantly higher on average than girls, whereas there was a trend in the opposite direction for Notel. Again, analyses conducted separately for the older and younger longitudinal groups were not enlightening.

Conclusions Regarding Vocabulary Results

Taken as a whole, the vocabulary results do not support the hypothesis that TV viewing has a positive influence on children's vocabulary. There were, however, some hints in that direction. First, there was a marginally significant difference in raw S–B vocabulary scores favoring Phase 1 Unitel children in kindergarten over their peers in Notel. However, there was no difference in PPVT scores for children in either kindergarten or grade 1. The PPVT is a less stringent test than the S–B or WISC vocabulary tests, since it makes fewer demands on memory and speech and does not require the child to produce a definition or even to respond verbally. Any positive influence of TV on vocabulary should be assessed more readily by the PPVT than the S–B or WISC. It also is difficult to explain why television might have a positive influence on S–B scores in kindergarten but no influence in grade 1. The children were tested in September, so the majority in both kindergarten and grade 1 were unable to read, and this is when television should be most beneficial for vocabulary. If the data from kindergarten and grade 1 are combined, which would make sense on conceptual grounds, none of the differences is even marginally significant with a liberal (one-tailed) test. In sum, the Phase 1 data for children in kindergarten and grade 1 failed to replicate Schramm et al.'s (1961) data from Radiotown and Teletown. Both studies involved comparisons between children entering school in towns with and without TV reception, and they yielded contradictory findings.

If the design of our study had been analogous to the Schramm et al. design and if we had compared our Phase 1 data for grades 4 and 7 with their findings for grades 6 and 10, we would again have concluded that the results were contradictory. Ours would have indicated a positive effect of TV on vocabulary, whereas theirs indicated none at grade 6 and grade 10 levels. However, the addition of our Phase 2 data revealed that if television did have a positive impact on Multitel children's vocabulary scores, it was fleeting. The lack of change in Notel children's scores and the decrease in Multitel scores suggest instead that the Phase 1 findings were not robust. This conclusion is reinforced by the finding, discussed earlier, that Multitel Phase 1 students who were not available for follow-up in Phase 2 had anomalously high vocabulary scores (see note 3).

The third hint that TV may have a positive influence on vocabulary arose in the longitudinal data. The finding that Multitel boys obtained higher vocabulary scores than Notel boys, averaging across the two phases, might be taken as an indication that TV has a positive impact for boys but not for girls, if the effect is long term. That is, one would have to explain why the arrival of television in Notel did not yield an increase in vocabulary scores for boys from Phase 1 to 2, if the better performance of Multitel boys is to be attributed to TV. The finding that the typical sex difference yielding higher vocabulary scores for girls than for boys (Maccoby, 1966; Maccoby & Jacklin, 1974) was reversed for the longitudinal Multitel sample suggests instead that the Phase 1 scores of Multitel boys were anomalously high.

If we view the vocabulary tests as measures of acquired knowledge, these three weak hints do not provide sufficient support to conclude that TV has a positive influence. If, on the other hand, we view the vocabulary tests as measures of intelligence, the pattern of results provides no evidence to support the hypothesis that television influences performance on verbal (or spatial) measures of intelligence, either positively or negatively.

With the advantage of hindsight we now see that the impact of television on vocabulary, a question that seems simple enough at first glance, is complex. It is possible that television has the potential to have a positive impact on the aspect of performance related to acquired knowledge. Whether this occurs, however, probably depends on what the child would be doing if she or he were not watching TV. If older children spend some of that time reading, or if younger children are read to (by siblings, parents, babysitters), then it becomes a question of which activity is most effective for teaching vocabulary knowledge. Meringoff et al. (1983) found that preschoolers' memory for figurative language increased dramatically after having a picture book read to them, by comparison with their language recall after watching a televised version of the same story. It also is necessary to consider the aspects of vocabulary measures which make them good measures of general intelligence. Again, what children do if they are not watching television is relevant. Certain types of experience, including both games and reflective thinking, probably facilitate performance on intelligence tests. Of course, performance on IQ measures, including vocabulary tests, also is in part constitutionally determined and to that extent not open to environmental influence. Perhaps the influence of television on children's performance varies according to their level of intelligence. In the absence of TV, perhaps brighter children are more likely than less intelligent children to spend their time in activities that enhance their performance on vocabulary and other measures of intelligence. In other words, a transactional process may occur, reminiscent of "the rich get richer."

Rather than asking whether television has an impact on some behavior or measure, we need to ask under what circumstances and for which people does it have an impact. This statement that the effects of television may be specific rather than general is not new; it was the conclusion reached by Schramm et al. (1961) and has been reiterated by Pearl et al. (1982). Unfortunately, qualified rather than absolute statements lead many people to conclude either that television has no influence, or that its effect cannot be determined. We would argue that this belief is mistaken, and that researchers and the public need to consider the impact of TV in all of its complexity.

CORRELATIONAL ANALYSES

Four questions prompted us to explore our data further using correlational and other techniques. These questions dealt with the stability of individual performance on our cognitive measures over time, the relationship between creativity and intelligence, the relationship within our sample between TV viewing and cognitive ability, and the relationship between creativity and participation in other leisure activities. The first two questions speak to methodological and conceptual issues with important ramifications for the last two questions.

Stability of Cognitive Abilities

If we want to assess the impact of the environment on human behavior, we need to know how stable an individual's performance is in that area over both the short and long run. This is especially important when correlations between variables such as TV viewing and cognitive ability are computed, since correlations between measures of two different behaviors assessed on either the same or different occasions would be expected to be lower than correlations between measures of the same behavior obtained on two different occasions.[19]

Students in the longitudinal sample who obtained high vocabulary scores in Phase 1 also tended to do so in Phase 2 ($r = .72$; Table 3.A5), and the same was true for block design scores ($r = .55$).[20] It also was true, although to a lesser degree, for the Alternate Uses ($r = .35$) and Pattern Meanings ($r = .38$) tasks.

Data on the short-term reliability of the creativity tasks unfortunately are difficult to locate, which makes it hard to evaluate our findings regarding stability over a 2-year interval. In their review of the creativity literature, Dellas and Gaier (1970) cite Guilford's (1966) attempt to explain "the low reliability of tests of divergent production" (p. 57). In a similar vein, Vernon (1979) states, "As scores on divergent thinking tests are rather unreliable (i.e., unstable over time), it seems unlikely that they will reveal any strong genetic component'' (p. 65). No evidence for these statements is cited, however. Wallach and Kogan (1965) reported split-half reliability coefficients for their creativity measures, but no test–retest reliability data.

Torrance (1974) reports the results of several studies involving his creativity tasks. Mackler (1962; cited in Torrance, 1974) used Torrance's Unusual Uses task, which is similar to the Alternate Uses task, and tested people on three occasions, 2 weeks apart. The means of the three correlations were .67 for fluency and .66 for originality scores. Williams and Fleming (1969) gave ideational fluency items from Wallach and Kogan's (1965) battery (including Alternate Uses, Pattern Meanings, and Line Drawing items) to 16 3- and 4-year-olds in two sessions, 4 to 6 weeks apart. Half the items were given in one session and half in the other, and performance across the two occasions was significantly correlated ($r = .42$, $p < .05$).

In sum, significant evidence of stability in the performance of individuals on all the cognitive measures was demonstrated over the 2-year interval between phases. Stability was greater for the measures of intelligence than for the measures of creativity, supporting Vernon's (1979) contention that ideational fluency is more open to environmental influence. This in turn is consistent with the results of our analyses of mean differences between the towns, which indicated that television has an impact on creativity as measured by the Alternate Uses task, but is not related systematically to performance on vocabulary or spatial ability measures.

Relationship between Creativity and Intelligence

Our findings concerning creativity and intelligence generally support their conceptualization as independent aspects of thinking (see Tables 3.A5 and 3.A6). The correlations among the verbal and figural ideational fluency measures tended to be high within and across the phases, as did the correlations among the measures of intelligence. By contrast, the correlations between the measures of creativity and intelligence tended to be low, although the pattern was not perfect. In sum, our results generally replicate those obtained by Wallach and Kogan (1965) in an urban U.S. setting and tend to support the conclusion that creativity and intelligence should be viewed as independent rather than similar aspects of thinking. They also conform fairly well to the criteria set forth by Campbell and Fiske (1959) for establishing convergent and discriminant trait validity.

TV Viewing and Cognitive Abilities

USE OF TELEVISION ACCORDING TO COGNITIVE ABILITY

The natural experiment enabled us to ask whether students who obtained high scores on the cognitive measures before television was available differed in their use of television 2 years after its arrival from students who initially obtained lower scores. We divided the Phase 1 Notel students at the median on each Phase 1 cognitive measure and then tested to see whether the groups differed in the amount of television they reported watching in Phase 2.[21] Notel students who scored above the median on the WISC Vocabulary subtest in Phase 1 reported watching less television (mean, 19 hours per week) in Phase 2 than students who had been below the Phase 1 median (mean, 26.3 hours per week). There were no significant differences for the other measures. This particular issue seemed best to address with data from Notel, but we did conduct a second set of analyses combining the Phase 1 cognitive data from the three towns and dividing the sample on each measure into those scoring one standard deviation or more above the mean, those scoring in the middle range, and those scoring one standard deviation or more below the mean.[22] No differences were found for the creativity measures or for the spatial ability task, but students who scored one standard deviation or more above the vocabulary mean reported watching significantly less television (mean, 19.0 hours per week) than those who scored in the middle range (27.05 hours) or one standard deviation below the vocabulary mean (29.2 hours). The latter groups did not differ, but there was a significant linear trend in the group means. The similarity between these findings and those for Notel alone tends to argue against chance as an explanation.

Our results indicating that TV use varies according to vocabulary scores are corroborated by some results reported in Chapter 5. Students in the three towns were divided into four groups on the basis of the group test IQ scores taken from the school records. There was a significant linear decrease in Phase 2 mean hours of TV viewing as IQ increased.[23] The negative correlations obtained in other studies between amount of TV viewing and school achievement or IQ (see Morgan & Gross, 1982, for a review) may, therefore, reflect differences between high and low scorers in use of television, rather than an influence of TV on achievement. The relationship also may be transactional, of course, as we discussed earlier.

The finding that students did not differ in amount of television watched in Phase 2 according to the Alternate Uses or Pattern Meanings scores they obtained in Phase 1 tends to argue against Wade's (1971) hypothesis that highly creative children use television differently than less creative children. Our data speak to this issue only in terms of amount of television, however, and it is possible that children who vary in creativity use TV differently in other ways. They may, for example, watch different kinds of programming, attend to and/or remember different material, process information differently, and so on. Our finding that Notel students obtained higher Alternate Uses scores than Unitel and Multitel children before television was available, but did not differ from them after 2 years of regular viewing, and did not use television differently according to their Phase 1 Alternate Uses scores, does tend to support our conceptual analysis emphasizing displacement rather than content for television's role in the development of creativity.

CORRELATIONS BETWEEN TV VIEWING AND COGNITIVE ABILITIES

Since most previous research has involved correlating exposure to television with performance on some measure of cognitive ability, we wanted to compare our findings with those obtained by other researchers for other samples. Correlational analyses also would indicate whether the results based on comparisons across the towns were corroborated by results based on comparisons among individuals within the towns. We approached these analyses with some trepidation, however. On the one hand, demonstration of a significant relationship between amount of viewing and performance on the cognitive measures would strengthen any conclusion arising from the natural experiment. On the other hand, as we and others have argued (Hornik, 1981; Williams, 1981; also see Chapter 1), the absence of significant correlations between television viewing and individual difference variables means only that a linear relationship does not hold, and we suspect a linear relationship may not be the most appropriate model for the impact of television.

Since most students in Notel watched no television in Phase 1 (median, 0 hours per week), all analyses involving Phase 1 hours of TV viewing were based only on Unitel and Multitel. Because Notel children's experience with television changed from Phase 1 to Phase 2, it seemed possible that relationships between television viewing and the cognitive measures would be more stable for students in Unitel and Multitel, whose experience had not changed. We therefore computed Phase 2 correlations separately for Notel students and for Unitel and Multitel (combined), as well as for all three towns combined. Since both TV viewing and cognitive ability scores varied with age, we controlled for age in these analyses.

The Phase 1 television-viewing data were not significantly related to performance by the Unitel and Multitel students on any of the cognitive ability measures (Table 3.A7).[24] The Phase 2 data yielded more interesting results. TV viewing was significantly negatively related to performance on the block design task and marginally negatively related to performance on the Pattern Meanings task, but only when all three towns were combined. Thus, there was no evidence to support Greenfield's (1984) contention that the visual nature of television may be positively related to performance on spatial ability or figural creativity tasks. The negative relationship between TV viewing and block design scores is not consistent with the evidence from the natural experiment which indicated that spatial ability does not vary as a function of television exposure. Since the WISC Block Design subtest is one component of a measure of general intelligence, the finding of a negative correlation between TV viewing and block design scores may simply reflect differential use of television according to IQ level. The lack of differences among the towns in mean scores tends to argue against a causal interpretation in the opposite direction.

The lack of significant correlations between amount of television watched and Alternate Uses scores suggests that the effect of television (seen previously in the town comparisons) is not linear, as we have hypothesized. Conversely, or in addition, television's impact may be more indirect than direct. That is, other activities may play an important role in the development of creativity by fostering mental elaboration and reflection or providing a wide range of experiences, and some of these activities may be displaced by TV. These speculations received some support from the analyses involving other activities and are discussed in more detail later on.

The finding that television viewing was not correlated with performance on the WISC Vocabulary subtest corroborates our finding of no relationship based on comparisons among the towns before and after Notel had television. It is not consistent, however, with the analyses involving median and third splits on vocabulary scores discussed earlier.

The relationship between group IQ test scores and TV viewing is described in Chapter 5. After age and sex were controlled, IQ was not significantly correlated with hours of TV viewing for Unitel and Multitel students (combined) in either Phase 1 or Phase 2. The relationship was significant ($r = -.31$, $p < .001$) for Notel in Phase 2.

In sum, our analyses exploring the relationship between TV viewing and cognitive abilities yielded mixed results. There was no evidence that amount of TV watched varies according to creativity scores obtained 2 years earlier, no evidence that students who obtain high Alternate Uses scores concurrently report watching more or less TV than those who obtain low scores, and only a hint that creativity Pattern Meanings scores

vary concurrently (negatively) with TV viewing. By contrast, there were
several indications that brighter students spend less time with TV than do
their less intelligent peers. These latter findings support the results of
numerous other studies. As the NIMH report (Pearl et al., 1982) pointed
out, however, they do not enable us to ascertain the direction of causation
underlying the negative relationship between IQ and amount of television
watched. It seems likely that the relationship occurs in part because
brighter children choose to spend less time watching television than do
their less intelligent schoolmates. It also is possible that children who
watch less television spend more of their time in activities which directly
or indirectly faciliate performance on cognitive measures. A transactional
model most likely applies. Children who participate in a wide variety of
activities are more likely to show enhanced performance on cognitive
measures than children whose experience is less varied, whatever their
initial level of intelligence. Since brighter children probably seek out more
varied experiences, however, they probably gain more than do slower
children, who fall further behind in part because they spend more time
with TV and less time in other activities. Whichever interpretation turns
out to be correct, the relationship, as reflected in the correlations and
mean differences among the towns, is not particularly strong. The bright-
est students in our sample watched about 5 hours less television per week
(or 45 minutes less per day) than the least intelligent group.

Cognitive Ability and Participation in Leisure Activities

Information from the study of participation in leisure activities (Chapter
4) enabled us to conduct an exploratory test of our hypothesis that television affects performance on creativity tasks by taking time away from
activities and experiences that otherwise would facilitate performance.

The community leisure activities were grouped into 12 categories; for
the purposes of this chapter we used the total score and the subtotal for
Sports. Students also indicated how often they had participated during the
previous year in each of 58 private leisure activities; we used the total as
well as frequency reports for the items "reading books" and "listen to
radio" for both phases. The relationships between the students' reports
for these leisure activities and the Phase 1 and Phase 2 cognitive ability
scores are shown in Table 3.A8.[25] Since both leisure activity participation
and performance on some cognitive measures vary with sex, we controlled for gender in one set of analyses; the results are in the bottom half
of Table 3.A8. Since intelligence might be a third variable related both to
participation in leisure activities and performance on the creativity tasks,
we also controlled for IQ in the analyses for the creativity tasks.[26]

The correlational analyses do provide some indication that participation in community and private leisure acitivities is related to performance on measures of creativity. Particularly provocative is the evidence that book reading is more strongly and more consistently related to creativity, vocabulary, and block design scores (as seen in Table 3.A8) than is amount of television viewing (as seen in Table 3.A7). Causal inferences cannot be made from these correlational findings alone, but when they are considered in the context of the results from comparisons among the towns based on the natural experiment, they provide some support for our hypothesis that television has a negative influence on ideational fluency because it displaces activities which otherwise might facilitate performance. At the same time, the fact that amount of book reading tended not to be correlated significantly with amount of television watched (the negative correlations for Notel in Phase 2 were the exception; see Chapter 5, Tables 5.A5 to 5.A7) suggests that a simple displacement hypothesis is inadequate. We shall elaborate on this point in the next section.

SUMMARY AND CONCLUSIONS

Our discussion of the relationship between TV viewing and cognitive abilities has covered a good deal of conceptual and empirical territory, so it may be useful to recapitulate the major findings and conclusions.

Summary of Results

CREATIVITY: ALTERNATE USES

Our findings for the Alternate Uses task were consistent and supported the hypothesis that television has a negative impact on creativity. Before their town had television, students in Notel obtained higher total and higher originality scores on the Alternate Uses task than students in Unitel and Multitel. Two years after the arrival of TV, the total scores of both the same Notel students (longitudinal sample) and same-aged Notel students (cross-sectional sample) had fallen to the level of students in the other towns. This pattern of results, which did not change when the effect of intelligence was removed, suggests that the availability of television and the acquisition of normal TV-viewing habits leads to a decline in mean level of performance on one of the most widely used measures of creativity available. The finding that Alternate Uses scores fell following the introduction of TV to Notel coupled with the finding that students with high versus low creativity scores in Phase 1 did not watch different amounts of TV in Phase 2 tends to rule out the interpretation that the negative relationship between TV viewing and creativity arises only because individuals who vary in creativity use TV differently.

The evidence from most of the analyses tends to converge on the conclusion that TV viewing has a negative influence on creativity, as measured by the Alternate Uses task. What theories have been offered to explain creative thinking, and how might television affect this process?

One major avenue of theorizing stems from psychoanalytic theory and its distinction between primary and secondary process. According to Suler (1980), both primary and secondary process thinking develop because infants must organize their perceptual world and integrate their needs with the environment (Holt, 1966). Primary process is an egocentric organizational mode which maintains the sense of self in the face of a changing environment, whereas secondary process is directed more to encounter and mastery (Noy, 1969). Under normal conditions, however, the two coordinate their efforts in maintaining self-identity and adapting to the environment. According to Suler (1980),

> The creative act can be conceptualized as a special form of interaction between primary and secondary process thinking in which a novel idea or insight is generated by the loose, illogical, and highly subjective ideation of primary process and is then moulded by secondary process into a context that is socially appropriate and meaningful to others. (p. 144)

He rejects the more traditional psychoanalytic view that creativity results from "regression in the service of the ego" (Kris, 1952), that is, that regression from secondary to primary process occurs in creative acts. Instead, Suler focuses on the access of secondary process to primary process.

The extent to which primary process is involved will, according to Suler, vary with the type of creative act involved. "Divergent thinking alone may not require any special access to primary process but may instead rely on those cognitive functions developed through the permanent integration of primary process styles into secondary process" (p. 160). Further, "the ability to think loosely, as required by tests of divergent thinking, is not necessarily a manifestation of primary process but may perhaps reflect cognitive faculties derived from primary process in the course of development" (p. 155). Suler differs with other theorists on the question of whether creativity is a stable personality characteristic.

> A more accurate assumption is that creative thinking is, for some people, a stable characteristic across situations but that for others creativity is a sporadic or situation-specific phenomenon. . . . Creativity is not some mysterious, invariable trait but a cognitive function shaped both by the immediate environment and by the larger cultural and historical context in which we live. (p. 161)

Most people who study creativity talk at some point about fluency of ideas, thinking that flits between ideas, and so on. Suler's analysis provides a theoretical context for these concepts. Although based on psychoanalytic ideas, his formulation is strongly cognitive. He argues that although creativity may be in part constitutionally derived, environmental factors also play a major role. He does not, unfortunately, spell out how, so we shall speculate.

If creativity is associated with receptive openness to experience, and if primary process becomes integrated with secondary process thinking as development proceeds (at least in highly creative as opposed to less creative individuals), then it would make sense that individuals who have a greater variety of experience will have more experiences to draw upon, and more emotion or affect (primary process) associated with memories of those experiences.

Suler's (1980) linking of affect or emotion to cognition via the concepts of primary and secondary process in psychoanalytic theory is reminiscent of Piaget's (1981) contention that thinking and affect are inextricably intertwined. Moreover, both emphasize the role of experience. It is our hypothesis, based in part on both of these theoretical positions, that television has a negative impact on creativity because of the kinds of experience it displaces. The several hours spent watching television each day by most North Americans probably results in an impoverished bank from which they can draw when in a situation that requires creative thinking or ideational fluency.

The format and content of television may not be optimal for development of the kinds of information-processing skills which facilitate creative thinking. Salomon (1983) contends that watching television does not require mental elaboration, so TV teaches viewers to process information only at lower levels (encoding, chunking). These information-processing skills are then used with material (e.g., print) and in situations (e.g., problem-solving tasks) for which they are inadequate or inappropriate. Collins (1982) contends that the pace and format of television discourage reflection. Both elaboration and reflection are important aspects of creative thinking. Dellas and Gaier's (1970) review of research on creativity led them to conclude that an individualistic rather than sociocentric orientation is important for creative performance, that is, an ability to tolerate aloneness with one's thoughts and ideas, to deal with the "anxiety of separateness." Wallach's (1970) review of research on creativity led him to conclude that "the crux of the matter revolves around the process of generating or producing associates without regard to evaluating them for relevance or applicability to a problem or task" (p. 1254). What is required, he suggested, is "breadth of attention deployment," and spontaneous fantasy or daydreaming "represents a form of attentional wandering par excellence" (p. 1261). Whereas television presents considerable fantasy to its viewers (and, indeed, sometimes is criticized for presenting too much), it may not encourage spontaneous fantasy (Singer & Singer, 1981, 1983). If anything, its attraction tends to be that it provides an alternative—instead of daydreaming, perhaps in part because of boredom, the individual seeks entertainment. The "constant television" phenomenon (keeping the TV on all day for company; Medrich, Roizen, Rubin, & Buckley, 1982) seems unlikely to encourage the ability to tolerate aloneness with one's thoughts and ideas.

In addition to displacing internal or mental experiences which otherwise might facilitate creative thinking, television may displace problem solving in games or situations encountered during other pursuits. Chapter 8 provides some evidence that television may have a negative impact even for adults on creative problem-solving performance and persistence.

Television apparently narrows the range and number of other leisure activities (Chapter 4), but a simple displacement explanation is inadequate, since there is evidence in both this and other studies (Medrich et al., 1982) that amount of TV viewing is not necessarily linearly related to participation in leisure activities or performance on cognitive measures. A nonlinear relationship may obtain, and/or as Medrich et al. suggest, the effect may be more motivational than directly time related. That is, the availability of television and the habit of being a regular viewer may make children less likely to think of alternative activities, and this effect may not be linear. The other options vary from time to time and person to person. Children (and adults) tend not to recognize that watching television involves choosing not to do other things. In addition, the content and format of television may encourage convergent rather than divergent thinking, and viewers may develop a "let you entertain me" orientation rather than a reflective orientation and motivation to persevere with difficult tasks. The common practice of time-sharing other activities with television viewing (Anderson, 1983) also may fractionate attention rather than encourage the development of concentration and the kinds of skills required for problem solving. As the habit of watching television during "free time" develops, alternative activities may come to mind less frequently.

Our hypothesis that television viewing displaces activities that might otherwise facilitate the development of creativity received some preliminary support. Involvement in other leisure activities tended to be positively correlated with performance on the creativity tasks. The contrast between the results for book reading and television provides a provocative starting point for further research on the role of leisure and other activities in the development of creativity.

CREATIVITY: PATTERN MEANINGS

The findings for the figural creativity task were less clear cut than those for the Alternate Uses task. Our major analyses yielded no evidence that performance on the Pattern Meanings task was related to the availability of television. In Phase 2, however, hours of TV viewing was marginally negatively correlated with Pattern Meanings scores when all three towns were combined. Why might the Alternate uses and Pattern Meanings tasks yield different patterns of results in relation to television viewing?

The Alternate Uses task requires the individual to think of all the different ways in which a common item could be used. General problem-solving skills, experience in similar situations, and experience with such items all probably would be helpful, as would flexibility in thinking. Although the figural tasks also require flexibility in thinking, they may draw more upon visual-spatial perceptual skills and less upon a broad range of experience. For some children, TV viewing may displace other activities which might facilitate performance on the Alternate Uses task, in the ways outlined above. Ward, Kogan, and Pankove (1972) suggested that tasks such as Alternate Uses may favor individuals with richer experiential repertoires, whereas figural tasks may have more to do with the organization and accessibility of repertoires. It is possible that experience with television facilitates performance on the visual-spatial aspect of figural tasks, but also displaces some activities that otherwise would facilitate problem-solving skills, and hence the results are less interpretable. Another possibility is that the verbal presentation of items in the Alternate Uses task favored children with less television experience. Perhaps a visual presentation of the item (e.g., a photograph of a key) would yield a different pattern of results. Finally, the Pattern Meanings task may not be as reliable a measure as the Alternate Uses task, which has a more eminent history as a measure of ideational fluency.

SPATIAL ABILITY

The major analyses focusing on mean differences for the block design task yielded little or no evidence that availability of television affects spatial ability. The only relevant piece of evidence was the finding for the longitudinal sample that a sex difference (favoring males) is characteristic of children who grow up with television but not those who grow up without it.

The correlational analyses conducted at the individual rather than the group level tended to reveal a negative relationship between hours of TV viewing and block design scores. This is consistent with the conclusion drawn in the NIMH (1982) review of research concerning the relationship between intelligence and TV viewing.

VOCABULARY

The weight of the evidence from comparisons among the towns did not support our hypothesis that television has a positive impact on vocabulary for children in the early grades. The correlational analyses corroborated this finding, yielding no evidence of a concurrent relationship between WISC vocabulary scores and hours of TV viewing. However, the median split and third analyses indicated that students in Phase 1 who obtained high vocabulary scores tended to watch less TV 2 years later than those who obtained low scores. Participation in other leisure activities, most notably book reading, tended to be positively related to performance on the WISC Vocabulary subtest.

Children undoubtedly do learn some vocabulary from television. The question is whether they learn as much or more than they would from activities they would be engaging in if they were not watching TV. Television may be more likely to have a positive impact on vocabulary for young children than for older children, because the former cannot read. This is consistent with the findings of Schramm et al. (1961), although data obtained in our own study by Mary Morrison did not support this hypothesis. In future research, information concerning the frequency with which young children are read to (by older siblings, baby-sitters, parents, and the like) should be obtained along with other measures of the reading and vocabulary environment of the home. Roberts, Bachen, Hornby, and Hernandez-Ramos (1984) found that the home environment in terms of both print and television contributes significantly to reading achievement at the grade 3 and grade 6 levels. We would be surprised if it did not also contribute to performance on vocabulary tests.

Finally, we might expect that television would be a more positive teacher of vocabulary when the language used on television is a second rather than a first language, particularly if children usually converse with adults in their first language. The general role of television in the adjustment of immigrants to a new culture strikes us as another important avenue for further research.

Conclusions

Our first conclusion is that television has a negative influence on creativity, as reflected in ideational fluency and measured with the Alternate Uses task. Integration of several results from this study and from Chapters 4 and 5 indicates, however, that the effect of television is more indirect than direct. Alternate Uses scores were higher in the absence than in the presence of television, as was participation in community activities (Chapter 4). Creativity scores generally were not concurrently correlated with hours of TV viewing, and children who had high versus low Phase 1 creativity scores did not watch different amounts of TV 2 years later. By contrast, creativity scores were significantly and positively correlated with participation in other leisure activities, both within and across the phases, even after sex and IQ were controlled. This set of findings suggests that television displaces other activities (although probably not linearly). In short, TV may displace both internal (information processing) and external (activity) experiences which otherwise would facilitate creativity. We earlier discussed some theoretical perspectives on creativity, but none took a developmental approach. What is needed now is longitudinal research designed to assess the role of various experiences, including television, in the development of creative thinking and performance.

Our results regarding verbal ability and spatial ability were mixed. On the one hand, comparisons among the towns in the natural experiment yielded no evidence that television affects spatial ability, and the few hints that it may have a positive impact on vocabulary were not sufficient to warrant that conclusion. On the other hand, vocabulary scores were not concurrently related to hours of TV viewing, but students with low Phase 1 vocabulary scores watched more TV 2 years later than students with high Phase 1 scores. The opposite was true for spatial ability; block design scores were significantly negatively correlated with hours of TV viewing, but Phase 1 scores were not predictive of Phase 2 TV-viewing reports. To complicate matters further, group test IQ scores were negatively related to amount of TV watched (Chapter 5), as other researchers have found (Pearl et al., 1982). Finally, vocabulary and block design scores were positively related to book reading. Since both measures are known to be reliable, and performance in this study was stable from Phase 1 to Phase 2, chance or error in measurement are unlikely explanations of the somewhat mixed results regarding TV and the block design and vocabulary scores. We are inclined to think the dual purpose of the measures is at fault; both assess intelligence as well as acquired knowledge. Some aspects of the results indicate that brighter students read more and watch less television than do less intelligent students (see Chapter 2 for further discussion). Fetler's (1982) research indicates they also watch different programs. Television teaches some vocabulary and provides some visual-spatial experiences. Whether its role as a teacher in these areas is positive or negative, however, depends upon what students would be doing if they were not watching TV, and this varies with age, IQ, socioeconomic status, and so on. In short, the paradox is that television may be both positively and negatively related to performance on vocabulary and spatial ability tests. Teasing out the transactional nature of the relationships among TV viewing, other activities, intelligence, vocabulary, performance on spatial tasks, and school achievement will not be easy.

However indirect are the processes involved, our results indicate that television plays a more inhibiting than facilitative role in the aspects of children's thinking that we studied. Whether changes in the format (for example, interactive systems), the content, or the use of North American television will yield more optimistic conclusions remains to be seen.

APPENDIX: TABLES

TABLE 3.A1
Means for the Cross-Sectional Creativity Data

	Total			Phase means	Uniqueness		
	Notel	Unitel	Multitel		Notel	Unitel	Multitel
Alternate Uses raw scores[a]							
Phase 1	31.79	22.63	23.35	25.92	4.09	2.32	2.25
Phase 2	22.32	24.51	20.22	22.35			
Town means	27.06	23.57	21.78				
Pattern Meanings raw scores[b]							
Phase 1	19.91	16.92	20.97	19.27	4.37	3.86	5.06
Phase 2	22.38	22.12	18.46	20.98			
Town means	21.15	19.52	19.72				
Pattern Meanings adjusted scores[c]							
Phase 1	19.50	15.73	20.20	18.48			
Phase 2	22.60	21.94	20.00	21.51			
Town means	21.05	18.84	20.10				

[a] IQ was not a significant covariate for either total scores or uniqueness scores.
[b] IQ was a significant covariate for total scores but not for uniqueness scores.
[c] Adjusted for IQ.

TABLE 3.A2
Means for the Longitudinal Creativity Data

	Notel	Unitel	Multitel	Means
Alternate Uses total scores				
Phase 1	15.17	11.46	13.17	13.27
Phase 2	11.80	12.21	11.99	12.00
Town means	13.49	11.83	12.58	
Pattern Meanings total scores				
Girls	13.44	10.90	10.37	11.57
Boys	11.18	9.75	15.01	11.98
Town means	12.31	10.33	12.69	

TABLE 3.A3

Means from the Cross-Sectional and Longitudinal Analyses
of the WISC Vocabulary and Block Design Data

	Cross-sectional				Longitudinal			
	Notel	Unitel	Multitel	Means	Notel	Unitel	Multitel	Mean
ocabulary scaled scores								
Phase 1	10.47	10.91	11.75	11.05	10.22	10.81	11.43	10.82
Phase 2	10.69	10.01	10.17	10.29	9.40	9.32	9.94	9.56
Town means	10.58	10.46	10.96		9.81	10.06	10.69	
Males	10.42	10.46	11.43	10.77	9.18	10.32	11.46	10.32
Females	10.74	10.46	10.48	10.56	10.44	9.81	9.91	10.06
Town means	10.58	10.46	10.96		9.81	10.06	10.69	
ock design scaled scores								
Males	11.48	11.46	11.40	11.45	11.69	11.39	12.57	11.88
Females	10.62	10.03	9.70	10.12	11.27	9.96	9.53	10.25
Town means	11.05	10.75	10.55		11.48	10.67	11.05	

TABLE 3.A4

Mean Phase 1 Stanford–Binet (S–B) and Peabody Picture Vocabulary Test (PPVT)
Scores for Notel and Unitel Children in Kindergarten and Grade 1

	Notel	Unitel	t	p (one-tailed)
Kindergarten				
S–B raw vocabulary score	5.93	6.79	−1.37	.09
PPVT raw score	50.07	52.29		ns
PPVT IQ score	95.60	100.21		ns
Age in months	65.00	63.79		ns
n	15	14		
Grade 1				
S–B raw vocabulary score	7.63	7.25		ns
PPVT raw score	59.25	56.69		ns
PPVT IQ score	104.06	99.81		ns
Age in months	75.19	75.31		ns
n	16	16		

TABLE 3.A5

Within-Phase and Across-Phase Partial Correlations among Creativity and Intelligence Measures for the Longitudinal Sample, Controlling for Age: Notel, Unitel, and Multitel Combined

	Phase 2					
	Creativity				Intelligence	
	Uses	Similarities	Patterns	Lines	Vocabulary	Block design
Phase 1						
Creativity						
Uses	.39***	.27***	.27***	.26**	.19*	.07
Patterns	.41***	.37***	.35***	.31***	.26**	.07
Intelligence						
Vocabulary	.22**	.43***	.26**	.25**	.70***	.37***
Block design	.11	.26**	.16	.18*	.36***	.55***
Phase 2						
Creativity						
Uses						
Similarities	.67***					
Patterns	.62***	.64***				
Lines	.53***	.56***	.86***			
Intelligence[a]						
Vocabulary	—	.42***	—	.28***		
Block design	—	.26**	—	.02	—	

[a] Dashes indicates correlations were computed for the larger sample in each phase (see Table 3.A6).
* $p < .05$; ** $p < .01$; *** $p < .001$; $n = 134$; two-tailed.

TABLE 3.A6

Within-Phase Partial Correlations among Creativity and Intelligence Measures for the Cross-Sect Sample, Controlling for Age: Notel, Unitel, and Multitel Combined[a]

	Creativity		Intelligence		
	Uses	Patterns	Vocabulary	Block design	I
Creativity					
Uses		.60*** (157)	.12 (157)	.17* (157)	.10
Patterns	.65*** (143)		.20* (157)	.14 (157)	.18*
Intelligence					
Vocabulary	.17* (143)	.15 (143)		.36*** (157)	.62**
Block design	.08 (143)	.11 (143)	.37*** (280)		.47**
IQ	−.01 (122)	.14 (122)	.68*** (250)	.57*** (250)	

[a] Phase 1 above the diagonal; Phase 2 below. Parentheses enclose the number of students on which each co is based.
* $p < .05$; ** $p < .01$; *** $p < .001$; two-tailed.

TABLE 3.A7

Partial Correlations between Cognitive Measures and
Reported Weekly Hours of TV Viewing, Controlling for Age[a]

	Alternate uses	Patterns	Vocabulary	Block design	
Phase 1					
Unitel, Multitel	−.02 (83)	.01 (83)	.11 (83)	.02	(83)
Phase 2					
Notel, Unitel, Multitel	−.07 (130)	−.15* (130)	−.04 (256)	−.20***	(156)
Unitel, Multitel	−.12 (80)	−.16 (80)	.03 (161)	−.18**	(161)
Notel	−.02 (47)	.13 (47)	−.15 (92)	−.21**	(92)

[a] Parentheses enclose the number of students on which each correlation is based.
* $p < .10$; ** $p < .05$; *** $p < .01$; two-tailed.

TABLE 3.A8

Zero-Order and Partial Correlations between Cognitive Measures and Leisure Activities, Controlling for Both IQ and Gender[a]

	Phase 1		Phase 2						Phase 1		Phase 2	
	Uses	Patt	Uses[b]	Uses[c]	Sim[c]	Patt[b]	Patt[c]	Lines[c]	Vocab	Blks	Vocab	Blks
					Zero-order correlations							
Phase 1												
Total community activities	.27**	.22**	—									
Sports	.30***	.20*	—									
Total private activities	.21*	.24**	—			—		.22*	.27**			
Book reading			—	.34***	.49***	—	.31**	.32**	.51***	.34***	.32***	.28**
Radio			—			—		.26**				-.21*
Phase 2												
Total community activities	.21*				.20*	.31***	.28**					
Sports	.24**					.28**						
Total private activities			.34***	.21*	.33***	.38***	.28***	.25**	.22*		.29***	
Book reading				.21*		.22*						
Radio			.20*		.19*	.29**						

Controlling for both IQ and Gender   _Controlling for gender only_

	Controlling for both IQ and Gender					Controlling for gender only				
	Uses	Patt	Sim	Vocab	Blks	Uses	Patt	Sim	Vocab	Blks
Phase 1										
Total community activities	.26**	.21*								
Sports	.30***	.19*								
Total private activities										
Book reading	—	.28**	.36***			.20*	.54***	.32***	.36***	.30***
Radio	—	—	.26**	.27**			.21*	.29***		
Phase 2										
Total community activities	.20*		.32***							
Sports	.24**		.28**							
Total private activities	.36***	.28**	.37***	.27**	.20*					
Book reading	.24*	.22*	.22*			.25**	.22*	.33***		
Radio	.25**		.32***							

[a] Key to column head abbreviations: Uses, Alternate Uses; Patt, Pattern Meanings; Sim, Similarities; Vocab, vocabulary; Blks, Block design.
[b] Cross-sectional sample.
[c] Longitudinal sample.
* $p < .10$; ** $p < .05$; *** $p < .01$; all two-tailed tests. Dashes indicate sample size was less than 10.

NOTES

[1] $r = .48$ at age $11\frac{1}{2}$.

[2] This portion of the study was conducted by Mary Morrison and is reported here with her permission.

[3] Mean Phase 1 scores of students who were and were not available for follow-up were:

	Nonre-tained group		Retained group				
	M	SD	M	SD	t	df	p
Vocabulary	12.17	2.69	10.67	2.41	2.72	158	.007
Block design	11.30	2.58	11.06	3.15	0.35	158	ns
Alternate Uses	26.78	13.40	25.43	14.99	0.41	158	ns
Pattern Meanings	19.61	6.92	18.89	9.75	0.34	158	ns

[4] Based on a standardization sample of 100 girls and 100 boys aged $10\frac{1}{2}$, the vocabulary subtest was correlated .82 with the verbal score and .83 with the full scale score. The block design test was correlated .66 with the performance score and .64 with the full scale score. These correlations have been corrected for spuriousness by the formula recommended by McNemar (1949). The split-half reliability at age $10\frac{1}{2}$ was .91 for the vocabulary test and .87 for the block design test. The test–retest reliability over a 1-month interval was .85 for the vocabulary test and .86 for the block design test. The source for all of these data is the WISC manual (Wechsler, 1974).

[5] Calculated as

$$\frac{2(\text{number of agreements between independent scorers})}{\text{total for scorer 1} + \text{total for scorer 2}}.$$

[6] A cross-sectional MANOVA of the vectors of uses, patterns, vocabulary, and block design scores for the factors Town, Sex, Grade, and Phase yielded an overall significant effect, $F(230,2211) = 1.76$, $p < .001$. In addition, the Hotelling's tests were significant for Sex, $F(4,256) = 4.80$, $p < .001$; Grade, $F(4,256) = 7.28$, $p < .001$; Phase, $F(4,256) = 4.89$, $p < .001$; Town $\times$ Phase, $F(8,512) = 2.85$, $p < .004$; and Sex $\times$ Grade $\times$ Phase, $F(4,256) = 3.14$, $p < .02$.

[7] In an unweighted means cross-sectional ANOVA on the Alternate Uses total scores for Town $\times$ Phase $\times$ Sex $\times$ Grade, the Town $\times$ Phase interaction, $F(2,282) = 4.07$, $p < .02$ was significant, as were the town, $F(2,282) = 3.62$, $p < .03$; and phase, $F(1,282) = 4.82$, $p < .03$ main effects (see Table 3.A1 for means). Simple main effects analyses of the interaction revealed that the towns differed in Phase 1, $F(2,282) = 6.53$, $p < .01$, but not in Phase 2. Tukey tests revealed that in Phase 1, Notel students obtained higher scores than both Unitel and Multitel ($p < .01$ for both) students, who did not differ. Between Phases 1 and 2, only the scores of Notel students changed significantly, and they decreased, $F(1,282)$, $= 11.28$, $p < .01$.

The only other significant result was the Sex $\times$ Grade $\times$ Phase interaction, $F(1,282) = 6.77$, $p < .01$. Simple main effects analyses revealed no readily interpretable pattern. There was no sex difference in either phase for seventh graders or in Phase 2 for fourth graders. In

Phase 1 the mean for girls (27.72) was higher than the mean for boys (21.36), but this was only marginally significant, $F(1,282) = 3.81, p < .10$. In grade 4, there was no phase difference in the scores of grade 4 boys and grade 7 girls, but Phase 1 scores were higher than Phase 2 scores for grade 4 girls (27.72 vs. 19.68), $F(1,282) = 4.61, p < .05$ and grade 7 boys (29.26 vs. 22.27), $F(1,282) = 7.83, p < .01$. Finally, there was a grade difference only in the case of Phase 1 boys, with seventh graders obtaining higher Alternate Uses scores (29.26) than fourth graders (21.36), $F(1,282) = 5.88, p < .05$. Since this Sex × Grade × Phase interaction was not readily interpretable and was not central to the hypotheses, we did not pursue it further.

A Town × Phase cross-sectional analysis of covariance was run to determine whether IQ was a significant covariate for the Alternate Uses scores, and it was not.

[8] In an unweighted means cross-sectional ANOVA on Phase 1 Alternate Uses uniqueness (originality) scores for Town × Sex × Grade, the only significant result was the town main effect, $F(2,148) = 4.74, p < .01$. Tukey analyses revealed that Notel students obtained higher scores than children in both Unitel and Multitel ($p < .05$ in both cases), who did not differ. A Town × Phase covariance analysis was run to determine whether IQ was a significant covariate for the Alternate Uses uniqueness scores, and it was not.

[9] The mean Phase 1 scores for shoe (4.72), key (4.57), and button (4.07) did not differ in a Tukey test following a repeated measures ANOVA on all five uses items from Phase 1, $F(4,544) = 23.82, p < .001$. The mean Phase 2 scores for chair (4.14), shoe (3.95), and button (3.88) did not differ in a Tukey test following a repeated measures ANOVA on all six verbal creativity items from Phase 2, $F(5,680) = 9.41, p < .001$. In Phase 1, $r = .71, .71,$ and $.61$, all $p < .001$, and Cronbach's alpha = .85 for shoe, key, and button. In Phase 2, $r = .56, .66,$ and $.65$, all $p < .001$ and Cronbach's alpha = .82 for chair, shoe, and button.

[10] A preliminary analysis of the longitudinal Alternate Uses total scores revealed no effect of sex and no interaction of sex with other factors. Accordingly, the major analysis was an unweighted means ANOVA with Town and Grade as between-subject factors and repeated measures on Phase.

The Town × Phase interaction was marginally significant, $F(2,131) = 2.88, p < .06$. Since this was the hypothesized effect, we conducted simple main effects analyses to break down the interaction. Notel scores decreased significantly from Phase 1 to Phase 2, $F(1,131) = 7.71, p < .01$, and no changes occurred in the other towns. The towns differed in Phase 1, $F(2,131) = 3.16, p < .05$, but not in Phase 2. Tukey tests revealed that in Phase 1, Notel students obtained higher Alternate Uses fluency scores than Unitel students, $p < .05$. Multitel students were in between and not different from Notel or Unitel.

The Grade × Phase interaction, $F(1,131) = 5.24, p < .03$ was significant. Simple main effects analyses revealed that the Alternate Uses scores of students who went from Grade 7 to 9 decreased from Phase 1 (14.15) to Phase 2 (11.29), $F(1,131) = 8.38, p < .005$, but no change occurred for students who went from grade 4 (12.38) to grade 6 (12.72).

[11] In an unweighted means cross-sectional ANOVA on the Pattern Meanings total scores for Town × Phase × Sex × Grade, the grade main effect was significant, $F(1,282) = 3.98, p < .05$, reflecting a higher mean score for grade 7 (21.38) than for grade 4 (18.87). The only other significant finding was the Town × Phase interaction, $F(2,282) = 3.21, p < .04$. Simple main effects analyses revealed no town differences in either phase, and only the scores of Unitel students changed significantly, $F(1,282) = 5.67, p < .05$; they increased from 16.92 to 22.12.

IQ served as a significant covariate for the cross-sectional Pattern Meanings total score in a Town × Phase analysis, $F(1,263) = 6.22, p < .02$. The only significant effect in this analysis was the phase main effect, $F(1,263) = 5.01, p < .03$, reflecting a higher score in Phase 2 (21.51) than in Phase 1 (18.48).

[12] In an unweighted means cross-sectional ANOVA on the Pattern Meanings uniqueness scores for Town × Sex × Grade, the grade main effect, $F(1,148) = 6.67$, $p < .02$ reflected a higher mean score for seventh graders (5.38) than fourth graders (3.48). The grade main effect was qualified by the Town × Grade interaction, $F(2,148) = 3.50$, $p < .04$. Simple main effects analyses revealed that the higher scores of seventh over fourth graders occurred largely because of Multitel, $F(1,148) = 10.23$, $p < .01$ (7.09 vs. 3.02), but seventh graders also scored marginally higher in Notel, $F(1,148) = 3.19$, $p < .10$ (5.50 vs. 3.23). Differences among the towns occurred only in grade 7, $F(2,148) = 3.91$, $p < .05$, with Multitel students (7.09) obtaining higher scores than Unitel students (3.54; $p < .05$ by Tukey test). Notel was in between and not different from either Unitel or Multitel. A Town × Phase covariance analysis was run to determine whether IQ was a significant covariate for the Pattern Meanings uniqueness scores, and it was not.

[13] The mean Phase 1 scores for patterns a(3.96), b(3.74), and c(3.89) did not differ in a Tukey test following a repeated measures ANOVA on all five figural creativity items from Phase 1, $F(4,544) = 23.51$, $p < .001$. The mean Phase 2 scores for patterns a(4.02), b(4.08), and f(3.43) did not differ in a Tukey test following a repeated measures ANOVA on all six figural creativity items given in Phase 2, $F(5,680) = 25.33$, $p < .001$. In Phase 1, $r = .72, .73$, and .64, all $p < .001$; and Cronbach's alpha = .87 for patterns a, b, and c. In Phase 2, $r = .75$, .73, .82, all $p < .001$; and Cronbach's alpha = .90 for patterns a, b, and f.

[14] In an unweighted means ANOVA on the Pattern Meanings scores with Town, Grade, and Sex as between-subject factors and repeated measures on Phase, only the Town × Sex interaction was significant, $F(2,125) = 4.88$, $p < .01$. Simple main effects analyses revealed town differences for boys, $F(2,125) = 5.24$, $p < .05$, but not for girls. Tukey tests revealed that Multitel boys (15.01) scored higher than Unitel boys (9.75; $p < .01$); Notel boys were in between (11.18) and not different from Unitel or Multitel boys. A sex difference occurred only for Multitel, $F(1,125) = 7.65$, $p < .01$, with boys obtaining higher scores than girls (15.01 vs. 10.37).

[15] In an unweighted means cross-sectional ANOVA on the block design scaled score for Town × Phase × Sex × Grade, only the sex main effect was significant, $F(1,282) = 14.73$, $p < .001$. Boys obtained a higher mean score (11.45) than girls (10.12).

[16] The longitudinal block design scaled scores were analyzed in an unweighted means ANOVA with Town, Sex, and Grade as between-subject factors and repeated measures on Phase. The sex main effect was significant, $F(1,125) = 12.62$, $p < .001$, again reflecting a higher mean score for boys (11.88) than for girls (10.25). In addition, the Town × Phase interaction, $F(2,125) = 2.38$, $p < .10$; Town × Sex interaction, $F(1,125) = 2.76$, $p < .07$; and Sex × Grade interaction, $F(1,125) = 3.58$, $p < .07$ were marginally significant. Since town differences were of primary interest, we conducted simple main effects analyses on the Town × Phase and Town × Sex interactions. In the former case, significant phase differences did not occur for any town, but there was a marginally significant town difference in Phase 2, $F(2,125)$, $p < .10$. Tukey tests revealed that Notel students, who obtained the highest mean block design scores in Phase 2 (mean 11.77), scored significantly higher than students in Unitel, who obtained the lowest Phase 2 mean score (10.30; $p < .05$). Multitel students, who were in between (11.30), did not differ from Notel but were marginally higher than Unitel ($p < .10$). Analyses of the Town × Sex interaction revealed no sex difference in Notel (boys' mean, 11.69, girls' mean, 11.27); a marginally significant difference in Unitel, $F(1,125) = 3.27$, $p < .10$, reflecting a higher mean for boys (11.39) than for girls (9.96); and a significant difference in the same direction in Multitel, $F(1,125) = 14.62$, $p < .01$ (boys' mean, 12.57, girls' mean, 9.53). There were no differences among the towns in the boys' mean scores, but the town difference for girls was marginally significant, $F(2,125) = 2.58$, $p < .10$. Tukey tests indicated that Notel girls had a marginally higher mean block design

score than Multitel girls ($p < .10$). Unitel girls were in between and not different from Notel or Multitel girls.

[17] In an unweighted means cross-sectional ANOVA on the WISC vocabulary scores for Town × Phase × Grade × Sex, the phase main effect was significant, $F(1,282) = 7.42$, $p < .01$ but was qualified by the Town × Phase interaction, $F(2,282) = 3.60$, $p < .03$. Simple main effects analyses revealed that the towns differed in Phase 1, $F(2,282) = 3.56$, $p < .05$, but not in Phase 2. In Phase 1, Multitel students (mean 11.75) scored signficantly higher than Notel students (10.47; $p < .05$ by Tukey test), and marginally higher than Unitel students (10.91; $p < .10$ by Newman–Keuls test). The scores of Notel students did not change from Phase 1 to Phase 2 (10.69), those of Unitel students decreased marginally (to 10.01), $F(1,282) = 3.46$, $p < .10$, and those of Multitel students decreased significantly (to 10.17), $F(1,282) = 10.86$, $p < .01$.

The only other significant result in the cross-sectional analysis of the vocabulary data was a grade main effect, $F(1,282) = 22.31$, $p < .001$, reflecting a higher mean scaled score for grade 4 (11.32) than for grade 7 (10.01).

[18] An unweighted means ANOVA of the longitudinal WISC vocabulary scaled scores was run for Town, Sex, and Grade as between-subject factors and repeated measures on Phase. The phase main effect, $F(1,125) = 67.16$, $p < .001$ reflected a decrease from Phase 1 (10.82) to Phase 2 (9.56). The grade main effect, $F(1,125) = 4.14$, $p < .05$ reflected a higher mean score for the younger (grade 4 to grade 6; 10.56) than the older (grade 7 to grade 9; 9.82) age-group. The Town × Sex interaction also was significant, $F(2,125) = 4.98$, $p < .008$. Simple main effects analyses revealed that Multitel boys (11.46) scored higher than Multitel girls (9.91), $F(1,125) = 5.93$, $p < .05$; the sexes did not differ in Unitel (girls, 9.81, boys, 10.32); and in Notel, girls (10.44) scored marginally higher than boys (9.18), $F(1,125) = 3.87$, $p < .10$. There were town differences in the scores of boys, $F(2,125) = 6.45$, $p < .005$, but not girls. Multitel boys obtained higher scores on average than Notel boys ($p < .01$ by Tukey test). Unitel boys were in between and not different from either Notel or Multitel boys.

[19] This also relates to one of Rogosa's (1980) arguments against the use of cross-lag panel correlations. The cross-lags (between two variables measured at two different time points) will be misleading if the stability coefficients for the two variables differ, which is usually the case.

[20] The stability coefficient over 2 years for vocabulary (.72) is substantial when evaluated in light of the short-term (1 month) reliability coefficients for the vocabulary subtest reported in the WISC manual (Wechsler, 1974). For a sample of 102 U.S. children aged $10\frac{1}{2}$–$11\frac{1}{2}$ the test–retest reliability was .85, and for a sample of 104 $14\frac{1}{2}$–$15\frac{1}{2}$-year-olds it was .89. The short-term reliability of the block design test over 1 month is .86 at age $10\frac{1}{2}$–$11\frac{1}{2}$ and .78 at age $14\frac{1}{2}$–$15\frac{1}{2}$ (Wechsler, 1974).

[21] Phase 2 hours of television viewing per week for Notel students who were below or above the Phase 1 median were:

	Below		Above				
	M	SD	M	SD	t	df	p
Uses	21.77	13.13	23.69	9.50	−.59	46	ns
Patterns	23.52	13.05	22.16	9.46	.42	46	ns
Vocabulary	26.32	11.74	19.00	9.46	2.37	46	.03
Block design	24.23	11.31	22.03	11.28	.65	46	ns

[22] When the combined data from Notel, Unitel, and Multitel were divided on each Phase 1 cognitive measure into those who scored one standard deviation or more above the mean,

those in the middle range, and those who scored one standard deviation or more below the mean, and the reported Phase 2 weekly hours of television viewing was calculated for each group, the only significant overall difference occurred for vocabulary, $F(2,125) = 5.24, p <$ .007. Students with high vocabulary scores in Phase 1 watched less TV in Phase 2 (mean 19.0 hours) than those with mid-range (mean 27.05 hours) or low scores (29.22; $p < .05$ by Tukey or Scheffé test for both comparisons). The latter groups did not differ but there was a significant (weighted) linear term, $F(1,125) = 8.51, p < .005$ for the means.

[23] Students in the three towns were divided into four IQ groups, those scoring one standard deviation or more below the mean (i.e., below 85), between 85 and 100, between 100 and 115, and above 115 (one standard deviation or more above the mean). Mean Phase 2 weekly hours of TV viewing for the four groups were 29.4, 28.0, 25.8, and 23.7, respectively, forming a significant linear trend, $F(1,632) = 15.22, p < .0001$. The highest IQ group watched less TV than the lowest ($p < .01$ by Tukey test) and second lowest ($p < .05$ by Tukey test) groups, and the 100–115 group also watched less TV than the lowest group ($p < .05$ by Tukey test).

[24] Despite having made specific predictions about the direction of the relationship between amount of television viewing and performance on the vocabulary and creativity measures, we have reported two-tailed levels of significance for all correlations. One-tailed levels (that is, directional tests) can be calculated by halving the level of significance for the two-tailed test (e.g., the correlation of $-.14$ for TV and Pattern Meanings reported in the top line of Table 3.A7 would be significant at $p < .05$ by one-tailed test).

[25] Two-tailed tests of significance have been used for all correlations between leisure activities and cognitive scores reported in Table 3.A8, even when our hypotheses would have justified the use of one-tailed tests, because of the exploratory nature of these analyses. For the same reason, and because the samples for some correlations were small (20–30 students), we have reported correlations significant at $p < .10$ or less. The level of significance for one-tailed tests is half that for two-tailed tests, so correlations significant at $p < .10$ by two-tailed test are significant at $p < .05$ by one-tailed test, and so on.

[26] IQ was used as a control for the creativity scores but not for the vocabulary or block design scores, since both were highly correlated with the group test IQ scores for these students and both are measures of intelligence. It is not clear what it means conceptually to partial out general IQ from correlations involving vocabulary and block design Scores.

REFERENCES

Anderson, D. R. Home television viewing by preschool children and their families. In A. C. Huston (Chair), *The ecology of children's television use.* Symposium presented at the meeting of the Society for Research in Child Development, Detroit, April 1983.

Andrews, F. M. Social and psychological factors which influence the creative process. In I. A. Taylor & J. Getzel (Eds.), *Perspectives in creativity.* Chicago: Aldine Publishing Company, 1975.

Bailyn, L. Mass media and children: A study of responsive habits and cognitive effects. *Psychological Monographs: General and Applied,* 1959, *73*(1), 1–48.

Ball, S., & Bogatz, G. A. Summative research on *Sesame Street:* Implications for the study of preschool children. In A. D. Pick (Ed.), *Minnesota Symposium on Child Psychology* (Vol.6). Minneapolis: University of Minnesota Press, 1972.

Barron, F. *Creativity and psychological health: Origins of personality and creative freedom.* Princeton, N.J.: Van Nostrand, 1963.

Barron, F., & Harrington, D. M. Creativity, intelligence, and personality. *Annual Review of Psychology,* 1981, *32,* 439–476.

Butcher, H. J. Intelligence and creativity. In P. Kline (Ed.), *New approaches in psychological measurement.* New York: Wiley, 1973.

Campbell, D. T., & Fiske, D. W. Convergent and discriminant validation by the multitrait–multimethod matrix. *Psychological Bulletin,* 1959, *56,* 81–105.

Cattell, R. B. *Abilities: Their structure, growth, and action.* Boston: Houghton Mifflin, 1971.

Collins, W. A. Cognitive processing and television viewing. In D. Pearl, L. Bouthilet, and J. Lazar (Eds.), *Television and behavior: Ten years of scientific progress and implications for the eighties.* Vol. 2. Rockville, Md.: NIMH, 1982.

Comstock, G. A., Chaffee, S., Katzman, N., McCombs, M., & Roberts, D. *Television and human behavior.* New York: Colombia University Press, 1978.

Cook, T. D., Appleton, H., Conner, R. F., Shaffer, A., Tabkin, G., & Weber, J. S. Sesame Street *revisited.* New York: Russell Sage, 1975.

Cropley, A. J., & Maslany, G. W. Reliability and factorial validity of the Wallach–Kogan creativity tests. *British Journal of Psychology,* 1969, *60,* 305–398.

Dellas, M., & Gaier, E. L. Identification of creativity: The individual. *Psychological Bulletin,* 1970, *73,* 55–73.

French, J. W. The description of aptitude and achievement tests in terms of rotated factors. *Psychometric Monographs,* No. 5, Chicago: University Chicago Press, 1951.

Furu, T. *The function of television for children and adolescents.* Tokyo: Sophia University, 1971.

Galton, F. *Hereditary genius: An inquiry into its law and consequences.* London: Macmillan, 1869.

Getzels, J. W. Creativity: Prospects and issues. In I. A. Taylor & J. W. Getzels (Eds.), *Perspectives in creativity.* Chicago: Aldine Publishing Company, 1975.

Getzels, J. W., & Csikszentmihalyi, M. From problem solving to problem finding. In I. A. Taylor and J. W. Getzels (Eds.), *Perspectives in creativity.* Chicago: Aldine Publishing Company, 1975.

Getzels, J. W., & Jackson, P.W. *Creativity and intelligence.* New York: Wiley, 1962.

Golann, S. E. Psychological study of creativity. *Psychological Bulletin,* 1963, *60,* 548–565.

Greenfield, P. M. *Mind and media: The effects of television, video games, and computers.* Cambridge, Mass.: Harvard University Press, 1984.

Greenfield, P. M., Geber, B., Beagles-Roos, J., Farrar, D., & Gat, I. *Television and radio experimentally compared: Effects of the medium on imagination and transmission of content.* Paper presented at the meeting of the Society for Research in Child Development, Boston, April 1981.

Guilford, J. P. Creativity. *American Psychologist,* 1950, *5,* 444–454.

Guilford, J. P. The structure of intellect. *Psychological Bulletin,* 1956, *53,* 267–293.

Guilford, J. P. Measurement and creativity. *Theory into Practice,* 1966, *5,* 186–189.

Guilford, J. P. Creativity: A quarter century of progress. In I. A. Taylor & J. W. Getzels (Eds.), *Perspectives in creativity.* Chicago: Aldine Publishing Company, 1975. pp. 37–59.

Hakstian, A. R., & Cattell, R. B. The checking of primary ability structure on a broader basis of performance. *British Journal of Education Psychology,* 1974, *44,* 140–154.

Himmelweit, H. T., Oppenheim, A. N., & Vince, P. *Television and the child.* London: Oxford University Press, 1958.

Holt, R. R. The development of the primary process: A structural view. In R. R. Holt (Ed.), *Motives and thought: Psychoanalytic essays in honor of David Rapaport.* New York: International Universities Press, 1966.

Horn, J. L. Organization of abilities and the development of intelligence. *Psychological Review*, 1968, *75*, 242–259.

Horn, J. L., & Cattell, R. B. Refinement and test of the theory of fluid and crystallized intelligence. *Journal of Educational Psychology*, 1966, *57*, 253–270.

Horn, J. L., & Knapp, J. R. On the subjective character of the empirical base of Guilford's structure-of-intellect model. *Psychological Bulletin*, 1973, *80*, 33–43.

Hornik, R. Out-of-school television and schooling: Hypotheses and methods. *Review of Educational Research*, 1981, *51*, 193–214.

Hornik, R. C., Gould, J., & Gonzalez, M. *Susceptibility to media effects.* Paper presented at the meeting of the International Communication Assocation, Acapulco, Mexico, May 1980.

Huston, A. C., & Wright, J. C. Children's processing of television: The informative functions of formal features. In J. Bryant & D. R. Anderson (Eds.), *Children's understanding of television: Research on attention and comprehension.* New York: Academic Press, 1983.

Kogan, N., & Pankove, E. Creative ability over a five-year span. *Child Development*, 1972, *43*, 427–442.

Kris, E. *Psychoanalytic explorations in art.* New York: International Universities Press, 1952.

Lesser, G. S. *Children and television: Lessons from* Sesame Street. New York: Random House, 1974.

Lyle, J., & Hoffman, H. R. Children's use of television and other media. In E. A. Rubinstein, G. A. Comstock, & J. P. Murray (Eds.), *Television and social behavior: Vol. 4. Television in day-to-day life: Patterns of use.* Washington, D.C.: U.S. Government Printing Office, 1972.

Maccoby, E. E. Television: Its impact on school children. *Public Opinion Quarterly*, 1951, *15*, 421–444.

Maccoby, E. E. (Ed.), *The development of sex differences.* Stanford: Stanford University Press, 1966.

Maccoby, E. E., & Jacklin, C. N. *The psychology of sex differences.* Stanford: Stanford University Press, 1974.

Maslow, A. *Motivation and personality.* New York: Harper, 1954.

Maslow, A. *Toward a psychology of being.* Princeton: Van Nostrand, 1962.

McLuhan, M. *Understanding media.* New York: McGraw-Hill, 1964.

McNemar, Q. *Psychological statistics.* New York: Wiley, 1949.

McNemar, Q. Lost: Our intelligence? Why? *American Psychologist*, 1964, *19*, 871–882.

Medrich, E. A., Roizen, J. A., Rubin, V., & Buckley, S. *The serious business of growing up: A study of children's lives outside school.* Berkeley: University of California Press, 1982.

Mednick, S. A. The associative basis of the creative process. *Psychological Review*, 1962, *69*, 220–232.

Meline, C. W. Does the medium matter? *Journal of Communication*, 1976, *26*(3), 81–89.

Meringoff, L. K. The influence of the medium on children's story apprehension. *Journal of Educational Psychology*, 1980, *72*, 240–249.

Meringoff, L., Vibbert, M. M., Char, C. A., Ferme, D. E., Banker, G. S., & Gardner, H. How is children's learning from television distinctive? Exploiting the medium methodologically. In J. Bryant & D. R. Anderson (Eds.), *Children's understanding of television: Research on attention and comprehension.* New York: Academic Press, 1983.

Milgram, R. M., & Milgram, N. A. Creative thinking and creative performance in Israeli students. *Journal of Educational Psychology*, 1976, *68*, 255–259.

Milgram, R. M., Milgram, N. A., Rosenbloom, G., & Rabkin, L. Quantity and quality of creative thinking in children and adolescents. *Child Development*, 1978, *49*, 385–388.

Morgan, M., & Gross, L. Television and educational achievement and aspiration. In D. Pearl, L. Bouthilet, & J. Lazar (Eds.), *Television and behavior: Ten years of scientific progress and implications for the eighties*. Vol. 2. Rockville, Md.: NIMH, 1982.

Noy, P. A. A revision of the psychoanalytic theory of the primary process. *International Journal of Psychoanalysis*, 1969, *50*, 155–178.

Pankove, E., & Kogan, N. Creative ability and risk taking in elementary school children. *Journal of Personality*, 1968, *36*, 420–439.

Pearl, D., Bouthilet, L., & Lazar, J. *Television and behavior: Ten years of scientific progress and implications for the eighties*. Vols. 1 and 2. Rockville, MD.: NIMH, 1982.

Piaget, J. *Intelligence and affectivity*. Annual Reviews Monograph. Palo Alto, Calif.: Annual Reviews Inc., 1981.

Roberts, D. F., Bachen, C. M., Hornby, M. C., & Hernandez-Ramos, P. Reading and television: Predictors of reading achievement at different age levels. *Communication Research*, 1984, 11, 9–49.

Salomon, G. *Interaction of media, cognition, and learning*. New York: Jossey-Bass, 1979.

Salomon, G. Television watching and mental effort: A social psychological view. In J. Bryant & D. R. Anderson (Eds.), *Children's understanding of television*. New York: Academic Press, 1983.

Schramm, W., Lyle, J., & Parker, E. B. *Television in the lives of our children*. Stanford: Stanford University Press, 1961.

Singer, D. G. Television and the developing imagination of the child. In D. Pearl, L. Bouthilet, & J. Lazar (Eds.), *Television and behavior: Ten years of scientific progress and implications for the eighties*. Vol.2. Rockville, Md.: NIMH, 1982.

Singer, J. L., & Singer, D. G. *Television, imagination and aggression: A study of preschoolers' play*. Hillsdale, N.J.: Erlbaum, 1981.

Singer, J. L. & Singer, D. G. Psychologists look at television: Cognitive, developmental, personality, and social policy implications. *American Psychologist*, 1983, *38*, 826–834.

Suler, J. R. Primary process thinking and creativity. *Psychological Bulletin*, 1980, *88*, 144–165.

Taylor, C. W. A factorial study of fluency in writing. *Psychometrika*, 1947,*12*, 239–262.

Thorndike, R. L. Some methodological issues in the study of creativity. In *Proceedings of the 1962 International Conference on Testing Problems* (pp. 40–54). Princeton, N.J.: Educational Testing Service, 1963.

Thorndike, R. L. Some methodological issues in the study of creativity. In A. Anastasi (Ed.), *Testing problems in perspective*. Washington, D.C.: American Council on Education, 1966.

Thurstone, L. L. Primary mental abilities. *Psychometric Monographs*, No. 1. Chicago: University of Chicago Press, 1938.

Thurstone, L. L. *Creative talent*. (University of Chicago Psychometric Laboratory Report No. 61). Chicago: University of Chicago, 1950.

Torrance, E. P. *Torrance tests of creative thinking: Norms—technical manual*. Lexington, Mass.: Xerox, 1974.

Torrance, E. P. Creativity research in education: Still alive. In I. A. Taylor & J. W. Getzels (Eds.), *Perspectives in creativity*. Chicago: Aldine Publishing Company, 1975.

Vernon, P. E. Ability factors and environmental influences. *American Psychologist*, 1965, *20*, 723–733.

Vernon, P. E. *Intelligence: Heredity and environment*. San Francisco: W. H. Freeman, 1979.

Wade, S. E. Adolescence, creativity and media. *American Behavioral Scientist*, 1971, *14*, 341–351.

Wallach, M. A. Creativity. In P. H. Mussen (Ed.), *Carmichael's manual of child psychology*, (3rd ed.). New York: Wiley, 1970.

Wallach, M. A., & Kogan, N. *Modes of thinking in young children*. New York: Holt, Rinehart & Winston, 1965.

Wallach, M. A., & Wing, C. W., Jr. *The talented student: A validation of the creativity-intelligence distinction*. New York: Holt, Rinehart & Winston, 1969.

Ward, W. C. Reflection-impulsivity in kindergarten children. *Child Development*, 1968, *39*, 867–874.

Ward, W. C. Creativity in young children. *Journal of Creative Behavior*, 1974, *8*, 101–106.

Ward, W. C., Kogan, N., & Pankove, E. Incentive effects in children's creativity. *Child Development*, 1972, *43*, 669–676.

Watt, J. H., Jr., & Welch, A. J. Effects of static and dynamic complexity on children's attention and recall of televised instruction. In J. Bryant & D. R. Anderson (Eds.), *Children's understanding of television*. New York: Academic Press, 1983.

Wechsler, D. *Wechsler intelligence scale for children: Manual* (Rev. ed.). New York: Psychological Corporation, 1974.

Williams, T. M. How and what do children learn from television? *Human Communication Research*, 1981, *7*(2), 180–192.

Williams, T. M., & Fleming, J. W. Methodological study of the relationship between associative fluency and intelligence. *Developmental Psychology*, 1969, *1*, 155–162.

Woolf, V. *A room of one's own*. New York: Harcourt Brace & World, 1929.

Wright, J. C., & Huston, A. C. The forms of television: Nature and development of television literacy in children. *New Directions for Child Development*, 1981, No. 13.

Zuckerman, D. M., Singer, D. G., & Singer, J. L. Television viewing, children's reading, and related classroom behavior. *Journal of Communication*, 1980, *30*(1), 166–174.

$$4$$

TELEVISION AND OTHER LEISURE ACTIVITIES

Tannis MacBeth Williams
A. Gordon Handford

INTRODUCTION

Most researchers interested in the effects of television have assessed the skills, behavior, or attitudes of individuals or groups. In this study we asked whether TV also has indirect, second-order effects. Television is the most popular leisure activity in North America; both children and adults spend more time watching TV than in any other single discretionary pastime (Comstock, Chaffee, Katzman, McCombs, & Roberts, 1978). Does the presence of television influence the number and kinds of community activities available? Does it affect patterns of participation and social interaction? As Comstock et al. (1978) noted, information about the ways in which television has altered other behavior is limited because "what is needed, but hard or impossible to obtain now, are data reflecting behavior before television or without television" (p. 152). Notel, Unitel, and Multitel provided this opportunity.

Having decided to study television's effects at the molar level rather than at the more typical individual or molecular level, we looked for an appropriate method of characterizing the communities. Subjective approaches were discarded because of the problem of experimenter bias

(Rosenthal, 1966). We knew how the towns varied with regard to television, so our perceptions and descriptions probably would be influenced by our preconceived notions. A more objective method was needed, one which quantified the characteristics of the towns into meaningful, manageable units. We chose a system developed by Barker and his associates (Barker, 1968; Barker & Gump, 1964; Barker & Wright, 1955), called *psychological ecology,* or *behavior settings analysis.*

In their now classic study of a town in the United States called "Midwest" (a town slightly larger than Notel, Unitel, or Multitel), Barker and Wright (1955) used the behavior setting concept. They theorized that human behavior is a result not only of the enduring characteristics of individuals and their motivations of the moment but also is determined by characteristics of their environment. Each environmental unit, or setting, places limits on the range and type of behavior likely to occur there, sometimes for physical reasons (e.g., it is impossible to swim in a place with no water) but also because of social and other conventions (e.g., people behave differently at weddings and funerals). Prediction of behavior requires knowledge of the behavior settings as well as the individuals involved. This notion is reminiscent of the more recent person–situation controversy in psychology. The particular system devised by Barker and his colleagues has the advantage of specifying environmental units in a way that can be applied to an entire community.

We conducted behavior settings analyses of all three towns both before and after the arrival of television in Notel. In addition, we surveyed participation in what we have termed *private leisure activities.* Some usually take place indoors (e.g., knitting, listening to records), whereas others occur out-of-doors (e.g., bicycling, hiking), but all tend to be planned by individuals and are not organized community activities.

If TV displaces other leisure pursuits more or less directly, a town without television might have more community activities. On the other hand, perhaps community events are less dependent on the behavior of the majority than on a small minority of "organizers" or "activists," and perhaps these people function relatively independently of television. In that case, the mean level of participation, but not the number of activities, might vary with the availability of television. Even then, television might have greater influence in some areas than in others (e.g., sports vs. civic affairs). In addition, television's impact may vary according to age and sex.

We hypothesized that, in general, television negatively affects participation in other leisure activities because discretionary time budgets are limited. We also believed, however, that television's content might stimulate interest in specific leisure pursuits and lead to increased participation in certain activities. Although we took a relatively simplistic displacement perspective when this study was designed, we now believe that more complex conceptualizations of the process of displacement are required. Researchers who have videotaped families in their homes while they watched television (e.g., Allen, 1965; Anderson, 1983; Bechtel, Achelpol, & Akers, 1972) have found that viewers usually do not conform to the "mesmerized" stereotype. They frequently leave the room and also engage in many other activities while "watching" TV. As we have noted in other chapters of this book, some activities probably can be time-shared with television more readily than others. We hoped that our survey of private leisure activities would shed light on this issue.

PREPARING THE COMMUNITY ACTIVITIES SURVEYS

The first task was to identify the community activities or behavior settings of each town. Two methods were available. The first was used by Barker and Wright (1955) to study Midwest: A team of participant observers noted all the activities and places over the course of a year, including the number and characteristics of people in attendance, their patterns of behavior and levels of involvement, constraints on participation, and so on. Lack of funds and the impending arrival of television in Notel ruled out this approach. We used a second method, one Barker and Gump (1964) developed to survey the behavior settings used by high school students. It involves first identifying the settings and then presenting them to their users, asking people to indicate which settings they entered in the preceding year and what they did there. Although some information is lost (e.g., if 50% of the respondents who report entering a particular bar are female, we cannot assume that at any given time, half the clientele is female), it still is possible to ascertain the proportion of people in each town who participated in each setting, their level of involvement, and the function the setting plays in the community.

Identifying Potential Community Activities or Settings

On an initial visit, the second author explored each town and its vicinity, chatting with residents and asking about the locale, sights to see, places to meet, parks, and so on. The use of local rather than map terminology yielded hangouts such as the steps of the theater, airstrip, and sand mines, which would not be discovered with a more geographical orientation. Names of people with specialized information about topics such as the town's activities and social events, businesses, civic government and police, church organizations, clubs and other meetings, and school-related activities also were sought. Interviews were conducted with people in each of the following categories: clergy, retailers, town clerks and elected officials, club officers, recreation commission personnel, school teachers, editors of local newspapers, police, and children. They were asked for schedules of sports and social event meeting dates; names of organizations, boards, councils, and so on; hours of operation; practice session schedules; out-of-town sports events attended by the locals; church service times; and the existence of gathering-places such as open areas and campgrounds. The information requested was straightforward, unambiguous, and designed to be nonthreatening: What are the public places, events, businesses, services, entertainments, and so on that have existed in this town during the past year? Perhaps because of this approach, people volunteered much more information than was requested. The second author also obtained and perused the weekly town newspapers (available in Notel and Unitel in both phases and in Multitel in Phase 2), the Multitel section of the regional newspaper published in a larger nearby community, the Chamber of Commerce business calendars, and the business license records for the preceding year.

A consistent pattern of diminishing returns was found after six to eight key informants were interviewed; new potential settings emerged less and less frequently. This attests to the validity of behavior settings as units of the psychological environment; they are spontaneously identified by the users, widely known, and therefore of some importance. Further evidence that this method identified most of the important settings in each town was obtained when the questionnaires were completed. Respondents were asked to list settings missing in each category (e.g., sports, businesses), but very few were elicited.

Discarding Settings That Do Not Meet the Criteria

Barker's (1968) structure test for defining a genuine behavior setting requires that it have a dominant pattern of behavior which is anchored to a particular milieu and must occur at a specific time in a special relationship to that space. In addition, the milieu space must define the boundaries of the activity. "The fishing hole by big rock" meets these guidelines, but "gone fishing" does not. "Steps of the theater" in Notel qualified because they are a well-known hangout for teenagers, whereas "steps of the arena" are not, and therefore simply constitute a physical structure. "The grade 7 homeroom" meets the structure criterion, but "the elementary school" does not, because it is a conglomerate of individual settings, each having its own distinct patterns of behavior.

The structure test was applied to the potential settings for each town, and some were deleted. We did, however, purposely include some behavior setting conglomerates (e.g., 4-H club; the high school gymnasium) because the questionnaires otherwise would have been too long. For example, the behavior settings identified in Midwest by Barker and Wright (1955) included the telephone booth, each academic school class, and the school lunchroom. Our decision rule was that if an event had several reasonably autonomous parts which would not automatically come to mind when the conglomerate was mentioned, then the discrete settings were individually stated. "Crowning the Carnival Queen" might have been missed if only "Winter Carnival" was mentioned, but "Lion's Sports Day" was a sufficient reminder of the events it encompassed. Decisions of this sort were made on the basis of interviews with residents.

Potential settings passing our interpretation of the structure test were then subjected to Barker's "internal" and "external dynamic" tests. These ascertain the degree of independence and interdependence of two or more activities or events. For example, is the magazine rack in the drugstore an independent setting (because people use it somewhat independently of the rest of the drugstore), or is it sufficiently similar to other counters that it is simply an interdependent part of the drugstore setting? Seven scales are used to rate each pair of potential settings on the degree (1 to 7 points for each of the seven scales) to which the same inhabitants tend to enter the settings; the same leaders are active; the settings occur at similar times; similar objects are used; similar behavior occurs; and so on. Any two settings can range from being maximally interdependent (a score of 7) to maximally independent (a score of 49), and Barker (1968) established the cutoff point of 21 (or greater) as defining a genuine behavior setting which "appeared to identify community parts with phenomenal reality and with dynamic significance for behavior" (p. 45). Using tables provided by Barker we found it relatively easy, without calculating specific scores, to determine which potential settings were components of a single discrete setting (and thus would be given scores below 16), and which potential settings were clearly independent (scores of 22 or greater). This left a relatively small number of potential settings in each town which would fall in the 17–21 range. On-site inspections were made to each of these remaining possibilities. For example, Unitel had a large store with three major areas (meat market, grocery section, and hardware). Were these discrete settings or was the store one setting? As a different example, several people identified the take-out area of a café as a different place than the booth area. In practice, however, during all but the summer months, people ordering take-out food had coffee with friends in the booth area while waiting for their order. These on-site visits resolved all the remaining problems and yielded a list of discrete behavior settings for each town.

Constructing the Questionnaires

The list of community activities and events unique to each town was organized into the categories used by Barker and Wright (1955) to describe Midwest. The categories and examples of activities, events, and locations follow.

1. Sports: leagues, tournaments, general (e.g., skiing)
2. Open areas: parks, playgrounds, swimming holes, hangouts
3. Businesses: stores, offices
4. Civic: post office, town hall
5. Educational: adult classes, school open houses, music lessons
6. Clubs and meetings—for both children and adults
7. Medical: hospital, doctors' offices, health unit
8. Dances (public or club), parties, suppers
9. Special days: weddings, funerals, elections
10. Religious: churches, bible camps
11. Entertainment: special movies, parades, bingo
12. Other: clean-up campaigns, fund-raising events

In Phase 1, separate lists for children and adults were developed in each town. This enabled us to break down some of the conglomerates without producing a questionnaire that was overly lengthy. For example, the hotel cocktail bar was listed separately from the hotel pub on the adult lists, but the child lists mentioned only the hotel. Conversely, the child lists contained more detailed information about the schools. The weakness of this approach is that it eliminates unusual responses by adults or children who enter settings intended primarily for the other group. In Phase 2, we produced only one list for each town.

The validity of our catalog of community activities and events for each town was checked in two ways. At the end of each category, space was provided for respondents to list settings we had missed. This opportunity was rarely taken, which bolstered our confidence that the settings had been adequately covered. In Notel and Unitel in Phase 1 we also included a red herring, or lie, scale of six fictitious community activities sprinkled throughout the questionnaire (e.g., "men's handball at school" under Sports; "Wilson's Stationery" under Businesses). This proved to be an unnecessary distraction, resulting in numerous written comments (e.g., "there is no such place!") and raised hands by the students, which made *us* liars ("we must have made a mistake") rather than detecting liars amongst the townspeople. Less than 4% of the Phase 1 responses in Notel and Unitel were red herrings. We therefore did not include a lie scale in the Phase 1 Multitel questionnaires or in any of the Phase 2 questionnaires.

Generation of the behavior settings lists in Phase 2 followed the procedures outlined for Phase 1, but were facilitated by the availability of the lists from Phase 1.

The questionnaires began by explaining, "This is a list of places to go and things to do in (actual town name) and the surrounding area." Beside each item, Phase 1 respondents circled yes if they went there during the preceding year and no if they did not. If yes, they answered the question "What did you do?" in a few words on a line next to that item. Phase 2 respondents checked for each item how frequently they went to the place in the last year (never, once, six times a year, monthly, twice a month, weekly, twice a week, every day) and then wrote answers to "What did you do?". Examples were provided in both phases. The change in response format meant that in Phase 1 we could determine whether or not an individual had participated in a particular activity during the preceding year, but not how often, whereas both kinds of information were available in Phase 2.

PREPARING THE PRIVATE LEISURE ACTIVITIES LIST

The behavior settings survey provided information about behavior in public or community activities. This does not exhaust the range of molar behavior, since some leisure activity occurs in private settings, in wide-ranging, ill-defined milieux, and/or in surroundings not tied to the activity occurring there (e.g., playing cards, fishing, and car repairing, respectively). Our starting point was the Leisure Activity Blank (LAB) developed by McKechnie (1973). However, some of the LAB items already had been tapped in our behavior settings lists (e.g., skiing, swimming, and volleyball). Others were not possible in Notel, Unitel, or Multitel for geographical reasons (e.g., skin diving) or because they required special facilities (e.g., horse races, scuba diving, squash). The final list of 58 private leisure items appeared on a sheet at the end of the behavior settings list. Whereas the community activities lists were specific to each town and phase of the study, the same list of 58 private activities was used in both phases in all three towns. In Phase 1, respondents indicated whether they never, occasionally, or regularly engaged in each activity during the preceding year. In Phase 2, they indicated whether they had done so never, once, six times, monthly, twice monthly, weekly, twice weekly, or every day during the preceding year. The change in response format meant we could make comparisons only within each phase, not longitudinally.

SCORING

Participation in community activities was scored from two perspectives, the number of settings entered and the participant's level of involvement. In Phase 1, each item for which yes was circled, or for which the respondent had circled neither yes nor no but had written a sensible response to "what did you do there?" received an *entry* score of 1. In Phase 2, each item for which a frequency of once or more was checked, or for which the respondent had checked no frequency but had written a sensible response to "what did you do there?" received an entry score of 1. The entry scores in each category were summed and then weighted according to the number of items in that category for that questionnaire. This ensured that differences between the towns in the number of items per category (e.g., sports), which might reflect differences related to the availability of television, did not get confounded with differences in participation rates. Each individual thus had 12 category scores, which were summed to yield a *total* entry score.

Some additional scores were calculated only in Phase 2, based on the information provided about frequency of participation (ranging from never to daily). The *mean frequency* score for each of the 12 categories was calculated by adding the frequency scores for each item (range, 0–7) and dividing by the number of items in that category for that town. The *weekly frequency* score for each category was the number of items per category in which the individual participated weekly or more often. The *total mean frequency* and *total weekly frequency* scores were calculated by summing the scores across the 12 categories.

Scoring the behavior settings for level of involvement was based on responses to the question "what did you do there?" A response qualified as a *performance* if it indicated that the individual was personally essential to the activity (e.g., a clerk in a store) rather than being more peripherally involved (e.g., a customer). These scores were added within each category and weighted according to the number of items to yield a performance score for each category. A *total performance* score was then calculated by summing the category scores. Two additional scores reflecting level of involvement were calculated for the Sports category. The *active sport* score consisted of the number of sports activities in which the individual was an active participant, divided by the number of sports activities in that town. The *passive sport* score consisted of the number of sports activities the individual attended as a spectator or onlooker (e.g., drove a child to hockey practice; watched women's softball games), but not as an active participant.

Each private leisure activity was scored for *frequency* as 1, 2, or 3 (never, occasionally, regularly) in Phase 1, and 0–7 (never to daily) in Phase 2. Each person also received a score reflecting the total *number* (variety) of private leisure activities (0–58) in which she or he participated.

When scorers had finished assigning entry and performance scores to the behavior settings section of a questionnaire, they made a judgment about the quality of the responses. This identified incomplete questionnaires, instances in which the respondent did not seem to have taken the task seriously (e.g., students who wrote "got drunk" beside every setting), and instances in which the instructions were so poorly followed that the meaning was obscure. A similar but independent judgment was made for the private leisure activities section.[1]

All scorers were trained to the level of 90% agreement for the entry, performance, and private leisure activity scores, and reliability was rechecked periodically as the scoring proceeded in each phase.

DESCRIPTION OF RESPONDENTS AND QUESTIONNAIRE ADMINISTRATION

The main participants were adolescents and adults. The numbers of respondents in each age group in each town and phase are shown in Tables 4.A1 and 4.A2.

Students in grades 7–12 completed the questionnaires under supervision in their classes at school. Those who were absent were followed up later, so almost all the teenaged students in each town participated in this study.

Adults in the three towns were sampled via mail. Every third name was taken from the electoral lists for each village (which in each case included the surrounding district), and the list was recycled until approximately 500 names had been selected for each town. A $2 inducement to complete the questionnaire was offered.

The response rates to the mailed questionnaire in Phase 1 were 25%, 20%, and 40% for Notel, Unitel, and Multitel, respectively. The most likely explanation for the higher response rate in Multitel relates to our methodology for the project as a whole. One of the other studies (Chapter 8, this volume) involved personal contact through door-to-door recruitment of a randomly preselected sample of residents. This study was conducted prior to our mailed survey in Multitel but after the survey in Notel and Unitel. We suspect that the personal contact provided informal public relations for the project, led to increased interest and/or allayed apprehension, and thereby resulted in a higher Phase 1 return rate in Multitel. We have no satisfactory explanation for the smaller difference between Notel and Unitel. It may reflect chance variation or may instead indicate that Unitel residents are less likely than residents of the other towns to participate in surveys and similar kinds of events. Contradictory evidence regarding this hypothesis comes from voting behavior information. On the one hand, the proportions of residents in Notel, Unitel, and Multitel on the voters' lists who voted in the previous provincial election were 64%, 59%, and 73%, respectively, indicating a slightly lower turnout in Unitel. On the other hand, the turnouts for the previous federal election (federal and provincial elections in Canada are held independently, and neither occurs on a regular schedule) were 69%, 66%, and 70%, respectively. These figures indicate similar voting patterns.

In Phase 2, the response rates for the mailed questionnaires were 33%, 32%, and 39% for Notel, Unitel, and Multitel, respectively. Based on Phase 1 experiences, we scheduled the door-to-door interviews for the Suedfeld et al. study (Chapter 8, this volume) prior to mailing our questionnaires in all three towns in Phase 2. We also sent follow-up reminders in Phase 2. The response rates in Notel and Unitel were higher than in Phase 1 and more similar to the rate for Multitel, which did not change. This indicates that our hypothesis concerning the general public relations effect of the personal contact involved in the interview study may be correct. The fact that the Phase 2 Notel and Unitel response rates were similar suggests the Phase 1 difference may have been due to chance.

Like other researchers, we would have preferred to have higher response rates for our mailed sample. However, in absolute terms our adult samples were large (see Tables 4.A1 and 4.A2). The adolescent sample is clearly better, since we included almost all teenagers in the area served by each town.

Since we assessed all students in grades 7–12 in each town but only attempted to systematically sample the older residents, teenagers are over-represented and adults are slightly under-represented.[2] This does not pose major problems but should be kept in mind when age-related differences are discussed. In addition, our samples for Multitel are larger than those for Notel and Unitel. Multitel is a slightly larger town, with larger school enrollments, so it is not surprising that our samples reflect this fact, especially since the adult response rates were highest for Multitel. In our opinion, the more important point is that the samples were large enough (indeed, unusually so) to warrant comparisons. Also important is the fact that the proportions of the samples for each phase which fell in each of the age ranges used in the analyses were comparable.[3]

Some of the individuals who participated in the Phase 1 leisure activities survey also participated in Phase 2. This longitudinal sample of 528 residents consisted of 93 Notel youths, 57 Notel adults, 69 Unitel youths, 46 Unitel adults, 154 Multitel youths, and 109 Multitel adults. The longitudinal sample did not differ significantly from those who were not followed up in number of community activities participated in during the year prior to Phase 1.[4]

RESULTS FOR COMMUNITY ACTIVITIES

In the interest of brevity, we have focused on similarities and differences among the towns in describing our results in the text. Sex- and age-related differences are indicated in the notes but mentioned in the text only when of special interest.

Number of Community Activities in Each Town

As we mentioned earlier, television might affect the number of other leisure activities available in a community, participation in those activities, both, or neither. The number of behavior settings in each category for each town and phase of the study is shown in Table 4.1. In Phase 1 the number of community activities in Notel and Unitel was greater than the number in Multitel, but only by about 10%. We identified the settings first in Notel, next in Unitel, and last in Multitel in each phase, so this aspect of our methodology is unlikely to account for the small differences which occurred in Phase 1. The most probable pattern to occur because of the order in which we went to the towns would be the opposite, since awareness of certain kinds of settings in one community would be likely to unearth similar settings in another community. The similarity between Notel and Unitel in Phase 1, coupled with the similarity in the changes between Phase 1 and Phase 2 in all three towns, indicates that television is not an important determinant of the absolute number of organized community activities available.

TABLE 4.1

Number of Community Activities in Each Category in Each Town and Phase

	Phase 1						Phase 2		
	Notel		Unitel		Multitel		Notel	Unitel	Multitel
	Youths	Adults	Youths	Adults	Youths	Adults			
Sports	35	40	28	33	32	33	41	47	51
Open areas	15	13	11	11	17	14	19	14	21
Businesses	41	53	52	66	40	40	56	55	48
Civic buildings	7	9	8	7	5	5	7	7	6
Educational	19	10	15	9	25	8	48	33	36
Clubs, meetings	14	35	13	22	6	30	44	43	44
Medical	4	4	4	4	3	4	4	3	4
Dances, parties, suppers	12	21	12	18	10	16	27	33	36
Special days	4	5	3	3	6	5	5	5	7
Religious	7	6	9	9	6	8	9	10	8
Entertainment	8	7	14	14	7	6	6	9	11
Other	5	9	10	9	8	12	13	16	8
	171	212	179	205	164	181	279	275	280

Total Number of Community Activities Participated In

In assessing the impact of television on participation rates, we first asked whether the total number of community activities (settings) participated in (entered) during the previous year, summed across the 12 categories, varied according to town, sex, or age level in each phase. Residents were grouped into six age-groups: 11–12, 13–15, 16–19, 20–35, 36–55, and 56 years and over. Conceptually, this provided a sensible breakdown with respect to stages of development. Empirically, it yielded reasonably sized groups which were roughly comparable across the towns. This ensured that any town differences obtained did not arise because of a disproportionate number of residents in a particular age-group in any one town.

PHASE 1 CROSS-SECTIONAL RESULTS FOR
ENTRY SCORES

During the year before television arrived, Notel residents participated in more community activities than was the case in Unitel, and Unitel residents participated in more activities than was the case in Multitel, averaging across the age-groups (see Figure 4.1 and Table 4.A3).[5] Differences among the towns occurred at every age level, with only slight variations in the pattern. Notel residents participated in more community activities than did residents of both Unitel and Multitel at every age level except 20–35 years. In addition, Unitel residents participated in more activities than did Multitel residents at the 13–15, 20–35, and 36–55 year age levels. With the exception of the 20–35 year age-group, the towns were consistently ordered, with Notel residents most active, Unitel residents next, and Multitel residents least active. The differences between Notel and the other towns were larger and more consistent than differences between Unitel and Multitel. When we turned the question around and asked about the pattern of age differences within each town, an interesting result came to light. In the towns with television reception there was a substantial drop in participation in community activities by people aged 56 and older, but this drop did not occur in the town without television. As we shall see shortly, it did occur in Notel 2 years after the inception of television, although not to such a marked degree.

In contrast to the towns with television, the anomalous Phase 1 group in Notel was the 20–35-year-olds. They were anomalous, however, only by comparison with the other Notel age-groups; their participation was at the same level as the 20–35-year-olds in the towns with television. For most people, leisure time is governed by a ceiling, and this ceiling fluctuates with life's stages, as well as with demands from other sources such as paid

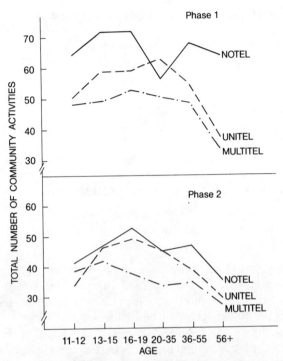

FIGURE 4.1   Mean number of total community activities participated in during the previous year by town, phase, and age group (all participants in each phase).

and unpaid work. In North American culture, available leisure time, especially for activities outside the home, is probably lowest during the years 20–35 when job and child rearing demands are greatest. We suspect the similarity between Notel and the other towns for this age-group is due to this ceiling effect.

PHASE 2 CROSS-SECTIONAL RESULTS FOR ENTRY SCORES

During the second year after television arrived in Notel, participation still was greater than that in Unitel, and Unitel participation was greater than that in Multitel, but the differences were smaller than in Phase 1 (Figure 4.1 and Table 4.A3).[6] Fewer age-group differences were statistically significant. In addition, the drop-off in participation by older residents evident in Phase 1 for the towns with television was now also evident in Notel.

LONGITUDINAL RESULTS FOR ENTRY SCORES

We next asked whether participation in total community activities changed between Phase 1 and Phase 2. The longitudinal sample was smaller than the cross-sectional samples within each phase, so only two age categories were used: 18 and under (youths or students), and 19 and over (adults). Participation varied according to town, age, and phase of the study, as can be seen in Figure 4.2.[7]

For youths, participation decreased significantly following the arrival of television in Notel, but no change occurred over the same period in Unitel and Multitel. Among adults, participation decreased significantly from Phase 1 to Phase 2 in all three towns, but the decrease in Notel was 33% greater than that in Unitel and 40% greater than that in Multitel. The most likely explanation for a decrease in participation by adults in all three communities is that they were 2 years older. Especially among those beyond age 55 or so, there is a general trend for participation to decrease with increasing age, as the cross-sectional analyses revealed earlier. We also considered the possibility that the decrease reflected methodological variance, due to change in the questionnaire or in the way people re-

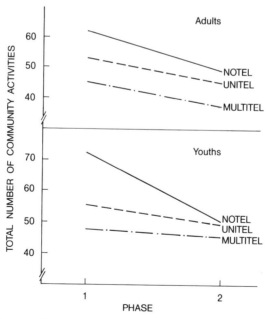

FIGURE 4.2 Mean number of total community activities participated in by youths and adults in the longitudinal sample for each town and phase.

sponded to it, between Phase 1 and Phase 2. This explanation, however, would predict a decrease for Unitel and Multitel adolescents as well as adults, which did not occur. The magnitude of the decrease in participation by Unitel and Multitel adults was exactly the same, 15% (calculated as a proportion of the Phase 1 mean for each town), which tends to support the first argument. Two years apparently is sufficient time in which to detect a decrease with age in participation in community activities in a large sample spanning the adult years.

Careful readers will notice that the significant decrease from Phase 1 to 2 for all three towns in the longitudinal sample also can be seen in visual comparisons of the total scores for all Phase 1 and 2 respondents (Figure 4.1 and Table 4.A3). It seemed important to understand why, so we pursued the matter further by looking at the longitudinal results for each age in each town in each of the 12 activity categories. Significant decreases in participation for both age groups in all three towns occurred for only three categories—medical, open areas, and businesses. For the other categories, participation increased or remained constant for at least one age-group in Unitel or Multitel. A general methodological explanation would require a more pervasive effect. It is possible that methodological change (e.g., in response format) was related to the decreases for these three categories, but other explanations applicable to all three communities also seem likely (e.g., economic recession, weather). In any event, these three categories are not part of the pattern of results involved in our conclusions regarding the effects of television. Moreover, when the contribution of these categories to the Phase 1 and Phase 2 total participation means is removed, the pattern of a substantial decrease in Notel with little or no change in Unitel and Multitel is clear.

SUMMARY OF RESULTS FOR PARTICIPATION IN TOTAL COMMUNITY ACTIVITIES

The cross-sectional and longitudinal comparisons present a consistent picture. Residents of a town without television reported participating in more of their community's activities than did residents of towns with television, and participation dropped off following television's arrival. Belson (1959) observed a similar decrease with the advent of television in Greater London, where involvement in frequent public and private leisure activities remained depressed up to 6 years after the set was obtained. In contrast, involvement in infrequent activites tended to recover to the pre-television level. In our study, residents of Unitel, which had had one television channel for 8–10 years, participated more in community activities than did residents of Multitel, which had had four channels for 10–12 years.

The finding that the participation rate for Notel remained higher than the rates for both Unitel and Multitel in the second year following television's arrival should be considered from both a methodological and a conceptual perspective. Small differences may be statistically significant in large samples, so it is important to ask not only whether differences are significant but whether they are important. In this case, the difference between Notel and Unitel was statistically significant when all 1376 Phase 2 respondents were included, but not when only the 528 in the longitudinal sample were included. From this methodological perspective, one might be inclined to downplay the finding that participation remained higher in Notel than in the other towns 2 years after the arrival of television, especially since the magnitude of the differences was much smaller than in Phase 1 (4.2 activities by comparison with Unitel and 8.9 by comparison with Multitel, vs. 11.9 and 19.3 in Phase 1). On the other hand, there are theoretical reasons to expect that if the arrival of television led to a drop in participation in community activities, the drop would not necessarily be rapid. One of the theoretical tenets of psychological ecology is that settings constrain and influence people's behavior. An organization, the library, a business, or an organized sport might tolerate some decrease in participation, but when the existence of the activity became threatened, pressure would be exerted on those involved. The pressure might be formalized, for example a fine for missed meetings, or it might be more informal. For example, someone present at a meeting might mention another person's absence upon encountering the absentee on the street or might mention it to a mutual acquaintance. In addition, the habit of participating in activities outside the home may, at least for some people, be fairly resistant to change. The finding in the longitudinal analyses that the drop in participation was greater for Notel youths than for Notel adults is consistent with these hypotheses. Youths probably are less likely than adults to participate in organizations with formal pressure to participate, and they probably are more likely to engage in activities which involve less pressure (e.g., visiting open areas, places students "hang out"). In addition, the habits involved in going out to meetings, sports, and other activities would be less firmly entrenched.

PHASE 2 RESULTS FOR FREQUENCY OF PARTICIPATION IN TOTAL COMMUNITY ACTIVITIES

We realized after collecting the Phase 1 data that we could assess television's impact on the number of community activities in which individuals were involved, but had no way of knowing whether television affects frequency of participation. Perhaps television narrows the range of other leisure activities but does not affect, or perhaps even stimulates, frequency of participation for this reduced range of events. This sort of theorizing prompted a slight change in methodology to obtain frequency information in Phase 2. What did that information reveal?

First, there was a very strong relationship between the number of community activities in which individuals participated and the frequency with which they did so, a finding which argues against the reduction-in-range-but-not-frequency hypothesis.[8] This was especially true for mean frequency across all activities (within or across categories). It also held true for activities in categories comprised primarily of recurrent rather than one-time events.

We asked next whether total mean frequency of participation varied according to town, sex, or age level, and then did the same thing for activities participated in weekly or more often.[9] The results corroborated rather than detracted from the results based on number of community activities. This finding, coupled with the strong relationship between our frequency and number measures for each of the 12 categories, means the lack of frequency data for Phase 1 is not worrisome.

Individual Community Activity Categories

So far we have been discussing total participation, summing across a wide variety of community activities. Are different kinds of activities affected similarly or differently by television? In each phase, the pattern for the 12 category participation scores for each town differed from the patterns for both of the other towns, and this was true for both youths (aged 18 and under) and adults (19 and over), as well as when all ages were combined.[10] With 12 activity categories and potential differences related to town, age level, and phase of the study, as well as systematic variations among these three factors, we could spend several hundred pages providing details of the results. Instead, we will consider each category in turn, in each case briefly summarizing the answers to four questions. What were the important similarities and differences in Phase 1? Was there evidence of change over the 2 years between the phases?[11] What were the important similarities and differences in Phase 2? What does the pattern of results suggest about the effects of television on this type of leisure activity? The results are shown in Tables 4.A4–4.A8 and in Figures 4.3–4.12, and are discussed in decreasing order of importance. It is necessary to remember for the longitudinal analyses that the individuals were 2 years older in Phase 2 than in Phase 1, and depending upon the activity involved, maturational changes as well as television-related changes might be expected. To further complicate matters, the direction of change expected with increasing age might be similar or different for youths and adults.

Sports

The results for sports were reasonably dramatic. In Phase 1, when youths and adults were combined, Notel residents participated in more sports activities than did Unitel residents, who in turn participated in more than Multitel residents. This also was true for youths and adults separately, but whereas all differences among the towns were significant for youths, only the difference between Notel and Multitel was significant for adults. In all three towns youths participated more than adults, but as Figure 4.3 and the means in Tables 4.A3–4.A5 indicate, Notel adults actually were more active in sports than Multitel youths prior to the arrival of TV in Notel. Over the next 2 years, participation in sports decreased significantly for Notel youths, increased significantly for Unitel and Multitel youths, decreased significantly for Notel adults, and remained constant for Unitel and Multitel adults.[12] These results are shown in Figure 4.4 and in Table 4.A7. In the second year after the arrival of television in Notel, participation in sports by youths no longer differed

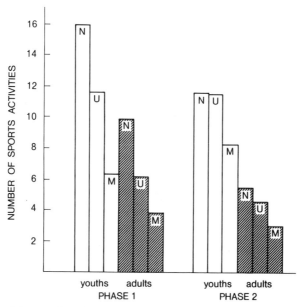

FIGURE 4.3   Mean number of sports activities participated in by youths and adults, by town and phase (all participants in each phase; N, Notel; U, Unitel; M, Multitel).

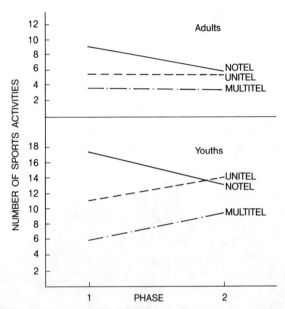

FIGURE 4.4 Mean number of sports activities participated in by youths and adults in the longitudinal sample, for each town and phase.

from that of youths in the other towns (see Table 4.A5). Notel adults were now similar to Unitel adults, although they still were more active in sports than Multitel adults.

A more detailed age breakdown (Figure 4.5, Table 4.A8) revealed that sports participation was greater in a town without television than in towns with television at every age level except 20–35 years, which echoes the finding for total community activities described earlier.[13] Television interacts with other constraints in the process of displacement. During the developmental stage of young adulthood (20–35 years in this study), job demands and/or those involved in raising young children apparently set a limit on the time available for leisure activities outside the home, and participation in sports is an important activity in this regard.

Two years after television arrived in Notel, there were significant differences among the towns in sports participation only for the 13–15 and 16–19 year age groups. In both age groups Notel and Unitel youths, who did not differ, participated more than did Multitel youths.

It is interesting that residents of towns with access to only one channel of Canadian television tended to participate more than residents of a town with access to four channels, one Canadian and three from the United States. A similar finding, namely a linear decrease in playing and watching sports with increasing availability of television, was obtained in Australia by Murray and Kippax (1978). In their study of the introduction of television to 18 children in a small village in Scotland, Brown, Cramond, and Wilde (1974) found that rule-governed outdoor activity (including sports) was more subject to displacement by TV than were other outdoor activities. In contrast, Himmelweit, Oppenheim, and Vince (1958) found that children's participation in unorganized outdoor activities suffered with the advent of television, but sports and watching sports were much less affected.

Theoretically, differences in sports participation could have arisen either because the number of sports activities differed (due to television-related factors or some other unknown reason) or because the numbers were comparable but participation rates were lower. The evidence in this study points more to the second explanation than to the first.

From the perspective of a displacement hypothesis it is not surprising to find that television affects participation in community sports activities. Both children and adults in the television towns spent an average of more than 20 hours per week with television. Activities which cannot be time-

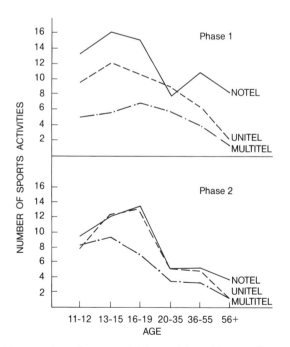

FIGURE 4.5   Mean number of sports activities participated in according to age group, for each town and phase (all participants in each phase).

shared with television would be affected most, and sports fall in that category. From another perspective, however, it is surprising that television has a negative influence, particularly in Multitel by comparison with Unitel (where the difference in weekly viewing, although significant, was only about 5 hours per week). Sports programming on television is extensive, and might well encourage participation. Anecdotal evidence that membership in gymnastics clubs increased following televised coverage of Olga Korbut's and Nadia Comaneci's Olympic victories provides one example. Certain sports such as gymnastics were not available in these communities, but the usual team sports seen on TV such as hockey, baseball, basketball, and soccer were well represented, along with individual sports such as skiing, tennis, bowling, and golf. Other team and individual sports not usually seen on television also were available, most notably curling, a winter sport popular in Canada, especially in small communities. Badminton, volleyball, and snowmobiling also were available. Although television theoretically could encourage participation in sports activities, the evidence from this study suggests instead that its overall effect is decreased participation.

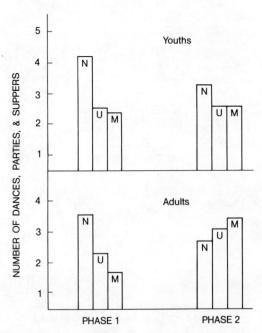

FIGURE 4.6 Mean number of dances, parties, and suppers attended by youths and adults according to town and phase (all participants in each phase; N, Notel; U, Unitel; M, Multitel).

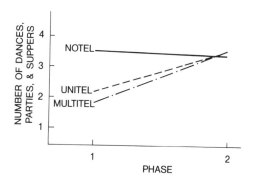

FIGURE 4.7 Mean number of dances, parties, and suppers attended by the longitudinal sample according to town and phase.

DANCES, PARTIES, AND SUPPERS

Both the cross-sectional and longitudinal results imply that television affects attendance at community dances, parties, and suppers (see Figures 4.6 and 4.7). Before television arrived, Notel residents attended more community social events than did residents of both Unitel and Multitel, who did not differ (Table 4.A4). This finding for adults and youths combined also held true for the youths alone (Table 4.A5). For the adults alone (Table 4.A6), the means followed the same pattern, with Notel highest and Multitel lowest, but only the difference between Notel and Multitel was statistically significant (Figure 4.6). Over the next 2 years there was an increase in attendance by members of the longitudinal sample residing in Unitel and Multitel, but no change in Notel (Figure 4.7).[14] The increases in Unitel and Multitel would be expected because attendance at social events such as parties, dances, and suppers or banquets would normally increase during the adolescent and early adult years. The relatively high level of attendance in Phase 1 in Notel and lack of subsequent increase indicate that in the absence of television, younger people attend more events of this sort. By Phase 2, attendance by both youths and adults in Notel was similar to that for Unitel and Multitel.

One other interesting finding regarding attendance at dances, suppers, and parties was revealed in the longitudinal analyses. Averaging across the phases, the mean number of events attended was similar for youths and adults in Unitel and Multitel, but higher for youths than for adults in Notel (see note 14). This reinforces the impression that television has a greater impact on attendance at dances, parties, and banquets for adolescents than for adults. It also provides another indication that one of the effects of television on community activities may be increased age segregation.

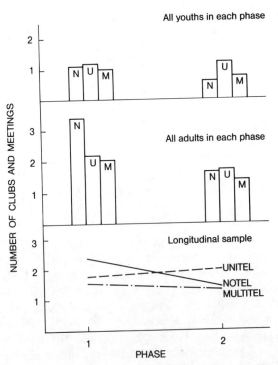

FIGURE 4.8   Mean number of clubs and meetings attended according to town and phase (N, Notel; U, Unitel; M, Multitel).

CLUBS AND MEETINGS

There was some evidence implicating television in attendance drop-off at clubs or other organizations and meetings, an intuitively likely prospect, but it was not as strong as that for sports and dances, parties, and suppers. The results for the longitudinal sample were clearer than those for the comparisons within each phase, so they will be described first (see Figure 4.8).[15] Before Notel had television, residents in the longitudinal sample attended a greater variety of club and other meetings than did residents of both Unitel and Multitel, who did not differ. There was a significant decline in Notel following the introduction of television, but no change in either Unitel or Multitel. In Phase 2, Unitel residents attended a greater variety of club and other meetings than did residents of both Notel and Multitel. These longitudinal results mirror fairly well the pattern predicted by a displacement hypothesis. When we included people who provided information only in Phase 1 or Phase 2, however, the picture was not as clear (see Tables 4.A4–4.A7). When youths and adults were combined, no difference among the towns was statistically significant in either phase of the study, although the means were ordered in the same way as for the longitudinal sample. This also was true when just the adults were considered. For youths there were no significant differences among the towns in Phase 1, and in Phase 2, Unitel youths attended a greater variety of clubs than did Notel youths, with Multitel youths in between and not different from Notel or Unitel.

Why might the results differ slightly for the longitudinal and cross-sectional samples? First, people in the longitudinal sample may be more likely to attend club and other meetings because they are more likely to be longer-term residents of their community than people who provided data only in Phase 1 or Phase 2. This hypothesis has some empirical support; the mean for the longitudinal adults was 2.47 by comparison with a mean of only 1.91 for adults present only in Phase 1 or Phase 2. The same explanation may apply to the students' responses. In addition, attendance at club and other meetings was more characteristic, on average, of adults than youths, and it was the youths who were the exception to an otherwise consistent ordering of means. Finally, the pattern of results for the adults in the cross-sectional sample was the same as for the longitudinal sample, but not statistically significant. The longitudinal statistical test has more power to detect differences, and we used a slightly less conservative test than for the cross-sectional comparisons within each phase (where the sample size was larger).

The relationship in Phase 2 between number of clubs and meetings attended (on which the analyses described thus far have been based) and those attended frequently (that is, weekly or more often) was only moderate, so we analyzed the frequency data to see if they yielded a different pattern of results.[16]

The pattern of differences and similarities among the towns in frequent Phase 2 attendance (weekly or more often) varied with age level. For the adult (20–35, 36–55, and 56 and over) age-groups there were no significant differences among the towns, but among the three youngest age-groups, frequent club attendance was highest in Unitel (higher than in both of the other towns), next highest in Multitel, and lowest in Notel. How should we interpret these results? They may reflect chance variation, but the consistency of the pattern within the three youngest and oldest age-groups argues otherwise. The difference in the involvement of Unitel and Multitel youths in clubs may reflect the differences in amount of time spent with television (see Chapter 5), and/or differences in the nature of the programming or number of channels available. The lesser involvement of Notel youths in clubs may be a result of the relatively recent arrival of television in the community. If so, an increase to the level characteristic of Unitel youths would be expected over subsequent years. If this interpretation is correct, it reflects one of only a handful of instances in this project in which the shorter-term impact of television in Notel differs from the longer-term impact of television in Unitel. The results of two studies conducted in the United Kingdom during the 1950s provide some evidence to support these speculations. Himmelweit et al. (1958) found that a year of television viewing effected little change in club membership and attendance for adolescents, but 11–12-year-olds went less often than they had previously. Belson (1959) studied adults in the Greater London area and found that strength of interest in clubs did not change in the first year of set ownership, decreased substantially during the second year, returned to its pre-TV level between the second and fourth year, and after about 5 years of set ownership, increased. Unfortunately, Belson did not conduct a similar analysis of trends in attendance.

Special Days

Residents were asked whether they had attended certain special ceremonies or days during the preceding year. Some items referred to categories of private events (e.g., weddings), and some referred to specific public events (e.g., Remembrance Day ceremonies, elections). In Phase 1, adults in Notel attended more such events than did adults in Multitel, who in turn attended more than adults in Unitel (Table 4.A7). For youths there were no significant differences among the towns in Phase 1, but the means followed the same pattern (Table 4.A5). When youths and adults in Phase 1 were combined (Table 4.A4), Notel and Multitel residents, who did not differ, attended more special days on average than did Unitel residents. A significant decrease in attendance at special days occurred between Phase 1 and Phase 2 for both the Notel youths and Notel adults (Figure 4.9). There was no change for either youths or adults in Multitel, and no change for Unitel youths, but a significant increase in attendance occurred for Unitel adults.[17] In Phase 2, there were no significant differences among the towns for youths, adults, or for the two combined (Tables 4.A4–4.A7).

These results provide some evidence that in the absence of television, adults attend more special days, and attendance drops for both youths and adults when television becomes available, but a couple of irregularities are puzzling. It is not clear why there was an increase in attendance by Unitel adults from Phase 1 to Phase 2. The most anomalous mean is that for Unitel adults in Phase 1 (see Figure 4.9), since the Phase 2 means for Notel and Unitel adults are similar to those for Multitel adults in both phases. The fact that the Multitel mean was not different from that for

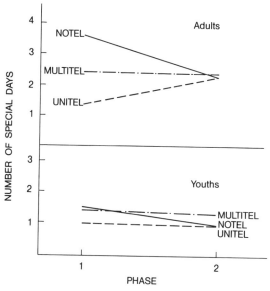

FIGURE 4.9 Mean number of special days attended by youths and adults in the longitudinal sample for each town and phase.

Notel in Phase 1 when all residents were combined also indicates the need for caution if television is invoked as a factor in attendance at special days.

ENTERTAINMENT

On the one hand, the significant decrease in attendance at entertainment events (e.g., bingo evenings, Christmas concerts) following the introduction of television to Notel suggests that television may play a negative role in participation in such activities (Tables 4.A4–4.A7).[18] On the other hand, the increase in Multitel and the pattern of Phase 2 town differences suggests that television may play a positive role in attendance. In our view, the increase in Multitel, decrease in Unitel, and lack of differences among the towns in the Phase 1 cross-sectional sample all suggest that other factors probably are more important. We suspect that town-specific traditions are especially relevant for this category. For example, in Phase 2, Multitel had a July 1st parade (honoring Dominion Day, the anniversary of Canadian confederation) and Unitel had a Winter Carnival parade. Aside from the seasonal differences which might affect attendance, one event may be a longer-standing tradition and, therefore, better (or more poorly) attended than the other. The ecologies of small towns are complex, and television is only one of many influences on community life.

MEDICAL

The towns were more similar than different in their use of medical settings (Tables 4.A4–4.A7). Frequency of attendance seemed to us to be a more appropriate measure than number of settings attended, so we also examined our Phase 2 data from this perspective.[19] Attendance was highest in Notel, significantly higher than in both the other towns, and the frequency for Unitel also was higher than in Multitel. In the absence of Phase 1 frequency data these results are difficult to interpret. It is possible that the arrival of television resulted in an increase in attendance at medical facilities, but other explanations are more likely. In both phases Notel was the only community with a hospital. A hospital would have more employees than the kinds of medical facilities available in the other towns, and residents also would be more likely to visit friends there.

It is not clear how television could affect the variety of medical settings or the frequency with which they are used in Canada, and our results support the conclusion that it does not. This is not to say, however, that television has no impact in the medical realm. We would be surprised if regular viewers of medically oriented television programs, either those intended for educational purposes (e.g., "The Body in Question" or other programs in the "Nova" series), those intended primarily for entertainment (e.g., older programs such as "Marcus Welby, M.D." or more recent ones such as "St. Elsewhere"), were not more knowledgeable about some medically related topics than people who rarely or never watch such programs. We have heard anecdotally from intensive care personnel that whereas they still warn visiting relatives that patients have many tubes and equipment attached to them and this may be upsetting, the comment "Oh, it's just like on television" is common, and people seem better prepared than in the past. It would be interesting to compare the medical knowledge and attitudes, of people who are and those who are not regular viewers of medically oriented programs, toward medical facilities and personnel. Self-selection would pose problems for such research, but controls for education could be included, and it might be possible to locate groups without access to such programming.

RELIGIOUS ACTIVITIES

The variety of religious activities attended varied according to town, age level, and phase of the study, but not in a meaningful way in relation to television (Tables 4.A4–4.A7).[20] Instead, the primary result was developmental; the variety of religious activities attended dropped during the adolescent years. Since most people who attend religious community activities probably do so primarily at one institution, however, variety of activities attended is probably a poor measure.

The Phase 2 frequency information was examined from the perspective of both mean frequency of attendance and number of religious activities attended weekly or more often. The results differed only slightly.[21] On the average, females reported attending religious community activities more often than did males, and differences among the towns occurred only for females. In terms of mean frequency of attendance, Unitel and Notel females did not differ, and both attended religious community activities more often than did Multitel females. Among 11–12-year-olds and 13–15-year-olds, Unitel youths more often attended religious activities than did Notel and Multitel youths, who did not differ. Among adults aged 56 and over, Notel residents attended religious events more often than did Multitel and Unitel residents, who did not differ.

Theoretically, religious and other television programming could encourage attendance at religious activities; could serve as an adjunct to attendance but not affect it; could displace attendance; or could be used primarily by people who are unable to attend religious community activities. Based on UNESCO time-budget studies from a number of countries, Robinson (1972) concluded that television reduces the amount of time devoted to religion. Our results are not entirely clear on this matter, but the frequency data from Phase 2 provide some indication that attendance tends to decrease as television is increasingly available. We are inclined to believe, however, that television played little or no role in this pattern of results, and that other factors were more important. This was the conclusion reached by Himmelweit et al. (1958), based on their study of the advent of television in the United Kingdom. Interviews we conducted in the three communities 2 years after Phase 2 did indicate that more Multitel residents than Notel or Unitel residents went to other communities for religious activities. In addition, Unitel had more fundamentalist church organizations than the other towns.

OPEN AREAS

There was no evidence that television has an impact on open area activities. Each town had several well-known outdoor places to which children and adults went for outings, to meet others, or to play games. The number of areas used by residents did vary by town, but not in a way that would implicate television (Tables 4.A4–4.A7).[22] Youths apparently go to more open areas than do adults, and residents of some towns typically use more of their open areas than do residents of other towns, but television does not seem to be a major factor in these patterns of use.

BUSINESSES

In both phases, Notel and Unitel residents, who did not differ, patronized significantly more of their community's businesses than was the case in Multitel. This held true separately for both youths and adults as well as when the two were combined (see Tables 4.A4–4.A6 and Figure 4.10). The longitudinal data revealed a significant decrease in the number of businesses attended over the 2 years between the phases for both youths and adults in all three towns.[23]

The most likely explanation for the lesser use of community businesses by Multitel residents is that they were closer to larger communities with more shopping facilities. Two towns with populations of 10,000 and 15,000 could each be reached (via different highways) in about 40 minutes' driving time. In contrast, Notel residents had to drive about 2½ hours and Unitel residents about 3½ or 4 hours before reaching a community with better shopping facilities. Some information obtained in Phase 2 lends indirect support to this explanation. Multitel residents reported

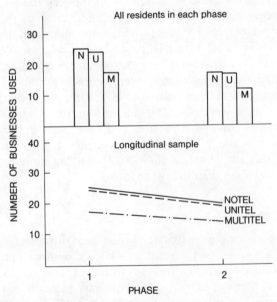

FIGURE 4.10   Mean number of businesses patronized during the previous year according to town and phase (N, Notel; U, Unitel; M, Multitel).

more frequently going to other communities (for any purpose) than did residents of both Notel and Unitel, who did not differ in this regard.[24]

Since the decrease in business use between Phase 1 and Phase 2 occurred at both age levels in all three towns, the most probable explanation is the mild recession in the Canadian economy which occurred during that period.

There is no evidence in this study to link business use to the availability of television. On the one hand this is not surprising, since people use businesses primarily for specific purposes (e.g., to buy groceries, have the car repaired). Television would be more likely to affect leisure or discretionary behaviors than behaviors involving maintenance. From another perspective, however, it would be surprising if it did *not* influence consumer behavior, since so much money is spent on television advertising. Unfortunately, we did not assess purchasing behavior (e.g., brand choices) in this study.

Civic

The pattern of results for civic activities (e.g., various types of court, the town office) is not readily interpretable in relation to the availability of television (see Tables 4.A4–4.A7).[25] The finding that among the adults in both phases, Notel residents were highest and Multitel residents lowest in number of civic activities attended could possibly be interpreted as evidence of greater civic interest on the part of adults residing in a town without television. If such interest is slow to change, this would explain why Notel adults still were highest in number of civic activities in Phase 2, even though there was a significant drop following the introduction of television. The lack of clarity in the pattern of results for youths could have arisen if one or more of the school classes was taken on a tour of the town jail, Royal Canadian Mounted Police station, or other civic locale. However, the conclusion that television affects civic activities would require us to dismiss the results for youths for that or some other reason. It seems just as likely that the results for both adults and youths reflects chance variation which is statistically significant because of the large samples involved or systematic variation related to factors other than television.

Educational Activities

Participation in educational activities which were not specifically part of the school curricula (e.g., first aid classes, teacher aide meetings, parent–teacher interviews, piano lessons, school concerts) varied according to town, age, and phase of the study, but not in an easily interpretable pattern (Tables 4.A4–4.A7).[26]

Two competing hypotheses regarding the influence of TV on participation in community educational activities seem plausible. Television might broaden its viewers' range of interests and lead to an increase in participation. The increase following the arrival of television in Notel which occurred for adults is consistent with this hypothesis, but an increase also occurred for Unitel adults, which is more difficult to explain. It seems unlikely but is conceivable that the improved reception in Unitel accounted for this increase. If this hypothesis is correct, however, we would expect the Phase 1 means for Unitel and Multitel to be higher than that for Notel, and they were not (Unitel was lower, and Multitel was equal to Notel). In addition, there is no evidence in the youths' data to support this first hypothesis. A second possibility is that television displaces educational community activities; residents may stay home to watch TV rather than going out to lessons, meetings, or other education-related activities. The decrease in participation by Notel youths between Phase 1 and Phase 2 is consistent with this hypothesis, but a decrease also occurred for Multitel youths, and in the case of Notel adults, there was a significant increase. This displacement hypothesis would predict a higher Phase 1 mean for Notel than for both Unitel and Multitel, which did not occur. It is possible that television displaces educational activities for some individuals (e.g., youths) and encourages participation for others (e.g., adults), but the pattern of results is not even consistent with this more complicated hypothesis or with the correlational results (discussed later and shown in Table 4.A9). When the kinds of activities we assessed are combined in one category and scores are based on the number of activities attended, participation in educational community activities seems idiosyncratic or, at least, unrelated to television. The Phase 2 frequency data are consistent with this conclusion.[27]

OTHER ACTIVITIES

We would have preferred to avoid a catchall category of Other, but in each community there were several events and activities that could not be readily classified. These included fund-raising events such as bake sales and walkathons, volunteer work on the ski hill, senior citizens' events, Girl Guide caroling, open house at the senior citizen's residence, and so forth. The results do not follow any readily interpretable pattern (see Tables 4.A4–4.A7), which suggests the events are disparate and specific to each town and phase of the study.[28] They add to our conclusions only by indicating that systematic differences in some categories were not balanced by systematic differences in the opposite direction in the Other category.

Correlations between Hours of TV Viewing and Participation in Community Activities

As we have seen, comparisons among the towns indicated that television may affect participation in some community activities. Did this relationship hold true for individuals? We correlated reported hours of TV viewing with the number of community activities participated in for each of the 12 categories, both within and across the phases (see Table 4.A9). Correlations involving Phase 1 hours of TV viewing were based on Unitel and Multitel only; inclusion of the Notel Phase 1 data would spuriously affect the results because the majority of Notel residents watched no television in Phase 1. The results for Phase 2 were calculated separately for Notel and the two other towns combined because the recent arrival of television in Notel might yield a relationship different than that typical of communities which have had television over a longer period, a possibility supported by the results. The correlations for youths and adults are shown separately (along with those for the combined samples) because of the possibility that the relationship between amount of TV viewing and participation in community activities differs by age level.

Both within and across the phases, individuals in Unitel and Multitel who reported watching more hours of television tended to report participating in fewer community activities. This evidence corroborates the results based on comparisons among the towns. It should be noted, however, that although a reasonable number of the correlations computed were statistically significant, none was large. This is not surprising. First, as we have emphasized in the other chapters of this book and elsewhere (Williams, 1981), the relationship between hours of TV viewing and other behaviors may not be linear. Second, as we also have emphasized, a simple displacement hypothesis regarding the effects of television is inappropriate. In the case of leisure activities, other demands constrain the amount of leisure time available. For example, an individual with no paid work and few domestic labor responsibilities might participate in many community activities and still have considerable time to spend watching television. Another person who spent the same amount of time with television might have no additional leisure time to spend in community activities because of domestic or other work responsibilities. Detailed time budgets are required to ascertain more precisely the ways in which television, other leisure activities, and paid and unpaid work responsibilities interact. Unfortunately, we were unable to obtain such information in this project.

The correlations for Notel residents (Table 4.A9) between Phase 2 hours of television viewing and participation in community activities do not form the same pattern as those for Unitel and Multitel. Relatively few were statistically significant, and of those that were, most were positive. How can we explain the apparent discrepancy between these positive correlations and the evidence discussed earlier that the mean level of participation decreased in Notel following the introduction of television? One possibility is that the advent of TV stimulated participation in the short run for certain kinds of activities. For example, some evidence discussed later in this chapter suggests that the introduction of television to Notel may have led to an increase in *passive* participation in sports at the expense of *active* participation, especially for adults (see note 32). The other possibility is that rather than indicating an effect of television, the positive correlations for Notel in Table 4.A9 indicate that people who tend to participate in certain kinds of activities (for example, passive involvement in sports) tend to watch more television after it becomes available. Whatever the explanation for the pattern of correlations in Notel 2 years after the arrival of television, the pattern of differences among the town means within and across the phases, coupled with the negative correlations for Unitel and Multitel between amount of TV viewed and participation in community activities, indicates that in the long run television leads to decreased participation.

Level of Involvement in Total Community Activities

Does television affect participation by people whose role is central to community activities, or does it only affect those more peripherally involved?

As we described earlier, people who completed our survey indicated not only whether they attended each activity, but what they had done there. Each description was scored to ascertain whether it met the criterion of a *performance,* defined as someone who was personally essential to the continuation or existence of the activity. For example, the clerk in a store would receive a performance score for that business, but a customer would not.

We first asked whether the total number of performances, summing across the 12 activity categories, varied by town, sex, or age-group (11–12, 13–15, 16–19, 20–35, 36–55, 56+) within each phase.

In Phase 1, Notel residents were centrally involved in more activities than were Unitel and Multitel residents, who did not differ.[29] The pattern

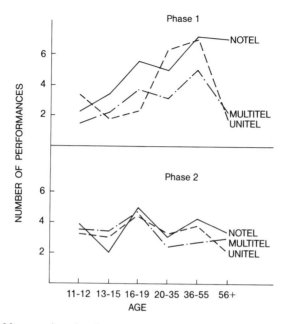

FIGURE 4.11   Mean number of performances (i.e., participant is essential to the community activity) according to age group for each town and phase (all participants in each phase).

of town differences varied by age level, however, as Table 4.A10 and Figure 4.11 indicate. There were no town differences for the two youngest age-groups. For 16–19-year-olds, Notel had more performances than Unitel; for 20–35-year-olds, Unitel had more than Multitel; for 36–55-year-olds, Notel and Unitel both had more than Multitel; and for adults 56 and over, Notel had more performances than both Unitel and Multitel. Not only were older Notel residents active in more of their community's activities than was the case in Unitel and Multitel, they played a more central role in their community's activities prior to the introduction of television.

In Phase 2, there were no longer any significant overall differences among the towns, and the only specific difference was that in the oldest age group, females in Notel had more performances than females in both Unitel and Multitel, who did not differ (Table 4.A10 and Figure 4.11).[30]

The number of performances increased significantly between Phase 1 and Phase 2 for Unitel and Multitel residents, but did not change for Notel residents (Figure 4.12).[31] This suggests that the arrival of television counteracted the normally expected increase in performances with increasing age (see in Figure 4.11 for the cross-sectional samples in each phase). The fact that performances increased on average between Phase 1 and Phase 2 for youths but did not change for adults supports this interpretation.

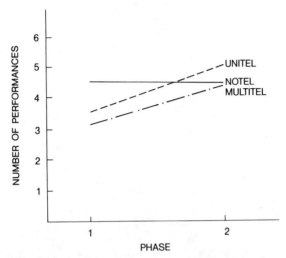

FIGURE 4.12   Mean number of performances (i.e., participant is essential to the community activity) by the longitudinal sample for each town and phase.

Before Notel had television, performances there were equally high for females and males, whereas in Unitel they were higher for males than for females, and in Multitel, equally low for both. In Phase 2, there were sex differences in all three towns among residents aged 56 and over, reflecting more performances by men than by women in both Unitel and Multitel, but more for women than for men in Notel. These results provide a hint that behavior may follow more traditional sex-role patterns in towns with television than in a town without television. We would not want to make much of these findings in and of themselves, but they are consistent with some of the findings obtained by other researchers in this project for reading and sex-role attitudes.

In sum, television apparently affects participation in community activities for individuals who are central to those activities, not just those who are more peripherally involved. Residents are more likely to be centrally involved in their community's activities in the absence than in the presence of television.

Level of Involvement in Sports

The category of leisure activities most strongly affected by television in this study was sports. Did television reduce active involvement in sports, spectator activities, or both? We classified each response to a sports item as either active (played, coached, was a regular participant, and so on) or passive (watched, drove a child to a practice session, and so on), and we calculated the mean for each type of response.[32]

A displacement hypothesis would predict that television has a negative impact on active involvement in community sports. Our results for both the town comparisons and the correlations between active sports participation and amount of TV viewed support this prediction; there was no evidence to indicate that television stimulates active participation in sports. Predicting television's influence on passive attendance at sports activities is more difficult, as Comstock et al. (1978) have discussed. On the one hand, Belson (1959) found that in the Greater London area television led to increased interest in, and attendance at, horse racing or jumping events and major soccer matches. On the other hand, he also found a decrease in interest in going to see general sports events but no change in reported attendance. These contrasting results occurred in the same sample. Bogart (1972) concluded that the advent of television in North American led to a decline in attendance at minor league baseball games and motion pictures. Murray and Kippax (1978) obtained evidence in Australia that television displaces both active and passive sports involvement. Our data provide some indication that the advent of television may lead to an increase in passive sports participation at the expense of active involvement, particularly for adults. Amount of TV watched was significantly positively correlated with passive sports participation for Notel adults in Phase 2, but there was no relationship for Unitel and Multitel adults.

RESULTS FOR PRIVATE LEISURE ACTIVITIES

Was there any evidence that television influences participation in what we have termed private leisure activities? There were 8 (of 58) private leisure activities which youths and adults of both sexes in all three towns indicated they did rarely, if ever, so they were eliminated from subsequent analyses (car racing, sculpture, darkroom work, flower arranging, horseshoes, volunteer fire fighting, weaving, and model building). We would have liked to reduce the remaining 50 activities to clusters which made sense both conceptually and empirically, but this was impossible because there were large differences in participation related to age and gender.[33] For example, bicycling was a common activity among youths but not common for adults, and sewing was a common activity for females but rare for males. If we ignored sex and age we would have obtained clusters due more to differences between groups than to different patterns of participation in the three towns, which was our primary interest. We therefore abandoned these attempts at data reduction and reported the results for all 50 activities, focusing on similarities and differences among the towns but also mentioning differences related to age and sex, especially when they varied by town. The means for Phase 1 are shown in Table 4.A11 and for Phase 2, in Table 4.A12.

We first asked whether the lists or vectors of 50 private leisure activity means varied in Phase 1, and found there were overall differences related to town, age, gender, the combination of town and age, and the combination of age and gender. The same pattern of results occurred in Phase 2.[34] We then looked in each phase at each of the 50 activities to determine where these differences arose. Since we had changed the response options on the questionnaire between Phase 1 and Phase 2, it was not possible to conduct longitudinal analyses.

PHASE 1: TOWN DIFFERENCES AND SIMILARITIES IN FREQUENCY OF PARTICIPATION

Averaging across age, Notel residents in Phase 1 reported exercising more frequently than did Unitel residents, and along with Multitel residents, read newspapers more often than Unitel residents. (Multitel was the only town with daily newspaper delivery.) Multitel residents rode bicycles more frequently than Notel residents. Other differences among the towns were specific to one age level. Notel youths traveled and jogged more often than Unitel youths, rode motorcycles more than both Unitel and Multitel youths, and, along with Multitel youths, hiked more than Unitel youths. Multitel youths also climbed and sunbathed more often than Unitel youths, played table tennis more often than both Unitel and Notel youths, and along with Unitel youths, played cards and visited to watch TV more often than Notel youths. Unitel youths reported writing letters more often than Notel youths and reading books more often than both Notel and Multitel youths. Notel adults reported climbing more often than Multitel adults, playing cards more often than Unitel adults, and eating with friends more often than both Unitel and Multitel adults. Along with Unitel adults they also read books and bird-watched more often than Multitel adults. Unitel adults, in addition, reported sight-seeing and writing letters more often than Multitel adults, whereas Multitel adults reported playing cards more often than Unitel adults. In absolute terms, irrespective of whether the differences were statistically significant or not, Notel residents had the highest mean for 20 of the 48 private leisure activities which were not directly related to television, were second for 17, and lowest for 11. The analogous figures for Unitel were 9, 23, and 16, and for Multitel, 15, 12, and 21. By chance, a distribution of 16, 16, and 16 would be expected in each town, and only the distribution for Unitel departs significantly from that expectation.

These results do not present a picture of numerous and systematic differences among the towns in involvement in private leisure activities prior to the arrival of television in Notel. The activities which Notel residents did more often than Unitel and/or Multitel residents probably include more which cannot be time-shared with television, whereas, the activities Multitel and/or Unitel residents did more often probably are easier to time-share with TV. We would not want to make much of this pattern, however, since the majority of private leisure activities on our list revealed no significant differences among the towns. Differences related to gender and age clearly were more overwhelming, as we shall document shortly.

PHASE 2: TOWN DIFFERENCES AND SIMILARITIES IN FREQUENCY OF PARTICIPATION

Averaging across age, Notel residents in Phase 2 reported listening to records and sewing more frequently than did Unitel residents, who reported jogging more often than Notel residents. In addition, both Unitel and Multitel residents reported traveling and social drinking more often than did Notel residents. The remaining general differences favored Multitel residents, who more often bicycled and visited to watch TV than did residents of Notel and more often boated, looked after pets, played cards, read newspapers (Multitel was the only town with home delivery), sunbathed, talked on the telephone, and window-shopped than did residents of both Notel and Unitel. Some differences among the towns occurred for only one age level. Multitel youths reported reading magazines, watching TV, and listening to the radio more often than did Notel and Unitel youths, and along with Unitel youths, reported playing table tennis more often than Notel youths. Notel adults reported writing letters more frequently than Multitel adults, home decorating more frequently than Unitel and Multitel adults, and along with Unitel adults, reported reading books more often than Multitel adults. These Phase 2 results indicate that, if anything, Multitel residents were more active in private leisure activities than were residents of Notel and Unitel. Most (but not all) of these could be time-shared with television, and two (watching TV and visiting to watch TV) directly involved television. Just as we found in Phase 1, however, there were no town-related differences for the majority (30) of the activities on our list, and the differences related to gender and age level were more numerous.

DIFFERENCES RELATED TO GENDER AND AGE LEVEL

In both phases there were significant differences in participation in most of the leisure activities we assessed related to age, sex, or both. These results are shown in Table 4.A13. They contain a few surprises (for example, parents of adolescents may be startled to see that youths and adults report talking on the telephone with the same frequency), but by and large correspond to patterns we would expect based on empirical and anecdotal evidence. The gender- and age-related results were consistent across the towns and phases, and contribute to our conclusions by indicating that residents of the three towns in this natural experiment were more typical than atypical. Consistency across the phases occurred despite the different scales used to obtain information (never, occasionally, and regularly in Phase 1; never, once only, six times, monthly, twice a month, weekly, twice a week, and every day in Phase 2). This suggests that even if we had used a more detailed scale in Phase 1, we would not have uncovered many more significant town-related differences.

TOWN DIFFERENCES AND SIMILARITIES RELATED TO NUMBER OF PRIVATE LEISURE ACTIVITIES

So far we have been discussing frequency of participation in individual private leisure activities. The total number, or variety, of private leisure activities in which residents reported participating also was similar, with no more than two activities' difference between any pair of towns in both phases of the study.

SUMMARY AND CONCLUSIONS

What were our major findings, and what do they imply regarding the processes involved in television's effects on community life?

Television apparently has little if any impact on the number of community activities available, but it has a noticeable negative effect on participation in those activities. Involvement in community activities, summing across the categories, was greatest in the absence of television and fell significantly following its arrival in Notel. There also was some evidence of greater participation in towns with one channel of CBC than in a town with four channels, CBC and the three major U.S. networks. Television affected central as well as peripheral involvement in community activities and active involvement in sports. Patterns of participation across the 12 categories varied by town, and television seemed to be related to participation for some kinds of community activities, but not for others.

Television's negative impact was greatest for sports, and the effect was stronger for youths than for adults. There also was reasonably clear evidence to implicate television in decreased attendance at dances, suppers, and parties, and again, the effect was stronger for youths than adults. In contrast, television seemed to result in decreased attendance by adults at clubs and other meetings, but the evidence for youths was less clear. For these three categories—sports, dances, and clubs—the pattern of findings was consistent enough to warrant the conclusion that television has a negative impact on participation. For two other categories, special days and entertainment, there was some evidence to suggest that television affects participation, again negatively, but the results were less clear, and we are more cautious in drawing that conclusion. If television does have an impact for these five categories, we suspect it does so primarily via displacement. None of these activities can be time-shared with television, and leisure time is limited.

For some categories the evidence indicated consistent town differences which were not related in any sensible way to the continuum of television's availability. We are inclined to think that the few systematic differences among Notel, Unitel, and Multitel for open areas, businesses, and civic, educational, and other activities occurred because of unique characteristics of one or more of these towns which were not related to television. Although one might reasonably hypothesize that television advertising would encourage use of businesses, that news programming would encourage participation in civic affairs, and that both educational and entertainment programming would encourage participation in educational activities, there was no evidence to indicate that it does. This study was not designed specifically to address these hypotheses, however, and other kinds of measures might yield different answers.

For the medical category, similarities among the towns seemed to outweigh any differences. For the religious category the data from both phases concerning variety of activities attended also yielded more evidence of similarities than differences. The Phase 2 reports of frequency of attendance were consistent with the hypothesis that television displaces participation in religious community activities, but also were amenable to other explanations.

The finding that the pattern of results varied in a sensible way across the categories strengthens our conclusions. It helps to rule out the possibility of response bias in the reports, that is, the possibility that a tendency by individuals to check off a lot of activities or only a few activities accounts for the results obtained.

It is noteworthy that participation in total community activities, and in sports in particular, was greater in Unitel than in Multitel in both phases.

This is one of the few results in the project indicating that the number and/ or origin of the channels available and differences in the way people use them, have an effect over and above the effect due to television's presence or absence. It should be possible to ascertain in further research both the generality of this finding and whether it arises more because of some distinction between the content of CBC and the three U.S. networks or because of differences in the number of channels and/or hours of programming available.

Another major finding concerned age. When television was not available, the oldest group of Notel residents (aged 56 and over) participated as much in their community's activities as did younger residents, and much more than did comparably aged Unitel and Multitel residents. Two years later, the substantial drop in participation by the oldest group seen earlier in the towns with television also was evident in Notel. This held true for both the total number of community activities attended during the previous year and the number of sports activities (the only individual category for which we examined age differences in this way). These age-related findings are provocative, since other research (reviewed by Iso-Ahola, 1980, Chapter 8) indicates that active leisure pursuits help the elderly to age more successfully than do passive pursuits.

Our age-related findings also suggest that television may affect the degree of age segregation characteristic of a community. If the older people attend fewer community activities, younger people who do attend have less opportunity to interact with older people. Further evidence that television may lead to increasing age segregation came from the results for the category of dances, suppers, and parties, except in this case younger people seemed to be most affected. Before Notel had television, adolescents there attended more community dances, and the like, than did adolescents in the towns with television, and the longitudinal results indicated they did so at a rate which did not become characteristic of Unitel and Multitel youths until they were 2 years older. In a sense, these age-related results suggest a qualitative component to the quantitative changes in community life associated with the impact of television.

Whereas the effect of television on participation in community activities, especially active participation in sports, was substantial, its impact on participation in private leisure activities, as assessed by either frequency or number, was minimal. There were more similarities than differences among the towns in both phases of the study, and only a few of the differences which did occur seemed to be related to the availability of television. At the same time, however, correlational results reported elsewhere in this book indicate that participation in some private leisure activities, especially those involving print use, is positively related to creativity (see Chapter 2) and negatively related to amount of time involved with television (see Chapter 5). Taken together, these findings indicate that the relationship of television to participation in other private leisure activities may be more obtuse than its relationship to participation in community leisure activities. Researchers wishing to untangle the complexities of this relationship should obtain detailed time-budget information and distinguish between activities which can and cannot be time-shared with television.

Belson (1959) investigated television's impact on the strength of adults' interest in other leisure activities, as well as the frequency of their actual involvement. His list of 50 activities overlapped with those covered in our lists of private and community activities but was more similar to the former than to the latter. He concluded that an initial decline in other activities following the advent of television is followed by a long-term recovery (over 4 to 6 years of TV ownership) in diversity or variety of interests, but at a lower level of frequency. Our findings concerning participation in private leisure activities are not consistent with this explanation, nor are our findings concerning community activities, since we observed differences between relatively long-term owners (Unitel and Multitel residents). As we have noted, however, Belson tapped relatively few community activities. On one point our results are in complete agreement: "Despite the nature of television's effects on interests *as a whole,* there is considerable variation in what happens to *specific* interests" (Belson, 1959, p. 155).

Some aspects of our results are consistent with those obtained by Murray and Kippax (1977, 1978) in a natural experiment in Australia, but others are not. They studied 98 families in a town without television (No-TV), 102 in a town with 1 year's experience with the Australian government-owned channel (Low-TV), and 82 in a town with 5 years' experience with the government channel and 2 years' experience with a commercial channel (High-TV). Parents were interviewed about the amount of time they and their children spent in each of 17 categories of leisure activities. Children in their No-TV town spent more time in other leisure activities than did children in the television towns. The main contributors to this effect were playing sports, watching sports, and other outdoor activities; linear decreases occurred as amount of television increased. The similarity between these results and ours for both total participation and sports activities is striking. In addition, there were linear decreases in the Australian study from the No- to Low- to High-TV towns in certain media activities (cinema attendance, radio listening, record playing). The results for adults indicated that involvement in other leisure activities differed overall by town. Specific differences occurred for both mothers and fathers in radio listening, cinema attendance, listening to records and tapes, theater attendance, and hobbies; in addition, fathers differed in watching sport, reading, and listening to public talks. The pattern of involvement in relation to television varied with the activity, which led Murray and Kippax (1978) to conclude that television "induces a major restructuring of one's conception of the media and patterns of daily activities" (p. 42). The differences in sample size, type of television available, and method of assessing participation make it difficult to assess reasons for disparities between our results and those obtained by Murray and Kippax, but both studies indicate that television displaces some kinds of leisure activities and not others. A similar conclusion was reached by Medrich, Roizen, Rubin, and Buckley (1982) and by Brown et al. (1974).

Medrich et al. (1982) conducted a study of time use by 764 sixth graders in Oakland, California. During the 7-hour period between about 3:00 and 10:00 P.M. on school days, these children spent 3–4 hours watching television, 2–3 hours on their own in various unorganized activities, less than $1\frac{1}{2}$ hours with their parents (including some television time), and less than 1 hour doing chores, related responsibilities, or jobs outside the home. In addition, most participated in some kind of organized activity (e.g., team sports, lessons), but this comprised only 4–5 hours per week, on average.Almost half (41%) of these sixth graders reported they "often feel bored and do not know what to do after school and on weekends," but children who played team sports were less likely (37%) to say so than children who did not play team sports (48%). Almost twice as many light as heavy viewers took fine arts lessons or belonged to sports or other groups. Nonetheless, Medrich et al. concluded that, overall, there was only limited evidence that light viewers spend their time in activities which make them otherwise different from their peers.

Brown et al. (1974) studied 18 children 4 months before and 8 months after their Scottish village obtained TV, comparing them with 18 children growing up in a community with TV and 11 children growing up in a community still without TV (except for daytime educational broadcasts). Their results led them to reject the functional equivalence or similarity hypothesis of mass media uses and effects and to argue instead that the displacement process is one of functional reorganization. That is, television affects the *structure* of leisure, it is not simply a question of one medium displacing another on the basis of whether they serve similar functions. Along with Murray and Kippax (1978), we are inclined to agree.

It is clear from our results and those obtained by other researchers that television's role in facilitating or hindering participation in other leisure activities is complex. Some, such as active participation in sports, apparently are displaced more or less directly, but others, especially those which can be time-shared with television, are not. To what extent, how, and for whom does television displace other activities simply because it is so readily available? What are the processes involved in choosing to watch television versus playing sport, reading, or attending a club meeting? We suspect that most people do not typically consider 5 or 10 activities and choose television as the preferred option. Rather, they think immediately of television, and the other possibilities never surface. Dorr (1980) cites the response of a second grader who was asked why television programs are available. "To entertain people. And to help me think. If they don't have TV, when you come in and you sit down and you just want to do something, you don't have anything to do".

In a sense, television may displace other leisure activities because its ready availability means the experience of finding something to do when bored—a game to play, something to make—has become alien. The senior author recalls numerous rainy Sunday afternoons when her parents sat around reading, and time moved inexorably slowly. On one of these occasions she discovered her mother's recorder and a book which described the fingering for it, and she spent the afternoon learning to play the instrument (she already knew how to read music). If television had been available, would this have happened? Does it matter (since she rarely played it again)? She can still remember clearly a strong sense of pride in accomplishment, a feeling of "I did it!" She also enjoyed the afternoon, and as a result may have been more likely when bored in the future to think of different things to do.

What we are suggesting is that participation in leisure activities may operate in a self-perpetuating upward or downward spiral. Medrich et al. (1982) contend that the easy availability of television attenuates the choice process, and this constitutes television's primary negative effect.

> If television were a scarce resource, as it is in some homes, the value of an hour spent watching would have to be measured against the value of an hour spent doing something else. Easy access to television means that most children do not even recognize that choices and trade-offs are involved in their viewing decisions. (p. 227)

The same is probably true of adults.

It is important to acknowledge that for some people, access to leisure activities is seriously limited by other factors. Some families do not have the option of participating in community sports activities because they cannot afford the equipment. For others, it may be safer to stay home. There, alternatives to TV may or may not be available. Television's effects on other leisure pursuits undoubtedly vary with SES.

Intuitively, it seems likely that television could stimulate participation in other leisure activities. Viewers might see an activity portrayed as enjoyable and as a result, try it themselves. This may well happen, but if we consider the nature of television and the ways in which ordinary people are depicted, it seems less likely. One rarely sees television characters playing board games, reading, and the like. They are portrayed in social interaction in their workplace or at home but rarely in leisure pursuits either in or out of their homes. The sports seen on television involve professionals. The content of most North American programming does not help viewers think of other possible leisure activities. Educationally oriented television might have a different effect; Murray and Kippax (1978) found that 66% of the children in their High-TV town said they watched television because they were bored, but only 39% of the children in their Low-TV town did so. The Low-TV town had access only to the government-owned channel on which 34% of the programming was intended for use in the schools, and an additional 20% involved news and documentaries. In addition, the commercial channel available in the High-TV town broadcast 98.8 hours per week versus 59.5 for the national channel in the Low-TV town. Our contention that television not only displaces other leisure activities but makes it less likely they will come to mind as options is supported by another finding reported by Murray and Kippax (1978). The amount of time parents reported their children spent sitting around doing nothing increased linearly from the No-TV, to the Low-TV, to the High-TV town.

Interactive television also might have a different effect on involvement in community activities. The HI-OVIS experiment in Japan is a good example (Slaby, personal communication, April, 1984). Residents of a small community have video equipment in their homes which enables them to participate via television in (live) discussions with town officials and other residents. For example, they might express their views on a plan to relocate the town's waste disposal site or they might discuss a hobby with other people who have similar interests. Anecdotal evidence indicates there will be numerous positive effects of this exciting new experiment.

Our speculations regarding the processes involved in television's negative effect on participation in other leisure activities, particularly community activities, may or may not stand up to empirical test. What *is* clear is that television affects the leisure pursuits of both children and adults. The results of other studies reported in this book, most notably those dealing with creativity, reading skills, and problem-solving skills, indicate that some of the activities displaced by television probably play an important role in fostering achievement, at least in certain areas and for certain people. By influencing how people play, television also may influence how people think and work.

APPENDIX: ADDITIONAL TABLES

TABLE 4.A1

Number of Participants in the Community Activities Surveys in Each Phase

	Age group[a]						All ages
	12 and under	13–15	16–19	20–35	36–55	56+	
Phase 1							
Notel	45	83	40	32	53	25	278
Unitel	34	97	28	30	42	21	252
Multitel	70	121	101	63	89	49	493
	149	301	169	125	184	95	1023
Phase 2							
Notel	65	100	61	66	86	38	416
Unitel	45	86	50	75	69	42	367
Multitel	78	142	102	99	96	69	586
	188	328	213	240	251	149	1369

[a] Two additional adults in Phase 1 and seven in Phase 2 did not provide age information. They were included in analyses which compared adults with youths, but not in analyses based on these more detailed age breakdowns.

TABLE 4.A2

Number of Participants in the Private Leisure Activities Surveys in Each Phase

	Youths (18 and under)	Adults (19 and over)	All ages
Phase 1			
Notel	145	95	240
Unitel	138	73	211
Multitel	254	153	407
	537	321	858
Phase 2			
Notel	210	173	383
Unitel	164	171	335
Multitel	292	235	527
	666	579	1245

TABLE 4.A3

Total Community Activity Participation: Phase 1 and Phase 2 Cross-Sectional Means:
All Respondents in Each Phase

| | Age group | | | | | | |
	12 and under	13–15	16–19	20–35	36–55	56+	Means
Phase 1							
Notel	64.03	71.65	72.09	56.10	67.77	64.23	65.98
Unitel	50.20	48.84	59.05	62.87	54.71	38.47	54.03
Multitel	48.08	49.41	52.91	50.47	45.35	33.73	46.66
Age means	54.11	59.97	61.35	56.48	55.95	45.48	
Phase 2							
Notel	41.38	56.73	52.28	44.92	45.86	35.88	44.68
Unitel	33.87	56.22	49.02	45.23	38.73	29.80	40.48
Multitel	39.09	41.79	37.46	33.99	34.85	27.38	35.76
Age means	38.11	44.91	56.25	41.38	40.15	31.02	
Phase 1							
Females	55.11	64.44	58.90	55.89	55.46	41.42	55.20
Males	53.10	55.50	63.79	57.08	56.44	49.54	55.91
Phase 2							
Females	38.32	50.26	47.69	45.91	41.54	27.51	38.74
Males	37.90	39.57	44.82	36.85	38.75	34.54	41.87

TABLE 4.A4

Mean Participation for Each Community Activity Category:
All Respondents in Phase 1 and All in Phase 2[a]

| | Phase 1 | | | Phase 2 | | |
	Notel	Unitel	Multitel	Notel	Unitel	Multitel
Sports	13.552[b]	9.588[c]	5.306[d]	8.688[b,d]	7.862[d]	5.817[c,d]
Open areas	6.263[d]	4.927[b,d]	6.651[c,d]	5.417[b]	3.642[c]	4.964[b]
Businesses	25.512[b]	24.292[b]	17.513[c]	17.789[b]	17.222[b]	12.243[c]
Civic	2.043[b]	2.442[b]	1.464[c]	1.417	1.415	1.120
Educational	4.160[b]	2.473[c]	3.935[b]	3.125	2.835	2.670
Clubs	2.056	1.650	1.424	1.115	1.477	1.085
Medical	2.139[b,d]	1.596[c,d]	1.708[d]	1.364[b]	0.797[c]	0.861[c]
Dances	3.961[b]	2.481[c]	2.097[c]	3.010	2.859	3.014
Special days	2.274[b]	1.211[c]	1.819[b]	1.242	1.095	1.470
Religious	0.907	0.973	0.564	0.607	0.591	0.346
Entertainment	2.505	2.838	2.292	0.796[b]	1.504[c]	2.353[d]
Other	2.103[b]	1.565[b]	3.128[c]	1.007[b,d]	0.612[d]	0.472[c,c]

[a] Within each phase, the multivariate analysis indicated all three towns were significantly differentiated overall. The superscript letters indicate which pairs of towns differed significantly within each phase of the study; town which do not share the same letter are significantly different at $p < .05$ by Scheffé test.

TABLE 4.A5

Mean Participation for Each Community Activity Category:
All Youths (Age 18 and under) Assessed in Each Phase [a]

	Phase 1			Phase 2		
	Notel	Unitel	Multitel	Notel	Unitel	Multitel
Sports	16.012[b]	11.620[c]	6.310[d]	11.577	11.517	8.305
Open areas	7.512[b]	5.563[b,d]	8.607[c,d]	6.686[b]	4.465[c]	7.116[b]
Businesses	24.693[b]	21.823[b]	16.931[c]	15.277[b]	15.201[b]	10.965[c]
Civic	1.681[b]	2.551[c]	1.359[b]	1.127	1.328	1.280
Educational	5.867[b]	3.538[c]	5.665[b]	3.504	3.661	3.640
Clubs	1.120	1.171	0.976	0.632[b,d]	1.213[c,d]	0.785[d]
Medical	1.976	1.500	1.500	1.154[b]	0.678[c]	0.653[c]
Dances	4.235[b]	2.557[c]	2.372[c]	3.295	2.603	2.621
Special days	1.548[b]	1.139	1.410	0.795	0.793	1.039
Religious	0.910	0.905	0.579	0.482	0.736	0.309
Entertainment	2.753	2.962	2.538	0.786[b]	1.655[c]	2.540[d]
Other	1.632	1.494	2.114	0.854[b]	0.374[c]	0.460[c]

[a] Within each phase, the multivariate analysis indicated all three towns were significantly differentiated overall. The superscript letters indicate which pairs of towns differed significantly within each phase of the study; towns which do not share the same letter are significantly different at $p < .05$ by Scheffé test.

TABLE 4.A6

Mean Participation for Each Community Activity Category:
All Respondents in Each Phase

	Phase 1			Phase 2		
	Notel	Unitel	Multitel	Notel	Unitel	Multitel
Sports	9.812[b,d]	6.181[d]	3.872[c,d]	5.462[b,d]	4.642[d]	3.058[c,d]
Open areas	4.446	3.947	3.857	4.000[b,d]	2.917[d]	2.578[c,d]
Businesses	26.866[b]	27.723[b]	18.345[c]	20.594[b]	19.031[b]	13.705[c]
Civic	2.589[b,d]	2.255[d]	1.616[c,d]	1.741[b,d]	1.497[d]	0.945[c,d]
Educational	1.643	0.777	1.463	2.700	2.114	1.651
Clubs	3.384	2.191	2.064	1.655	1.715	1.425
Medical	2.384	1.681	2.005	1.599[b]	0.896[c]	1.098[c]
Dances	3.562[b,d]	2.266[d]	1.704[c,d]	2.690	3.083	3.454
Special days	3.330[b]	1.372[c]	2.404[d]	1.741	1.368	1.956
Religious	0.875	1.043	0.542	0.746	0.461	0.389
Entertainment	2.116	2.596	1.941	0.807[b]	1.368[b]	2.149[c]
Other	2.696[b]	1.681[b]	4.576[c]	1.178[b,d]	0.824[d]	0.487[c,d]

[a] Within each phase, the multivariate analysis indicated all three towns were significantly differentiated overall. The superscript letters indicate which pairs of towns differed significantly within each phase of the study; towns which do not share the same letter are significantly different at $p < .05$ by Scheffé test.

TABLE 4.A7

Mean Participation in Each Community Activity Category for the
Longitudinal Sample

	Youths		Adults	
	Phase 1	Phase 2	Phase 1	Phase 2
Sports				
Notel	17.26	13.20	8.96	5.88
Unitel	11.25	14.14	5.70	5.33
Multitel	5.94	9.49	3.62	3.28
Open areas				
Notel	7.69	6.99	4.54	3.75
Unitel	5.09	4.32	3.37	2.91
Multitel	8.40	7.61	4.00	2.83
Businesses				
Notel	24.63	16.88	25.82	22.09
Unitel	21.78	16.64	27.22	19.24
Multitel	15.38	12.99	18.34	15.05
Civic				
Notel	1.59	1.34	2.54	2.09
Unitel	2.39	1.55	2.37	1.93
Multitel	1.15	1.46	1.70	1.19
Educational				
Notel	5.93	2.93	1.65	3.26
Unitel	3.65	3.91	0.76	2.24
Multitel	6.16	4.10	1.51	2.09
Clubs, meetings				
Notel	1.24	0.55	3.46	2.30
Unitel	1.20	1.19	2.28	2.70
Multitel	0.93	0.73	2.14	1.93
Medical				
Notel	2.10	1.24	2.30	1.61
Unitel	1.35	0.72	1.59	0.74
Multitel	1.49	0.75	2.06	1.27
Dances, suppers				
Notel	4.45	4.31	2.61	2.56
Unitel	2.26	3.39	2.15	3.76
Multitel	2.06	3.35	1.64	3.82
Special days				
Notel	1.50	0.90	3.60	2.25
Unitel	1.00	0.87	1.37	2.26
Multitel	1.39	1.29	2.38	2.35
Religious				
Notel	0.93	0.50	0.82	0.96
Unitel	1.00	0.55	1.39	0.80
Multitel	0.63	0.33	0.52	0.43

TABLE 4.A7 (Continued)

	Youths		Adults	
	Phase 1	Phase 2	Phase 1	Phase 2
Entertainment				
Notel	2.76	0.95	2.56	0.93
Unitel	2.85	1.81	2.52	1.28
Multitel	2.32	3.06	1.86	2.35
Other				
Notel	1.84	0.95	2.91	1.67
Unitel	1.33	0.51	1.65	1.35
Multitel	2.08	0.50	4.66	0.76

TABLE 4.A8

Mean Participation in Sports According to Town and Age Group:
All Respondents in Each Phase

	Age Group[a]						
	12 and under	13–15	16–19	20–35	36–55	56+	Means
Phase 1							
Notel	13.45^b	15.99^b	15.02^b	7.73	10.88^b	8.62^b	11.95
Unitel	9.67^c	11.81^c	10.64^c	8.98	6.42^c	2.44^c	8.33
Multitel	5.10^d	5.58^d	6.91^d	5.77	4.01^c	1.54^c	4.82
Age means	9.41	11.13	10.86	7.49	7.10	4.20	
Phase 2							
Notel	9.62	11.83^b	13.28^b	5.40	5.40	3.81	8.22
Unitel	7.24	11.97^b	12.92^b	5.39	5.04	1.57	7.36
Multitel	7.57	9.14^c	7.43^c	3.64	3.32	1.50	5.43
Age means	8.14	10.98	11.21	4.81	4.59	2.30	

[a] Within each age-group in each phase, towns which have differently lettered superscripts differ significantly at $p < .05$ or less by Tukey test. Similarities and differences among age groups within each town and phase follow.

Phase 1. Notel: 20–35 < 12 and under, 16–19, and 13–15; 56+ < 12 and under, 16–19, and 13–15; 36–55 < 16–19 and 13–15. Unitel: 56+ < 20–35, 12 and under, 16–19, and 13–15; 36–55 < 16–19 and 13–15. Multitel: 56+ < 13–15, 20–35, and 16–19.

Phase 2. Notel: 56+ < 12 and under, 13–15, and 16–19; 36–55 < 12 and under, 16–19, and 13–15; 20–35 < 12 and under, 13–15, and 16–19; 12 and under < 16–19. Unitel: 56+ < all others; 36–55 < 13–15 and 16–19; 20–35 < 13–15 and 16–19; 12 and under < 13–15 and 16–19. Multitel: three oldest groups all less than three youngest.

TABLE 4.A9

Correlations between Hours of Television Viewing and Participation in Community Activities

| | Unitel and Multitel combined | | | | | | Notel[a] | | |
| | Phase 1 TV hours | | | Phase 2 TV hours | | | Phase 2 TV hours | | |
	Youths	Adults	All residents	Youths	Adults	All residents	Youths	Adults	All residents
Phase 1									
Sports		-.17**	-.08	-.23***	-.20*	-.23***		.40**	
Open areas		-.18**	-.10**	-.18**		-.13*			
Businesses		-.15*	-.10*			-.11*			
Civic		-.13*							
Educational	.15**	-.13*							
Clubs									
Medical									
Dances				-.22***		-.16**			
Special days									.19*
Religious	-.10*	.13*	.09*			-.12*			
Entertainment			-.09*					.27*	.24**
Other		-.16*		-.20**		-.17***			
Total	-.12*	-.23**	-.14*						
Phase 2									
Sports	-.19***	-.21*		-.11*		-.10**		.18*	
Open areas		-.28***			-.11*	-.09**			
Businesses		-.19*		-.12*	-.11*	-.10**			
Civic		-.20*			-.12*	-.11**		-.25**	
Educational						-.07*			
Clubs									
Medical									
Dances				-.15**			-.16*		
Special days						.09**			
Religious	-.17**		-.14**					.29***	.11*
Entertainment								.39***	.18**
Other									
Total	-.12*		-.14**	-.12*		-.11*			

[a] Correlations with Phase 1 hours of TV viewing could not be computed for Notel because the town lacked television.

TABLE 4.A10
Total Performance Means for All Residents in Each Phase

	Age group						
	12 and under	13–15	16–19	20–35	36–55	56+	Means
Phase 1							
Notel	2.327	3.391	5.583	4.951	7.144	6.922	5.053
Females							4.872
Males							5.234
Unitel	3.254	1.790	2.272	6.328	7.078	1.887	3.768
Females							2.444
Males							5.093
Multitel	1.546	2.166	3.734	3.071	4.882	2.287	2.948
Females							2.754
Males							3.142
Phase 2: females							
Notel	3.036	2.450	5.536	3.057	3.939	5.000	3.836
Unitel	4.167	3.523	4.773	3.024	3.030	0.938	3.242
Multitel	3.636	4.169	4.857	2.625	2.500	1.148	3.156
Phase 2: males							
Notel	4.667	1.596	4.269	2.957	4.567	1.842	3.316
Unitel	2.120	2.500	3.917	3.469	4.370	3.524	3.317
Multitel	3.297	2.676	4.600	2.206	2.895	4.774	3.408

TABLE 4.A11

Differences and Similarities among the Towns in Phase 1 Participation in Private Leisure Activities

	Means[a]			$F(2,633)$	p	Tukey tests[b]
	Notel	Unitel	Multitel			
	Activities with the same pattern of significant town differences for both youths and adults					
Bicycling	2.014	1.930	2.097	3.40	.04	
Exercising	2.048	1.873	2.020	3.10	.05	
Reading newspapers	2.373	2.181	2.372	4.80	.009	
	Activities with significant town differences for youths					
Climbing	1.886	1.692	2.028	5.11	.01	M > U, .01
Hiking	2.439	2.135	2.562	12.07	.01	M > U, .01; N > U, .01
Jogging	1.783	1.577	1.728	3.00	.05	N > U, .05
Motorcycling	2.022	1.654	1.688	8.12	.01	N > U, .01; N > M, .01
Playing cards	2.006	2.308	2.348	6.59	.01	M > N, .01; U > N, .01
Reading books	2.226	2.519	2.238	4.72	.01	U > N, .05; U > M, .05
Sunbathing	1.551	1.423	1.740	5.82	.01	M > U, .01
Table tennis	1.630	1.538	1.952	10.08	.01	M > U, .01; M > N, .01
Traveling	1.779	1.481	1.648	4.25	.05	M > U, .01
Visit to watch TV	1.579	1.962	2.011	11.08	.01	M > N, .01; U > N, .01
Writing letters	1.896	2.173	2.056	3.72	.05	U > N, .05
	Activities with significant town differences for adults					
Bird-watching	1.638	1.545	1.248	12.22	.01	N > M, .01; N > U, .01
Climbing	1.658	1.483	1.400	5.11	.01	N > M, .05
Eat at friends'	2.066	1.824	1.719	6.37	.01	N > M, .01
Playing cards	2.060	1.824	2.171	6.73	.01	M > U, .01; M > N, .05
Reading books	2.593	2.515	2.173	9.36	.01	N > M, .01; U > M, .01
Sight-seeing	1.987	2.117	1.818	4.35	.05	U > M, .01
Writing letters	2.096	2.280	1.910	7.82	.01	U > M, .01

[a] Based on a scale of 1 (never) to 3 (regularly). Activities for which no town-related differences occurred were: car repairing, boating, camping, carpentry, checkers/chess, collecting, cooking, crosswords, fishing, gardening, home decorating, jigsaw puzzles, keeping pets, kite flying, knit/crochet, leather work, listen to radio, motorboating, needlework, paint/draw, playing records, play instrument, reading magazines, sewing, singing, social drinking, taking pictures, talk on phone, visit to chat, window-shop, write poem/story, woodworking.

[b] Decimal numbers denote the significance level of the comparison by the Tukey tests.

TABLE 4.A12

Differences and Similarities among the Towns in Phase 2 Participation in Private Leisure Activities

	Means[a]			$F(2,633)$	p	Tukey tests[b]
	Notel	Unitel	Multitel			
	Activities with the same pattern of significant town differences					
	for both youths and adults					
Bicycling	2.724	3.057	3.385	6.57	.002	M > N, .01
Boating	1.544	1.597	1.870	6.04	.003	M > N, .01; M > U .05
Jogging	1.652	1.996	1.816	3.50	.03	U > N, .05
Keeping pets	3.358	3.506	4.192	7.41	.001	M > N, .01; M > U, .01
Playing cards	3.298	3.215	3.761	5.53	.004	M > U, .01; M > N, .01
Playing records	4.432	3.091	4.061	3.47	.04	N > U, .05
Reading						
newspapers	4.348	3.914	5.530	33.69	.001	N > U, .01
Sewing	2.743	2.231	2.514	7.23	.001	M > N, .01; M > U, .05
Social drinking	2.528	3.000	3.017	5.73	.004	M > U, .01; M > N, .05
Sunbathing	1.597	1.564	1.943	5.59	.004	M > N, .01; M > U, .01
Talk on phone	4.745	4.920	5.924	19.11	.001	M > N, .01; M > U, .01
Traveling	2.603	3.009	3.185	8.10	.001	M > N, .01; U > N, .05
Visit to watch TV	1.827	2.016	2.184	3.33	.04	M > N, .05
Window-shop	1.789	1.885	2.288	7.28	.001	M > N, .01; M > U, .05
	Activities with significant town differences for youths					
Listen to radio	4.385	3.874	5.378	11.33	.001	M > U, .01; M > N, .01
Read magazines	2.807	3.019	3.869	7.90	.001	M > N, .01; M > U, .01
Table tennis	1.503	1.894	2.201	10.69	.001	M > N, .01; U > N, .05
Watching TV	5.549	5.785	6.693	9.04	.001	M > N, .01; M > U, .01
	Activities with significant town differences for adults					
Listen to radio	1.726	1.400	1.422	4.37	.03	N > U, .05; N > M, .05
Read magazines	5.114	4.996	4.288	4.39	.03	N > M, .05; U > M, .05
Table tennis	3.622	3.248	2.922	5.84	.004	N > M, .01

[a] Based on a scale of 1 (never) to 8 (daily). Activities for which no town-related differences occurred were: car pairing, bird-watching, camping, carpentry, checkers/chess, climbing, collecting, cooking, crosswords, exercising, —hing, gardening, hiking, jigsaw puzzles, kite flying, knit/crochet, leather work, motorboating, motorcycling, nee—work, paint/draw, play instrument, sight-seeing, singing, taking pictures, visit to chat, eat at friends', write poem/—ry, woodworking.

[b] Decimal numbers denote the significance level of the comparison by the Tukey tests.

TABLE 4.A13

Sex- and Age-Related Differences in Participation in Private Leisure Activities Which
Were Consistent across the Phases[a]

Activities for which more frequent participation occurred in both phases among

Youths	Adults	Females	Males
Bicycling	Carpentry	Bird-watching (adults)	Carpentry
Boating	Cooking	Cooking	Car repairing
Camping	Home decorating	Crosswords	Fishing
Climbing	Knit/crochet	Exercising	Motorcycling
Eat at friends'	Needlework	Gardening	Motorboating
Fishing	Listen to radio	Keeping pets	Social drinking
Hiking	Reading magazines	Knit/crochet	Woodworking
Jogging	Reading newspapers	Needlework	
Keeping pets		Paint/draw	
Kite flying		Listen to radio	
Leather work		Playing records	
Motorcycling		Reading books	
Paint/draw		Reading magazines	
Playing cards		Sewing	
Play instrument		Singing	
Playing records		Sunbathing	
Table tennis		Talking on phone	
Visit to watch TV		Visit to chat	
Woodworking		Window-shopping	
		Writing letters	
		Write poem/story	

[a] Activities for which there was no sex difference in either phase were: jogging, leather work, visiting
to watch TV, and table tennis. Activities for which there were no age-related differences in either phase
were: car repair, crossword puzzles, and talking on the telephone.

NOTES

All significant effects are indicated in these notes, but post hoc analyses
are reported only for effects involving town. Others are available from the
senior author.

[1] Of the 1081 Phase 1 community activities questionnaires completed, 1025 (95%) provided adequate information regarding the number of activities participated in, and 966 (89%)
provided adequate information regarding level of involvement. Only 25 (2.3%) were judged
to be completely unusable. Of the 1079 private leisure activities questionnaires completed in
Phase 1, 863 (80%) were of adequate quality. In Phase 2, 1432 community activities questionnaires were completed, of which 1376 (96%) provided adequate information regarding
number of activities, and 1259 (88%) did so for level of involvement. Only 9 questionnaires

(1%) were completely unusable. All 1261 (100%) of the Phase 2 private leisure activities questionnaires completed were judged to be of adequate quality for analysis.

[2] The proportion of the sample (summing across the three towns) in the adolescent and preadolescent years was 60.5% in Phase 1 and 53.2% in Phase 2, by comparison with 36.4% for census data. The proportions of our samples in the 20–35 year age range were 12.2% and 17.5% for Phase 1 and Phase 2 versus 19.8% for the census data. For 36–55-year-olds the analogous figures were 18.0%, 18.3%, and 23.9%, and for the 56 and older group, 9.3%, 10.9%, and 18.4%, respectively. For adults combined, the figures are 39.5% for Phase 1, 46.7% for Phase 2, and 42.1% for the census data.

[3] For the 11–12, 13–15, 16–19, 20–35, 36–55, and 56+ age-groups the Phase 1 sample proportions were 14.6%, 29.4%, 16.5%, 12.2%, 18.0%, and 9.3%, respectively; the Phase 2 proportions were 13.7%, 24.0%, 15.6%, 17.5%, 18.3%, and 10.9%, respectively.

[4] The longitudinal sample did not differ in either mean level of variation in Phase 1 participation from residents assessed only in Phase 1.

	Phase 1 mean	SD	F	t	df	p
Longitudinal youths	56.51	22.64	1.15	0.41	622	ns
Phase 1 youths only	57.28	24.24				
Longitudinal adults	50.58	22.36	1.10	1.25	408	ns
Phase 1 adults only	53.42	23.48				

Longitudinal analyses were not done for the private leisure activities because the response scales were not comparable across phases.

[5] In an unweighted means cross-sectional ANOVA on Phase 1 participation in total community activities (summing across the 12 categories) for Town × Sex × Age Level (11–12, 13–15, 16–19, 20–35, 36–55, and 56+), the town main effect, $F(2,987) = 54.72, p < .001$; age main effect, $F(5,987) = 9.08 \ p < .001$; Town × Age interaction, $F(10,987) = 3.07, p < .001$; and Sex × Age interaction, $F(5,987) = 2.49, p < .03$ were significant.

Averaging across age and sex, before television arrived in Notel, residents participated in more of their community's activities (mean 65.98) than was the case for Unitel residents (54.03), who in turn participated more than was the case in Multitel (46.66; $p < .01$ by Tukey test for all comparisons). Averaging across town and gender, both the 13–15-year-old and 16–19-year-old age-groups participated more than the 56+ age group ($p < .05$ by Tukey test for both comparisons), but no other age differences were significant.

Simple main effects analyses of the Town × Age interaction revealed town differences at all age levels. For the 12 and under group, $F(2,987) = 7.19, p < .01$, Notel (64.02) participated more ($p < .01$ by Tukey test) than both Unitel (50.20) and Multitel (48.08), which did not differ. Among 13–15 year olds, $F(2,987) = 11.95, p < .01$, the Notel mean (71.65) was higher than both the Unitel (58.84; $p < .05$ by Tukey test) and Multitel (49.41; $p < .01$ by Tukey test) means, and Unitel also was higher than Multitel ($p < .05$ by Newman–Keuls test). Among 16–19-year-olds, $F(2,987) = 9.21, p < .01$, the Notel mean (72.09) was higher than both the Unitel (59.05; $p < .05$ by Tukey test) and Multitel (52.91; $p < .01$ by Tukey test) means. Among 20–35-year-olds, $F(2,987) = 3.70, p < .05$, the Unitel mean (62.87) was higher than that for Multitel (50.47; $p < .05$ by Tukey test); Notel (56.10) was in between and not different from the other town means. Among 36–55-year-olds, $F(2,987) = 12.16, p < .01$, Notel participation (67.77) was greater than that in both Unitel (54.71; $p < .05$ by Tukey test) and Multitel (45.35; $p < .01$ by Tukey test), and the Unitel–Multitel difference was significant at $p < .05$ by Newman–Keuls test. Among those 56 and older, $F(2,987) = 25.83$, $p < .01$, Notel participation (64.23) was greater than that in both Unitel (38.47) and Multitel (33.73; $p < .01$ by Tukey test for both comparisons). Age differences occurred in all three towns. In Notel, $F(5,987) = 3.40$, $p < .01$, both the 13–15-year-olds and 16–19-year-olds participated in more community activities than did the 20–35-year-olds, who were least active. No other differences were significant. In Unitel, $F(5,987) = 7.37$, $p < .01$, the oldest age group (56+) participated less than all other age groups ($p < .05$ by Newman–Keuls test for comparison with the 12 and under group, and $p < .01$ by Tukey test by comparison with all others). In addition, the 20–35-year-olds participated more than the 11–12 age-group. All other comparisons were nonsignificant. In Multitel, the oldest age group (56+) participated less than all other groups ($p < .05$ by Newman–Keuls test in comparison with 36–55-year-olds; $p < .05$ by Tukey test for comparison with the 12 and under group; and $p < .01$ by Tukey test for 13–15, 20–35, and 16–19-year-olds). No other comparisons were significant.

[6] In an unweighted means cross-sectional ANOVA on Phase 2 total participation for Town × Sex × Age Level (11–12, 13–15, 16–19, 20–35, 36–55, and 56+), the town, $F(2,1333) = 19.72$, $p < .001$; sex, $F(1,1333) = 7.28$, $p < .001$; and age, $F(5,1333) = 14.74$, $p < .001$ main effects were significant and were qualified by significant Town × Age, $F(10,1333) = 2.02$, $p < .03$; and Sex × Age, $F(5,1333) = 5.025$, $p < .001$ interactions.

Averaging across sex and age, mean participation was highest for Notel (44.68), lowest for Multitel (35.76), and Unitel was in between (40.48; all $p < .01$ by Tukey test). Averaging across town and sex, the 56+ age-group participated less than all other age groups ($p < .01$ by Tukey test for all comparisons), and the 16–19-year-olds participated more than all age groups but the 13–15-year-olds ($p < .01$ by Tukey test in comparison with the oldest and youngest groups; $p < .01$ by Tukey test in comparison with the oldest and youngest groups; $p < .05$ by Tukey test in comparison with 36–55-year-olds; and $p < .05$ by Newman–Keuls test in comparison with 20–35-year-olds). The 13–15-year-olds participated more than the 36–55-year-olds ($p < .05$ by Newman–Keuls) in addition to the already mentioned 56+ and 11–12 age groups. Simple main effects analyses revealed that the towns differed at the 11–12, $F(2,1333) = 4.88$, $p < .01$; 16–19, $F(2,1333) = 20.03$, $p < .01$; 20–35, $F(2,1333) = 13.55$, $p < .01$; 36–55, $F(2,1333) = 12.42$, $p < .01$; and 56+, $F(2,1333) = 6.33$, $p < .01$ age levels. There were no town differences for 13–15-year-olds, and although the F test for the 11–12-year-old group was significant, no pair of towns differed at that age level by either Newman–Keuls or Tukey test. Among 16–19- and 20–35-year-olds, both Notel and Unitel residents, who did not differ, participated more than Multitel residents. Among 36–55-year-olds, Notel participated more than both Multitel ($p < .01$ by Tukey test) and Unitel residents ($p < .05$ by Newman–Keuls test), who did not differ. Among the 56+ age group, only the Notel–Multitel difference was significant (Notel higher; $p < .05$ by Tukey test). Age differences occurred in all three towns. In Notel, $F(5,1333) = 5.13$, $p < .01$, the 56+ age group participated less than the 20–35 ($p < .05$ by Newman–Keuls test), 13–15 ($p < .05$ by Tukey), 36–55 ($p < .05$ by Tukey), and 16–19 ($p < .01$ by Tukey) age-groups. The 16–19-year-olds also participated more than the 11–12 age group ($p < .05$ by Tukey). In Unitel, $F(5,1333) = 9.56$, $p < .01$, the 56+ group participated less than the 36–55 ($p < .05$ by Newman–Keuls), 20–35, 13–15, 16–19 (all $p < .01$ by Tukey) age-groups. The 11–12 group also participated less than the 20–35 ($p < .05$ by Tukey), and 13–15 and 16–19 ($p < .01$ by Tukey for both) age groups. Finally, the 16–19-year-olds also participated more than the 36–55-year-olds ($p < .05$ by Tukey). In Multitel, $F(5,1333) = 4.12$, $p < .01$, the 56+ age-group participated less than the 16–19, 11–12 ($p < .05$ by Tukey for both), and 13–15 ($p < .01$ by Tukey) age groups.

[7] For the longitudinal sample, total number of community activities participated in was

analyzed in a Town × Sex × Age Group (18 and under, youths; 19 and over, adults) × Phase unweighted means ANOVA, with repeated measures on phase.

The town, $F_{(2,516)} = 24.33, p < .001$; age, $F_{(1,516)} = 8.22, p < .004$; and phase, $F_{(1,516)} = 97.50, p < .001$ main effects were significant, as was their three-way interaction, $F_{(2,516)} = 4.39, p < .015$, and the interaction of Town and Phase, $F_{(2.516)} = 15.46, p < .001$. Simple main effects analyses on the three-way interaction asked first whether participation changed from Phase 1 to Phase 2 for each town and age combination. Among youths, a significant decrease (71.60 to 50.42) occurred in Notel, $F_{(1.516)} = 39.09, p < .001$, but the decreases in Unitel (55.16 to 49.48) and Multitel (47.71 to 45.33) were not significant. Among adults, a significant decrease occurred in all three towns: for Notel (61.82 to 49.08), $F_{(1,516)} = 14.14$, $p < .01$; for Unitel (52.90 to 44.91), $F_{(1,516)} = 5.55$, $p < .05$; and for Multitel (44.35 to 37.34), $F_{(1,516)} = 4.28$, $p < .05$. We next asked whether the towns differed for each combination of phase and age, and all four tests were significant. Among youths in Phase 1, $F_{(2.516)} = 58.15, p < .001$, those in Notel participated more than those in both Unitel and Multitel ($p < .01$ by Tukey test for both), who did not differ. Although the overall test was significant for the youths in Phase 2, $F_{(2,516)} = 3.65, p < .05$, no pair of town means differed significantly by Tukey or Newman–Keuls test. Among adults in Phase 1, $F_{(2,516)} = 13.30$, $p < .01$, those in Notel participated more than those in both Unitel ($p < .05$ by Tukey test) and Multitel ($p < .01$ by Tukey), and adults in Unitel also participated more than those in Multitel ($p < .05$ by Tukey). Among adults in Phase 2, $F_{(2,516)} = 6.17, p < .01$, only the difference between Notel and Multitel was significant ($p < .01$ by Tukey test).

The only other significant effects were the Sex × Town, $F_{(2,516)} = 3.79, p < .03$; and Sex × Age Group, $F_{(1,516)} = 7.47, p < .007$ interactions. Participation by females (61.77) was greater than that by males (54.68) in Notel, $F_{(1,516)} = 5.80, p < .05$, but there was no difference in Unitel (48.48 vs. 52.74) or Multitel (45.18 vs. 42.18). Among males, $F_{(2,516)} = 10.42, p < .01$, those in Notel and Unitel participated in more community activities ($p < .01$ by Tukey test in both cases) than those in Multitel. Among females, $F_{(2,516)} = 17.74, p < .01$, those in Notel participated in more activities than those in both Unitel and Multitel ($p < .01$ by Tukey test in both cases).

[8] Averaging across all three towns in Phase 2, the total number of community activities in which individuals participated (total entry score) was significantly correlated with both mean frequency of participation in total activities, $r(1372) = .89, p < .001$, and with weekly frequency of participation (total number of activities done weekly or more often), $r(1372) = .62, p < .001$. The mean frequency and weekly frequency scores also were significantly related, $r(1372) = .88, p < .001$. The correlations were similar when computed separately by town.

For each category, the correlation between Phase 2 number of activities participated in and Phase 2 mean frequency of participation is given first and the correlation between Phase 2 number of activities and Phase 2 weekly or more frequent participation is given second in the following list; all are for the total sample of 1374 children and adults in the three towns, and all are significant at $p < .01$ or better.

1. Sports: $r = .89$; $r = .70$
2. Open areas: .86, .65
3. Businesses: .85, .52
4. Civic: .82, .35
5. Educational: .83, .64
6. Clubs and meetings: .88, .43
7. Medical: .82, .26
8. Dances, parties and suppers: .85, .12

9. Special days: .89, .07
10. Religious: .90, .65
11. Entertainment: .73, .18
12. Other: .74, .18

These correlations follow a sensible pattern. The number of activities participated in is strongly related to mean frequency of participation for all 12 categories. Number of activities is strongly related to frequent participation (weekly or more often) for ongoing activities (sports, open areas, businesses, educational, religious), moderately related for categories which include a mixture of ongoing and one-time events (clubs and meetings) or which are used relatively rarely (civic, medical) and only minimally related for categories in which one-time events predominate (dances, parties and suppers, special days, entertainment, and other).

[9] An unweighted means cross-sectional ANOVA on total mean Phase 2 frequency scores was run for Town × Sex × Age Level (11–12, 13–15, 16–19, 20–35, 36–55, 56+). The town, $F(2,1332) = 17.35$, $p < .001$; and age, $F(5,1332) = 34.59$, $p < .001$ main effects were significant and were qualified by significant Town × Age, $F(10,1332) = 2.21$, $p < .02$; and Town × Sex, $F(2,1332) = 3.71$, $p < .03$ interactions.

Overall, Notel ($M = 0.430$) and Unitel ($M = 0.421$) residents, who did not differ, participated more often in community activities than Multitel residents ($M = 0.351$, $p < .01$ by Tukey test for both comparisons).

Simple main effects analyses of the Town × Age interaction revealed that the towns differed at all but the youngest (Notel, .407; Unitel, .373; Multitel, .414) and oldest (Notel, .314, Unitel, .265, Multitel, .234) age levels. Among 13–15-year-olds, $F(2,1332) = 3.24$, $p < .05$, Unitel (.527) and Notel (.526), which did not differ, both had marginally higher means than Multitel (.447, $p < .10$ by Tukey test in both cases). Among 16–19-year-olds, $F(2,1332) = 13.65$, $p < .01$, Unitel (.564) and Notel (.528) did not differ, and both ($p < .01$ by Tukey test) had higher means than Multitel (.393). Among 20–35-year-olds, $F(2.1332) = 6.04$, $p < .01$, Unitel (.425) and Notel (.401), which did not differ, both had higher means ($p < .01$ for Unitel and $p < .05$ for Notel by Tukey test) than Multitel (.312). Among 36–55-year-olds, $F(2,1332) = 4.01$, $p < .05$, Notel (.406) had a higher mean ($p < .05$ by Tukey test) than Multitel (.306); Unitel was in between (.374) and not different from Notel or Multitel. There were age differences in all three towns: for Notel, $F(5,1332) = 11.07$, $p < .01$; for Unitel, $F(5,1332) = 19.16$, $p < .01$; and for Multitel, $F(5,1332) = 9.91$, $p < .01$. In Notel, 13–15- and 16–19-year-olds, which did not differ, had higher means than all other age groups ($p < .05$ or less by Tukey test), and no other differences were significant. In Unitel, the 13–15- and 16–19-year-olds participated more frequently than the 56+, 11–12, and 36–55 year age groups, and 16–19-year-olds also participated more than 20–35 year-olds. In addition, the oldest age group participated less than all other age groups. In Multitel, the oldest age group participated less frequently than all others, the 36–55 year age group less than the three youngest groups, the 20–35-year-olds less than 11–12- and 13–15-year-olds, and the 16–19-year-olds less than 13–15-year-olds.

Simple main effects analyses of the Town × Sex interaction revealed a sex difference only in Unitel, where males (.436) participated in community activities more often than females (.407; $p < .05$ by Tukey test). The significant Town difference for males, $F(2,1332) = 15.62$, $p < .01$ reflected a higher mean frequency of participation for both Unitel (.436) and Notel (.410) than Multitel (.331; $p < .01$ by Tukey test for both comparisons). The significant town difference for females, $F(2,1332) = 9.11$, $p < .01$ reflected more frequent participation in Notel (.450) than in Multitel (.371) and marginally more frequent participation than in Unitel ($p < .10$ by Tukey test and $p < .05$ by Newman–Keuls test).

An unweighted means cross-sectional ANOVA on total Phase 2 weekly frequency scores was run for Town × Sex × Age Level (11–12, 13–15, 16–19, 20–35, 36–55, and 56+). The town, $F(2,1332) = 7.59$, $p < .001$; and age, $F(5,1332) = 52.31$, $p < .001$ main effects were significant and were qualified by significant Town × Age, $F(10,1332) = 1.99$, $p < .04$; and Town × Sex, $F(2,1332) = 3.92$, $p < .02$ interactions.

Overall, Unitel (mean 10.37) and Notel (9.96) residents, who did not differ, participated weekly or more often in more community activities than did Multitel residents (8.56; $p < .01$ by Tukey test for both comparisons).

Simple main effects analyses of the Town × Age interaction revealed that this held true specifically at only two age levels, however. There were no town differences for the 11–12 (Notel, 10.02; Unitel, 9.99; Multitel, 11.26); 20–35 (N, 7.97; U, 8.80; M, 7.15); 36–55 (N, 7.55; U, 8.14; M, 5.98); and 56+ (N, 6.12; U, 4.60; M, 4.35) age-groups. Among 13–15-year-olds, $F(2,1332) = 3.59$, $p < .03$, Unitel (15.23) youths participated frequently in more activities than Multitel youths (12.24; $p < .05$ by Tukey test), and the Notel mean was marginally higher (14.74) than that for Multitel ($p < .10$ by Tukey and $p < .05$ by Newman–Keuls test). Among 16–19-year-olds, $F(2,1332) = 9.16$, $p < .01$, both the Unitel (15.47; $p < .01$ by Tukey) and Notel (13.34; $p < .05$ by Tukey) youths participated frequently in more activities than did Multitel (10.39) youths.

Simple main effects analyses of the Town × Sex interaction revealed that significant town differences occurred among males, $F(2,1332) = 9.22$, $p < .01$, reflecting a higher mean for Unitel (11.11) than for both Multitel (8.16; $p < .01$ by Tukey test) and Notel (9.47; $p < .05$ by Tukey test). The town differences for females were not significant (Notel, 10.44; Unitel, 9.64; Multitel, 8.97). There was a sex difference only in Unitel, $F(1,1332) = 4.54$, $p < .05$, reflecting a higher mean for males than for females.

[10] A MANOVA on the vectors of 12 community activity categories for all Phase 1 respondents indicated that averaging across age, the three town vectors of category means differed significantly, $F(24,2040) = 58.56$, $p < .001$, and all three towns were significantly differentiated: For Notel by comparison with Unitel, $F(12,1020) = 24.97$, $p < .001$; Notel by comparison with Multitel, $F(12,1020) = 76.12$, $p < .001$; and Unitel by comparison with Multitel, $F(12,1020) = 78.82$, $p < .001$. When the analyses were conducted separately for youths (18 and under) and adults (19 and over), similar results were obtained: MANOVA for youths, $F(24,1200) = 40.37$, $p < .001$; Notel differed from both Unitel, $F(12,600) = 19.03$, $p < .001$ and Multitel, $F(12,600) = 54.06$, $p < .001$; and Unitel differed from Multitel, $F(12,600) = 50.94$, $p < .001$; MANOVA for adults, $F(24,790) = 27.12$, $p < .001$; Notel differed from both Unitel, $F(12,395) = 16.1$, $p < .001$ and Multitel, $F(12,395) = 29.9$, $p < .001$; and Unitel differed from Multitel, $F(12,395) = 35.69$, $p < .001$. Scheffé tests were then conducted for each activity category to determine which pairs of towns differed significantly for that category, for example, Sports. These tests controlled the error rate at $p < .05$ or less for each category. The results are shown in Tables 4.A4–4.A6.

A MANOVA on the vectors of 12 activity categories for all Phase 2 respondents indicated that, averaging across age, the three town vectors of category means differed significantly, $F(24,2722) = 45.35$, $p < .001$, and all three towns were significantly differentiated; for Notel by comparison with Unitel, $F(12,1361) = 24.57$, $p < .001$; Notel versus Multitel, $F(12,1361) = 72.01$, $p < .001$; and Unitel versus Multitel, $F(12,1361) = 41.39$, $p < .001$. When the analyses were conducted separately for youths and adults, similar results were obtained: MANOVA for youths, $F(24,1382) = 30.64$, $p < .001$; Notel differed from both Unitel, $F(12,691) = 19.98$, $p < .001$ and Multitel, $F(12,691) = 42.59$, $p < .001$; and Unitel differed from Multitel, $F(12,691) = 29.04$, $p < .001$; MANOVA for adults, $F(24,1302) = 22.38$, $p < .001$; Notel differed from both Unitel, $F(12,651) = 10.76$, $p < .001$ and Multitel, $F(12,651) = 39.85$, $p < .001$; and Unitel differed from Multitel, $F(12,651) = 19.94$, $p < .001$. Scheffé tests were then conducted to determine which towns differed significantly within each category, controlling the error rate at a maximum of $p = .05$. The results are shown in Tables 4.A4–4.A6.

[11] The question of whether significant changes occurred between Phase 1 and Phase 2 for each activity category was addressed using a series of unweighted means ANOVAs on the data from the longitudinal sample. For each category, town and age were between-subject variables and phase was a repeated measure (within-subject) variable. The results are reported for each category, focusing on change between the phases. (These analyses also yielded information concerning similarities and differences between the towns within each phase, but we have not reported those results here; such information is available for the larger cross-sectional sample in each phase in the multivariate results [see note 10] and town comparisons reported in Tables 4.A4–4.A6.) For each category, the Town × Age × Phase means are shown in Table 4.A7.

[12] The longitudinal analysis (see note 11) for Sports revealed significant town, $F(2,522) = 42.43$, $p < .001$; and age, $F(1,522) = 156.52$, $p < .001$ main effects, as well as significant Town × Age, $F(2,522) = 4.54$, $p < .02$; Town × Phase, $F(2,522) = 26.26$, $p < .001$; Age × Phase, $F(1,522) = 10.02$, $p < .002$; and Town × Age × Phase, $F(2,522) = 5.47$, $p < .004$ interactions.

Simple main effects analyses of the three-way interaction revealed that from Phase 1 to Phase 2, sports participation decreased for Notel youths, $F(1,522) = 25.74$, $p < .01$; increased for Unitel, $F(1,522) = 13.16$, $p < .01$ and Multitel, $F(1,522) = 19.76$, $p < .01$ youths; decreased for Notel adults, $F(1,522) = 14.93$, $p < .01$, and did not change for Unitel or Multitel adults.

[13] Within each phase, cross-sectional unweighted means analyses of variance for Town × Sex × Age Group (12 and under, 13–15, 16–19, 20–35, 36–55, and 56+) were conducted on the Sports participation scores.

In Phase 1, the main effects of both town, $F(2,1022) = 86.42$, $p < .001$; and Age-Group, $F(5,1022) = 23.53$, $p < .001$ were significant, as was their interaction, $F(10,1022) = 3.35$, $p < .001$. Simple main effects analyses revealed significant age differences for each town; for Notel, $F(5,1022) = 13.17$, $p < .001$; for Unitel, $F(5,1022) = 13.14$, $p < .001$; and for Multitel, $F(5,1022 = 3.92$, $p < .05$. The means and significant differences between the towns are shown in Table 4.A8. There were significant town differences for all but the 20–35 year age-group: 12 and under, $F(2,1022) = 19.83$, $p < .001$; 13–15, $F(2,1022) = 31.48$, $p < .001$; 16–19, $F(2,1022) = 18.69$, $p < .001$; 36–55, $F(2,1022) = 13.74$, $p < .001$; and 56+, $F(2,1022) = 16.83$, $p < .001$.

In Phase 2, the main effects of town, $F(2,1344) = 19.15$, $p < .001$; and age, $F(5,1344) = 63.60$, $p < .001$ were significant, along with their interaction, $F(10,1344) = 2.11$, $p < .025$. Simple main effects analyses revealed town differences only at the 13–15, $F(2,1344) = 3.96$, $p < .05$; and 16–19, $F(2,1344) = 16.88$, $p < .01$, age groups. The means and significant differences are shown in Table 4.A8. There were age-group differences in all towns: for Notel, $F(5,1344) = 23.82$, $p < .001$; for Unitel, $F(5,1344) = 29.76$, $p < .001$; and for Multitel, $F(5,1344) = 14.25$, $p < .001$.

[14] The longitudinal analysis (see note 11) for dances, parties, and suppers revealed significant town, $F(2,522) = 4.36$, $p < .02$; age, $F(1,522) = 6.03$, $p < .02$; and Phase, $F(1,522) = 59.07$, $p < .001$ main effects, as well as significant Town × Age, $F(2,522) = 7.88$, $p < .001$; and Town × Phase, $F(2,522) = 18.39$, $p < .001$ interactions.

Simple main effects analyses of the Town × Phase interaction revealed that attendance at dances, and the like, increased from Phase 1 to Phase 2 in both Unitel, $F(1,522) = 36.88$, $p < .001$ and Multitel, $F(1,522) = 58.95$, $p < .001$, but did not change in Notel. There were town differences in Phase 1, $F(2,522) = 15.74$, $p < .001$, reflecting a higher mean for Notel than for Unitel and Multitel ($p < .01$ by Tukey test in both cases), but no town differences in Phase 2.

Simple main effects analyses of the Town $\times$ Age interaction revealed a significant age difference in Notel, $F(1,522) = 21.63$, $p < .001$, reflecting a higher mean for youths than adults, but no age difference in the other towns. Among the youths, $F(1,522) = 11.80$, $p < .01$, Notel participation was greater than that for both Unitel and Multitel ($p < .01$ by Tukey test in both cases), which did not differ. There were no town differences for adults.

[15] The longitudinal analysis (see note 11) for Clubs and meetings revealed significant town, $F(2,522) = 3.41$, $p < .04$; age, $F(1,522) = 91.02$, $p < .001$; and phase, $F(1,5220 = 11.99$, $p < .001$ main effects, as well as a significant Town $\times$ Phase, $F(2,522) = 13.55$, $p < .001$ interaction.

Simple main effects analyses of the interaction revealed that the towns differed in both Phase 1, $F(2,522) = 7.32$, $p < .01$ and Phase 2, $F(2,522) = 4.47$, $p < .05$. In Phase 1, the mean for Notel was higher than that for both Unitel ($p < .05$ by Tukey test) and Multitel ($p < .01$ by Tukey), which did not differ. In Phase 2, the mean for Unitel was higher than the means for both Notel and Multitel ($p < .05$ by Tukey test for both), which did not differ. Between Phase 1 and Phase 2, participation in clubs by Notel residents decreased significantly, $F(1,522) = 35.71$, $p < .01$; there was no change in Unitel or Multitel.

[16] In Phase 2 (but not in Phase 1) we obtained information about frequency of attendance at clubs and other meetings. In an unweighted means cross-sectional ANOVA for Town $\times$ Sex $\times$ Age Level (11–12, 13–15, 16–19, 20–35, 36–55, and 56+) on number of clubs and meetings attended frequently (weekly or more often), the town, $F(2,1332) = 10.73$, $p < .001$; and age, $F(5,1332) = 12.50$, $p < .001$ main effects were significant and were modified by a significant Town $\times$ Age interaction, $F(10,1332) = 3.55$, $p < .001$. The only other significant result was the sex main effect, $F(1,1332) = 4.73$, $p < .03$, reflecting a higher mean for females (.087) than for males (.073).

Simple main effects analyses of the interaction revealed that differences among the towns occurred only for the three youngest age groups. Among 11–12-year-olds, $F(2,1332) = 4.84$, $p < .01$, Unitel youths (mean .590) frequently attended more clubs than both Multitel (.442; $p < .05$ by Tukey test) and Notel (.261; by Tukey $p < .01$) youths; Multitel youths also attended more than Notel youths (by Tukey $p < .01$). Among 13–15-year-olds, $F(2,1332) = 17.01$, $p < .001$, the Unitel mean (.859) was higher than both the Multitel (.322) and Notel (.320) means ($p < .01$ by Tukey test for both comparisons), which did not differ. Among 16–19-year-olds, $F(2,1332) = 3.98$, $p < .05$, the Unitel mean (.414) was higher than the Notel mean (.116; by Tukey $p < .01$) and marginally higher than the Multitel mean (.286; $p < .05$ by Newman–Keuls test); the Multitel mean also was higher than the Notel mean (by Tukey $p < .05$).

[17] The longitudinal analysis (see note 11) for Special days revealed significant town, $F(2,522) = 17.64$, $p < .001$; age, $F(1,522) = 155.52$, $p < .001$; and phase, $F(1,522) = 11.06$, $p < .001$ main effects, as well as significant Town $\times$ Age, $F(2,522) = 7.11$, $p < .001$; Town $\times$ Phase, $F(2,522) = 36.24$, $p < .001$; and Town $\times$ Age $\times$ Phase, $F(2,522) = 14.87$, $p < .001$ interactions.

Simple main effects analyses of the three-way interaction revealed that attendance at special days decreased from Phase 1 to Phase 2 for Notel youths, $F(1,522) = 13.73$, $p < .001$ and for Notel adults, $F(1,522) = 69.07$, $p < .001$, and increased over the same period for Unitel adults, $F(1,522) = 30.01$, $p < .001$.

[18] The longitudinal analysis (see note 9) for Entertainment revealed significant town, $F(2,522) = 7.50$, $p < .001$; age, $F(1,522) = 8.88$, $p < .003$; and phase, $F(1,522) = 56.80$, $p < .001$ main effects, as well as a significant Town $\times$ Phase, $F(2,522) = 50.66$, $p < .001$ interaction.

Simple main effects analyses of the interaction revealed that the number of entertainments attended decreased significantly from Phase 1 to Phase 2 for Notel, $F(1,522) = 98.68$,

$p < .001$ and Unitel, $F(1,522) = 45.99$, $p < .001$ residents, but increased over the same period for Multitel residents, $F(1,522) = 13.45$, $p < .001$.

[19] The longitudinal analysis (see note 11) for Medical settings revealed a significant decrease in the number of settings attended between Phase 1 and Phase 2, $F(1,522) = 159.40$, $p < .001$, which did not vary by town. Overall, attendance was greater for adults than for youths, $F(1,522) = 16.13$, $p < .001$.

An unweighted means cross-sectional ANOVA for Town × Sex × Age Level was run on the Phase 2 data regarding frequency of use of medical facilities. The town, $F(2,1332) = 38.86$, $p < .001$; sex, $F(1,1332) = 42.50$, $p < .001$; and age, $F(5,1332) = 7.99$, $p < .001$ main effects were significant, along with the Age × Sex, $F(5,1332) = 6.00$, $p < .001$ interaction.

Overall, Notel residents (0.745) attended medical facilities more frequently than Unitel (0.499) and Multitel (0.392) residents ($p < .01$ by Tukey test for both comparisons), and the Unitel–Multitel difference also was significant ($p < .01$ by Tukey test).

[20] The longitudinal analysis (see note 11) for Religious activities revealed significant town, $F(2,522) = 9.81$, $p < .001$; and phase, $F(1,522) = 26.59$, $p < .001$ main effects, as well as significant Town × Phase, $F(2,522) = 4.44$, $p < .02$; and Town × Age × Phase, $F(2,522) = 3.39$, $p < .04$ interactions.

Simple main effects analyses of the three-way interaction revealed that the number of religious activities attended decreased between Phase 1 and Phase 2 for youths in all three towns—$F(1,522) = 10.01$, $p < .01$ for Notel; $F(1,522) = 10.91$, $p < .01$ for Unitel; and $F(1,522) = 4.84$, $p < .01$ for Multitel—as well as for Unitel adults, $F(1,522) = 18.65$, $p < .001$. There was no change for Notel or Multitel adults.

[21] An unweighted means cross-sectional ANOVA for Town × Sex × Age Level (11–12, 13–15, 16–19, 20–35, 36–55, 56+) was run on the Phase 2 data regarding mean frequency of attendance at religious activities. The town main effect, $F(2,1332) = 9.17$, $p < .001$ was significant, reflecting more frequent attendance by Unitel (mean 0.209) and Notel (0.194) residents than by Multitel residents (0.114; $p < .01$ by Tukey test for both comparisons). The sex main effect, $F(1,1332) = 32.40$, $p < .001$ indicated females (0.228) attended religious community events more frequently than males (0.117). The age main effect, $F(5,1332) = 9.79$, $p < .001$ also was significant, but was qualified by the significant Town × Age interaction $F(10,1332) = 4.75$, $p < .001$. The towns differed for the 11–12 year age level, $F(2,1332) = 17.88$, $p < .01$, at which the Unitel mean (0.492) was significantly higher than the Notel (0.223) and Multitel (0.165) means ($p < .01$ by Tukey test for both comparisons). The towns also differed for the 13–15 year age level, $F(2,1332) = 5.58$, $p < .01$, at which the Unitel mean (0.291) was significantly higher than the Notel (0.151) and Multitel (0.100) means ($p < .01$ by Tukey test for both comparisons). At the 56 and over age level, $F(2,1332) = 5.91$, $p < .01$, Notel residents (0.326) attended more often than both Multitel (0.163; $p < .05$ by Tukey test) and Unitel (0.145; $p < .01$ by Tukey test) residents. Finally, simple main effects analyses of the Town × Sex interaction, $F(2,1332) = 3.50$, $p < .03$ revealed that females attended religious events more often than males in both Notel, $F(1,1332) = 17.10$, $p < .001$ and Unitel, $F(1,1332) = 21.70$, $p < .001$, but not in Multitel. The towns did not differ among males (Notel, 0.124; Unitel, 0.132; Multitel, 0.094), but among females, $F(2,1332) = 12.04$, $p < .01$, the Unitel (0.287) and Notel (0.264) means were higher than the Multitel mean (0.133).

An unweighted means cross-sectional ANOVA comparable to the analysis described above was run on the mean number of religious activities attended frequently (weekly or more often) in Phase 2. The town main effect, $F(2,1332) = 10.41$, $p < .001$ reflected more frequent attendance by Unitel (0.256) than Notel (0.171; $p < .05$ by Tukey test) and Multitel

(0.104; $p < .01$ by Tukey test) residents; the Notel mean was also higher than the Multitel mean ($p < .05$ by Newman–Keuls test). The age main effect was also significant, $F(5,1332) = 9.79$, $p < .001$, as was the Town × Age interaction, $F(10,1332) = 4.45$, $p < .001$. Town differences occurred at the 11–12 year age level, $F(2,1332) = 16.34$, $p < .01$, with the Unitel (0.610) mean higher than the Notel (0.214) and Multitel (0.192) means ($p < .01$ by Tukey test for both comparisons); the 13–15 year age level, $F(2,1332) = 10.40$, $p < .01$, with the Unitel mean (0.420) higher than the Notel (0.116) and Multitel (0.079) means ($p < .01$ by Tukey test for both comparisons); and the 56 and over age level, $F(2,1332) = 4.21$, $p < .05$, with the Notel mean (0.381) higher than the Multitel (0.188) and Unitel (0.167) means ($p < .05$ by Tukey test for both comparisons). The sex main effect, $F(1,1332) = 19.07$, $p < .001$ reflected frequent attendance at more religious activities by females (0.237) than males (0.117) overall, but simple main effects analyses of the significant Town × Sex interaction, $F(2,1332) = 3.39$, $p < .04$ revealed that this sex difference occurred only in Notel, $F(1,1332) = 6.63$, $p < .01$; and in Unitel, $F(1,1332) = 19.19$, $p < .01$, not in Multitel. The town differences were specific to females, $F(2,1332) = 12.64$, $p < .01$, with the mean for Unitel (0.359) higher than that for both Notel (0.232; $p < .05$ by Tukey test) and Multitel (0.119; $p < .01$ by Tukey test); the Notel–Multitel difference also was significant ($p < .05$ by Tukey test).

[22] The longitudinal analysis (see note 11) for Open areas revealed significant town, $F(2,522) = 17.74$, $p < .001$; age, $F(1,522) = 118.85$, $p < .001$; and phase, $F(1,522) = 19.78$, $p < .001$ main effects, as well as a significant Town × Age interaction, $F(2,522) = 9.40$, $p < .001$.

Participation in open area activities was greater on the average in Phase 1 (5.52) than in Phase 2 (4.74).

Simple main effects analyses of the interaction revealed a higher mean for youths than adults in all three towns: For Notel, $F(1,522) = 41.49$, $p < .001$; for Unitel, $F(1,522) = 9.99$, $p < .01$; and for Multitel, $F(1,522) = 86.10$, $p < .001$. Town differences occurred only for youths, $F(2,522) = 24.86$, $p < .001$, reflecting higher means for Multitel and Notel, which did not differ, than for Unitel ($p < .01$ by Tukey test in both cases).

[23] The longitudinal analysis (see note 11) for Businesses revealed significant town, $F(2,522) = 52.01$, $p < .001$; age, $F(1,522) = 29.78$, $p < .001$; and phase, $F(1,522) = 176.37$, $p < .001$ main effects, as well as significant Town × Phase, $F(2,522) = 8.81$, $p < .001$; and Town × Age × Phase, $F(2,522) = 7.19$, $p < .001$ interactions.

Simple main effects analyses revealed a significant decrease between Phase 1 and Phase 2 for all groups: for Notel youths, $F(1,522) = 69.28$, $p < .001$; for Unitel youths, $F(1,522) = 30.52$, $p < .001$; for Multitel youths, $F(1,522) = 6.58$, $p < .001$; for Notel adults, $F(1,522) = 16.10$, $p < .05$; for Unitel adults, $F(1,522) = 73.38$, $p < .001$; and for Multitel adults, $F(1,522) = 12.50$, $p < .01$.

[24] In Phase 2 (but not Phase 1), residents indicated the frequency with which they went to each of several other towns in the area. In an unweighted means cross-sectional ANOVA for Town × Sex × Age Level (11–12, 13–15, 16–19, 20–35, 36–55, and 56+), the town main effect, $F(2,1332) = 173.00$, $p < .001$; age main effect, $F(5,1332) = 21,89$, $p < .001$; and Sex × Age interaction, $F(5,1332) = 5.57$, $p < .001$ were significant.

Multitel residents ($M = 1.385$) more often went to other towns than did residents of both Notel (.612) and Unitel (.587), who did not differ ($p < .001$ by Tukey test for both comparisons).

[25] The longitudinal analysis for Civic activities revealed significant town, $F(2,522) = 15.10$, $p < .001$; age, $F(1,522) = 13.45$, $p < .001$; and phase, $F(1,522) = 22.70$, $p < .001$ main effects, as well as significant Town × Age, $F(2,522) = 4.66$, $p < .01$; Town × Phase, $F(2,522) = 4.23$, $p < .015$; and Town × Age × Phase, $F(2,522) = 5.39$, $p < .005$ interactions.

Simple main effects analyses of the Town $\times$ Phase interaction revealed decreases between Phase 1 and 2 for Notel, $F(1,522) = 7.16$, $p < .01$ and Unitel, $F(1,522) = 23.44$, $p < .001$, but no change for Multitel.

[26] The longitudinal analysis for Educational activities (those which were not part of the school curricula) revealed significant town, $F(2,522) = 6.60$, $p < .001$; and age, $F(1,522) = 143.30$, $p < .001$ main effects, as well as significant Town $\times$ Age, $F(2,522) = 3.71$, $p < .025$; Town $\times$ Phase, $F(2,522) = 10.76$, $p < .001$; Age $\times$ Phase, $F(1,522) = 76.62$, $p < .001$; and Town $\times$ Age $\times$ Phase, $F(2,522) = 9.33$, $p < .001$ interactions.

Simple main effects analyses of the three-way interaction revealed that between Phase 1 and Phase 2, participation in educational activities decreased for Notel youths, $F(1,522) = 57.70$, $p < .001$; did not change for Unitel youths; decreased for Multitel youths, $F(1,522) = 27.18$, $p < .001$; increased for Notel adults, $F(1,522) = 16.70$, $p < .01$ and Unitel adults, $F(1,522) = 14.01$, $p < .01$; and did not change for Multitel adults.

[27] In Phase 2 (but not Phase 1) we obtained information about frequency of attendance at educational (extracurricular) activities. In an unweighted means cross-sectional ANOVA for Town $\times$ Sex $\times$ Age Level (11–12, 13–15, 16–19, 20–35, 36–55, and 56+), the town, $F(2,1332) = 3.13$, $p < .05$; and age, $F(5,1332) = 59.33$, $p < .001$ main effects were significant, as was their interaction, $F(10,1332) = 2.05$, $p < .03$. Overall, the Notel (.906; $p < .10$ by Tukey test) and Unitel (.893; $p < .10$ by Tukey test and .05 by Newman–Keuls test) means, which did not differ, were marginally higher than the Multitel mean.

Simple main effects analyses of the interaction revealed that town differences were specific to the 13–15 year age-group, $F(2,1332) = 9.06$, $p < .01$, reflecting higher means for both (Tukey $p < .01$) Unitel (1.970) and Notel (1.94), which did not differ, than for Multitel (1.171).

[28] The longitudinal analysis (see note 11) of Other activities revealed that all effects were significant: town, $F(2,522) = 20.74$, $p < .001$; age, $F(1,522) = 83.22$, $p < .001$; Town $\times$ Age, $F(2,522) = 5.38$, $p < .005$; phase, $F(1,522) = 328.69$, $p < .001$; Town $\times$ Phase, $F(2,522) = 66.73$, $p < .001$; Age $\times$ Phase, $F(1,522) = 19.91$, $p < .001$; and Town $\times$ Age $\times$ Phase, $F(2,522) = 27.33$, $p < .001$. Simple main effects analyses of the three-way interaction revealed no indication of any meaningful pattern in the results.

[29] An unweighted means ANOVA on total Phase 1 performance scores for Town $\times$ Sex $\times$ Age-Group (12 and under, 13–15, 16–19, 20–35, 36–55, and 56+) revealed significant town, $F(2,888) = 12.58$, $p < .001$; sex, $F(1,888) = 10.76$, $p < .001$; and age, $F(5,888) = 12.66$, $p < .001$ main effects, which were qualified by significant Town $\times$ Sex, $F(2,888) = 4.81$, $p < .008$; Town $\times$ Age, $F(10,888) = 3.57$, $p < .001$; and Sex $\times$ Age, $F(5,888) = 5.12$, $p < .001$ interactions. The means are shown in Table 4.A10.

Overall, Notel residents ($M = 5.05$) had more performances in Phase 1 than both Unitel (3.77) and Multitel (2.95) residents ($p < .01$ by Tukey test for both comparisons), which did not differ.

Simple main effects analyses of the Town $\times$ Age interaction revealed town differences at all but the two youngest age levels. For 16–19-year-olds, $F(2,888) = 5.13$, $p < .01$, Notel had more performances than Unitel ($p < .01$ by Tukey test). For 20–35-year-olds, $F(2,888) = 4.96$, $p < .01$, Unitel had more performances than Multitel ($p < .01$ by Tukey test). For 36–55-year-olds, $F(2,888) = 3.09$, $p < .05$, both Notel and Unitel had more performances than Multitel ($p < .05$ by Tukey test in both bases). For adults 56 and over, $F(2,888) = 14.58$, $p < .001$, Notel had more performances than both Unitel and Multitel ($p < .01$ by Tukey test for both comparisons). There were age differences in all three towns. In Notel, $F(5,888) = 6.84$, $p < .01$, the yougest age group had fewer performances than the 16–19-year-olds ($p < .05$ by

Tukey), 56+ group ($p < .01$ by Tukey), and 36–55-year-olds ($p < .01$ by Tukey). The 13–15-year-olds also had fewer performances than the two oldest groups ($p < .01$ by Tukey test for both). In Unitel, $F(5,888) = 10.22$, $p < .01$, the 36–55-year-olds were again highest, with significantly more performances than all but the 20–35-year-olds ($p < .01$ by Tukey test for all other comparisons) who were next; the 20–35-year-olds had more performances than the 13–15 ($p < .01$), 56+ ($p < .01$), 16–19 ($p < .01$), and 12 and under ($p < .05$) age groups (all Tukey tests). In Multitel, $F(5,888) = 2.75$, $p < .05$, 36–55-year-olds had more performances ($p < .05$ by Tukey) than the youngest group, and no other differences were significant.

Simple main effects analyses of the Town × Sex interaction revealed that performances were equally high for women and men in Notel, equally low in Multitel, and differed only in Unitel, $F(1,888) = 19.59$, $p < .001$, reflecting a higher mean for men than women. Among males, $F(2,888) = 7.64$, $p < .01$, Notel and Unitel residents both had more performances ($p < .01$ by Tukey test for both) than Multitel residents. Among females, $F(2,888) = 9.73$, $p < .01$, Notel residents had more performances than both Unitel and Multitel residents ($p < .01$ by Tukey test for both).

[30] An unweighted means ANOVA on total Phase 2 performance scores for Town × Sex × Age Group (12 and under, 13–15, 16–19, 20–35, 36–55, and 56+) revealed a significant age, $F(5,1218) = 4.05$, $p < .001$ main effect, which was qualified by the significant Town × Sex × Age interaction, $F(10,1218) = 2.24$, $p < .02$. The means are shown in Table 4.A11.

Simple main effects analyses of the three-way interaction revealed that significant town differences occurred only for the oldest (56+) group of females, $F(2,1218) = 7.09$, $p < .01$, reflecting a higher mean for Notel than for both Unitel and Multitel ($p < .01$ by Tukey test for both comparisons). From another perspective, gender differences occurred only for the oldest age-group in all three towns, reflecting a higher mean for females than for males in Notel, $F(1,1218) = 4.86$, $p < .05$, but the opposite pattern (males higher) in Unitel, $F(1,1218) = 4.53$, $p < .05$; and Multitel, $F(1,1218) = 8.91$, $p < .01$.

[31] In an unweighted means ANOVA on total performances for the longitudinal group, with Town and Age (18 and under, youths; 19 and over, adults) as between-subject factors and repeated measures on phase, the age, $F(1,464) = 15.40$, $p < .001$; and phase, $F(1,464) = 10.96$, $p < .001$ main effects were significant and were qualified by Town × Phase, $F(2,464) = 3.39$, $p < .04$; and Age × Phase, $F(1,464) = 20.46$, $p < .001$ interactions.

Simple main effects analyses of the Town × Phase interaction revealed no change from Phase 1 to Phase 2 for Notel (4.50 to 4.41) but increases in both Unitel (3.58 to 5.06), $F(1,464) = 10.68$, $p < .01$ and Multitel (3.15 to 4.35), $F(1,464) = 17.03$, $p < .01$.

Simple main effects analyses of the Age × Phase interaction revealed a significant increase from Phase 1 to Phase 2 for youths (2.23 to 4.28), $F(1,464) = 130.58$, $p < .001$, and no change for adults (5.58 to 4.93).

[32] The level of involvement data concerning what the respondent did at each sports activity were scored as reflecting either *active* or *passive* involvement. Both scores took into account the number of sports activities available, but they were not comparable across the phases.

In an unweighted means cross-sectional ANOVA for Town × Sex × Age level (11–12, 13–15, 16–19, 20–35, 36–55, and 56+) on the Phase 1 active sports scores, the town, $F(2,926) = 61.86$, $p < .001$; and Age, $F(5,926) = 26.42$, $p < .001$ main effects were significant, as was their interaction, $F(10,926) = 4.23$, $p < .001$. Planned comparisons of the town main effect revealed that all three towns were significantly differentiated ($p < .01$ by Tukey test), with Notel highest ($M = .285$), Unitel next ($M = .240$), and Multitel lowest ($M = .119$). Simple main effects analyses of the interaction revealed the following:

| Age group | Means | | | $F(2,926)$ | p | Tukey comparisons[a] |
	Notel	Unitel	Multitel			
<12	.337	.311	.128	18.89	.001	N > M, .01; U > M, .01
13–15	.407	.346	.140	26.99	.001	N > M, .01; U > M, .01
16–19	.366	.330	.154	17.28	.001	N > M, .01; U >M, .01
20–35	.168	.230	.150	2.21	ns	
36–55	.239	.172	.106	6.43	.01	N > M, .01; N >U*, U>M*
56+	.192	.048	.035	10.50	.01	N > U, .01; N > M .01

[a] Decimal numbers denote significance level of comparisons, by Tukey test.
*$p < .10$ by Newman–Keuls test; ns, nonsignificant by Tukey test.

Age differences occurred in all three towns but the pattern varied. In Notel, $F(5,926) = 13.45$, $p < .001$, the means for the age groups were ordered as follows: 13–15 (.407), 16–19 (.366), 11–12 (.337), 36–55 (.239), 56 and over (.192), and 20–35 (.168), with the means for 13–15 and 16–19-year-olds greater than those for the three adult groups, and that for 11–12-year-olds greater than the 20–35 and the 56 and over group ($p < .05$ or better, by Tukey test). In Unitel, $F(5,926) = 18.07$, $p < .001$, the means were ordered as follows: 13–15 (.346), 16–19 (.330), 11–12 (.311), 20–35 (.230), 36–55 (.172), and 56 and over (.048), with the 56 and over mean lower than all others, the 36–55 mean lower than the means for all three youth groups, and the 13–15 mean higher than all others ($p < .05$ or better, by Tukey test). In Multitel, $F(5,926) = 2.71$, $p < .05$, the means were ordered as follows: 16–19 (.154), 20–35 (.150), 13–15 (.140), 11–12 (.128), 36–55 (.106), and 56 and over (.035), with the 20–35 and 16–19 means higher than that for the oldest group ($p < .05$ by Tukey test) and no other differences.

In an analogous ANOVA on Phase 2 active sports scores, the town, $F(2,1332) = 9.03$, $p < .001$ main effect was significant, reflecting higher mean scores for Notel (0.078) and Unitel (0.072), which did not differ, than for Multitel (0.056; $p < .01$ by Tukey test for both comparisons). The sex main effect, $F(1,1332) = 4.41$, $p < .04$ reflected higher scores for males (0.073) than for females (0.064), on average. The age main effect, $F(5,1332) = 58.4$, $p < .001$ also was significant, with the age-groups ordered from most to least active as follows: 16–19 (0.111), 13–15 (0.110), 11–12 (0.084), 20–35 (0.948), 36–55 (0.040), and 56 and over (0.018). All age-groups were significantly differentiated at $p < .01$ by Tukey test or better, with the exceptions that 13–15- and 16–19-year-olds did not differ, 20–35- and 36–55-year-olds did not differ, and 36–55-year-olds were more active than adults 56 and over ($p < .05$ by Tukey test). None of the interactions was statistically significant.

In a similar unweighted means cross-sectional ANOVA for Town × Sex × Age Level on the Phase 1 passive sports scores, only the age main effect, $F(5,926) = 8.92$, $p < .001$ was significant. The means were ordered as follows: 16–19 (.052), 13–15 (.043), 11–12 (.028), 56 and over (.022), 20–35 (.018), and 36–55 (.012). The 16–19-year-olds were passively involved in more sports than all but the 13–15-year-olds, who were in turn involved in more sports than the three adult groups ($p < .05$ or better, by Tukey test).

In an analogous ANOVA on Phase 2 passive sports scores, the town, $F(2,1332) = 40.63$, $p < .001$; and age, $F(5,1332) = 26.58$, $p < .001$ main effects were significant, and were qualified by significant Town × Age, $F(10,1332) = 1.99$, $p < .04$; Sex × Age, $F(5,1332) = 6.04$, $p < .001$; and Town × Sex × Age, $F(10,1332) = 1.94$, $p < .04$ interactions.

Simple main effects analyses of the three-way interaction revealed the following results:

| | Means | | | | | |
	Notel	Unitel	Multitel	$F(4,1332)$	p	Tukey comparisons[a]
Males						
11–12	.135	.097	.054	2.63	.05	N > M, .01
13–15	.122	.104	.063	1.53	ns	
16–19	.151	.157	.048	5.51	.01	U > M, .01; N > M, .01
20–35	.053	.056	.033	1	ns	
36–55	.058	.050	.043	1	ns	
56+	.123	.028	.025	4.62	.01	N > M, .01; N > U, .01
Females						
11–12	.140	.069	.061	2.87	.05	N > M, .01; N > U, .05
13–15	.218	.154	.106	5.03	.01	N > M, .01; N > U, .05
16–19	.175	.139	.076	3.81	.01	N > M, .01; U > M, .05
20–35	.091	.081	.034	1.30	ns	
36–55	.116	.067	.031	2.87	.05	N > M, .01
56+	.012	.004	.019	1	ns	

[a] Decimal numbers denote significance level of comparisons, by Tukey tests; ns, nonsignificant.

Correlations computed on the Phase 2 data between hours of TV viewed per week and the active and passive sports scores revealed that active participation in sports was significantly negatively (though weakly) related to amount of TV viewing for Unitel and Multitel residents, r (798) = −.15, p < .0001. The relationship was nonsignificant for Notel residents, r (345) = .02, though when they were added to the Unitel and Multitel sample the relationship for all three towns was still significant (and negative), r (1145) = −.11, p < .001. The relationship between active sports participation and amount of TV viewing was also stronger (though still weak) for adults, r (508) = −.14, p < .002, in the three towns combined than for youths, r (631) = −.07, p < .08. The relationship between Phase 2 passive sports participation and TV viewing varied more clearly by town and age group. It was nonsignificant for Unitel and Multitel youths and adults, even when all were combined, r (798) = −.05. For Notel youths the relationship also was nonsignificant, r (197) = .07, but for Notel adults, the correlation was significant and positive, r (146) = .22, p < .01.

[33] We attempted to reduce the set of 50 private leisure activities to a manageable number of categories using factor analyses, and intended to use the factor scores to examine patterns of similarities and differences among the towns. We abandoned this plan because there were such large age and gender differences that we were unable to find a homogeneous group on which to establish the factor structure. We would have obtained factors which were determined more by between-group differences (e.g., age or sex) than by differences in patterns of participation by individuals. Furthermore, even if we had been able to find a group that was homogeneous across the towns (e.g., adult males), the factor structure appropriate for them would be inappropriate for other groups (e.g., female youths).

[34] An unweighted means MANOVA on the vectors of 50 private leisure activity means for Phase 1 for Town × Sex × Age Level (youths, 18 and under; adults, 19 and over) yielded

significant town, $F(100,227) = 4.30$, $p < .001$; sex, $F(50,614) = 33.05$, $p < .001$; and age, $F(50,614) = 19.52$, $p < .001$ main effects, as well as significant Town $\times$ Age, $F(100,227) = 1.76$, $p < .001$; and Age $\times$ Sex, $F(50,614) = 3.54$, $p < .001$ interactions. The results are further described in the text and in Table 4.A13.

An unweighted means MANOVA on the vectors of 50 private leisure activity means for Phase 2 for Town $\times$ Sex $\times$ Age Level (youths, adults) yielded significant town, $F(100, 367) = 3.54$, $p < .001$; sex, $F(50,184) = 4.71$, $p < .001$; and age, $F(50,184) = 25.80$, $p < .001$ main effects, as well as significant Town $\times$ Age, $F(100,367) = 1.27$, $p < .05$; and Sex $\times$ Age, $F(50,184) = 4.71$, $p < .001$ interactions. The results are further described in the text and in Table 4.A14.

REFERENCES

Allen, C. L. Photographing the TV audience. *Journal of Advertising Research,* 1965, *5,* 2–8.
Anderson, D. R. Home television viewing by preschool children and their families. In A. C. Huston (Chair), *The ecology of children's television use.* Symposium presented at the meeting of the Society for Research in Child Development, Detroit, April 1983.
Barker, R. G. *Ecological psychology: Concepts and methods for studying the environment of human behavior.* Stanford, Calif. Stanford University Press, 1968.
Barker, R. G., & Gump, P. V. *Big school, small school.* Stanford, Calif.: Stanford University Press, 1964.
Barker, R. G., & Wright, H. R. *Midwest and its children.* Hamden, Conn.: Archon Books, 1971. (Originally published, 1955.)
Bechtel, R. B., Achelpol, C., & Akers, R. Correlates between observed behavior and questionnaire responses on television viewing. In E. A. Rubinstein, G. A. Comstock, & J. P. Murray (Eds.), *Television and social behavior. Vol. 4. Television in day-to-day life: Patterns of use.* Washington, D.C.: U.S. Government Printing Office, 1972.
Belson, W. A. Effects of television on the interests and initiative of adult viewers in Greater London. *British Journal of Psychology,* 1959, *50,* 145–158.
Bogart, L. *The age of television* (3rd ed.). New York: Frederick Ungar, 1972.
Brown, J. R., Cramond, J. K., & Wilde, R. J. Displacement effects of television and the child's functional orientation to media. In J. G. Blumler & E. Katz (Eds.), *The uses of mass communications: Current perspectives on gratifications research.* Beverley Hills, Calif.: Sage, 1974.
Comstock, G., Chaffee, S., Katzman, N., McCombs, M., & Roberts, D. *Television and human behavior.* New York: Columbia University Press, 1978.
Dorr, A. When I was a child I thought as a child. In S. B. Withey & R. P. Abeles (Eds.), *Television and social behavior: Beyond violence and children.* Hillsdale, N.J.: Erlbaum, 1980.
Himmelweit, H. T., Oppenheim, A. N., & Vince, P. *Television and the child.* London: Oxford University Press, 1958.
Iso-Ahola, S. E. *The social psychology of leisure and recreation.* Dubuque, Iowa: William C. Brown, 1980.
McKechnie, G. E. *Manual for the Leisure Activities Blank.* Unpublished manuscript, 1973.
Medrich, E. A., Roizen, J. A., Rubin, V., & Buckley, S. *The serious business of growing up: A study of children's lives outside school.* Berkeley: University of California Press, 1982.

Murray, J. P., & Kippax, S. Television diffusion and social behaviour in three communities: A field experiment. *Australian Journal of Psychology,* 1977, *29*(1), 31–43.

Murray, J. P., & Kippax, S. Children's social behavior in three towns with differing television experience. *Journal of Communication,* 1978, *30*(4), 19–29.

Robinson, J. P. Television's impact on everyday life: Some cross-national evidence. In E. A. Rubinstein, G. A. Comstock, & J. P. Murray (Eds.), *Television and social behavior: Vol. 4. Television in day-to-day life: Patterns of use.* Washington, D.C.: U.S. Government Printing Office, 1972.

Rosenthal, R. *Experimenter effects in behavioral research.* New York: Appleton-Century-Crofts, 1966.

Williams, T. M. How and what do children learn from television? *Human Communication Research,* 1981, *7*(2), 180–192.

TELEVISION-VIEWING PATTERNS AND USE OF OTHER MEDIA

Tannis MacBeth Williams
Michael C. Boyes

INTRODUCTION

Our research project in Notel, Unitel, and Multitel was designed primarily to investigate television's effects. Our principal findings and conclusions are based on a gross measure of exposure—the presence versus absence of television reception. Although we did not have to rely solely upon measures of the amount and/or content of television viewed, we did ask participants about their media use. The major purpose of this chapter is to describe that information. In addition to being helpful in interpreting some of the effects discussed in other chapters, these results also carry some implications regarding media uses and gratifications in general.

DESCRIPTION OF TELEVISION AVAILABLE IN THE THREE TOWNS

Variations in the amount and type of television programming available in Notel, Unitel, and Multitel are described in detail in Chapter 1, so only a brief overview is provided here. The major way in which the CBC programming available in Unitel in both phases and in Notel in Phase 2 differed from the extra programming available to Multitel residents in both phases (via ABC, CBS, and NBC) was that there was less of it.[1] Programming started later and ended earlier each day, with the result that television was available to Notel and Unitel residents in Phase 2 approximately 16.8 hours per day compared with 19.8 hours for Multitel residents.[2]

Two aspects of CBC policy that differed from ABC, CBS, and NBC policy have special relevance for children. CBC does not carry advertising on programming intended primarily for children less than 12 years of age, and CBC does not carry Saturday morning cartoons.[3] The only cartoons shown in Unitel (and Notel, Phase 2) were "Bugs Bunny," specials (e.g., "Charlie Brown"), and those on "Wide World of Disney." The cartoon difference provides one indication that CBC may portray less aggression than is characteristic of the U.S. networks (Williams, Zabrack, & Joy, 1977, 1982). Certainly, the Saturday morning programming available to children in Notel and Unitel, which began later and was in French[4] until 10:00 A.M. or later, differed from the cartoons shown for several hours on the U.S. networks available in Multitel.

Other similarities and differences in aggressive content between CBC and the U.S. networks (Williams et al., 1977, 1982) are discussed in Chapter 1, as is the evidence concerning sex-role portrayals. These are two of the areas in which effects studied in this project were hypothesized to be related primarily to the content of television. Unfortunately, there has been very little research comparing Canadian and U.S. television, and more is needed. The available evidence indicates that CBC does differ in some ways from ABC, CBS, and NBC, but all four networks emphasize entertainment and the similarities may be greater than the differences.

MEASUREMENT OF MEDIA USE: OVERVIEW AND RATIONALE

In both phases we obtained information about the television habits of both children and adults, and in Phase 2 we obtained information about other media as well. These data were used to address several questions. To what extent was Notel a town without television in Phase 1? Did Unitel residents, who were restricted to one channel, differ in their use of the media from Multitel residents, who could choose among four channels? Notel and Unitel had similar programming in Phase 2; was 2 years of television sufficient to establish viewing habits in Notel comparable to those in Unitel? How did media use by residents of our three communities compare generally with the media habits reported by other researchers for other North American residents?

Before describing our data and results, however, we would like to discuss some general issues concerning measurement of media use. In examining our data we confronted a number of issues concerning two major questions about media use information. First, how confident should we and other researchers be that our methods yield reliable data? That is, do the same people provide similar answers about their use of TV and other media when asked on different occasions, and/or when asked with different methods? Second, how confident should we be that our methods are valid? That is, do they provide answers that accurately reflect actual media use? These questions are central to all research on media effects.

We are least confident about the reliability and validity of information obtained from children in the early grades. At this stage of development, children's sense of time is still poor (Fraisse, 1963; Piaget, 1970). Many youngsters in our study answered "a little" or "a lot" when asked how many hours of television they usually watched, even when the questions were broken down into segments (e.g., on weekday mornings before school, at lunchtime, after school until supper, and after supper until bedtime). Asking about the number of programs watched was not particularly helpful, because programs, especially children's shows, vary considerably in length. We even found that reading a list of programs shown the previous day was not ideal, because many children in the early grades do not know the program names; they remember them by central characters. Perhaps the best method would be to have a photograph of a typical scene from each show and ask children whether they saw that show yesterday. How accurately they would remember what they'd seen "yesterday" as opposed to "usually" is not clear, but that problem may occur at all age levels. Preschoolers are even less reliable informants than school-age children, of course, and for that reason many researchers consult parents. Unfortunately, many (perhaps most) parents do not know what their children watch. Asking parents to keep a log or diary circumvents this problem but requires high motivation and assumes they are home whenever their children watch TV. Researchers studying preschoolers are familiar with all of these issues, but we suggest that concern about the accuracy of media information should extend upward to about 9 years of age. Although this discussion has centered on hours of television viewed, we also are skeptical about estimates of frequency or amount for other media behaviors. First or second graders probably are accurate informants about whether or not they use the public library, but perhaps not about how often or how many books they check out per week or month.

Some findings reported by Anderson (1983) raise other serious and more general questions about the accuracy of television-viewing reports. He videotaped families while they watched TV at home, using a time-sampling technique over a 10-day period. Preliminary analyses indicate that 5-year-olds were in the room while the set was turned on an average of 1.9 hours per day, but one month earlier their parents had estimated that these same children watched television an average of 3.3 hours per day, and the correlation between the two estimates was only .21. Anderson suggests that estimates of amount of television viewing obtained in previous research, based on parental or self-reports, are too high, in part because children (and adults) frequently leave the room and, therefore, watch television intermittently. His results have important implications for any displacement hypotheses regarding the effects of television, as we discussed in Chapter 1.

Perhaps some of the issues related to validity of media use measures can be clarified by considering how "amount of TV viewing" is conceptualized and measured. It seems important to distinguish among at least five possibilities. The first we have chosen to call "time spent with TV." This is probably how most people conceptualize their TV viewing, unless otherwise instructed. They base their estimates on program length, irrespective of whether they have time-shared TV viewing with other activities in the same or other rooms. "Time in the room with the set on" is a second way of thinking about amount of TV viewing. This is how Anderson instructed the parents in his study to record their child's TV viewing for the diary. He obtained a high correlation (.84) between parents' diary reports and his time-sampled videotape observations. The low correlation (.21) between his time-sampled observations and the parents' more global estimates is in our view not surprising. His instructions for the diary specified a "time in the room" conceptualization, but we suspect that parents' global estimates were based on a "time spent with TV" conceptualization. Data obtained by Huston and Wright (personal communication, November, 1983) are consistent with this interpretation. They asked parents of preschoolers to estimate the time their child usually spent watching television during different segments of the week (global estimates) and then asked them to keep a diary, giving the same instructions Anderson used (i.e., time in the room with the set on). The diary data correlated .35 with the global estimates for 3-year-olds and .55 for 5-year-olds. (Anderson's comparable correlation for 5-year-olds was .60.) The difference may indicate that 3-year-olds leave the room more often than do 5-year-olds, a likely prospect, given age differences in comprehension and attention reported in other research (see Bryant & Anderson, 1983). It is not surprising that measures of "time in the room with the set on" are only moderately related to more global estimates, which probably reflect a different conceptualization of TV viewing ("time spent with TV"). There undoubtedly are large individual and situational differences in frequency and duration of periods spent out of the room when "watching TV."

Unfortunately, although Anderson (1983) does have videotapes of the parents' home viewing behavior, he did not ask them to estimate or keep a diary of their own TV use. The issues we are raising about the validity of TV-use measures and the different ways of conceptualizing TV use apply to adults as well as to children.

The third and fourth ways amount of television viewing can be conceptualized and measured are "time looking at the screen" and "time cognitively involved with TV." These need to be distinguished because, as we have noted, people process information from television auditorally as well as visually. Conversely, they sometimes stare at the set without processing much, if any, information. We are thinking here of Salomon's (1981, 1983) notion of amount of invested mental effort (AIME), which posits that individuals vary in the amount of effort they expend in processing information from different media, which in turn affects how much they learn and retain.

Finally, television use sometimes is measured in terms of "time the set is on," for example, by researchers interested in the "constant TV" phenomenon (Medrich, 1979). Some people keep the set on most of the time, for background noise or company, and watch intermittently. At what point does leaving the room during "time spent with TV" become entering the room intermittently during "time the set is on"? The common practice of time-sharing other activities with television deserves more careful research attention. A variation of "time the set is on," that is, "time the set is tuned to a specific channel" is used in the United States as one determinant of the TV ratings.

Once researchers have chosen a method of conceptualizing and measuring TV use, how confident can they be that their data are reliable? We obtained several kinds of evidence on this question, some from children and some from adults.

In Phase 1, 239 of the students in grades 7–12 provided two different sets of estimates for the amount of television they usually watched. On one occasion they were interviewed individually, and on another they completed a questionnaire in the classroom. The interview questions were more finely segmented (e.g., typical viewing before school, after school, and after supper) than the questionnaire questions (e.g., typical weekday), but despite the different format and context the answers were highly reliable.[5] We feel confident, therefore, that the data from older students provide a reliable assessment of "time spent with TV," which is how we concepualized and measured television use. We did not obtain reliability data from the younger children, but for the reasons raised earlier, we are less confident of our data from children in the early grades. Accordingly, we have omitted or de-emphasized those results.

In Phase 2, we obtained media-use information from adults via both individual interviews conducted in the home and mailed questionnaires. These were two different samples, but a subset of 63 adults provided both kinds of data. The time between these occasions varied from a few days to a few weeks. Again, the two methods yielded evidence of test–retest reliability.[6] This finding is noteworthy because mailed surveys have been widely criticized as a method of data collection. The circumstances under which questionnaires are completed are quite variable, respondents may collaborate in answering, response rates typically are very low, and some questions may be poorly or incorrectly understood. When possible, it is preferable to obtain data through interviews. However, the personnel costs can be enormous and, as in this study, prohibitive. People also are more likely to give socially desirable responses when an interviewer is present, and this may be relevant to some questions regarding media use. Administering questionnaires in a supervised setting alleviates most of these difficulties, but the presence of the researchers still may increase the social desirability bias. Our findings indicate that some misgivings about mailed questionnaires may not be well founded.

In addition to assessing reliability for the subset of adults who provided data via both interviews and mailed questionnaires, we asked whether the two different kinds of samples yielded similar results, that is, results which would lead to comparable conclusions. The two groups in each town were compared on their reports of hours spent watching television at different times of the week and day; their reading habits (books, magazines, and newspapers); restriction of their children's TV viewing, and so on.[7] Only 5 of 72 comparisons yielded statistically significant differences. Since approximately this many differences would occur by chance, and there was no pattern to the differences, we concluded that the interviews and mailed questionnaires yielded similar results. This enabled us to combine the data from the two groups in each town for subsequent analyses. This finding also has a methodological implication. It strengthens conclusions drawn in this and other studies from mailed questionnaires regarding media use, since it is based on three different towns and thus was replicated twice. The return rate for our mailed questionnaire was substantially lower (about 40%) than the rate of agreement to participate for individuals approached in person (more than 80%), as is usually the case. Despite this difference the samples did not differ in media use, a noteworthy finding, given the considerably greater expense of interviews.

It is clear that although much of the research on the effects of television has involved correlating amount of television watched with other behaviors, research on how best to measure television use is as badly needed as research on its ramifications (see Roberts, Bachen, Hornby, & Hernandez-Ramos, 1984, for further discussion). In this study we took care to avoid the more obvious pitfalls, for example, by asking for specific rather than global estimates and questioning extreme answers given in interviews. Moreover, the estimates we obtained for older students and adults were reliable. Our data are, however, based on self-report rather than behavioral measures and therefore subject to the limitations of all studies of this genre. Measurement difficulties and the phenomenon of time-sharing also may explain in part why correlations between amount of television viewed and other behaviors, even when statistically significantly different from zero, are rarely large. These problems underscore the advantage of our natural experiment for assessing the effects of television.

With these caveats concerning measurement in mind, what did we learn about media use by the residents of Notel, Unitel, and Multitel?

PHASE 1: DESCRIPTION OF TV-USE DATA COLLECTED

Children

Information about TV use in Phase 1 was obtained from 340 children in Notel, 325 in Unitel, and 493 in Multitel. In Notel and Unitel each student was interviewed individually. In Multitel, students in grades 1–8 were interviewed individually and those in grades 9–12 described their TV-viewing habits on the leisure activities questionnaire which they completed in class (see Chapter 4). Preliminary analyses indicated these methods yielded comparable information, so the data were combined (see note 5).

Adults

In Phase 1, information about the TV-viewing habits of adults in all three communities was obtained via the mailed survey of participation in leisure activities (see Chapter 4). This questionnaire was sent to a random sample of residents on the municipal voters' list in each town. Unfortunately, the section dealing with television was omitted from all of the questionnaires distributed in Notel and from many of those distributed in Unitel, so the Phase 1 adult sample for Unitel is small. Since the children's sample in all three towns included all children attending school, this did not endanger the major question of interest in Phase 1, which was the availability of television to Notel residents by comparison with residents of Unitel and Multitel. The analyses of adults' Phase 1 TV-viewing habits are based on the responses of 43 Unitel and 196 Multitel residents.

PHASE 1: AMOUNT OF TV VIEWING

Children

Students in all three towns were asked whether they had a working television set at home and how many hours they usually watched television during different weekday and weekend periods. Their responses were combined to yield totals for the average weekday, weekend day, and week. Because of our reservations about the quality of the Phase 1 data for first through third graders, we have focused on students in grade 4 and beyond. In addition, because the Unitel school did not go beyond grade 10 in Phase 1, some of our analyses do not include grades 11 or 12. The children's mean and median Phase 1 hours of TV viewing are shown in Figure 5.1 and in Table 5.A1.

Although the geographic location of Notel denied television reception to most homes prior to the installation of the repeating transmitter, a few homes in the area did receive one channel (CBC) on a more or less regular basis. The quality of reception varied from day to day, and was never good. Nonetheless, anecdotal reports indicated that families with TV sets

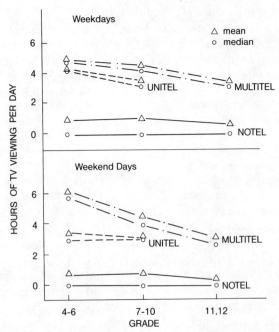

FIGURE 5.1 Mean and median Phase 1 reported hours of TV viewing per weekday and weekend day for children, by town and grade in school.

who were able to pick up even a weak signal tended to watch regularly. This made it less likely that we would find differences between Notel and the other towns. That is, it provided a conservative test.

In Phase 1, 76% of the Notel students in grades 1–12 reported watching 0 hours of TV per week, by comparison with 8% of Unitel children and 3% of Multitel children. The median levels of viewing (the point above and below which 50% of the children were distributed) were similar to the means for Unitel and Multitel. For Notel, the means were higher than the medians because of the small number of children with typical North American viewing habits. These data establish clearly that for most residents in Phase 1, Notel was a town without television. In contrast, the proportions of Unitel and Multitel children who reported watching 0 hours of TV per week were very close to the figure of 5% reported by Hirsch (1980), based on 1975, 1976, and 1977 data from a large representative sample of U.S. residents.

How similar were the Phase 1 hours of TV viewing reported by Unitel and Multitel children? There were no differences related to gender, but amount of TV viewing did vary according to town and grade level (Figure 5.1 and Table 5.A1).

We omitted the data from students in grades 1 to 3 because of concerns discussed earlier about their validity. Based on previous reports of age trends in viewing patterns (e.g., Comstock et al., 1978), we combined the reports of students in grades 4–6 and did the same for students in grades 7–10.[8] As other researchers have found, the younger groups in both towns reported watching more total hours of television per week than the older group. On average, Multitel students reported watching more television (mean, 33.6 hours per week) than Unitel students (25.4 hours). When each grade level (4–10) was included separately in the analysis, the same pattern of findings obtained.[9] Overall, Multitel students watched more than Unitel students and the weekly totals varied according to grade level. No specific pair of grades differed significantly, however.

We next looked separately at weekday and weekend hours of viewing.[10] The only significant difference for weekdays was that Multitel students reported watching more than Unitel students. There was no evidence that viewing varied by grade level on weekdays, but on weekends, Multitel students in grades 4–6 watched more than those in grades 7–10. Multitel students watched more weekend TV than Unitel students at both grade levels.

Do Multitel children watch more TV because the variety of programming is greater or because more hours of programming are available? (TV signals from the United States are broadcast more hours per day than CBC; see Chapter 1 for details.) The weekday difference in TV viewing by Multitel and Unitel students (.92 hours per day, multiplied by 5 equals 4.6 hours) accounts for 55% of the weekly difference (8.28 hours). In Phase 1 we did not ask Multitel students specifically about their viewing before school, when Unitel children were unable to watch, but in Phase 2, Multitel children reported watching an average of 0.2 hours of television on an average weekday morning, that is, 1 hour per week. In addition, some of the differences between Multitel and Unitel weekend viewing probably arose because English-language programming in Unitel did not begin on Saturday mornings until about 10:00 A.M. Whereas Multitel fourth through sixth graders watched more weekend television than Multitel seventh through tenth graders, there was no grade difference in Unitel. This finding is consistent with our speculation, since the early Saturday programming shown on the U.S. networks would be more likely to appeal to the younger students.

If we take into account the difference in hours of programming available during early mornings, when many children watch television, the remaining difference between Unitel and Multitel children is not large. Indeed, given that Unitel students had access only to CBC programming, whereas Multitel students had the three U.S. networks in addition to CBC, the difference reasonably attributable to variety rather than availability of programming is surprisingly small. When all channels emphasize entertainment, the amount of time children spend with television apparently differs relatively little according to the number of channels available. This finding for Phase 1 was corroborated by the Phase 2 data for children and the information obtained from adults in both phases. Together, these results demonstrate the attractiveness of television as a leisure pursuit. Even when no choice is available, viewers spend almost as much time with TV as they do when they can choose among four channels. This underscores the importance of considering television's displacement effects in addition to its content effects.

Adults

The Phase 1 information regarding TV viewing by adults was used principally to assess the similarity between Unitel and Multitel residents (Figure 5.2 and Table 5.A2).

On average, Multitel adults reported watching more television per week (mean, 29.7 hours) than did Unitel residents (21.4 hours), and women reported watching more (30.3 hours) than men (20.9 hours).[11] This sex difference occurred in both towns. Total weekly viewing did not vary according to whether the individual was over or under 50 years of age, but

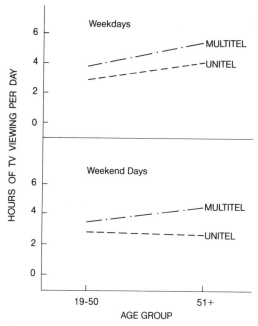

FIGURE 5.2   Mean Phase 1 reported hours of TV viewing per weekday and weekend day for Unitel and Multitel adults, by town and age group.

for weekdays, older adults reported watching more television than younger adults, women reported watching more than men, and Multitel residents reported watching more than Unitel residents.[12] For weekends, Multitel residents said they watched more than Unitel residents, and women more than men, but there were no age-related differences.[13]

This pattern of results related to age and sex probably reflects differences in the flexibility with which individuals can plan their leisure and work activities. In 1973, in the province in which these three towns were located, 78% of adult men by comparison with 39% of adult women were in the labor force (Statistics Canada, 1974). More women than men thus would be able to time-share their work with television viewing, since it would be done primarily at home. Similarly, more adults under age 50 than those over 50 were in the labor force, and this may explain the age difference in weekday hours of television viewing. The younger adults apparently watched more television on weekends, (although not significantly more than older adults) and this extra amount resulted in our failure to find an age difference for the weekly total.

One important question with ramifications for both content and displacement effects is the relationship between the availability of television and its use. Does amount of TV viewing increase linearly with the number of channels available? Our data indicate that it does not. Multitel residents, who could choose among four channels, did report watching more television than Unitel residents (an average of 9 hours per week), but they did not watch four times or even twice as much. TV viewing apparently leaps exponentially when just a single channel is available, and perhaps due to a ceiling affect, does not increase much thereafter. Unitel and Multitel were similar enough that the same patterns of television use according to age and gender occurred for the three comparison periods (weekday, weekend, total).

PHASE 2: DESCRIPTION OF TV-USE DATA COLLECTED

The TV-use information obtained in Phase 2 was more detailed than the Phase 1 data. The use of other media (radio, magazines), book-reading habits, and parental control of children's television viewing also were assessed.

Children

In Phase 2, children in grades 1–12 in all three towns were interviewed individually. The analyses are based on data from 373 Notel students, 369 Unitel students, and 464 Multitel students.

Adults

Information about adults' Phase 2 media habits was obtained for two different samples in each town. The first group comprised the representative sample of households studied by Suedfeld, Little, Rank, Rank, and Ballard (see Chapter 8, this volume) and were interviewed individually in their homes. This interview sample consisted of 63 Notel residents, 55 Unitel residents, and 56 Multitel residents. The second group, the mailed questionnaire sample, comprised adults who responded to the survey of participation in community and private leisure activities (see Chapter 4). The media-use questionnaire was presented at the end of that survey, and both were distributed by mail to a random sample of adults in each town. The mailed media-use questionnaire sample consisted of 150 adults in Notel, 170 in Unitel, and 247 in Multitel. Since preliminary analyses (see note 6) indicated the interview and questionnaire samples yielded comparable results, the data were combined.

PHASE 2: TV-USE RESULTS

The design of this project assumed that by Phase 2 most Notel residents would be regular television viewers, and that turned out to be true. Averaging across the three towns, almost all school children (93.3%) reported having a working television set in their home, and the same was true of the adults (92%). In Notel, 93.8% of the students reported having a working TV set, and only 11% reported watching 0 hours of TV per week (by comparison with 76% in Phase 1). The analogous figures for Unitel were 86.3% and 13.8%, and for Multitel, 98.3% and 2.8%.[14] These town differences are of a different order of magnitude than the Phase 1 results. By Phase 2, Notel had changed dramatically—become a town with television—and was similar in that regard to Unitel and Multitel.

Children's Amount of Viewing

We approached the issue of television in a variety of ways during the Phase 2 children's media-use interviews. First, an overall estimate of the number of hours per week the child usually spent watching television was obtained. This question was not asked directly, however, since a global estimate would be less reliable than one based on shorter periods. Instead, we asked, "How many hours of television do you usually watch on weekdays before school?" Similarly, we asked about the number of hours characteristically watched on weekdays after school, weekdays after supper, and on Saturdays and Sundays. Further questioning of improbable responses ensured that these estimates were as accurate as possible. For example, students who reported watching long hours in the evening were quizzed about what they watched. If they said "the late movies," we asked which ones they had seen that week and what the movies were about. (The interviewers watched in their motel so they would know if the answer was correct.) The total number of hours of television usually watched per week was calculated by summing the responses to the separate questions. There were no differences related to gender, so the results reported next focus on similarities and differences among the grades.[15]

The number of hours children spent watching television per week varied according to both town and grade, but the same pattern of differences among the grades occurred for both sexes in each town (see Figure 5.3 and Table 5.A3). Averaging across grades, children in Multitel reported watching more television (26.9 hours per week) than children in Unitel (21.0 hours per week) and Notel (20.9 hours per week), who did not differ (see note 15). This is not surprising, since television was available more

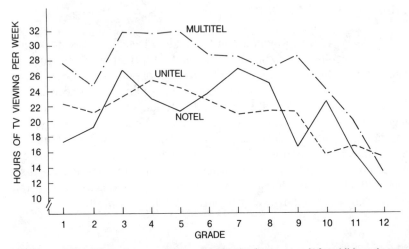

FIGURE 5.3   Mean Phase 2 reported hours of TV viewing per week for children, by town and grade in school.

hours in Multitel than in Notel or Unitel, as we discussed earlier. In particular, Notel and Unitel children could not watch television before school on weekdays (when Multitel children reported watching an average of 0.2 hours per day or 1.0 hours total Monday to Friday) or before 9:00 A.M. on weekends. We asked whether children usually watched TV on Saturday morning, but not how many hours. Multitel students reported watching more television overall on Saturdays and Sundays (mean difference of 1.8 hours on Saturday and 0.1 hours on Sunday when compared with Notel, and 1.5 hours on Saturday and 0.4 hours on Sunday when compared with Unitel). Saturday morning television on the U.S. networks is aimed specifically at children, whereas Sunday morning programming is not, which probably explains the greater difference between Multitel and the other towns on Saturdays than on Sundays. If these average differences for Saturday and Sunday viewing are added to the amount of before-school viewing reported by Multitel children, the total is 2.9 hours per week, yielding a modified Multitel weekly total of 24.0 hours. Thus, children with access to four television channels only watched an average of 3 hours more per week at times when programming was available in all three towns than did children with access to only one channel. Himmelweit, Oppenheim, and Vince (1958) obtained a similar finding in the United Kingdom, as did Murray and Kippax (1977) in Australia. Specifically, Multitel children watched, on the average, 15 more minutes of afternoon television and 20 more minutes of evening television per weekday, than did Notel and Unitel children.[16]

The same age trends in TV viewing over grades 1–12 occurred in all three towns, and for both sexes. Hours of TV viewing increased in the early grades and decreased in high school, forming an inverted U-shaped pattern (see Figure 5.3). This provides another indication that after 2 years of viewing, Notel children's TV habits were similar to those of children in the other towns. Similar age trends have been reported for several other North American samples (Comstock et al., 1978).

Children's Saturday Morning Viewing

We asked whether students usually watched television on Saturday morning, since that period on the U.S. networks is unique in being aimed almost exclusively at children. By contrast, CBC programming in Unitel and Notel began later and was in French until 10:00 A.M. This was usually followed by one non-animated English-language children's program, and then sports (e.g., a football game).

Averaging across all grades, significantly more Multitel (59%) than Unitel (49%) children reported usually watching Saturday morning TV, and both proportions were significantly greater than that for Notel (34%).[17] The greater availability of children's programming in Multitel probably accounts for the difference between Unitel and Multitel. Although programming was the same in Notel and Unitel, more Unitel children watched Saturday morning TV. Indeed, almost half the Unitel children siad they watched TV on Saturday mornings even though there was little programming intended for them.

We next asked how Saturday morning viewing varied with age.[18] Fewer Notel children than Multitel children watched Saturday morning TV at every age level except 11–12 years; at that point there were no town differences. At ages 5–7 and 8–10, only the Multitel–Notel difference was significant; at age 13–15 all three towns were differentiated significantly; and at age 16–18 the difference between Notel and both Unitel and Multitel was significant.

These results suggest that, notwithstanding a general effect due to greater availability of children's programming, experience with television makes a difference. Children who grew up with television continued to watch Saturday morning programming into their teenage years. In contrast, children who were 11 or older when TV arrived in Notel did not watch much Saturday morning TV, even though they watched as much as their Unitel peers at other times of the week. If children develop the habit of watching Saturday morning programming, which is aimed at a fairly young age level, a reasonable proportion apparently continue to do so even when they are beyond the age level at which the programming is aimed. Apparently, they are a captive audience and will watch whatever is provided on Saturday morning. This finding is consistent with our results for both children and adults that greater variety in programming (i.e., in Multitel by comparison with the other towns) has little influence on amount of viewing.

Adults' Amount of Viewing

Adults in the three towns were asked in Phase 2 for separate estimates of usual hours of viewing for weekday mornings, weekday afternoons, weekday evenings, Saturdays, and Sundays. Variations in media use across the adult years were examined by dividing the sample into young adult (19–35 years), middle-age (36–55 years), and mature adult (56 years and over) categories. This more detailed age breakdown was possible because the Phase 2 adult sample was larger than the Phase 1 sample. The results are shown in Figure 5.4 and in Table 5.A3.

For adult weekly viewing totals, there were town, sex, and age differences in Phase 2, but the differences due to sex and age were the same in

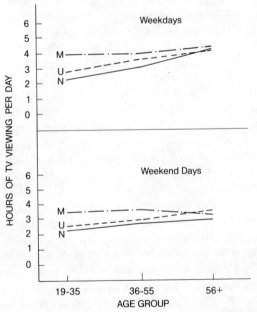

FIGURE 5.4 Mean Phase 2 reported hours of TV viewing per weekday and weekend day for adults, by town and age group (M, Multitel; U, Unitel; N, Notel).

all three towns.[19] Multitel adults reported watching more television than did adults in both Unitel and Notel, who did not differ. Again, these totals include reports of early morning viewing (before 9:00 A.M.) when programming was not available in Notel and Unitel. A revised weekly viewing estimate was calculated for each town by removing the reported usual weekday morning hours from the total (0.092 hours per weekday morning in Notel, 0.177 in Unitel, and 0.290 in Multitel). Unfortunately, it was not possible to similarly adjust the Saturday and Sunday totals, since those reports were based on the entire day. However, since Saturday morning programming on U.S. networks is aimed primarily at children, it seems reasonable to assume that relatively few Multitel adults watched television early Saturday morning before programming began in Unitel and Notel. Analyses based on the adjusted total yielded smaller differences, but Multitel adults still reported watching more television than both Unitel and Notel adults. In this case, however, only the difference between Notel and Multitel was significant.[20] The results again indicate that adults who can choose among four channels watch only slightly more TV than adults who have only one channel; Unitel and Multitel did not differ in the revised analysis. This consistent finding in our study could be interpreted as support for the contention of Gerbner and his colleagues (Gerbner, Gross, Signorielli, Morgan, & Jackson-Beeck, 1979) that North American audiences more often turn on the set to "watch TV" than to watch a specific program. This does not preclude the possibility that viewers are selective once the set is on (when more than one channel is available), but it does indicate that factors other than the possibility of choice are the major determinant of amount of time spent with TV.

Given that more hours of morning programming were available in Multitel than in Notel and Unitel, it is not surprising that Multitel adults reported watching more weekday morning television than Notel adults and marginally more than Unitel adults. The results for weekday afternoon viewing in Phase 2 are not confounded by differential availability, and there were no town differences.[21] The age- and sex-related results for weekday mornings and afternoons probably reflect different levels of flexibility in scheduling work and leisure time (see note 21). People who are retired or do the bulk of their work at home may be able to watch some television during the day, whereas people with less flexible work schedules cannot.

This hypothesis receives further support from the results for after-dinner, weekday viewing.[22] Hours of viewing varied according to town and age, but not sex. The finding that Multitel adults reported watching more weekday evening TV than Notel adults, and marginally more than Unitel adults, may reflect the greater variety of programming available in that community. It also may be due in part to the Notel adults' years of experience without television. Although Notel adults participated in fewer community activities after TV's arrival than before it was available, they still participated more than adults in Unitel and Multitel (Chapter 4). The difference in time spent in these activities may explain the difference between Notel and Multitel in Phase 2 TV viewing.

Taken together, the findings for adults' evening television viewing suggest that when the option to watch TV is equally available, the sex difference observed at other times of the day is no longer found. What is most striking about the levels of evening viewing, averaging across town and age, is that despite programming differences and intuitive expectations regarding the relationship between age and TV use, the results are remarkably consistent. The reports of Notel adults, who had had television for just 2 years, were very similar to those of Unitel adults.

There were no town, age, or sex differences among adults in Sunday viewing. The Saturday question yielded only a significant difference among the towns.[23] Multitel adults reported more Saturday viewing than did both Notel and Unitel adults, who once again did not differ.

In sum, 2 years after their town obtained television, Notel adults watched about the same amount of television as Unitel adults, who had similar programming. Both towns watched less than Multitel, but after availability was controlled, the difference between Unitel and Multitel disappeared and only the Multitel–Notel difference was significant. Women watched more TV than men, and older adults watched more than younger adults. Although these differences are statistically significant, in absolute terms they are not large. For all practical purposes there was relatively little variation among the towns, sexes, and adult age groups in hours of television watched per week.

STABILITY OF TV USE FROM PHASE 1 TO PHASE 2

Some participants provided information about their use of television in both Phase 1 and Phase 2, so we assessed stability of reported viewing over this 2-year period.

Adults

There were 17 Unitel adults and 107 Multitel adults who provided TV-use information in both phases.[24] Individuals who reported watching many hours of television in Phase 1 also tended to report watching a lot of television in Phase 2. This was true for weekday viewing, weekend viewing, and total viewing over the week. In addition, the mean levels of reported viewing did not change (see Figure 5.5). There were no differences related to town, sex, or age. In effect, these results add longitudinal evidence of reliability to the cross-sectional evidence reported earlier for media-use reports by adults.

Children

The question of stability in the children's reports is somewhat more complex, since our own data and findings obtained by other researchers indicate that significant changes in television use occur over the school years. Thus, the amount of TV viewing for students in the longitudinal sample might be expected to have increased or decreased depending upon their initial age level. The opportunity to assess whether an apparent developmental trend seen in cross-sectional research holds true for a longitudinal sample was important.

Longitudinal data were available for 143 students in Unitel and 209 in Multitel.[25] The grades 1–3 Phase 1 group was in grades 3–5 in Phase 2, grade 4–7 in 6–9, 8–9 in 10–11, and tenth graders were in grade 12 in Phase 2. The inverted U-shaped pattern of viewing seen in the cross-sectional samples and reported as typical by Comstock et al. (1978) led us to expect an increase in hours of viewing for the youngest group and a

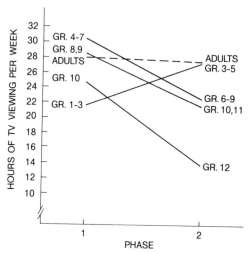

FIGURE 5.5   Mean Phase 1 and Phase 2 reported hours of TV viewing per week for Unitel and Multitel adults and children in the longitudinal sample.

decrease for the older students. The results supported this expectation (see Figure 5.5). Only the youngest group reported watching significantly more television in Phase 2 than in Phase 1; the other groups all watched significantly less. This indicates that the decrease in television viewing beyond about grade 6 typically found in cross-sectional research reflects a true developmental trend rather than a cohort effect. Most children *do* watch less TV during the teenage years; the decrease seen in cross-sectional samples does not occur merely because hours of viewing have tended to increase for each successive cohort growing up over the last decade (Comstock et al., 1978). The change in mean levels of viewing with age is accompanied by only moderate stability for individual children as heavy or light viewers, as the correlation of .44 between hours of TV viewing in Phase 1 and Phase 2 in Table 5.A4 indicates.

RELATIONSHIPS AMONG MEASURES OF TV USE

Some additional information about television use and attitudes toward television was obtained in the leisure activity questionnaires given to students in grades 7–12 and to adults in both phases (see Chapter 4). In Phase 1 Unitel and Multitel residents indicated the frequency with which they watched television (the code for this question used in Table 5.A4 is WATCH TV), and in Phase 2 residents of all three towns did so. In both phases residents of all three towns indicated the frequency with which they visited friends to watch television (VISIT TO WATCH TV) and the extent to which they liked television (LIKE TV). Since television-viewing habits varied according to age and gender, we partialled out the effects of both age and sex in computing the relationships among these measures of TV use. The results are shown in Table 5.A4. Since the television environment changed radically in Notel between Phase 1 and Phase 2, the results for Notel are shown separately. These findings add support to the reliability and stability evidence discussed earlier for our measure of hours of TV viewing. Both children and adults who on one occasion reported they watched a lot of television tended to give similar responses to different but related questions asked within a month of the first occasion, and they also responded similarly to questions about amount of TV viewing asked 2 years apart. Individuals who indicated they liked television also tended to say they watched more television than those who indicated less liking for TV. In general, the measures of TV use were more strongly interrelated for Unitel and Multitel than for Notel.

FAMILY INTERACTION REGARDING TV USE

Living with television has certain interpersonal consequences, and although we did not study the role of television in family interaction patterns in any detail, several questions in Phase 2 were designed to tap this domain.

Children said they rarely watched TV alone; 90.2% reported usually watching TV with others, a figure which did not vary with age.[26] This raises the possibility of conflict.

Conflict over what to watch could not arise in Notel because there was only one channel. In Phase 2, Unitel residents had two CBC channels, but most of the programming was the same. Multitel residents could choose among four different channels. A precise comparison of parents' and children's reports on this issue would require matching parents with their own children, and this was not possible. Nonetheless, if we assume the parent and child samples are equally representative of families in these towns, an intriguing, though tentative, finding emerges. The percentage of children who reported that their parents chose the channel (33.3%) was comparable to that reported by the adults (39.3%), but the proportions of children reporting "democratic" (17.6%) and "child-centered" (30.7%) methods of conflict resolution were roughly the reverse of the parental reports (41.3% and 10.7%). Two explanations seem plausible. Perhaps children include occasions on which only children are watching TV, in which case, unless the parents intervene, the viewing choice will be made by children no matter what. It also seems likely, however, that children and adults have different conceptual frameworks for decision making and democracy. What adults may label as a democratic process, children may label either as a parental or child choice depending upon who had the last word. This would account for the large discrepancy between the percentage of parents (41.3%) and children (17.6%) who report that viewing decisions are arrived at democratically. The question of how parents and children construe decision making in their families seems a fruitful topic for research in general, not merely with regard to decisions involving television viewing. The general role of television in family conflicts also is worth pursuing (Chaffee, 1977).

Beyond knowing how decisions are made about what to watch, we were interested in whether parents monitored their children's viewing habits. Parental control over children's viewing is more palatable to most North Americans than is control of television's content via government or other decree. We asked whether parents ever prevented children from watching TV. Averaging across the towns, the proportion of children who said yes decreased with age from 70.1% under age 7 to 13.9% of those over 16 years.[27] According to children, frequency of parental intervention did not vary by age, town, or sex; 25.8% reported that their parents intervened often, 54.7% reported it occurred once in a while, and 19.5% said it hardly ever happened. By contrast, marginally more Notel parents (25.4%) than Multitel parents (7%) reported often stopping their children from watching TV; Unitel parents (17.9%) were in between and differed neither from Notel nor Multitel. Most parents gave a combination of reasons for curtailing children's viewing, making comparisons difficult. The majority (54.2%) mentioned program content. The next largest category (35.8%) involved general rules such as a restriction on total hours watched or contingencies such as homework or chores which must be done before children may watch TV. Such contingencies could apply to any leisure activity; it would be interesting to know whether parents are more or less likely to have rules for television.

PHASE 2: USE OF OTHER MEDIA

Two years after television arrived, did Notel residents use other media in ways similar to or different from Unitel and Multitel residents? How comparable in media use were these towns to other North American samples? Relationships among the different media also were of interest. Do people who spend a lot of time watching television report less use of magazines, newspapers, books, and the like? Are they heavy users of all media? Is there no particular relationship? Residents were specifically asked about their use of a variety of information sources including radio, newspapers, magazines, comic books (for children), and the town's public library.[28]

Children's Use of Other Media

Each town received two daily papers from a major center some distance away. In Notel and Unitel both papers could be purchased daily in a number of retail outlets. Only Multitel had home delivery. In addition, a small local paper was published weekly in each town. Children were asked how often they read a paper of any kind; first through third graders were not included because of their limited reading skills. When the range of responses from "every day" to "never" was divided into two categories, "once a week or more" and "monthly or less," more Multitel (78.5%) than Unitel (66.3%) children reported reading papers once a week or more. Notel children (72.8%) were in between and not different from Unitel or Multitel.[29] A similar pattern of results occurred for magazine reading. More students in Multitel than in Unitel reported ever reading magazines; Notel did not differ from either Unitel or Multitel.[30]

Slightly more Notel children reported ever going to their local library than did Multitel children; Unitel children did not differ from either Notel or Multitel. Library users were asked how often they took books out; there were no town differences, and overall, 57% of the children said they did so weekly or more often. The number of students going to the library decreased with age.[31] Multitel children were slower to start using their public library, and among older children, Notel students were the heaviest library users. The greater availability of television in Multitel may play a role in the delayed use there, but other factors also may be involved. The results for older Notel students suggest that library habits may be well entrenched by age 11 or so and maintained in the advent of competition from television.

Overall, girls reported reading more books per month than boys, and number of books read per month decreased with age.[32] This decrease probably occurs because books for older children tend to be longer than those for younger children, which points up the difficulty of measuring book reading (Roberts et al., 1984). It may also be the case, however, that book reading falls off with age because older students spend more of their leisure time with peers and music (Lull, 1983). Von Feilitzen (1976) contends that television fails to meet the needs of adolescents because it represents the family from which they are trying to withdraw, that is, to establish their independence. Perhaps it also represents the values and society in which they are trying to establish their unique identity. The popularity with adolescents of certain "anti-establishment" programs (e.g., "Monty Python," "Saturday Night Live," and "SCTV") is consistent with this hypothesis.

Adults tend not to view comic books as central media sources. From the child's point of view, however, they may be quite important. Comics are widely read; 80.4% of all students reported ever reading comic books (as opposed to 58.5% who reported reading magazines). The differences among towns were relatively small, but more Unitel than Multitel children reported reading comics; Notel children did not differ from the other towns.[33] In this sample, comic reading did not vary by age. This finding is less surprising if one views comic books as children's magazines intended for a wide age range (e.g., *Donald Duck* for young children, *Archie* for children in the middle years, and the more complex plots and characters of such *Marvel* heros as Thor and Spiderman for older children).

Since one important media function is to provide information about world events, we asked children how they usually found out about the news. The major categories provided were TV, radio, print, and people, and more than one source could be indicated. Of those who indicated only one news source (approximately half the students), about half (45.8%) reported usually getting their news from television. One-fifth (19.2%) named radio, another fifth (20.5%) reported getting it from people, and the remainder (14.5%) reported usually using print. Among children who indicated only one primary news source, more Notel (53.1%) and Unitel children (46%) reported that TV was their usual news source than was the case for Multitel children (32.8%).[34] This latter finding complements the evidence discussed earlier that more Multitel students reported frequently (weekly or more often) reading a newspaper. The easier access to a newspaper in Multitel via home delivery makes it difficult to draw conclusions about variations in use of news sources across the three towns.

An oft-cited finding is that 65% of adult U.S. residents report they obtain most of their news from TV (Roper Organization, 1975). Comstock et al. (1978) point out that this figure includes both local and national news. Our findings also include both, but the percentage of children reporting TV as their sole primary news source (45.8%) is somewhat lower. When children who indicated that TV is *one* of their usual ways of finding out about the news were included, the combined figure rose to 60.1%, which more closely approaches the level cited by the Roper Organization. Asking people how they usually find out about the news may reveal more about the perceived salience of various news sources than about the real use of various media.

In describing the effects of the introduction of TV on the use of other media, Comstock et al. (1978) contended that the "displacement of one medium by another is caused by the interplay of several functions—such as content, inherent properties, and the audiences to which they appeal" (p. 167). Another important complicating factor is time-sharing. People do many other things while watching TV, including using other media. Some print materials (e.g., comics) undoubtedly are easier to share with TV than are others (e.g., books). Other media with audio channels are especially difficult to time-share with TV (e.g., radio, records). These speculations about time-sharing receive some empirical support from the correlations shown in Table 5.A6. Children who watched more television reported reading fewer books and less radio listening, but more comic reading. In addition to being more readily time-shared, television and comics provide access to fantasy with less mental effort (Salomon, 1981, 1983) than do other sources such as books. Moreover, their content is often redundant (some cartoons and comics have the same characters). Conversely, or perhaps in addition, use of books, magazines, and newspapers versus comics and television probably varies according to reading skill and/or intelligence.

Two years after the arrival of television, Notel children were more similar to than different from children in the other towns in their media use. They did differ in some instances, most notably in their greater library use, but the absolute differences were small. Any adjustments in children's media habits related to television apparently had taken place within 2 years of its arrival, and media habits had stabilized at levels comparable to those for children who had grown up with television.

Use of Other Media by Adults

Radio use by adults was more similar than different across the towns. About half (56.2%) reported listening to the radio frequently, and most (64%) said they did so at one or two characteristic times of day. The news was mentioned by 79% of radio listeners, followed by music (69%), talk shows (34%), and sports events (17%).

Multitel adults reported reading fewer books per month than did adults in both Notel and Unitel.[35] There were age and sex differences in these reports, and the age trends in book reading varied by sex, but the pattern did not vary by town. There were no significant differences for women in the age groups 19–35, 36–55, and 56 and older. By contrast, men in the mature age group reported reading more books than men in the middle-aged group. Young male adults did not differ from either of the other older groups in this regard. Whereas middle-aged men read fewer books than women of the same age, the reverse was true of mature men and women. It may be helpful to recall out hypothesis regarding flexibility of schedules for work and leisure. The absence of age differences among women may reflect similarity in scheduling flexibility across age. The hypothetical increase in this type of flexibility for older males would lead to just the kind of difference in book reading reported between the middle and mature age groups.

Fewer Multitel adults (25.5%) than adults in both Unitel (40.4%) and Notel (34.1%) reported ever checking books out of the library for their own use.[36] Among library users, frequency of checking out books did not vary by town (65% at least monthly vs. 35% less than monthly). The library-use results corroborate the book-reading data in indicating that Multitel adults read books less often than Notel and Unitel adults, who did not differ. One possible explanation is that Multitel adults spent 4–5 hours more per week watching television than did Unitel and Notel residents, and some of this time may displace book reading. Conversely, perhaps CBC television, by contrast with the U.S. networks, is more of a stimulus to book reading. These two interpretations are not, of course, mutually exclusive. It also is possible that the Notel and Unitel libraries do a better job than the Multitel library of stimulating book reading and lending, but this seems unlikely, since the probability that effectiveness would occur equally in the two communities is small. Other unknown factors also may be relevant, of course, and it is unfortunate that we did not obtain analogous information about book reading and library use in Phase 1. The correlations among media-use measures (discussed earlier for children and next for adults) provide some additional evidence that TV viewing may to some extent displace book reading, in contradiction to Robinson's (1980) conclusion that TV viewing displaces newspaper but not book or magazine reading.

Most adults reported reading magazines, but more in Notel (92%) than in Unitel (84%) did so; Multitel (89%) adults were in between and not different from either Notel or Unitel residents.[37] Most adults (60%) reported reading magazines at least weekly as opposed to less than weekly.

When residents were asked about the frequency with which they read newspapers, the pattern was similar across the towns; most (86%) reported reading some kind of paper several times a week or more often.[38] The only town differences involved Multitel adults, who more often (74%) reported daily newspaper reading than did adults in either Notel (38%) or Unitel (21%). The modal response (56%) in these latter towns was several times per week. These results are consistent with the town differences in availability of newspapers. Multitel was the only town with home delivery; in Unitel and Notel, daily papers were available for purchase at local stores.

Just as the children had done, most adults tended to give a variety of sources when asked how they characteristically obtained the news. Only 19% named one source, and of those adults, 47.2% named television, 26.4% named radio, and 12% named newspapers. If we consider all adults who mentioned TV as *one* news source, the percentage rises to 80.8%. The percentage who included radio as one of their sources was 72.5% and newspapers, 62%. In our sample, most adults and children said they preferred to obtain their news from a variety of sources. Most adults listened to the radio regularly, and when asked what they listened to, the single most frequent response was news (79%). Most adults reported reading newspapers (86%), and 62% listed newspapers as one of their news sources. In one sense these findings are commensurate with the Roper Organization (1975) report that 65% of U.S. adults report TV as a primary news source. At the same time, the variety of sources typically used by adults in this study underscores the potential for confusion when source salience is confounded with source use.

Relationships among Measures of Media Use

Do individuals who watch a lot of television tend also to be heavy users of other media? Do some media, but not others, "hang together," and if so, which ones?

In addition to the questions already disucssed, a few media questions were included in the leisure activities questionnaires given in both phases to adults and students in grades 7–12 (see Chapter 4). These included frequency of radio listening, record listening, book reading, magazine reading, and newspaper reading. We therefore assessed the relationships among answers to the media questions from the two different question-naires. Since other analyses had indicated that media use varies according to both age and gender, we controlled for both of these factors (as well as their interactive effect) when computing the correlations. The results for Phase 1 are shown in Table 5.A5, for Phase 2 in Table 5.A6, and the relationships between Phase 1 and Phase 2 are shown in Table 5.A7. We will not discuss these results in detail, but will try to draw some general conclusions.

As was the case for TV use, individuals tended to respond similarly to different questions regarding the same medium. For example, both children and adults who said they read books frequently on the leisure activi-ties questionnaire also tended to say on the TV questionnaire that they read many books per month, relative to other individuals.

Reported use of media other than television tended to be stable from Phase 1 to Phase 2 for both children and adults in Unitel and Multitel. It was less stable for Notel adults and not at all stable for Notel children. This suggests that the introduction of television to Notel disrupted pat-terns of use of other media. Although we do not have Phase 1 data regard-ing use of other media, this finding that the relative rankings of Notel individuals as heavy or light users of other media changed following the introduction of TV does suggest that TV affected patterns of use of other media. This interpretation gains strength from the stability of media use in Unitel and Multitel, which indicates that major change is atypical.

Heavy viewers of television do not seem to be heavy users of all media; indeed, television viewing seems relatively independent of the use of many other media. The exceptions were that children who reported watching more hours of television were more likely to be comic readers (even after age was controlled), and there was some evidence that amount of TV viewing was negatively related to book reading as well as to listen-ing to records and radio.

The "functional equivalence" hypothesis (e.g., von Feilitzen, 1976) contends that media replace other media and other activities in general when they satisfy the same needs. By comparison, for example, with video games (which have already passed a zenith and are declining in popularity in North America), television seems especially powerful at displacing other activities. Proponents of the functional equivalence argument contend this is because television is the least specialized medium and therefore able to satisfy the most needs, or to satisfy them best. This may be true, but several other factors strike us as equally if not more important. The first is time-sharing. People are likely to spend more time with a medium that can be time-shared with other activities, including other media, than with one which cannot (e.g., ironing can be done while watching TV or listening to the radio, but not while reading; reading can be done while watching TV, but listening to records cannot). The second is perceived ease of the medium. Salomon (1983) has shown that by comparison with print media, children perceive television to be an easier medium and one at which they are more expert. (They retain more information from print, but since North Americans use television primarily for entertainment, this is unlikely to be an important determinant of use.) In addition to ease of time-sharing, ease of access undoubtedly is important. For example, we found (Chapter 4) that television displaced participation in community activities outside the home, but there was little evidence to indicate it displaced private leisure activities, including ones typically conducted inside the home. Participation in organized community activities requires more effort than watching television, whereas some indoor leisure activites can be time-shared with TV.

In contrast to the relationship between television and other media, heavy users of one print medium tend to be heavy users of other print media; the relationships between book reading and other print media are particularly strong. It also is interesting to note that radio listeners tend to use print media fairly heavily, and this holds true for both children and adults. The contrast between radio and television in relationship to print use is striking. It is possible that either intelligence or perceived ease of the medium (Salomon, 1983) accounts for this contrast. That is, people who perceive print to be relatively difficult for them may use radio (especially CBC radio) less than people who find print easier. And of course, we expect ease of print use to be related to intelligence.

RELATIONSHIP BETWEEN INTELLIGENCE
AND MEDIA USE

The National Institute of Mental Health (NIMH) review of research on television and human behavior conducted during the 1970s (Pearl, Bouthilet, & Lazar, 1982) concluded there is consistent evidence of a negative relationship between intelligence and television use, but insufficient evidence to determine the direction of causation. Some of the findings from this natural experiment concerning television and intelligence have been discussed in Chapter 3. For this chapter we looked at additional evidence concerning the relationship between IQ and TV use, and also asked whether IQ plays a role in the use of other media.

We began by asking whether children's reports of the amount of television they watched per week in Phase 2 varied according to IQ level (dividing IQ at 100 into an above average and below average group), and whether any IQ-related difference varied by town or grade level (3–5, 6–8, 9–12).[39] This analysis was restricted to children in grade 3 or above, since IQ scores were not available for a sufficient number of younger children. We also excluded children who did not have a working TV set at home, since they were likely to represent an anomalous group with respect to socioeconomic status and perhaps IQ. Independent of the finding reported earlier that Multitel children watched more TV than children in Notel and Unitel, and the finding that viewing levels tended to be lower for students in grades 6–8 and 10–12 than for those in grades 3–5, children with IQ scores above 100 reported watching less television (24.9 hours per week) on average than their peers with lower IQ scores (27.8 hours per week). The difference in TV viewing according to IQ level was due largely to Notel students in grades 3–5 and 6–8.

We did find an interesting pattern of TV viewing in relation to IQ that varied by town and grade level (see note 39). The brighter students in grades 6–12 in the three towns watched approximately equal amounts of television, but the brighter grade 3–5 Notel students watched less TV than their peers in Unitel and Multitel. Conversely, among the less intelligent students there were no town differences among the two younger age groups, but the falloff in amount of TV viewing typical of adolescents (Comstock et al., 1978) did not occur in Multitel, with the result that the less intelligent Multitel students in grades 9–12 watched more TV than their peers in Notel and Unitel. Perhaps greater variety and amount of programming has the potential to maintain TV viewing at a high level among less intelligent adolescents.

In an attempt to examine the shape of the relationship between IQ and TV viewing, we divided students in the three towns into four, rather than just two, IQ groups. The lowest group obtained IQ scores of one standard deviation or more below the test mean of 100 (i.e., had scores below 85); the next group's scores were between 85 and 100; the third group, between 100 and 115; and the highest group scored above 115 (i.e., one standard deviation or more above the mean). The mean reported weekly hours of TV viewing for these four groups were 29.4, 28.0, 25.8, and 23.7, respectively, forming a significant linear trend.[40] The lowest IQ group watched significantly more TV than the two highest IQ groups. The second lowest IQ group also watched more TV than the highest group.

Since the relationship between IQ and TV viewing seemed to be linear, we used correlational analyses to examine the relationship between IQ and use of other media. The results for media use in Phase 1 are shown in Table 5.A5 and for Phase 2, in Table 5.A6. When age and gender were controlled, IQ was not significantly related to hours of TV viewing for Unitel and Multitel students in either Phase 1 or Phase 2. Thus, although there was a mean difference in TV viewing according to IQ, as we reported earlier, the systematic variation among individuals was not strong for Unitel and Multitel. In contrast, brighter students in Unitel and Multitel tended to report reading books more often than their less intelligent peers in both phases of the study, and in Phase 2 they reported more magazine and newspaper reading as well as more radio listening, but less comic reading. In short, the correlational analyses indicated that IQ was positively related to reading and to use of media other than television by Unitel and Multitel students, but not to TV viewing. The opposite was true for Notel.

The relationship between IQ and use of media other than television apparently varies according to whether television is unavailable (Notel, Phase 1), recently has become available (Notel, Phase 2), or was available throughout childhood (Unitel and Multitel, both phases). It seems important in future research to tease out the relationships among use of television, use of other media (especially print), reading competence, and IQ. Among children who have grown up with TV, brighter students are better readers (Chapter 2) and heavier users of print and radio. Do they become better readers because they read more; do they read more because they're more skilled; or is the relationship transactional? Among children who have grown up without television, IQ tends to be more independent of print use, and brighter children tend to watch less TV after it arrives. Do less intelligent children who have grown up with TV more readily abandon media that require greater mental effort (attention, concentration, evaluation, and thought) in favor of television? The finding that reading comics, which like television could be described as an easier medium, is positively related to TV viewing and, among children who have grown up with TV, negatively related to IQ is consistent with this hypothesis.

It is tempting to speculate that when television is available, the less intelligent students, who have the most difficulty learning to read, most readily abandon reading practice in favor of TV viewing. As they grow older they continue to watch more television and read less print because they are poor readers. They do, however, read more comics by comparison with their brighter peers, since these are less demanding of reading skill and mental effort. In the absence of television, less intelligent children do practice reading enough that, on average, their competence does not differ from that of their brighter peers. They also use print media similarly. When television arrives, however, they watch more than their brighter classmates. Two years after the arrival of TV, they also read books and newspapers less frequently. These speculations, derived from our findings, are offered as hypotheses to be pursued in further research (also see Chapter 2).

SUMMARY AND CONCLUSIONS

How might we summarize the use of television and other media by residents of our three towns?

For all practical purposes, Notel was a town without television in Phase 1. The median number of hours watched by Notel school children in Phase 1 was 0, and fully 76% of Notel students reported watching no television. By contrast, only 8% of Unitel students and 3% of Multitel students watched 0 hours of television per week in Phase 1.

Two years after one channel of CBC television arrived, Phase 2 Notel residents were very similar in their use of TV to residents of Unitel, who had had CBC for 10 years. The only notable difference was that fewer Notel than Unitel children said they usually watched television on Saturday mornings. The most interesting aspect of this finding, however, was that more than 45% of the Notel and Unitel children reported watching Saturday morning TV when there was little, if any, programming at that time intended for children. This tends to support the argument that young children are a captive audience, and will watch whatever is available, at least during certain popular viewing periods. The same may be true for adults during the evening hours. That is, the important decision is whether to watch, not what to watch. Once the set has been turned on, perhaps as much out of habit as anything else, the viewer searches for the most attractive alternative (or, as the industry says, the least objectionable programming).

On average, Multitel residents, who could choose among four channels, did report watching more television than Unitel residents in both phases of the study, and more than Notel residents in Phase 2. In absolute terms, however, the differences were less striking than the similarities, especially if hours of availability are considered. Canadians complain loudly and regularly that CBC does not provide the quantity and quality of entertainment fare available on the U.S. networks. (A small minority complains, conversely, that CBC is too much like the U.S. commercial networks and should try instead to model itself after BBC in the United Kingdom or the U.S. Public Broadcasting System.) We were surprised, therefore, to find that residents of towns receiving only CBC watch almost as much television as residents of a town with access in addition to ABC, CBS, and NBC from the United States. Their favorite programs also were similar. These findings support the results described in the other chapters regarding the effects of television, which are consistent in pointing to the difference between presence and absence of television as greater than the difference between one channel, CBC, and four channels, ABC, CBC, CBS, and NBC. Together, these results support our contention that the effects of television due to displacement of other activities deserve as much research attention as effects due to its content.

Reports of television viewing by residents of our three Canadian towns generally were similar to those obtained by other researchers in the United States (see Comstock et al., 1978, for a review). Mean hours of viewing by children and adults were in the expected ranges. In addition, we found that older adults watched more TV than younger adults, and women watched more than men, but among school children the viewing habits of girls and boys were similar. The peak in amount of TV viewing by children in the grades 3–5 age range, followed by a decrease during adolescence, also has been characteristically reported. Our longitudinal data indicate this is not a cohort effect. The typical viewing habits of students and adults in this study indicate they are representative of North Americans in their use of television.

One could argue that the hypothesis, new media alter old (Comstock et al., 1978), was supported by the finding that the advent of television in Notel seemed to affect relationships among the use of other media there. That is, the use of other media tended to be more strongly interrelated in Unitel and Multitel than in Notel in Phase 2, and this was especially true of children. Even in Unitel and Multitel, however, certain media tended to cluster better than others. Most notable in this regard were the print media, especially newspapers and magazines, which also were strikingly independent of television. Indeed, amount of television watched was not strongly related to the use of any other media, although there was some evidence of a negative relationship to book reading and radio listening, and for children, a positive relationship to comic reading. What implications does this pattern of results have for our hypotheses regarding television's displacement effects? We suspect that television's role in the use of other media is more complex than has been acknowledged. Earlier studies (e.g., Allen, 1965; Bechtel, Achelpol, & Akers, 1972) and later research conducted by Anderson (1983) in which people have been videotaped in their homes reveal they often are not looking at the screen or are not even in the same room when the television set is on. Moreover, both children and adults engage in many other activities while watching television. Certain media (perhaps comics, newspapers, and magazines) may be relatively easy to time-share with television, whereas others (radio, records, and books seem salient) are likely to make time-sharing more difficult. In addition, the efficiency with which any particular activity can be time-shared with television probably varies according to age, skill at the activity, television literacy, and intelligence; it undoubtedly also varies with the type of programming involved. Television does not displace other activities in a simplistic manner, and this may in part explain the typically low and often nonsignificant correlations between hours of TV viewing and other behaviors. When individuals are asked how much time they spend watching television, their estimates are likely to be based on program hours, not time in the room during the program. We would be more accurate to use the phrase "time spent with television" and to acknowledge that such time is shared with other activities. Considerably more research is needed before we can hope to understand what activities (media and otherwise) television displaces, for whom, and at what benefits and costs.

Our findings regarding the role of intelligence in media use underscore the complexities involved in understanding their impact. Amount of television viewed decreased linearly when students were grouped according to IQ. Among children who grew up without television, IQ was positively correlated with book reading, not related to use of other media, and was negatively related to amount of television watched 2 years after its inception. Conversely, among children who grew up with TV, IQ was correlated with the use of other media, but not with the amount of television watched. These findings and those reported in Chapters 2 and 3 support the tentative hypothesis that children vary less according to intelligence in their use of print (and perhaps radio as well) in the absence than in the presence of television. When TV is available, the less intelligent students tend to drop some activities in favor of TV viewing, especially those which require most mental effort (books). All children may do this to some extent, but those who find print most difficult probably do so most readily. This hypothesis needs to be assessed empirically in a longitudinal study.

Before we can make serious inroads at untangling this complex web of questions, better methods of assessing television use must be devised. The work underway at Stanford (Roberts et al., 1984) indicates the importance of considering the larger context of the television environment (e.g., parental rules, behavior, and attitudes regarding television; the child's orientation toward TV as a medium for entertainment vs. learning). Good measures of amount of television viewing also are needed. In this study we interviewed children individually, asked about television viewing during specific periods of the day, and questioned implausible answers. We assessed the reliability of the estimates given by older children and by adults, and the results were encouraging. For reasons outlined at the beginning of this chapter, however, we are less than satisfied with this method of obtaining TV-use information from children in the early elementary grades. It is then, of course, and also during the preschool years that relationships among television use, print use, school achievement, and intelligence may be most interesting, because they have the greatest consequences for later development. The tedious and expensive job of testing different methodologies for obtaining reliable and valid data regarding media use by young children is not enticing. Nonetheless, it must be undertaken if we wish to advance our understanding of both the displacement and content effects of television.

APPENDIX: TABLES

TABLE 5.A1

Phase 1 Hours of TV Viewing: Children[a]

	Notel		Unitel		Multitel	
	Median	Mean	Median	Mean	Median	Mean
Grades 4–6						
Weekdays	0	0.793	4.0	4.077	4.8	4.864
Weekend days	0	0.708	3.0	3.497	5.8	6.075
Total for week	0	3.559	26.0	26.948	35.0	35.765
Grades 7–10						
Weekdays	0	1.041	3.3	3.557	4.0	4.607
Weekend days	0	0.826	3.0	3.163	3.9	4.585
Total for week	0	5.726	22.5	23.764	29.8	31.507
Grades 11, 12						
Weekdays	0	0.586	—	—	3.3	3.516
Weekend days	0	0.457	—	—	2.8	3.302
Total for week	0	3.845	—	—	23.5	24.187
Grades 4–12						
Weekdays	0	0.897	4.0	3.739	4.0	4.322
Weekend days	0	0.735	3.0	3.184	4.0	4.782
Total for week	0	4.690	23.5	25.061	29.3	31.173

[a] Dashes indicate that information was not obtained.

TABLE 5.A2
Phase 1 Hours of TV Viewing: Adult Means[a]

| | Age (in years) | | | | | |
| | Notel | | Unitel | | Multitel | |
	19–50	51+	19–50	51+	19–50	51+
Weekdays	—	—	2.852	4.000	3.816	5.352
Weekend days	—	—	2.820	2.615	3.496	4.471
Total for week	—	—	20.038	24.846	25.661	35.451

[a] Dashes indicate that information was not obtained.

TABLE 5.A3
Phase 2 Mean Hours of TV Viewing

	Notel	Unitel	Multitel
Children			
Weekday mean	3.119	3.212	3.961
Before school[a]	—	—	0.185
After school	1.193	1.240	1.426
After supper	1.926	1.972	2.350
Weekend mean	2.695	2.797	3.634
Saturday	2.383	2.839	4.168
Sunday	3.007	2.755	3.100
Total for week	20.991	21.668	27.076
Adults			
Weekday mean	3.327	3.549	4.115
Mornings	0.092	0.177	0.290
Afternoons	0.895	0.868	0.959
Evenings	2.340	2.504	2.866
Weekend mean	2.709	3.052	3.515
Saturday	2.400	2.682	3.449
Sunday	3.018	3.422	3.580
Total for week	22.038	23.783	27.604

[a] Television was not available before school on weekdays in Notel and Unitel.

TABLE 5.A4

Partial Correlations among Measures of Television Use, Controlling for Age and Gender[a]

	Phase 1				Phase 2			
	Total hours	WATCH TV	VISIT TO WATCH TV	LIKE TV	Total hours	WATCH TV	VISIT TO WATCH TV	LIKE TV
Unitel and Multitel								
Phase 1								
Total hours		.27**		.38***	.44***	.18**		.21**
WATCH TV	.44***		.38***	.42***	.22**	.22*		
VISIT TO WATCH TV	.26*	.55***		.22*	.26***	.25*		.22*
LIKE TV					.21***			
Phase 2								
Total hours	.70***	.35***		.41***		.30***		.45***
WATCH TV	.27**	.54***					.16**	.30***
VISIT TO WATCH TV						.23***		
LIKE TV	.47***	.38***		.44***	.47***			
Notel[b]								
Phase 1								
VISIT TO WATCH TV	—	—						.38**
LIKE TV	—	—	.38*					
Phase 2								
Total hours	—	—	.37*	.36*				.22**
WATCH TV	—	—	.36*	.47**	.40***			.18*
VISIT TO WATCH TV	—	—						.20*
LIKE TV	—	—			.39***			

[a] Correlations for children above the diagonal, for adults below.

[b] Dashes indicate television was not available in Notel so correlations could not be computed.

* p < .05; ** p < .01; *** p < .001; all tests two-tailed.

TABLE 5.A5

Partial Correlations among Phase 1 Measures of Media Use,
Controlling for Age and Gender[a]

	Total TV hours	Radio	Records	Books	Magazines	Newspapers
			Unitel and Multitel			
IQ				.18*		
Total TV hours		−.19*				
Radio					.23**	
Records	−.21*					
Books					.40***	.29***
Magazines		.19*		.43***		.61***
Newspapers		.20*			.57***	
			Notel[b]			
IQ	—					
Radio	—					
Records	—					
Books	—					.24*
Magazines	—					.46***
Newspapers	—				.39**	

[a] Correlations for children above the diagonal, for adults below.

[b] Dashes indicate television was not available in Notel so correlations could not be computed. IQ data were available only for children.

* $p < .05$; ** $p < .01$; *** $p < .001$; all tests two-tailed.

TABLE 5.A6

Partial Correlations among Phase 2 Measures of Media Use, Controlling for Age and Gender[a]

Unitel and Multitel

	Total TV[b]	Radio[c]	Radio[b]	Records[c]	Books[c]	Books[b]	Library[b]	Magazine[c]	Magazine[b]	News-paper[c]	News often[b]	Comics[b]
IQ		.20***	.14**		.32***			.16**	.19***	.29***	.19***	-.11*
Total TV hours per week[b]			-.12***									.13***
Radio[c]			.44***	.27***	.29***		.18***	.34***	.14**	.33**	.14**	
Radio[b]		.15***		.25***	.10*		.21***	.20***	.18***	.17***	.16***	
Records[c]		.11*	.11*		.28***	.27***	.22***	.34***	.16**	.29***	.11*	
Books[c]			.12*			.30***	.09**	.38***		.42***		
Books[b]			.13*		.37***			.17***			.13***	
Library[b]	-.10*				.26***	.16**		.17***	.27***	.17**	.20***	
Magazines[c]		.22***	.14**	.22***	.40***		.18**		.36***	.57***	.17***	
Magazines[b]		.14**		.11*	.16**		.14**	.48***		.19***	.41***	
Newspaper[c]		.29***		.19***	.20***		.11*	.17**	.22***		.29***	
News often[b]					.16**							

Notel

	Total TV[b]	Radio[c]	Radio[b]	Records[c]	Books[c]	Books[b]	Library[b]	Magazine[c]	Magazine[b]	News-paper[c]	News often[b]	Comics[b]
IQ	-.31***				.19*	-.12*				.22*		
Total TV hours per week[b]			-.19***									.20***
Radio[c]			.36***		.20**		.21***	.36***	.18*	.41***		
Radio[b]	-.19*	.48***		.27***			.22***	.18*	.18*	.25***		
Records[c]		.30***	.19*		.24***			.19**		.49***		
Books[c]		.23**	.17*			.38***	.29***	.28***	.15*	.16*		
Books[b]		.21*						.17*	.31***	.58***		
Library[b]		.30***	.19*	.22**	.19*			.34***		.31***		.11*
Magazines[c]		.23**	.31***		.33***	.21*	.16*		.34***			
Magazines[b]		.39***			.19*			.33***	.28***			
Newspaper[c]	.22*				.20*			.33***	.23**			
News often[b]		.16**										

[a] Correlations for children above the diagonal, for adults below. IQ data were available only for children.

[b] Item from interview (grades 1–12) or questionnaire (adults) re media use.

[c] Item from questionnaire given in grades 7–12 and mailed to adults re leisure activities.

Table 5.4

Longitudinal Partial Correlations (across the Phases) among Measures of Media Use, Controlling for Age and Gender[a]

Phase 1	Phase 2											
	TV hours[b]	Radio[c]	Radio[b]	Records[c]	Books[c]	Books[b]	Library[b]	Magazine[c]	Magazine[b]	News[c]	News often[b]	Comics[b]
Unitel and Multitel: Children												
TV hours[b]	.44***								.17**		.14**	—
Radio[c]		.27**	.20**		.19*			.26**				—
Records[c]		.24***	.24**		.34***	.26***	.17*			.18*		—
Books[c]		.33***	.24**				.26***	.21*	.18*	.21*		—
Magazines[c]		.23**	.24**							.29***		—
Newspaper[c]												—
Unitel and Multitel: Adults												
TV hours[b]	.70***											
Radio[c]	−.19*	.26*	.40***	.34***							.21*	
Records[c]				.34***	.53***	.34***	.30**	.26*	.36***	.25*	.39***	
Books[c]				.24*	.26*		.23*	.42***	.29**	.30**	.36***	
								.22*				
Notel: Children												
Radio[c]											.21*	
Records[c]				−.27*								—
Books[c]							.33**		.31***			—
Magazines[c]							.35**					—
Newspaper[c]												—
Notel: Adults												
Radio[c]	.31*	.36*	.37***									
Records[c]												—
Books[c]		.43**		.51***	.51***		.38**	.31*	.32*	.37*		—
Magazines[c]				.44**	.33*			.45**		.31*		—
Newspaper[c]												—

[a] Adults were not asked about reading comics so correlations were not computed. [b] Item from interview (grades 1–12) or questionnaire (adults) re media use. [c] Item from questionnaire given in grades 7–12 and mailed to adults re leisure activities. * $p < .05$; ** $p < .01$; *** $p < .001$; all tests two-tailed.

253

NOTES

[1] CBC is the Canadian government-owned network. When television came to Notel it was the only channel. Unitel had only CBC reception in both phases of the project, one channel in Phase 1, and two (with similar programming except for local news, and the like) in Phase 2. More than 80% of Multitel residents received CBC, ABC, CBS, and NBC via cable reception in both phases of the study. Those who did not have cable reception received only one channel, a network affiliate of CBS (i.e., U.S. but not Canadian TV).

[2] Even in the fall of 1983 in Vancouver, the third largest city in Canada, CBC did not begin its programming on the English network until 9:15 A.M. on weekdays, 9:30 A.M. on Saturdays, and 8:30 A.M. on Sundays. The French network began at 9:00 A.M. weekdays and 8:30 A.M. on both Saturdays and Sundays.

[3] It should be noted that the major commercial network in Canada, CTV, was not available in Notel, Unitel, or Multitel in either phase of this project. The description of CBC programming does not apply to CTV. We are currently studying differences and similarities between CBC and CTV as well as the three major commercial U.S. networks and PBS, the U.S. public broadcasting network.

[4] Very few preschool or elementary school children in Notel or Unitel spoke or understood French.

[5] Results regarding reliability of individual interviews versus supervised questionnaires for obtaining TV viewing data for children in grades 7–12 are:

| | Means | | | | | | |
	Interview	Questionnaire	df	t	p	r	p
Notel							
Weekend hours	1.30	1.23	115	.5	ns	.865	.001
Weekday hours	0.68	0.66	116	.62	ns	.951	.001
Total hours (computed)	4.24	4.09	111	.51	ns	.943	.001
Unitel and Multitel							
Weekend hours	7.37	6.88	118	1.86	ns	.832	.001
Weekday hours	3.72	3.79	119	−.60	ns	.857	.001
Total hours (computed)	25.60	25.53	116	.11	ns	.873	.001

The high correlation coefficients indicate that individual children who reported high levels of viewing on the questionnaire also did so when interviewed, and the lack of significant difference between the means (t tests) indicates that the scale on which students responded was equivalent with the two methods.

[6] Reliability of adult responses for Notel, Unitel, and Multitel combined was assessed with paired observation t tests, which indicate whether respondents used the same scale on the two occasions, and Pearson product-moment correlations, which indicate whether individuals who reported high levels of viewing relative to others in the group (and vice-versa for low levels) did so on both occasions:

	Inter-view	Question-naire	df	t	p	r	p
Morning hours	0.36	0.64	61	−2.17	.035	.897	.001
Afternoon hours	2.93	4.44	61	−3.32	.002	.788	.001
Evening hours	12.18	10.76	61	1.90	ns	.748	.001
Saturday hours	2.86	2.56	61	1.07	ns	.512	.001
Sunday hours	3.50	3.47	61	0.12	ns	.653	.001
Total hours	21.84	21.87	61	−0.03	ns	.758	.001

The availability of detailed information regarding adults' viewing patterns in Phase 2 allowed for an analysis of reliability of questionnaire versus interview responses for more fine-grained viewing measures than was possible in Phase 1. The significant differences noted in the table for reported hours of morning and afternoon viewing may, however, be misleading. Many adults worked outside the home during the day. Almost all (60 out of 63) reporting watching *no* morning TV and nearly half (29 out of 63) reported watching 0 hours of afternoon TV. The consequence of so many reports of 0 hours is that even minor variations can result in significant differences when the two sources of data are compared. A more accurate estimate of reliability is reflected in such variables as total hours of viewing per weekday, since these include a better range of answers.

[7] Comparability of the results from the two samples was assessed in the following manner: For interval variables (e.g., number of hours of television usually watched on weekday mornings; number of books usually read per month) the significance of the difference between the interview and mailed questionnaire groups in each town was assessed with *t* tests (two-tailed), based on either a pooled variance estimate for the two groups or separate variance estimates, depending upon the outcome of a preliminary homogeneity of variance test for each variable. For nominal and ordinal variables (e.g., whether the family included a child under 18; how often library books were checked out), the significance of the difference between the interview and mailed questionnaire groups was assessed with chi-square tests. Raw chi squares were computed when the degrees of freedom were greater than 1; corrected chi-square tests were used when there was 1 degree of freedom. Only 5 of 72 comparisons yielded statistically significant differences, and these were not systematic.

[8] In an unweighted means cross-sectional ANOVA on the Phase 1 total hours of television watched per week for Town (Unitel, Multitel) × Sex × Grade (4–6, 7–10), only the town, $F(1,436) = 29.81$, $p < .001$; and grade, $F(1,436) = 6.02$, $p < .02$ main effects were significant. Multitel students ($M = 33.64$) watched more than Unitel students (25.36), and the younger grade group ($M = 31.36$) watched more than the older grade group (27.64).

[9] In an unweighted means cross-sectional ANOVA on the Phase 1 total hours of television watched per week for Town × Sex × Grade in which each of grades 4–10 was included, the results were similar to those reported above (see note 8). In this case the grade main effect was significant, $F(6,416) = 2.17$, $p < .045$, but there were no significant differences between any pair of grade means by either Tukey or Newman–Keuls tests. The means for grades 4, 5, 6, 7, 8, 9, and 10 were 31.73, 29.61, 31.30, 31.47, 25.25, 28.11, and 23.87, respectively.

[10] In an unweighted means cross-sectional ANOVA on Phase 1 weekday hours of TV viewing for Town (Unitel, Multitel) × Sex × Grade (4–6, 7–10), only the town main effect was significant, $F(1,470) = 16.58$, $p < .001$, reflecting a higher mean for Multitel (4.735) than Unitel (3.817). For Phase 1 weekend hours, in an unweighted means cross-sectional ANOVA for Town (Unitel, Multitel) × Sex × Grade (4–6, 7–10), the town main effect,

$F(1,442) = 53.67$, $p < .001$; grade main effect, $F(1,442) = 11.16$, $p < .001$; and their interaction, $F(1,442) = 4.48$, $p < .035$ all were significant. Overall, Multitel students ($M = 5.33$ hours per weekend day) watched more than Unitel students (3.33), and younger students watched more (4.79) than older students (3.87). Simple main effects analyses of the Town × Grade interaction revealed that this grade level difference was specific to Multitel, $F(1,442) = 14.89$, $p < .001$ ($M = 6.08$ hours for grades 4–6 vs. 4.59 hours for grades 7–10); the difference in Unitel (3.50; 3.16) was not significant. At both grade levels Multitel students watched more than Unitel students; for grades 4–6, $F(1,442) = 44.60$, $p < .001$ and for grades 7–10, $F(1,442) = 13.78$, $p < .001$.

[11] In an unweighted means cross-sectional ANOVA on total viewing hours per week reported by adults in Phase 1 for Town (Unitel, Multitel) × Sex × Age (50 years or younger vs. over 50), only the main effects for town, $F(1,229) = 7.19$, $p < .008$; and sex, $F(1,229) = 9.12$, $p < .003$ were significant. Multitel adults watched more (29.75 hours per week) than Unitel adults (21.40 hours), and women watched more (30.27) than men (20.88).

[12] In an unweighted means cross-sectional ANOVA on weekday viewing by Phase 1 adults for Town (Unitel, Multitel) × Sex × Age (50 or younger vs. over 50), all main effects, but none of their interactions, were significant. The town main effect, $F(1,231) = 32.16$, $p < .02$ reflected more weekday viewing by Multitel (4.45 hours) than Unitel (3.43 hours) adults. The sex main effect, $F(1,231) = 47.54$, $p < .004$ reflected more viewing by women (4.56 hours) than men (3.32 hours). The age main effect, $F(1,231) = 28.88$, $p < .03$ reflected more weekday viewing by people over 50 (4.43 hours) than by younger people (3.46 hours).

[13] In an unweighted means cross-sectional ANOVA on weekend viewing by Phase 1 adults for Town (Unitel, Multitel) × Sex × Age (50 or younger vs. over 50) only the main effects for town, $F(1,224) = 185.29$, $p < .002$; and sex, $F(1,224) = 3.99$, $p < .05$ were significant. On average, Multitel adults watched more TV on the weekends ($M = 3.98$ hours per weekend day) than Unitel adults (2.72 hours), and women watched more (3.68 hours) than men (2.79 hours).

[14] There was a significant difference among the towns in Phase 2 in the proportions of children who reported having a working television set in their homes, $\chi^2(2) = 48.5$, $p < .001$. More Multitel children had TV sets (98.3%) than was true for Notel, 93.8%, $\chi^2(2) = 11.55$, $p < .003$; or Unitel, 86.3%, $\chi^2(2) = 41.57$, $p < .001$. The Notel–Unitel proportions also were significantly different, $\chi^2(2) = 11.70$, $p < .003$.

The post hoc comparisons among the towns following the significant overall test in this case and in all others in this chapter were based on the Scheffé theorem as outlined by Marascuilo (1966). This procedure constructs confidence intervals for the set of all possible pair-wise comparisons in the contingency table such that the Type I (alpha) error rate is controlled at $p < .05$ for the set of comparisons as a whole. Significant comparisons are those for which the confidence interval does not bracket zero.

[15] In an unweighted means cross-sectional ANOVA on Phase 2 total hours of television watched per week for Town × Grade × Sex, the town main effect, $F(2,1170) = 31.13$, $p < .001$; and the grade main effect, $F(11,1170) = 9.56$, $p < .001$ were significant. Neither the sex main effect nor any of the interactions was significant.

Multitel children watched more television per week (26.9 hours) than both Unitel (21.01 hours) and Notel children (20.88 hours), who did not differ ($p < .01$ by Tukey test in all cases).

Averaging across the towns, the pattern of television viewing by grade followed an inverted U-shaped curve (see Figure 5.3), replicating the age trends reported for several other North American samples (Comstock et al., 1978). Students in grade 12 watched significantly fewer hours of television per week (14.7) than students in all other grades except grade 11, and eleventh graders also watched significantly fewer hours per week (17.5) than students in the middle grades (grades 3, 4, 5, 6, and 7 watched 27.2, 26.7, 25.9, 25.2, and 25.7 hours per week, respectively). A similar trend was evident for tenth graders, who watched less television (21.0 hours per week) than third graders (27.2 hours per week), who, in absolute terms, watched more television than children in any other grade. However, as we noted earlier, tenth graders still watched more television than did twelfth graders.

[16] In an unweighted means cross-sectional ANOVA on hours of television watched after school for Town × Grade × Sex, only the main effects for town, $F(2,1170) = 9.12, p < .001$; and grade, $F(11,1170) = 14.40$, $p < .001$ were significant. Multitel children watched more hours ($p < .01$ by Tukey test in both cases) of after school television (1.426 hours per day) than children in Notel (1.193 hours) and Unitel (1.240 hours), who did not differ. For hours of television watched after supper, in an unweighted means cross-sectional ANOVA for Town × Grade × Sex, only the main effects for town, $F(2,1170) = 10.44$, $p < .001$; and Grade, $F(11.1170) = 7.57$, $p < .001$ were significant. The Multitel children watched more television ($p < .01$ by Tukey test in both cases) after supper (2.350 hours per day) than did children in Unitel (1.972 hours) or Notel (1.926 hours), who did not differ.

[17] A Town (3) × Saturday Morning Viewing (yes/no) contingency table yielded an overall significant difference, $\chi^2(2) = 49.68$, $p < .004$. Post hoc comparisons indicated that the proportion of Multitel children reporting usual Saturday morning viewing (58.8%) was greater than the proportions of both Unitel (48.9%) and Notel (34.2%) children, and the Unitel proportion was also significantly greater than that for the Notel children.

[18] In a series of Town (3) × Saturday Morning Viewing (yes/no) contingency tables, age was controlled by constructing a separate table for each age group. The overall χ^2 values for the following age groups were significant: 5–7 years, $\chi^2(2) = 10.92$, $p < .005$; 8–10 years, $\chi^2(2) = 13.96, p < .001$; 13–15 years, $\chi^2(2) = 48.69, p < .001$; and 16–18 years, $\chi^2(2) = 11.17$, $p < .01$.

Within each age level, similarly lettered (in superscripts) percentages are similar (i.e., do not differ significantly), and differently lettered percentages *do* differ significantly in the following table showing percentages of students who said they usually watched TV on Saturday morning in Phase 2.

Age	Notel	Unitel	Multitel
5–7	59.6[a]	72.3[a,b]	86.4[b]
8–10	67.1[a]	83.1[a,b]	90.5[b]
11–12	46.0[a]	57.1[a]	60.9[a]
13–15	14.7[a]	34.5[b]	42.4[c]
16–18	0[a]	23.3[a]	15.5[b]

[19] An unweighted means cross-sectional ANOVA on hours of television watched per week for Town × Sex × Age (19–35, 36–55, and 56+) yielded significant town, $F(2,564) = 4.62$, $p < .01$; sex, $F(1,564) = 13.67$, $p < .001$; and age main effects, $F(2,564) = 9.23$, $p < .001$. None of the interaction terms was significant. Multitel adults reported watching significantly more hours of TV per week (27.41 hours) than did Notel adults (22.04 hours; $p < .01$ by Tukey test) and Unitel adults (23.78 hours; $p < .05$ by Newman–Keuls test). Notel and Unitel adults' reports did not differ. Women (27.14 hours) watched more than men (21.69 hours). The mature adults watched more (26.9 hours) than the young adult group (20 hours; $p < .01$ by Tukey test), and the youngest group watched less than the middle-aged group (23.6 hours per week; $p < .05$ by Newman–Keuls), which did not differ significantly from the mature adult group.

[20] In an unweighted means cross-sectional ANOVA on adjusted hours of TV viewing per week for Town × Sex × Age, there were significant main effects for town, $F(2,564) = 3.77$, $p < .05$; sex, $F(1,564) = 10.58$, $p < .001$; and age (19–35, 36–55, and 56+), $F(2,564) = 8.47$, $p < .001$, but no significant interactions. Multitel adults reported watching more TV (26.04 hours per week) than Notel adults (21.56 hours per week; $p < .05$ by Tukey test). Unlike the analysis which did not adjust for availability of morning television, however, Unitel adults (22.90 hours per week) did not differ from either Notel or Multitel adults. Women (25.72) watched more than men (21.27). The oldest age group (26.87) watched more than the youngest (19.98); 36–55-year-olds were in between (23.64) and not different from the other groups.

[21] An unweighted means cross-sectional ANOVA on hours of television watched by adults on weekday mornings for Town × Sex × Age 19–35, 36–55, and 56+) yielded a significant town main effect, $F(2,570) = 4.46$, $p < .02$; sex main effect, $F(1,570) = 14.48$, $p < .001$; and age main effect, $F(2,570) = 4.72$, $p < .01$. None of the interaction terms was significant. Multitel adults reported more morning viewing (0.290 hours per weekday morning) than Notel adults (0.092 hours; $p < .01$ by Tukey test) and marginally more than Unitel adults (0.177 hours; $p < .10$ by Newman–Keuls). Adults over 55 years reported more morning viewing (0.304 hours) than both the 36–55 year group (0.132 hours; $p < .05$ by Tukey test) and the 19–35 year group (0.124 hours; $p < .05$ by Tukey test). Finally, women (0.290) reported watching more morning TV than men (0.083). For hours watched by adults on weekday afternoons, an unweighted means cross-sectional ANOVA for Town × Sex × Age yielded significant effects for sex, $F(1,569) = 35.52$, $p < .001$; and age, $F(2,569) = 9.25$, $p < .001$, but not for town. The Age × Sex interaction also was significant, $F(2,569) = 5.00$, $p < .007$. The mature adult group (56+) reported watching more afternoon television (1.2 hours per weekday afternoon) than adults in both the middle-age group (0.871 hours; $p < .05$ by Tukey test) and the young adult group (0.65 hours; $p < .01$ by Tukey test). Simple main effects analysis of the Sex × Age interaction revealed that the young adult male group watched fewer hours of weekday afternoon TV (0.26 hours) than women of the same age (1.04 hours, $F(1,569) = 18.41$, $p < .001$), and the same was true of middle-aged men (0.404 hours) compared to middle aged women (1.34 hours), $F(1,569) = 26.29$, $p < .001$. No differences were found between men and women in the mature adult group. There were no age differences for women, but there were for men, $F(1,569) = 25.49$, $p < .001$. The oldest group of men reported more weekday afternoon viewing (1.118 hours) than both the middle-aged male group ($p < .01$ by Tukey test) and the young adult male group, ($p < .01$ by Tukey).

[22] An unweighted means cross-sectional ANOVA on reported hours of evening weekday viewing for Town × Sex × Age yielded significant main effects for town, $F(2,567) = 4.18$, $p < .02$; and age, $F(2,567) = 5.51$, $p < .0005$, but not for sex. There were no significant interactions. Multitel adults watched more weekday evening television (2.87 hours per evening) than Notel (2.34 hours; $p < .05$ by Tukey test) and Unitel adults (2.50 hours; $p < .05$ by Newman–Keuls). Notel and Unitel adults did not differ. The adults over 55 reported watching more evening television (2.84 hours per weekday evening) than did the 19–35-year-olds (2.24 hours; $p < .01$ by Tukey test), but they did not differ significantly from 36–55-year-olds (2.64 hours). The middle-aged adults reported more evening viewing than the younger adult group ($p < .05$ by Newman–Keuls test).

[23] An unweighted means cross-sectional ANOVA on reported hours of Saturday TV viewing for Town × Sex × Age yielded only a significant main effect for town, $F(2,569) = 8.05$, $p < .001$. Multitel adults reported more Saturday viewing (3.45 hours) than both Notel adults (2.4 hours; $p < .01$ by Tukey test) and Unitel adults (2.68 hours; $p < .05$ by Tukey test), who did not differ. A similar analysis of Sunday viewing yielded no significant effects.

[24] In an unweighted means longitudinal ANOVA on weekly total hours of TV viewing with Town (Unitel, Multitel), Sex, and Age (19–35, 36–55, and 56+ in Phase 1) as between-

subject factors and repeated measures on Phase, there were no significant main effects or interactions. The mean hours of TV viewing for this longitudinal sample was 28.1 hours in Phase 1 and 27.5 hours in Phase 2.

The stability coefficients for individuals from Phase 1 to Phase 2 (raw Pearson correlations) were .64 for weekday viewing, .70 for weekend viewing, and .74 for the weekly total (all $p < .001$, $df = 122$).

[25] An unweighted means repeated measures (Phase 1 and 2) ANOVA was run first for Town (Unitel, Multitel) $\times$ Grade (1–3, 4–7, 8–9, and 10) $\times$ Sex on total reported hours of TV viewing per week. The main effect for sex was not significant so the analysis was rerun after collapsing across sex. This second analysis yield significant main effects for town, $F(1,344) = 20.75$, $p < .001$; grade, $F(3,344) = 4.31$, $p < .005$; and phase, $F(1,344) = 25.35$, $p < .001$, as well as a significant Grade $\times$ Phase interaction, $F(3,344) = 12.69$, $p < .001$. On average, Multitel students (27.23 hours) watched more than Unitel students (20.34 hours), and students in this longitudinal group watched more TV (26.32 hours per week) in Phase 1 than in Phase 2 (21.25 hours).

Averaging across both phases, both the grades 4–7 and 1–3 groups (determined by Phase 1 grade status) reported more weekly viewing than the Grade 10 group (26.51 and 24.92 vs. 19.27 hours per week; $p < .01$ by Tukey test). Simple main effects analyses of the Grade $\times$ Phase interaction revealed grade differences in both phases; in Phase 1, $F(2,344) = 6.76$, $p < .005$; and in Phase 2, $F(2,344) = 13.84$, $p < .001$. From Phase 1 to Phase 2 there was a significant increase in viewing for the students initially in grades 1–3, $F(1,344) = 4.27$, $p < .05$. The remaining groups decreased significantly; grade 4–7, $F(1,344) = 9.57$, $p < .005$; grade 8–9, $F(1,344) = 6.75$, $p < .01$; and grade 10, $F(1,344) = 18.20$, $p < .001$. The means for this analysis of the Grade $\times$ Phase interaction follow.

Grade in		Phase	
Phase 1	Phase 2	1	2
1–3	3–5	21.77	27.12
4–7	6–9	30.47	22.56
8–9	10–11	28.30	21.55
10	12	24.75	13.79

[26] Chi-square tests were used to assess whether children in the three towns differed according to whether they usually watched TV alone or with others. There was a difference only for 11–12-year-olds, $\chi^2(2) = 8.13$, $p < .02$. Fewer Unitel (81.5%) than Notel 11–12-year-olds (96.7%) usually watched with others; Multitel children (89.7%) were similar to both Notel and Unitel in this regard ($p < .05$ for entire set of comparisons).

[27] There were significant differences among the towns in the proportion of children who said their parents prevented them from watching television at the 11–12 year and 13–15 year age ranges.

Fewer Unitel 11–12-year-olds (37.9%) reported their parents ever prevented them from watching TV than did children either in Notel (62.3%; $\chi^2(2) = 8.04$, $p < .02$) or Multitel (60.2%; $\chi^2(2) = 7.94$, $p < .02$), who did not differ. At the 13–15 year level there were differences among all three towns; Notel (55.3%) versus Unitel (21.7%), $\chi^2(2) = 25.47$, $p < .001$; Notel versus Multitel (37.4%), $\chi^2(2) = 8.05$, $p < .02$; and Unitel versus Multitel, $\chi^2(2) = 6.80$, $p < .04$.

There were significant differences among the towns in the proportions of adults who said they often (as opposed to sometimes or hardly ever) stopped their children from watching TV, $\chi^2(2) = 10.26, p < .01$. Fewer Multitel (7%) than Notel (25.4%) parents said they did this often; Unitel parents were in between (17.9%) and not different from Notel or Multitel.

[28] Because of space limitations we can only highlight some of our media-use results.

[29] The proportion of children in grades 4–12 who reported reading newspapers at least once a week varied significantly across town, $\chi^2(2) = 11.42, p < .04$ (72.8% for Notel, 78.5% for Multitel, and 66.3% for Unitel). Only the difference between Multitel and Unitel, $\chi^2(2) = 11.27, p < .04$ was significant.

[30] More Multitel (62%) than Unitel children (52.3%) reported ever reading magazines, $\chi^2(2) = 7.82, p < .02$. Notel children (60.3%) did not differ from either Unitel or Multitel children.

[31] A Town (3) × Library Use (2; yes/no) contingency table yielded a significant $\chi^2(2)$ value of 6.62, $p < .04$. The percentage of Notel children (76.3%) who reported using their library was greater than that for Multitel (68.0%); the Unitel proportion (70.4%) did not differ from Notel or Multitel.

A Library Use (2; yes/no) by Age Level (5) contingency table yielded a significant overall $\chi^2(4)$ value of 176.31, $p < .0001$. The age groups which differed significantly in library use are indicated by asterisks in the following table.

	Age in years				
	6–7	8–10	11–12	13–15	16–18
Percentage who use library	86.1	93.8	79.0	58.1	43.6
8–10	ns				
11–12	ns	*			
13–15	*	*	*		
16–18	*	*	*	*	

Town differences at each age level were assessed by first calculating an overall χ^2 value for each age group. If this was significant, paired comparisons were conducted with the alpha level set at .05 for each set of comparisons. Town differences were found at the following age levels: 6–7 years, $\chi^2(2) = 19.22, p < .0001$, Multitel (70.7%) less than both Notel (92.7%) and Unitel (98.1%); 8–10 years of age, $\chi^2(2) = 13.90, p < .001$, Multitel (100%) greater than Unitel (86.5%), and Notel not different from the other towns (95.8%); 13–15 years, $\chi^2(2) = 9.75, p < .01$, Notel (70.4%) greater than both Unitel (51.5%) and Multitel (53.4%).

[32] An unweighted means cross-sectional ANOVA on the reported number of books read per month for Town × Sex × Age Level yielded significant main effects for sex, $F(1,1174) = 17.82, p < .001$; and age, $F(4,1174) = 18.32, p < .001$. The Town × Age interaction, $F(8,1174) = 2.60, p < .008$ also was significant. Girls reported reading more books per month (8.09) than boys (5.72). The means for the 6–7, 8–10, 11–12, 13–15, and 16–18 year age groups were 9.93, 9.40, 6.60, 4.25, and 4.35, respectively. The youngest group reported reading more books than all but the 8–10 year group ($p < .01$ by Tukey test in each case). The 8–10-year-olds also read more books than the three oldest groups ($p < .01$ by Tukey test by comparison with 13–15- and 16–18-year-olds; $p < .05$ by comparison with 11–12-year-olds).

Simple main effects analyses on the Town × Age interaction revealed significant town differences for the 6–7 year age group, $F(2,1174) = 5.97$, $p < .005$ and the 11–12-year-olds, $F(2,1174) = 3.34$, $p < .05$. In the youngest group, Multitel students (12.88 books per month) reported reading more books than both Unitel (9.21 books; $p < .05$ by Tukey test) and Notel (7.70 books; $p < .01$ by Tukey test) students. Among 11–12-year-olds, Unitel children reported more book reading (8.29 books per month) than Multitel children (4.40 books per month; $p < .05$ by Tukey test). Notel children did not differ (7.09 books per month) from either Unitel or Multitel.

[33] More Unitel children (84.7%) than Multitel children (77.7%) reported ever reading comic books, $\chi^2(2) = 7.38$, $p < .04$). Notel children (79.6%) did not differ from children in the other towns.

[34] There were significant differences among the towns for children who indicated they usually found out about the news from one source, $\chi^2(2) = 19.88$, $p < .001$. Fewer Multitel children (32.8%) than Notel children (53.1%); $\chi^2 = 18.82$, $p < .001$) and Unitel children (46%; $\chi^2 = 8.78$, $p < .02$) named television as their usual sole source.

[35] In an unweighted means cross-sectional ANOVA on number of books read per month for Town × Sex × Age (19–35, 36–55, and 56+) there was a significant main effect for town, $F(2,539) = 8.61$, $p < .001$. The Sex × Age interaction also was significant, $F(2,539) = 6.96$, $p < .001$. Multitel adults reported reading significantly fewer books per month (2.36) than adults in both Notel (4.68) and Unitel (4.39; $p < .01$ by Tukey test for both comparisons).

Simple main effects analyses of the Sex × Age interaction revealed that book reading by women did not differ significantly by age (4.51, 4.47, and 3.14 books per month for the 19–35, 36–55, and 56+ age groups, respectively) but for men it did, $F(2,539) = 6.63$, $p < .005$. Males over 55 years of age read more books (5.15 books per month) than middle-aged males (2.01 books per month; $p < .01$ by Tukey test). Young males (19–35 years old) did not differ from either of the other groups (3.57 books per month). Middle-aged women read more books than middle-aged men, $F(1,539) = 8.19$, $p < .005$, but mature men read more than mature women, $F(1,539) = 5.42$, $p < .05$.

[36] A Town (3) by Library Use (yes/no) contingency table resulted in a significant overall $\chi^2(2) = 10.51$, $p < .005$. Fewer Multitel (25.5%) than Unitel (40.4%) and Notel (34.1%) adults reported using their town library.

[37] A Town (3) by Magazine Use (yes/no) contingency table resulted in a significant overall effect, $\chi^2(2) = 6.54$, $p < .04$. Multitel adults did not differ from the other towns in this regard (89% reported ever reading magazines), but more Notel adults reported reading magazines (92%) than did Unitel residents (84%; $p < .04$).

[38] A Town (3) × Frequency of Newspaper Reading (daily vs. less than daily) contingency table yielded a significant overall effect, $\chi^2(2) = 137.9$, $p < .001$. More Multitel adults (74%) reported reading the paper daily than was the case for Notel adults (38%), of whom more reported such reading than adults in Unitel (21%).

[39] An unweighted means cross-sectional ANOVA was run on Phase 2 hours of TV viewed per week for Town × IQ Level (100 or below vs. 101 or above) × Grade Level (3–5, 6–9, and 10–12). This analysis was restricted to students with a working TV set at home. Significant main effects were found for town, $F(2,618) = 10.97$, $p < .001$; IQ level, $F(1,618) = 10.82$, $p < .001$; and grade level, $F(2,618) = 10.99$, $p < .001$. Multitel students (29.29 hours per week) reported watching more TV than both Notel (24.79 hours; $p < .005$ by Tukey test) and Unitel (25.02 hours; $p < .005$ by Tukey test) students, who did not differ.

The three-way interaction of town, IQ, and grade also was significant, $F(4,618) = 2.57$, $p < .04$. When simple main effects analyses were conducted to determine whether there were IQ differences for each town and grade level combination, significant differences occurred only for Notel third to fifth graders, $F(1,618) = 6.75$, $p < .01$ (above average IQ students watched 22.56 hours per week by comparison with 29.45 for below average IQ students) and sixth to eighth graders, $F(1,618) = 7.85$, $p < .01$ (higher IQ mean, 23.2 hours; lower IQ mean, 30.6 hours per week). When simple main effects analyses were conducted to determine whether the towns differed at any combination of IQ and grade level, significant differences were found for the grade 3–5 above average IQ group, $F(2,618) = 5.99$, p .01: Multitel (31.63 hours) watched more than Notel (22.56 hours; $p < .01$ by Tukey test); and Unitel (28.31 hours; $p < .05$ by Newman–Keuls) differed from Notel, but not from Multitel. Town differences also occurred for the grade 9–12 below average IQ group, $F(2,618) = 7.88$, $p < .001$. Here, Multitel students (29.98 hours) watched more than both Notel (19.53 hours; $p < .01$ by Tukey test) and Unitel students (23.56 hours; $p < .05$ by Tukey test), who did not differ.

[40] The sample size for students with IQ data did not enable us to conduct the preceding ANOVA on more than two IQ groups. We therefore did a separate analysis on four IQ groups (85, 85–100, 101–115, and 115), asking whether there was a significant linear or quadratic relationship in the mean hours of TV viewing for these four groups. The main effect of IQ group was significant, $F(3,632) = 5.85$, $p < .001$, and the means (from lowest to highest IQ) of 29.41, 28.01, 25.79, and 23.73 hours, respectively, formed a significant linear trend, $F(1,632) = 15.22$, $p < .0001$. The highest IQ group watched less TV than the lowest ($p < .01$ by Tukey test) and second lowest ($p < .05$ by Tukey test) IQ groups, and the second highest IQ group also watched less than the lowest IQ group ($p < .05$ by Tukey test).

REFERENCES

Allen, C. L. Photographing the TV audience. *Journal of Advertising Research*, 1965, 5, 2–8.

Anderson, D. R. Home television viewing by preschool children and their families. In A. C. Huston (Chair), *The ecology of children's television use*. Symposium presented at the meeting of the Society for Research in Child Development, Detroit, April 1983.

Bechtel, R. B., Achelpol, C., & Akers, R. Correlates between observed behavior and questionnaire responses on television viewing. In E. A. Rubinstein, G. A. Comstock, & J. P. Murray (Eds.), *Television and social behavior: Vol. 4. Television in day-to-day life: Patterns of use*. Washington, D.C.: U.S. Government Printing Office, 1972.

Bryant, J., & Anderson, D. R. *Children's understanding of television: Research on attention and comprehension*. New York: Academic Press, 1983.

Chaffee, S. H. Mass media effects: New research perspectives. In D. Lerner & L. Nelson (Eds.), *Communication research—a half century appraisal*. Honolulu: East–West Center Press, 1977.

Comstock, G., Chaffee, S., Katzman, N., McCombs, M., & Roberts, D. *Television and human behavior*. New York: Columbia University Press, 1978.

Fetler, M. *Television viewing habits and school achievement*. Paper presented at the meeting of the American Educational Research Association, New York, March 1982.

Fraisse, P. *The psychology of time*. New York: Harper & Row, 1963.

Gerbner, G., Gross, L., Signorielli, N., Morgan, M., & Jackson-Beeck, M. The demonstration of power: Violence profile no. 10. *Journal of Communication*, 1979, 29(3), 177–196.

Himmelweit, H. T., Oppenheim, A. N., & Vince, P. *Television and the child*. London: Oxford University Press, 1958.

Hirsch, P. The "scary world" of the nonviewer and other anomalies: A reanalysis of Gerbner et al.'s findings of cultivation analysis. *Communication Research*, 1980, 7, 403–456.

Lull, J. *The origins and consequences of adolescent mass media use*. Paper presented at the meeting of the International Communication Association, Dallas, May 1983.

Marascuilo, L. A. Large-sample multiple comparisons. *Psychological Bulletin*, 1966, *65*, 280–290.

Medrich, E. A. Constant television: A background to daily life. *Journal of Communication*, 1979, *29*(3), 171–176.

Murray, J. P., & Kippax, S. Television diffusion and social behaviour in three communities: A field experiment. *Australian Journal of Psychology*, 1977, *29*(1), 31–43.

Pearl, D., Bouthilet, L., & Lazar, J. (Eds.), *Television and behavior: Ten years of scientific progress and implications for the eighties*. Vols. 1 and 2. Rockville, Md.: NIMH, 1982.

Piaget, J. *The child's conception of time* (A. S. Pomerans, Trans.). New York: Basic Books, 1970. (Translation originally published, 1969.)

Roberts, D. F., Bachen, C. M., Hornby, M. C., & Hernandez-Ramos, P. Reading and television: Predictors of reading achievement at different age levels. *Communication Research*, 1984, *11*, 9–49.

Robinson, J. P. The changing reading habits of the American public. *Journal of Communication*, 1980, *30*(1), 141–152.

Roper Organization, Inc. *Trends in public attitudes toward television and other mass media, 1959–1974*. New York: Television Information Office, 1975.

Salomon, G. Introducing AIME: The assessment of children's mental involvement with television. *New Directions for Child Development*, 1981, No. 13, 89–102.

Salomon, G. Television watching and mental effort: A social psychological view. In J. Bryant & D. R. Anderson (Eds.), *Children's understanding of television: Research on attention and comprehension*. New York: Academic Press, 1983.

Statistics Canada. *The labour force* (Catalogue Number 71-001). December, 1974.

von Feilitzen, C. The functions served by the media. In R. Brown (Ed.), *Children and television*. Beverly Hills, Calif.: Sage, 1976.

Williams, T. M., Zabrack, M. L., & Joy, L. A. A content analysis of entertainment television programming. In *Report of the Ontario Royal Commission on Violence in the Communications Industry*, Vol. 3. Toronto, 1977.

Williams, T. M., Zabrack, M. L., & Joy, L. A. The portrayal of aggression on North American television. *Journal of Applied Social Psychology*, 1982, *12*(5), 360–380.

$$6$$

TELEVISION AND
SEX-ROLE ATTITUDES

Meredith M. Kimball

INTRODUCTION

Television has become an important agent of socialization in North American culture (Rushton, 1982). When we ask how television teaches its viewers about social relationships and social beliefs, we are asking about the effects of television's content rather than its effects via displacement. The content of television and its impact have been studied in terms of at least five social roles—sex roles, family roles, race roles, job roles, and age roles (Greenberg, 1982). This chapter focuses on sex roles, that is, guidelines for each sex in the realms of behavior, dress, attitudes, aspirations, and achievement.

The ways in which women, men, boys, and girls are portrayed on television have been well documented. The impact of these portrayals has been less well documented, but some effects of television on sex-role stereotypes have been demonstrated. One difficulty in evaluating long-term effects, however, is that other media sources and real life also provide sex-role models, and to the extent that portrayals on TV coincide with these other sources, their separate influence is difficult to ascertain (see Pingree & Hawkins, 1980; Siegel, 1982). Almost all of the research dealing with television's influence on sex-role attitudes and behavior has been conducted on regular viewers. Indeed, Pingree and Hawkins (1980) note that unexposed, representative control groups are impossible to find.

Thus, the opportunity to study Notel, Unitel, and Multitel before and after the arrival of television in Notel promised to shed new light on television's impact on children's sex-role attitudes and perceptions relatively independently of the impact of other influences.

Television is one of the most important sources of models in North American society. Children probably are exposed to more models through television than through any other medium, and some children may spend more time watching TV than they spend in the presence of their parents. How important are these models?

Although theorists differ on other details of the process, most assume models play a central part in children's sex-role development by providing examples of behavior which children imitate as they take on the roles established by society for their sex (Bem, 1981; Kagan, 1958; Kohlberg, 1966; Martin & Halverson, 1981; Mischel, 1970). Maccoby and Jacklin (1974) have raised some questions about the effects of models on preschool children's learning of specific sex-role behaviors, based in part on the fact that young children express sex-typed attitudes and behaviors before they imitate same-sex models in the laboratory. Nevertheless, there is general agreement that sex-role models exist and are important for sex-role development.

It is not sufficient, however, to state that models are important. Understanding the links between observing a model and the child's (or adult's) resulting attitudes and behaviors requires two kinds of information: what is shown and how that affects the observer. First, it is important to know, in as much detail as possible, what models are available. How do the models behave? What roles do they portray? What attitudes do they express? The next section of this chapter addresses this point. A subsequent section, "The Effects of Televised Portrayals on Sex-Role Attitudes and Behavior," summarizes what is known about the effects of televised models on the attitudes and behaviors of people who watch them. Finally, we describe how we studied television's impact on the sex-role attitudes of children in Notel, Unitel and Multitel, what we found, and the implications of those results.

THE PORTRAYAL OF WOMEN AND MEN ON TV

Researchers interested in objectively analyzing television's portrayal of the sexes have conducted numerous studies documenting the behavior of women and men on TV. Over a period of more than 25 years (Greenberg, 1980, 1982; Head, 1954), content analyses have revealed that the portrayal of men and women on TV has remained remarkably constant, providing a traditional and conservative view of sex roles in our society.

Preponderance of Male Characters

One of the most consistent findings is the percentage by which men outnumber women on television.[1] This holds true for programming aimed at both children and adults. In 1954, Head reported that 68% of the major characters in adult television programs were men. This imbalance has not changed; the percentage of male characters has remained remarkably close to 70% over the intervening years (Greenberg, Richards, & Henderson, 1980; McNeil, 1975; Tedesco, 1974; Turow, 1974; Williams, Zabrack, & Joy, 1977).

There is some variation in the ratio of men to women according to type of program involved, but women never exceed men. Females are more under-represented in drama and crime programs than in comedy and variety programs (Henderson, Greenberg, & Atkin, 1980; McNeil, 1975; Williams et al., 1977). The only category of adult programming in which men and women tend to appear in equal numbers is the daytime serial, or soap opera. Katzman (1972) found 192 male characters and 179 female characters in a sample of daytime programs. Downing (1974) found 129 female and 127 male characters on daytime serial programs.

In children's programming male characters are, if anything, even more over-represented than in adult programming. Williams et al. (1977) found that 74% of the characters in cartoons and 76% of the characters in non-animated children's programs were male. Busby (1974) reported that 80% of the minor characters and 72% of the major characters were males, and Sternglanz and Serbin (1974) found that 67% of the characters in children's shows were male.[2]

Some researchers have asked whether the proportions of men and women on television have changed over the years. Dominick (1979) surveyed the number of male and female starring characters from 1953 to 1977. The highest percentage of female starring characters occurred in 1955 (slightly over 40%). Since then the percentage of female characters has averaged right around 30%. Other studies over shorter time spans also have found that the percentage of female characters may vary slightly but never exceeds 31% (Greenberg et al., 1980; O'Donnell & O'Donnell, 1978; Seggar, 1977).

In sum, there are more than twice as many male as female models on TV, and when women do appear, they are most frequently found in comedy and light entertainment programs. Furthermore, this situation has remained constant over time.

Sex-Role Stereotypes on Television

Male and female characters on television tend to be portrayed in stereotyped ways. For example, women on TV are more likely than men to be younger (Aronoff, 1974; Katzman, 1972; Williams et al., 1977) and to be uniformly attractive (Long & Simon, 1974). Two other types of TV sex-role stereotypes on which researchers have focused are occupational stereotypes and family role stereotypes.

OCCUPATIONAL STEREOTYPES

Women on TV are employed less often than either men on TV or their female counterparts in real life. Several researchers have studied employment patterns portrayed on prime-time television, that is, programs aired during the evening hours when the TV audience peaks. De Fleur (1964) found that women made up 16% of the occupational portrayals on television. Nine years later Seggar and Wheeler (1973) found the situation to be essentially the same at 18%. Female TV characters are more likely to be employed if they are unmarried (up to 60%) than if they are married (up to 21%) (Busby, 1974; Long & Simon, 1974; McNeil, 1975; Tedesco, 1974). By comparison with the television figures, Canadian data for 1982 indicated that 51.6% of all Canadian women and 48.9% of all married women were employed (Armstrong, 1984). Data for the United States indicate that 50.1% of married women were employed in 1979 (*Statistical Abstract of the United States*, 1980).

The kinds of jobs held by TV characters also tend to be stereotyped. Women on TV are employed primarily in clerical, nursing, entertainment, and service jobs (Downing, 1974; Katzman, 1972; McNeil, 1975; Seggar & Wheeler, 1973). In contrast, men are employed as professionals (mostly physicians and lawyers), law enforcement officers, and managers (Downing, 1974; Katzman, 1972; McNeil, 1975). Further, men are portrayed in a wider range of occupations and roles than are women (Busby, 1974; Seggar & Wheeler, 1973). Men are less likely to be supervised (33%) than women (56%), and 90% of the supervisors seen on television are male (McNeil, 1975). A man's employment status is more likely to be clearly indicated than is a woman's (Downing, 1974), implying that it is more important to know employment status for men than for women. Finally, Dominick (1979) found that the occupational roles of men and women on television changed very little between 1953 and 1979.

FAMILY STEREOTYPES

One societal stereotype holds that family and personal relationships are more important for women than for men. Television reinforces this stereotype by more frequently indicating marital status for women (Downing, 1974; McNeil, 1975; Williams et al., 1977). Katzman (1972) found that women's TV conversations tended to focus on family, romantic, health, and domestic issues; men more often discussed professional and business concerns. Similarly, McNeil (1975) found that 74% of female interactions by comparison with 38% of male interactions focused on personal concerns, and 39% of male interactions by comparison with 15% of female interactions focused on professional concerns. In the world of television, "Men are often without family connections but rarely without a career; women are rarely without personal ties but often without a career" (McNeil, 1975, p. 268).

STEREOTYPES ABOUT PERSONALITY CHARACTERISTICS AND SOCIAL INTERACTION

The personalities of women and men on television also reflect cultural stereotypes. Women are less likely to be portrayed as bad; men are the aggressors and women the victims. For children's shows, Sternglanz and Serbin (1974) found that 27% of the males played evil characters compared with 4% of the females. Williams et al. (1977) found that women were more likely to be portrayed as emotional, predictable, clean, good, nonviolent, sexually attractive, interesting, and warm, whereas men were portrayed more often as unemotional, dishonest, immoral, bad, violent, and competent.

Personality traits have been assessed in three content analyses of children's programming. Sternglanz and Serbin (1974) found that males were more likely to be aggressive, constructive, and provide aid to those in need, whereas women were more likely to behave deferentially and to be punished for high levels of activity. Busby (1974) rated each character in children's programs on a number of dimensions, (e.g., strong versus weak, good versus bad). She found two distinct groups of men—husbands and heroes. By comparison with heroes, husbands were less helpful, less cultured, less intelligent, more quarrelsome, less logical, and less patient. However, both groups of men differed from women more than they did from each other. Of 40 items, 24 were rated differently for male and female characters. Of these 24 items, 13 are similar or identical to those used by Broverman, Vogel, Broverman, Clarkson, and Rosenkrantz (1972) to study sex-role stereotypes (e.g., males are more aggressive, logical, unemotional; females are more sensitive, submissive, and tied to the home). The others fit well with generally accepted stereotypes (e.g., males are more knowledgeable, brave, bold; females are more timid, fragile, romantic). Busby (1974) found that female villains were often portrayed as sex-role reversed, that is, they were physically larger than the males and scored high on dominance, aggression, and activity. McArthur and Eisen (1976) found that male characters on children's programs displayed more autonomy and aggression and received more consequences for their behavior than did female characters. Female characters were more likely than male characters to display nurturant and social behavior.

The possible exception to this picture is the daytime serial, the only type of program in which women appear as frequently as men. In addition, the setting is domestic, traditionally a place in which women exercise power. Downing (1974) concluded that women in soap operas are respected, act independently, participate as responsible members of their families, and exercise judgments respected by others. They are stronger than the typical woman on prime-time or children's programs. However, it may be that the woman in the daytime serial looks different only because she conforms to a different stereotype. Downing says, "Serial housewives—always immaculately groomed and coiffed—have as a major goal the happiness and well-being of their families. They exhibit never-ending understanding toward members of both older and younger generations, and offer continuous comfort to their husbands, all of whose concerns they insist on sharing" (1974, p. 136). In her study of who gives advice in prime-time and daytime television, Turow (1974) concluded that although women are more central and have a larger percentage of the parts in daytime programs, the stereotypes remain as strong. Women are given as little chance in daytime as in prime-time programs to display superior knowledge, and when they are given a chance it is often in traditional areas, for example, nursing.

The televised interactions of women and men over a 3-year period (1975–1977) were studied by Greenberg et al. (1980). They found that males were more likely than females to give orders, especially when in positions of authority. The difference was largest for crime and adventure programs and on Saturday morning (i.e., children's) programming and smallest for situation comedies. Women were found to request emotional support significantly more often than men, whereas male characters were significantly more likely not to request support in situations in which they might have done so. Overall, females constituted 27% of the TV characters but they displayed 40% of the emotional support needs. The stereotyping of women and men with regard to giving orders and asking for support from others did not change over time, leading Greenberg et al. to comment, "Sex-role stereotyping does not appear to have undergone any deliberate, accidental, or even random changes in the three years reflected in these data" (p. 86).

STEREOTYPES ABOUT EVERYDAY BEHAVIORS

Stereotyping in the portrayal of common, everyday behaviors was studied by Henderson and Greenberg (1980). Females were portrayed doing disproportionately more entertaining of others, preparing and serving food, and performing indoor housework. Taking into account the proportions of each sex on television, females did less driving, participating in sports, conducting of business on the phone, drinking, and smoking, and they also used firearms less.

VICTIMIZATION

Although women are less likely to be bad or aggressive and violent on television, they are more likely to be victims. Tedesco (1974) found that twice as many men as women were killers, and three times as many women as men were killed. Gerbner (1972) reported that a decline in the number of violent characters on prime-time and Saturday morning television from 1967 to 1969 consisted of a decrease in the number of violent females and male victims, thereby increasing the differential. In his view, this only further strengthened the symbolic function of violence as a demonstration of social power. Gerbner (as reported in Liebert & Schwartzberg, 1977) also found that among women, the single woman is victimized most of all. One exception to this picture is hostile humor. Stocking, Sapolsky, and Zillmann (1977) found that like men, women in prime-time programs made hostile humorous comments as often as they received them.

COMMERCIALS

The traditional view of sex roles presented in TV programs is further emphasized in commercials. Women and men are represented more equally in commercials than in programs (Halpern & Ethier, 1977; McArthur & Resko, 1975), but women seldom appear as authorities in commercials unless the ad is one for food, domestic products, or feminine-care products (Marecek et al., 1978).

Portrayals on CBC versus ABC, CBS, and NBC

Almost all of the content analyses of North American television have focused on the three major U.S. networks. The scanty evidence available indicates that sex-role portrayals on CBC are fairly similar to those on ABC, CBS, and NBC. First, many of the programs shown on CBC are from the U.S. networks, especially during the prime-time evening hours. Second, Halpern and Ethier (1977) examined several facets of sex-role portrayals on Canadian and U.S. channels, using programs taped in May 1976. There was some indication that Canadian-produced commercials may be less strongly sex-typed than those produced in the United States, but there also was considerable evidence of similarity (see Chapter 1 for further details).

Summary of Televised Sex-Role Portrayals

In commercials and in programs aimed at both children and adults, the personalities, interests, and concerns of women and men reflect quite accurately the cultural stereotypes of masculinity and femininity (Busby, 1974; Sternglanz & Serbin, 1974; Williams et al., 1977). Television implicitly furthers these stereotypes by misrepresenting the proportions of men and women who lead active lives in the real world. Both sexes are stereotyped on television, but females may be more stereotyped than males. If so, this may be because they are outnumbered; more female roles might result in more varied characterizations (Greenberg, 1982). Sex-role portrayals on CBC probably do not differ markedly from those an ABC, CBS, and NBC, but the evidence is limited and more content comparisons are needed.

THE EFFECTS OF TELEVISED PORTRAYALS ON SEX-ROLE ATTITUDES AND BEHAVIOR

How does the repetitive presentation of traditional sex roles affect the children and adults who watch then?

Investigators have used two different approaches to studying the effects of TV viewing on sex-role attitudes and behaviors. The first is based on the idea that the more people watch TV, the more closely will their ideas about sex roles match what is presented on TV. The results of several studies support this hypothesis. Beuf (1974) found that 3–6-year-old, heavy TV viewers were more likely than moderate viewers to say they would choose stereotyped careers when they grew up. Frueh and McGhee (1975) reported that children in kindergarten through sixth grade who were heavy TV viewers were more likely to make same-sex toy choices on a projective test than were light viewers. In a later study using the same children, McGhee and Frueh (1980) found that by comparison with light viewers, heavy viewers gave more stereotyped answers to questions about sex-role stereotypes on the Williams and Bennett (1975) scale.

One problem with this kind of research is the difficulty of disentangling the effects of television from the influences of the rest of society. The messages offered by books, school, peers, parents, and television are similar. A second problem is the difficulty of making causal inferences. Morgan's (1982) 2-year longitudinal study of sixth through ninth graders dealt with both problems. For girls, amount of television viewing in the first year significantly predicted higher sexism scores in the second year, even after the influences of demographic variables (grade, IQ, socioeconomic status) and earlier sexism scores were controlled. Earlier TV viewing did not predict later sex-role attitudes for boys, but higher sexism scores in the first year did predict more TV viewing in the second year, even after earlier TV viewing and demographic variables were controlled. These results suggest that the causal connections between television viewing and sex-role stereotypes can operate in both directions. That is, television viewing may lead to more stereotypic attitudes, and people with more stereotypic attitudes may watch more television than do those with less stereotypic attitudes. Television viewing was most likely to influence the sex-role attitudes of groups who held the least traditional views (more intelligent girls and those of higher socioeconomic status) and least likely to influence groups with the most traditional views (boys, lower socioeconomic status girls and less intelligent girls). It may be that the sexism scores of the children who held very traditional views were so high to begin with that there was very little chance for TV to produce an effect.

The second approach to studying the effects of television on sex-role attitudes isolates the influence of television by portraying women and men in counter-stereotypical roles (e.g., women taking charge, men looking after babies) and observing whether changes in attitude or behavior occur following exposure to these nontraditional models. This kind of research has been done with special programming both in the laboratory and in field studies.

The results of the studies involving nontraditional models also have been consistent. Davidson, Yasuna, and Tower (1979) found that 5- and 6-year-old girls who watched a $\frac{1}{2}$-hour children's program in which sex roles were reversed gave less stereotyped answers to the Williams and Bennett scale (1975) than girls who had seen either a neutral or a highly stereotyped children's program. The lower scores of the girls who saw the role reversals were due mainly to less stereotyped answers on the feminine items of the scale. McArthur and Eisen (1976) showed preschool children a 9-minute TV skit in which the sex roles were either traditional or reversed. After viewing one of the skits, the child was given a chance to play with the toys seen in the film, questioned to find out how well she or he remembered what had happened in the film, and asked which activities in the film they liked best. The boys recalled and reproduced more activities of the male model even when he engaged in sex-role reversal behavior. The results for the girls were similar but not as strong. Atkin and Miller (1975) found that grade-school children who saw a $\frac{1}{2}$-hour cartoon in which role-reversed commercials had been inserted were more likely to describe the nontraditional occupations portrayed in the commercials as appropriate for women than were children who saw the same cartoon but with stereotypical commercials. Pingree (1978) also obtained some evidence that children exposed to commercials portraying women in nontraditional occupations gave less traditional responses to questions about appropriate sex-role behavior. Miller and Reeves (1976) found that third through sixth graders who recognized female characters who played counter-stereotypical roles on TV (two police officers, a park ranger, a high school principal, and a TV news producer) were more likely to consider these occupations to be appropriate for women than were children who did not recognize the characters. Another attempt to study the effect of counter-stereotypical altitudes was the series "Freestyle," which was designed to reduce sex-role stereotyping by 9- and 12-year-olds and to increase awareness of career possibilities for girls. An evaluation of this series indicated that, relative to control groups, students from different U.S. sites became more approving of nontraditional roles for girls and less stereotypical in their perceptions of nontraditional sex-role behavior for both females and males (Johnston & Ettema, 1982). A follow-up indicated that when the program was seen in school and accompanied by classroom discussion, the effect persisted for more than 60% of the students up to 9 months after exposure.

The counter-stereotype approach has been used with adults as well as children. Jennings, Geis, and Brown (1980) showed female undergraduates commercials that were either sex-role traditional or sex-role reversed and found that women who saw the role-reversed commercials were more independent in their judgments of cartoons and behaved more confidently than women who saw the traditional commercials. Geis et al. (1979, cited in Jennings et al., 1980) reported that women shown traditional commercials expressed fewer career aspirations than those seeing role-reversed commercials. There were no effects for men.

In sum, researchers have demonstrated that television characters are stereotyped in terms of both the proportions and ways in which men and women are portrayed. These portrayals have been remarkably consistent over time. Studies conducted both with traditionally oriented material and counter-stereotypical content indicate that children and adults are influenced by these portrayals.

THE DESIGN OF THIS STUDY

The design of this study involves a third kind of approach to asking whether exposure to television influences viewers' sex-role attitudes. It was a naturalistic, or field, study in that we assessed the effects of exposure to normal television diets rather than special programming involving counter-stereotypical portrayals. It differed from earlier studies, however, because in Phase 1, Notel residents did not regularly watch television. It was therefore possible to assess television's influence on residents' sex-role attitudes relatively independently of other influences.

Measures and Hypotheses

Sex-role perceptions were measured with part of the Sex Role Differentiation (SRD) scale developed by Lambert (1971). This scale has two sections, a set of Peer Scales asking children to rate how appropriate or frequent certain behaviors are for boys and girls their own age, and a set of Parent Scales asking children to rate how frequently their own mother and father perform certain tasks.

We hypothesized that before the introduction of television, Notel children would express less traditional sex-role attitudes on the SRD Peer Scales than students in Unitel and Multitel. We also expected that after Notel had had television for 2 years, children's (Peer Scale) sex-role attitudes would have become more stereotyped, whereas no such change would occur in Unitel or Multitel. Predictions about students' perceptions of their parents' division of household and child-rearing tasks were more difficult to make. It is possible that stereotyped portrayals on television affect parents' behavior in these areas, but this would not necessarily imply a change in children's perceptions of their parents' behavior. Conversely, children's perceptions might change even if their parents' behavior was not influenced by television.

Peer Scales.   The Peer Scales consist of 61 items spread across five subscales (Traits, Behaviors, Jobs, Peer Relations, and Authority Relations). The items require the child to rate how typical certain behaviors and characteristics are of boys their own age and how typical those same behaviors are of girls their own age. For each of the 61 items the child must say how true that item is (ranging from 1, not true, to 7, very true) for boys their age, and then again rate the item for girls their age. The instructions, a sample item, and a list of all the items are in the Appendix.

Scoring.   The items are scored as the absolute difference between the two ratings. For example, a child might have thought that girls their age are quite hardworking and rate them as 6. The same child might believe boys to be less hardworking and rate them as 2. The child's score for that item would be 4. Similarly, if a child rated girls as 2 and boys as 6, his or her score also would be 4. The maximum score for an item is 6, the minimum, 0. The scores are summed across the items to produce a score for each of the five peer subscales and a total peer score.

High scores on the SRD scales reflect a tendency to segregate the sexes socially and psychologically, whereas low scores indicate a tendency to perceive the sexes more equally or similarly. In other words, the Peer Scales measure gender salience, not gender stereotypes, in the sense discussed by Bem (1981). She contends that for highly sex-typed people, gender is a dominant organizer or schema applied to many situations, whereas gender is less salient for people who are not strongly sex typed. Although it is theoretically possible for a high score on the SRD scale to result from either stereotyped or counter-stereotyped responses, the majority of the responses in which different ratings were given to girls and boys in this study were, as expected, in the stereotyped direction (between 60% and 90%, depending upon the subscale).

Parent Scale.   The same procedure is used for rating and scoring the 41 Parent Scale items, except in this case children are asked about their own mother's (or stepmother's) behavior and their own father's (or stepfather's) behavior. The Parent Scale has four subscales, Activities, Discipline, Support, and Power. The instructions and items for the Parent Scales are in the Appendix.

Procedures and Children Tested

The SRD scales were administered to all students in grades 6 and 9 in each of the three towns both before and 2 years after television reception began in Notel. To ascertain the generalizability of our findings to urban populations we also analyzed data for a group of fifth- and eighth-grade

Vancouver children who had previously completed the SRD scale (Kimball & Harrison, 1973).[3] The Vancouver students were tested in March 1973, 8 months prior to the first phase of testing in Notel, Unitel, and Multitel.

All children completed the questionnaire in their classrooms, taking about 40 minutes to do both scales. Their questions, if any, were answered by the researchers administering the questionnaire.

Occasionally, students left one or several items blank. If only 1 item in one of the five Peer or four Parent subscales was blank, the average score for the other items on that subscale was assigned to the missing item. If more than 1 item was blank, we omitted both that subscale for that child and the relevant total score (peer or parent) from the analyses. Because of missing data, 27 peer scores (14 from Notel, 6 from Unitel, and 7 from Multitel) and 38 parent scores (16 from Notel, 11 from Unitel, and 11 from Multitel) were eliminated. In addition, occasionally a child used only the extreme ends of the 1–7 scale to answer all or most of the items, and sometimes a child used only a single response (most often 1 or 7). These students either did not understand the instructions or took the task less seriously than was expected; in either case their answers were not meaningful and could be misleading. Accordingly, if more than 85% of the peer or parent items on any questionnaire were answered in this way, we did not use the relevant score in the analyses. Following this rule, 15 peer scores (6 from Notel and 9 from Unitel) and 23 parent scores (6 from Notel, 16 from Unitel, and 1 from Multitel) were eliminated. For the analyses done separately for each sex, we also eliminated three Notel children who did not put their sex on the questionnaire.

After some peer and parent scores had been eliminated according to the guidelines outlined above, a total of 536 children completed the Peer Scales (130 from Notel, 135 from Unitel, 166 from Multitel, and 105 from Vancouver), and a total of 517 children completed the Parent Scales (129 from Notel, 123 from Unitel, 160 from Multitel, and 105 from Vancouver).

In a departure from the procedures used in other studies in this project, the students' responses in this study were completely anonymous. This was done because the children were asked questions about their parents' behavior. As a result, only cross-sectional comparisons could be made. In addition, we could not examine the sex-role data in relation to information obtained in other studies from the same students.

RESULTS FOR PEER SCALES

In analyzing the data, we first asked whether the Peer total scores varied according to the child's town, sex, grade, and/or the phase of the study. There was an overall sex difference. In general, averaging across

Meredith M. Kimball

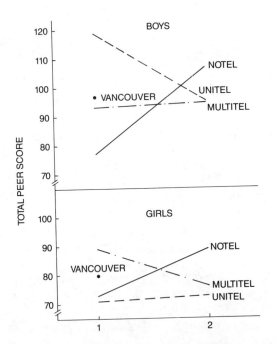

FIGURE 6.1   Peer sex-role perception mean total scores for girls and boys in each town and phase.

towns, grades, and phases of the study, girls held less strongly sex-typed attitudes than boys and perceived the sexes to be more similar. Specifically, this sex difference occured in Unitel in Phase 1 and in all three towns in Phase 2.[4] The remaining analyses, which examined differences among the three towns and between the two phases of the study, were done separately for girls and boys.[5]

For girls, Peer total scores varied according to the town and phase of the study.[6] These results are shown in Figure 6.1; the means are presented in Table 6.A1. Before Notel had television, gender was a less salient dimension of girls' sex-role perceptions than it was for girls in Multitel. The girls in Unitel also had less strongly sex-typed views that the Multitel girls. Two years after the introduction of TV, the Notel girls' perceptions had become significantly more sex typed and were now, along with those of Unitel girls, similar to the perceptions of Multitel girls. The scores of the Unitel girls did not change significantly between Phase 1 and Phase 2. Although there was a marginally statistically significant decrease ($p < .10$) for the Multitel girls, since this change had not been predicted, it was not interpreted as significant.[6] Taken together, the results for girls were consistent with the hypothesis that television affects sex-role perceptions.

The boy's Peer total scores also varied according to the town and phase of the study (Figure 6.1; the means are in Table 6.A1).[7] Before television, the boys in Notel were less sex typed than boys in both Unitel and Multitel. The very high Phase 1 scores for Unitel boys are anomalous; possible explanations are discussed in the summary of this section, but we have no ready explanation for them. Two years after Notel obtained TV, gender had become significantly more salient for Notel boys and less salient for Unitel boys, by comparison with their age-mates assessed in Phase 1. In Phase 2 there were no significant differences in the perceptions of boys in the three towns. These findings also provide some support for the hypothesis that television affects sex-role attitudes.

The Peer total score was derived from the scores on five different Peer subscales. To ascertain how the different subscales contributed to the findings for the Peer total score just discussed, we analysed these subscale scores and found several differences (see Table 6.A2 for means).[8] The students' perceptions of their peers were most sex typed on the Jobs and Behaviors subscales, next most sex typed on the Traits subscale, and least sex typed on the Peer Relations and Authority Relations subscales. As with the Peer total scores, we found sex differences. In particular, boys' attitudes about peer behavior were more sex typed than the girls' attitudes on the Behaviors, Jobs, and Peer Relations subscales. Other differences in the subscale scores depended on the town, sex of the child, and phase of the study. The changes for Notel from Phase 1 to Phase 2 all involved increases in gender salience, whereas the changes in Unitel and Multitel involved decreases in sex typing. The following specific changes were statistically significant:

1. Notel girls' perceptions had become more sex typed on the Peer Relations and Authority Relations subscales;
2. Notel boys' perceptions had become more sex typed on the Behaviors and Jobs subscales;
3. The perceptions of Unitel boys and Multitel girls had become less sex typed on the Jobs subscale.

There were no significant changes from Phase 1 to Phase 2 for Unitel girls or Multitel boys.

Summary of Peer Results

Taken together, the bulk of the evidence for the Peer Scales lends support to both hypotheses. As predicted, before their town had television Notel students held more egalitarian sex-role attitudes than students who viewed television regularly. This was true of Notel boys compared with boys in Unitel and Multitel, and for Notel girls compared with girls in Multitel. The only inconsistency in Phase 1 was that Unitel girls' attitudes did not differ from Notel girls' attitudes, and thus girls in both towns gave less sex-typed responses than did Multitel girls. In Phase 2, girls in the three towns obtained similar scores, and the same was true for boys. The second hypothesis, that Notel students' sex-role perceptions would become more sex typed following the introduction of television, whereas the attitudes of Unitel and Multitel students would not change over the same period, also was generally borne out. The one exception was that the Unitel boys' perceptions became less sex typed over the 2 years.

The major anomalous finding for the Peer Scales was the extremely high Phase 1 scores and their subsequent decrease for Unitel boys. Might this decrease reflect a societal change in attitudes toward sex roles over the historical span of this study? Minimal support for this hypothesis can be found in the marginally significant decrease in the overall sex-typing score of the Multitel girls' attitudes, and significant decreases in sex typing on the Jobs subscale for Unitel boys and Multitel girls. There was, however, no decrease for Unitel girls or Multitel boys on any subscale or overall (total), as would be required to support clearly the hypothesis of historical change. The second anomaly was the finding that in Phase 1, Unitel girls' perceptions were less sex typed than those of Multitel girls, and not different from those of Notel girls. This might indicate that the content of CBC is less stereotypical than that of ABC, CBS, and NBC, but this hypothesis would require a different pattern of Phase 2 results. Although there is no obvious explanation for these two discrepant results (Unitel girls and boys in Phase 1), the weight of the findings support our hypotheses that the sex-role attitudes of Notel children would be initially less sex typed than the attitudes of students who had grown up with television, and would become more stereotyped following the introduction of television. The results were consistent with the hypotheses for 10 of the 12 data points involved.

RESULTS FOR PARENT SCALES

The only differences obtained for the Parent Scales related to gender, that is, whether it was girls or boys who were rating their parents' behavior.[9] The results are graphed in Figure 6.2; the means for significant effects are in Table 6.A3. On average, boys had more sex-typed perceptions than girls. That is, for the Parent total score (sum of the four Parent subscales), boys reported less sharing of various household and child-

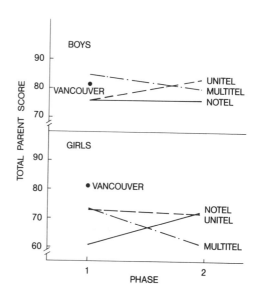

FIGURE 6.2 Parent sex-role perception mean total scores for girls and boys in each town and phase.

rearing tasks by their parents than did girls. This sex difference, however, was specific to grade 6 and did not occur in grade 9.

Some variations in the pattern of sex differences occurred among the four Parent subscales.[10] (The means are in Table 6.A4). Students rated their parents as sharing least on the Activities subscale, more on the Power and Discipline subscales, and most on the Support subscales. On all subscales, however, boys' perceptions of their parents' behavior were more stereotyped than girls' perceptions. Further analysis of the complex relationship among the Parent subscale scores showed that there was a sex difference for grade 6 students in both phases on the Activities subscale, and in Phase 2 in addition on the Discipline and Power subscales. For grade 9 students the only sex differences occurred in Phase 1 on the Activities subscale. In each case the boys' scores were higher than the girls', indicating they thought their parents shared less in each of these areas.

How might we explain the consistent sex difference in the children's perceptions of their parents' activities? One possibility is that parents of girls share more equitably than do parents of boys. Since many if not most of the children had siblings, many of whom would be of the opposite sex, this explanation seems unlikely. The finding that the sex difference in children's perceptions of their parents' behavior occurred for sixth graders but not for ninth graders lends weight instead to the hypothesis that the behavior of parents of sons and daughters is similar but is perceived differently by their children during middle childhood.

The Parent total scores did not vary according to the town or phase of the study. In other words, there was no evidence that exposure to television is associated with children's perceptions of their parents' behavior.

SEX DIFFERENCES

One of the most striking results was the consistency of sex differences in children's scores. On all of the Peer Scales except Authority Relations, girls considered the sexes to be more similar than did boys (i.e., girls' scores were lower than boys'). Sex differences also were found for the Parent total score and on all the Parent subscales. Using the same measures, Lambert (1971) also obtained higher scores for boys.

Why would gender be less salient for girls than for boys? One possible explanation is that females have more to gain from seeing the sexes as similar, since greater value traditionally has been accorded to masculine traits and behaviors in our society. Children learn this very early. Haugh, Hoffman, and Cowan (1980) found that 3-year-olds described an infant they had been told was a boy as smart, strong, hard, big, mad, fast, loud, and mean. Other 3-year-olds, who were told the same infant was a girl, described the baby as dumb, weak, soft, little, scared, slow, quiet, and nice. Since their sex is valued less, girls and women may be more willing than boys and men to engage in cross-sex behavior and to perceive the sexes as more similar.

Other research supports this argument. Brown (1958) found that only 2–4% of adult men compared to 20–31% of adult women recall having been consciously aware of wanting to be the opposite sex at some point in their life. Maccoby and Jacklin (1974) report several studies demonstrating that boys are less likely to play with attractive "opposite-sex" toys than are girls, especially if they know an adult is watching. Frueh and McGhee (1975) found that boys made more masculine toy choices than girls made feminine ones on a projective doll play test. Miller and Reeves (1976) found that boys were more likely to nominate same-sex TV characters as desirable models than were girls. None of the boys nominated opposite-sex characters, but 27% of the girls nominated one or more male models. When she asked 3–6-year-olds what they would want to be if they were the other sex, Beuf (1973) found that all of the girls had an answer, but many of the boys hadn't ever thought about it and were suspicious of the question. A typical comment by boys was, "That's a weird question, you know." Huston (1983) reviews additional studies demonstrating that boys' choices consistently are more extremely sex typed than those of girls.

Kohlberg (1966) has explained these and similar findings by invoking the concept of cognitive conflict in the sex-role development of girls. Working from Piaget's general theory of development, Kohlberg contends that all young children tend to value their own sex because of their egocentric nature. They see the world from their own point of view and are not yet able to take a variety of perspectives. At the same time, however, even very young children realize that society expects males and females to behave differently and are aware that masculinity usually is accorded higher prestige than femininity. Kohlberg argues that as a result of this value difference, girls experience cognitive conflict. Because of their egocentrism they value their own sex but at the same time they realize society places more value on males and on stereotypically masculine characteristics. Boys do not experience this conflict and therefore are less likely to choose opposite-sex activities or to think they would like to be a member of the other sex.

URBAN COMPARISON

The availability of SRD data collected in Vancouver enabled us to compare the sex-role attitudes of children in this study with the perceptions of children growing up in a large urban center (see note 3).

The Vancouver data were obtained from fifth and eighth graders, 8 months prior to the first phase data obtained from sixth and ninth graders in Notel, Unitel, and Multitel. Our analyses focused on whether Unitel, Multitel, and Vancouver children, all of whom had had television for several years, differed in their perceptions of peer and parent sex roles. Notel students were omitted since they were unique in having grown up without television. The results indicated that children who grow up with TV generally hold similar sex-role attitudes, whether they live in a small community or large metropolitan area.

When we asked whether scores on the SRD Peer and Parent scales differed according to town, sex, and grade, there were no differences related to grade.[11] We therefore felt justified in analyzing the Vancouver, Unitel, and Multitel data together even though the Vancouver students had been one grade level below the others when tested.

We next asked whether Peer and Parent total scores differed by town and/or sex. For the Peer scales we found that, just as was the case for Notel, Unitel, and Multitel, Vancouver boys had more traditional sex-role perceptions than Vancouver girls.[12] We also found that peer perceptions varied according to town, with Unitel students holding significantly more traditional sex-role attitudes than Multitel students. Vancouver students were in between and not significantly different from either Unitel or Multitel (see Figure 6.1 and Table 6.A5). The higher scores of Unitel students were, as discussed earlier, due to the anomalously high scores of Unitel boys.

On the Parent Scales, we found only marginally significant differences among the towns.[13] Vancouver and Multitel students were similar, and both perceived their parents as sharing household and child-rearing tasks marginally more equally than did Unitel students (see Figure 6.2 and Table 6.A5).

The analyses involving the Vancouver data indicate that students in the small towns we studied were generally similar to students in a large urban center, at least in terms of their sex-role perceptions.

HOW DO CHILDREN LEARN SEX ROLES FROM TV?

The results of this study offer some support for the hypothesis that television influences sex typing. The strongest results are those for the Notel students whose attitudes became more stereotyped after the introduction of television. What are the mechanisms or processes through which television affects sex-role perceptions and behavior? Does TV affect boys and girls differently? What ages are most susceptible to TV sex-role content? How does the form of the message influence children's understanding?

The common conception of the child viewer glued to the set passively taking in everything is being challenged by studies of how children watch TV and how much they understand of what they watch. Research conducted by Anderson and his colleagues (Anderson & Lorch, 1983; Lorch, Anderson, & Levin, 1979) indicates that children actively select what they watch according to their ability to process the information depicted. Krull and Husson (1979) also have offered a model to account for children's attention to television. Both models suggest it is unlikely that children learn sex-role attitudes from TV automatically; more likely the child actively attends to what are for her or him the relevant aspects of the program, one of which is the sex of the characters.

There is considerable evidence that both children and adults prefer same-sex characters and more accurately remember same-sex characters and their actions. Lyle and Hoffman (1972a) asked first graders if they liked each of 13 characters appearing on the most popular children's shows. More boys than girls reported liking all 11 male characters, whereas more girls than boys reported liking each of the 2 female characters. The girls and boys questioned spent an equal amount of time watching television. Joy, Kimball, and Zabrack (1977) showed grade 1 and grade 2 children a 3-minute videotape of two adults engaged in dramatic action. After viewing the film, the children were asked a series of questions including, "Who did you like better—John or Mary?" Of the boys, 71% chose John, and 85% of the girls chose Mary. Maccoby and Wilson (1957) found that grade 7 girls and boys identified with the same-sex character in a movie. They were asked: Which character is most like you? Which part would you most like to play? Which character would you most like to be? Ninety percent of the girls and 84% of the boys answered the majority of these questions with the same-sex character from the movie. Sprafkin and Leibert (1978) found that when the theme of a television program dealt with sex-typed content, children attended to programs featuring a central character of their own sex more than one featuring the other sex. Maccoby, Wilson, and Burton (1958) found that in each of two movies, adult men spent more time watching the male character while women spent more time watching the female character. This difference was accounted for by a time lag in shifting attention to the opposite-sex character when he or she began to talk and by momentary shifts back to the same-sex character while the other was talking. In other words, the time preference for the same-sex character occurred because viewers watched the same-sex character's reactions to what was being said by the opposite-sex character.

Researchers also have found that children are better able to recognize same-sex characters and behaviors. Lyle and Hoffman (1972b) found that more 3–5-year-old boys than girls correctly recognized 13 of 15 male characters tested, and more girls than boys correctly identified 5 female characters. Maccoby and Wilson (1957) found that after viewing a film, grade 7 boys remembered more of the material in which only a boy was depicted. They also remembered more of the aggressive content if the boy had been the agent of aggression. The girls remembered more of the content depicting girls alone and more depicting girls in interaction. Donahue (1976) reported that adult women found a violent film more disorganized than did men. It may be that differential perception of aggression occurs because males pay more attention to it and thus see more consistency and organization in violent episodes.

In sum, there is evidence that both children and adults attend differentially to TV characters according to their sex, prefer same-sex characters, and more accurately remember same-sex characters and their actions. This is especially true when the portrayals fit traditional sex stereotypes (Huston, 1983), which is the norm on television. What happens when the portrayals do not fit traditional stereotypes? Rather than changing the stereotype to fit the evidence, the opposite tends to occur; the incoming information is transformed to match the stereotype. For example, Martin and Halverson (1983) found that 5–6-year-olds, asked to recall pictures they had seen one week earlier, changed the sex of actors for pictures that contravened traditional sex roles (e.g., they remembered they had seen a girl when they had been shown a boy cooking). They also were more confident of memory for pictures they remembered as sex-role consistent, even when this was a distorted memory, than they were for sex-role inconsistent pictures. Cordua, McGraw, and Drabman (1979) found that more than half the children who saw a film about a female doctor and a male nurse recalled the opposite, and only 22% identified both correctly. In contrast, all children who saw a film involving a male doctor and female nurse recalled both correctly.

Schema-based theories of sex typing (e.g., Bem, 1981; Martin & Halverson, 1981) help to explain why stereotype-consistent information is remembered better than stereotype-inconsistent information, once the stereotypes have been established. In these information-processing models, a stereotype is considered to be a *schema,* a naive or ill-structured theory which organizes and structures experience by telling the perceiver the kinds of information to look for in the environment and how to interpret it. Once established, schemata tend to be self-perpetuating because they direct attention and influence memory, as Martin and Halverson (1981, 1983) emphasize. The salience of gender schemata, and therefore their power in organizing experience as well as their content, varies from individual to individual (Bem, 1981). Children who hold less traditional or weaker sex-role stereotypes remember information portrayed on television differently from children who hold more traditional or stronger stereotypes. List, Collins, and Westby (1981) showed third graders who held either conventional sex-role expectations or less stereotyped expectations a program featuring a traditional female character and a second program featuring a nontraditional female. The recognition errors of high-stereotyped children tended to reflect traditional sex-role expectations, whereas low-stereotyped viewers more often made errors consistent with less traditional expectations. This study suggests that television content activates viewers' sex-role expectations, and these, in turn, influence children's perceptions of that content (Collins, 1983).

In general, schema theories account quite well for the data from studies of television's influence on sex typing. To date, however, most research and theorizing has focused more on television's role in the maintenance of stereotypes than on its role in their formation. Since most North American children begin to watch television at an early age, probably are exposed to more sex-role models via television than via any other avenue during their early years, and rarely see females or males in other than traditional roles on television, it seems reasonable to hypothesize that television plays a central role in the initial formation of gender schemata. Because of the resistance of these schemata to change, occasional nontraditional portrayals are not likely to have much effect, but if such portrayals were commonplace, their influence on young children's expectations might be substantial.

The second question we raised about how sex roles are learned from TV concerns the effects of televised sex-role messages on girls and boys. The evidence to date is mixed. Some researchers have found girls and boys to be similarly affected (Beuf, 1974; Frueh & McGhee, 1975; McGhee & Frueh, 1980; Miller & Reeves, 1976). This consistency is noteworthy because of the preponderance of male models on TV. In addition, it calls into question the argument that boys rely more on general culture than their own parents for sex-role models, since fathers are much less available than mothers as models for young children (Lynn, 1966). Lynn's theory implies that TV should affect boys' attitudes more than girls' attitudes. That this apparently does not happen may be due to the strong preference typically expressed from the age of 5 or 6 onward for same-sex characters (Joy et al., 1977; Lyle & Hoffman, 1972a; McArthur & Eisen, 1976; Maccoby & Wilson, 1957; Maccoby et al., 1958; Schramm et al., 1961) and the concomitantly greater attention to and recognition of same-sex characters and their behavior (Lyle & Hoffman, 1972b; McArthur & Eisen, 1976; Maccoby & Wilson, 1957). In other words, although girls have fewer female models from which to choose, they may selectively attend to the female models available. Selective attention to and preference for same-sex models is one of the hallmarks of the cognitive-developmental theory of sex-role development (Kohlberg, 1966). Salomon's (1981) proposal that learning from television is dependent in part on amount of invested mental effort also may be relevant here.

Other researchers have obtained different effects of television for males and females. McGhee & Frueh (1980) found a sex difference among their heavy viewers on the masculine items of the Williams and Bennett (1975) scale. Specifically, first-grade boys who were heavy viewers had highly stereotyped views, and this remained true for students through grade 7. On the other hand, first-grade girls who were heavy TV viewers gave very few stereotyped responses to the masculine items, and seventh-grade girls who were heavy viewers gave the most stereotyped answers. McArthur and Eisen (1976) found that both sexes tended to recall and to imitate more of the activities of a same-sex model, but even when the model displayed role-reversed behavior, preschool boys recalled and imitated more than did preschool girls. Geis et al. (cited in Jennings et al., 1980) found that viewing nontraditional commercials influenced the expressed career aspirations of college women but not of college men. Morgan (1982) found that earlier TV viewing was related to later sexism for girls but not for boys.

The bulk of the evidence from this study indicates that television's influence on sex typing is similar for girls and boys.[14] Attitudes about peer behavior became significantly more sex typed for both girls and boys following the introduction of television to Notel, and before their town had television, gender was less salient to both girls and boys in Notel than it was to their counterparts in Multitel. Our conclusion that television affects the sexes similarly is less surprising if one considers that we measured gender salience or degree of sex typing of sex-role perceptions, not stereotypical or schematic content. As Huston (1983) points out, research based on schema theory demonstrates that social learning and cognitive-developmental theories are slightly off target in emphasizing the child's learning of same-sex patterns. Rather, children seem to learn (and encode for further observation) the stereotyped patterns for both genders, and then elaborate their schemata for their own gender. Selection of sex-typed behavior occurs not at the level of acquisition, but at the level of cognitive elaboration and performance.

Possible sex differences in the effect of TV on sex-role attitudes needs to be investigated further. In future research, it may be important to distinguish between gender salience or degree of sex typing and content or knowledge of sex-role schemata.

Does TV influence children differently at different ages? More research is needed to investigate possible developmental effects. The students in this study were older (grades 6 and 9) than children in most other research. Despite their greater age and longer history of attitudinal learning, and despite the resistance of gender schemata to change, TV still significantly influenced their sex-role perceptions. Even adults may not be immune to the influence of television. Jennings and her colleagues (1980) found that adult women showed more independence of judgment and nonverbal self-confidence if they saw role-reversed as opposed to traditional commercials. As we noted earlier, the very early end of the developmental spectrum also deserves attention, particularly with regard to the role of television in the initial establishment of gender schemata and stereotypes.

In all of these studies the emphasis has been on the effects of the content of television. What about the impact of the techniques used in programming? Welch, Huston–Stein, Wright, and Plehal (1979) found that commercials aimed at girls were characterized by fades, soft music, slow changes, lack of aggression, and inactivity. In contrast, commercials aimed at boys were characterized by action, inanimate objects, more cuts, more variability in changes to new scenes, more noise, and more music. Thus, even if the content of television programs is not stereotyped, the techniques used in presenting the content may convey stereotyped messages.

Finally, the impact of television on all social roles should be studied behaviorally (Siegel, 1982).

SUMMARY OF MAJOR FINDINGS

We hypothesized that the sex-role attitudes of Notel children would be initially less strongly sex typed than the perceptions of students who had grown up with television in Unitel and Multitel, and would become more stereotyped following the introduction of television to their community. The pattern of results was not perfect, but the weight of the evidence from the peer perception scales supported both hypotheses. Only 2 of the 12 data points formed by the means for the three towns, two sexes, and two phases were anomalous. In Phase 1, Unitel boys obtained inexplicably high scores and Unitel girls obtained inexplicably low scores. Otherwise, Notel girls' and boys' perceptions were less strongly sex typed than those of Multitel students in Phase 1, increased significantly following the introduction of television, and did not differ from Unitel or Multitel students' perceptions in Phase 2. By contrast, there was no evidence that television affects students' perceptions of their own parents' behavior. As other researchers have found, girls in this study held less strongly sex-typed attitudes than did boys. This, coupled with the evidence that the scores of Unitel and Multitel students were in the same range as scores obtained from students residing in Vancouver, a large urban center, indicates that the students in our three towns were typical rather than atypical. On the whole, these findings are consistent with those of numerous other studies; together they provide converging evidence of the importance of television for sex-role socialization. Since sex roles are portrayed on television in narrow and traditional ways, as content analyses have demonstrated, this conclusion is, in one sense, not surprising. However, since parents, peers, schools, books, and other media also usually present traditional models and messages, it is noteworthy that the introduction of television to Notel added enough to these messages to produce an increase in sex typing.

CONCLUSIONS AND IMPLICATIONS

What can we conclude about the effect of television programming on children's sex-role attitudes and perceptions? What kinds of changes might be recommended? Several studies, including this one, have documented links between TV viewing and stereotyped sex-role attitudes. The evidence for same-sex preferences in viewing television, greater recognition of same-sex characters and behaviors, and the role of gender schemata in processing sex-role information probably account for the effects of TV viewing. In light of this information we recommend that more female characters be portrayed in more varied roles on television. This may be particularly important for young children.

In addition to recommending that more women appear on television, there is the important issue of how they appear. Ultimately, one's political preference will determine whether more flexible roles are desired or not. The finding that the portrayal of counter-stereotypes is effective in producing less stereotyped attitudes for both boys and girls suggests that television has the potential for changing attitudes. Whether TV will continue to support, through example, highly sex-typed roles for women and men or whether a greater variety of roles and opportunities will be portrayed is an important decision. This decision should be made with the knowledge that television is a major source of models and information for socialization.

APPENDIX: INSTRUCTIONS TO RESPONDENTS AND TABLES

Peer Scale Instructions

PEER SCALE: TRAITS

Instructions. In this part of the questionnaire, we are interested in how you think boys and girls your age *actually act*. We want to know what they are *really like*. Look at item #1 below. We want to know in this item how *tough* boys and girls your age really are. If it is *very true* that boys your age are generally tough, then you would circle "7," the highest number on the boy's scale. If it is *not true* that boys your age are generally tough, then you would circle "1," the smallest number on the boy's scale. Or, if you think that it is *partly true* that boys your age are tough, then you would circle one of the numbers between "1" and "7" depending on *how true* you think it is. After that you tell us how tough girls your age generally are. And then you would go on to the next item.

Please do not skip any items or any scales.

Sample peer scale item:

	Boys your age	Girls your Age
1. Tough	1 2 3 4 5 6 7	1 2 3 4 5 6 7

Other items. Hardworking, sneaky, generous, noisy, outgoing and friendly, awkward and clumsy, trustworthy, obedient, mischievous, careful, and bossy.

PEER SCALE: BEHAVIORS

Instructions. In the following items, we would like to know whether these are the sorts of things boys and girls your age should or should not do. How suitable are they for boys your age? How suitable are they for girls your age? If you think something is alright for boys your age to do, or something they should do, then you would circle "7," the highest number on the boy's scale. But if you think it is something which is really not suitable or is something which should not be done, then you would circle "1" on the boy's scale. Or you would circle a number between "1" and "7," depending on how suitable it is for boys your age to do. Then tell us about girls your age. Please do not skip any items or any scales.

Items. Cry when hurt, do dishes, play rough sports, dance, play softball, go out alone after dark, swear, learn to cook and bake, show-off, make their own beds, go on dates, go on a long trip alone.

PEER SCALE: JOBS

Instructions. Next, we would like to know how suitable some jobs are for boys and girls when they grow up. Circle "7" if you think a job is really quite suitable, "1" if you think it isn't suitable, and a number between "1" and "7" if it is only partly suitable. The more suitable the job is, the higher the number you would circle. Do this for boys and for girls. Do not skip any items or any scales.

Items. Medical doctor, cashier in a restaurant, bus driver, librarian, grade school teacher, cook, clerk in a store, scientist, Prime Minister of Canada, usher in a movie theater, principal of a school, a judge.

PEER SCALE: AUTHORITY RELATIONS, PEER RELATIONS

Instructions. We are interested in this section in how boys and girls your age behave with other people. Remember, "7" means *often,* "1" means *never,* and the numbers between "1" and "7" mean *sometimes.*

The higher the number you circle, the more often boys or girls do what you are describing. Circle only one number on each scale. Do not skip any items or any scales.

Items: Authority Relations. Do what their parents say, try hard to please the teacher, help parents with household chores, tell parents where they are going, come in when they are supposed to, ask their parents for money, wear what they want to school, tell their parents when they think they are wrong, pick their own friends, decide for themselves what they want to be when they become adults.

Items: Peer Relations. Stick up for their brothers and sisters, obey older sisters, help younger brothers and sisters, keep secrets which their friends tell them, share things with boys and girls their age, tell younger brothers and sisters what to do, tell off girls your age, swear in front of boys, tell girls your age what to do, tell boys your age what to do.

Parent Scale Instructions

PARENT SCALES

Instructions. In this part of the questionnaire, we would like you to tell us about the kinds of things your mother and father do around the house. Use the scales in the first column to describe your father or stepfather. Use the scales in the second column to describe your mother or stepmother. For example, look at the first item below. If your father *often* "does the shopping," then circle "7" on the father's scale. If he *never* does the shopping, then circle "1" on the fathers' scale. Or, if he shops some of the time, then circle a number between "1" and "7," depending on *how often* he shops. Then tell us about your mother on the mother's scale. And then go on to the next item.

Do not skip any items or any scales in the two columns.

Sample parent scale item:

	Father	Mother
1. Does the shopping	1 2 3 4 5 6 7	1 2 3 4 5 6 7

Other items: Activities. Gets father's breakfast on work days, repairs things around the house, cleans up the house after visitors leave, does the evening dishes, moves heavy furniture, looks after the children in the evening and on the weekends, does the family laundry, drives the family car, helps the children with their schoolwork, writes excuse notes when children are absent from school, visits relatives, talks with the neighbors, goes to meetings and clubs, goes out with his or her friends, goes to church, answers the telephone when both are at home.

Items: Discipline. Scolds or punishes the children when they don't behave, threatens or warns the children, tells the children when to come in the house, sees to it that the children do their homework, tells the children what they can and can't do, explains to the children what is expected of them and why, finds out when you do something you shouldn't have done, sees to it that the children do their errands, makes you feel guilty or bad when you do something you shouldn't have, whose punishment or disapproval you dislike or fear the most.

Items: Support. Takes the children places, enjoys and takes time to talk with the children, notices when the children are unhappy and tries to cheer them up, does things with the children, makes you feel that what you do and think is important, says "hello" when the children come in and says "good night" when they go to bed, helps you with things when you're having trouble with it.

Items: Power. Has the most to say about how the children are to be punished, has the most to say about where to go on family outings, has the most to say about what jobs are to be done around the house and who is to do them, has the most to say about how much allowance the children will get, has the most to say about who to have into the house, has the most to say about what you will wear.

Tables

TABLE 6.A1

Peer Total Means for Girls and Boys, by Town and Phase

	Phase 1	Phase 2
Girls		
Notel	72.74	88.70
Unitel	70.93	72.58
Multitel	88.94	76.13
Boys		
Notel	76.84	106.73
Unitel	118.78	95.40
Multitel	93.27	94.94

TABLE 6.A2

Peer Subscale Means, by Town, Sex, and Phase

	Girls		Boys	
	Phase 1	Phase 2	Phase 1	Phase 2
Notel				
Traits	1.40	1.79	1.50	1.96
Behaviors	1.57	1.32	1.70	2.44
Jobs	2.00	1.94	1.70	2.42
Peer Relations	0.60	1.46	0.89	1.30
Authority Relations	0.70	1.34	0.91	1.19
Unitel				
Traits	1.76	1.27	2.21	1.81
Behaviors	1.32	1.49	2.69	2.20
Jobs	1.44	1.77	2.52	1.96
Peer Relations	0.80	1.93	1.74	1.23
Authority Relations	0.87	1.89	1.24	1.15
Multitel				
Traits	1.88	1.89	1.84	1.65
Behaviors	1.57	1.51	2.10	2.04
Jobs	1.93	1.28	1.96	2.14
Peer Relations	1.34	0.97	1.20	1.35
Authority Relations	1.10	1.03	1.05	1.16

TABLE 6.A3

Parent Total Means, by Sex and Grade

	Girls	Boys	Grade means
Grade 6	64.08	81.74	72.91
Grade 9	73.05	77.54	75.30
Sex means	68.57	79.64	

TABLE 6.A4

Parent Subscale Means, by Sex, Grade, and Phase

	Phase 1		Phase 2	
	Girls	Boys	Girls	Boys
Grade 6				
Activities	2.30	2.55	2.19	2.70
Discipline	1.43	1.58	1.02	1.82
Support	0.79	1.05	0.72	1.10
Power	1.18	1.90	1.21	1.72
Grade 9				
Activities	2.22	2.85	2.52	2.55
Discipline	1.43	1.25	1.56	1.40
Support	1.08	1.03	1.09	1.12
Power	1.62	1.52	1.31	1.59

TABLE 6.A5

Phase 1 Peer and Parent Total Means for Vancouver,
Unitel, and Multitel

	Girls	Boys	Town means
Peer means			
Unitel	70.93	118.78	97.80
Multitel	88.94	93.27	80.50
Vancouver	80.09	96.77	89.03
Sex means	76.87	101.35	
Parent means			
Unitel	60.79	76.34	68.57
Multitel	73.29	85.14	79.22
Vancouver	80.94	81.71	81.33
Sex means	71.67	81.06	

NOTES

[1] The frequency with which the proportions—about 70% men and 30% women—appear over time and across a variety of media is impressive. For example, Jones (1942) studied movies and found that 67% of the major characters were male; Child, Potter and Levine (1946) studied children's books and discovered that 73% of the major characters and 63% of the noncentral characters were male.

[2] This figure was biased downward due to selection procedures involved in the study, since programs were chosen only if at least one female and one male character appeared in

the show. Four of the most popular children's television shows were eliminated from the study because they had no female characters at all.

[3] Vancouver is the third largest city in Canada. At the time of this study, the population of its metropolitan area was 1 million, and most residents received the major Canadian (CBC, CTV) and U.S. (ABC, CBS, NBC) television networks, as well as PBS (Public Broadcasting System) from the United States.

[4] In Tables 6.A1, 6.A3, and 6.A5, as well as in the statistical analyses on total Peer and Parent scores, the means were based on scores totalled across all subscales. The subscale means in Tables 6.A2 and 6.A4, as well as the statistical analyses of subscale scores, are based on the average rather than the total score for the subscale, which is why the subscale means do not add up to the total means. Average rather than total scores were used for the subscale analyses because the subscales consisted of varying numbers of items and it was necessary to use scores which were comparable across the various subscales. In an unweighted means cross-sectional ANOVA on Peer total scores for Town × Phase × Sex × Grade, the following effects involving sex were significant: sex main effect, $F(1,407) = 27.74, p < .001$ (girls' mean, 78.34 and boys' mean, 97.66); Town × Sex interaction, $F(2,407) = 4.76, p < .009$; Town × Sex × Phase interaction, $F(2,407) = 3.18, p < .04$; and Town × Sex × Grade interaction, $F(2,407) = 3.53, p < .03$.

A simple main effects analysis of the Town × Sex × Phase interaction revealed that a significant sex difference, with gender more salient for boys than for girls, occurred in Phase 1 for Unitel, $F(1,407) = 28.35, p < .001$. A similar sex difference occurred in Phase 2 for Notel, $F(1,407) = 4.03, p < .05$; Unitel, $F(1,407) = 6.45, p < .05$; and Multitel, $F(1,407) = 4.38, p < .05$.

[5] This method of analysis was chosen because of the consistent sex difference in the scores. It was assumed that the unequal numbers of girls and boys in the sample did not reflect unequal numbers of males and females in the population but were accidental results of the sampling procedure, that is, the class size. Therefore, unweighted means ANOVAs were conducted. However, since there was a sex difference, the unequal numbers of males and females contributed differentially to any interaction not involving sex. To control for this bias, Town × Phase × Grade ANOVAs were run separately for each sex. The results reported here separately for the sexes are the same as those found for the Town × Sex × Phase interaction in the overall ANOVA in which sex was included as a factor.

[6] For girls, an unweighted means cross-sectional ANOVA on Peer total scores for Town × Phase × Grade revealed a significant Town × Phase interaction, $F(2,192) = 3.59, p < .03$. Simple main effects analyses revealed a significant increase from Phase 1 to Phase 2 in sex typing of peer perceptions for Notel girls, $F(1,192) = 4.42, p < .05$; no change for Unitel girls; and a marginally significant decrease, $F(1,192) = 2.85, p < .10$, for Multitel girls. In Phase 1, Multitel girls ($M = 88.94$) had more stereotyped perceptions than girls in both Notel (72.74; $p < .05$ by Newman–Keuls test) and Unitel (70.93; $p < .05$ by Tukey test), who did not differ. In Phase 2, there were no significant differences among the towns (Notel mean, 88.70, Unitel, 72.58, and Multitel, 76.13).

[7] For boys, an unweighted means cross-sectional ANOVA on Peer total scores for Town × Phase × Grade revealed a significant Town × Phase interaction, $F(2,215) = 7.27, p < .001$. Simple main effects analyses revealed that Notel boys' perceptions became more sex typed from Phase 1 ($M = 76.84$) to Phase 2 ($M = 106.73$), $F(1,215) = 9.15, p < .005$; and Unitel boys' perceptions became less sex typed (means of 118.78 and 95.40, respectively), $F(1,215) = 5.59, p < .05$. Multitel boys' perceptions did not change (means of 93.27 and 94.94, respectively).

In Phase 1, $F(2,215) = 9.14, p < .01$, Unitel boys had more strongly sex-typed views than both Multitel and Notel boys ($p < .01$ by Tukey test), and Multitel boys also held more sex-typed perceptions than Notel boys ($p < .05$ by Tukey test). In Phase 2, there were no significant differences among the towns.

[8] In an unweighted means cross-sectional ANOVA for Town × Sex × Phase × Grade × Peer Subscale Score, the peer subscale main effect was significant, $F(4,1628) = 118.56, p < .001$. Tukey tests revealed that gender was more salient for the Jobs, Behaviors, and Traits subscales than for the Peer Relations and the Authority Relations subscales ($p < .01$ for all comparisons), and perceptions for the Jobs subscale also were more sex typed than for the Traits subscale ($p < .01$).

Simple main effects analyses of the significant Sex × Subscore interaction, $F(4,1628) = 10.54$, $p < .001$ revealed that boys held more stereotyped perceptions than girls on the Behaviors, $F(1,407) = 41.01, p < .001$; Jobs, $F(1,407) = 11.74, p < .01$; and Peer Relations, $F(1,407) = 5.46, p < .05$ subscales.

Simple main effects analyses of the significant Town × Sex × Phase × Subscale interaction, $F(8,1628) = 5.02, p < .001$ revealed the following. For Notel students several significant increases in gender salience occurred from Phase 1 to Phase 2, whereas only two significant changes, both decreases, occurred for Unitel and Multitel students over the same period. Specifically, significant increases in sex typing occurred from Phase 1 to Phase 2 for Notel girls for the Peer Relations, $F(1,407) = 9.34, p < .01$; and Authority Relations, $F(1,407) = 5.28, p < .05$ subscales, and for Notel boys for the Behaviors, $F(1,407) = 6.87, p < .01$; and Jobs, $F(1,407) = 6.67, p < .01$ subscales. Significant decreases in sterotyping of peer perceptions from Phase 1 to Phase 2 occurred on the Jobs subscale for Unitel boys, $F(1,407) = 4.08, p < .05$ and for Multitel girls, $F(1,407) = 5.47, p < .05$. There were no changes for Unitel girls or Multitel boys.

[9] In an unweighted means cross-sectional ANOVA on Parent total scores for Town × Sex × Phase × Grade, the only significant results were the sex main effect, $F(1,388) = 12.59, p < .001$ (girls' mean, 68.57, and boys' mean, 79.64); and the Sex × Grade interaction, $F(1,388) = 4.45, p < .04$.

Simple main effects analyses of the Sex × Grade interaction revealed that boys ($M = 81.74$) had more sex-typed views of their parents' behavior than did girls ($M = 64.08$) in grade 6, $F(1,388) = 16.00, p < .001$, but there was no sex difference in grade 9 (boys' mean, 77.54, and girls' mean, 73.05).

[10] In an unweighted means cross-sectional ANOVA for Town × Sex × Phase × Grade × Parent Subscale Score, the parent subscale main effect was significant, $F(3,1164) = 276.66$, $p < .001$. Tukey tests revealed that students' perceptions of their parents' behavior were more stereotyped for the Activities subscale ($M = 2.484$) than for the Power (1.505), Discipline (1.436), and Support (0.999) subscales ($p < .01$ in all cases), and they also were more stereotyped for the Power and Discipline subscales than for the Support subscale ($p < .01$).

Simple main effects analyses of the significant Sex × Phase × Grade × Parent Subscale Score interaction, $F(3,1164) = 4.65, p < .003$ revealed that boys held less egalitarian views of their parents' behavior than did girls in the following specific instances: Phase 1, grade 6, for the Power subscale, $F(1,388) = 12.31, p < .01$; Phase 1, grade 9, for the Activities subscale, $F(1,388) = 9.48, p < .01$; and Phase 2, grade 6, for the Activities, $F(1,388) = 5.91$, $p < .05$; Discipline, $F(1,388) = 14.73, p < .01$; and Power, $F(1,388) = 6.19, p < .05$ subscales.

[11] In an unweighted means cross-sectional ANOVA on Peer total scores for Town × Sex × Grade, neither the grade main effect nor any interaction involving grade was statistically significant. The same was true for a similar analysis on the Parent total scores.

[12] In an unweighted means cross-sectional ANOVA on Peer total scores for Town × Sex, the sex main effect was significant, $F(1,288) = 23.60, p < .001$, reflecting more sex-typed perceptions for boys ($M = 101.35$) than for girls ($M = 76.87$). The town main effect was also

significant, $F(2,288) = 3.92$, $p < .03$. Unitel students' peer sex-role perceptions were more stereotyped ($M = 97.8$) than those of students in Multitel ($M = 80.50$; $p < .05$ by Tukey test). Vancouver students ($M = 89.03$) differed from neither Unitel nor Multitel.

[13] In an unweighted means cross-sectional ANOVA on Parent total scores for Town × Sex, the town main effect was significant, $F(2,281) = 3.13$, $p < .05$, but paired comparisons revealed only marginally significant differences. Vancouver students' perceptions of their parents' behavior ($M = 80.89$) did not differ from Multitel students' perceptions ($M = 80.68$), and both were marginally more sex typed than Unitel students' perceptions ($M = 70.80$; $p < .10$ by both Tukey and Newman–Keuls tests for both comparisons).

[14] Although the magnitude of the increase in sex typing was greater in absolute terms for Notel boys (29.90 points on the SRD scale) than for Notel girls (15.96 points), from a statistical perspective the difference should not be given much credence, since both sexes in Notel were less sex typed than Multitel students in Phase 1, since both increased significantly, and since neither differed from Multitel students in Phase 2.

REFERENCES

Anderson, D. R., & Lorch, E. P. Looking at television: Action or reaction? In J. Bryant & D. R. Anderson (Eds.), *Children's understanding of television*. New York: Academic Press, 1983.

Armstrong, P. *Labour pains*. Toronto: Women's Press, 1984.

Aronoff, C. E. Old age in prime time. *Journal of Communication*, 1974, *24*(4), 86–87.

Atkin, C. K., & Miller, M. *The effects of television advertising on children: Experimental evidence*. Paper presented at the meeting of the International Communication Association, Chicago, 1975.

Bem, S. Gender schema theory: A cognitive account of sex typing. *Psychological Review*, 1981, *88*, 353–364.

Beuf, A. Doctor, lawyer, household drudge. *Journal of Communication*, 1974, *24*(2), 142–145.

Broverman, K., Vogel, S. R., Broverman, D. M., Clarkson, F. E., & Rosenkrantz, P. S. Sex-role stereotypes: A current appraisal. *Journal of Social Issues*, 1972, *28*, 59–78.

Brown, D. G. Sex role development in a changing culture. *Psychological Bulletin*, 1958, *55*, 232–243.

Busby, L. J. Defining the sex-role standard in network children's programs. *Journalism Quarterly*, 1974, *51*, 690–696.

Child, I. L., Potter, E. M., & Levine, E. M. Children's textbooks and personality development. *Psychological Monographs*, 1946, *60*(3), 1–54.

Collins, W. A. Interpretation and inference in children's television viewing. In J. Bryant & D. R. Anderson (Eds.), *Children's understanding of television*. New York: Academic Press, 1983.

Cordua, G., McGraw, K., & Drabman, R. Doctor or nurse: Children's perceptions of sex-typed occupations. *Child Development*, 1979, *50*, 590–593.

Davidson, E. S., Yasuna, A., & Tower, A. The effects of television cartoons on sex-role stereotyping in young girls. *Child Development*, 1979, *50*, 597–600.

De Fleur, M. L. Occupational roles as portrayed on television. *Public Opinion Quarterly*, 1964, *28*, 57–74.

Dominick, J. R. The portrayal of women in prime-time, 1953–1977. *Sex Roles*, 1979, *5*, 405–411.

Donahue, T. R. Perceptions of violent TV newsfilm: An experimental comparison of sex and color factors. *Journal of Broadcasting*, 1976, *20*, 185–195.

Downing, M. Heroine of the daytime serial. *Journal of Communication*, 1974, *24*(2), 130–137.

Frueh, T., & McGhee, P. Traditional sex role development and amount of time spent watching television. *Developmental Psychology*, 1975, *11*, 109.

Gerbner, G. Violence in television drama: Trends and symbolic functions. In G. A. Comstock & E. A. Rubinstein (Eds.), *Television and Social Behavior* (Vol. 1). *Media content and control*. Washington, D.C.: U.S. Government Printing Office, 1972.

Greenberg, B. S. *Life on television: Content analyses of U.S. TV drama*. Norwood, N.J.: Ablex Publishing, 1980.

Greenberg, B. S. Television and role socialization: An overview. In D. Pearl, L. Bouthilet, & J. Lazar (Eds.), *Television and behavior: Ten years of scientific progress and implications for the eighties*. Vol. 2. Rockville, Md.: NIMH, 1982.

Greenberg, B. S., Richards, M., & Henderson, L. Trends in sex-role portrayals on television. In B. S. Greenberg (Ed.), *Life on television: Content analysis of U.S. TV drama*. Norwood, N.J.: Ablex Publishing, 1980.

Halpern, S., & Ethier, B. *The portrayal of men and women in Canadian and U.S. television commercials*. Unpublished manuscript, University of British Columbia, Department of Psychology, 1977. (Available from T. M. Williams).

Haugh, S. S., Hoffman, C. D., & Cowan, G. The eye of the very young beholder: Sex typing of infants by young children. *Child Development*, 1980, *51*, 598–600.

Head, S. W. Content analysis of television dramatic programs. *Quarterly of Film, Radio and Television*, 1954, *9*, 175–194.

Henderson, L., & Greenberg, B. S. Sex-typing of common behaviors on television. In B. S. Greenberg (Ed.), *Life on television: Content analyses of U.S. TV drama*. Norwood, N.J.: Ablex Publishing, 1980.

Henderson, L., Greenberg, B. S., & Atkin, C. K. Sex differences in giving orders, making plans, and needing support on television. In B. S. Greenberg (Ed.), *Life on television: Content analyses of U.S. TV drama*. Norwood, N.J.: Ablex Publishing, 1980.

Huston, A. Sex-typing. In P. H. Mussen & E. M. Hetherington (Eds.), *Handbook of child psychology: Vol. 4. Socialization, personality, and social development* (4th ed.). New York: Wiley, 1983.

Jennings (Walstedt), J., Geis, F. L., & Brown, V. Influence of television commercials on women's self-confidence and independent judgement. *Journal of Personality and Social Psychology*, 1980, *38*, 203–210.

Johnston, J., & Ettema, J. S. *Positive images: Breaking stereotypes with children's television*. Beverly Hills, Calif.: Sage, 1982.

Jones, D. B. Quantitative analysis of motion picture content. *Public Opinion Quarterly*, 1942, *6*, 411–428.

Joy, L., Kimball, M., & Zabrack, M. *Television exposure and children's aggressive behaviour*. Paper presented at the meeting of the Canadian Psychological Association, Vancouver, June 1977.

Kagan, J. The concept of identification. *Psychological Review*, 1958, *65*, 296–305.

Katzman, M. Television soap operas: What's been going on any way? *Public Opinion Quarterly*, 1972, *36*, 200–212.

Kimball, M. M., & Harrison, L. F. *A study of sex differences in fear of success, attitudes toward sex roles, and performance in competitive and non-competitive tasks*. Paper presented at the Canadian Psychological Association meetings, Victoria, June 1973.

Kohlberg, L. A cognitive developmental analysis of children's sex-role concepts and attitudes. In E. E. Maccoby (Ed.), *The development of sex differences*. Stanford, Calif.: Stanford University Press, 1966.

Krull, R., & Husson, W. Children's attention: The case of TV viewing. In E. Wartella (Ed.), *Children communicating*. Sage Annual Reviews of Communication Research, Vol. 7. Beverly Hills, Calif.: Sage, 1979.

Lambert, R. D. *Sex role imagery in children: Social origins of the mind*. Studies of the Royal Commission on the Status of Women in Canada, No. 6, Ottawa: Information Canada, 1971.

Liebert, R. M., & Schwartzberg, N. S. Effects of mass media. *Annual Review of Psychology*, 1977, *28*, 141–173.

List, J., Collins, W. A., & Westby, S. *Comprehension and inferences from traditional and nontraditional sex-role portrayals*. Unpublished manuscript, University of Minnesota, 1981.

Long, M. L., & Simon, R. J. The roles and status of women on children and family TV programs. *Journalism Quarterly*, 1974, *51*, 107–110.

Lorch, E. P., Anderson, D. R., & Levin, S. R. The relationship of visual attention to children's comprehension of television. *Child Development*, 1979, *50*, 722–727.

Lyle, J., & Hoffman, H. R. Children's use of television and other media. In E. A. Rubinstein, G. A. Comstock, & J. P. Murray (Eds.), *Television and Social Behavior* (Vol. 4). *Television in day-to-day life: Patterns of use*. Washington, D.C.: U.S. Government Printing Office, 1972a.

Lyle, J., & Hoffman, H. R. Explorations in patterns of television viewing by preschool-age children. In E. A. Rubinstein, G. A. Comstock, & J. P. Murray (Eds.), *Television and Social Behavior* (Vol. 4). *Television in day-to-day life: Patterns of use*. Washington, D.C.: U.S. Government Printing Office, 1972b.

Lynn, D. B. The process of learning parental and sex-role identification. *The Journal of Marriage and the Family*, 1966, *28*, 466–470.

McArthur, L. Z., & Eisen, S. V. Television and sex-role stereotyping. *Journal of Applied Social Psychology*, 1976, *6*, 329–351.

McArthur, L. Z., & Resko, B. G. The portrayal of men and women in American television commercials. *Journal of Social Psychology*, 1975, *97*, 209–220.

McGhee, P. E., & Frueh, T. Television viewing and the learning of sex-role stereotypes. *Sex Roles*, 1980, *6*, 179–188.

McNeil, J. C. Feminism, femininity and the television series: A content analysis. *Journal of Broadcasting*, 1975, *19*, 259–271.

Maccoby, E. E., & Jacklin, C. N. *The psychology of sex differences*. Stanford, Calif.: Stanford University Press, 1974.

Maccoby, E. E., & Wilson, W. C. Identification and observational learning from films. *Journal of Abnormal and Social Psychology*, 1957, *55*, 76–87.

Maccoby, E. E., Wilson, W. C., & Burton, R. V. Differential movie-viewing behavior of male and female viewers. *Journal of Personality*, 1958, *26*, 259–267.

Marecek, J., Piliavin, J. A., Fitzsimmons, E., Krogh, E. C., Leader, E., & Trudell, B. Women as TV experts: The voice of authority? *Journal of Communication*, 1978, *28*(1), 159–168.

Martin, C. L., & Halverson, C. F. A schematic processing model of sex-typing and stereotyping in children. *Child Development*, 1981, *52*, 1119–1134.

Martin, C. L., & Halverson, C. F., Jr. The effects of sex-typing schemas on young children's memory. *Child Development*, 1983, *54*, 563–574.

Miller, M. M., & Reeves, B. Dramatic TV content and children's sex-role stereotypes. *Journal of Broadcasting*, 1976, *20*, 35–50.

Mischel, W. Sex differences. In P. Mussen (Ed.), *Carmichael's Manual of Child Psychology* (Vol. 2) (3rd ed.). New York: Wiley, 1970.

Morgan, M. Television and adolescents' sex role stereotypes: A longitudinal study. *Journal of Personality and Social Psychology*, 1982, *43*, 947–955.

O'Donnell, W. J., & O'Donnell, K. J. Update: Sex-role messages in TV commercials. *Journal of Communication*, 1978, *28*(1), 156–158.

Pingree, S. The effects of nonsexist television commercials and perceptions of reality on children's attitudes about women. *Psychology of Women Quarterly*, 1978, *2*, 262–277.

Pingree, S., & Hawkins, R. P. Children and media. In M. Butler & W. Paisley (Eds.), *Women and the mass media: Source book for research and action.* New York: Human Sciences Press, 1980.

Rushton, J. P. Television and prosocial behavior. In D. Pearl, L. Bouthilet, & J. Lazar (Eds.), *Television and behavior: Ten years of scientific progress and implications for the eighties.* Vol. 2. Rockville, Md.: NIMH, 1982.

Salomon, G. *Interaction of media, cognition, and learning.* New York: Jossey-Bass, 1979.

Salomon, G. Introducing AIME: The assessment of children's mental involvement with television. *New Directions for Child Development*, 1981, No. 13, 89–102.

Schramm, W., Lyle, J., & Parker, E. B. *Television in the lives of our children.* Stanford, Calif.: Stanford University Press, 1961.

Seggar, J. F. Television's portrayal of minorities and women, 1971–75. *Journal of Broadcasting*, 1977, *21*, 435–446.

Seggar, J. F., & Wheeler, P. World of work on TV: Ethnic and sex representation in TV drama. *Journal of Broadcasting*, 1973, *17*, 201–214.

Siegel, A. Introductory comments to chapters on social beliefs and social behavior. In D. Pearl, L. Bouthilet, & J. Lazar (Eds.), *Television and behavior: Ten years of scientific progress and implications for the eighties.* Vol. 2. Rockville, Md.: NIMH, 1982.

Sprafkin, J. N., & Liebert, R. M. Sex-typing and children's television preferences. In G. Tuchman, A. K. Daniels, & J. Benét (Eds.), *Hearth and home: Images of women in the mass media.* New York: Oxford University Press, 1978.

Statistical Abstract of the United States. Washington, D.C.: U.S. Department of Commerce, Bureau of the Census, 1980.

Sternglanz, S. H., & Serbin, L. A. Sex-role stereotyping on children's television programs. *Developmental Psychology*, 1974, *10*, 710–715.

Stocking, S. H., Sapolsky, B. J., & Zillmann, D. Sex discrimination in prime time humor. *Journal of Broadcasting*, 1977, *21*, 447–457.

Tedesco, N. S. Patterns in prime-time. *Journal of Communication*, 1974, *24*(2), 119–124.

Turow, T. Advising and ordering: Daytime, prime-time. *Journal of Communication*, 1974, *24*(2), 138–141.

Welch, R. L., Huston–Stein, A., Wright, J. C., & Plehal, R. Subtle sex-role cues in children's commercials. *Journal of Communication*, 1979, *29*, 202–209.

Williams, J. E., & Bennett, S. M. The definition of sex-role stereotypes via the Adjective Check List. *Sex Roles*, 1975, *1*, 327–337.

Williams, T. M., Zabrack, M. L., & Joy, L. A. A content analysis of entertainment television programming. In *Report of the Ontario Royal Commission on Violence in the Communications Industry*, Vol. 3. Toronto, 1977.

TELEVISION AND CHILDREN'S AGGRESSIVE BEHAVIOR

Lesley A. Joy
Meredith M. Kimball
*Merle L. Zabrack**

INTRODUCTION

Of all the areas of concern over the effects of television's content on children's behavior, aggression has received most attention from researchers. This is because the concentration of violence portrayed on television has the potential of generating aggressive behavior, both immediately and in the long term (Greenberg, Edison, Korzenny, Fernandez-Collado, & Atkin, 1980; Signorelli, Gross, & Morgan, 1982; Williams, Zabrack, & Joy, 1977, 1982). We are not talking about the kind of assertive or competitive behavior sometimes described as "aggressive" in, for example, the business community (Siegel, 1980). We are referring to physical aggression, with the potential to injure, and verbal abuse, including threats.

---

*Order of authors is alphabetical to reflect their equal contribution.

THE IMPACT OF TELEVISION
A Natural Experiment in Three Communities

303

Television and its relation to aggressive behavior has been the subject of many lengthy reviews (e.g., chap. 8 in Comstock et al., 1978; Cook, Kendzierski, & Thomas, 1983; Lefkowitz & Huesmann, 1980; Pearl, Bouthilet, & Lazar, 1982). Before describing our own research in this area, it may be helpful to provide the theoretical and methodological context in which it was conducted. In highlighting previous work, special attention will be paid to different research approaches taken to this topic.

METHODOLOGICAL PARADIGMS

Several methods have been used to study the relationship between television viewing and children's aggressive behavior: the laboratory experiment, the field experiment, and the naturalistic study. Each has advantages and disadvantages, but as Comstock (1980) notes, laboratory experiments are especially suited to testing the processes through which television affects its viewers and to testing competing theoretical models, whereas field experiments and naturalistic studies are better suited to testing whether effects observed in the laboratory also occur in real life.

Laboratory Experiments

The most widely used methodology has been the laboratory experiment. Typically, children are randomly assigned to watch either a short film portraying violence, a nonviolent film, or no film. The child is then observed, usually alone, and often in the presence of toys or objects the same as, or similar to, those used in the film. Observers record the child's behavior, paying special attention to aggression. The results of such experimental studies have been clear: Children who watch a film with aggressive content imitate aggressive behavior seen in the film, show an increase in other aggressive behaviors, and are more aggressive than children who see either a neutral film or no film at all (e.g., Bandura, Ross, & Ross, 1963a, 1963b; Bandura, 1965).

In addition to measuring aggression against inanimate objects, various researchers have observed aggression toward adults (Hanratty, Liebert, Morris, & Fernandez, 1969) and toward other children (Feshbach, 1972; Hartmann, 1965; Liebert & Baron, 1972; Stoessel, 1972). The results have been consistent: Children who view films with violent or aggressive content behave more aggressively after viewing than children who do not see such films.

The major advantage of laboratory experiments is that participants can be assigned randomly to film-viewing conditions, thereby ensuring that numerous other factors, such as socioeconomic status, intelligence, and previous TV viewing experience, do not systematically influence the results. These conditions allow causal inferences to be made. The experimenter can say that in a particular situation, viewing a film with aggressive content caused the children who saw it to behave more aggressively than the children who did not see it.

The major disadvantage of laboratory experiments is that the researcher cannot be certain how realistic the setting is. Does the laboratory parallel the situation of a child who watches TV at home and behaves aggressively in interactions with other children and adults? A number of factors present in laboratory studies differ from those in naturalistic settings. For example, a short segment of a film is used rather than a full-length TV show; only short-term or one-shot exposure can be assessed, rather than the typical long-term exposure to TV that children experience; and only immediate performance of aggressive behavior is measured—people who may learn aggressive behaviors from TV, but do not display these behaviors until later, are not shown to have been affected. In addition, the situation in which aggression is measured is generally very permissive: The child is alone, and the experimenter says the child may do anything he or she wants. Peer retaliation and adult sanctions, typical consequences of aggressive behavior, are absent. Finally, the behavior measured as an indicator of aggression is often unrealistic. It may involve aggression against inanimate objects or responses such as pressing a lever to hurt someone. The extent to which these behaviors are representative of naturally occurring aggression is unclear. Nevertheless, and despite these criticisms, laboratory experiments are an important facet of research on television and aggression because they enable casual inferences to be made and the learning process to be analyzed.

Field Experiments

To avoid some of the problems associated with the laboratory study, but to retain some of the advantages of control, scientists have conducted field experiments. Children are randomly assigned to view violent or nonviolent television programming for a period of a few days to a few weeks. Measures of aggressive behavior, fantasy, and/or attitudes are taken before, during, and after the period of controlled viewing. Studies using this design have been conducted with children in nursery schools and with adolescent boys living in residential schools or institutions. The findings tend to be similar to those for laboratory experiments—increases in aggressive behavior have been found for children exposed to televised aggression. However, methodological problems associated with several of the field studies have led some reviewers to conclude that these studies produce little consistent evidence (notably Cook et al., 1983). In addition, effects are sometimes limited to populations that were initially more aggressive.

Steuer, Applefield, and Smith (1971) matched five pairs of preschool children and showed one child of each pair a 10-minute aggressive cartoon each day for 11 days, while the other child in the pair watched a nonaggressive cartoon. The children who had watched the aggressive cartoons behaved more aggressively during a free-play situation than the children who had watched nonaggressive cartoons. Stein and Friedrich (1972) exposed preschool children to 10–20 minutes per day of aggressive, neutral, or prosocial television. During the 4 weeks of controlled viewing, increased levels of aggressive behavior in a free-play situation were found for children who saw the violent programs. However, this held true only for children initially high in aggressive behavior, and, furthermore, Saurin (1973) failed to replicate this finding.

Field studies of adolescent boys have been conducted in private schools, boys' homes, or institutions for juvenile delinquents. In the most controversial of these studies, Feshbach and Singer (1971) found that boys from boys' homes who were initially high in aggressive behavior and low in fantasy aggression displayed more aggression when they viewed *nonviolent* TV shows for 6 weeks. This finding contradicts the results obtained in the laboratory, as well as in other field experiments. The authors argued that for boys who are aggressive and do not have the resources to express that aggression through fantasy (that is, boys who are low on measures of fantasy aggression), violence on TV serves as an outlet for aggressive feelings. This decreases the boys' needs to behave aggressively. In essence, they propose a catharsis model. However, their conclusions have been challenged on several points. First, Feshbach and Singer found that boys liked aggressive shows better than nonaggressive shows. An alternative explanation for their results is therefore possible. The boys assigned to view only the nonaggressive, less well liked shows may have been frustrated and resentful and, as a result, displayed more aggression than boys in the other group. This explanation is supported by the fact that boys in both groups were allowed to watch "Batman," a highly aggressive show, because the boys in the nonviolent viewing group objected so strongly to not being allowed to see this program. It is not surprising that adolescent boys who were denied their favorite television shows for several weeks would be unhappy. Indeed, this may be a problem common to all studies in which the viewers' television diet is restricted.

Perhaps the most important challenge to the Feshbach and Singer findings is in a replication of their study, by Wells (1973), who found the opposite and more usual effect; that is, boys viewing aggressive TV content showed an increase in aggressive behavior. This was especially true for the boys who were initially aggressive. Other field studies have found either an increase in aggression for boys watching violent TV and/or an increase in aggression among those boys initially high in aggression who viewed violent shows (Leyens, Camino, Parke, & Berkowitz, 1975; Parke, Berkowitz, Leyens, West, & Sebastian, 1977).

The field experiment has some of the advantages of the laboratory study, in particular, random assignment of viewers to viewing conditions. It also avoids some of the disadvantages of the laboratory in that real TV shows are used, the shows are viewed in a natural setting, and aggressive behavior occurs in a situation where consequences may follow. However, field experiments have drawbacks. Because there is not as much control as in the laboratory, the researcher cannot be as certain that the only difference between groups is the kind of TV viewed. Moreover, the people studied in field experiments often represent an unusual group; for example, they may be living in an institutional setting. This may allow for stricter control over the TV programming viewed, but draws into question the representativeness of the results.

Naturalistic Studies

Yet another type of investigation, the naturalistic study, examines the relationship between TV viewing and aggression in a natural environment. In these studies, people are not randomly assigned to groups as in a true experiment. Rather, their behavior is examined on the basis of how much TV they watch, their preferences for certain kinds of programming, or because they reside in a town or home without TV reception. What the naturalistic study loses in the way of control, and thereby the possibility of drawing causal conclusions, is offset by gains in the realism and the validity of the study for assessing effects in real life.

Again, the results of naturalistic studies, especially those using measures of how much violent TV is watched, have tended to support the conclusion drawn from the laboratory and field experiments: TV viewing is positively related to aggressive behavior. However, the results are less definitive than the results of laboratory and field experiments, since television exerts its effects in a complex milieu of other influences.

Two early studies did not find a relationship between the presence of absence of TV in the home and teacher reports of aggressive behavior (Himmelweit, Oppenheim, & Vince, 1958) or scores on an antisocial aggression scale (Schramm, Lyle, & Parker, 1961), although in the latter study, tenth-grade boys who were heavy TV viewers and read very little obtained higher aggression scores than boys without TV.

Among the researchers who have assessed the relationship between self-reports of favorite shows and self-report or peer ratings of aggression, some found a positive relationship between the preference for violent programs and ratings of aggressive behavior (Eron, 1963; Huesmann, Lagerspetz, & Eron, 1984; McIntyre & Teevan, 1972; Robinson & Bachmann, 1972), some found no relationship (Lefkowitz, Eron, Walder, & Huesmann, 1972; McLeod, Atkin, & Chaffee, 1972), and in one case, a negative relationship was found (Friedman & Johnson, 1972). The naturalistic studies demonstrating the strongest connection between TV viewing and aggression have examined the relationship between self-reports of amount of violent TV viewed and self-reports of positive attitudes toward aggression (Dominick & Greenberg, 1972) or self-reports of positive attitudes toward aggression (Dominick & Greenberg, 1972) of self-reports of actual aggressive behavior (Belson, 1978; McCarthy, Langer, Gersten, Eisenberg, & Orzeck, 1975; McLeod, et al., 1972).

Several researchers have used naturalistic, longitudinal panel studies in an attempt to make causal inferences about the relationship between TV viewing and aggression over time (Eron, 1982, Eron, Huesmann, Lefkowitz, & Walder, 1972; McLeod, et al., 1972; Milavsky, Kessler, Stipp, & Rubens, 1982a, 1982b; Rosengren, Roe, & Sonesson, 1983; Singer & Singer, 1980). Eron et al. (1972) used the cross-lagged panel technique, which involves measuring both TV viewing and aggressive behavior at two points in time and then comparing the strength of the relationships between TV viewing and aggression. They found that among boys, TV viewing in grade 3 was more strongly correlated with peer nominations of aggressiveness 10 years later than with peer ratings of aggression in grade 3. Furthermore, there was no relationship between early aggression and later TV viewing. Whether such correlational information can be used to infer a causal connection is a matter of debate (Cook & Campbell, 1979; Howitt, 1972; Huesmann, Eron, Lefkowitz, & Walder, 1973; Kaplan, 1972; Rogosa, 1980). Milavsky et al. (1982a, 1982b) conducted a panel field study over a 3-year period (1970–1973) and found no support for a relationship between TV viewing and aggression. Aggression was assessed by peer nominations for the 2400 elementary school children and by self-reports for the 800 teenage boys in the study. All students were interviewed about their television-viewing habits. Milavsky et al. (1982a, 1982b) concluded that earlier television viewing did not predict later aggressive behavior because the number of positive relationships obtained was no more than would be expected by chance. However, their interpretation has been criticized by Cook et al. (1983), who contend that Milavsky et al. did not fully probe all possible interactions and used statistical tests with questionable power for skewed distributions. The high rate of attrition for this study, and the fact that more high-aggression than low-aggression students were lost by attrition, also raise doubts about the validity of the causal inferences drawn from the longitudinal analyses.

Eron and Huesmann and their colleagues collected data from elementary school children in the United States, Finland, Poland, Australia, and Holland. Huesmann (1982) has reported on the results for the first three countries. This study, which used a peer nomination measure for aggression and self-reports on the viewing of television violence, focused on children who were initially in grades 1 and 3. They were re-assessed 2 years later. Longitudinal analyses for the U.S. sample revealed positive relationships between earlier TV viewing and later aggressive behavior and between earlier aggression and later TV viewing. Cook et al. (1983), on reexamining the data from the two aforementioned studies (Huesmann, 1982; Milavsky, 1982a, 1982b), claim that early measures of viewing TV violence add to the predictability of later aggression over and above the predictability afforded by measures of earlier aggression only. That is, the lagged effects are consistently positive and statistically significant.

Rosengren and his colleagues in Sweden have obtained data from 6-, 9-, and 11-year-olds in their Media Panel Program (Rosengren et al., 1983). For boys, teachers' ratings of aggressiveness at ages 6 and 11 were significantly related to concurrent amounts of television viewing, and there was some evidence that boys who were rated as more aggressive at age 6 watched more TV at age 9. Rosengren suggests these data fit an "addiction model," one in which the mass media have short-term effects on attitudes and related behavior of the individual. This leads to a craving for more of the same kind of media content, which again has short-term effects, and so on. The Swedish data, along with that obtained by Eron and Huesmann and their colleagues (Eron, 1982), suggest that the relationship between television and aggression is likely to be circular; that is, television may lead to an increase in the viewer's aggressive behavior, but more aggressive children also may watch more television in general and more violent television in particular.

The only longitudinal data involving observations rather than ratings were obtained by Singer and Singer (1980), who studied 3 and 4-year-olds during the course of a year. Observers rated the children on overt aggression after watching them individually for two 10-minute periods, and parents kept a log of their TV-viewing behavior. These two measures were significantly correlated when taken concurrently, and earlier TV viewing was significantly correlated with later aggressive behavior. Singer and Singer concluded that the results pointed to a causal link between watching TV—especially programs with violent content—and subsequent aggression. However, this causal inference was based on cross-lagged panel analysis and, therefore, may be questionable.

Two other naturalistic studies have provided evidence on the relationship between television and aggressive behavior. Belson (1978) interviewed 1565 teenaged boys in England to determine both the magnitude and type of their exposure to violent television between 1959 and 1971. In addition, each boy gave information about his own level of violent behavior, including the frequency and nature of aggression in the preceding 6-month period. The boys reported a range of violence from minor aggravation to threats to kill. After carefully matching boys with high and low exposure to television, Belson found that viewers who watched high amounts of violence reported greater involvement in serious violent behavior. In addition, interpersonal violence was associated with long-term exposure to plays or films featuring verbal and physical violence, gratuitous violence, fictional violence presented realistically, depictions of violence for a good cause, and violent westerns. Interestingly, Belson found that exposure to violence in cartoons, sports, science fiction, or slapstick comedy programs was not related to the boys' reports of aggressive behavior.

Belson proposed that viewing TV violence leads to disinhibition. As this disinhibition continues, the boys slip more easily and spontaneously into violent forms of behavior in response to their environment. In support of Belson's findings, McCarthy et al. (1975) found that children's conflict with parents, fighting, and delinquency all were positively correlated with frequency of exposure to violent television. Amount of television viewed was related to aggressive behavior as well.

The fact that researchers conducting naturalistic studies have obtained results congruent with the laboratory and field experimental findings lends strength to the conclusion that viewing violent TV can lead to an increase in aggression. The correlations obtained in the naturalistic studies are often relatively small, and, therefore, it is important to acknowledge that outside the laboratory, television is only one of many influences on aggression. For example, Eron and Huesmann and their colleagues (Eron, 1982) have some data suggesting that children in grades 1 and 3 who are reported as aggressive by their peers are likely to have parents who are aggressive themselves, use physical punishment, and are rejecting toward their children. Thus, more research is needed on the interaction of television with other socializing agents.

THE ROLE OF TELEVISION IN MORE SERIOUS AGGRESSION AND VIOLENCE

Taken together, the laboratory experiments, field experiments, and naturalistic studies support the hypothesis of a causal link between television and aggressive behavior; but what is the evidence that the aggression is sufficiently serious to warrant concern? This is another area in which more research is needed.

Some limited evidence does link television to serious acts of violence. Hennigan *et al.* (1982) found that the introduction of television in the United States was associated with increases in larceny. This was tentatively attributed to factors such as frustration or relative deprivation associated with viewing programs showing high levels of consumption rather than social learning of larceny, since larceny is not shown on TV very often. There was no consistent evidence that the introduction of TV affects violent crime, burglary, or auto theft rates. Phillips (1982) found an increase in the United States in 1977 of at least 127 suicides and 161 motor vehicle fatalities immediately following soap opera suicide stories, and Belson's (1978) study of teenage males in London led him to conclude that "high exposure to television violence increases the degree to which boys engage in serious violence" (p. 520). Stanley and Riera (1977) and Comstock (1983) have documented a number of "bizarre replications," in which violent acts seen on television seem to be imitated in real life. These have included instances of murder. Given that almost all North Americans watch television daily, but very few engage in delinquent or criminal acts, it would be surprising to find much evidence of a direct link between more serious aggression and TV viewing. However, there is good evidence that aggressive behavior remains stable over time (Huesmann, Eron, Lefkowitz, & Walder, 1984) and some evidence for males that peer nominations for aggressiveness at age 8 predict number and seriousness of criminal convictions at age 30 (Huesmann & Eron, 1985). This illustrates the need to understand how television's effects interact with the social controls of the family and broader systems in which individuals live.

In sum, it is the consensus of most researchers working in this area that the relationship between television and aggressive behavior established in laboratory studies is maintained in the field, and that the potential long-term effects of television on aggression may be sufficiently serious to warrant concern (see Comstock et al., 1978; Cook et al., 1983; Palmer & Dorr, 1980; Pearl et al., 1982; and Roberts & Bachen, 1981, for extensive reviews).

DESIGN OF OUR STUDY

The opportunity to study children's behavior in Notel, Unitel, and Multitel was advantageous because it enabled us to conduct longitudinal research of observed aggressive behavior in a naturalistic setting. The study was designed with the shortcomings of the various methodological approaches in mind. To date, only the Singer and Singer (1980) study has included actual observations of children's aggressive behavior. Other researchers have relied on either self-reports of aggressive behavior or ratings by peers and adults. Unfortunately, such measures depend upon the raters' ability to remember their perceptions of past events and on their willingness to report such events. Therefore these measures may be less reliable than observations.

We observed children's aggressive behavior during free play and also obtained teacher and peer ratings of aggression. Since observations for Notel children were made both before and 2 years after regular TV viewing began, we were able to study long-term effects. Because this was a natural experiment, we could not randomly assign children to TV-viewing conditions (towns), but we could design the study so as to minimize threats to internal validity. Some of these potential threats do not apply to this study (see Chapter 1 for a more detailed explanation), and others could be ruled out on the basis of either the data obtained or the design of the study (e.g., quirks of history, maturation, and statistical regression toward the mean). In essence, observing children's aggressive behavior before and after they became regular television viewers represented an important opportunity to assess the direction of the relationship between television and aggression.

HYPOTHESES

In the introduction of this book, the point was made that television may affect its viewers in two possible ways: by displacing other activities and through its content. Although they differ in other ways, all theoretical conceptualizations of the impact of television on aggressive behavior emphasize the influence of content. Social learning and information-processing theorists stress observational learning, that is, modeling and imitation of what is portrayed on the screen. Theorists with a psychoanalytic orientation also focus on the effect of television's content, arguing that TV either triggers pent-up aggressive impulses or allows viewers to vicariously release aggression through their emotional involvement with the televised portrayals. The bulk of empirical evidence does not support this latter catharsis hypothesis (Wells, 1973; also see our discussion of Feshbach & Singer's (1971) study in the previous section, "Field Experiments"). Theorists who emphasize the role of arousal, either in the physiological sense or in terms of cognitive involvement with the medium, also focus on television's content. In sum, whatever their differences, all conceptualizations of the processes whereby TV affects the aggressive behavior of its viewers emphasize content rather than displacement effects. We investigated several hypotheses about these effects.

The most important question was whether the aggressive behavior of Notel children would change following the inception of television in their community. Our prediction, based on the findings obtained in most previous research, was that it would increase. We expected this pattern to hold true for both the longitudinal comparisons involving children observed in both phases of the study, and the cross-sectional comparisons involving children observed only in the first or second phase. It was less clear, however, what to predict concerning the behavior of Unitel and Multitel children. Would continued exposure to aggressive content on television be associated with an increase in aggressive behavior, or would an asymptote be reached, and would we, therefore, see little evidence of change in the aggressive behavior of Unitel and Multitel children? It also was difficult to predict relative levels of aggression for each town. On the one hand, we might expect Notel children to be less aggressive than children in the other two towns in Phase 1 because of their less frequent exposure to television. On the other hand, we were aware that aggressive behavior depends upon numerous factors and processes involving complex interactions among members of a group. Television is only one infulence among many.

Second, if increases in aggression did occur, we were interested in the initial characteristics of the children. In some previous studies, increases in aggression following exposure to aggressive content occurred only for children initially high in aggression. These findings have been used on occasion to argue that violence on TV only affects people who are already highly aggressive. However, most of these previous studies involved short-term assessments. Learning aggressive behavior involves two steps, acquisition and performance (Bandura, 1978), but only performance is observable. If performance is delayed and does not occur until the person has left the experiment, there is no way of knowing whether acquisition occurred. Immediately following exposure to an aggressive model, the people most likely to perform the aggressive behavior they have just acquired may be those with fewest inhibitions against it, that is, those initially most aggressive. The natural experiment in Notel provided a unique opportunity to assess whether the long-term impact of regular television viewing was a change in aggressive behavior only for children initially high in aggression, or whether it was a more general phenomenon.

Related to the question of who, if anyone, increases in aggressive behavior is the issue of who watches what kind of television and how much. Do children initially high in aggression watch more television than children initially low in aggression? Do they prefer more violent programming? The data from previous research are mixed on this issue; both Rosengren (1983) and Eron (1982) have argued that the relationship between television and aggressive behavior goes both ways.

We also hypothesized that the repertoire of aggressive behaviors displayed by Notel children might change from the first to the second phase of the study so as to more closely resemble the repertoires of the Unitel and Multitel children. This hypothesis was based on evidence that children learn *specific* behaviors they see portrayed on television.

Finally, we hypothesized that boys would display more aggressive behavior than girls, since consistent sex differences in aggression are reported in the literature (Maccoby & Jacklin, 1974). This hypothesis was not central to the purpose of our study, but the replication of well-established findings obtained by other researchers with other samples would indicate that the children in the towns we studied were not unusual. This would lend external validity to our findings concerning the impact of television.

MEASURES AND PROCEDURES

We measured aggression in three different ways: through observations of physical and verbal aggression during free play, through teacher ratings, and through peer ratings. Direct observations were chosen not only because, at that time, they had never been used in a naturalistic study, but also because they have several advantages over peer and teacher ratings. First, other than having memorized the children's names, the people observing free-play aggression did not know the children and, therefore, could not be influenced by irrelevant factors such as how much they liked a child or knew about his or her home life, and so on. Second, the observers assessed actual free-play aggression and did not rely on retrospective and, therefore, perhaps, selective reporting. Third, as we note later in this chapter, sex-role and other stereotypes may affect peer and/or teacher judgments. The peer and teacher ratings were gathered primarily to see how well they related to our observations of aggressive behavior.

Observational Measures and Procedures

There has been considerable debate in the literature over the definition of aggression. Some researchers (e.g., Milavsky et al., 1982a, 1982b), have restricted themselves to behaviors which specify intention to hurt (trying to hurt by pushing and shoving; by hitting and punching; by saying mean things; lying to get someone in trouble; stealing; and damaging property). In her discussion of the development of aggression, Maccoby (1980) also emphasizes intentional acts of aggression. She points out, however, that unconscious aggression also occurs, that humans of all ages aggress without knowing why, and that they also act in ways that do not seem aggressive to themselves but to objective observers seem motivated to hurt. The coding system we used was chosen because the defined behaviors were reasonably clear examples of aggression. It would be difficult, if not impossible, for observers to judge intent reliably and we did not attempt to do so. However, coders do not recall observing or coding an aggressive act for which a child apologized. Thus, accidental aggression was not included in our data.

A second facet of the debate over the definition of aggression centers on "rough-and-tumble play." This issue arises most often with respect to preschool children, because of the problem of determining when children begin to have sufficient understanding of the self and others that intent to hurt becomes possible. Rough-and-tumble play, in which children roll around on the ground wrestling and punching each other, was very rare in our study, perhaps because the data in both phases were collected during the winter months and the ground was typically snow covered. Therefore, we do not think our data contain much of what has been described as rough-and-tumble play.

No definition of aggression or coding system is unassailable. For the reasons outlined here and earlier in this chapter, we believe our data appropriately measure children's aggressive behavior. The children were observed on the school playground during free-play periods (before school, during recess, at lunchtime, and after school). A time-sampling procedure was used: each child was observed for 21 1-minute intervals, but no child was observed for any 2 consecutive minutes. Order of observations was randomly predetermined rather than dictated by the action of the moment. All the observations in any one town were gathered over a 2-week period and each child was observed on several days. These procedures meant that the vicissitudes of daily life, for example, an argument with parents or siblings at breakfast, would not bias a child's scores. Observations in both phases of the study were made during the same month of the year to keep constant any effects weather might have on children's aggression.

A checklist of 14 physical and 9 verbal aggressive behaviors was used.[1] (Detailed descriptions of each aggression cateogry are provided in Table 7.A1). Physical aggression included behavior such as hitting, pushing, and chasing. Verbal aggression included threatening, arguing, and insulting. If the child exhibited any of the physical or verbal categories of aggression during the 1-minute observation period, the observer checked the appropriate category. Within a 1-minute period, any aggression category could be checked more than once.

The observers were as unobtrusive as possible. They were introduced in each classroom and said they would be walking around the playground to see how children play together. There was no mention of either television or aggression. During the first few days, when the observers were learning the children's names (no coding was done during this time), the children seemed aware of the observers, but began to ignore them when it became evident that the observers were not going to interfere with their play. The children were aware that two women were on the playground, but were not aware of which particular child was being observed at any time. Moreover, the children were accustomed to adults (the teachers) wandering around the playground. Although the presence of observers probably affected the children's behavior in some minor ways, these procedures seemed to be successful and made it less likely that the observers were unduly inhibiting the children's behavior.

None of the observers in Phase 1 participated in Phase 2 of the study. Within each phase, all observations in all three towns were made by the same pair of observers. Each child was observed by both members of the pair on different days. The extent to which the observers were scoring the same behaviors in the same way was checked periodically by having both observers watch the same child concurrently. High levels of agreement were reached; the inter-observer reliability for Phase 1 was .86 and for Phase 2, .80 (perfect agreement would be 1.00).[2]

The criteria used for including a child in the observational part of this study were the following: (1) the child was not substantially below average in ability according to a teacher rating; (2) the child had not repeated a grade; (3) the child had lived more than 3 years in the town; and (4) no sibling had been selected to be in the observational study.[3] We included this last criterion because potential environmental or genetic similarities in aggression that would be more likely to occur among siblings might have affected the results. Once these criteria had been met, children were randomly selected for observation.

A total of 240 children from all three towns and both phases of the study were observed. In Phase 1, observations were made in each town for five girls and five boys in each of grades 1, 2, 4, and 5. Grades 1 and 2 were chosen because we wanted to study the youngest elementary school children possible, and, whereas some families did not send their children to kindergarten, almost all sent them to grade 1. Grades 4 and 5 were chosen because we wanted to know whether the onset of regular viewing would affect aggressive behavior differently depending upon the age of the child when TV first became available.

In Phase 2, we would have preferred to re-observe all of the same children, that is, the longitudinal sample, as well as a complete cross-sectional sample of same-aged children. This was not possible for several reasons. First, pilot work suggested that by the time children reach grades 6 and 7, their patterns of behavior have changed enough that trying to observe aggressive behavior on school playgrounds would be fruitless. At this stage they do not play, but "hang out"; that is, they stand around and talk. We, therefore, restricted our longitudinal sample to students in grades 3 and 4 in Phase 2 who had been among the 60 first and second graders observed in Phase 1 and who were still available. The longitudinal analyses were based on 45 such children, 16 from Notel, 15 from Unitel, and 14 from Multitel. These 45 children did not differ in physical or verbal aggression from the other 15 children with whom they had been observed during Phase 1, who were not available for observation in Phase 2.[4]

The second constraint we faced was that the observations were time consuming. Two weeks were required in each town to observe 40 children in each phase of the study. It simply was not possible to spend the additional time that would have been necessary to obtain complete longitudinal and cross-sectional samples. Accordingly, in each town during Phase 2, we observed five boys and five girls in each of grades 1, 2, 3, and 4. The first and second graders provided a between-phase, cross-sectional comparison with first and second graders provided a between-phase, cross-sectional comparison with first and second graders in Phase 1. Most (75%) of the third and fourth graders observed in Phase 2 constituted the longitudinal sample. To these 45 children we added 15 third and fourth graders so that we would also be able to make cross-sectional comparisons between students in grades 4 and 5 in Phase 1 and those in grades 3 and 4 in Phase 2.[5] This meant we observed five girls and five boys in each town, in each of four grades, within each phase of the study.

Peer and Teacher Ratings

The peer ratings of aggression were obtained in both phases for all children in grades 1–5, including the children who were observed on the playground. For the peer ratings, each child nominated the three class-mates whom she or he perceived as the bossiest, fighting the most, talking back to the teacher the most, arguing and disagreeing the most, and pushing, shoving, and poking the most. In each case the child named first received a score of 3 points for that item, the child named second received a score of 2 points and the child named third received a score of 1 point. These scores were then totaled for each child. Since children in grades 1 and 2 would have had difficulty reading the forms and writing their answers, they were interviewed individually. The older children completed the forms in the classroom with assistance if it was required.

The teachers were asked to rate each child in their class on 10 7-point scales. For each behavior listed, the teacher indicated to what extent the behavior was very characteristic or not at all characteristic of the child being rated. Both positive and negative behaviors were included. For the analyses, the 10 individual items were grouped into four composite teacher ratings: (1) aggressive, argumentative, bossy, and hostile; (2) active and loud; (3) competitive and dominant; (4) friendly and honest.

TV-Viewing Habits

All of the children in the schools, including those involved in this study, were interviewed individually about their television-viewing and other media habits. The information obtained and the results of these interviews are described in detail in Chapter 5. In this chapter, we will discuss some of the TV-viewing data in relation to the measures of aggression for the children in this study.

RESULTS: LACK OF GRADE DIFFERENCES

All of the analyses of the observational data were based on the mean number of aggressive acts per minute. The first question asked was whether aggression varied according to the child's grade. These analyses were conducted separately for each phase of the study.

There were no differences in either physical or verbal aggression due to grade level.[6] This finding is important for two reasons. First, it enabled us to combine the data from the various grade levels for the longitudinal and cross-sectional analyses in which we asked about the impact of television. This increased the size of the groups for these analyses. The second, and more important, implication of the lack of differences among grade levels, is that maturation can be eliminated as an explanation of any increase in aggressive behavior observed in the longitudinal sample.

RESULTS: DIFFERENCES RELATED TO TELEVISION
EXPOSURE AND SEX

We next asked whether aggressive behavior was related to exposure to television. We began with the observational study, looking first at the longitudinal sample and then making cross-sectional comparisons between and within the phases. We then analyzed the peer and teacher ratings to ascertain whether they corroborated the observational data.

Longitudinal Group Comparisons

The longitudinal sample consisted of the 45 children observed when they were in grade 1 or 2, before Notel had television, and again 2 years later when they were in grade 3 or 4. The first step in the longitudinal analyses was a multivariate analysis in which both the physical and verbal aggression scores were included. The results indicated that, overall, the combination of these scores varied according to town, sex, and phase of the study, and, in addition, the phase difference varied according to town.[7] These significant overall findings justified the next step, which was to conduct separate univariate analyses on the physical and verbal aggression scores in order to delineate the results.

For the longitudinal sample, the *pattern* of findings regarding television exposure did not differ according to sex. However, in both phases of the study and in all three towns, boys were on average more physically aggressive than girls. The boys did not differ from girls in their mean level of verbal aggression.[8]

The most important question was whether the aggressive behavior of Notel children increased from Phase 1 to Phase 2. We found that Notel children increased in both physical and verbal aggression, while Unitel and Multitel children did not change significantly in either physical or verbal aggression (see note 8). These findings are depicted in Figure 7.1; the means are presented in Table 7.A2.

Before their town had television, Notel children in the longitudinal sample did not differ in physical aggression from children in the other towns, but 2 years later the same children were observed to be significantly more physically aggressive than children in both Unitel and Multitel. Unitel and Multitel children did not differ from each other in physical aggression in either phase of the study. The same pattern of results occurred for verbal aggression. The towns did not differ in Phase 1, but 2 years later, when the same Notel children were observed again, they had become significantly more verbally aggressive than their peers in Unitel and Multitel.

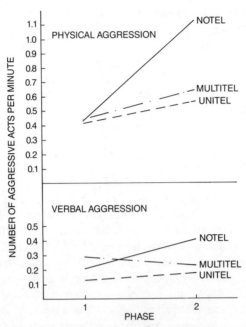

FIGURE 7.1   Mean number of verbal and physical aggressive acts per minute by town, sex, and phase for the longitudinal sample.

The significant increases observed in Notel children's physical and verbal aggressive behavior cannot be attributed to maturation, since Unitel and Multitel children's behavior did not change over the same 2-year period. Moreover, as pointed out earlier, aggressive behavior did not differ according to grade level in either phase of this study.

Cross-Sectional Group Comparisons

Did the cross-sectional comparisons involving same-aged children observed only in Phase 1 or Phase 2 support the longitudinal findings? To determine whether children in Phase 2 differed in aggressive behavior from the same-aged children in Phase 1, we began with a multivariate analysis, comparing the combination of physical and verbal aggression of first and second graders in Phase 1 with the behavior of first and second graders observed 2 years later. In another multivariate analysis we compared fourth and fifth graders from Phase 1 with third and fourth graders from Phase 2 (see note 5).[9] Then we made specific comparisons for each town for physical and verbal aggression.[10]

On average, first and second graders residing in Notel 2 years after TV arrived had higher mean physical and verbal aggression scores that first and second graders residing in Notel before the inception of television (see note 10). This was also true when Notel third and fourth graders in Phase 2 were compared with Notel fourth and fifth graders in Phase 1. The greater incidence of physical aggression in Phase 2 was true of both girls and boys in grades 3 and 4 and of girls in grades 1 and 2 when they were compared with their peers from Phase 1, and the greater incidence of verbal aggression in Phase 2 was true of both girls and boys in grades 3 and 4 and of boys in grades 1 and 2 when they were compared with their peers from Phase 1. In sum, 10 of the 12 cross-sectional comparisons revealed a statistically significant increase in aggression 2 years after the arrival of television. In the other two instances the means were higher in Phase 2, but the differences were not large enough to be statistically significant.

In contrast to the increase in both verbal and physical aggression in Notel between Phase 1 and Phase 2 (see note 10), none of the 12 comparisons was significant in Unitel. In Multitel, a decrease was found for girls' verbal aggression (grades 1 and 2) and an increase was found for physical aggression for both sexes combined (grades 3 and 4) (see note 10).

We next examined whether there was evidence in the cross-sectional data that the towns differed in either phase of the study and explored more fully the question of sex differences in aggressive behavior.[11] The longitudinal sample had provided some answers to these questions, but the cross-sectional samples, consisting of all children observed in each phase of the study, provided a better test because of the larger sample size (120 children in each phase in comparison to 45 children in the longitudinal sample).

Before their town had television reception, Notel and Unitel children exhibited significantly less verbal aggression than Multitel children. The towns did not differ in physical aggression in Phase 1. Two years later Notel children exhibited the most physical aggression, significantly more than Unitel children, who were lowest. Multitel children's level of aggression was in the middle and was not different from either Notel or Unitel. Notel children also exhibited the most verbal aggression, significantly more than children in both Multitel and Unitel, who did not differ. These results (see note 11) are depicted in Figure 7.2.

The pattern of findings regarding the impact of television was the same for girls and boys, but on the average, boys exhibited more physical aggression than did girls in both phases of the study, and in Phase 2, they also exhibited more verbal aggression than did girls (see note 11). There was no sex difference in verbal aggression in Phase 1.

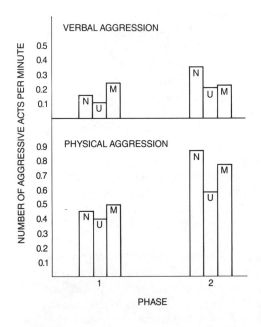

FIGURE 7.2 Mean number of verbal and physical aggressive acts per minute by town, sex, and phase for all participants in each phase. (Cross-sectional samples; N, Notel; U, Unitel; M, Multitel.)

Median Analyses

The aggressive behavior of children in this sample did not conform to a bell-shaped curve, or normal distribution. Instead, it was J shaped, with most children exhibiting relatively low levels of aggression and a smaller number of children exhibiting relatively high levels. Milavsky et al. (1982) have reported the same type of distribution for their peer and self-report data on aggression. As Table 7.A2 indicates, one consequence is that the median tends to be lower than the mean.

Many statistical procedures, typically the most powerful ones, assume that the behavior to be analyzed is normally distributed. Since these procedures also tend to be fairly robust, they often are used to analyze data which are not normally distributed. Indeed, a review of the research on aggressive behavior indicates that violation of the assumption of normality has been routinely ignored. We also have taken this approach, but only after ascertaining that a more conservative approach would lead to the same general conclusions. We asked whether there was a change in the median levels of physical and verbal aggression in Notel from Phase 1 to Phase 2, comparing separately the two lower and upper grades in the study, and repeated this for Unitel and Multitel.[12] The results of these analyses generally pointed to the same conclusions as those based on the means (see note 10).

Summary of Results Based on Group Comparisons of Observations

Taken together, the analyses of the observational data indicated that Notel children increased in both verbal and physical aggression following the introduction of television into their community, as we had hypothesized. However, rather than being initially less aggressive than the children in Unitel and Multitel, and then increasing to the level of children in those towns, Notel children exhibited similar levels of aggression and then increased to the extent that 2 years after the arrival of television in their town they were more aggressive than children who had grown up with TV. The only instance in which Notel children exhibited less aggression in Phase 1 was in the cross-sectional analyses of verbal aggression, in which they were less aggressive than Multitel, but not Unitel, children. One tentative explanation of this pattern of findings is that the social constraints which operate in children's play groups may have effectively controlled the behavior of children on the playground in all three towns in Phase 1, but the introduction of television to Notel broke down these controls, resulting in an increase in both verbal and physical aggression in that community. This impact was not short lived, since it was observable 2 years later.

We will discuss these findings in more detail later. Before doing so, we will consider the results of some additional analyses.

Relationship between TV Viewing and Aggression for Individuals

In addition to comparing groups differing in exposure to television, we were able to compare individuals differing in reported exposure, since we obtained information about usual hours of TV viewed per week. The details of the methods used to obtain these data are outlined in Chapter 5. It should be noted that we did not have Phase 1 TV-viewing data for some of the children. This reduced the size of the sample on which analyses of Phase 1 TV viewing could be based.

Regression analyses were conducted to determine the extent to which our measures of aggressive behavior and TV viewing were related for individuals in this study. We chose regression, rather than correlational, analyses because they enabled us to ask whether two measures were related and also whether a given measure (e.g., TV viewing) added significantly to prediction from other measures (e.g., aggression).

The regression analyses involved prediction within each phase of the study, as well as prediction from Phase 1 to Phase 2. The six measures of aggression used as predictor variables in the regression analyses were: (1) observed physical aggression (mean per minute); (2) observed verbal aggression (mean per minute); (3) sum of peer nominations (for bossiest, gets into fights, talks back to the teacher, argues and disagrees with the other children, and pushes, shoves, and pokes other children); (4) peer nomination for the specific item "gets into fights"; (5) sum of teacher ratings for aggressive, argumentative, bossy, and hostile; and (6) sum of teacher ratings for friendly and honest. The measures of TV viewing consisted of the reported hours viewed per week in Phase 1 and hours viewed per week in Phase 2. We asked whether observed physical aggression, observed verbal aggression, and self-reports of amount of TV viewing could be predicted by any combination of the other measures, both within and across the phases. The analyses were conducted twice, first for all three towns combined and then for only Unitel and Multitel. (This was done because Notel residents' experience with television differed from the experience of Unitel and Multitel residents.) The results of the regression analyses are presented in detail in Tables 7.A3–7.A5 and summarized briefly next. Whenever the predictors included hours of TV viewing in Phase 1, the analysis was restricted to Unitel and Multitel (since most Notel children watched 0 hours of television in Phase 1).

Summary of Regression Analyses

Perhaps the strongest conclusion to be drawn from the regression analyses is evidence of validity for our observational measures of aggression. The judgments of other observers, especially the children's peers but also, in some instances, their teachers (in the concurrent Phase 1 analyses), tended to corroborate our observations. In addition, the regression analyses also yielded some evidence to support the hypothesis that children who watch more TV tend to be more physically aggressive (see Tables 7.A4 and 7.A5). Given the fairly strong relationships among different measures of aggression and the stability of aggressive behavior over time, it is interesting to find that, at least in some instances, amount of TV viewing does add significantly to prediction of aggressive behavior.

In sum, we consider these regression analyses to be an adjunct to our main findings of mean differences among the towns and of mean increases in aggression for Notel children from Phase 1 to Phase 2 of the study. The fact that the regression results support these findings strengthens any conclusions we might draw concerning the impact of television on children's aggressive behavior.

Summary of Sex Differences

Both the longitudinal and cross-sectional analyses revealed consistent sex differences in physical aggression; in both phases of the study boys had a higher mean physical aggression score than girls. The findings for verbal aggression were less consistent, but when a sex difference appeared, in particular, in the Phase 2 cross-sectional comparisons, boys exhibited higher levels of verbal aggression than did girls.

This pattern of sex differences replicates findings obtained by other researchers. Literature reviews point to the greater physical aggressiveness of boys as one of the most consistently found sex differences in human behavior (Feshbach, 1970; Maccoby & Jacklin, 1974). The same reviewers also report that when sex differences in verbal aggression are found, boys score higher than girls. Our replication of this established pattern indicates that the children in the three towns we studied were similar in this regard to children in samples drawn from larger urban populations. This permits greater confidence in generalizing from our results.

SUMMARY OF DIFFERENCES IN AGGRESSION RELATED TO TV EXPOSURE

On the whole, the findings from the longitudinal analyses and the cross-sectional comparisons from Phase 1 to Phase 2 were consistent and supported the hypothesis that Notel children would exhibit increases in aggressive behavior following the inception of television in their community. Increases in Notel were observed in both physical and verbal aggression for both sexes and for children at all age levels. There was less change in the aggressive behavior of children in Unitel and Multitel. This is not to say that TV had no impact in Unitel and Multitel, since we did find a relation between amount of TV viewing and observed physical aggression in these two towns in Phase 2.

Comparisons made among the towns in the two phases of the study, in both the longitudinal and cross-sectional analyses, also yielded a consistent pattern of results. In Phase 1, cross-sectional comparisons among the towns indicated that Notel children (along with Unitel children) were less verbally aggressive than Multitel children, but there was no evidence of differences among the towns in physical aggression. After 2 years of regular TV viewing, Notel children were more physically and verbally aggressive than children in the other towns.

The lack of differences among the towns in the levels of physical aggression exhibited on the school playgrounds prior to the arrival of TV reception in Notel should not be surprising given that television is only one factor to influence the acquisition of aggressive behavior. As we noted earlier, television does not affect its viewers in a vacuum. Rather, the wider milieu of aggressive behavior and prohibitions for such behavior must be considered when comparisons are made among social groups. For example, children can learn to behave aggressively from modeling each other; in self-defence or retaliation against another child's aggression; from parental teaching, sanctions, and modeling; from other media sources; and from the general acceptance of violence as a method of conflict resolution in our society.

DOES TV ONLY AFFECT CHILDREN INITIALLY HIGH IN AGGRESSION?

Did most Notel children increase in aggressive behavior following the inception of TV in their community, or was the increase specific to highly aggressive children?

Because several other researchers have reported that violent programs have their greatest, and perhaps only, impact on children who are already highly aggressive (Leyens et al., 1975; Parke et al., 1977; Stein & Friedrich, 1972; Wells, 1973), we assessed whether this was the case in our study. We first determined, for each town, the median scores on physical and verbal aggression in Phase 1, that is, the score above and below which 50% of the sample fell. We then classified each Notel child in the longitudinal sample as either initially high in physical aggression (above the median in Phase 1) or initially low in physical aggression (below the median in Phase 1). We repeated this procedure for each town and for verbal aggression. We then looked at Phase 2 behavior and compared the mean levels of Phase 2 aggressive behavior for the groups above and below the Phase 1 median.

If the children in Notel who were highly aggressive before they became regular TV viewers were most affected by the arrival of television, we would have found that their Phase 2 scores were higher than the scores of the Notel children who were initially low in aggression. This did not happen. The groups did not differ in either physical or verbal aggression 2 years after the arrival of television, indicating that increases for children initially below the median were on average as large as the increases for children intially above it. A similar pattern of results was found for children in Unitel and Multitel.[13]

Why might our findings run counter to the research showing that television affects the aggressive behavior of only those viewers who are already high in aggression? The most plausible explanation is that we examined long-term effects of television. Researchers who have found a greater impact of TV for highly aggressive children measured aggression during and/or immediately following a change in the children's television diet. As we noted earlier, children who are least inhibited about behaving aggressively might be most likely to exhibit aggression soon after observing such behavior.

It is certainly possible that the immediate effect of the inception of TV in Notel was an increase in the aggressive behavior of children initially high in aggression, with no change for those initially low in aggression. This might occur if all children *acquired* aggressive behaviors from TV, but because of differences in their inhibitions against behaving aggressively, only those initially high in aggression *performed* the behaviors. If so, we might speculate that, over time, the more aggressive children served as models for the less aggressive children. Or, the initially less aggressive children might have become more aggressive as a result of interacting with their now highly aggressive peers. In other words, the change in the behavior of the children intially low in aggression could result from their own observations of models on TV, from copying their more aggressive peers, and/or for reasons of self-defense; they may simply have retaliated against aggression directed at them. Most likely all three of these processes were operating. The possibility that exposure to television has a greater effect on highly aggressive children who, in turn, affect less aggressive children, receives support from two studies (Murray, Hayes, & Smith, 1978; Thomas & Drabman, 1975).

It is, of course, possible that the effect of television was similar for Notel children who were initially high or low in aggressiveness, an effect that might have been present immediately following the arrival of television or that might have developed over time. The experience of Notel children changed from occasional exposure (when they visited families with television) to being able to watch TV daily. This is a greater change than is typical of the field experiments in which regular TV diets are altered (Cameron & Janky, 1971; Feshbach & Singer, 1971; Wells, 1973) or aggressive or nonaggressive programming or films are added to regular TV-viewing schedules (Leyens, et al., 1975; Parke et al., 1977; Stein & Friedrich, 1972; Steuer et al., 1971).

TV-VIEWING PREFERENCES

The question of who was affected by the inception of television in Notel leads logically to the question of whether Notel children's preferences for television in the second phase of the study varied according to their initial level of aggressive behavior. This question deals with the important issue of whether television exposure is related to aggressive behavior because TV causes an increase in aggression, because aggressive people choose to watch a lot of aggression on television, or both. We pursued this in two ways, through median split and regression analyses. The results of the regression analyses are shown in Tables 7.A3–7.A5. In Phase 2, observed physical aggression was a significant predictor of hours of TV viewing, but only for Unitel and Multitel. When Phase 2 TV viewing was analyzed in relation to Phase 1 aggression measures, the peer nomination item "gets into fights" was a significant predictor when the three towns were combined, but not when Notel children were omitted. In sum, the regression analyses yielded some evidence that more aggressive children tend to watch more television, but it was not strong.

For the median split analyses we divided the children observed in Phase 1 into groups according to whether they were above or below the physical aggression median for their town. We then calculated the mean number of hours of television watched per week by each group in Phase 2. This procedure was repeated for verbal aggression. There was no evidence in any town that children above the median in Phase 1 in either physical or verbal aggression watched more TV in Phase 2 than their classmates who had been below the median.[14] In addition, there was no evidence that Notel children, who were more physically aggressive than their peers before they became regular TV viewers, named more violent programs as favorites 2 years later.[15] This finding is consistent with the results obtained by Eron et al. (1972), who found no relationship in their longitudinal study between aggression at 8 years of age and preference for violent TV at 18 years of age. However, the data obtained by Eron and Huesmann and their colleagues in their subsequent 3-year longitudinal study have led Eron (1982) to conclude that aggressive children tend to watch more television in general and more violent television in particular. The relationship between aggressive behavior and preference for violent TV was found to be stronger than the relationship between aggressive behavior and amount or frequency of TV viewing. Our findings are based on a general measure of television exposure, irrespective of content, and therefore may provide a relatively weak test.

TEACHER AND PEER RATINGS OF AGGRESSION

As we have emphasized, behavioral observations have several methodological advantages over ratings. Nevertheless, we obtained teacher and peer ratings of aggression because they provided an external validity check on our observations, and, in addition, several researchers have relied on teacher and/or peer ratings. These measures are easier to obtain, and beyond about age 10, observation of aggressive behavior becomes difficult, if not impossible. Therefore, we assessed the extent of agreement between ratings and behavioral observations. The regression analyses described earlier (see Tables 7.A3–7.A5) also provided information concerning this issue.

Agreement among Different Measures of Aggression

Correlations were computed among the aggression measures within each phase of the study. As Table 7.A6 indicates, correlations among individual items within each type of measure (teacher ratings, peer ratings, and observations) were generally significant, and there was evidence of agreement among the different measures. When correlations were computed separately for each town in each phase (Table 7.A7), the relationships among the measures were maintained with only a few exceptions. The peer and teacher ratings in Unitel were not related in Phase 1, and in Phase 2, neither the peer nor the teacher ratings in Notel were related to observations of aggressive behavior. The ratings were examined in more depth in an effort to explain some of these discrepancies (see Tables 7.A6–7.A8).[16]

We found that relatively few children were named by their peers in response to the five questions asked, and the same children tended to be named in response to all of the questions. In other words, even though some of the items were designed to assess physical aggression (fights; pushes, shoves, and pokes), other items to assess verbal aggression (argues and disagrees; talks back to the teacher), and one to assess dominance (bossy), the children did not tend to discriminate in responding to the different items. Moreover, the peer ratings were more consistently related to observed physical aggression than to observed verbal aggression (especially in Phase 1). This seems to indicate that the children define *aggression* as *physical aggression* and make judgments about their peers based on physical rather than verbal aggressive behavior. Because the children tended to name the same youngsters in response to each item of the peer ratings and to nominate relatively few children in total, the peer ratings formed a J-shaped distribution which was more severely skewed than the observations. This lack of variation among the peer ratings means that significant correlations with other variables are less likely to be obtained. Given the skewed nature of both the peer ratings and the observations, the number of obtained significant correlations is noteworthy and indicates that observed physical aggression and peer ratings of aggression were indeed related.

The teachers' ratings for the items that related to aggression (i.e., all but friendly and honest) were in agreement with the peer ratings in both phases of the study (see Tables 7.A7–7.A9). They also were related to our observations of aggression in Phase 1, but the relationships were not as strong in Phase 2.

The most interesting lack of relationship between the ratings and observations occurred for Notel in Phase 2. As can be seen in Table 7.A7, none of the peer or teacher ratings correlated significantly with either physical or verbal observations of aggression. In explaining this lack of correlation we considered two possibilities. The first was experimenter bias (see discussion on p. 333). A systematic bias on the part of the observers to rate Notel children as more aggressive in Phase 2 would have influenced the mean level of aggression observed, but it would not have changed the rank order of the children. An unsystematic bias would have resulted in lower inter-observer reliability in Phase 2, and this was not found. Thus, observer bias is an unlikely explanation of the lack of relationship between ratings and observations for Notel in Phase 2. On the other hand, increased social disorganization resulting from the introduction of television could have led to just such a lack of relationship. For both children and adults, the disruption of social structures, as well as increased overall levels of aggression, may have changed expectations about who was aggressive and in what situations they were expected to be aggressive. This explanation gains strength from the fact that all the children in Notel, not just those initially high in aggression, became more aggressive following TV's arrival. The lack of correspondence between ratings and observations in Notel in Phase 2 thus provides further evidence of the effect of the introduction of television on social structures, on aggressive behavior, and on perceptions of aggression. In sum, although they were not in complete agreement, the weight of the evidence indicates that our observations were consistent with peer and teacher ratings of aggression.

Possible Bias in Ratings of Aggression

In the process of examining the distribution of peer ratings, we noticed the children seldom nominated girls. This led us to suspect that peer ratings and, for that matter, ratings by teachers and adults in general may be subject to bias because boys are on average more physically aggressive than girls. This stereotype is well founded; our data, and the results of many other studies, indicate that the mean physical aggression score for boys tends to be higher than that for girls. This does not mean, however, that girls are never physically aggressive. In other words, knowledge of a mean difference does not make prediction accurate in individual cases, but people may be influenced by this when rating individuals.

As can be seen in Table 7.A9, observations of physical aggression were consistently and significantly related to the peer nominations for boys but generally unrelated to the peer nominations for girls. As Table 7.A8 indicates, when the towns and sexes were combined, the peer nominations were generally not related to observed verbal aggression. However, girls in Phase 1 who were observed to be verbally aggressive tended to be nominated by their peers as bossy, talking back to the teacher, and arguing and disagreeing. They were *not* nominated for fighting or pushing, shoving, and poking, even though the observations indicated that girls high on verbal aggression also tended to be high on physical aggression in both phases (see Table 7.A9). In addition, the item "fights" was not correlated with the other peer rating items for girls in Phase 1, a surprising finding in view of the tendency discussed earlier for children to rate a few of their peers as high on everything (yielding Cronbach's alpha coefficients of .91 and .90 overall). All of these results suggested to us that children may be reluctant to judge girls as physically aggressive.

In order to examine this reluctance, the children within each town and phase were ordered from highest to lowest on observed physical aggression. As Table 7.A10 indicates, more than two-thirds of the children in both the top 10% and the top 15% of physically aggressive children in each group were boys. However, when we ordered the same children from highest to lowest on the peer nomination items "fights" and "pushes, shoves, and pokes," the proportions were even higher. The data for "fights" are particularly noteworthy.

When the children were ordered from highest to lowest on observed verbal aggression, boys were not particularly over-represented among the top 10 or 15% (with the exception of Multitel in Phase 2). However, as can be seen in Table 7.A10, boys were generally over-represented among the children identified by their peers as constituting the top 10 and 15% on the items "argues and disagrees," and "talks back to the teacher." This suggests that children may be reluctant to judge girls as high in verbal aggression as well.

In sum, the data suggest that when peer nominations are used to assess aggression, they may be biased by sex stereotypes about aggressive behavior.

CONCLUSIONS REGARDING MEASURES OF
AGGRESSION

Most of the evidence from the analyses comparing relationships among the different measures of aggression indicates that the aggressive behavior observed on the school playgrounds was representative of the children's usual behavior. However, the relationship between observed behavior and the judgments by the children's teachers and peers was not perfect. The pattern of inconsistencies, and our examination of the peer ratings in particular, suggest that judgments may be biased for a variety of reasons. The *lack* of variation in the peer ratings further suggests the correlations between peer ratings on aggression and exposure to television may underestimate the degree of relationship. Investigators who rely on peer nominations should consider potential sources of bias. For all of these reasons we continue to hold the opinion that researchers studying aggression in the preschool and early elementary years should obtain observational data if at all possible.

QUALITATIVE ANALYSES OF CHANGES IN
AGGRESSIVE BEHAVIOR

In addition to predicting quantitative changes in Notel children's aggressive behavior as a consequence of exposure to television, we assessed possible qualitative changes as well. The observational data were examined to see whether there were differences among the towns or changes between Phases 1 and 2 in the kinds of physical or verbal aggression displayed. There were not. The most frequent types of physically aggressive behaviors in the first phase of the study, in all three towns, were "pushes," "hits above the waist," and "interferes with the activity of another child." The first two of these behaviors were also noted most frequently in all three towns in the second phase. "Interferes with the activity of another child" was replaced as the third most frequent physically aggressive behavior by "chasing" in Notel, by "throwing an object at someone" in Unitel, and by "kicking and tripping" in Multitel. For verbal aggression there were no changes between Phase 1 and Phase 2; in all three towns the most frequent examples of verbal abuse were "makes disparaging remarks," "argues," and "commands in a loud and angry voice," in that order.

The lack of differences in the types of aggressive behavior displayed does not mean that differences did not exist but, rather, that they did not occur for the types of behaviors included in our observational system and the settings in which observations occurred.

We know from other research conducted in the laboratory, and from instances of "copycat crimes" (for example, hijacking threats following showing of the movie *Doomsday Flight*), that people do learn specific aggressive behaviors from television (see Stanley & Riera, 1977, for a review). The optimal way of documenting such learning, however, is in laboratory or field studies in which the presentation of specific content is monitored, and viewers are subsequently observed to see whether they display those specific behaviors. Bachen (personal communication, April, 1984) is currently conducting such research. The long-term nature of our study and the very general measure of exposure to television precluded this possibility.

ALTERNATIVE POSSIBLE EXPLANATIONS OF OUR FINDINGS

In any naturalistic study of television's effects, it is difficult to control all possible relevant factors. Thus it is important to consider potential alternative explanations of the results. Three such possibilities for our study are experimenter bias, changes in school personnel, and mediating variables.

The observers could not have been "blind" to, that is, unaware of, television reception in the towns in which they were observing. Nevertheless, we believe that experimenter bias did not significantly influence the results. First, observers in both phases of the study did not know the specific hypotheses being tested. Second, different people served as observers in the two phases of the study. The observers in Phase 2 were unaware of the results from the first phase, including the specific levels of aggression observed in each town. Because of this, and because we hypothesized a pattern of results involving change in Notel but were unsure whether to expect a change in Unitel and Multitel, it would have been difficult for experimenter bias to produce such a pattern. Third, the high levels of inter-observer agreement (.86 for Phase 1 and .80 for Phase 2) offers evidence of the consistency of the ratings and reduces the possibility that experimenter bias was a systematic factor. Fourth, some of our hypotheses were not supported by the data. For example, our expectation that the repertoire of aggressive behavior would vary with the town and phase of the study was not borne out. Finally, as we have already discussed in some detail, our observations of aggression generally were corroborated by the peer and teacher ratings. All of these considerations make us reasonably confident that experimenter bias does not account for the results.

Changes in school personnel, which could have resulted in alterations of playground rules concerning aggression, constitute another potential explanation of our findings. This alternative would require that the rules in Unitel and Multitel changed less than those in the Notel school playground. Moreover, the change in Notel would have to have been such that the rules were more lenient in Phase 2 than in Phase 1. This possibility can be eliminated on several grounds. Most important is the fact that our findings occurred for verbal aggression as well as physical aggression, but in all three towns and in both phases of the study, playground rules concerned physical aggression and not verbal aggression. Teachers would intervene in a physical fight, but would not attempt to control verbal abuse. Moreover, the same rules held in all three towns—fights were stopped if it appeared that a child was being physically hurt or about to be hurt. The principals of the elementary schools in all three towns changed between the first and second phases of the study. The Notel principal during Phase 2 was not noticeably more lenient in dealing with physical aggression on the playground than the Phase 1 Notel principal. If anything, a change might have been expected in Unitel, since the Phase 2 principal had a rather strict policy regarding physical aggression, and when he appeared on the playground, physical aggression tended to decrease. Even this apparent influence did not result in Unitel children behaving less aggressively in the second than in the first phase of the study. Therefore, it is highly unlikely that playground rules accounted for the pattern of results found in this study.

IQ and socioeconomic status were considered as mediating variables. In our study, IQ was not related to observed physical or verbal aggression, and as the children were sampled randomly and the towns were economically comparable, socioeconomic status also can be discounted.[17]

SUMMARY OF RESULTS

To summarize, there was a significant increase in the aggressive behavior of Notel children following the inception of television in their community. This increase occurred for both physical and verbal aggressive behavior; it occurred for both boys and girls; it occurred at more than one age level; it occurred for children who were initially low in aggressive behavior as well as those who were initially high in aggressive behavior; and it occurred for the same children studied longitudinally and same-aged children compared cross-sectionally. The evidence from this natural experiment suggests, therefore, that television led to an increase in Notel children's aggressive behavior. Before considering the possible processes involved and our interpretation of the results of this study, we would like to make two additional points.

First, we measured both physical and verbal aggression and found evidence of increases for both. Before they became regular TV viewers, Notel children exhibited less verbal aggression than Multitel children. Two years after the arrival of TV, both the same Notel children and same-aged Notel children were more verbally aggressive than children in the other towns. However, most of the research dealing with television and aggression has focused on physical aggression, even though North American television also contains high levels of verbal abuse, as has now been documented through content analyses (Greenberg, 1980; Williams et al., 1977, 1982). It should not be surprising to find that viewers may be affected by the verbal abuse and threats that are characteristic of television fare, as Wotring and Greenberg (1973) found for adolescent boys. As Greenberg (1980) points out, verbal aggression is less prone than physical aggression to negative sanctions if imitated or modeled, and it also is easier to practice.

A second noteworthy point about our results is that Notel children's aggressive behavior changed following exposure to only one channel of programming, the Canadian government-owned channel, CBC. Between the first and second phases of this study, CBC carried only two crime–detective shows per week: "Police Story" (U.S.-produced) and "Sidestreet" (Canadian-produced). However, content analyses have revealed that although the mean level of aggression in CBC programming is lower than the mean level for the U.S. networks ABC, CBS, and NBC, it is still substantial (Williams et al., 1977, 1982). The levels of verbal aggression in situation comedies on CBC were relatively high, and the most explicit physical violence depicted in the content sample analyzed by Williams and her colleagues came from documentaries shown on CBC. The finding that exposure to CBC was sufficient to bring about the changes observed in Notel brings us back to the threshold argument put forth in Chapter 1. Given typical North American TV diets, that is, many hours of viewing repetitive content, a consistent linear relationship between TV exposure and the viewer's behavior seems unlikely.

PROCESSES INVOLVED IN TV'S IMPACT

Although our study was designed to assess the impact of television in a naturalistic setting rather than to evaluate competing theoretical models of the processes through which TV affects it viewers, an examination of those models with respect to our findings seems in order.

Several different processes, operating either directly or indirectly, have been hypothesized to account for television's influence on children's aggressive behavior. Of these processes, the most widely discussed, and the one for which most empirical evidence has been accumulated, is observational learning. Through laboratory experiments, Bandura and others (Bandura, 1965; Bandura et al., 1963a, 1963b; Feshbach, 1972; Hanratty et al., 1969; Hartman, 1965; Liebert & Baron, 1972; Stoessel, 1972) have documented that people who view filmed aggression imitate what they have seen and heard. This kind of learning is sometimes termed *vicarious* because it occurs in the absence of any apparent reinforcement for the viewer. Mere exposure to a model may be sufficient, although certain aspects of the portrayal have been shown to increase the likelihood that imitation will occur. These have been summarized by Comstock (1980) under four categories: social approval for the model and/or behavior; the efficacy or successfulness of the behavior; the relevance of the behavior and the model's characteristics to the viewer; and whether the portrayal optimizes arousal for the viewer. Huesmann (1982) has reviewed several theoretical and empirical attempts to link observational learning more closely to theorizing in cognitive psychology. The evidence suggests that viewers who see aggressive behavior on television can store and, subsequently, retrieve and perform the behavior when the appropriate cues are present. Even minor and seemingly irrelevant cues may serve as triggers. Thus, one process whereby TV affects its viewers consists of teaching aggressive styles of conduct (Bandura, 1978; Comstock, 1980; Comstock et al., 1978; Lefkowitz & Huesmann, 1980). It is likely that at least some children in Notel were affected by television through observational learning.

An important facet of observational learning is *disinhibition*, another mechanism through which TV has been hypothesized to affect its viewers (Lefkowitz & Huesmann, 1980). According to this view, TV alters restraints over acting aggressively (Bandura, 1978), thus affecting people's willingness to behave in an aggressive manner. The high levels of both physical and verbal aggression on television tend to be presented repeatedly with the same messages. For example, aggression is the most common method of conflict resolution portrayed (arbitration or conciliation, for example, are rarely seen), and it is depicted as successful (victims give in or witnesses are passive; Williams et al., 1977, 1982). Accordingly, viewers do not just learn specific types of aggressive behavior from television; they also learn that aggression is a successful and accepted method of achieving goals. This message is received not only by an individual child who watches TV, but also by that child's siblings, parents, peers, and teachers. It is likely, therefore, that inhibitions against behaving aggressively are altered not only through direct learning from television but also indirectly through the impact of television on other viewers with whom the child interacts.

There is a growing body of evidence concerning the role of arousal in television's impact. Krull and Watt (1973) have demonstrated that the excitatory attributes of television, apart from any violence portrayed, and the violence, apart from television's excitatory attributes, each *independently* relates to viewer aggressiveness. Wright and Huston (1983) have conducted research designed to measure the independent effects of television's violent content and its form (that is, its noncontent aspects such as action, pace, visual techniques and auditory features). Their results indicate that what maintains children's attention to television is salient form rather than violent content, a finding which suggests that much of the violent content could be eliminated without reducing audience interest.

Other research suggests that optimal levels of arousal, achieved through media effects, facilitate learning from TV (e.g., Tannenbaum & Zillman, 1975; see Comstock et al., 1978, for a more detailed review). The notion of an *optimal* level of arousal is important. As is the case for other areas of human behavior (Berlyne, 1965), very low or very high levels of arousal result in less learning than does some middle range of arousal. Of course, that middle range and, therefore, what is optimal undoubtedly vary with age and from one individual to another.

In the case of the impact of television, the term *arousal* refers to both physiological and cognitive processes. Arousal would not be optimal if the viewer was asleep (low physiological arousal) or not listening to and/ or looking at the screen (low cognitive involvement or attention). Salomon (1979) has discussed the relationships among cognition, media, and learning in greater detail. He emphasizes the role of attentive involvement in learning from television (Salomon, 1981, 1983). In the case of our natural experiment in Notel, it is likely that arousal played an important role in television's impact on the children's aggressive behavior. At least initially, Notel children probably were very attentive to and cognitively involved with the programming. Because it was a new phenomenon for most of them, it also would be exciting. All of this would facilitate learning from television.

TV may desensitize and habituate people to violence and verbal abuse, and, as a consequence, their tolerance for such behavior may increase (Bandura, 1978; Comstock, 1980; Lefkowitz & Huesmann, 1980). It is possible that, as a result of increased exposure to aggression by means of television, people in Notel, including teachers, parents, and peers, were more willing to tolerate aggression by Notel children. However, as Comstock (1980) notes, the empirical studies of desensitization to date have shown only that people exposed to televised violence increase their tolerance for further televised violence (Cline, Croft, & Courrier, 1972; Drabman & Thomas, 1974). Research is needed to determine whether media experience affects tolerance for real-life violence as well.

In considering the processes by which television affects aggressive behavior, some additional points regarding cognitive involvement with television, specifically, attention and comprehension, should be made. Attention clearly facilitates learning from television, as stated earlier. In addition, lack of understanding of the motives and consequences for aggressive behavior makes it even more likely the behavior will be imitated. Researchers have found that, when simple, short, film sequences are shown in the laboratory, imitation of aggression decreases if negative consequences are shown (Bandura et al., 1963a; Bandura, 1965; Hicks, 1968; Leifer & Roberts, 1972). However, in real television programs, motives and consequences for aggression, if depicted at all, are widely separated in time from the aggressive act (for example, the violence may occur at the beginning and punishment at the end, a half-hour or an hour later). In addition, children of similar ages to those in our study attend sporadically to the set, paying attention when the action is attractive and often looking away (Anderson, 1977; Anderson, Alwitt, Lorch, & Levin, 1979; Anderson & Levin, 1976; Anderson & Lorch, 1983; Lorch, Anderson, & Levin, 1979). Indeed, Anderson and his colleagues have reported (Anderson, 1983) that although the 5-year-olds in their study spent 2.2 hours per day in the room with the television set, they were looking at the screen only 1.3 hours per day and often did other things while watching television. Furthermore, they frequently left the room. These data help explain why children understand little of what they see on television (e.g., Collins, 1981, 1983; Friedlander, Wetstone, & Scott, 1974; Williams, 1981). They tend to remember important and unimportant events to an equal degree, and their understanding of motives and consequences is tenuous and easily disrupted. They may remember individual actions and events but often do not understand the inter-scene relationships. Collins (1983) finds that this holds true for children in the second and third grades as well. Substantial improvement in comprehension occurs between that age level and the fifth grade. What this means is that young children may learn the aggressive behavior shown on television without necessarily comprehending or learning negative sanctions when they are depicted. This makes it more likely that the various processes involved in learning from television will be effective.

As noted earlier, aggression is a very complex phenomenon. It is likely that no one process accounts for the relationship between television and aggressive behavior; rather, the processes outlined above are intricately interwoven. What is missing from these accounts is consideration of the social structure in which the television viewer exists. The findings of this study make it clear that in order to understand the long-term effects of television on aggressive behavior as it occurs in naturalistic settings, we should consider the child's social milieu.

Several researchers (Maccoby, 1980; Strayer, 1977; Strayer & Strayer, 1978) have proposed the existence of dominance hierarchies in children's social systems. According to Maccoby (1980), these hierarchies, once established, serve to reduce the amount of fighting among children. It is possible that one effect of TV within the child's social milieu is the disruption of these hierarchies, and, thus, an increase in aggression might follow until the hierarchy is once again established.

SUMMARY AND CONCLUSION

The finding that Notel children displayed more aggression 2 years after the introduction of television into their town further strengthens the evidence for a relationship between television and aggression demonstrated previously in laboratory, field, and naturalistic studies. Particularly striking about the results of this study is that the effects of television were not restricted to a subset of children. Boys and girls, children initially high and low in aggression, and those watching more or less TV were equally likely to show increased aggressive behavior.

Television supports and perpetuates prevailing societal values including the general acceptance of violence and aggression. Since content analyses have shown that violence is often gratuitous (Williams et al., 1977, 1982), surely it would be advantageous to produce television programming that promotes prosocial instead of aggressive modes of interacting.

The processes whereby aggressive content influences attention, comprehension, and subsequent behavior are still unclear. We would suggest that future research focus less on demonstrating the relationship between television and aggressive behavior, which has already received considerable attention. Instead, let us turn our research forces to the investigation of processes that would complete our understanding of the impact of television on our lives.

APPENDIX: TABLES

TABLE 7.A1

Checklists of Aggressive Behaviors Used in Observations

Physical
1. Hits, slaps, punches, or strikes with body part above waist
2. Hits, slaps, punches, or strikes with a held object
3. Kicks, steps on, sits on, lies on, or trips with body part below waist
4. Bites or spits
5. Pushes, holds, pulls, grabs, drags, or chokes
6. Snatches property of another (without damage to that property)
7. Damages the property of another
8. Tries to create a reaction, that is, teases, annoys, or interferes in the activity of another (except where chasing is involved and 11 or 12 is scored)
9. Threatens with some part of the body
10. Threatens with a held object
11. Chases another
12. Chases with a held object
13. Growls, grimaces, or makes sounds of dislike or anger toward another
14. Throws or kicks an object at another, except as required (e.g., ball in game)

Verbal
1. Disparages; makes remarks of dislike; finds fault with or censures; condemns; humiliates; laughs at the misfortune of; mocks; attributes bad qualities to; or curses another; or expresses the desire that he or she be the victim of imperious events
2. Verbally tries to claim a possession of another
3. Rejects or denies some activity, privilege, or object to another
4. Threatens to hurt
5. Commands or demands another to do or not to do something in a loud, vigorous, or angry tone of voice
6. Argues with or is at cross-purposes with another, when this involves more than one statement separated by a rejoinder
7. Tells an authority figure about another's behavior (which the subject of observation apparently considered negative)
8. Shifts the blame for some activity (apparently considered negative) to another
9. Tries to cause injury to another via an agent

TABLE 7.A2

Mean and Median Physical and Verbal Aggression Scores per Minute

	Physical aggression				Verbal aggression			
	Phase 1		Phase 2		Phase 1		Phase 2	
	Mean	Median	Mean	Median	Mean	Median	Mean	Median
Longitudinal children only[a]								
Notel	.431	.452	1.122	1.086	.205	.143	.405	.365
Unitel	.419	.286	.564	.524	.124	.095	.177	.143
Multitel	.444	.405	.640	.405	.287	.268	.244	.118
All children observed in each phase[b]								
Notel	.454	.405	.876	.780	.163	.143	.354	.286
Unitel	.399	.286	.586	.452	.116	.095	.212	.143
Multitel	.498	.476	.764	.619	.244	.238	.224	.143
Females	.284	.238	.498	.786	.173	.190	.188	.143
Males	.616	.524	.986	.905	.175	.190	.290	.238

[a] $n = 45$.
[b] $n = 120$ per phase.

TABLE 7.A3

Forward Stepwise Regression Analysis: Concurrent Phase 1 Predictions[a]

Predictors				Analysis of regression			
Equation variables	β	p	Partial corre-lation	F	df	p	R^2
Predicting Phase 1 observed physical aggression							
Notel, Unitel, Multitel[b]				24.29	2,113	.0001	.30
Constant	0.139						
Peer fights	0.021	.0001	.44				
Teach agg	0.017	.003	.28				
Unitel, Multitel[c]				19.47	1,44	.0001	.31
Constant	0.266						
Peer sum	0.017	.0001	.55				
Predicting Phase 1 observed verbal aggression							
Notel, Unitel, Multitel[b]				6.09	1,114	.02	.05
Constant	0.088						
Teach agg	0.006	.02	.22				
Unitel, Multitel[c]				4.88	1,44	.04	.10
Constant	0.136						
Obs phys agg	0.128	.04	.32				

[a] The set of possible predictors used in these analyses was: Observed physical aggression per minute (Obs phys agg); Observed verbal aggression per minute (Obs verb agg); Sum of peer nominations (Peer sum); Peer nomination score for item "gets into fights" (Peer fights); Sum of teacher ratings for all but the positive items (Teach agg); Sum of teacher ratings for positive items, "friendly" and "honest" (Teach pos); Hours of TV viewing per week (TV hours).

[b] Hours of TV viewing was not included because most Notel residents watched 0 hours.

[c] Hours of TV viewing was included.

TABLE 7.A4

Forward Stepwise Regression Analysis: Concurrent Phase 2 Predictions[a]

Equation variables	β	p	Partial corre-lation	F	df	p	R^2
	Predictors			Analysis of regression			
Predicting Phase 2 observed physical aggression							
Notel, Unitel, Multitel				14.07	3,99	.0001	.30
Constant	0.245						
Peer sum	0.008	.0001	.42				
Obs verb agg	0.696	.002	.32				
TV hours	0.008	.05	.20				
Unitel, Multitel				20.38	3,60	.0001	.50
Constant	0.173						
Peer sum	0.010	.0001	.63				
Obs verb agg	0.602	.006	.35				
TV hours	0.009	.03	.28				
Predicting Phase 2 observed verbal aggression							
Notel, Unitel, Multitel				13.42	1,101	.0004	.12
Constant	0.143						
Obs phys agg	0.141	.001	.34				
Unitel, Multitel				8.99	1,62	.004	.13
Constant	0.077						
Obs phys agg	0.155	.004	.36				
Predicting Phase 2 hours of TV viewing per week							
Notel, Unitel, Multitel[b]							
Unitel, Multitel				4.21	1,62	.05	.06
Obs phys agg	6.012	.05	.25				

[a] See Table 7.A3 for key to predictors used in the analyses.

[b] The regression analysis was not statistically significant; that is, none of the possible predictors was significant.

TABLE 7.A5

Forward Stepwise Regression Analysis: Predicting Phase 2 Aggression and
Hours of TV Viewing from Phase 1 and Phase 2 Measures[a]

	Predictors			Analysis of regression			
Equation variables	β	p	Partial correlation	F	df	p	R^2
Predicting Phase 2 observed physical aggression from Phase 1 and Phase 2 aggression measures and Phase 2 hours of TV viewing							
Notel, Unitel, Multitel[b]				12.66	1,33	.002	.28
Constant	0.586						
Peer sum 1	0.021	.002	.53				
Unitel, Multitel[c]				10.29	3,15	.001	.67
Constant	−0.148						
TV hours 2	0.016	.003	.69				
Peer sum 1	0.014	.03	.53				
Obs phys agg 1	0.425	.04	.50				
Predicting Phase 2 observed verbal aggression from Phase 1 and Phase 2 aggression measures and Phase 2 hours of TV viewing							
Notel, Unitel, Multitel[b]				6.52	1,33	.02	.16
Constant	0.184						
Peer sum 1	0.007	.02	.41				
Unitel, Multitel[c]				7.63	2,16	.005	.49
Constant	−0.176						
Peer sum 1	0.014	.02	.57				
Obs phys agg 1	1.273	.03	.53				
Predicting Phase 2 hours of TV viewing from Phase 1 aggression measures and hours of TV viewing							
Notel, Unitel, Multitel[b]				5.80	1,93	.02	.06
Constant	23.729						
Peer fights 1	0.377	.02	.24				
Unitel, Multitel				4.71	1,34	.04	.12
Constant	14.612						
TV hours 1	0.328	.04	.35				

[a] See Table 7.A3 for key to predictors used in the analyses. The number to the right of the variable indicates the phase in which it was measured (Phase 1 or 2).

[b] Phase 1 hours of TV viewing was not included here because most Notel residents watched 0 hours per week.

[c] Phase 1 hours of TV viewing was not included here because the number of children with scores for all measures was too small when it was included.

TABLE 7.A6

Correlations among Teacher Ratings, Peer Ratings, and Observational Measures of Aggression, Collapsed across Towns[a]

	Teach 1	Teach 2	Teach 3	Teach 4	Peer 1	Peer 2	Peer 3	Peer 4	Peer 5	Physical	Verbal
Teach 1		.61***	.48***	-.66***	.27**	.24**	.37***	.32***	.28**		
Teach 2	.78***		.22**	-.40***	.31***	.35***	.40***	.27**	.43***	.21**	.23**
Teach 3	.58***	.64***									
Teach 4	-.26**	-.16*	.27**				-.19*		-.17*		
Peer 1	.41***	.47***	.28**			.74***	.72***	.71***	.74***	.31***	.21**
Peer 2	.26**	.36***			.59***		.62***	.63***	.78***	.40***	
Peer 3	.43***	.46***	.19*		.74***	.60***		.65***	.72***	.32***	.21**
Peer 4	.38***	.47***	.24**		.85***	.69***	.74***		.65***	.37***	
Peer 5	.39***	.46***	.18*	-.23**	.65***	.63***	.61***	.63***		.41***	.20*
Physical	.37***	.35***	.26**		.27***	.49***	.36***	.40***	.38***		.38***
Verbal	.22**	.31***	.28**		.17*			.17*		.19*	

[a] Phase 1 below the diagonal; Phase 2 above. Key to abbreviations used in Tables 7.A6, 7.A7, and 7.A9: Teach 1—sum of teacher rating measures aggressive, argumentative, bossy, hostile; Teach 2—sum of teacher rating measures active, loud; Teach 3—sum of teacher rating measures competitive, dominant; Teach 4—sum of teacher rating measures friendly, honest; Peer 1—Peer rating for bossy; Peer 2—Peer rating for fights; Peer 3—Peer rating for talks back; Peer 4—Peer rating for argues, disagrees; Peer 5—Peer rating for push, shove, poke; Physical—Observational measure of physical aggression; Verbal—Observational measure of verbal aggression.

* p < .05; ** p < .01; *** p < .001; all two-tailed tests.

TABLE 7.A7

Correlations among Teacher Ratings, Peer Ratings, and Observational Measures of Aggression within Each Town and Phase[a]

	Teach 1	Teach 2	Teach 3	Teach 4	Peer 1	Peer 2	Peer 3	Peer 4	Peer 5	Physical	Verbal
Notel											
Teach 1											
Teach 2	.78***										
Teach 3	.58***	.70***									
Teach 4	-.31*	.78***	.46**								
Peer 1	.62***	.63***	.53***	.40*							
Peer 2	.39**	.47***		.34*	.55***						
Peer 3	.60***	.55***	.36*	-.38**	.76***	.58***					
Peer 4	.57***	.61***	.46***	-.36*	.91***	.63***	.80***				
Peer 5	.68***	.62***	.55***	-.45**	.73***	.73***	.69***	.75***			
Physical	.39**	.37**		-.35*	.36*	.61***	.41**	.71***	.50***		
Verbal		.46***	.50***	-.45**	.27*	.75***	.29*	.54***	.72***	.28*	
Unitel											
Teach 1					.39*		.44*		.51**		.36*
Teach 2	.75***						.47**		.43**		
Teach 3	.68***	.72***									
Teach 4		.48**	.49***		-.41**		-.35*		-.39**		

346

Peer 1						.98***	.89***	.65***	.85***	.48***	
Peer 2					.70***		.86***	.63***	.85***	.53***	
Peer 3					.49***	.44**		.53***	.85***	.45**	
Peer 4					.59***	.66***	.47***		.64***	.49***	
Peer 5					.42**	.64***	.46***	.51***		.49***	
Physical	.45**	.40**	.39**				.42**	.33*			.38**
Verbal							.35*			.27*	
Multitel											
Teach 1		.77***	.47**	−.70***	.34*	.37*	.27*	.39**	.36*		
Teach 2	.82***		.39**	−.61***	.32*	.37*	.29*		.43**		.39**
Teach 3	.55***	.54***			.34*	.44**	.33*	.33*			
Teach 4	−.41**	−.41**									
Peer 1	.33*	.28*				.76***	.66***	.66***	.64***	.49***	.31*
Peer 2	.31*	.46**		−.31*	.53***		.79***	.74***	.80***	.55***	
Peer 3	.54***	.52***		−.32*	.53***	.46**		.61***	.64***	.45**	
Peer 4	.40**	.41**			.59***	.34*	.42**		.55***	.55***	
Peer 5		.38*		−.43**	.64***	.74***	.42**	.36*		.56***	.27*
Physical	.32*	.35*			.38*	.42**	.52***		.36*		.39**
Verbal	.42**	.36*						.33*			

[a] Phase 1 below the diagonals; Phase 2 above. See Table 7.A6 for key to abbreviations.
* $p < .05$; ** $p < .01$; *** $p < .001$; all two-tailed tests.

TABLE 7.A8

Correlations among the Sum of the Peer Ratings, the Teacher Ratings, and
Observational Measures of Aggression[a]

	Teacher agg	Teacher pos	Peer sum	Physi-cal	Verbal
All towns combined					
Teacher agg		−.56***	.38***		
Teacher pos					
Peer sum	.46***			.42***	
Physical	.38***		.45***		.38***
Verbal	.29**			.19*	
Notel					
Teacher agg		−.42**	.44**		
Teacher pos					
Peer sum	.68***				
Physical	.37*	−.35*	.58***		.28*
Verbal	.40**				
Unitel					
Teacher agg			.37*	.32+	
Teacher pos					
Peer sum				.54***	
Physical	.47**				.38**
Verbal				.27*	
Multitel					
Teacher agg		−.62***	.46**		
Teacher pos	−.30+				
Peer sum	.47**			.60***	
Physical	.35*		.49**		.39*
Verbal	.35*				

[a] Phase 1 below the diagonals, Phase 2 above. Teacher agg—sum of active, aggressive, argumentative, bossy, hostile, loud, dominant, and competitive ratings; Teacher pos—sum of friendly and honest ratings; Physical—observational measure of physical agression; Verbal—observational measure of verbal aggression. See note 16.

$+ p < .10$; $* p < .05$; $** p < .01$; $*** p < .001$; all two-tailed tests.

TABLE 7.A9

Correlations among Aggression Measures Separately for Girls and Boys within Each Phase[a]

	Teach 1	Teach 2	Teach 3	Teach 4	Peer 1	Peer 2	Peer 3	Peer 4	Peer 5	Physical	Verbal
Girls											
Teach 1		.67***	.46***	-.64***				.38**	.37**		
Teach 2	.77***		.60***	-.42**			.28*		.32*		
Teach 3	.64***	.60***									
Teach 4	-.35**	-.26*									
Peer 1	.44***	.43***	.37**				.51***	.47***	.50***		
Peer 2								.36**	.43***		
Peer 3	.45**	.54***	.44***		.78***			.27*	.65***		
Peer 4	.39**	.45***	.32*		.85***		.72***		.49***		
Peer 5	.50***	.44***	.33*		.86***		.73***	.79***			
Sum	.48***	.49***	.39***		.96***		.86***	.92***	.91***		
Physical	.39**	.43***	.38**				.27*				.37*
Verbal	.40**	.43***	.36**		.27*		.30*	.33**		.39**	
Boys											
Teach 1		.53***	.50***	-.65***	.31*		.40**				
Teach 2	.76***		.68***	-.32*	.34*		.37**		.35**		
Teach 3	.53***	.68***									
Teach 4			.44***								
Peer 1	.36*	.50***				.82***	.76***	.76***	.79***	.29*	
Peer 2	.27*	.39**			.84***		.57***	.66***	.77***	.34**	
Peer 3	.44***	.44***			.76***	.57***		.69***	.68***	.26*	
Peer 4	.36*	.45***			.88***	.62***	.69***		.66***	.32*	
Peer 5	.32*	.42***			.66***	.62***	.57***	.58***		.30*	
Sum	.40**	.50***			.95***	.89***	.85***	.91***	.78***	.35**	
Physical	.28*	.30*			.34*	.46***	.34**	.47***	.28*		.29*
Verbal											

[a] Phase 1 below diagonals, Phase 2 above. See Table 7.A6 for key to abbreviations.
* $p < .05$; ** $p < .01$; *** $p < .001$; all two-tailed tests.

Lesley A. Joy, Meredith M. Kimball, and Merle L. Zabrack

TABLE 7.A10
Percentage of Children Who Were Male among Highly Aggressive Children[a]

	Observed aggression			Peer ratings		
	Physical aggression		Fights		Pushes, shoves, pokes	
	Top 10%	Top 15%	Top 10%	Top 15%	Top 10%	Top 15%
Phase 1						
Notel	100	100	100	100	75	83
Unitel	75	83	100	83	100	100
Multitel	75	67	100	100	100	100
Phase 2						
Notel	100	83	100	100	100	100
Unitel	100	100	100	100	100	83
Multitel	75	83	100	100	100	83
	Verbal aggression		Argues, disagrees		Talks back to teacher	
Phase 1						
Notel	25	50	75	67	75	67
Unitel	25	33	75	83	75	50
Multitel	50	67	75	67	100	100
Phase 2						
Notel	50	50	100	83	100	100
Unitel	25	50	75	83	75	67
Multitel	100	83	75	50	100	100

[a] This table indicates what percentage of the top 10% and top 15% of children, ordered in terms of aggression, were male. For example, in Notel in Phase I, when the children were ordered from highest to lowest on observed verbal aggression, 25% of the top 10% and 50% of the top 15% were male. However, when the same children were ordered on the peer rating item ''argues and disagrees'', 75% of the top 10% and 67% of the top 15% were male.

NOTES

[1] The coding scheme was a modified form, developed and validated by Jo-Anne McFadden, of the Walters, Pearce, and Dahm (1957) scheme.

[2] Interrater reliability was calculated by dividing the number of responses on which both observers agreed by the total number of responses. In the first phase of the study the reliability of .86 represents a mean based on 40 1-minute observations. In the second phase of the study the reliability of .80 represents a mean based on 51 1-minute observations.

[3] The purpose of the first criterion was to exclude children who, in a larger community, would be classified as retarded and placed in special classes for slow learners. In these towns there were no such classes until the high school grades, and, since the towns were relatively distant from residential homes for the retarded, families typically chose to keep mentally handicapped children at home and send them to the local school.

[4] T tests were used to determine whether the 45 children in the Phase 1 longitudinal sample differed in either physical or verbal aggression from the other 15 children observed in Phase 1 who were not still available in Phase 2, and they did not: physical aggression, $t(58) = .89, p = .38$; verbal aggression, $t(58) = -.04, p = .97$.

[5] It was legitimate to compare fourth and fifth graders from Phase 1 with third and fourth graders from Phase 2 because there were no differences in aggressive behavior due to grade level (see note 6).

[6] Cross-sectional Town × Grade ANOVAs were run for each phase of the study on the total physical and total verbal aggression scores. No significant grade main effect and no significant Grade × Town interaction was found for either physical or verbal aggression in either phase of the study.

[7] When the physical and verbal aggression scores from the longitudinal sample were combined in a MANOVA, Hotelling's tests yielded significant town, $F(4,74) = 2.9, p < .03$; sex, $F(2,38) = 8.63, p < .001$; and phase, $F(2,38) = 6.55, p < .004$ main effects, using a unique sums of squares solution. In the unique solution the analysis simultaneously solves the equation. The Town × Phase interaction closely approached significance when a unique solution was used, $F(4,74) = 2.42, p = .056$ and was significant when a sequential solution was used, $F(4,74) = 2.87, p < .03$. A sequential solution solves the equation according to an ordering scheme set up by the experimenter. Since the Town × Phase interaction was of primary interest in this study, and even the unique solution closely approached statistical significance, we followed up this multivariate analysis with analyses designed to specify the relations among the variables separately for physical and verbal aggression.

[8] When the longitudinal physical aggression data were analyzed using a Town × Phase × Sex repeated measures ANOVA with an unweighted means solution, the sex main effect was statistically significant, $F(1,39) = 17.70, p < .001$, reflecting higher mean physical aggression for boys than for girls (means, .810 and .397 acts per minute, respectively). In addition, the phase main effect, $F(1,39) = 13.45, p < .001$; and Town × Phase interaction, $F(2,39) = 3.44, p < .05$ were significant. The town main effect, $F(2,39) = 3.20, p = .052$ closely approached significance. No other interactions were statistically significant.

Simple main effects analyses used to break down the Town × Phase interaction revealed that only the scores of Notel children changed from Phase 1 to Phase 2, $F(1,39) = 17.49, p < .001$, increasing from .432 to 1.122 acts per minute. There were significant differences among the towns in physical aggression in Phase 2, $F(2,39) = 6.72, p < .01$, but not in Phase 1. In Phase 2, Notel children ($M = 1.122$) were more physically aggressive than children in both Unitel ($M = .564; p < .01$ by Tukey test) and Multitel ($M = .640; p < .01$ by Tukey test), and the latter two did not differ.

When the longitudinal verbal aggression data were analyzed using a Town × Phase × Sex repeated measures ANOVA with an unweighted means solution, the town main effect, $F(1,39) = 3.77, p < .04$ was statistically significant, and the Town × Phase interaction was marginally significant, $F(2,39) = 3.07, p = .058$. Since this was a major hypothesized finding, we conducted simple main effects analyses to break down this interaction. The pattern of results was the same as for physical aggression. As hypothesized, only Notel children's verbal aggression changed from Phase 1 to Phase 2, $F(1,39) = 6.52, p < .05$, increasing from .205 to .405 acts of verbal aggression per minute. The differences among the towns in Phase 1 were not significant, but in Phase 2, $F(2,39) = 4.67, p < .05$, Notel children were more verbally aggressive than children in both Unitel ($M = .178$; $p < .01$ by Tukey test) and Multitel ($M = .224$; $p < .10$ by Tukey and $.05$ by Newman–Keuls test). Neither the sex main effect nor any interactions of sex with other factors was statistically significant.

[9] We could not use just one set of analyses with the cross-sectional data to ask whether aggressive behavior changed following the inception of television in Notel and whether the towns differed in each phase of the study as we had done for the longitudinal sample, since most (75%) of the children in grades 3 and 4, who were observed in Phase 2, were the same children we had observed in Phase 1 when they were in grades 1 and 2. To do so would mean we were treating the longitudinal children, who were observed in both phases, as if they were different children, and this would violate the assumption of the statistics used in cross-sectional analyses that the measurements are independent. We first used multivariate analyses to compare children in grades 1 and 2 from the first phase with children in grades 1 and 2 from the second phase, and then we did a similar analysis for children in the two higher grades (grades 4 and 5 in Phase 1 versus grades 3 and 4 in Phase 2). We then used t tests to assess changes in physical and verbal aggression from Phase 1 to Phase 2 (note 10) and ANOVAs to ask whether aggressive behavior varied according to town and sex within each phase of the study (note 11).

When the physical and verbal aggression scores from the cross-sectional samples of first and second graders were combined in a MANOVA, the main effects for town, $F(4,212) = 4.44, p < .002$; sex, $F(2,107) = 12.23, p < .001$; and phase, $F(2,107) = 3.26, p < .05$; and the Sex × Time interaction, $F(2,107) = 3.10, p < .05$ all were significant. When the scores from fourth and fifth graders from Phase 1 were analyzed by comparison with the scores from third and fourth graders from Phase 2 in a similar MANOVA, the main effects for sex, $F(2,107) = 14.40, p < .001$; and phase, $F(2,107) = 11.81, p < .001$; and the Town × Phase interaction, $F(4,212) = 3.42, p < .01$ all were significant, and the town main effect was marginally significant, $F(4,212) = 2.30, p = <.06$. These MANOVA results involving town and phase justified moving on to more specific comparisons.

[10] One-tailed t tests were used to evaluate cross-sectionally whether Notel children in Phase 2 displayed more aggression than their same-aged Notel peers in Phase 1. Depending on the outcome of the homogeneity of variance test for the two groups being compared, pooled variance estimates (in which case degrees of freedom are expressed as an integer or whole number) or separate variance estimates (in which case degrees of freedom are expressed as a non-integer) were used. The results follow.

| | Means | | | | |
	Phase 1	Phase 2	t	df	p(one-tailed)
Grades 1 and 2 versus 1 and 2					
Physical					
Both sexes	.469	.705	−1.80	38	.04
Girls	.243	.653	−2.61	11.88	.01
Boys	.696	.757	−.32	18	ns
Verbal					
Both sexes	.215	.345	−1.91	38	.03
Girls	.281	.295	−.15	18	ns
Boys	.148	.395	−2.58	10.68	.01

(Con't.)

	Means				
	Phase 1	Phase 2	t	df	p(one-tailed)
Grades 4 and 5 versus 3 and 4					
Physical					
Both sexes	.438	1.047	−2.87	30.59	.01
Girls	.229	.625	−2.84	12.5	.01
Boys	.648	1.470	−2.36	18	.02
Verbal					
Both sexes	.112	.363	−4.25	38	.001
Girls	.062	.358	−3.75	12.94	.001
Boys	.162	.369	−2.32	18	.02

Two-tailed t tests were used to evaluate cross-sectionally whether Unitel and Multitel children in Phase 2 displayed more aggression than their same-aged Unitel and Multitel peers in Phase 1, since it was unclear whether the most appropriate hypothesis predicted an increase or no change. Depending on the outcome of the homogeneity of variance test for the two groups being compared, pooled variance estimates (degrees of freedom shown as an integer or whole number) or separate variance estimates (degrees of freedom shown as a non-integer) were used. The 12 tests conducted for Notel were also run for both Unitel and Multitel, but only results that were statistically significant using a two-tailed test are shown in the following table.

	Means				
	Phase 1	Phase 2	t	df	p(two-tailed)
Grades 1 and 2 versus 1 and 2					
Multitel girls, verbal	.273	.133	2.24	18	.04
Grades 4 and 5 versus 3 and 4					
Multitel, both sexes, physical	.436	.887	−2.74	25.73	.05

[11] Cross-sectional differences among the towns within each phase of the study were tested in Town × Sex univariate ANOVAs, summing across the grades.

For physical aggression in Phase 1, only the sex main effect was significant, $F(1,114) = 32.33$, $p < .001$, with the boys' mean (.616) higher than that for girls (.284). For verbal aggression in Phase 1, only the town main effect was significant, $F(2,114) = 8.39$, $p < .001$, with Tukey tests indicating that Multitel children ($M = .244$) exhibited more verbal aggression than both the Notel children ($M = .163$; $p < .05$ by Tukey test) and Unitel children ($M = .116$; $p < .01$ by Tukey test), who did not differ.

For physical aggression in Phase 2, the sex main effect was significant, $F(1,114) = 24.59$, $p < .001$, again reflecting a higher mean for boys (.986) than for girls (.498). The town main effect, $F(2,114) = 2.94$, $p = .057$ approached significance, and Tukey tests indicated that Notel children (.876) were more physically aggressive than Unitel children (.586; $p < .05$) with Multitel children (.764) in between and not different from either Notel or Unitel. For verbal aggression in Phase 2, the sex main effect was significant, $F(1,114) = 6.85$, $p < .01$, once again reflecting a higher mean for boys (.290) than for girls (.188). The town main effect was also significant, $F(2,114) = 9.45$, $p < .001$, and Tukey tests revealed that Notel children ($M = .354$) were more verbally aggressive than both the Multitel children ($M = .224$; $p < .05$) and the Unitel children ($M = .212$; $p < .01$) who did not differ.

[12] The analyses described in note 10 were repeated using median rather than mean levels of aggression, since the J-shaped nature of the distribution of aggressive behavior meant the medians tended to be lower than the means. All results for which at least one test was significant at $p < .05$ or better are shown in the following table.

	n	Median		Median test p(one-tailed)	Mann–Whitney U	p
		Phase 1	Phase 2			
Notel						
Grades 1 and 2 versus 1 and 2						
Physical, girls	10	.238	.500	.02	15.00	.01
Verbal, both sexes	20	.190	.262	.02	126.5	.05
Verbal, boys	10	.143	.286	.02	21.00	.03
Grades 4 and 5 versus 3 and 4						
Physical, both sexes	20	.262	.881	.02	93.5	.01
Physical, girls	10	.214	.514	.04	20.0	.03
Physical, boys	10	.476	1.300	.04	21.5	.04
Verbal, both sexes	20	.024	.352	.01	66.0	.001
Verbal, girls	10	.000	.309	.02	7.5	.01
Verbal, boys	10	.143	.400	.09	22.0	.04
Unitel						
Grades 1 and 2 versus 1 and 2						
Physical, boys	10	.357	.857	.02	24.0	.05
Multitel						
Grades 1 and 2 versus 1 and 2						
Verbal, both sexes	20	.238	.127	.01	137.0	.09
Verbal, girls	10	.286	.119	.09	24.0	.05
Grades 4 and 5 versus 3 and 4						
Physical, both sexes	20	.452	.809	ns	121.0	.04

[13] In each town, the children in the longitudinal sample were divided at the median into two groups on the basis of their physical aggression scores in Phase 1, and then the difference between their mean Phase 2 physical aggression scores was tested using one-tailed t tests. Similar tests were then run for verbal aggression. No significant differences in Phase 2 aggressive behavior were found in any town between the groups initially below and above the median on Phase 1 aggression.

[14] In each town, the children in the longitudinal sample were divided at the median into two groups on the basis of their physical aggression scores in Phase 1. The difference between these two groups, in terms of hours of TV viewed per week in Phase 2, was then tested using one-tailed t tests. Similar tests were also run for verbal aggression. No significant differences in Phase 2 hours of TV viewing were found in any town between the groups initially below and above the median on Phase 1 physical or verbal aggression.

[15] When asked about their favorite TV programs in the second phase of the study, Notel children above the median in aggression in Phase 1 most frequently named "Forest Rangers," "The Partridge Family," "The Waltons," and "Coming up Rosie." Those initially below the median named "The Partridge Family," "All in the Family," "Walt Disney," and "Forest Rangers."

[16] As can be seen in Tables 7.A6 and 7.A7, the children's responses to the five peer items were strongly interrelated in each phase. The internal consistency of these ratings was assessed statistically, and very high estimates were obtained; Cronbach's alpha for Phase 1 was .91 and for Phase 2, .90. Since a coefficient of .60 is considered high enough to warrant combining the items into a single score, we reduced the data and the number of tests conducted in further analyses by summing the five peer items.

The teacher rating items had been combined previously to assess aggression (aggressive, argumentative, bossy, hostile), activity level (active, loud), dominance (competitive, dominant), and positive characteristics (friendly, honest). As Table 7.A6 indicates, the teachers' ratings for these four categories were significantly intercorrelated, so we assessed the degree of internal consistency among the teacher ratings, as we had done for the peer ratings. When all four categories were included, Cronbach's alpha was .61 in Phase 1. It was only .24 in Phase 2, so we eliminated the "friendly and honest" category, which was negatively correlated with the other three, and computed Cronbach's alpha for the remaining three categories. The coefficients were .78 for Phase 1 and .68 for Phase 2 (the standardized item, alpha coefficients were .86 and .70, respectively). These coefficients were high enough to warrant reducing the data and number of tests conducted by combining the teachers' ratings for these three categories in the subsequent analyses. This combined rating will be referred to as the teachers' aggression rating.

[17] The correlations between IQ and observed physical and verbal aggression were low and nonsignificant. IQ was negatively related to the teachers' rating for aggressive, argumentative and bossy, hostile, $r(98) = -.24$, $p < .02$; positively related to the teachers' rating for friendly, honest, $r(98) = .29$, $p < .004$; and negatively related to peer ratings for the item push, shove, poke, $r(100) = -.32$, $p < .002$, as well as the sum of peer nominations, $r(99) = -.21$, $p < .04$. These findings may be another indication of potential bias in peer and teacher ratings.

REFERENCES

Anderson, D. R. *Children's attention to television.* Paper presented at the Biennial meeting of the Society for Research in Child Development, New Orleans, March 1977.

Anderson, D. R. Home television viewing by preschool children and their families. In A. C. Huston (Chair), *The ecology of children's television use.* Symposium presented at the meeting of the Society for Research in Child Development, Detroit, April 1983.

Anderson, D. R., Alwitt, L. F., Lorch, E., & Levin, S. R. Watching children watch television. In G. Hale & M. Lewis (Eds.), *Attention and the development of cognitive skills.* New York: Plenum, 1979.

Anderson, D. R., & Levin, S. R. Young children's attention to "Sesame Street." *Child Development,* 1976, *47,* 806–811.

Anderson, D., & Lorch, E. P. Looking at television: Action or reaction. In J. Bryant & D. R. Anderson (Eds.), *Children's understanding of television.* New York: Academic Press, 1983.

Bandura, A. Influence of model's reinforcement contingencies on the acquisition of imitative responses. *Journal of Personality and Social Psychology,* 1965, *1,* 589–595.

356 Lesley A. Joy, Meredith M. Kimball, and Merle L. Zabrack

Bandura, A. Social learning theory of aggression. *Journal of Communication.* 1978, *28*(3), 12–29.

Bandura, A., Ross, D., & Ross, S. A. Imitation of film-mediated aggressive models. *Journal of Abnormal and Social Psychology,* 1963a, *66,* 31–11.

Bandura, A., Ross, D., & Ross, S. A. A comparative test of the status envy, social power and secondary reinforcement theories of identificatory learning. *Journal of Abnormal and Social Psychology,* 1963b, *67,* 527–534.

Belson, W. A. *Television violence and the adolescent boy.* Westmead, England: Saxon House, 1978.

Berlyne, D. *Conflict, arousal, and curiosity.* New York: McGraw-Hill, 1965.

Cameron, P., & Janky, C. The effects of TV violence on children: A naturalistic experiment. *Proceedings of the 79th Annual Convention of the American Psychological Association.* Washington, D.C.: American Psychological Association, 1971.

Cline, V. B., Croft, R. G., & Courrier, S. Desensitization of children to television violence. *Journal of Personality and Social Psychology,* 1972, *27,* 360–365.

Collins, W. A. Schemata for understanding television. *New Directions for Child Development,* 1981, No. 13, 31–46.

Collins, W. A. Interpretation and inference in children's television viewing. In J. Bryant and D. R. Anderson (Eds.), *Children's understanding of television.* New York: Academic Press, 1983.

Comstock, G. New emphases in research on the effects of television and film violence. In E. L. Palmer & A. Dorr (Eds.), *Children and the faces of television.* New York: Academic Press, 1980.

Comstock, G. A. Media influences on aggression. In A. Goldstein (Ed.), *Prevention and control of aggression: Principles, practices and research.* New York: Pergamon Press, 1983.

Comstock, G., Chaffee, S., Katzman, N., McCombs, M., & Roberts, D. *Television and human behavior.* New York: Columbia University Press, 1978.

Cook, T. D., & Campbell, D. T. *Quasi-experimentation: Design and analysis issues for field settings.* Chicago: Rand McNally, 1979.

Cook, T. D., Kendzierski, D. A., & Thomas, S. V. The implicit assumptions of television research: An analysis of the NIMH report on Television and Behavior. *Public Opinion Quarterly,* 1983, *47,* 161–201.

Dominick, J. R., & Greenberg, B. S. Attitudes toward violence: The interaction of television exposure, family attitudes, and social class. In G. A. Comstock & E. A. Rubinstein (Eds.), *Television and social behavior: Vol. 3. Television and adolescent aggressiveness.* Washington, D.C.: U.S. Government Printing Office, 1972.

Drabman, R. S., & Thomas, M. H. Does media violence increase children's tolerance of real-life aggression? *Developmental Psychology,* 1974, *10,* 418–421.

Eron, L. D. Relationship of TV viewing habits and aggressive behavior in children. *Journal of Abnormal and Social Psychology,* 1963, *67,* 253–263.

Eron, L. D. Parent–child interaction, television violence, and aggression of children. *American Psychologist,* 1982, *37,* 197–211.

Eron, L. D., Huesmann, L. R., Lefkowitz, M. M., & Walder, L. Does television violence cause aggression? *American Psychologist,* 1972, *27,* 253–263.

Feshbach, S. Aggression. In P. Mussen (Ed.), *Carmichael's manual of child psychology* (Vol. 2). New York: John Wiley & Sons, 1970.

Feshbach, S. Reality and fantasy in filmed violence. In J. P. Murray, E. A. Rubinstein, & G. A. Comstock (Eds.), *Television and social behavior: Vol 2. Television and social learning.* Washington, D.C.: U.S. Government Printing Office, 1972.

Feshbach, S., & Singer, R. D. *Television and aggression*. San Francisco: Jossey-Bass, 1971.

Friedman, H. L., & Johnson, R. I. Mass media use and aggression: A pilot study. In G. A. Comstock and E. A. Rubinstein (Eds.), *Television and social behavior: Vol. 3. Television and adolescent aggressiveness*. Washington, D.C.: U.S. Government Printing Office, 1972.

Friedlander, B. Z., Wetstone, H. S., & Scott, C. S. Suburban preschool children's comprehension of an age-appropriate information television program. *Child Development, 1974, 45,* 561–565.

Greenberg, B. S. *Life on television: Content analyses of U.S. TV drama*. Norwood, N.J.: Ablex, 1980.

Greenberg, B. S., Edison, N., Korzenny, F., Fernandez-Collado, C., & Atkin, C. K. Antisocial and prosocial behavior on television. In B. S. Greenberg (Ed.), *Life on television: Content analyses of U.S. TV drama*. Norwood, N.J.: Ablex, 1980.

Hanratty, M. A., Liebert, R. M., Morris, L. W., & Fernandez, L. E. Imitation of film-mediated aggression against live and inanimate victims. *Proceedings of the 77th Annual Convention of the American Psychological Association*. Washington, D.C.: American Psychological Association, 1969.

Hartmann, D. P. *The influence of symbolically modeled instrumental aggression and pain cues on the disinhibition of aggressive behavior*. Unpublished doctoral dissertation, Stanford University, 1965.

Hennigan, K. M., Del Rosario, M. L., Heath, L., Cook, T. D., Wharton, J. D., & Calder, B. J. Impact of the introduction of television on crime in the United States: Empirical findings and theoretical implications. *Journal of Personality and Social Psychology, 1982, 42,* 461–477.

Hicks, D. L. Effects of co-observer's sanctions and adult presence on imitative aggression. *Child Development, 1968, 39,* 303–309.

Himmelweit, H. T., Oppenheim, A. N., & Vince, P. *Television and the child*. London: Oxford University Press, 1958.

Howitt, S. Television and aggression: A counter argument. *American Psychologist, 1972, 27,* 969–970.

Huesmann, L. R. Television violence and aggressive behavior. In D. Pearl, L. Bouthilet, & J. Lazar (Eds.), *Television and behavior: Ten years of scientific progress and implications for the eighties*. Vol. 2. Rockville, Md.: NIMH, 1982.

Huesmann, L. R., & Eron, D. Structural models of the development of aggression. In D. Magnusson (Chair), *Development of aggressive behavior*. Symposium presented at the meeting of the International Society for the Study of Behavioural Development, Tours, July 1985.

Huesmann, L. R., Eron, L. D., Lefkowitz, M. M., & Walder, L. O. Television violence and aggression: The causal effect remains. *American Psychologist, 1973, 28,* 617–620.

Huesmann, L. R., Eron, L. D., Lefkowitz, M. M., & Walder, L. O. Stability of aggression over time and generations. *Developmental Psychology, 1984, 20,* 1120–1134.

Huesmann, L. R., Lagerspetz, K., & Eron, L. D. Intervening variables in the television violence—aggression relation: Evidence from two countries. *Developmental Psychology, 1984, 20,* 746–775.

Kaplan, R. M. On television as a cause of aggression. *American Psychologist, 1972, 27,* 968–969.

Krull, R., & Watt, J. H., Jr. *Television viewing and aggression: An examination of three models*. Paper presented at the meeting of the International Communication Association, Montreal, April 1973.

Lefkowitz, M. M., & Huesmann, L. R. Concomitants of television violence viewing in children. In E. L. Palmer & A. Dorr (Eds.), *Children and the faces of television*. New York: Academic Press, 1980.

Lefkowitz, M. M., Eron, L. D., Walder, L. O., & Huesmann, L. R. Television violence and child aggression: A follow-up study. In G. A. Comstock & E. A. Rubinstein (Eds.), *Television and social behavior. Vol. 3. Television and adolescent aggressiveness*. Washington, D.C.: U.S. Government Printing Office, 1972.

Leifer, A. D., & Roberts, D. F. Children's responses to television violence. In J. P. Murray, E. A. Rubinstein, & G. A. Comstock (Eds.), *Television and social behavior: Vol. 2. Television and social learning*. Washington, D.C.: U.S. Government Printing Office, 1972.

Liebert, R. M., & Baron, R. A. Short-term effects of televised aggression on children's aggressive behavior. In J. P. Murray, E. A. Rubinstein, & G. A. Comstock (Eds.), *Television and social behavior. Vol. 2. Television and social learning*. Washington, D.C.: U.S. Government Printing Office, 1972.

Leyens, J., Camino, L., Parke, R., & Berkowitz, L. The effects of movie violence on aggression in a field setting as a function of group dominance and cohesion. *Journal of Personality and Social Psychology*, 1975, *32*, 346–360.

Lorch, E., Anderson, D., & Levin, S. The relationship of visual attention to children's comprehension of television. *Child Development*, 1979, *50*, 722–727.

Maccoby, E. E. *Social development: Psychological growth and the parent–child relationship*. New York: Harcourt Brace Jovanovich, 1980.

Maccoby, E. E. & Jacklin, C. N. *The psychology of sex differences*. Palo Alto, Calif.: Stanford University Press, 1974.

McCarthy, E. D., Langer, T. S., Gersten, J. C., Eisenberg, V. G., & Orzeck, L. Violence and behavior disorders. *Journal of Communication*, 1975, *25*(4), 71–85.

McIntyre, J. J., & Teevan, J. J. Television violence and deviant behavior. In G. A. Comstock & E. A. Rubinstein (Eds.), *Television and social behavior. Vol. 3. Television and adolescent aggressiveness*. Washington, D.C.: U.S. Government Printing Office, 1972.

McLeod, J., Atkin, C., & Chaffee, S. Adolescents, parents and television use: Adolescent self-report measures from Maryland and Wisconsin samples. In G. A. Comstock & E. A. Rubinstein (Eds.), *Television and social behavior. Vol. 3. Television and adolescent aggressiveness*. Washington, D.C.: U.S. Government Printing Office, 1972.

Milavsky, J. R., Kessler, R., Stipp, H., & Rubens, W. S. *Television and aggression: Results of a panel study*. New York: Academic Press, 1982a.

Milavsky, J. R., Kessler, R., Stipp, H., & Rubens, W. S. Television and aggression: Results of a panel study. In D. Pearl, L. Bouthilet, & J. Lazar (Eds.), *Television and behavior: Ten years of scientific progress and implications for the eighties*. Vol. 2. Rockville, Md.: NIMH, 1982b.

Murray, J. P., Hayes, A. J., & Smith, J. E. Sequential analysis: Another APPROACH to describing the stream of behaviour in children's interactions. *Australian Journal of Psychology*, 1978, *30*, 207–215.

Palmer, E. L., & Dorr, A. *Children and the faces of television: Teaching, violence, selling*. New York: Academic Press, 1980.

Parke, R., Berkowitz, L., Leyens, J., West, S., & Sebastian, R. Some effects of violent and non-violent movies on the behavior of juvenile delinquents. In L. Berkowitz (Ed.), *Advances in Experimental Social Psychology* (Vol. 10). New York: Academic Press, 1977.

Pearl, D., Bouthilet, L., & Lazar, J. *Television and behavior: Ten years of scientific progress and implications for the eighties*. Vols. 1 and 2. Rockville, Md.: NIMH, 1982.

Phillips, D. P. The impact of fictional television stories on U.S. adult fatalities: New evidence on the effect of the mass media on violence. *American Journal of Sociology,* 1982, *87,* 1340–1349.

Roberts, D. F., & Bachen, C. M. Mass communication effects. In M. R. Rosenzweig & L. Porter (Eds.), *Annual Review of Psychology,* 1981, *32,* 307–356.

Robinson, J. P., & Bachman, J. G. Television viewing habits and aggression. In G. A. Comstock & E. A. Rubinstein (Eds.), *Television and social behavior. Vol. 3. Television and adolescent aggressiveness.* Washington, D.C.: U.S. Government Printing Office, 1972.

Rogosa, D. A. A critique of cross-lagged correlation. *Psychological Bulletin,* 1980, *88,* 245–258.

Rosengren, K. E., Roe, K., & Sonesson, I. *Finality and causality in adolescents: Mass media use.* Paper presented at the meeting of the International Communication Association, Dallas, May 1983.

Salomon, G. *Interaction of media, cognition, and learning.* New York: Jossey-Bass, 1979.

Salomon, G. Introducing AIME: The assessment of children's mental involvement with television. *New Directions for Child Development,* 1981, No. 13, 89–102.

Salomon, G. Television watching and mental effort: A social psychological view. In J. Bryant & D. R. Anderson (Eds.), *Children's understanding of television.* New York: Academic Press, 1983.

Saurin, D. B. *Aggressive behavior among children in small polygroup settings with violent television.* Unpublished doctoral dissertation, University of Minnesota, 1973.

Schramm, W., Lyle, J., & Parker, E. B. *Television in the lives of our children.* Stanford, Calif.: Stanford University Press, 1961.

Siegel, A. E. Research findings and social policy. In E. L. Palmer & A. Dorr (Eds.), *Children and the faces of television.* New York: Academic Press, 1980.

Signorielli, N., Gross, L., & Morgan, M. Violence in television programs: Ten years later. In D. Pearl, L. Bouthilet, & J. Lazar (Eds.), *Television and behavior: Ten years of scientific progress and implications for the eighties.* Vol. 2. Rockville, Md.: NIMH, 1982.

Singer, J. L., & Singer, D. G. *Television, imagination and aggression: A study of preschoolers' play.* Hillsdale, N.J.: Erlbaum, 1980.

Stanley, P. R. A., & Riera, B. Replications of media violence. In *Report of the Ontario Royal Commission on Violence in the Communications Industry,* Vol. 5. Toronto, 1977.

Stein, A. H., & Friedrich, L. K. TV content and young children's behavior. In G. A. Comstock & E. A. Rubinstein (Eds.), *Television and social behavior. Vol. 3. Television effects: Further explorations.* Washington, D.C.: U.S. Government Printing Office, 1972.

Steuer, F. B., Applefield, J. M., and Smith, R. Televised aggression and the interpersonal aggression of preschool children. *Journal of Experimental Child Psychology,* 1971, *11,* 442–447.

Stoessel, R. E. *The effects of televised aggressive cartoons and children's aggressive behavior.* Unpublished doctoral dissertation, St. John's University, 1972.

Strayer, F. F. Peer attachment and affiliative subgroups: In F. F. Strayer (Ed.), *Ethological perspectives on preschool social organization.* Thème de recherche #5, l'Université de Québec à Montréal, Départment de Psychologie, Avril 1977.

Strayer, J., & Strayer, F. F. Social aggression and power relations among preschool children. *Aggressive Behavior,* 1978, *4,* 173–183.

Tannenbaum, P. H., & Zillman, D. Emotional arousal in the facilitation of aggression through communication. In L. Berkowitz (Ed.), *Advances in experimental social psychology* (Vol. 8). New York: Academic Press, 1975.

Thomas, M. H., & Drabman, R. S. *Some new faces of the one-eyed monster*. Paper presented at the meeting of the Society for Research in Child Development, Denver, 1975.

Walters, J., Pearce, D., & Dahm, L. Affectional and aggressive behavior of preschool children. *Child Development*, 1957, *28*, 14–28.

Wells, W. D. *Television and aggression: Replication of an experimental field study*. Unpublished manuscript, University of Chicago, Graduate School of Business, 1973.

Williams, T. M. How and what do children learn from television? *Human Communication Research*, 1981, *7(2)*, 180–192.

Williams, T. M., Zabrack, M. L., & Joy, L. A. A content analysis of entertainment television programming. In *Report of the Ontario Royal Commission on Violence in the Communications Industry*, Vol. 3. Toronto, 1977.

Williams, T. M., Zabrack, M. L., & Joy, L. A. The portrayal of aggression on North American television. *Journal of Applied Social Psychology*, 1982, *12(5)*, 360–380.

Wotring, C. W., & Greenberg, B. S. Experiments in televised violence and verbal aggression: Two exploratory studies. *Journal of Communication*, 1973, *23(4)*, 446–460.

Wright, J. C., & Huston, A. C. A matter of form: Potentials of television for young viewers. *American Psychologist*, 1983, *38*, 835–843.

8

TELEVISION AND ADULTS: THINKING, PERSONALITY, AND ATTITUDES

Peter Suedfeld
Brian R. Little
A. Dennis Rank
Darilynn S. Rank
Elizabeth J. Ballard

INTRODUCTION

Most research on television and human behavior has focused on children. When adults have been included, the emphasis has usually been on hypotheses and theories on the societal level. Some researchers have been concerned with television viewing as a function of demographic and individual characteristics (e.g., Israel & Robinson, 1972); others, with the effects of television on various aspects of life, including sports (Harmond, 1979; Kirby, 1979), family structure and functioning (reviewed by McLeod, Fitzpatrick, Glynn, & Fallis, 1982), political beliefs and behavior (reviewed by Comstock, Chaffee, Katzman, McCombs, & Roberts, 1978, chap. 7), consumer behavior (reviewed by Comstock et al., 1978, chap. 7; Atkin, 1982), conceptions of social reality (reviewed by Hawkins & Pingree, 1982), and the urban crisis (Muccigrosso, 1979).

Our own concerns were less global (or perhaps more elementary), focusing on changes within individuals. Individual change can lay the foundation for societal change; whether it does or not, it is of major psychological importance. A review of the literature revealed little previous research on the impact of television upon the thought processes, emotional reactions, attitudes, and personality characteristics of the general adult population, except in a few selected areas (e.g., politics, violence) with an intuitively obvious relationship to TV. It seems logical, however, that a medium so prominent in providing information and interpretation (see Comstock et al., 1978), role models and exemplars (Bandura, 1963), and what might be considered the folk myths and archetypal tales of our culture (Bruner & Olson, 1973) should have a measurable influence in these areas. We began by asking how adults might be affected by the dramatic change which occurred in Notel with the inception of television. We then selected relevant measures which had been tested in previous research to ask whether and how television affects the cognitive processes, personality characteristics, and attitude structures of adults.

SOME COMPONENTS OF TELEVISION'S INFLUENCE

What are the dimensions or characteristics through which television influences adult viewers? Four seemed especially salient to us: stimulation level, information structure, information content, and impact on behavior settings.

Stimulation level refers to changes in sensory stimulation that occur as a function of television viewing. On the one hand, ambient noise and visual stimulation would be expected to increase following the introduction of television, especially in "constant television" households (Medrich, 1979), in which the set is on most of the time. We would expect this to occur even though people's attention may not be fully—or at all—directed to the set all the time it is on. TV content may often be evaluated by a critic as boring or unoriginal, but from the sensory standpoint its rapidly changing components certainly add to the total stimulus array available in the environment. On the other hand, television viewing may displace involvement in other highly stimulating activities (e.g., participant sports, large social gatherings), thus decreasing the net level of stimulation experienced by family members.

Information structure refers to the characteristics of visual and auditory stimulation beyond mere load or amount. Increases in such structural or "collative" (Berlyne, 1960) variables as complexity, surprisingness, and incongruity might be expected to occur with the introduction of television. Again, it would be important to be sensitive to the distinction between net and gross changes in each aspect of information structure.

The *content* features of television have received considerably more research attention than its load and structural components (e.g., Comstock & Rubinstein, 1972). Television content can be categorized in several different ways. From the perspective of the kinds and range of objects to which individuals are exposed, television presents images of a greater number and variety of persons, objects, and places than are available otherwise. Viewers also are exposed to unfamiliar conduct such as violence or the customs of remote or deviant groups. The number and type of such secondhand experiences depends, of course, upon specific program selection, and their novelty varies with the viewer's real-life experience. It seems reasonable to assume, however, that the general level of exposure to these kinds of behavior would increase with the introduction of television. The content of television may affect a wide range of values and attitudes; for example, viewers of violent programs may perceive a high level of violence in society (see Hawkins & Pingree, 1982, for a review of this literature) or may acquire new perspectives on their own social and physical environment. As a result of comparing their experiences with those shown on TV, they may also acquire new evaluations and expectations about themselves and their community. For example, Hennigan et al. (1982) attributed the increase in thefts in the United States following the introduction of television to factors such as feelings of frustration and deprivation associated with viewing programs showing high levels of consumption.

The introduction of a television set results in a shift in the distribution and dynamics of household behavior settings (Barker, 1968), since television in itself constitutes a major new *behavior setting*.[1] Above and beyond its influence as an enclosed stimulus array, in many homes television serves as a focal point for various activities. Such activities, although social in the sense that several people are present, may be parallel rather than interactive; even when they are interactive, as often as not they revolve around television (LoSciuto, 1972). In addition, television displaces participation in behavior settings outside the household, as Williams and Handford found (Chapter 4, this volume).

EFFECTS INVESTIGATED IN THIS STUDY

Previous research has indicated that television influences both the behavior and the attitudes of its viewers. The relationship between attitudes and behavior and the direction of any causal link between them have been a topic of controversy in social psychology for many years. It is difficult to find unequivocal operational definitions and measures, either of attitudes or of the behaviors that might be related to those attitudes (see Fishbein & Ajzen, 1975). However, we agree with theorists who accept the intuitively appealing assumption that the two components are indeed related (Oskamp, 1977; Rajecki, 1982). We therefore used both behavioral and attitudinal (or quasi-attitudinal) measures to study three major domains: cognitive processes, perceptions of the self and community, and orientation toward the environment.

Cognition: Divergent Thinking

In *divergent thinking,* the cognitive steps taken toward solving a problem are not obvious, not previously overlearned, and they represent some novel departure from linear thinking. This kind of approach, one important component of creative problem solving, is of course most successful when the problem to be solved is complex and unfamiliar. By contrast, *convergent thinking* involves following well-practiced, logically sequential steps in reasoning. Both the ability to generate novel solutions to problems and the ability to apply well-tested solutions are societally important, and research on divergent and convergent thinking has a long history within experimental psychology.[2] Researchers have examined the types of problems that require one or the other kind of approach (e.g., open- versus closed-ended tasks; Bartlett, 1958) and devised performance and verbal tests to measure divergent problem solving and creativity (e.g., Vernon, 1970). The degree to which creativity is a function of innate talent, environmental facilitation, or an interaction between these two factors, is not well understood. The antecedent correlates of divergent thinking have not been established; there is little evidence that intelligence, educational level, age, or other demographic variables are strongly predictive of the ability to approach specific problems in this way. Nevertheless, the possibility that a major increase in environmental stimulation could affect the ability to persevere and succeed in developing creative solutions was worth investigating in Notel, Unitel, and Multitel. One often hears television blamed for stifling creativity, engendering lazy thinking, affecting children's ability or willingness to persist with difficult tasks, and so on. The natural experiment provided an opportunity to obtain empirical evidence against which to evaluate these anecdotally based statements.

Considerable theorizing and data have supported a curvilinear model of cognitive performance derived from animal research in the early part of the century (Yerkes & Dodson, 1908). This inverted U-shaped model posits differential effects on convergent and divergent thinking as the environment changes. In particular, the rate, complexity, and variability of information and stimulation in the environment, acting upon the general arousal level of the organism, should (1) curvilinearly first improve and then impair both kinds of performance; (2) lead to improvements on simple or convergent thinking at arousal levels too high for optimal creative thinking; and (3) provide a broader zone of optimal performance on tasks demanding simple solutions compared to those requiring complex ones (Schroder, Driver, & Streufert, 1967; Spence, 1956; Suedfeld, 1969).

One problem with these postulates is the difficulty of specifying optimal levels of stimulation for various tasks and individuals. No system of measuring either stimulation or arousal has been agreed upon, and so there is considerable imprecision in the theory. On the whole, however, tasks requiring divergent thinking should be more susceptible to environmental changes. As we noted earlier, the introduction of television may have increased the absolute level, rate of change, and complexity of stimulation and information provided by the environment in Notel. It therefore seemed appropriate to test its effect on creative problem solving. Two competing hypotheses were tested. Since television provides models of novel problems and solutions, it might facilitate divergent thinking by viewers. On the other hand, the increased level of arousal resulting from high stimulation levels induced by television would reduce the likelihood of divergent thinking by increasing the probability of the most dominant, familiar responses. It should be noted that we are here postulating changes that persist even when the individual is not actually watching TV, whether by an altered set-point for arousal, a new adaptation level, a change in chronic level of arousal, or some other mechanism.

Unfortunately, this is not a true strong-inference test of the hypotheses (Platt, 1964), since other explanations also are tenable. For example, it may be that television, in toto, provides few models of creative or unusual thinking, and more often presents conventional approaches to problem solving as successful.

We chose two tests of problem-solving flexibility to assess the impact of television on divergent thinking in adults.

The Duncker (1945) Candle Problem was used in Phase 1. Individuals were given a vertical cardboard surface and an array of common objects including a box of thumbtacks, a candle, and a book of matches (see Figure 8.1). They were told to "affix the candle to the cardboard wall, using any of the objects on the table, so it stays there and burns freely without being held." The correct solution is to empty the box of tacks, tack the box to the cardboard, and put the candle in or on the box. This is

366

Peter Suedfeld et al.

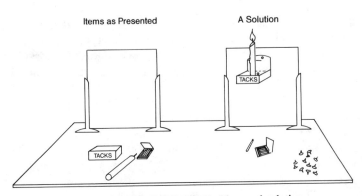

FIGURE 8.1 Duncker Candle Problem and solution.

difficult because people tend to think of each object only in relation to its obvious use (*functional fixedness*). In this case, the box typically is viewed only as something to hold the tacks, rather than something that could be emptied out and used to hold the candle. Presenting the box empty and with the tacks scattered on the table is an alternative, and easier, version of the task. In our study, the tacks were in the box (high functional fixedness version) for half the adults tested and out of the box (low fixedness version) for the other half. To measure the possible effect of additional motivation, half the adults were offered $20 or $10 prizes if they solved the problem quickly. This manipulation made no difference; it was therefore eliminated from further Phase 1 data analyses and was not used in Phase 2.

We could not use the same problem-solving task in Phase 2, since people would be likely to remember the solution. Instead we gave the Nine Dot Problem (Dworetzky, 1982). Participants were shown a piece of paper with nine dots forming a three by three square (see Figure 8.2) and

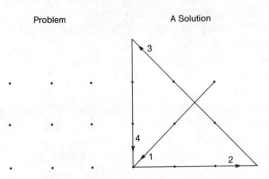

FIGURE 8.2 Nine Dot Problem and solution.

were asked to connect all the dots with no more than four straight pencil lines. The solution could include lines that cross each other, but the solver was not permitted to retrace any portion of any line or to lift the pencil off the paper. Again, the solution requires overcoming a strong assumption. The problem cannot be solved unless the pencil line goes outside the square twice, but because the sides of the square are typically considered to represent the boundaries of the solution, most people find this difficult to envision.

These problems were chosen for several reasons. First, they were non-verbal. We felt it desirable to break the monotony of the otherwise verbal measures; we also expected that even if some of the adults in this study were not highly articulate, they might be very competent in other realms. Second, the tests measure both the ability to engage in divergent, flexible, original thinking and the willingness to persist at trying to solve a problem which cannot be solved immediately. Third, these particular problems require very little equipment and do not involve major modifications of the environment. Last, they are both quite interesting, evoking a high degree of involvement and mental effort; thus, they are likely to measure the optimal performance.

Cognition: Cognitive Style

A second topic in which we were interested, cognitive style, relates cognition to personality and attitude structure. *Cognitive style* refers to stable ways of approaching problem solving in general, ranging across the wide spectrum from strictly cognitive tasks to those involving decision making in significant real-life domains such as choosing a career or dealing with interpersonal relationships (Goldstein & Blackman, 1978). The two aspects of cognitive style we investigated are both based on a great deal of empirical research, and are considered to be among the important cognitive personality variables (Schroder & Suedfeld, 1971).

Field dependence–independence (Witkin, Dyk, Faterson, Good-enough, & Karp, 1962), more recently relabeled *differentiation,* defines the degree to which an individual can distinguish gradations along a stimulus dimension. Field dependence (low differentiation) is reflected by judgments that depend upon environmental cues rather than upon internalized standards; it also involves a less clear sense of body boundaries and of the self and a greater use of global defense mechanisms. The degree of differentiation reflects the presence of subsystems for specific operations; how well these work together defines how integrated the system is.

We used the Embedded Figures Test (Gottschaldt, 1926) to assess field independence in both phases. Each item consists of a simple geometric figure and then a series of complex drawings. The task is to identify which of these more complex figures has the simple one hidden within it (see Figure 8.3). This test is purported to measure the degree to which people structure their perceptual field in an articulated or differentiated fashion (Goldstein & Blackman, 1978; Witkin et al., 1962). As a measure of field independence, it assesses the degree to which the individual can overcome distracting aspects of the environment and use internal processes to arrive at a correct answer. People who do well on this test—that is, are more highly differentiated or field independent—are theorized to have a better sense of individuality and more internalized standards of judgment and decision making. The degree to which field independence (or any other cognitive style) is modifiable by environmental characteristics after childhood is unknown. Haggard (1973) found no significant differences between rural and urban children in performance on the Embedded Figures task. Although cross-cultural differences have been reported (e.g., Berry, 1976; Witkin & Berry, 1975), the relationship between environment and culture is so confounded as to be pragmatically uninterpretable in this context.

Conceptual complexity (Harvey, Hunt, & Schroder, 1961; Schroder et al., 1967; Streufert & Streufert, 1978) goes two steps beyond differentiation. It, too, incorporates the degree to which individuals can distinguish among stimuli along a dimension but calls this "discrimination." A second component of complexity is the number of dimensions along which stimuli are scaled. This, unfortunately, is labeled "differentiation," which tends to lead to confusion when this theory is compared with the field independence approach. At the highest levels of cognitive complexity, the degree to which judgments made along different dimensions can be synthesized and combined into an integrated whole is called "integration."

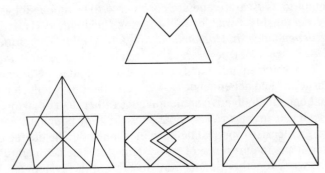

FIGURE 8.3   Example of an embedded figure from the Embedded Figures Test.

The conceptual complexity approach is unusual among the cognitive complexity and cognitive style theories in explicitly emphasizing all three of these components, and it is unique in measuring both differentiation and integration along the same axis in its major assessment technique (Schroder & Suedfeld, 1971). Measurement relies primarily on cognitive–affective judgments expressed in an open-ended verbal format rather than on perceptual judgments with a simple behavioral index (as in the case of field independence–dependence).

The Paragraph Completion Test (PCT; Schroder et al., 1967) was used in both phases to measure conceptual complexity. It measures the differentiation and integration of points of view expressed in the process of completing sentences related to central social and cognitive issues (see Table 8.A1). Level of conceptual complexity is defined as a dimension that ranges from rigid, all-or-none, restricted attitudes and approaches at the low end to flexible, combinatorial, highly information-based, finely graded approaches at the high end.

Attempts to relate both field independence and conceptual complexity to other measures of personality and cognition indicate they are relatively independent. Both tend to remain stable across adult age levels, although the former increases up to age 17 (Goldstein & Blackman, 1978). Both are moderately (.2 to .6) correlated with intelligence. The data currently available do not show generally reliable differences as a function of sex, socioeconomic status, or education. The few significant relationships reported have been complex rather than monotonic and are frequently contradicted by inconsistent findings in other studies.

We predicted that exposure to the rich stimulus and information array provided by television would increase fineness of information processing. Access to a wider array of points of view, situations, and stimuli was expected to result in better gradation and greater internalization of standards—in other words, greater field independence. The opportunity provided by television to examine, evaluate, and develop attitudes about a greater variety of frequently conflicting messages was expected to foster discrimination, differentiation, and integration, leading to higher conceptual complexity.

Perceptions of the Self and Community

In addition to assessing the influence of television on problem solving and cognitive style, we were interested in its impact on the ways individuals perceive themselves and their community. The measures we chose seemed particularly relevant to the hypothesized components of television influence discussed previously.

The Adjective Check List (Gough & Heilbrun, 1965) consists of 300 adjectives. Individuals indicate the degree to which they believe they possess each characteristic listed, and their responses are scored on a number of scales measuring such traits as aggressiveness, achievement orientation, and autonomy (see Table 8.A2). The inclusion of this measure, which was used in both phases, was exploratory, since we had no specific hypothesis concerning the effects of television on personality. It seemed possible, however, that exposure to TV could modify self-perception regarding some personality characteristics.

The Cantril Scales (Cantril, 1965) indicate major areas of human concern, on both micro- (individual, family) and macro- (community, nation) levels. The scales emphasize perception of one's present circumstances as compared to probable future conditions. Cantril hypothesized that the mass media strongly affect these evaluations, making his procedure particularly appropriate to our study. The test consists of "ladders," or dimensions, on which the person places a mark representing concerns or satisfactions with aspects of the past (5 years ago), present, and future (5 years from now). In another part of the test, the individual is asked to identify hopes and fears about various aspects of personal, family, community, national, and world conditions (see Table 8.A3). The Cantril Scales were given only in Phase 2. We predicted that the negative information frequently presented in graphic and dramatic forms on television would engender concern about both personal and community outcomes, with a possibility that the latter would be more marked.

Orientation to the Environment

Individual differences in response to the everyday environment, a topic which combines cognition, personality traits, attitudes, and interests, is of relatively recent interest to psychologists (e.g., Craik, 1976; Craik & McKechnie, 1977; Little, 1972, 1976).

The Environmental Response Inventory (McKechnie, 1974), given in both phases, assesses perception of desirable qualities in the environment. The emphasis is not on specific situational features, but rather on attitudes related to the individual's preferred level and kind of environmental exposure. We predicted that people who were not regular TV viewers would have attitudes less marked by what might be called a technological–urban pattern. We expected them to score lower on the Urbanism, Stimulus Seeking, and Mechanical Orientation scales and higher on the Pastoralism, Environmental Adaptation, Environmental Trust, Antiquarianism, and Need for Privacy scales (see Table 8.A4).

Our last measure, given in both phases, was an index of Thing–Person Orientation (Little, 1972, 1976). It contrasts an emphasis on inanimate objects with an emphasis on people as sources of information, standards, and reinforcers. Two possible hypotheses concerning the effects of television on Thing–Person orientation seemed possible, assuming television displaces some activities of a nonsocial nature (e.g., mechanical tasks, solitary hobbies). If the Thing-orientation score reflects the amount of (presumably satisfying) experience with such activities, it might be expected to be highest when TV is not available. On the other hand, if Thing-orientation scores reflect an unfilled need for encounters with the inanimate domain rather than satisfaction of this need, then we would expect individuals without access to television to score lower. Analogous predictions were possible for person orientation. If this index measures the degree to which social stimuli are present and attended to in the individual's environment, TV viewers should score relatively high; if the measure is one of need for such stimuli, they should score relatively low. Alternatively, Thing and Person orientations may be stable personality traits, in which case we would expect television to have little effect in adulthood.

SELECTION OF PARTICIPANTS, TESTING PROCEDURE, AND DATA ANALYSIS

In Phase 1, each of the three towns was subdivided into several geographical areas. Within each area, 60 to 65 households were selected by a random process. The same process was used in Phase 2, which meant some households were recontacted (longitudinal sample), and others were contacted for the first time. A total of 167 adults participated in Phase 1, and 179 in Phase 2. As Table 8.A5 indicates, 62 of these adults were tested at both time periods (longitudinal sample); the rest participated in only one phase (cross-sectional sample). The mean age for all communities was 40.3 years for males and 38.8 years for females; 41.0 years in Notel, 36.4 years in Unitel, and 41.0 years in Multitel.

Once the households had been selected, pairs of research assistants went to each house, explained the study, and requested participation. Most of the participants were married couples living in the same household. If it was convenient, the tests were administered immediately. If not, or if one of the potential participants was not at home, the research assistants made an appointment to return at a more appropriate time.

There had been sufficient informal publicity about the presence of researchers from the University that relatively little additional explanation was needed. Over 95% of the households selected through the random procedure agreed to cooperate. The interview sessions were conducted over approximately a week in each community in each phase of the study.

The tests were administered individually. During the problem-solving tasks, other people were asked to leave the room. For the written measures, the two participants were permitted to be in the same room, but not to discuss their answers. The tests took approximately 1 hour for each participant.

At the end of the session, the research assistants answered questions about the purpose of the study and the tests, asked the participants not to discuss the procedures with any other townspeople until the data collection was completed, and thanked the participants for their help. Summaries of the results were made available at the end of the study to interested participants.

A general statement regarding the criteria adopted for interpreting the findings may be helpful. We had the most confidence in results that were statistically significant for both the longitudinal and cross-sectional samples. Next came effects found to be significant with the longitudinal sample but not replicated with the cross-sectional sample. Because there is uncertainty about the equivalence of the participants involved in only one phase of the research, we place less credence in the cross-sectional than in the longitudinal results. Interpretation will occasionally be made of cross-sectional results that were not replicated with the longitudinal sample and of results in either sample reaching only borderline statistical significance but of particular theoretical or practical interest.

We considered several possible procedures for analyzing the data. One was to analyze our data for the longitudinal sample and to use the cross-sectional people studied only in Phase 1 or Phase 2 as a second (replication) sample. The other was to compare both groups in Phase 1 and combine them if their data were similar; to do the same for Phase 2; to analyze the longitudinal data; and then present all of the cross-sectional data as a replication. The cross-sectional and longitudinal groups differed on more measures than would be expected by chance, so we took the first approach.[3]

RESULTS: COGNITIVE PERFORMANCE

Because we wanted to avoid practice effects, which would have made it impossible to evaluate the impact of television per se, different problem-solving tasks were given in Phase 1 and Phase 2. This precluded comparisons across the phases.

Prior to the introduction of television to Notel, 40.4% of the adults tested solved the Duncker Candle Problem, compared to 25.5% of Unitel residents and 30% of Multitel residents. The differences among these proportions are not statistically significant, but there were significant differences among the towns in the speed with which the problem was solved and in the amount of time that residents who were eventually unsuccessful persisted in trying to solve it.[4] Notel adults who solved the problem did so more quickly than adults in the towns with television; indeed, they were almost twice as fast. Among those who were not successful, Notel residents continued to try significantly longer than Unitel residents (who gave up most quickly) and marginally longer than Multitel residents. Sex did not make a difference in performance. As other researchers have found, the low functional fixedness version of the task (box empty, tacks on the table) was significantly easier to solve than the high functional fixedness version (tacks in the box).

Information about television-viewing habits, which was obtained in another study in this project (see Chapter 5), was available for some of the participants in this study. We therefore conducted additional analyses relating amount of TV viewing to performance on the Duncker Candle Problem. We cannot specify whether the findings are due to individual cognitive differences which in turn lead to differential TV viewing, to cognitive changes which result from differential viewing, or to a transactional relationship. Nevertheless, the results are compatible with the evidence, based on our comparisons among the towns, that television has a negative impact on divergent problem solving.[5] Unitel and Multitel residents who solved the candle problem reported watching significantly fewer hours ($M = 18.1$) of television per week than did residents who failed to solve the problem ($M = 33.4$ hours). In addition, among the Unitel and Multitel adults who failed to solve the problem, those who persisted relatively longer in trying tended to watch less television than those who gave up sooner. This latter finding was not statistically significant; TV-viewing information was available for only a relatively small number of the nonsolvers.

How confident are we that our results are due to television rather than other factors and/or differences among the towns? One possible confound is age. Although longitudinal studies of the same individuals over the adult years (at least up to the 50s) indicate that cognitive functioning does not deteriorate, cross-sectional studies of different-aged individuals studied at the same time indicate that older people do more poorly than younger people (e.g., Horn & Cattell, 1966). This kind of cohort effect in cross-sectional samples is usually attributed to the historical periods in which the age groups were raised, most likely involving the different educational experiences of the older and younger groups tested (Schaie & Strother, 1968). Since our study was cross-sectional, it was important to rule out cohort differences as a possible explanation of our results. Age did not vary according to town or sex.[6] We did not obtain specific educational information from the participants, but the census data as well as information regarding parental occupation obtained in interviews with the school children (see Chapter 1) indicated that the towns were fairly similar in this regard. We therefore feel confident in concluding that the Duncker Candle Problem results for Phase 1 indicate that over the long run, television has a negative influence on divergent problem solving by adults, in terms of both the speed of solution and persistence in trying to find a solution.

The Nine Dot Problem given in Phase 2 proved to be so difficult that only 7 of 188 adults tested in the three towns solved it. Our analyses, therefore, centered on the amount of time participants spent at the task—that is, how long they continued to try. Notel residents persisted significantly longer than Unitel residents, and marginally longer than Multitel residents.[7] Although direct comparisons between the Duncker Candle and Nine Dot problems are not possible, the difference in persistence between Notel and the mean for the other towns was substantially larger before television arrived (95 seconds) than 2 years later (22.5 seconds).

Since so few people managed to solve the Nine Dot Problem, we looked at the data again and rescored the drawings. Individuals who went outside the boundary of the square formed by the dots in attempting to link them were scored as having "broken set." In Notel, 25% of the adults did so, compared to 15% in Unitel and 9.4% is Multitel.[8] This was a marginally significant difference.

Averaging across the three towns, residents who solved the Nine Dot Problem reported watching significantly fewer hours of television per week ($M = 12.8$) than did those who failed to solve it ($M = 23.4$). The same was true for those who broke set ($M = 17.2$ hours of television) by comparison with those who did not ($M = 24.7$).[9]

Summary of Cognitive Performance Results

Results from the Duncker Candle Problem given prior to the arrival of television in Notel and the Nine Dot Problem given 2 years later were consistent in pointing to a negative impact of television on divergent thinking by adults. In the absence of TV, Notel residents solved the Duncker Candle Problem more quickly than residents of towns with television, and those who did not succeed tended to keep trying longer. When the Nine Dot Problem was given 2 years later, the differences among the towns were smaller, but Notel residents still persisted longer. The finding that Unitel and Multitel residents did not differ on any of the problem-solving measures supports the conclusion that television was a major factor in the differences between those towns and Notel. Further support comes from the evidence in both phases that people who did well on the problem-solving tasks tended to watch less television than those who did poorly. These results concerning problem solving by adults are consistent with results obtained for children by Harrison and Williams (see Chapter 3), who used a different measure of creativity and controlled for intelligence.

RESULTS: COGNITIVE STYLE

On the Gottschaldt Embedded Figures Test, participants in Phase 2 were significantly less dependent on external cues for solving the problem (i.e., were more field independent) than were those tested in Phase 1. This was true of both the longitudinal and the cross-sectional samples.[10] There were no other stable differences.

The Paragraph Completion Test revealed little evidence of differences among the towns.[11] In both phases, conceptual complexity was greatest in Multitel, but the town differences were not significant in Phase 1 and only marginally significant in Phase 2. Our hypothesis had been that television might foster better discrimination among concepts because it exposes the viewer to a wide variety of views, ways of thought, life-styles, personalities, and the like. Thus, we predicted lower conceptual complexity in Notel than in the other towns in Phase 1, with an increase in Notel in Phase 2. The absence of such a change and the weakness of the evidence for higher conceptual complexity in Multitel indicate that television has little or no impact on conceptual complexity.

RESULTS: PERCEPTIONS OF SELF AND COMMUNITY

The Adjective Check List consists of 21 scales, plus 3 scales constructed from these 21 (number of adjectives checked, number of favorable adjectives, and number of unfavorable adjectives). Significant differences were found on 8 scales for the longitudinal sample and on 18 when data from the longitudinal and cross-sectional samples were combined in each phase. The pattern of results differed between longitudinal and cross-sectional participants for 7 of the 21 adjectives in Phase 1 and for 6 in Phase 2; the number of adjectives checked also varied in Phase 2 (see note 3). For adjectives reflecting both favorable (e.g., achievement) and unfavorable (e.g., abasement) characteristics, as well as for the number of positive adjectives checked, the scores for the three towns tended to be similar for people who participated in only one phase of the study (pure cross-sectional sample) and to differ for people who participated in both phases. Why might this occur? We cannot be sure, but longitudinal partic- ipants may have been more likely to be long-term residents of their re- spective communities, whereas those who participated in only one phase may have been more likely to be transient. If correct, this hypothesis would explain why the cross-sectional participants were more similar than different in the three communities.

In the longitudinal sample, averaging across the two phases, Multitel residents tended to describe themselves in the most positive light, Unitel residents did so in the most negative light, and Notel residents were in between.[12] For Adjective Check List responses referring to desirable at- tributes such as good personal adjustment, high achievement, change (novelty seeking), order, affiliation, and intraception, Multitel scores were highest and Unitel scores lowest, and this also was true for the number of favorable adjectives and total number of adjectives checked. Multitel residents also were highest in defensiveness, a measure of resis- tance to or stubbornness in taking the test. The finding that Unitel men scored higher on the measure of counseling readiness than did men in Notel and Multitel is further evidence of the pattern that Unitel residents tended to see themselves in the least favorable light. Since the towns were ordered consistently, but not in a sensible pattern in relation to the avail- ability of television, these results probably reflect other kinds of differ- ences.

The Cantril Scale data from Phase 2 supported Cantril's (1965) original finding that people living in rural areas generally do not express high levels of concern. Only 4 of the 38 categories were marked by more than 50% of the respondents as a personal concern. Hopes and fears for the general economic situation were highest, followed by concerns related to the respondent's personal economic situation and family.[13] There was little interest in non-economic problems of society in general, a finding which perhaps reflects the mild recession in the North American economy at that time. In the realm of personal concerns, Notel residents tended to express more satisfaction with both the present and future than did Multi- tel residents. Significant intertown differences were also found for feel- ings about the community in the past, with Unitel residents expressing less satisfaction than residents of both Notel and Multitel. The latter did not differ.[14]

Gerbner and his colleagues (e.g., Gerbner, Gross, Morgan, & Signorielli, 1972) argue that television tends to foster negative and fearful attitudes about a wide variety of social issues, especially among heavy viewers (see Hawkins & Pingree, 1982, for a review). Our finding that ratings of one's personal situation in the present and future were most positive in Notel and least positive in Multitel, with Unitel in between, might be taken as support for this position. Since these data were collected in Phase 2, however, we would have to argue that the effect develops so slowly that Notel residents had not yet been affected 2 years after the arrival of television. Moreover, the effect should be stronger for ratings concerning the community than for personal ratings. This was not the case. The only significant difference in the town ratings was that Unitel residents described their town as it had been in the past less positively than did Notel and Multitel residents, an apparently idiosyncratic finding. Taken together, our results tend to contradict, rather than support, the notion that television cultivates a negative conception of social reality. It may be that the rural nature of these communities outweighed any negative feelings aroused by television coverage of troublesome issues, particularly since television tends to emphasize problems more relevant to large cities. The portrayal of urban problems may have seemed so irrelevant that, if anything, a contrast effect may have occurred. That is, satisfaction may have been enhanced for viewers in these three towns. These speculations are highly tentative, of course, especially since we did not obtain ratings of these factors in the first phase of the study. They are, however, compatible with some other findings (reviewed by Hawkins & Pingree, 1982), including those obtained in Toronto by Doob and Macdonald (1979).

RESULTS: ORIENTATION TO THE ENVIRONMENT

For both the longitudinal and the cross-sectional samples, the Environmental Response Inventory scores revealed sex differences on several of the scales.[15] There also were some town- and phase-related differences, but these were more common for people who were assessed only in one phase than for those who participated in both phases. Since we are more confident about the meaningfulness of longitudinal results, we shall give them more emphasis.

Averaging across towns and phases, men in the longitudinal sample obtained higher scores than women for the Stimulus Seeking, Environmental Trust, and Mechanical Orientation scales, whereas women obtained higher Antiquarianism scores. These sex differences also occurred in the cross-sectional sample. We may conclude that they probably are characteristic of residents of such communities, and may be broadly generalizable.

Some evidence of differences among the towns was found in the longitudinal sample for four of the nine scales. For Environmental Trust, there were town differences only for women, with higher scores in Multitel than in Notel and marginally higher scores in Multitel than in Unitel. The hypothesis that television "cultivates a mean world view" (Gerbner et al., 1982) would predict the opposite pattern of town differences, which is what we found for the cross-sectional sample. However, since there was no evidence of change for any of the towns from Phase 1 to Phase 2, and since the longitudinal and cross-sectional results were inconsistent, the only reasonable conclusion is that the town differences are unrelated to the availability of television.

In the longitudinal sample, Need for Privacy was higher in Phase 1 in Unitel than in both Notel and Multitel. The latter towns did not differ. Unitel decreased from Phase 1 to Phase 2, at which point all three towns were similar. In the cross-sectional sample, the pattern was the same in both phases: Unitel and Notel did not differ, and both were higher than Multitel in Need for Privacy. Taken together, these results hint that expressed need for privacy may decrease as television is increasingly available. Again, however, the lack of change in Notel following the arrival of television and the inconsistency in the longitudinal and cross-sectional results make the evidence for that interpretation weak at best.

Averaging across the phases, the longitudinal sample yielded marginal evidence that the towns differed in Antiquarianism. There also were significant differences in the cross-sectional sample. Again the pattern was opposite to intuitive prediction, since Notel was the lowest in the former case and highest in the latter.

The final instance of town differences occurred for Stimulus Seeking. However, the patterns for the cross-sectional and the longitudinal samples differed. Within the latter sample, the order of means did not show a consistent relationship to the availability of television. Since we cannot attribute the results to the major factor being studied, we will not try to interpret them.

Taken together, the results obtained with the Environmental Response Inventory provide evidence of some stable sex differences but little if any reason to believe that television influences adult viewers' orientation toward their environment.

On the Person scale of Thing–Person Orientation, women in both the longitudinal and pure cross-sectional samples scored higher than men.[16] This was true of all three towns in both phases. Person-orientation scores were ordered from highest in Multitel to lowest in Notel, with Unitel in between. The Multitel–Notel difference was statistically significant, and the Multitel–Unitel difference was marginally significant. This pattern was consistent for the longitudinal and the cross-sectional samples, as well as for both sexes and both phases of the study. On Thing-orientation, men in both samples had higher mean scores than women. In the longitudinal sample, Unitel residents scored highest, significantly higher than Notel residents, who were lowest. Multitel residents were in between, not different from Unitel, and marginally higher than Notel. There were no town-related differences on Thing-orientation for the cross-sectional sample.

The finding that women in these towns tended to score higher than men on Person-orientation and lower on Thing-orientation is consistent with sex-role stereotypes in Western culture and with previous research. Note, however, that the mean scores showed both sexes to be more Person-oriented than Thing-oriented. These findings tend to support the idea that this test measures involvement and interest. What, then, are we to make of the differences among communities? Notel residents were relatively low on both Person- and Thing-orientation, whereas the towns with television were relatively high. Whether this reflects low levels of involvement or low levels of need to get involved (as discussed previously) must be left for further research. The absence of change in Notel following the introduction of television does suggest that if television or other aspects of the environment influence Person- and/or Thing-orientation among adults, the process of change is slow.

CONCLUSIONS

Our findings indicate that the effects of television viewing on adults in the areas we assessed are neither overwhelming nor straightforward. The tests were directed towards processes and functions that might logically be expected to be susceptible to environmental influence: divergent thinking to solve a novel problem; persistence when one is frustrated in solving it; the use of internal and external anchors in perceptual judgment; the ability to recognize, distinguish, and integrate different points of view concerning important social and personal topics; a long list of personality characteristics, values, opinions and attitudes; and ways of relating to various aspects of the environment. Given the degree to which television familiarizes its viewers with a greater range of specific contents (social norms, interpersonal behavior patterns, physical and social environments, and so on) and enlarges the scope of structural variables (e.g., level and complexity of stimulation and information, rate of environmental change), we would not have been surprised to find dramatic differences across the towns and phases of this study. This did occur, but not for the majority of the measures we used.

Some of our results probably *can* be ascribed to the effects of television. Most compelling is the evidence that television affects cognitive task performance by adults. Both across and within towns, less television viewing was associated with better performance and greater perseverance. Why and how might television affect problem-solving behavior?

Theoretically, increased exposure to a variety of problem situations via television might enhance problem solving by making it easier for people to break set and try novel approaches. But this is not what we found. It may be that television programs do not provide such model situations but emphasize instead a small number of relatively straightforward (convergent) solutions. In addition, it is possible that TV provides relatively high levels of stimulation and leads to increased arousal, and that as a result, viewers tend to fixate rigidly on well-learned responses. On the tasks we presented, familiar responses were bound to lead to failure; if such responses were made more probable by television viewing, solution of the problem would be made less probable. This hypothesis would explain the fact that adults who watched more television were less likely to succeed in solving either the Duncker Candle Problem or the Nine Dot Problem. Television also might influence adult problem-solving behavior in two other ways, as Harrison and Williams (Chapter 3) have argued for children. Perhaps television displaces activities which otherwise might facilitate performance in creative problem-solving tasks. These might include actual problem-solving situations or games. In addition, some activities displaced by TV might facilitate mindful information processing (Langer, 1982), whereas television viewing may require less invested mental effort (Salomon, 1983).

The effects of television on perseverance by adults in problem-solving tasks can be interpreted in at least three ways. Individuals who are used to watching television may develop a relatively short attention span and/or low frustration tolerance. When faced with a problem they are unable to solve, they may be less likely to continue working on it. Another possible explanation is that individuals who spend more time watching television have fewer alternative, non-obvious solution methods available to them, because of the narrowing effects of higher arousal, because they have less experience with problem solving, or both. They may therefore exhaust their repertoire sooner. A third and somewhat simpler explanation is that perseverance may be learned in part through experience with problem-solving situations, and that watching television may to some extent displace such experiences. Whatever the processes involved, the results of this natural experiment provide the first empirical evidence for adults to support the frequently stated concern that television may over the long run affect concentration or willingness to persist in the face of difficulty.

If further research consistently demonstrates that television has long-term negative effects on problem solving, the implication that it has the potential to change stable and broadly relevant personality–cognitive characteristics of the adult population is thought-provoking. Developmental research also seems worthwhile, since most theories of cognitive development imply that environmental influences have greater impact during childhood and adolescence than in adulthood.

Whereas performance on concrete, open-ended, problem-solving tasks apparently is adversely affected by television, our results regarding general cognitive style support the conclusion that television does not affect stable levels of conceptual complexity or field independence.

In the realm of attitudes, the accessibility of several television channels in Multitel was associated with greater desire to affiliate with other people, as measured by the Person-orientation task. On the other hand, individuals with such access showed less general satisfaction with their personal circumstances than did individuals for whom television had only recently become available. Like some other researchers (e.g., Doob & Macdonald, 1979), we failed to replicate findings (reviewed by Hawkins & Pingree, 1982) that television engenders an increasingly fearful and negative attitude toward the external world, but the measures we used were not designed specifically for that purpose.

Orientation to the environment showed a stereotyped sex difference. Women reported themselves as more oriented toward other people than did men, and the opposite was true for things and mechanical processes.

In examining whether our results indicate that television influences adult behavior and attitudes, we looked for consistent patterns. Were the towns ordered in relation to the continuum of television availability? Was the introduction of television to Notel associated with changes which did not occur in Unitel and Multitel? The results that we have emphasized and that we have been willing to attribute to television were those that yielded positive answers to one or both of these questions. In several instances, however, differences among the towns were not a simple function of the introduction of television to Notel or the number of channels available in the three communities. Results for which the order of differences was not linearly related to the number of TV channels available (i.e., the order of towns was other than Notel–Unitel–Multitel) may indicate one of several things. The most conservative interpretation, and the one we favor, is that television has no influence in those areas. A second possibility is that aspects of television other than its availability make a difference. For example, something in the specific content of CBC might have produced an effect in Unitel in both phases or in Notel in Phase 2. Note, however, that Multitel residents also had access to CBC, so this interpretation would require evidence that they were less exposed to the specifically non-U.S. CBC content in question. The favorite programs of adults and children in the three towns were quite similar. The evidence from content analyses of similarities and differences between CBC and the three U.S. networks is mixed (Halpern & Ethier, 1977; Longstaffe & Williams, 1985; Williams, Zabrack, & Joy, 1977, 1982). On balance, we are inclined to reject the hypothesis that content differences account for these particular results. Television content may, however, explain some of the results obtained by Murray and Kippax (1977, 1978) in their study of three Australian communities, since the media diets of residents of their Low-TV and High-TV towns differed substantially in terms of both amount and type (educational vs. entertainment) of programming watched. A third potential explanation for the lack of a clear Notel–Unitel–Multitel continuum in many of our results is that Unitel residents in both phases and Notel residents in Phase 2 watched almost as much television as did Multitel residents and had similar favorite programs, even though they had access to only one channel (see Chapter 5). It also is possible that lack of choice in programming has psychological effects quite aside from any content effects, in the same way that perceived control can affect the evaluation of, and response to, other stimuli (e.g., Glass & Singer, 1972).

Perhaps the best summary of our findings would be that the effects of television on adults are not necessarily uniform, linear, overwhelming, or all bad. These results, like those reported in the other chapters of this book, confirm that there are no simple answers to the question of how television affects its viewers.

APPENDIX: TABLES

TABLE 8.A1

Items on the Paragraph Completion Test

When I am in doubt . . .	When a friend acts differently
Rules . . .	toward me . . .
When others criticize me it usually	Policemen . . .
means . . .	When I don't know what
Confusion . . .	to do . . .

TABLE 8.A2

Traits Measured by the Adjective Check List (ACL)

Trait	Description
Abasement	To express feelings of inferiority through self-criticism, guilt, or social impotence.
Achievement	To strive to be outstanding in pursuits of socially recognized significance.
Affiliation	To seek and sustain numerous personal friendships.
Aggression	To engage in behaviors which attack or hurt others.
Autonomy	To act independently of others or of social values and expectations.
Change	To seek novelty of experience and avoid routine.
Counseling readiness	A special scale developed to identify those individuals who would seem likely to profit from counseling. High scorers are reported to be high in anxiety, complicated, and ambivalent about their status in contrast to low scorers who enjoy life in an uncomplicated way.
Defensiveness	Resistance in taking the ACL. High scorers are regarded as resolute and even stubborn in pursuing their objectives.
Deference	To seek and sustain subordinate roles in relationship to others.
Dominance	To seek and sustain leadership roles in groups or to be influential and controlling in individual relationships.
Endurance	To persist in any task undertaken.
Exhibitionism	To behave in such a way as to elicit the immediate attention of others.
Heterosexuality	To seek the company of and derive emotional satisfaction from interactions with opposite-sex peers.
Intraception	To engage in attempts to understand one's own behavior or the behavior of others.
Lability	A disposition to be spontaneous, restless, adventurous, and rejecting of convention and routine.
Nurturance	To engage in behaviors which extend material or emotional benefits to others.
Order	To place special emphasis on neatness, organization, and planning one's activities.
Personal adjustment	A disposition towards a positive, optimistic, and adaptable approach to life.
Self-confidence	A disposition to be outgoing, poised, and self-assured, particularly in social encounters.
Self-control	A disposition to be conscientious, dependable, and responsible.
Succorance	To solicit sympathy, affection, or emotional support from others.

TABLE 8.A3
Categories of the Cantril Scales[a]

Own personal character	International situation and world
Personal economic situation	General
Job or work situation	National political concerns
Other references to "self"	National economic concerns
Other references to family	National social concerns
Political concerns (general, community)	Social morality and population concerns
General economic situation	International relations, cold war, peace, etc.
Social	Independence, status and importance of nation
Environment	General international concerns
Religion, morality and public service	

[a] Subject is asked to identify hopes and fears in each category.

TABLE 8.A4
Environmental Response Inventory Scales

Scale	Description
Antiquarianism	Enjoyment of antiques and historical places; preference for traditional vs. modern design; aesthetic sensitivity to built environments and to landscape; appreciation of cultural artifacts of earlier eras; tendency to collect objects for their emotional significance.
Environmental Adaptation	Modification of the environment to satisfy needs and desires, and to provide comfort and leisure; opposition to governmental control over private land use; use of technology to solve environmental problems; preference for stylized environmental details.
Environmental Trust	General environmental openness, responsiveness, and trust; competence in finding one's way about the environment versus fear of potentially dangerous environments; security of home versus fear of being alone and unprotected.
Mechanical Orientation	Interest in mechanics in its various forms; enjoyment in working with one's hands; interest in technological processes and basic principles of science; appreciation of the functional properties of objects.
Need for Privacy	Need for physical isolation from stimuli; enjoyment of solitude; dislike of neighbors; need for freedom from distraction.
Pastoralism	Opposition to land development; concern about population growth; preservation of natural resources, including open space; acceptance of natural forces as shapers of human life; sensitivity to pure environmental experiences; self-sufficiency in the natural environment.
Stimulus Seeking	Interest in travel and exploration of unusual places; enjoyment of complex and intense physical sensations; breadth of interests.
Urbanism	Enjoyment of high density living; appreciation of unusual and varied stimulus patterns of the city; interest in cultural life; enjoyment of interpersonal richness and diversity.

TABLE 8.A5
Number of Participants in Each Town and Phase

| | | Phase 2 | | |
| | | | | |
Town	Phase 1	Previously tested (longitudinal)	New (cross-sectional)	Total
Notel	58	19	41	60
Unitel	54	21	38	59
Multitel	55	22	38	60
	167	62	117	179

NOTES

[1] A *behavior setting* is an environmental unit which places limits on the range and type of behavior likely to occur in it. See Chapter 4 (this volume) for a more detailed explanation.

[2] See Chapter 3 (this volume) for a more detailed discussion, including evidence and speculation regarding the impact of television on both convergent and divergent thinking.

[3] A proportional means ANOVA for Town (T; Notel, Unitel, Multitel) × Sex (S) × Group (G; cross-sectional, longitudinal) was run on the data from each phase (1, 2) for the Thing–Person, Environmental Response Inventory, and Adjective Check List measures. The significant effects involving Group are indicated in the following table:

| | Phase 1 | | Phase 2 | |
| | | | | |
Measure	Significant effects	F	Significant effects	F
Thing–Person				
Person Scale			S × G	3.9*
Thing Scale	T × G	5.3**		
Environmental Response Inventory[a]				
Antiquarianism	T × G	4.3*		
Environmental Adaptation			G	9.4***
Environmental Trust	T × G	3.2*	T × G	3.8*
Mechanical Orientation	S × G	4.1*		
Pastoralism	T × G	4.3*		
Stimulus Seeking	T × S × G	4.6**		

(*Continued*)

	Phase 1		Phase 2	
Measure	Signi- ficant effects	F	Signi- ficant effects	F
Adjective Check List[b]				
Total number checked	T × G	3.8*		
Achievement	T × G	3.4*		
Affiliation	T × G	4.2*	T × G	4.4*
Defensiveness	T × G	3.8*		
Dominance	T × G	4.2*		
Number favorable checked	T × G	3.4*	T × G	3.1*
Intraception			G	4.2*
			T × G	3.7*
Personal adjustment	T × G	5.4**	T × G	3.7*
Self confidence	T × G	3.7*		
Succorance	T × G	4.5*		

[a] See Table 8.A4 for definitions.
[b] See Table 8.A2 for definitions.
* $p < .05$; ** $p < .01$; *** $p < .005$.

[4] For adults who solved the Phase 1 Duncker Candle Problem, a least squares solution ANOVA on their speed (in seconds) was run with town (Notel, Unitel, Multitel), sex, and functional fixedness (low, box empty, tacks on the table; high, tacks in the box) as between-subject variables. The town main effect, $F(2,43) = 3.22$, $p < .05$ was significant. Notel residents ($M = 150.6$ seconds) solved the problem significantly faster ($p < .05$ by Newman–Keuls test) than Unitel ($M = 251.0$ seconds) and marginally significantly faster than Multitel residents ($M = 263.1$ seconds; $p < .10$ by both Tukey and Newman–Keuls test). Unitel and Multitel did not differ. The significant functional fixedness main effect, $F(1,43) = 5.60$, $p < .03$ confirmed that the low functional fixedness condition was easier ($M = 179.5$ seconds) than the high functional fixedness condition ($M = 271.4$ seconds). The sex main effect and all interactions were nonsignificant.

For residents who did not solve the Duncker Candle Problem, a least squares ANOVA was run on the length of time (in seconds) they persisted in trying, with town, sex, and functional fixedness as between-subject variables. Only the town main effect was significant, $F(2,105) = 4.16$, $p < .02$. Planned comparisons revealed that Notel residents ($M = 401.0$ seconds) persisted significantly longer than Unitel residents ($M = 279.9$ seconds; $p < .01$ by Tukey test) and marginally longer than Multitel residents ($M = 332.4$ seconds; $p < .10$ by Newman–Keuls test). Unitel and Multitel did not differ.

[5] Unitel and Multitel residents who solved the Duncker Candle Problem reported watching fewer hours ($M = 18.1$) of television per week in Phase 1 than did residents who failed to solve it ($M = 33.4$ hours of TV viewing), $t(33) = 3.79$, $p < .001$.

For Unitel and Multitel residents who did not solve the problem, time (in seconds) spent trying was negatively but not strongly related to hours of reported TV viewing in both Phase 1, $r(22) = -.27$, $p < .20$ and Phase 2, $r(37) = -.29$, $p < .08$.

[6] In an unweighted means ANOVA on the ages of Phase 1 Duncker Candle Problem participants for Town × Sex, none of the effects approached significance.

[7] In a least squares ANOVA on time (in seconds) spent trying to solve the Nine Dot Problem in Phase 2 for Town × Sex × Solution (solved vs. not), the town main effect was significant, $F(2,178) = 5.17, p < .007$. Notel residents ($M = 292.8$ seconds) persisted significantly longer than Unitel residents ($M = 263.8$); $p < .01$ by Tukey test) and marginally longer than Multitel residents ($M = 277.3$; $p < .10$ by Newman–Keuls test). Unitel and Multitel did not differ. The significant solution main effect, $F(1,178) = 22.01, p < .001$ indicated (as expected) that people who solved the problem spent less time at the task ($M = 190.9$ seconds) than people who did not ($M = 281.7$ seconds). No other effects approached significance.

[8] In Phase 2 on the Nine Dot Problem, 16 of 64 participants in Notel (25%) broke set (took their pencil line outside the boundary formed by the nine dots) by comparison with 9 of 60 Unitel residents (15%) and 6 of 58 Multitel residents (9.4%). The difference in these distributions is marginally significant, $\chi^2(2) = 5.47, p < .07$.

[9] For the Nine Dot Problem given in Phase 2, averaging across the three towns, people who were successful reported watching less television ($M = 12.75$ hours per week) than those who were not ($M = 23.39$ hours), $t(85) = 4.90, p < .001$. Those who broke set on the problem also reported watching less TV ($M = 17.18$ hours) than those who did not break set ($M = 24.65$), $t(95) = 2.52, p < .01$.

[10] In an unweighted means ANOVA on the Gottschaldt Embedded Figures Test for longitudinal participants, with town and sex as between-subject variables and repeated measures on phase, only the phase main effect, $F(1,55) = 20.20, p < .001$ was significant, reflecting a higher mean score (greater field independence) in Phase 2 (8.04) than in Phase 1 (5.69). The analysis restricted to those who participated in only one phase (true cross-sectional subjects) revealed similar results, but the phase main effect was only marginally significant, $F(1,219) = 3.62, p < .06$; Phase 1 mean, 6.01, Phase 2 mean, 7.24.

[11] In an unweighted means ANOVA for Town × Sex on the Phase 1 Paragraph Completion Test scores of all participants, none of the effects approached significance. The means were 1.38 for Notel, 1.33 for Unitel, and 1.42 for Multitel. In a similar analysis on Phase 2 scores, the town main effect, $F(2,163) = 2.29, p = .104$ approached significance. Since such an effect had been hypothesized, planned comparison tests were run on the means (1.35 for Notel, 1.36 for Unitel, 1.50 for Multitel). The Multitel mean was higher than the Unitel mean ($p < .05$ by Newman–Keuls test), and no other differences approached significance. None of the effects involving sex was significant in either phase of the study. Because of the way the data were scored it was not possible to separate longitudinal from cross-sectional participants.

[12] A series of Town × Sex × Phase unweighted means ANOVAs was run for longitudinal participants on the Adjective Check List scores. The town main effect was significant in nine of these analyses, and the results are as follows:

Type of score	Town means			$F(2,40)$	Tukey comparisons[a]
	Notel	Unitel	Multitel		
Total number checked	47.26	38.06	55.11	7.38**	M > U, .01
Favorable number checked	46.78	38.61	52.28	8.00***	M > U, .01; N > U, .05
Achievement	48.80	45.03	53.58	4.03*	M > U, .05
Affiliation	46.17	39.92	52.45	7.71***	M > U, .01; M > N, .05, N > U, .05

(Continued)

Type of score	Town means			$F(2,40)$	Tukey comparisons[a]
	Notel	Unitel	Multitel		
Change	47.99	41.36	47.20	3.85*	N > U, .10; M > U, .10
Defensiveness	47.88	42.64	53.42	5.91**	M > U, .01
Intraception	46.38	40.33	52.69	7.53**	M > U, .01; M > N, .05
Order	48.81	45.86	55.25	4.64*	M > U, .01
Personal adjustment	45.26	41.94	52.44	7.83***	M > U, .01; M > N, .05

[a] Decimal numbers denote significance level of comparisons, by Tukey test.
* $p < .05$; ** $p < .01$; *** $p < .001$.

In only three analyses were other effects significant. The analysis for order revealed a significant phase main effect, $F(1,40) = 4.26$, $p < .05$, reflecting a higher mean in Phase 2 (51.14) than in Phase 1 (48.59).

The analysis for personal adjustment also revealed significant interactions for Town × Phase, $F(2,40) = 3.93$, $p < .03$; and for Town × Sex × Phase, $F(2,40) = 4.85$, $p < .02$. Simple main effects analyses of the three-way interaction revealed that differences among the towns were specific to men in Phase 1, $F(2,40) = 7.61$, $p < .01$ and women in Phase 2, $F(2,40) = 3.92$, $p < .05$. In Phase 1 the mean for Unitel men (36.33) was significantly lower than that for both Notel (48.5; $p < .05$ by Tukey) and Multitel (51.89; $p < .01$ by Tukey) men, who did not differ. In Phase 2 the mean for Multitel women (53.78) was significantly higher than that for Unitel women (42.89; $p < .05$ by Tukey) and marginally higher than that for Notel women (44.5; $p < .10$ by Tukey and .05 by Newman–Keuls test).

The analysis for counseling readiness revealed a significant Town × Sex interaction, $F(2,40) = 3.65$, $p < .04$. The towns differed only for males, $F(2,40) = 5.60$, $p < .01$, with the mean for Unitel (60.67) significantly higher than that for both Notel (50.75) and Multitel (50.28; $p < .01$ by Tukey test for both comparisons).

[13] Averaging across the towns in Phase 2, the concerns most frequently expressed had to do with the general economic situation (hopes expressed by 94.9%, fears by 82.4%), the respondent's personal economic situation (hopes 53.1%, fears 23.3%), and non-economic references to the family (hopes 43.2%, fears 59.7%). The Cantril categories for which concerns were least often expressed in this sample were independence, status, and importance of the nation (hopes 0.6%, fears 0%) and general international concerns (hopes 0%, fears 0.6%).

[14] Unweighted means cross-sectional ANOVAs were conducted on the Phase 2 scores from the series of Cantril scales (ladders) on which respondents rated themselves (personal) and their town in the past, present, and future. For the personal ratings, the town main effect was marginally significant for the present, $F(2,173) = 3.02$, $p < .06$ and future, $F(2,173) = 2.47$, $p < .09$. Notel residents ($M = 7.15$) rated their personal situation in the present better than did Multitel residents ($M = 6.41$; $p < .05$ by Newman–Keuls test); Unitel residents ($M = 6.79$) were between the other two groups and not significantly different from them. The same pattern occurred for the future personal ratings (Notel, 8.17; Unitel, 8.02; Multitel, 7.37). For the community or town ratings, the town main effect was significant for the past, $F(2,173) = 4.47$, $p < .02$. Both Notel ($M = 5.25$) and Multitel ($M = 5.07$) residents, who did not differ, rated their town as better in the past than did Unitel residents ($M = 4.18$; $p < .05$ by Newman–Keuls test for both comparisons). There were no significant results for the town-present or town-future ratings.

[15] A series of unweighted means ANOVAs was run for the longitudinal sample on the nine Environmental Response Inventory scale scores, with town and sex as between-subject

variables and repeated measures on phase. None of the effects was significant for the Pastoralism, Urbanism, Environmental Adaptation, and Communality scales. The scales yielding significant sex differences are shown in the following table, along with the analogous results from the cross-sectional sample.

Scale	Males	Females	F^a
Antiquarianism			
Longitudinal	61.89	69.51	12.20***
Cross-sectional	63.50	66.91	6.32*
Environmental Trust			
Longitudinal	61.58	57.48	5.37*
Cross-sectional	61.15	55.46	21.01***
Mechanical Orientation			
Longitudinal	71.04	63.53	14.92***
Cross-sectional	71.95	60.47	76.46***
Stimulus Seeking			
Longitudinal	60.49	55.49	4.59*
Cross-sectional	63.99	57.83	18.73***

^{a} df for longitudinal analyses: 1,49; for cross-sectional: 1,209.
* $p < .05$; ** $p < .01$; *** $p < .001$.

There were some additional significant results. The Environmental Trust longitudinal ANOVA revealed a significant Town × Sex interaction, $F(2,49) = 3.88$, $p < .03$. The town means differed for women, $F(2,49) = 4.05$, $p < .05$, but not for men. Women in Multitel scored significantly higher (62.19) than those in Notel (53.35; $p < .01$ by Tukey test) and marginally higher than those in Unitel (56.91; $p < .10$ by Newman–Keuls test). The Environmental Trust cross-sectional ANOVA also revealed a significant town main effect, $F(2,209) = 5.63$, $p < .005$, reflecting a higher mean in Notel (60.33) than in Multitel (55.27; $p < .01$ by Tukey test). The Unitel mean (58.04) was marginally higher than the Multitel mean ($p < .10$ by Newman–Keuls test).

The Need for Privacy longitudinal ANOVA revealed a significant Town × Phase interaction, $F(2,49) = 5.84$, $p < .005$. Simple main effects analyses indicated the phase difference was specific to Unitel, $F(1,49) = 9.43$, $p < .01$, reflecting a decrease from Phase 1 (60.00) to Phase 2 (55.44). There was no change in Notel (53.43, 55.79) or Multitel (54.60, 55.14). The towns differed in Phase 1, $F(2,49) = 5.00$, $p < .05$, the mean for Unitel being higher than those for both Notel ($p < .01$ by Tukey test) and Multitel ($p < .05$ by Tukey test), but the towns did not differ in Phase 2. The Need for Privacy cross-sectional ANOVA revealed a significant town main effect, $F(2,209) = 5.20$, $p < .007$, reflecting the same pattern—a higher mean in Unitel (56.94) than in both Notel (56.54; $p < .05$ by Tukey test) and Multitel (52.69; $p < .01$ by Tukey test).

The Antiquarianism longitudinal ANOVA revealed a marginally significant town main effect, $F(2,49) = 3.14$, $p = .052$, reflecting a higher mean in Unitel (68.18) than in Notel (61.89; $p < .05$ by Tukey test); the Multitel mean (67.02) also was marginally higher than the Notel mean ($p < .10$ by Newman–Keuls test). The Antiquarianism cross-sectional ANOVA revealed a significant town main effect, $F(2,209) = 3.96$, $p < .03$, reflecting a higher mean in Notel (67.94) than in Multitel (63.81; $p < .05$ by Tukey test); the Notel mean also was marginally higher than the Unitel mean (64.15; $p < .10$ by Tukey and .05 by Newman–Keuls test). In addition, the significant phase main effect, $F(1,209) = 6.15$, $p < .02$ reflected an increase from Phase 1 (63.67) to Phase 2 (67.02).

The Stimulus-Seeking ANOVA for the longitudinal sample also yielded a significant Town × Sex × Phase interaction, $F(2,49) = 8.18$, $p < .001$. Simple main effects analyses indicated that from Phase 1 to Phase 2 the scores of Notel men decreased significantly (64.25 to 58.75), $F(1,49) = 4.19$, $p < .05$, Multitel men increased significantly (57.50 to 65.20), $F(1,49) = 7.99$, $p < .01$ and Multitel women decreased marginally (61.75 to 56.50), $F(1,49) = 3.81$, $p < .10$. There was no change for Unitel men (58.75, 58.38), Notel women (50.70, 54.10), or Unitel women (56.27, 53.64). The towns did not differ significantly at any combination of sex and phase. The Stimulus-Seeking ANOVA for the pure cross-sectional sample yielded a significant Town × Sex interaction, $F(2,209) = 4.83$, $p < .009$, in addition to the sex main effect described in the table above. Simple main effects analyses revealed that the towns differed significantly among females, $F(2,209) = 4.90$, $p < .01$, with the mean for Notel (61.26) higher than that for Multitel (53.47; $p < .01$ by Tukey test). The Unitel mean (58.03) was between the other two and marginally higher than the Multitel mean ($p < .10$ by Newman–Keuls test). The town means for males did not differ.

All of the significant effects from the longitudinal ANOVAs have been described in this note, and the significant effects in the cross-sectional analyses for Antiquarianism, Environmental Trust, Mechanical Orientation, Stimulus Seeking, and Need for Privacy also have been described in full. There were some additional significant effects in the cross-sectional analyses for Pastoralism, Urbanism, and Environmental Adaptation. Since these were not corroborated in the longitudinal sample, which we consider to be more representative of the communities studied, they have not been discussed.

[16] In an unweighted means ANOVA on the longitudinal Person-orientation scores with town and sex as between-subject factors and repeated measures on phase, the sex main effect, $F(1,56) = 11.45$, $p < .001$ was significant, reflecting a higher mean for women (26.30) than for men (20.77). The town main effect also was significant, $F(2,56) = 3.78$, $p < .03$, reflecting a higher mean in Multitel (26.59) than in Notel (21.25; $p < .05$ by Tukey test). The Unitel mean (22.75) was between the other two and marginally different from the Multitel mean ($p < .10$ by Newman–Keuls test). In an unweighted means ANOVA on the Person-orientation scores of the pure cross-sectional sample with town, sex, and phase as between-subject variables, the same pattern of results was obtained. The sex main effect, $F(1,214) = 22.32$, $p < .05$ reflected a higher mean for women (25.80) than for men (20.68). The town main effect, $F(2,214) = 3.05$, $p < .05$ reflected a higher mean in Multitel (25.06) than in Notel (21.88; $p < .05$ by Tukey test) and a marginally higher mean in Multitel than in Unitel (22.77; $p < .10$ by Newman–Keuls test).

In the analogous ANOVA on the longitudinal Thing-orientation scores, the sex main effect was marginally significant, $F(1,56) = 3.89$, $p = .054$, reflecting a higher mean for men (20.08) than for women (16.91). The significant town main effect, $F(2,56) = 3.90$, $p < .03$ reflected a higher mean in Unitel (20.93) than in Notel (15.51; $p < .05$ by Tukey test). The Multitel mean (19.05), which did not differ from the Unitel mean, also was marginally higher than the Notel mean ($p < .10$ by Newman–Keuls test). In the analogous ANOVA on the cross-sectional Thing-orientation scores, only the sex main effect was significant, $F(1,214) = 21.97$, $p < .001$, reflecting a higher mean for men (21.29) than for women (16.25).

REFERENCES

Atkin, C. K. Television advertising and socialization to consumer roles. In D. Pearl, L. Bouthilet, & J. Lazar (Eds.), *Television and behavior: Ten years of scientific progress and implications for the eighties.* Vol. 2. Rockville, Md.: NIMH, 1982.

Bandura, A. *Social learning and personality development.* New York: Holt, Rinehart & Winston, 1963.

Barker, R. G. *Ecological psychology: Concepts and methods for studying the environment of human behavior.* Stanford, Calif.: Stanford University Press, 1968.

Bartlett, F. C. *Thinking: An experimental and social study.* London: Allen & Unwin, 1958.

Bayley, N., & Oden, M. H. The maintenance of intellectual ability in gifted adults. *Journal of Gerontology,* 1955, *10,* 91–107.

Berlyne, D. E. *Conflict, arousal, and curiosity.* New York: McGraw-Hill, 1960.

Berry, J. W. *Human ecology and cognitive style: Comparative studies in cultural and psychological adaptation.* Beverly Hills, Calif.: Sage, 1976.

Bruner, J. S., & Olson, D. R. Learning through experience and learning through media. In G. Gerbner, L. P. Gross, & W. H. Melody (Eds.), *Communications technology and social policy.* New York: Wiley, 1973.

Cantril, H. *The pattern of human concerns.* New Brunswick, N.J.: Rutgers University Press, 1965.

Comstock, G., Chaffee, S., Katzman, N., McCombs, M., & Roberts, D. *Television and human behavior.* New York: Columbia University Press, 1978.

Comstock, G. A., & Rubinstein, E. A. *Television and social behavior: Vol. 1. Media content and control.* Washington, D.C.: U.S. Government Printing Office, 1972.

Craik, K. H. The personality paradigm in environmental psychology. In S. Wapner, S. Cohen, & B. Kaplan (Eds.), *Experiencing the environment.* New York: Plenum, 1976.

Craik, K. H., & McKechnie, C. E. Personality and the environment. *Environment and Behavior,* 1977, *9,* 155–276.

Doob, A., & Macdonald, G. Television viewing and fear of victimization: Is the relationship causal? *Journal of Personality and Social Psychology,* 1979, *37,* 170–179.

Duncker, K. On problem-solving. *Psychological Monographs,* 1945, *58,* No. 270.

Dworetzky, J. P. *Psychology.* St. Paul, Minn.: West, 1982.

Fishbein, M., & Ajzen, I. *Belief, attitude, intention and behavior: An introduction to theory and research.* Redding, Mass.: Addison-Wesley, 1975.

Gerbner, G., Gross, L., Morgan, M., & Signorielli, N. Charting the mainstream: Television's contributions to political orientations. *Journal of Communication,* 1982, *32*(2), 100–127.

Glass, D. C., & Singer, J. E. *Urban stress.* New York: Academic Press, 1972.

Goldstein, K. M., & Blackman, S. *Cognitive style: Five approaches and relevant research.* New York: Wiley, 1978.

Gottschaldt, K. Concerning the influence of experience on the perception of figures, I. *Psychologische Forschung,* 1926, *8,* 261–317.

Gough, H. G., & Heilbrun, A. B. Jr. *The Adjective Check List manual.* Palo Alto, Calif.: Consulting Psychologists Press, 1965.

Haggard, E. A. Effects of isolation in natural settings. In J. E. Rasmussen (Ed.), *Man in isolation and confinement.* Chicago: Aldine, 1973.

Halpern, S., & Ethier, B. *The portrayal of men and women in Canadian and U.S. television commercials.* Unpublished manuscript, University of British Columbia, Department of Psychology, 1977. (Available from T. M. Williams).

Harmond, R. Sugar daddy or ogre? The impact of commercial television on professional sports. In F. J. Coppa (Ed.), *Screen and society.* Chicago: Nelson-Hall, 1979.

Harvey, O. J., Hunt, D. E., & Schroder, H. M. *Conceptual systems and personality organization.* New York: Wiley, 1961.

Hawkins, R. P., & Pingree, S. Television's influence on social reality. In D. Pearl, L. Bouthilet, & J. Lazar (Eds.), *Television and behavior: Ten years of scientific progress and implications for the eighties.* Vol. 2. Rockville, Md.: NIMH, 1982.

Hennigan, K. M., Del Rosario, M. L., Heath, L., Cook, T. D., Wharton, J. D., & Calder, B. J. Impact of the introduction of television on crime in the United States: Empirical findings and theoretical implications. *Journal of Personality and Social Psychology*, 1982, *42*, 461–477.

Horn, J. L., & Cattell, R. B. Age differences in primary mental ability factors. *Journal of Gerontology*, 1966, *21*, 210–220.

Israel, H., & Robinson, J. P. Demographic characteristics of viewers of television violence and news programs. In E. A. Rubinstein, G. A. Comstock, & J. P. Murray (Eds.), *Television and social behavior: Vol. 4. Television in day-to-day life: Patterns of use*. Washington, D.C.: U.S. Government Printing Office, 1972.

Kirby, W. L. The influence of television on social relations: Some personal reflections. In F. J. Coppa (Ed.), *Screen and society*. Chicago: Nelson-Hall, 1979.

Langer, E. J. Playing the middle against both ends: The usefulness of adult cognitive activity as a model for cognitive activity in childhood and old age. In S. R. Yussen (Ed.), *The development of reflection*. New York: Academic Press, 1982.

Little, B. R. *Person–thing orientation: A provisional manual for the T–P scale*. University of Oxford, Department of Experimental Psychology, 1972.

Little, B. R. Specialization and the varieties of environmental experience. In S. Wapner, S. B. Cohen, & B. Kaplan (Eds.), *Experiencing the environment*. New York: Plenum, 1976.

Longstaffe, S., & Williams, T. M. *Content analysis of informative television programming on the major English networks available in Canada*. Paper presented at the meeting of the Canadian Communication Association, Montreal, June 1985.

LoSciuto, L. A. A national inventory of television viewing behavior. In E. A. Rubinstein, G. A. Comstock, & J. P. Murray (Eds.), *Television and social behavior: Vol. 4. Television in day-to-day life: Patterns of use*. Washington, D.C.: U.S. Government Printing office, 1972.

McLeod, J. M., Fitzpatrick, M. A., Glynn, C. J., & Fallis, S. F. Television and social relations: Family influences and consequences for interpersonal behavior. In D. Pearl, L. Bouthilet, & J. Lazar (Eds.), *Television and behavior: Ten years of scientific progress and implications for the eighties*. Vol. 2. Rockville, Md.: NIMH, 1982.

McKechnie, G. E. *Manual for the Environmental Response Inventory*. Palo Alto, Calif.: Consultant Psychologists Press, 1974.

Medrich, E. A. Constant television: A background to daily life. *Journal of Communication*, 1979, *29*(3), 171–176.

Muccigrosso, R. Television and the urban crisis. In F. J. Coppa (Ed.), *Screen and society*. Chicago: Nelson-Hall, 1979.

Murray, J. P., & Kippax, S. Television diffusion and social behaviour in three communities: A field experiment. *Australian Journal of Psychology*, 1977, *29*(1), 31–43.

Murray, J. P., & Kippax, S. Children's social behavior in three towns with differing television experience. *Journal of Communication*, 1978, *30*(4), 19–29.

Oskamp, S. *Attitudes and opinions*. Englewood Cliffs, N.J.: Prentice-Hall, 1977.

Platt, J. R. Strong inference. *Science*, 1964, *146*, 347–353.

Rajecki, D. W. *Attitudes: Themes and advances*. Sunderland, Mass.: Sinauer, 1982.

Salomon, G. Television-watching and mental effort: A social psychological view. In J. Bryant & D. R. Anderson (Eds.), *Children's understanding of television: Research on attention and comprehension*. New York: Academic Press, 1983.

Schaie, K. W., & Strother, C. R. A cross-sequential study of age changes in cognitive behavior. *Psychological Bulletin*, 1968, *70*, 671–690.

Schroder, H. M., & Suedfeld, P. (Eds.). *Personality theory and information processing*. New York: Ronald, 1971.

Schroder, H. M., Driver, M. J., & Streufert, S. *Human information processing.* New York: Holt, Rinehart & Winston, 1967.

Spence, K. W. *Behavior theory and conditioning.* New Haven: Yale, 1956.

Suedfeld, P. Changes in intellectual performance and susceptibility to influence. In J. P. Zubek (Ed.), *Sensory deprivation: Fifteen years of research.* New York: Appleton-Century-Crofts, 1969.

Streufert, S., & Streufert, S. C. *Behavior in the complex environment.* Washington, D.C.: Winston, 1978.

Vernon, P. E. (Ed.). *Creativity.* New York: Penguin Books, 1970.

Williams, T. M., Zabrack, M. L., & Joy, L. A. A content analysis of entertainment television programming. In *Report of the Ontario Royal Commission on Violence in the Communications Industry,* Vol. 3. Toronto, 1977.

Williams, T. M., Zabrack, M. L., & Joy, L. A. The portrayal of aggression on North American television. *Journal of Applied Social Psychology,* 1982, *12,* 360–380.

Witkin, H. A., & Berry, J. W. Psychological differentiation in cross-cultural perspective. *Journal of Cross-Cultural Psychology,* 1975, *6,* 4–87.

Witkin, H. A., Dyk, R. B., Faterson, H. F., Goodenough, D. R., & Karp, S. A. *Psychological differentiation.* New York: Wiley, 1962.

Yerkes, R. M., & Dodson, J. D. The relation of strength of stimulus to rapidity of habit-formation. *Journal of Comparative and Neurological Psychology,* 1908, *18,* 459–482.

9

SUMMARY, CONCLUSIONS, AND IMPLICATIONS

Tannis MacBeth Williams

INTRODUCTION

What *did* this natural experiment reveal about the effects of television? The variety of topics studied and questions asked, coupled with the complexity of the results, make it difficult to provide a brief summary. Nevertheless, that is the first task of this final chapter.[1] The second task is to discuss processes through which television may influence its viewers and to present some of the broader implications of our findings.

Our first general conclusion is that television affects viewers negatively in a variety of areas via displacement. Since the majority of North American children and adults spend several hours each day with television and discretionary time is limited, choosing to watch TV inevitably displaces some other activities. This process is often indirect, however, and never simple. Many activities can be successfully time-shared with television, but others cannot. Most obvious are those conducted outside the home. For example, our results indicate that television negatively affects participation in community activities, especially sports. Some activities requiring concentration probably also cannot be effectively time-shared with television. Our results indicate that television may interfere with the acquisition of fluent reading skills and creative thinking by children, as well as creative problem solving by adults.

Television also affects its viewers more directly; the content of television may serve as a teacher. In our study children's aggressive behavior increased and their beliefs about appropriate behavior for girls and boys became more strongly sex typed. These content effects have been demonstrated by other researchers, but the design of this project as a natural experiment lends a new kind of data to the converging body of evidence.

Our third general conclusion is that the effects of television have more to do with its presence versus absence than whether one channel of CBC or four channels, including the three major U.S. networks, are available.[2] The differences between Notel and the other towns were more consistent and tended to be greater than the differences between Unitel and Multitel. In addition, the residents of Unitel and Multitel used television similarly despite the variations in source and number of channels. Since Himmelweit, Oppenheim, and Vince (1958) obtained a similar finding in the United Kingdom more than a decade ago, it is apparently robust.

These few comments cannot, of course, do justice to what we have learned about the effects of television. Indeed, our results underscore the importance of the statement made by Schramm, Lyle, and Parker (1961), "Effects are not that simple." Fortunately, researchers now have reached the exciting stage of unraveling some of the empirical and theoretical complexities of television's effects. Aware that oversimplification may be misleading, we turn now to the individual studies in this project. The results and our speculations regarding the processes through which television influences its viewers are summarized for each study.

CHAPTER SUMMARIES

Children's Reading Skills: Chapter 2

Comparisons among the towns just before and 2 years after the arrival of television in Notel indicated that TV probably slows down the acquisition of fluent reading skills. Once established, however, they do not deteriorate. Children who watch more hours of television per week tend to be poorer readers than those who watch fewer hours, even after the effects of intelligence are removed. Better readers also tend to be heavier users of print media (books, magazines, and newspapers) than are poorer readers.

The pattern of results we obtained was not perfect, but the weight of the evidence, when considered along with findings obtained by other researchers, is consistent with the following hypothetical scenario. In the absence of television most children practice reading enough to become fluent to the point that decoding letters, words, and phrases is automatic. Practice is hard work, and children cannot read during this stage for entertainment or information (Chall, 1983). Television provides a more attractive alternative for most children, but especially for those who have most difficulty learning to read and who need the practice most, namely, those who are less intelligent (or have a learning disability). The brighter children either need less practice and get enough in school or practice more. Differences related to socioeconomic status (SES) emerge (Roberts, Bachen, Hornby, & Hernandez-Ramos, 1984) because more children in higher SES families are given encouragement and assistance, raised in a print-oriented environment, and so on. In subsequent elementary and high school years, children who have not acquired good reading skills enjoy reading less than the better readers, so they spend less time reading and more time with television. This provides even less opportunity to hone their skills. This hypothesized chain of events results in the typical finding for high school students that poor readers are less intelligent, are of lower SES, read less, and watch more television than students who are better readers (Morgan & Gross, 1982). The chain begins because television displaces reading practice, and this leads to more reading "dropouts" in the long run. There always have been and will be people who do not become fluent readers, but the numbers may be greater when television is available. Parents and educators who want children to read well should ensure they practice enough in the early grades to become fluent and should foster positive attitudes toward print throughout childhood and adolescence. Television's influence is indirect; reducing the child's involvement with television may be necessary, but it is not likely to be sufficient.

Cognitive Development: Chapter 3

We studied television's relationship to several aspects of children's thinking: creativity, verbal ability as reflected in vocabulary, spatial ability, and general intelligence.

Before their town had television, Notel children obtained higher creativity scores, as measured with the Alternate Uses task, than Unitel and Multitel students. Two years later their scores were similar to those of students who grew up with TV. These results may have occurred in part because watching television requires little or no mental elaboration (Salomon, 1981, 1983). Children may learn to process information at the lower

levels required by television (encoding and chunking) and then use these
strategies in tasks (e.g., problem solving) that require more "mindful"
approaches. TV may encourage viewers to rely on ready-made ideas, that
is, to be mentally passive. In addition, time spent with television may
displace activities and experiences which otherwise would be helpful in
problem-solving situations. These hypotheses gain some support from
evidence that students who obtained higher creativity scores tended to
read more books and participate in a greater variety of leisure activities
than did students who obtained lower scores. Since creativity and intelligence were found to be unrelated, these results were not simply a reflection of intelligence. Finally, the orientation of television toward entertainment and a fast pace rather than reflection may play a role in its influence
on creative thinking. This conjecture receives some support from results
for the adult problem-solving tasks (see later summary and Chapter 8).

We hypothesized that television's content has a positive effect on vocabulary but found no evidence to support this hypothesis. Some children
undoubtedly do learn some vocabulary from television, especially children who cannot yet read and for whom other sources are limited. For
most children, however, television may be less important as a vocabulary
teacher than are other sources, especially print. We should point out,
however, that most vocabulary measures, including the ones we used,
also are measures of intelligence. Since our results (discussed next), as
well as other research, indicate amount of viewing is negatively related to
performance on measures of intelligence, this may mask any positive
influence it has in teaching vocabulary.

There was little evidence to link television to performance on a measure
of visual-spatial ability. The results regarding performance on the Pattern
Meanings task were mixed. The figural tasks have a less eminent history
as measures of creativity than does the Alternate Uses task, for which our
results (described earlier) were more clear cut.

Amount of television viewing was negatively related to performance on
a group measure of intelligence (or IQ; also see Chapter 5), as other
researchers have found, but this did not account for the results obtained
for other aspects of children's thinking or for the findings of other studies
in this project. We are inclined to think the negative relationship between
intelligence and TV viewing occurs primarily because brighter children
use their leisure time differently than do less intelligent children.

Other researchers have demonstrated the role of cognitive development
for children's understanding of television (see Bryant & Anderson, 1983,
for reviews). Our results point to the importance of television for the
development of children's thinking, to the transactional nature of the
relationship between cognitive development and television, and to the

need to consider the role of intelligence in television's influence in other areas.

Participation in Leisure Activities by Adolescents and Adults: Chapter 4

Television apparently is not a major determinant of the number of activities available in a community, but it does have a negative impact on participation in those activities. The effect is especially strong for sports, but our results also indicate television affects attendance at dances, suppers, and parties, particularly by youths, as well as attendance at meetings of clubs and other organizations, particularly for adults. There was some evidence that television affects participation, again negatively, for the categories "special days" and "entertainment," but these results were less clear. By contrast, there were no systematic differences among the towns in attendance at medical and religious activities, and the differences which occurred for open areas, businesses, civic affairs, educational (non-school), and other activities did not implicate television.

The displacement by television of community activities occurred for both adolescents and adults and was particularly strong for people aged 56 and over. When television was available, participation for the oldest age group was dramatically lower than that for younger adults and youths. This decrease with age was not evident in Notel before the arrival of television but did occur 2 years later and was seen in Unitel and Multitel in both phases. This, along with some other findings, suggests television may lead to greater age segregation and thus may have a qualitative influence on community life by reducing contact between young and old people. The negative effect of television on participation in community activities was apparent for residents who were centrally as well as peripherally involved, even for the oldest age group.

In contrast to the findings for community activities, there was little evidence that television affects participation in private leisure activities. These different patterns of results point to the need for further research on time-sharing and decision making in use of leisure time.

Use of Television and Other Media by Children and Adults: Chapter 5

What similarities and differences did we find in media use by residents of these three towns? In Phase 1, most Notel residents watched zero hours of television per week, but 2 years after its inception their TV-viewing habits were indistinguishable from those of Unitel residents. In both phases, children and adults who had one channel (CBC) reported watching fewer hours of television per week than residents of a town with four channels (CBC and the three commercial U.S. networks; see note 2). The similarity, however, was more striking than the difference (22 hours by comparison with about 27 hours, on average). Moreover, the television-viewing habits of residents of these communities generally were similar to those reported by other North American researchers. These findings regarding TV use therefore corroborate the evidence in other chapters regarding its effects; presence versus absence of television is more important than the number or content of channels available.

Our results indicate that use of television in relation to other media forms a complex pattern and is not merely a simple question of one medium displacing another, that is, functional equivalence. This may be in part because some media (e.g., magazines, newspapers, and comics) are easier to time-share with television than are others (e.g., radio, records, and books). Research on time-sharing of activities with television and how it varies with age and intelligence would be helpful in illuminating the effects of television on performance in several areas. In addition, more complex conceptualizations of "watching TV" and better ways of measuring it are needed.

Children's Sex-Role Attitudes: Chapter 6

Children's sex-role attitudes, that is, beliefs about appropriate and typical behavior for girls and boys, were more strongly sex typed in the presence than in the absence of television. On the one hand, this is not surprising, since content analyses have documented the predominance of traditional sex roles on television (e.g. Greenberg, 1982). On the other hand, since much of real-life experience corroborates these portrayals, it is surprising that the influence of television is strong enough to be noticeable.

Several factors may combine to make television an especially effective teacher of sex roles. Television provides more models than most children encounter in real life, and with rare exceptions they are presented in traditional roles in both programs and commercials. All theories of sex-role acquisition emphasize the importance of models. Children do not observe these models passively, however; they attend actively and differentially. Children and adults prefer same-sex characters and more accurately remember them. This would explain why girls as well as boys learn sex roles from television even though male characters outnumber female characters by a ratio of three to one. In addition, information about sex roles obtained from television is seldom contradicted and often reinforced by information the child obtains from real life. Finally, sex-role attitudes and behavior fit particularly well into theories which emphasize cognitive models or stereotypes (called schemata or scripts) for processing information and directing social attitudes and behavior. (These ideas are discussed in more detail later in the section, "Processes Involved in Television's Influence.")

Whereas the students' perceptions of appropriate behavior for girls and boys apparently were affected by television, their perceptions of their own parents' actual behavior apparently were not.

One implication of these findings is that television could serve a positive educational function if it provided a wider range of models regarding female and male behavior.

Children's Physical and Verbal Aggression: Chapter 7

The aggressive behavior of Notel children increased significantly following the introduction of television. This conclusion that TV viewing and aggression are linked has been reached by most other researchers, but several aspects of our results are new. They are based on observations of actual behavior rather than self-reports or ratings. Effects occurred for both girls and boys and for both physical and verbal aggression. Increases occurred for children initially low in aggression, not just a small subsample of highly aggressive children. The effects were substantial enough to be observable 2 years after the introduction of television to Notel. Finally, the design of our study as a natural experiment enabled us to be certain the relationship between television exposure and aggressive behavior did not occur merely because more aggressive children choose to watch more violence on television, although this also may be true.

How did the advent of television in Notel lead to increases in children's physical and verbal aggression? Without observing the process we cannot be sure, but some or even all of the processes demonstrated in previous research may have been involved. Imitation of aggressive models through vicarious learning is likely, especially in light of the evidence that young children attend sporadically to TV (e.g., Anderson & Lorch, 1983) and may not understand the links between aggressive actions and any punishments portrayed (e.g., Collins, 1983). Scenarios involving aggressive interaction, which are presented repeatedly and rarely counteracted on television (Williams, Zabrack, & Joy, 1977, 1982), therefore, are likely to be copied by young children. Physiological arousal, stimulated in part by the fast pace and high action typically associated with aggressive portrayals, and cognitive arousal, associated with attentiveness on the part of children for whom television was a novelty, also may have facilitated learning. The frequent portrayal of aggression as a successful method of resolving conflict may have reduced inhibitions against behaving aggressively, and this may have been coupled with desensitization, that is, increased tolerance for violence and verbal abuse on the part of both children and adults in the community. Just as television may teach sex-role stereotypes, it may teach scripts for behaving aggressively.

Finally, our results suggest the viewer's social milieu plays an important role in television's impact on aggression. When social controls are adequate, the behaviors and attitudes concerning aggression modeled on TV may be acquired but not performed. However, when the social milieu is disrupted in some way (in our study, by the introduction of television), the social controls may break down. The aggressive behaviors learned from television (as well as from other sources) then may be more likely to be performed. The adequacy of controls over aggression varies, so television will have a greater impact on some groups and individuals than on others. For exposure to television to result in actual performance of aggression, it must overcome inhibitions against behaving aggressively. Thus, research will yield only weak evidence of effects at best; behaviors may be acquired but, because of social controls, not performed during the study.

Adult Thinking, Attitudes, and Orientation toward the Environment: Chapter 8

One of our most surprising results is the evidence that television may affect performance by adults on creative problem-solving tasks. The solutions to the tasks given in this study required going beyond the initially obvious approach and thinking of less likely alternatives. Residents of a town without television solved the Duncker Candle Problem faster than did residents of towns with television, and those who were not successful kept trying longer. Two years after the arrival of television, Notel residents still persisted longer in trying to solve the Nine Dot Problem. Unfortunately, so few people solved this problem that performance comparisons could not be made. How would television affect success in problem solving by adults? Some or all of the hypotheses offered earlier to explain the children's creativity results may be relevant.

The apparent effect of television on persistence may occur because television leads to decreased attention and/or tolerance for frustration. Or, the displacement of problem-solving experiences may mean that people who watch more television have fewer non-obvious solution methods available and exhaust their repertoire more quickly. Perhaps perseverance is something which must be learned; the experience of solving problems after relatively long periods of trying may make it more likely that individuals will persist with subsequent problems. Whatever the explanation, this seems to be the first empirical evidence demonstrating that television may, over the long term, affect concentration or persistence by adults.

By contrast, there was relatively little evidence to suggest that television affects the cognitive style, perceptions of the self and community, or orientation toward the environment of adults in this study.

THE PROCESSES INVOLVED IN TELEVISION'S INFLUENCE

The summaries just provided describe briefly our major results and our speculations linking them to television. The relevant chapters provide amplified versions of these hypotheses but, there again, ones specific to the topics investigated. Can these theoretical notions be integrated into more general statements regarding the processes involved in television's influence? Several theories have been advanced by other researchers to account for television's effects in different areas, but they tend to be discussed in isolation. The following analysis is an attempt to integrate these ideas and introduce some new ones. These speculations, as well as the more specific ones described earlier and in each chapter, are included because we believe knowledge advances more rapidly when it is grounded in theory. The conceptual issues will remain whether or not these particular explanations of television's effects stand the test of time.

First, it is clear that television viewers are not entirely passive; even very young children attend (or not), select, and process the information presented (e.g., Anderson & Lorch, 1983; Collins, 1983; Dorr, 1980; Huston & Wright, 1983). In trying to account for television's effects, the cognitively active nature of the audience must be kept in mind.

Let us begin our analysis with what might be considered the "building blocks" of the system, the units of information obtained from television and the way in which this information is taken in, stored, and used to deal with new information (from television or other experience). Some concepts advanced by psychologists in a variety of fields seem helpful here, particularly the notion that human behavior is governed by mental models, beliefs, or expectations which are built up and modified through experience (Abelson, 1976, 1981; Schank & Abelson, 1977). Cognitive psychologists tend to call this kind of information-processing and behavior-directing model a *schema* (plural *schemata*).[3] Perceptual psychologists refer to a *prototype,* and social psychologists use *script* or *plan,* particularly to refer to schemata representing a sequence of events. We shall use the term *schema* when referring to relatively constant characteristics of people or scenes and the term *script* to refer to sequentially organized events. Whichever words are used, the basic ideas are similar. The model, belief, or expectation is actively constructed by the individual, based on experience. Once established, it is used to process new information—upon encountering something (which may be a social situation, a sight, a sound, or the like), the individual searches mentally for a schema or script into which to fit the information. These reflect what the person understands about the world and, thus, direct perceptions and behavior. If the knowledge (schema or script) is faulty—for example, too narrow—events will be perceived and/or remembered incorrectly. The everyday concept that most closely approximates these ideas is a stereotype.

In the realm of sex roles it has been shown that children who see a film about a female physician and a male nurse are likely to recall that the physician was male and the nurse female (Cordua, McGraw, & Drabman, 1979). The theoretical explanation (e.g., Bem, 1981; Martin & Halverson, 1981) is that children process the information through their gender-stereotyped schemata, which specify that doctors are male and nurses are female, and the mismatch goes unnoticed. Gender schemata are constructed by each child, based on his or her experiences, including what people tell them and what they see and hear. These experiences may be specific to the content of the schemata, for example, doctors and nurses encountered in real life, ones seen in the media, and ones discussed by others. More general experience also is important, however, and particular content is not necessary for expectations to exist. For example, a child's observations of a variety of individuals and situations (again, via real life, the media, conversations, and so on) might produce the stereotype "men are in charge, whereas women take orders and are helpers." This in turn would yield the expectation that doctors are male and nurses are female. Most general and specific experiences in the realm of sex roles are consistent. For example, most people refer to doctors of unknown sex as "he" and nurses of unknown sex as "she," even though they know that both men and women occupy both kinds of jobs. The theory would predict that children (or adults) whose experience is not consistent, for example, those who have encountered or heard of female physicians and/or male nurses, might be more likely to have more flexible schemata and less likely to recall the film incorrectly. Note, however, that although schemata and scripts are modified, however slightly, to fit new incoming data—and this is how they develop in complexity and number—there will be a tendency for stereotypes to be self-perpetuating.[4] That is, the individual has to notice the mismatch or the schema will not be altered. Real-world experiences that require actual interaction may be more likely than filmed or televised counterexamples to effectively alter stereotypes, although this has not to our knowledge been empirically tested. Schemata, scripts, and stereotypes are difficult to change, however, because they typically operate automatically, out of awareness. Even when mismatches are noticed, they usually are processed as exceptions, thus maintaining the stereotype or schema.

It may be useful to ask what role television plays in the formation and use of scripts and schemata (Collins, 1983; Janis, 1980; Salomon, 1983; Williams et al., 1982). North American children show interest in television as early as 6 months of age (Hollenbeck & Slaby, 1979) and begin to watch regularly around 2½ years. Television probably provides the child's first information about a variety of places, types of people, and social interactions; it is an "early window" (Liebert, Sprafkin, & Davidson, 1982) on the world. TV therefore may play a central role in the initial development of many of the child's schemata and scripts. If so, it will influence the child's perceptions and behavior for new real-world experiences, since subsequently encountered information will be processed through these schemata. The hypothesis that people's beliefs or concepts are initially established in part through television viewing and then used to process new information from all sources, including television, is consistent with a number of findings, some of which are difficult to explain otherwise.

For example, Hawkins and Pingree (1982) have found that adults' beliefs about social reality are most open to influence by television when they are not actively mentally involved in viewing. This apparent paradox may occur because a crude fit of a schema to incoming information will be acceptable under conditions of low involvement, whereas high involvement is likely to yield a more careful matching attempt (Williams et al., 1982). Viewers who carefully attend to the information will be more likely to notice discrepancies between their real-world experience and the model of reality seen on TV, will be more likely to question or reject the televised model, and thus will be influenced less by it. So far this analysis assumes the viewer has real-world data with which to compare the content of television and that real-world data have contributed to the development of the schemata. In the absence of such information, the impact of television will be stronger. This explains a widely accepted tenet, namely, that television's influence is strongest when it functions as a primary or sole source of information (Comstock, Chaffee, Katzman, McCombs, & Roberts, 1978). Hornik, Gould and Gonzalez (1980) add that susceptibility to media effects is greatest when the information is "distant," that is, cannot be checked easily against reality when it is sought; and it is perceived by viewers as likely to have to be acted upon, that is, as self-relevant. This analysis would predict, for example, that in North America television would play a major role in the development of children's conceptualizations of sexuality and appropriate sexual behavior.

Another facet of this analysis centers on the lack of variety in North American programming. Content analyses have demonstrated, for example, the lack of variety in character portrayals (in terms of age, sex, race, and occupation), and one hears often that producers tend to generate more of what is successful (at this writing, evening "soaps" and miniseries) rather than to try out new kinds of material. This means a schema or script developed primarily through experience with television rarely will encounter contradictory evidence on television.

Television has been shown to influence beliefs about social reality in a variety of areas (e.g., sex roles, age-related stereotypes, and family interactions), but its influence is most consistent and strongest in areas related to violence, especially demographic measures of the prevalence of violence (e.g., crime rate estimates) and interpersonal mistrust (Hawkins & Pingree, 1982). Again, this is not surprising from a theoretical standpoint. Most viewers have little personal experience with violence, but it is common on television. For many children, schemata and scripts about violence may be derived initially from television. Janis (1980) contends that recurrent television themes, those reinforced with multiple presentations and rarely contradicted or counteracted, are likely to have the most potent effects. The portrayal of aggression and violence meets these criteria. Williams et al. (1977, 1982) found that conflict was almost invariably solved via aggression, which was portrayed as highly successful. Arbitration, conciliation, and other methods of conflict resolution occurred rarely, and witnesses tended to assist the aggressor or remain passive. Thus, television is likely to play a major role in the initial formation of scripts about human conflict and thereby subsequently to influence viewers' beliefs and behavior related to aggression.

There is some evidence to suggest that schemata or scripts acquired from television compete successfully with those acquired from experience in the real world, at least when processing information from television. Young children tended to base their inferences on their own personal experiences when a story was read to them, but relied more heavily on visually presented material in the (same) story when it was shown on television (Meringoff, 1980). As Janis (1980) points out, the potentially cumulative effects of television (and other media) on the acquisition of personal scripts may be substantial.

In addition to playing a role in the establishment and maintenance of personal or individual scripts, Withey (1980) contends television may affect its viewers indirectly because it prescribes precedents and proposes acceptable aspirations. That is, the scripts portrayed may influence social institutions and the culture in broader ways, not just via explicit messages individually interpreted.

How do schemata and scripts fit in with other concepts which have been emphasized as theoretically important in television's influence?

Observational learning from television of both prosocial and antisocial behaviors has been demonstrated in both laboratory and field experiments (Bandura, 1977; see Chapter 7, this volume). As Bandura emphasizes, learning involves two steps, acquisition and performance, but only performance can be observed. His work and that of most other researchers has focused on performance. It seems plausible that acquisition consists of constructing a new schema or processing new information via established schemata, modifying them in the process. The likelihood that scripted knowledge then will lead to performance depends upon several other factors which have been summarized by Comstock (1980) in four categories: social approval for the model and/or behavior; the efficacy or successfulness of the behavior; the relevance of the behavior and the model's characteristics to the viewer; and whether the portrayal optimizes arousal for the viewer. We would point out in addition that performance of acquired behaviors is determined not just by factors related to the portrayal (in real life or the media) at the time the behavior was acquired, but by factors subsequently in effect, including the general and specific aspects of the individual's social milieu.

An optimal level of arousal has been shown to be an important determinant of learning from television (see Comstock et al., 1978). We are referring here to both physiological arousal (e.g., sleep–wakefulness, excitation) and cognitive arousal (e.g., attentiveness). They operate in tandem and both media and non-media sources influence both. Huston and Wright (1983) have summarized the formal or noncontent features of television (such as pace, action, and auditory features) found to increase and decrease attentiveness to the screen for children of varying age levels. In the realm of cognitive arousal, Salomon (1981, 1983) emphasizes the role of what he calls amount of invested mental effort (AIME) for learning from television. As Huston and Wright (1983) point out, most learning from television is incidental rather than intentional, since people more often watch for entertainment than for education. Typical viewing therefore involves relatively little AIME. The schemata and scripts learned incidentally in this way from television are subjected to relatively little mental scrutiny and elaboration. Moreover, as we noted earlier, relatively little AIME occurs as viewers process subsequent information from the media. The typical and optimal levels of arousal differ for incidental and intentional learning (from television or any source). They may also vary with the viewer's level of cognitive development and experience with the medium. These factors will determine in part whether new schemata or scripts are constructed, the extent to which old ones are modified, and the accuracy with which both match the incoming information.

So far we have emphasized content effects for the processes involved in television's influence, since most research on television and human behavior has dealt with content. One of our major findings, however, is that television also influences its viewers indirectly via displacement.

How does television displace other activities? First, we do not want to imply that all time spent with television otherwise would be spent at directly or indirectly productive tasks. Television may displace such tasks, but we suspect there are other important components of displacement. For example, many people say they watch television when bored, so television probably displaces "doing nothing." Doing nothing is not necessarily wasted experience; it may include reflecting upon ideas, looking for and thinking up things to do, and social interaction. Some of these activities may directly or indirectly facilitate such things as creativity, performance in problem-solving tasks, and social relationships.

People who grow up with unlimited access to television may construct the maxim "when bored, watch TV," whereas people who grow up with limited or no access may develop many solutions, for example, "when bored, make something, take something apart to see how it works, imagine what the clouds are, flood your backyard and skate (and perhaps daydream while skating), read, hit a tennis ball against a wall, play a board game, sell lemonade," and so on. Such experiences may provide a bank to be called upon to generate ideas and solve problems in the future. They also may make the individual more comfortable about being alone and thus indirectly encourage reflectiveness. In effect, we are suggesting that television may be an especially powerful behavior setting (Barker, 1968; also see Chapter 5, this volume) in the sense of placing limits on alternative behaviors. Choosing to watch television is a choice not to do other things, including "nothing." Over the long run, successive decisions of this sort may not be inconsequential.

In addition to providing experiences that can be called upon in future situations, activities displaced by television may be more likely to encourage the kind of mindful thinking that facilitates success in future tasks. Salomon (1983) contends that information processing entails three phases—encoding, chunking, and elaborating—and the skills involved in elaboration (e.g., making inferences) require greater mental effort. His evidence indicates children tend to process television at the first two levels, not the third. Moreover, they construct *metarules*, or knowledge of what is required (in terms of AIME) to process information, based on their television experiences. These metarules may then be transferred and used for processing other material, for example, print, for which they are inappropriate. In our view this is analogous to college students who read their mathematics text like a novel, not realizing they need to work out mentally the steps involved in statements such as "it follows that . . . ." Critical thinking requires reflection, including trying to think of reasons why statements might be wrong. Visual, quick presentations discourage this process. The material sounds fine at first encounter; with no time for reflection, counterexamples never arise.

In a sense, the content and displacement avenues of television's influence intersect in this theoretical analysis. The content of television constrains the content and scope of viewers' schemata and scripts for processing information and, thus, constrains their knowledge of appropriate and possible behaviors. Television's displacement of other experiences constrains their plans for their own behavior.

WHO IS AFFECTED BY TELEVISION?

Age Differences

Are television's effects greater at some points in development than at others? It is tempting to state simply that younger children are affected more than older children and adults, but careful consideration indicates the answer may depend in part on whether content or displacement effects are involved.

The theory outlined in the last section would predict that television's content has the greatest potential to influence people who have not yet developed a broader framework for integrating and interpreting the kind of information presented. If television's content is the primary source of information used to form the schema, its influence will be greater than if competing experiences form the basis of the schema. Subsequent information will be processed through that schema or script, and it will direct subsequent perception and memory. This notion was the basis for Kozinski's novel, *Being There*. Since young children's sphere of operation in the world, and thus their range of experience, is more limited than that of older children and adults, this theory would predict that television's content has its greatest effect on younger children. Other groups with limited access to other sources of information, for example people in institutions, people who are new to the culture, or the elderly, also may be more strongly influenced. Note that it is experience rather than age per se that is relevant. The skills involved in mindful information processing (elaboration, reflection, and the like), and perhaps the propensity to apply these skills, also must be acquired through experience.

Let us consider the content effects studied in this project. In the case of sex-role behaviors and attitudes, television is one of several sources of information about the ways in which females and males behave, dress, work, interact, and so on, but for very young children it provides more models than are encountered in real life. The child's parents, siblings, and other humans provide real-life models with which to compare the televised models. For most children, all of these sources are consistent in presenting traditional sex roles; relatively few children encounter explicit messages contradicting what they see on television. Although increasing numbers of implicit counterexamples are available (e.g., female engineers), once the traditional schemata are established, these counterexamples may go unnoticed, for the reasons discussed earlier. In short, for most children the content of television presents consistent messages regarding sex roles, and these tend to converge with real-life experience. Our results indicate that sex-role attitudes of students as old as 10–13 years of age may be influenced by television.

The messages children receive regarding violence and aggression are less consistent than sex-role messages. Television itself presents inconsistent messages. On the one hand, a good deal of violence is depicted, but on the other hand, "crime does not pay" is a frequent theme (Williams et al., 1977, 1982). Since aggression on television tends to be portrayed as immediately successful, if not in the long run, understanding the negative consequences portrayed requires attention and ability to comprehend the relationship between events separated in time and/or place. Young children may be more likely than older children to perform aggressive behaviors learned from television, since they are less likely to understand the negative consequences portrayed (see Collins, 1983, for a review of research on children's comprehension of television). As the reader may recall, social approval–disapproval was one of the four categories of factors shown to influence performance (Comstock, 1980).

The messages viewers receive about aggression from sources other than television also tend to be less consistent than messages about sex roles. On the one hand society has laws prohibiting violence, and many parents discourage hitting, kicking, and so on. On the other hand, most adults also encourage children to "stick up for yourself," and some parents punish their children's aggressive behavior with verbal and/or physical aggression, thus providing aggressive models to imitate. Some parents behave aggressively and even violently toward one another, and some children live in neighborhoods where aggression is commonplace, though relatively few encounter the extreme violence (e.g., murder) often seen on North American television. In short, real life also provides children with contradictory messages regarding violence and aggression. Our research indicates that the aggressive behavior of children in the early elementary grades increases as a result of exposure to television, and this is true for most children, not just special subgroups. Our results also indicate the importance of considering the social milieu in making predictions about television's effects on aggression. Television, as well as other influences, may disrupt social controls which otherwise serve to reduce aggression.

In sum, the empirical and theoretical evidence suggests that in general, the effects of television's content depend in part on the extent to which contradictory messages are available, understood, and consistent. In the case of sex-role attitudes, messages from television are consistent and either absent or reinforced in real life, whereas in the case of aggressive behavior, most viewers receive contradictory messages from both sources. All viewers may learn aggression from television, but whether they perform it will depend on a variety of factors. If we wish to predict behavior, that is, performance, we need to know something of the viewers' social milieu.

Are displacement effects of television stronger at some stages of development than at others? The answer probably depends on the task or behavior as well as age. Our results indicate that some skills, such as fluent reading, may be especially vulnerable during their acquisition, whereas others, such as creative thinking, may require more recent and/or consistent practice. Television apparently even has a substantial displacement influence on the elderly, at least for participation in community activities.

In the early years, television's displacement effects may be greater for less intelligent children and/or children of low SES because it is during these years that important basic skills (e.g., reading, mindful information processing) and motivation and attitudes regarding achievement (e.g., persistence) usually are acquired. Brighter children may manage despite the time television takes from other activities. Later on, television's displacement effects may be greater for the more intelligent children and/or those from families of higher SES. These children have the skills required for creative and other achievements, but television displaces experiences which otherwise could facilitate their performance. They may be more likely than less intelligent children and those of lower SES to have the opportunity to spend their non-television time to best advantage. Fetler's (1982) California school achievement data are consistent with this hypothesis.

Other Individual Differences

Television has been touted as "the great leveler." By bringing information into everyone's home, it supposedly provides the poor with the same advantages as the rich. In our view, the evidence indicates it more often has the opposite effect. We suspect television displaces reading practice for those who need it most, and this may be true in other areas of achievement as well. Less intelligent and/or more disadvantaged children may be more likely to time-share homework with television, in some instances because they are less likely to realize the costs in efficiency involved, and in other instances because there is no alternative (i.e., no quiet place to study available).

As Himmelweit et al. (1958) and Schramm et al. (1961) documented when television was relatively new, and as Fetler (1982) has subsequently confirmed, intelligent students tend to use television differently than less intelligent ones. They watch less, and they watch different programming. As Roberts et al. (1984) have demonstrated, children from neighborhoods varying in SES differ in their attitudes regarding print and television and their use of both media. In their study of children's leisure activities, Medrich, Roizen, Ruben, and Buckley (1982) found that children from the least advantaged homes were almost three times as likely to be heavy television viewers as children from the most advantaged homes, which Medrich et al. concluded, "further adds to their advantage deficit" (p. 228). Bryant, Alexander and Brown (1983) reported that disadvantaged children did make gains in the skills presented on "Sesame Street," but middle-class children made even greater gains and also were more likely to see the program. Hornik's (1978) results indicated that acquisition of television had a negative impact on general ability scores for students in his El Salvador cohort representing less urban and poorer homes, who entered grade 7 with lower general ability and reading scores. This effect did not occur for students in the other cohorts, who were relatively better off.

It must be acknowledged that for some children, the stimulation and education provided by television may be more beneficial than the limited kind and range of other experiences available. For example, playing out-of-doors or exploring the neighborhood may be unsafe, the home may contain few books or other reading materials, and the child may avoid bringing home library books for fear that siblings or pets will ruin them. To our knowledge, the impact of television on such specialized subgroups has not been studied. Taken together, the evidence suggests that television may create wider gaps in achievement between generally advantaged and disadvantaged children than would occur without television. Whether this could be remedied by different programming or education designed to alter media diets is not clear. What is clear is the need for longitudinal studies of the role of intelligence in media use and effects.

GENERALIZABILITY OF THE RESULTS

As Anderson and Bryant (1983) have emphasized, television is not a unitary entity but is constantly evolving in both technology and content. It therefore is difficult to know whether the effects of television demonstrated in one locale with the content available there are relevant to other locales where the television programming and technology are different, not to mention the social milieu and other relevant factors. This is why we studied both Unitel and Multitel rather than just one town with television. It seemed likely we would find differences between a town with one channel of CBC reception and a town with four channels (including CBC and the three U.S. networks) that were at least as large as differences between towns with and without television. Instead, there were relatively few differences between Unitel and Multitel by comparison with either the number and magnitude of differences between Notel and the other towns or the before and after observations made within Notel. This pattern of results occurred for behaviors hypothesized to be affected via both the content and displacement effects of television. Since the effects of television, as they occur in the long run in the field, do not depend closely on the number and content of channels available, our results are broadly applicable.

Several additional aspects of the findings substantiate the representativeness of our sample. First, results obtained by other researchers with urban samples in the United States and elsewhere were replicated. We found, for example, that boys were on average more physically aggressive than girls; the mean score for boys on the Wechsler Intelligence Scale for Children Block Design task was higher than that for girls; boys on average held more stereotyped sex-role attitudes than did girls; women obtained higher Person-orientation scores and lower Thing-orientation scores than did men; ideational fluency and originality scores were highly correlated; creativity and intelligence scores were relatively independent; creativity scores decreased during early adolescence; and the television-viewing habits of children and adults in our three towns were comparable to those reported by other researchers. Second, the average performance of children in Notel, Unitel, and Multitel on intelligence tests previously standardized on representative U.S. or Canadian samples was similar to the norms for those tests. Third, scores obtained with the sex-role attitude measure from an urban Canadian sample were in the same range as the scores of Unitel and Multitel students. Most important, our results tend to confirm and extend, rather than to contradict, findings obtained in laboratory and field studies by other North American and Western European researchers.

For all these reasons we believe our results are generalizable. Those who wish to argue otherwise must explain how and why the effects of television on the residents of Notel, Unitel, and Multitel differ from the effects of television experienced by other Canadians and by residents of the United States and other western cultures.

THE IMPACT OF NUMBER AND/OR ORIGIN OF TV CHANNELS AVAILABLE

As we have just discussed, differences associated with the presence versus absence of television were more consistent and substantial than differences associated with the numbers of channels available or network origin. What are the implications of this interesting result? One has to do with the design of this study as a natural rather than true experiment. In a true experiment participants are randomly assigned to groups. Other factors which might explain the results are assumed to vary randomly rather than systematically with group membership. When random assignment is not possible, as in our study, it is important to be alert to possible "third variable" explanations. Are there ways in which the groups vary systematically that might explain the results as well as or better than the "treatment," in this case the introduction of television? We took great care in choosing our comparison towns and believe Unitel and Multitel were as similar as possible to Notel, as the data reported in Chapter 1 indicate. However, it was impossible to find two control towns the same distance as Notel was from the United States. The major criterion in selecting Multitel was that it have U.S. as well as Canadian programming; the only towns in this category were close to the border. Had we found consistent differences between Multitel and the other towns, one possible explanation would have been that the proximity of Multitel to the United States rather than the availability of U.S. television and/or more channels accounted for the results. Since the results for Unitel and Multitel were more similar than different, this can be ruled out. A second, more minor difference between Multitel and the other towns was its proximity to larger communities. Multitel was about 25 miles from one Canadian town of 15,000 people and 25 miles in a different direction from another Canadian town of 9500. The nearest large city, located about 125 miles away in the United States, had a population of about 185,000. By contrast, the nearest larger community to Notel was 130 miles away and had a population of 35,000. That same city was 180 miles from Unitel; 200 miles from Unitel in a different direction was a city of 40,000. Both Notel and Unitel were at least 10 hours driving time away from a city of greater than 100,000 population. The finding that Multitel and Unitel residents were more similar than either group was to Notel residents in Phase 1 indicates that the availability of television had a stronger influence than did proximity to larger communities or proximity to the United States.

The initially surprising result that the number of channels available was not of major consequence becomes more understandable when patterns of television use are considered. The school-age children and adults in Unitel watched almost as many hours of CBC, the Canadian government-owned channel, as their Multitel counterparts watched of CBC and the three major U.S. networks combined (see Chapter 5). Two years after their town obtained television, Notel residents behaved similarly. This similarity in amount of viewing and concomitant similarity in the effects of television adds strength to our argument that the displacement effects of television deserve as careful consideration as the impact of its content.

The finding that the content of CBC apparently was similar in its impact to the content of the U.S. commercial networks also is thought-provoking. Again, however, consideration of other data, in this case previous content analysis studies, makes this result more understandable. There is some evidence that the U.S. networks display, on average, more aggression (Williams et al., 1977, 1982) and more stereotyped portrayals of sex roles (Halpern & Ethier, 1977) than does CBC. However, the similarities are more striking than the differences. The evidence that the introduction of CBC television to Notel was followed by an increase in children's aggressive behavior (Chapter 7) and increased stereotyping of children's sex-role attitudes (Chapter 6) is consistent with information obtained in previous research concerning the content of the programming available.

The finding that CBC television was more similar to than different from ABC, CBS, and NBC programming in its impact on viewers should be considered when comparing our results with those obtained elsewhere. For example, Murray and Kippax (1977, 1978) studied the introduction of television to an Australian community which acquired the government-owned channel. We are not aware of any content analyses in which Cana-

dian and Australian programming have been compared, but conversations
with Australians familiar with television in both countries convince us the
programming introduced to Kippax and Murray's No-TV town differed in
several respects from the TV introduced to Notel. The Australian government-owned channel is more explicitly oriented toward education,
whereas CBC focuses primarily on entertainment, as do the privately
owned Canadian network (CTV) and the U.S. commercial networks. The
programming on the Australian government-owned network probably is
more similar to that on the U.S. Public Broadcasting Service (PBS) channel and the British Broadcasting Corporation (BBC) channels in the
United Kingdom than to CBC programming. CBC seems to lie some-
where between these systems and the commercial North American systems, but more in the direction of the latter than the former. We are
currently conducting research to investigate empirically the content similarities and differences among the major North American channels available in Canada.

IMPLICATIONS REGARDING MEDIA DIETS

Our results were obtained for North American viewers and entertain-
ment-oriented programming. Different kinds of programming used similarly or differently might well produce different results. The Australian
study (Murray & Kippax, 1977, 1978) provides a good example. The Low-
TV town received only the Australian Broadcasting Commission's public
channel, which at that time devoted 34% of its programming to educational–instructional material intended for use in the schools. The High-
TV town received that channel plus a commercial channel which devoted
only 3% of its programming to educational–instructional material. Murray
and Kippax found that 66% of the 8–12-year-olds interviewed in their
High-TV town said they watched television because they were bored,
whereas only 39% of the Low-TV town's children said they did so. This
finding was interpreted by Murray and Kippax as a novelty effect, since
the Low-TV town had had their channel for only 1 year, whereas the
High-TV town had had TV for 5 years. Another explanation also seems
plausible; the children whose only channel devoted one-third of its broadcast time to educational programming may have conceptualized and used
television differently than High-TV children. Other data support this interpretation. First, Low-TV children were *least* likely to perceive television as like the cinema, and the boundaries of the functions of "television" and "school" were closer than in the other towns. Second, in the
High-TV town, viewing of "action–adventure–crime" programs in-

creased dramatically between the 5–7 and 8–12 age groups (an increase from about 8% to about 32% of viewing time, as reported by parents in a diary); the comparable percentages for the Low-TV town were less than 5% at both age levels. Over the same age range interest in "drama" programs increased from about 10 to 30% of viewing time in the Low-TV town but changed only from about 0 to 2½% in the High-TV town. As Murray and Kippax (1978) noted, these differences cannot be explained entirely by the differences in programming, since children in the High-TV town had access to the same public, educationally oriented television as Low-TV town residents. Since children in the two towns watched the same amount of television, different viewing patterns must have reflected differences in programming preferences.

These pieces of data clearly do not constitute sufficient evidence but should be helpful in formulating hypotheses for future research on how television's impact varies according to the media diets of its viewers. With the increasing availability of new technologies, in particular video recorders and cable channels, this question takes on added complexity. Some families we know have built video libraries of educational children's programs and restrict their young children's viewing to such material. The impact of television on these children probably is different from the impact we observed. The difficulty in studying such families, of course, is that they are not typical and differ in many ways from other families (Coffin, 1955; Robinson, 1972). This once again points up the advantage of a natural experiment for assessing the effects of television.

We have suggested that changes in the type of programming available and/or changes in patterns of television use might yield changes in television's effects. Unfortunately, this will be easier said than done. One of the major problems involved in the development of effective educational programming is its age specificity. Because comprehension, memory strategies, and even quality of thinking change so much with development over the preschool to adolescent years, educational programming appeals to and is effective for only a narrow age range. This in turn means that knowledge of child development is essential for the production of good educational programming. As Siegel (1980) points out, however, the people who are employed to produce such programs (writers, performers, producers, and executives) typically lack relevant formal education and are not expected to keep up with research in child development. Most are scientifically naive, but this is not necessarily their fault; researchers are notoriously poor at communicating their empirical findings to the lay public. The social scientists with advanced knowledge and/or degrees who *are* employed by the networks tend to have been trained in sociology or communications, not in psychology, and especially not in developmental psychology or child development. The exceptions serve to reinforce the point. "Mister Rogers," "Sesame Street" (and Children's Television Workshop programs in general), and "Freestyle" all are examples of successful collaborations between child development specialists and production experts. We hope this kind of collaboration will become the rule rather than the exception.

CRITICAL VIEWING SKILLS

In part for the reasons outlined, changes in television programming tend to evolve slowly, and the interested public has relatively little influence on the process. The concept of control by government or other decree is anathema in many countries. The prospect of changing how people use television is more palatable and seems easier to achieve than the prospect of changing television's content. To this end researchers and public action groups (such as Action for Children's Television in the United States and the Children's Broadcast Institute in Canada) distribute suggestions for parents interested in monitoring their children's viewing. More formal curricula also have been developed for use in the schools. Both have the goal of teaching *television literacy* and *critical viewing skills*.

Television literacy involves understanding television programming, including how it is produced and broadcast, familiarity with the formats used, ability to recognize overt and covert themes of programs and commercial messages, and appreciation of television as an art form (Corder-Bolz, 1982). Most critical viewing skills curricula cover these topics, and in addition, attempt to teach children to be critical of some of the material presented on television. Violence is the most common target, but stereotypes about different groups of people (e.g., women, people of other races, people from other countries, the elderly) and advertising also are often included.

Unlike J. Anderson (1983), we agree with many of the goals of television literacy and critical viewing skills curricula. Most of those we have seen, however, assume television's effects result primarily or even solely from its content, and therein lies the rub. Television also may have negative effects which occur via displacement. When television use is included in critical viewing curricula, however, it is usually in terms of choosing one kind of program versus another (focusing on content) rather than choosing to watch TV versus doing other things (focusing on displacement). Since these curricula do attempt to teach children a good deal about the medium, embed lessons about television in other (e.g., language) lessons, and involve homework which requires television viewing, the net effect might even be an increase in television viewing. Children may obtain the impression that watching television is a good way to spend one's leisure time and doing so can have only positive consequences.

We would suggest one or two additions to critical viewing skills curricula. First, children could be taught that some tasks require sufficient mental (and perhaps sensorimotor) concentration that they should not be time-shared with other activities, including television. Practicing reading, studying, and any other task for which achievement is important must be done on its own to be maximally effective. In effect, we are suggesting that metacognition or knowledge of AIME (Salomon, 1981, 1983) required by various tasks be incorporated into the curricula. The emphasis could be moved from critical viewing to critical perusal of information from a variety of sources, including print, which would provide an opportunity to explain and demonstrate the importance of mental reflection, elaboration, and so on. Second, children could be taught the concept of displacement; watching television is a choice not to do other things. Alternatives could be discussed; what can be done out-of-doors and indoors when "there's nothing to do"? What are the pros and cons of doing these other things versus watching television?

It would be interesting to compare the effects of the current curricula and one designed with more emphasis on the goal of reducing the child's involvement with television. We would suggest that all evaluations of critical viewing curricula assess their impact on television viewing as well as their indirect impact on other activities such as print use.

HINDSIGHT

As in any large project, especially longitudinal ones, hindsight and information available only after the data were collected have suggested ideas we wish we had pursued. Mentioning topics we did *not* study may help explain some unanswered questions and/or provide suggestions for future research.

Preschoolers

Perhaps most obvious is the absence of any data on preschool children. Other researchers have documented that by the age of about 2½ preschoolers watch a substantial amount of television (Comstock et al., 1978), and even infants attend to the set and express some interest (Hollenbeck &

Slaby, 1979). A great deal of the research dealing with aggression and most of that focused on prosocial behavior has been conducted with young children. Why did we focus on school-aged children and adults? The answer is largely pragmatic. It would have been very difficult to obtain data on a representative sample of preschoolers because they were not accessible via organized groups. Unfortunately, our budget did not allow for the personnel and time that would have been involved in identifying and individually contacting families with preschoolers.

Information and General Knowledge

We wish we had asked whether the availability of television affected the amount and/or type of general knowledge accrued by children and adults in Notel, Unitel, and Multitel. It seems commonly accepted that children who grow up with television are more knowledgeable and "worldly." This tenet reflects the belief that television's content serves as a teacher, and previous research indicates viewers consider television to be a good source of information. If we consider the content functions of television, it makes sense to hypothesize that regular TV viewers are better informed than nonviewers, particularly with regard to topics not encountered in their daily lives. If, on the other hand, we consider the displacement functions of television, it makes sense to hypothesize that people who do not spend several hours a day watching television might spend some of that time in activities that would inform them about topics remote from their daily experience. The two competing hypotheses would lead, in turn, to consideration of the content of television by comparison with the content of other information sources, especially print materials.

We did not assess television's role in the acquisition of information or general knowledge and are unable to shed light directly on this issue, but it may be helpful to consider briefly the data obtained in previous research. In their early North American study Schramm et al. (1961) asked, "Is television raising a better-informed generation?" They concluded that children are growing up better informed than used to be the case. "It is not at all certain, though, that television can be credited with much of the improvement" (p. 151). Arguing from a displacement perspective, they made specific predictions which varied with the child's level of intelligence and amount of viewing. Children of low intelligence who are relatively heavy viewers were predicted to be slightly better informed (than they would be without TV), and children of high intelligence who are relatively light viewers were predicted to be better informed if they chose to take advantage of the unusual opportunities television offers to see and hear famous people, hear issues discussed, see far places and important events, see demonstrations of science, and so on. By contrast, children of high intelligence who are relatively heavy viewers were predicted to be less well informed than comparable children who do not watch television. For children of average intelligence, irrespective of amount of viewing, and children of low intelligence who are relatively light viewers, television was predicted to make "probably not much difference." These predictions were based on Schramm et al.'s assessment that commerical television, which is rich in talent and money, focuses chiefly on offering fantasy experiences, whereas noncommercial educational television, which is devoted to offering reality experiences, is starved for talent and money. In addition, noncommercial television (e.g., PBS, the Public Broadcasting System in the United States) has a very small, restricted audience by comparison with the commercial channels. Schramm et al. concluded that television's accomplishment in raising a better-informed generation is nothing compared to what it could accomplish if more of its power were used for reality experiences.

Research conducted in the United Kingdom led Himmelweit et al. (1958) to similar conclusions. Children with regular access to television scored significantly higher than children who did not yet have television in knowledge of geography, science, sports, music, handicrafts, and household chores. They did not differ in their knowledge of English literature, history, nature or rural studies, art and architecture, current affairs, and religion. On the whole, television's benefits in the area of general knowledge were "confined to the younger, less intelligent children, whose access to other sources of general information is restricted" (p. 272). After testing children's knowledge by asking them to write down as many world events or happenings as they could think of, Himmelweit et al. also concluded that television does not increase children's breadth of knowledge.

Comparisons between adult viewers and nonviewers in the Greater London area in terms of both strength of expressed interest and frequency of actual involvement in certain activities were made by Belson (1959). After controlling for pre-viewing differences between the groups, he found that television was associated with significant decreases rather than increases in interest in theater, ballet, paintings, and events in different parts of the world. It also was associated with significant decreases in attendance at the theater and ballet, in visiting places of historic importance, and in reading about politics in Great Britain, modern developments in science, international and world affairs, and people in other countries (as well as decreased book reading in general). The only activity (related to general knowledge) which increased was visiting art galleries to look at paintings; this seemed to be the result of a particular series of programs and occurred for people who already had a relatively strong interest in paintings.

Roberts and Bachen's (1981) review of research on media transmission of knowledge and information to adults indicates that educational level tends to predict knowledge better than media use predicts, and print use is a better predictor than is television.

In sum, the evidence from previous research suggests that if television does increase the general knowledge of its viewers, the effect is selective in terms of both the kind of information imparted and the characteristics of those affected. It undoubtedly is the case that children growing up now are better informed than children from previous generations. In our view, this probably results more from the advances in general knowledge which accumulate with each succeeding generation and are transmitted via schooling and all media than from the influence of television alone. The belief that today's children are more knowledgeable than were their parents and grandparents at the same age probably reflects a cohort effect (Schaie, 1965, 1967; Schaie & Strother, 1968). Researchers who conduct cross-sectional studies tend to find that performance on intellectual or cognitive measures peaks in early adulthood (e.g., Horn & Cattell, 1966). In contrast, researchers who conduct longitudinal studies by following the same set of individuals for several years do not observe decreases, and some researchers have found increases beyond age 50 (e.g., Bayley & Oden, 1955). The discrepancy in these findings occurs because succeeding generations tend to be better schooled, on average, than earlier generations.

Impact of Commercials

Had we focused more on North American television's primary function, that is, its commercial marketing role, and less on its teaching and displacement functions, we might have studied consumer behavior. It would be reasonable to hypothesize that Notel residents' buying patterns would change following the introduction of television, since they would be exposed to more advertisements and hours of advertising via television than via any other medium.[5] Unfortunately, we did not collect any data relevant to this issue. We are considering the possibility of examining the records of shops in the three towns, but do not as yet know whether this will be feasible.

Physical Fitness

The evidence described in Chapter 4 concerning participation in community sports activities is clear; television has a negative effect. This suggests that television may play a direct role in physical fitness. If so, its impact may be greatest among adolescents and the elderly.

A displacement hypothesis and our findings for sports participation might predict that people who watch a lot of television are on average less fit than those who watch relatively little. On the other hand, some kinds of exercise can be time-shared with television. Moreover, yoga and other exercise programs are shown on television, and in Canada, the federal government sponsors advertisements intended to stimulate participation in sports and other exercise. It is possible, therefore, that television has a positive effect on physical fitness, and this may or may not be specific to certain groups of viewers. If we consider more indirect content effects, the snack foods, chocolate bars, and convenience foods advertised on television also might influence fitness and health, but in the opposite direction. Aside from research designed to evaluate the potential use of television for encouraging healthier eating habits and life-styles (see Solomon, 1982, for a review), and research by Gorn and Goldberg (1982) comparing the actual snack choices of children exposed to commercials for fresh fruit or candy, there seems to have been relatively little research in this area.

Hockey Games

How we wish we had videotaped hockey games in the children's leagues before and after the introduction of television to Notel! It would have made an interesting addition to the study of aggressive behavior, particularly since hockey is the national sport of Canada. One of the most popular programs on television is the regular Saturday evening broadcast, "Hockey Night in Canada." Concern has been expressed in North America over the increasing aggression in professional hockey, including the fights which now are commonplace. It would be interesting to know whether children who regularly watched hockey on TV differed in the way they played the game in their own leagues from children residing in a town where neither the children, the coaches, nor the parents could regularly watch hockey on TV. We have learned recently that records of penalties in organized hockey leagues are kept for many years, and if such records are available in Notel, Unitel, and Multitel it would be interesting to examine them.

IMPLICATIONS FOR THE NEW TECHNOLOGIES

The finding that residents of a town receiving only one channel of television were more similar to residents of a town receiving four channels than to those receiving no television may have some implications regarding the impact of pay-TV in North America. Indeed, Multitel residents who had access to the four channels (more than 80% of the homes in both phases) did so via a version of pay-TV; they paid a monthly fee to a cable company in order to obtain the additional channels.[6] Proportionately more Canadians than residents of any other country in the world subscribe to pay television, which until recently has provided access primarily to ABC, CBS, NBC, and, in many locations, PBS from the United States. Our results indicate that people who pay for access to four channels do watch more television than those who receive only one channel without paying a fee, but not much more (about 5 hours difference per week for school-age children and 4 hours per week for adults). This suggests there is a ceiling on the number of hours the average person will spend viewing television, which is not surprising since leisure time is limited for most people by their paid and domestic labor obligations and the time required for sleeping, eating, and so on.

How do individuals and families change their media behavior when they acquire the capability, via video recording, of viewing selected programming at their own convenience? Gerbner and his colleagues (Gerbner, Gross, Signorielli, Morgan, & Jackson-Beeck, 1979) contend most people watch TV by turning on the set and looking for the most attractive programming rather than by preselecting certain programs and watching when those programs are scheduled. This may or may not be an accurate description of most TV viewers (see Hawkins & Pingree, 1980, for a different viewpoint), but it probably is inappropriate for families with video recorders. Ownership of recorders will be confounded initially with SES, since only wealthier families are likely to purchase the necessary equipment. However, the availability of movies via rental may make video recorders especially attractive to certain segments of the population, and families purchasing machines may vary more in SES than would at first seem likely. For example, anecdotal evidence suggests recorders may be especially attractive to immigrants. We have heard of several families in which the following scenario has occurred. Prior to the purchase of a video recorder, the children (who speak English in addition to their native language) watch a good deal of regular TV programming, but the parents and grandparents (who speak little or no English) watch little. Following the purchase of a video recorder, the entire family spends considerable time watching movies from the old country in their native language. This family movie viewing occurs at the time of day (evenings) when the children previously watched scheduled prime-time television programming. This suggests a variety of questions we plan to pursue in future research. For both the non-video-recorder and video-recorder families, what is the role of television in the interaction patterns of immigrant families? What is the impact on learning English as a second language? What is the impact on assimilation to North American culture, and what is the impact on maintenance of the culture of origin?

What about home computers and video games? Greenfield (1984) has speculated about their potential for stimulating cognitive development and has some preliminary data indicating positive results (personal communication, July, 1985). Our results should provide additional hypotheses and ideas regarding avenues for future research, particularly in the area of "mindful" versus "mindless" information processing.

We have mentioned three recent technological developments likely to play an important future role in the effects of television—pay TV, video recorders, and home computers and video games. Whilst encouraging research involving these new technologies, however, we would not want to discourage further research on the uses, content, and effects of television itself. Hornik (1981) has said that research on TV often seems to be a fly-by-night enterprise; relatively few researchers have conducted more than one study. Those who have done so are now using sophisticated methodologies to understand the complexities involved in television's influence, and it is important that this effort not be abandoned (Pezdek, 1983).

FINAL THOUGHTS

As many reviewers have noted, most research on television and human behavior has dealt with immediate, direct effects of content. When long-term effects have been assessed, the data usually have been correlational. The opportunity to study the natural experiment comprising Notel, Unitel, and Multitel therefore was exciting. We were skeptical that effects would hold up in the field over such a long period, but the introduction of greater ecological validity did not significantly alter conclusions reached by other researchers based on laboratory studies, short-term field studies, and correlational evidence. No single study can be definitive, but converging evidence gives confidence in drawing conclusions. We refer here, of course, to evidence that the content of television leads to increased sex-role stereotyping and aggressive behavior. The methodological advantages of the natural experiment make these results important. They are no more interesting, however, than our results demonstrating television's effects via displacement in a number of areas less well studied in previous research—the thinking of both children and adults, acquisition of fluent reading skills, and participation in community activities.

We designed our research with the expectation that television has the potential to affect its viewers in a variety of ways, some positive and some negative. This summary of the results points to the conclusion that for the topics we studied, the net effects of North American television on regular viewers, especially children, are negative. Other possible explanations of our results have been carefully considered and rejected. It is possible, of course, that the effects we observed are due to some even more influential force we have not considered, but it is difficult to imagine one that would produce the same pattern of results. Moreover, even if such a "ghost in the machine" were identified, would it turn out to be robust in the face of the considerable scrutiny received by this and other research on television? We think not, and are left to conclude, therefore, that television does have some negative effects substantial enough to be documented over the long run in naturalistic settings.

This natural experiment provided a conservative test of television's effects. It was based on a gross measure of exposure, and although most Notel residents could not watch television regularly in Phase 1, a few could. In addition, we have taken a reasonably conservative approach in accepting findings as evidence of the effects of television by trying to avoid Type I error.[7] At the same time, however, we have been cognizant of Comstock's (1983) advice that

> avoidance of Type II error is the radical face of science. It imposes on those who invoke the label of science the obligation to speculate, entertain the improbable, trace obscure threads, elaborate fully alternative interpretations, experiment with varying criteria, and above all to seek as much meaning as possible from the data and evidence before them. (p. 11)

In additional to producing results we believe are important, this natural experiment has provided insight into the processes involved in television's influence and has generated many hypotheses we plan to test in future research in both laboratory and field settings. We hope it yields similar benefits for others.

NOTES

[1] Because this final chapter is a summary, the reader is referred to the preceding chapters for detailed findings, citations, and qualifying statements.

[2] Recall that CBC is the Canadian government-owned network. It was available in both

phases of the study in Unitel and Multitel and became available in Notel just after the Phase 1 data were collected. Multitel had ABC, CBS, and NBC channels (the three major U.S. networks), in addition to CBC, in both phases.

[3] Piaget, with whom the concept originated, distinguished between a cognitive structure which directs action (both internal action, i.e., thinking, perception, mental plans; and external action, i.e., sensorimotor behavior) and a mental image or figurative outline. As Furth (1981) and Mandler (1983) point out, English translations of Piaget's work sometimes use the word *scheme* (plural *schemes*) to refer to the cognitive structure and sometimes use the word *schema* (plural *schemata*), in either case using the other term for the figurative outline, which is the less important concept in Piaget's theory. Cognitive psychologists fairly consistently use schema for the cognitive structures they discuss. Following Mandler, we have used schema as a means of emphasizing the similarity between Piaget's conceptualization and that of many other cognitive psychologists.

[4] In Piaget's theory, schemata are modified through the process of adaptation, which has two aspects, assimilation and accommodation. Assimilation is the taking-in aspect of the process, the incorporation of the new information to the schema. Accommodation, the changing of the schema to fit the new information, occurs as a result. Assimilation and accommodation always occur together, and it is through this process of adaptation that development proceeds. Note that if the new information is too disparate from any available schemata, there will be no attempt to incorporate it; the information will not be recognized as assimilable.

[5] The major radio station available in Notel in both phases of the study was CBC. CBC radio carried commercials up to April 1975, when they were discontinued on all English-language programs except the "Metropolitan Opera." They have been retained on CBC television, but it has been CBC policy since September 1974 not to carry commercials on television programming aimed at children under 12 years of age.

[6] Multitel residents who did not subscribe to the cable received only CBS. In other words, they received no Canadian channels and only one from the United States.

[7] Type I error is a statistical term meaning that the researcher concluded there was a significant effect when there really wasn't one: The result (for example, a difference between two groups, or a correlation reflecting the relationship between two sets of scores) actually occurred by chance and would be unlikely to occur again if the study was replicated. Type II error is the opposite, that is, concluding there is no effect when there really is one.

REFERENCES

Abelson, R. P. Script processing in attitude formation and decision making. In J. Carroll & J. Payne (Eds.), *Cognition and social behavior*. Hillsdale, N.J.: Erlbaum, 1976.

Abelson, R. P. Psychological status of the script. *American Psychologist*, 1981, *36*, 715–729.

Anderson, D. R., & Bryant, J. Research on children's television viewing: The state of the art. In J. Bryant & D. R. Anderson (Eds.), *Children's understanding of television: Research on attention and comprehension*. New York: Academic Press, 1983.

Anderson, D., & Lorch, E. P. Looking at television: Action or reaction. In J. Bryant & D. R. Anderson (Eds.), *Children's understanding of television: Research on attention and comprehension*. New York: Academic Press, 1983.

Anderson, J. A. Television literacy and the critical viewer. In J. Bryant & D. R. Anderson (Eds.), *Children's understanding of television: Research on attention and comprehension*. New York: Academic Press, 1983.

428   Tannis MacBeth Williams

Bandura, A. *Social learning theory.* Englewood Cliffs, N.J.: Prentice Hall, 1977.

Barker, R. G. *Ecological psychology: Concepts and methods for studying the environment of human behavior.* Stanford, Calif.: Stanford University Press, 1968.

Bayley, N., & Oden, M. H. The maintenance of intellectual ability in gifted adults. *Journal of Gerontology,* 1955, *10,* 91–107.

Belson, W. A. Effects of television on the interests and initiative of adult viewers in Greater London. *British Journal of Psychology,* 1959, *50,* 145–158.

Bem, S. L. Gender schema theory: A cognitive account of sex typing. *Psychological Review,* 1981, *88,* 354–364.

Bryant, J., Alexander, A. F., & Brown, D. Learning from educational television programs. In M. J. A. Howe (Eds.), *Learning from television: Psychological and educational research.* London: Academic Press, 1983.

Bryant, J., & Anderson, D. R. *Children's understanding of television: Research on attention and comprehension.* New York: Academic Press, 1983.

Chall, J. S. *Stages of reading development.* New York: McGraw-Hill, 1983.

Coffin, T. E. Television's impact on society. *American Psychologist,* 1955, *10,* 630–641.

Collins, W. A. Interpretation and inference in children's television viewing. In J. Bryant & D. R. Anderson (Eds.), *Children's understanding of televison: Research on attention and comprehension.* New York: Academic Press, 1983.

Comstock, G. A. New emphases in research on the effects of television and film violence. In E. L. Palmer & A. Dorr (Eds.), *Children and the faces of television.* New York: Academic Press, 1980.

Comstock, G. A. *Scientific progress in the study of human aggression and the mass media.* In *Violence and Television: A National Health Issue?* Conference sponsored by the National Coalition on Television Violence, Washington, D.C., October, 1983.

Comstock, G., Chaffee, S., Katzman, N., McCombs, M., & Roberts, D. *Television and human behavior.* New York: Columbia University Press, 1978.

Corder-Bolz, C. Television literacy and critical television viewing skills. In D. Pearl, L. Bouthilet, & J. Lazar (Eds.), *Television and behavior: Ten years of scientific progress and implications for the eighties.* Vol. 2. Rockville, Md.: NIMH, 1982.

Cordua, G., McGraw, K., Drabman, R. Doctor or nurse: Children's perceptions of sex-typed occupations. *Child Development,* 1979, *50,* 590–593.

Dorr, A. When I was a child I thought as a child. In S. B. Withey & R. P. Abeles (Eds.), *Television and social behavior: Beyond violence and children.* Hillsdale, N.J.: Erlbaum, 1980.

Fetler, M. *Television viewing habits and school achievement.* Paper presented at the meeting of the American Educational Research Association, New York, March 1982.

Furth, H. G. *Piaget and knowledge: Theoretical foundations* (2nd ed.). Chicago: University of Chicago Press, 1981.

Gerbner, G., Gross, L., Signorielli, N. Morgan. M., & Jackson-Beeck, M. The demonstration of power: Violence profile no. 10. *Journal of Communication,* 1979, *29*(3), 177–196.

Gorn, G. V., & Goldberg, M. E. Behavioral evidence of the effects of televised food messages on children. *Journal of Consumer Research,* 1982, *9,* 200–205.

Greenberg, B. S. Television and role socialization: An overview. In D. Pearl, L. Bouthilet, & J. Lazar (Eds.). *Television and behavior: Ten years of scientific progress and implications for the eighties.* Vol. 2. Rockville, Md.: NIMH, 1982.

Greenfield, P. M. *Mind and media.* Cambridge, Mass.: Harvard University Press, 1984.

Halpern, S., & Ethier, B. *The portrayal of men and women in Canadian and U.S. television commercials.* Unpublished manuscript, University of British Columbia, Department of Psychology, 1977 (Available from T. M. Williams).

Hawkins, R. P., & Pingree, S. Some processes in the cultivation effect. *Communication Research*, 1980, *7*, 193–226.

Hawkins, R. P., & Pingree, S. Television's influence on social reality. In D. Pearl, L. Bouthilet, & J. Lazar (Eds.), *Television and behavior: Ten years of scientific progress and implications for the eighties*. Vol. 2. Rockville, Md.: NIMH, 1982.

Himmelweit, H. T., Oppenheim, A. N., & Vince, P. *Television and the child*. London: Oxford University Press, 1958.

Hollenbeck, A. R., & Slaby, R. G. Infant visual and vocal responses to television. *Child Development*, 1979, *50*, 41–45.

Horn, J. L., & Cattell, R. B. Age differences in primary mental ability factors. *Journal of Gerontology*, 1966, *21*, 210–220.

Hornik, R. C. Television access and slowing of cognitive growth. *American Educational Research Journal*, 1978, *15*, 1–15.

Hornik, R. Out-of-school television and schooling: Hypotheses and methods. *Review of Educational Research*, 1981, *51*, 193–214.

Hornik, R. C., Gould, J., & Gonzalez, M. *Susceptibility to media effects*. Paper presented at the meeting of the International Communication Association, Acapulco, May 1980.

Huston, A. H., & Wright, J. C. Children's processing of television: The informative functions of formal features. In J. Bryant & D. R. Anderson (Eds.), *Children's understanding of television: Research on attention and comprehension*. New York: Academic Press, 1983.

Janis, I. L. The influence of television on personal decision-making. In S. B. Withey & R. P. Abeles (Eds.), *Television and social behavior: Beyond violence and children*. Hillsdale, N.J.: Erlbaum, 1980.

Liebert, R. M., Sprafkin, J. N., & Davidson, E. S. *The early window: Effects of television on children and youth (2nd ed.)*. New York: Pergamon Press, 1982.

Mandler, J. M. Representation. In J. H. Flavell & E. M. Markman (Eds.), *Cognitive Development*. Vol. 2 of P. Mussen (Ed.), *Manual of child psychology*. New York: Wiley, 1983.

Martin, C. L., & Halverson, C. F. A schematic processing model of sex-typing and stereotyping in children. *Child Development*, 1981, *52*, 1119–1134.

Medrich, E. A., Roizen, J. A., Rubin, V., & Buckley, S. *The serious business of growing up: A study of children's lives outside school*. Berkeley: University of California Press, 1982.

Meringoff, L. K. The influence of the medium on children's story apprehension. *Journal of Educational Psychology*, 1980, *72*, 240–249.

Morgan, M., & Gross, L. Television and educational achievement and aspiration. In D. Pearl, L. Bouthilet, & J. Lazar (Eds.), *Television and behavior: Ten years of scientific progress and implications for the eighties*. Vol. 2. Rockville, Md.: NIMH, 1982.

Murray, J. P., & Kippax, S. Television diffusion and social behaviour in three communities: A field experiment. *Australian Journal of Psychology*, 1977, *29*(1), 31–43.

Murray, J. P., & Kippax, S. Children's social behavior in three towns with differing television experience. *Journal of Communication*, 1978, *30*(4), 19–29.

Pezdek, K. Comment. Presented in a discussion of research on television at the meeting of the Society for Research in Child Development, Detroit, April 1983.

Roberts, D. F., & Bachen, C. M. Mass communication effects. *Annual Review of Psychology*, 1981, *32*, 307–356.

Roberts, D. F., Bachen, C. M., Hornby, M. C., & Hernandez-Ramos, P. Reading and television: Predictors of reading achievement at different age levels. *Communication Research*, 1984, *11*, 9–49.

Robinson, J. P. Television's impact on everyday life: Some cross-natural evidence. In E. A. Rubinstein, G. A. Comstock, & J. P. Murray (Eds.), *Television and social behavior: Vol. 4. Television in day-to-day life: Patterns of use.* Washington, D.C.: U.S. Government Printing Office, 1972.

Salomon, G. Introducing AIME: The assessment of children's mental involvement with television. *New Directions for Child Development,* 1981, No. 13, 89–102.

Salomon, G. Television watching and mental effort: A social psychological view. In J. Bryant & D. R. Anderson (Eds.), *Children's understanding of television: Research on attention and comprehension.* New York: Academic Press, 1983.

Schaie, K. W. A general model for the study of developmental problems. *Psychological Bulletin,* 1965, *64,* 92–107.

Schaie, K. W. Age changes and age differences. *The Gerontologist,* 1967, *7,* 128–132.

Schaie, K. W., & Strother, C. R. A cross-sequential study of age changes in cognitive behavior. *Psychological Bulletin,* 1968, *70,* 671–680.

Schank, R. C., & Abelson, R. P. *Scripts, plans, goals, and understanding.* Hillsdale, N.J.: Erlbaum, 1977.

Schramm, W., Lyle, J., & Parker, E. B. *Television in the lives of our children.* Stanford, Calif.: Stanford University Press, 1961.

Siegel, A. E. Research findings and social policy. In E. L. Palmer & A. Dorr (Eds.), *Children and the faces of television.* New York: Academic Press, 1980.

Solomon, D. S. Health campaigns on television. In D. Pearl, L. Bouthilet, & J. Lazar (Eds.), *Television and behavior: Ten years of scientific progress and implications for the eighties.* Vol. 2. Rockville, Md.: NIMH, 1982.

Williams, T. M., Zabrack, M. L., & Joy, L. A. A content analysis of entertainment television programming. In *Report of the Ontario Royal Commission on Violence in the Communications Industry,* Vol. 3. Toronto, 1977.

Williams, T. M., Zabrack, M. L., & Joy, L. A. The portrayal of aggression on North American television. *Journal of Applied Social Psychology,* 1982, *12*(5), 360–380.

Withey, S. B. An ecological, cultural, and scripting view of television and social behavior. In S. B. Withey & R. P. Abeles (Eds.), *Television and social behavior: Beyond violence and children.* Hillsdale, N.J.: Erlbaum, 1980.

AUTHOR INDEX

Numbers in italics refer to the pages on which the complete references are cited.

A

Abelson, R. P., 403, *427, 430*
Achelpol, C., 145, *212,* 246, *262*
Akers, R., 145, *212,* 246, *262*
Ajzen, I., 364, *391*
Alexander, A. F., 40, *84,* 412, *428*
Allen, C. L., 145, *212,* 246, *262*
Allington, R. L., 70, *84*
Alwitt, L. F., 338, *355*
Anderson, D. R., 10, 13, *36,* 74, *84,* 124,
  138, 145, *212,* 217, 218, 219, 246, *262,*
  284, *298, 300,* 338, *355, 358,* 398, 401,
  403, 413, *427, 428*
Anderson, J. A., 418, *427*
Andrews, F. M., 91, *138*
Applefield, J. M., 306, 327, *359*
Appleton, H., 40–41, *84,* 88, *138*
Armstrong, P., 268, *298*
Aronoff, C. E., 268, *298*
Atkin, C. K., 21, *37,* 267, 274, *298, 299,*
  303, 308, *357, 358,* 361, *390*

B

Bachen, C. M., 43, 44, 45, 46, 50, 64, 67,
  69, 72, 73, *85,* 126, *140,* 220–221, 237,
  247, *263,* 311, *359,* 397, 412, 422, *429*
Bachman, J. G., 308, *359*
Bailyn, L., 98, *138*
Ball, S., 40, 41, *84,* 88, *138*
Bandura, A., 304, 313, 336, 337, 338, *355,
  356,* 362, *391,* 407, *427*
Banker, G. S., 114, *140*
Barker, R. G., 144, 145, 146, 147, 148,
  212, 363, *391,* 408, *427*
Baron, R. A., 304, 336, *358*
Barron, F., 89, 90, 91, 101, 109, *138*

Bartlett, F. C., 364, *391*
Bayley, N., *391,* 422, *428*
Beagles-Roos, J., 94, *139*
Bechtel, R. B., 145, *212,* 246, *262*
Belson, W. A., 158, 168, 179, 185, *212,*
  308, 310, 311, *356,* 421, *428*
Bem, S. L., 266, 276, 286, *298,* 404, *428*
Bennett, S. M., 273, 274, 287, *301*
Bensman, J., 26, *38*
Berkowitz, L., 307, 326, 327, *358*
Berlyne, D. E., 337, *356,* 362, *391*
Berry, J. W., 368, *391, 393*
Beuf, S., 272, 282, 287, *298*
Blackman, S., 367, 368, 369, *391*
Bogart, L., 179, *212*
Bogatz, G. A., 40, 41, *84,* 88, *138*
Bouthilet, L., 3, *37,* 88, 95, 115, 120, 127,
  140, 242, *263,* 304, 311, *358*
Broverman, D. M., 269, *298*
Broverman, K., 269, *298*
Brown, D., 40, *84,* 412, *428*
Brown, D. G., 282, *298*
Brown, J. R., 12, *36,* 163, 186, *212*
Brown, V., 274, 287, 288, *299*
Bruner, J. S., 362, *391*
Bryant, J., 40, *84,* 218, *262,* 398, 412, 413,
  427, 428
Buckley, S., 124, *140,* 186, 187, *212,* 412,
  429
Burton, R. V., 285, 287, *300*
Burton, S. G., 43, *84*
Busby, L. J., 267, 268, 269, 270, 272, *298*
Butcher, H. J., 89, *138*

C

Calder, B. J., 311, *357,* 363, *392*
Calonico, J. M., 43, *84*

431

SUBJECT INDEX

A

Age segregation, effect of TV on, 155, 165, 184, 399
Aggression
  as predictor of TV use, 308, 309, 314, 324, 326–327, 328
  definitions of, 35, 303, 315
  measures of
    observational measures, 304, 309, 315–317, 330, 332
    peer ratings, 308–309, 310, 317–318, 328–332
    self-reports, 308–309, 310
    teacher ratings, 307, 318, 328–330, 332
  portrayal on TV, 21–22, 216, 303, 335, 336, 401–402, 406, 410–411, 415
    physical, 22, 303, 335, 336, 401–402, 406, 410–411
    verbal, 22, 303, 335, 336, 402
  relation to TV exposure, 3–4, 9, 27, 30, 303–360, 396, 401–402, 410–411, 415
    design of this study, 312
    hypotheses of this study, 312–314
    measures used in this study, 6, 28, 312, 314–318, 340
    results, 318–335, 339, 401–402
      cross-sectional, 320
      longitudinal, 319–320
      observational data, 318–323, 325–326
      peer and teacher ratings, 328–332
      relation to amount of TV viewing, 323–324
      relation to TV viewing preferences, 327–328
      sex differences, 325
      summary, 334–335
    sample studied, 6, 316–318
    theoretical explanations, 309–311, 312–314, 335–339

research approaches, 304–311
  field experiments, 305–307
  laboratory experiments, 304–305
  naturalistic studies, 307–311
societal constraints on, 311, 326, 330, 339, 402, 407, 410–411
Amount of invested mental effort (AIME), in media use, 74, 95, 219, 242, 244, 247, 287, 380, 397–398, 407–408, 408–409, 419, 425
  relation to intelligence, 95, 247
Arousal, TV effects on, 313, 337, 338, 362, 365, 380, 401–402, 407–408
Attendance at community activities, see Leisure activities
Attention to television, 124, 337, 338, 339, 362, 402, 403, see also Comprehension of television

B

Before and after studies, see Quasi-experiment
Behavior setting, 144, 145–148, 149–150, 153, 363, 408
  definition of, 144
  identifying settings in the towns, 145–148, 149–150, 153
  TV as, 363, 408
Book reading
  by adults, 239–240, 244, 247
  by children, 41–42, 237, 238
  relation to intelligence, 244, 247
  relation to TV viewing, 238, 239

C

Cable TV, 4, 417, 424
Catharsis model, 306, 312–313